P9-DTQ-841

GLENCOE
STREET LAW

A Course in Practical Law

SEVENTH EDITION

Authors

Lee P. Arbetman, M.Ed., J.D.
Adjunct Professor of Law
Georgetown University Law Center

Edward L. O'Brien, J.D.
Adjunct Professor of Law
Georgetown University Law Center

The work of
Ed McMahon, our
colleague and co-author on
earlier editions of this text,
continues to focus and
strengthen this
new edition.

 **Glencoe**

New York, New York   Columbus, Ohio   Chicago, Illinois   Peoria, Illinois   Woodland Hills, California

Authors

Lee Arbetman is a graduate of Grinnell College, the University of Massachusetts (M.Ed.) and George Washington University's National Law Center (J.D.). He is the director of U.S. programs at Street Law and coordinator of the U.S. Department of Justice's national law-related education program, Youth for Justice. Along with Professor Diana Hess, he conducts the Supreme Court Summer Institute for Teachers. Arbetman has been an active member of the National Council for the Social Studies and a former chair of its citizenship committee. A former winner of the Isidore Starr Award from the American Bar Association, he is also co-author of *Great Trials in American History,* as well as numerous magazine and journal articles.

Ed O'Brien is a graduate of the University of Virginia and Georgetown University Law Center. Along with Professor Jason Newman, he co-founded the Street Law program in 1972 and now serves as its executive director. O'Brien has taken Street Law's message of law, democracy and human rights to more than 30 countries on every continent. He is the founder and director of the Black South African Lawyer's Program at Georgetown Law School and serves as president of the Friends of the University of Natal, Inc. Former chair of the Association of American Law Schools' Teaching Law Outside Law Schools Committee and a member of the American Bar Association's Division on Public Legal Education, O'Brien is also the co-author of *Human Rights for All, Democracy for All,* and numerous legal and educational articles.

Reviewers

James G. Adair
Prospect High School
Mount Prospect, Illinois

Pam Burley
Wasilla High School
Wasilla, Alaska

Janet Chandler
Hamilton Southeastern
   High School
Fishers, Indiana

Mark Elinson
Monroe High School
North Hills, California

Jackie Johnson
Center for Education in Law
   and Democracy
Denver, Colorado

Peggy Marko
Clarkston High School
Clarkston, Michigan

Tamera Schlegel
Cherry Creek School District
Englewood, Colorado

Glencoe

The *McGraw·Hill* Companies

Send all inquiries to:
Glencoe/McGraw-Hill
8787 Orion Place
Columbus, Ohio 43240-4027

ISBN 0-07-860019-7 (Student Edition)   ISBN 0-07-860020-0 (Teacher Manual)

Printed in the United States of America

8 9 058/055 08 07

The seventh edition of *Street Law: A Course in Practical Law* builds upon the success and popularity of earlier editions. Incorporating their best features, this edition provides new information, practical advice, and competency-building activities designed to provide students with the ability to analyze, evaluate, and resolve legal disputes.

Throughout the book we have added text and problems dealing with the most current law-related public issues, including terrorism and technology. We have continued our emphasis on promoting alternative (nonjudicial) forms of dispute resolution. We have also added a new feature—Law and Democracy—that challenges young people to consider legal aspects of some of the most difficult issues facing our democracy.

A Web site to complement the curriculum can be found at www.streetlaw.glencoe.com. The program includes a teacher manual, workbook, testing materials, transparencies, and a video with lesson plans.

Street Law's approach to law-related education is to provide practical information and problem-solving opportunities that develop in students the knowledge and skills necessary for survival in our law-saturated society. The curriculum includes case studies, mock trials, role-plays, small group exercises, and visual analysis activities. For optimal results, *Street Law* requires the use of community resource people such as lawyers, judges, law students, police officers, and consumer advocates. It also requires community experiences such as court tours and police ride-alongs. This methodology allows students to be active participants in their own education.

The authors gratefully acknowledge the teachers, law students, law professors, and others who have assisted in the development of our curriculum materials. Over the years, many people have provided valuable field-testing, research, editorial assistance, encouragement, and support.

Our colleagues at Street Law, Inc. provided useful input into this edition. Particular assistance was received from staff members Alex Ashbrook, Andrea Miotto, Erin Donovan

Hull, Matt Kavanagh, Mary Larkin, and Judy Zimmer. Lena Morreale Scott led the preparation of the teacher materials. Review of the student edition by Margaret Fisher of the Seattle University School of Law proved quite beneficial.

We were particularly fortunate to have the assistance of Joanne Lytle-Miller, at the time a third-year law student at Georgetown University Law Center. We also received research assistance from Sarah Shapiro, at the time a third-year law student at Boston University School of Law, and college interns Cullen Ann Drescher, Lauren Isaacoff, and Jaclyn Lonegan.

Legal experts whose review was absolutely essential to the creation of the new edition and whose contributions are most appreciated are: *Unit One:* Tom Krattenmaker and Michael Haas, Mintz Levin Law Firm; *Unit Two:* Professor John Copacino, Georgetown University Law Center, Professor Angela Davis, American University School of Law, Professor Orin Kerr, George Washington University Law School, and Kevin Driscoll, Senior Legislative Counsel, American Bar Association; *Unit Three:* Tom Krattenmaker and Michael Haas; *Unit Four:* Federal Trade Commission lawyers Claudia Simons, Carole Danielson, and Carole Reynolds, and Alan Korn, Esquire, from Safe Kids; *Unit Five:* Professor Margaret Berry, Catholic University School of Law, and Mary Bissell, Esquire, Children's Legal Defense Fund; and *Unit Six:* Tom Krattenmaker and Michael Haas, and Kerry O'Brien, Esquire, D.C. Employment Justice Center. Dr. Neil Ravin advises on matters of law and medicine.

Lee Arbetman
Ed O'Brien
Washington, DC

Advice to Readers: Law varies from state to state and is constantly changing. Therefore, someone confronted with a legal problem should not use this text as a substitute for legal advice from an attorney.

Contents

UNIT 2 Criminal Law and Juvenile Justice **72**

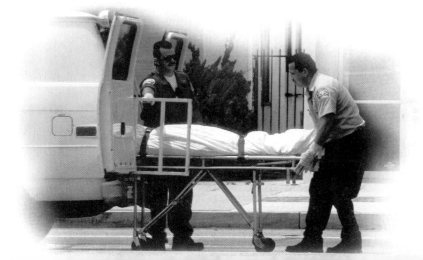

Contents

Contents

UNIT 3   Torts   210

UNIT 4 Consumer and Housing Law 274

Contents

UNIT 5 Family Law 368

Contents

Features

The Case of . . .

The Case of . . .

Unit 6

Features

For Your Information . . .

Steps to Take

You Be The Judge

Human Rights USA

Law & Democracy

Law in Action

The Street Law materials are a product of Street Law, Inc., a non-profit organization whose roots can be traced back to a Georgetown University Law Center program launched in 1971. In this program—which continues to this day—law students teach practical law courses in District of Columbia public high schools as well as community-based settings. More than 70 law schools now participate in the Street Law program nationwide.

Street Law, Inc. is dedicated to empowering people through law-related education (LRE). Law-related education is a unique blend of substance and instructional strategies. Students learn substantive information about law, democracy, and human rights through strategies that promote problem solving, critical thinking, cooperative learning, improved communication and conflict resolution skills, and the ability to participate effectively in society.

Street Law has also brought its educational message of law, democracy, and human rights to more than 30 countries around the world.

Street Law's many programs and materials are described in detail on the organization's Web site, www.streetlaw.org. Street Law and other law-related education programs are supported by a national network of statewide law-related education centers. These centers may have resources that can strengthen your program. To find your state's LRE center, go to the Street Law Web site and click on "state LRE centers."

Street Law staff and consultants provide training and technical assistance to school districts, law schools, bar associations, juvenile corrections, community-based organizations, and others wishing to implement its programs.

For additional information or assistance, contact
Street Law, Inc.
1010 Wayne Avenue
Suite 870
Silver Spring, Maryland 20910
301-589-1130
FAX 301-589-1131
www.streetlaw.org
clearinghouse@streetlaw.org.

Board of Directors

Over the years many corporations, foundations, government agencies, law firms, and individuals have helped to make Street Law's work possible. We appreciate their support and acknowledge their assistance. We particularly want to thank the following for their contributions:

Corporations

The Anschutz Corporation
C&P Telephone
Court TV
Exide Corporation
Exxon Corporation
IBM Corporation
Interactive Digital Software
    Association Foundation
Levi-Strauss
McDonald's Corporation
McGraw-Hill/Glencoe
Metropolitan Life Foundation
Microsoft Corporation
Nationwide Mutual Insurance Co.
Sterling Drug, Inc.
United States Trust Company of New York
West Publishing Company
Xerox Corporation

Foundations

Arizona Bar Foundation
The Atlantic Fund
George Batchelor Foundation
Morris & Gwendolyn Cafritz Foundation
Jim Casey Foundation
John J. Creedon Foundation
Dade Community Foundation
Cora and John H. Davis Foundation
Max and Victoria Dreyfus Foundation, Inc.
Fannie Mae Foundation
Ford Foundation
Philip Graham Fund
Harold Kohn Foundation
Anthony Lucas-Spindletop Foundation
Eugene and Agnes Meyer Foundation
Molner Foundation

New York Community Trust
Open Society Institute (Soros Foundation)
Dwight D. Opperman Foundation
Rotary Foundation of DC
The Stanley Foundation
Surdna Foundation

Government

Baltimore County Schools
Chicago Public Schools
Fairfax (VA) Schools
Montgomery County (MD) Human Relations
    Commission
Montgomery County (MD) Public Schools
National Highway Traffic Safety
    Administration (D.O.T.)
Public Schools of District of Columbia
Superior Court of the District of Columbia
U.S. Agency for International Development
U.S. Department of Education
U.S. Department of Defense
U.S. Department of Justice, Office of Juvenile
    Justice and Delinquency Prevention
U.S. Department of State
U.S. Information Agency

Law Firms

Arent, Fox, Kintner, Plotkin & Kahn
Arnold & Porter
Caplin & Drysdale
Collier, Shannon, Rill & Scott
Covington & Burling
Cypen & Cypen
Dewey Ballantine
Edlavitch & Tyser
Friday, Eldredge & Clark
Harmon, Curran, Spielberg & Eisenberg, LLP
Hogan & Hartson
Holland & Knight
Jones, Day, Reavis & Pogue
Latham & Watkins
McDermott, Will & Emery
Morrison & Foerster
O'Connor & Hannan
Oldaker, Biden & Belair

Paul, Weiss, Rifkind, Wharton & Garrison
Powell, Goldstein, Frazer & Murphy
Rider, Bennett, Egan & Arundel
Ruden, Barnett, McCloskey, Smith,
    Schuster & Russell, P.A.
Sidley & Austin
Spriggs & Hollingsworth
Venable, Baetjer, Howard & Civiletti
Verner, Liipfert, Bernhard, McPherson
    & Hand
Whyte, Hirschboek & Dudek
Williams & Connolly

Other (private support)

Alabama Center for Law and Civic Education
American Bar Association, The Central
    European and Eurasian Law Initiative
American Corporate Counsel Association
American Immigration Lawyers Association
Arizona School Resource Officers
Association of Trial Lawyers of America
Bar Association of the District of Columbia
Catholic University
Chemonics International
Cleveland Bar Foundation
Communities in Schools (Philadelphia)
Covenant House Washington
Development Services Group
Georgetown University Law Center
Goldman Fund
Hebrew University of Jerusalem
National Crime Prevention Council
National Endowment for Democracy
National Institute for Dispute Resolution
National Safety Council
National Youth Court Center
New Jersey Center for Law-Related Education
Northern Ireland Human Rights Commission
PipeVine, Inc.
Queens University of Belfast
RFK Memorial
Rotary Foundation of Washington, DC
Storm Internet Services
Supreme Court Historical Society

Temple University's Law, Education and
    Participation Program
United Way of the National Capital Area
Washington Metropolitan Area Corporate
    Counsel Assoc.
YMCA of Metropolitan Washington

Individuals

Jacqueline Allee
Aggie Alvez
Lee Arbetman
Clyde Atkins
Eleanor Barnard
Robert Barnett
Lowell Beck
Robert R. Belair
William Bell
Lee Roy Black
Jennifer Bloom
Bruce Bonar
Rebecca Bond
Kevin C. Boyle
David R. Brink
James Buchanan
Patrick Campbell
Arthur Catullo
Frank W. Clarke
A. Gus Cleveland
Thomas T. Cobb
Alice Collopy
Lawrence Dark
Tom Diemer
Lashonda Dixon
Charles Douglas
Gretchen Dykstra
Bert H. Early
Sue Eedle
David Ellwanger
Justice William J. Erickson
Robert M. Ervin
William W. Falsgraf
Beth Farnbach
John D. Feerick
Robert Floyd

Carolyn Galbreath
Mark Gelber
Brenda Girton
Judge Thomas Greene
Ruth Gutstein
Katherine Hagen
Dean Hansell
Julia Hardin
Geoffrey Hazard, Jr.
William Henry
Roger Hewitt
Christopher Hicks
Ruth Hinerfeld
A.P. and Mildred Hollingsworth
Benigno Hooker
Mark Hulsey
Leonard Janofsky
Douglas Jobes
Judge Norma H. Johnson
Judge Sam D. Johnson
T. Paine Kelly
Eric Klotz
Charles Kolb
John Kramer
Kim Kwang
Mary Curd Larkin
Liane Levetan
R. Stanley Lowe
Christopher McBride
Chief Justice Vincent L. McKusick
Abelardo Menendez
Elmer Merryman
Robert Meserve
Theodore Milbach
Charles E. Miller
Vivian Mills
Ricardo Morales
Mark Murphy
Jason Newman
Edward L. O'Brien
Alan Page

Richard Parker
Charles Peebles
Richard Pettigrew
Lissa Pierce
Justice Lewis F. Powell, Jr.
E. Barrett Prettyman, Jr.
Judge William Pryor
Ramon Rasco
Janet Reno
Linda Riekes
David Robinson
James Rohloff
Adam Ruehl
Donald Saint
Jack Lee Sammons
John Sauer
Benjamin Schneider
Bernard Segal
Debra Smith
Phillip Spector
Justin A. Stanley
Linda Start
Susan Stroud
Janet Studley
Theodore Tetzloff
Warren Thompson
Sabrina Toma
Lyman Tondel
Jerrol Tostrud
Mary Pat Toups
Sidney Tuchman
Dan Walbolt
Sharyll Watterson
Leroy Wevv
Fay Williams
Jarod Wood
K. Woods
Carlton Wright
Jamil Zainaldin
Judith Zimmer
Howard Zipser

UNIT
1

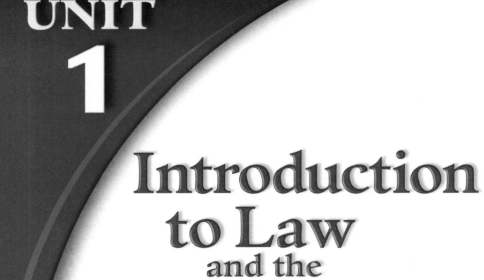

Introduction to Law
and the
Legal System

Street Law
online
Visit the *Street Law* Web
site at streetlaw.glencoe.com for
unit-based activities.

Unit 1, Introduction to Law and the Legal System, sets the stage for your study of Street Law. Chapters in this unit will help you learn important basic information including:

- What is law?
- How are laws made in the various branches of government?
- What roles can you play in influencing lawmakers?
- How is our legal system organized, including the difference between trials and appeals and between the state and federal court systems?
- How do you find and get help from a lawyer?

This unit also contains two chapters that help you develop skills you will need for the rest of your life. Chapter 3 discusses advocacy and will help you identify problems in your community, state, and country. As an effective advocate, you will be able to develop and implement plans (including voting and lobbying) for

The Apathetic Bystanders

Catherine "Kitty" Genovese was attacked and stabbed to death in 1964 in a highly populated area of Queens, New York. During the half-hour ordeal, 38 people heard Kitty's screams for help and watched from their windows. Twice the killer was scared off by the sound of voices and the realization that he was being watched. However, both times, when it became obvious that nobody was going to call the police, the killer returned to finish off his victim. Rather than give any aid to Kitty, such as calling the police or an ambulance, all 38 bystanders chose to pull their shades, draw their blinds, and ignore Kitty's urgent pleas for help as her life was taken by the deranged attacker.

Problem 1.6

a. Why do you think the bystanders took no action?

b. Did the bystanders commit a crime by not acting? Give your reasons.

c. Did the bystanders do the right thing?

d. Should the law hold citizens responsible for not helping out in cases such as this one?

Kinds of Laws

Laws fall into two major groups: criminal and civil. **Criminal laws** regulate public conduct and set out duties owed to society. A criminal case is a legal action that can only be brought by the government against a person charged with committing a crime. Criminal laws have penalties, and offenders are imprisoned, fined, placed under supervision, or punished in some other way. In the U.S. legal system, criminal offenses are divided into **felonies** and **misdemeanors.** The penalty for a felony is a term of more than one year in prison. For a misdemeanor, the penalty is a prison term of one year or less. Felonies, such as murder or robbery, are more serious crimes. Less serious crimes, such as simple assault or minor theft, are called misdemeanors.

Civil laws regulate relations between individuals or groups of individuals. A **civil action** is a lawsuit that can be brought by a person who feels wronged or injured by another person. Courts may award the injured person money for the loss, or they may order the person who committed the wrong to make amends in some other way. An example of a civil action is a lawsuit for recovery of damages suffered in an automobile accident. Civil laws regulate many everyday situations, such as marriage, divorce, contracts, real estate, insurance, consumer protection, and negligence.

Sometimes behavior can violate both civil and criminal laws and can result in two court cases. A criminal case is brought by the government against a **defendant,** the person accused of committing the crime. A civil case is brought by the **plaintiff**—the person or company harmed—against the defendant.

The O.J. Simpson trials attracted national and international media attention. *Did the public understand the difference between the civil and criminal law in these cases?*

"Reason is the life of law."

— Sir Edward Coke

In a famous series of cases, former star football player O.J. Simpson was prosecuted in connection with the deaths of his former wife, Nicole Brown Simpson, and her friend, Ron Goldman. The Los Angeles district attorney was the **prosecutor** in this criminal case. In order to win a conviction, the district attorney had to prove that O.J. Simpson was guilty **beyond a reasonable doubt.** This means that if the jury (or the judge in a case tried without a jury) has any reasonable doubts about the defendant's guilt, then it must vote not to convict. The jury verdict in Simpson's criminal case was *not guilty.*

Several months later, the parents of Ron Goldman brought a civil suit against O.J. Simpson to recover damages resulting from the wrongful death of their son. In a civil case, the plaintiff wins by convincing the jury (or the judge in a case tried without a jury) by a **preponderance of the evidence.** The jury (or judge) needs only to decide if it is more likely than not that the plaintiff's complaint is true. This is a lower requirement for proof than the beyond-a-reasonable-doubt standard used in criminal cases. The reason for the different standards of proof is that a defendant loses money in a civil case, but can suffer lengthy imprisonment or even the death penalty as a result of a criminal conviction. The Goldmans won their civil case against O.J. Simpson. Because the public tends not to understand the difference between civil and criminal cases, there was much confusion about how a person could be found not guilty in a criminal case and then responsible in a civil suit for damages for the same act.

You will learn much more about criminal law in Unit 2 of *Street Law* and much more about civil law in Units 3 through 6.

Problem 1.7

Matt and Kenji decide to skip school. They take Kenji's brother's car without telling him and drive to a local shopping center. Ignoring the sign "Parking for Handicapped Persons Only," they leave the car and enter an electronics shop.

After looking around, they buy a portable CD player. Then they buy some sandwiches from a street vendor and walk to a nearby park. While eating, they discover that the CD player does not work. In their hurry to return it, they leave their trash on the park bench.

When Matt and Kenji get back to the shopping center, they notice a large dent in one side of their car. The dent appears to be the result of a driver's carelessness in backing out of the next space. They also notice that the car has been broken into and that the car stereo has been removed.

They call the police to report the accident and theft. When the police arrive, they seize a small, clear bag containing illegal drugs from behind the car's back seat. Matt and Kenji are arrested.

a. List all the things you think Matt and Kenji did wrong.

b. What laws are involved in this story?

c. Which of these are criminal laws? Which are civil laws?

Our Constitutional Framework

The U.S. Constitution is the highest law of the land. Drafted more than two hundred years ago, this remarkable document is the longest-lasting written constitution in the world. It sets forth the basic framework of our government. It also lists the government's powers, the limits on those powers, and the people's freedoms that cannot be taken away by the government. (The text of the entire Constitution is provided on pages 570–599.)

Integral to the Constitution is the principle of **limited government.** Before the U.S. Constitution was written and ratified, the individual states were reluctant to give up power to the national government. After all, a revolution had just been fought against the government of the king of England to preserve individual liberty and the freedom to govern without interference. As a result, the Constitution created a national government of limited powers, with authority to pass laws only in the areas specifically listed in Article I of the Constitution. Those who criticize the power and reach of the federal government today often cite these historic reasons for limiting its power.

Perhaps nothing is more important in the Constitution than the division of lawmaking power among the three branches of government: the executive, the legislative, and the judicial. This division is known as the **separation of powers.** The executive branch, which includes the president and federal agencies, is primarily responsible for enforcing the law. However, the executive branch often issues

The Adoption of the Constitution by J.B. Stearns depicts the members of the Constitutional Convention formally endorsing their new plan of government. *What is the purpose of the U.S. Constitution?*

rules and executive orders that have the force of law. The legislative branch, or Congress, uses lawmaking power when it passes laws, or **statutes.** The judicial branch, or judiciary—the courts—clarifies, and in some instances establishes laws through its rulings. These rulings may interpret a provision of the Constitution, a statute, or a rule issued by an executive agency.

The three branches of government are independent, but each has the power to restrain the other branches in a system of **checks and balances.** The system was designed to prevent one branch from becoming too powerful and abusing its power. Examples of checks and balances include congressional investigations of actions by the president or other executive officials, the prosecution in court of members of Congress or the executive branch for violating the law, and impeachment. Another check is the president's power to **veto** (refuse to approve) laws passed by Congress.

One of the most visible and important checks of one branch on another is the courts' power of **judicial review.** Judicial review enables a court to declare unenforceable any law passed by Congress or a state legislature that conflicts with the nation's highest law, the Constitution. For example, Congress might pass a law prohibiting media criticism of elected officials. If challenged in court, this law would be declared invalid and unconstitutional because it violates the freedom of press guaranteed in the First Amendment. In general, the courts can declare a law **unconstitutional** either because (1) the government has passed a law which the Constitution does not give it the power to pass or (2) the government has passed a law that violates somebody's rights. Judicial review also gives the courts the power to declare an action of the executive or legislative branch to be unconstitutional. For example, the courts can strike down a regulation improperly issued by an executive branch agency. The courts may also prevent Congress from taking away the president's power to grant pardons.

Just as the Constitution restricts the power of the branches, it also reflects the view that the federal government as a whole should be limited by the power of the states. This division of power between the states and the federal government is known as **federalism.** The federal government's powers to make laws are listed in the Constitution, and the remaining powers are reserved for the states. This is why most civil and criminal laws are passed by state legislatures or local governments. Consequently, many legal differences exist among the states. For example, a 16-year-old boy can obtain a license to drive a car in some states but not in others.

The principle of limited government is also reflected in the **Bill of Rights,** the first 10 amendments to the Constitution. The Bill of Rights defines and guarantees the fundamental rights and liberties of all Americans, including the freedoms of religion, speech, and press; the freedom from unreasonable search and seizure; and other individual rights. Courts have decided that most provisions of the Bill of Rights limit the power of state and local governments as well as the federal government.

Every state has a constitution, and most state constitutions reflect the major principles of the U.S. Constitution. All provide for different branches of government, separation of powers, checks and balances, and judicial review. Some state constitutions provide greater protection of rights than the U.S. Constitution. Our federal system allows states to do this if they wish. For example, some state constitutions have equal rights amendments guaranteeing women greater rights than they have under the U.S. Constitution.

Federal troops enforce the Constitution and forcibly integrate Little Rock High School in September 1957 after members of the Arkansas National Guard prevented Elizabeth Ann Eckford from entering the school. *What is the role of the federal government in protecting individual rights?*

The U.S. Constitution and most state constitutions are difficult to change. This is because they were drafted with the belief that they should not be changed without careful thought, discussion, and debate. The idea was to make these documents as permanent as possible. However, allowances were made to accommodate necessary changes. The U.S. Constitution may be changed in two ways. A proposed amendment must be approved either by a two-thirds vote of both houses of Congress or at a convention called by two-thirds of the states. In either case, it must then be ratified, or approved, by three-fourths of the states.

People try to change the Constitution for many reasons. One of the most common reasons for change has been to extend rights that were not originally written into the Constitution. Although ratification is difficult, 27 amendments have been added to the Constitution. These extensions of rights often reflect the changing viewpoints of citizens and their elected representatives. For example, when the original Constitution was ratified in 1789, most states restricted voting to white males who owned property. Since then, various amendments have extended voting rights to minorities, women, persons without property, and persons aged 18 to 20.

Amendments for a range of issues have been discussed and proposed over the years. Some think there should be a constitutional amendment to extend statehood to the District of Columbia. Another proposed amendment would require the federal government to adopt a balanced budget. Other amendments have been proposed in recent years to punish flag burning, protect victims of crime, and ban abortions. The Equal Rights Amendment passed Congress in 1972. It prohibited discrimination on the basis of sex. However, it failed to be ratified by the required 38 states, so it did not become a part of the U.S. Constitution. In 1992, the Twenty-Seventh Amendment became part of the Constitution. This amendment, first proposed by James Madison in 1789, bans midterm congressional pay raises.

> *"All religions, laws, morals and political systems are but necessary means to preserve social order."*
>
> — Chien Tu-Hsiu

Problem 1.8

Examine each of the following situations and determine for each whether it involves the principle of separation of powers, checks and balances, judicial review, federalism, or some combination of these principles. Specify the principle or principles involved and explain your answer.

a. A state law requires that a prayer be said each day in public schools. The courts rule that the law violates a First Amendment clause that prohibits the government from establishing a religion.

b. The U.S. Congress passes a law that restricts the import of handguns from other countries. The legislature in one state allows the sale of handguns to anyone over age 18.

c. Because a prison is very old and overcrowded, a state court orders the state legislature to spend $10 million on a new prison.

Lawmaking

The laws that U.S. citizens are expected to obey come from many sources, including federal and state governments. Constitutions set forth laws and also establish the structure of government. Legislatures, of course, make laws. In some situations, voters can act directly as lawmakers. Administrative agencies make many laws. Finally, laws are sometimes made by courts when they decide appeals.

Legislatures

As you have seen, the U.S. Constitution divides the power to make laws between the federal government and the state governments. At both the federal and the state levels, legislatures are the primary lawmaking bodies. The U.S. Congress—the federal legislature—is made up of two houses. The Senate is composed of 100 members with two from each state, and the House of Representatives has 435 members with each state represented according to the size of its population. The U.S. Constitution gives Congress the power to pass laws that are binding on the people in every state. States have the power to pass laws that apply only within their boundaries.

The U.S. Capitol is home to the legislative branch of the federal government.

"Even when laws have been written down, they ought not always to remain unaltered."

— Aristotle

Street Law
online

Visit the *Street Law* Web site at streetlaw.glencoe.com for chapter-based information and resources.

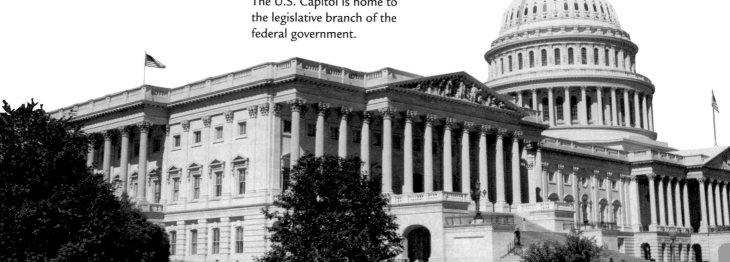

Segregated drinking fountains were common in the American South in the 1960s. *Why was the federal government concerned about this situation?*

The lawmaking authority of Congress is exercised through the passage of laws known as federal **statutes.** When Congress passes a federal statute, it affects people in every state. Federal statutes deal with issues of national impact, such as environmental quality, national defense, homeland security, labor relations, veterans' affairs, public health, civil rights, economic development, postal services, and federal taxes.

The states' lawmaking powers are vested in their legislatures, which pass laws called state statutes. Except for Nebraska, every state has a two-house legislature. Most states' legislatures meet on an annual basis; in a few states, the legislatures meet every two years. States pass laws with statewide impact in such areas as education, traffic, state taxes (including how they will be spent), marriage and divorce, most criminal laws, and the powers and duties of state government officials. Although tribal governments of Native Americans vary a great deal, many place legislative authority—and sometimes executive authority as well—in a body known as the tribal council.

The power of the federal government to pass laws is limited. Congress cannot legislate unless given the power to do so in the Constitution. The states, on the other hand, have broader power to legislate. In general, the states have power to legislate in all those areas over which the national government was not granted power by the Constitution. For example, a state could not enter into a treaty with another country or coin money, as those are among the powers assigned to the national government. However, states can pass marriage and divorce laws, as those are not powers assigned to the national government.

Sometimes federal laws conflict with state laws. However, unless it can be shown that Congress is legislating in an area the Constitution delegated to the states, the courts will usually follow the federal law and not the state law. For example, in the 1960s, federal laws against racial segregation in restaurants and hotels came into conflict with laws of some states that required separate accommodations for African Americans and whites. The courts ruled the state laws invalid based on Article VI of the Constitution, the **supremacy clause,** which states that "the Constitution and the Laws of the United States . . . shall be the supreme law of the land."

In addition to the U.S. Congress and state legislatures, cities, towns, and counties have lawmaking bodies such as county or city councils, boards of aldermen, or local boards of education. Local governments pass laws known as ordinances or regulations. Legislative issues that concern local governments include land use, parking, schools, and regulation of local business. Laws passed by local governments apply only to a county, city, or town. The local lawmaking body has been given the power to enact ordinances by the state. Many of the laws most important to us in our daily lives are passed by local governments.

Problem 2.1

Decide whether each of the following laws is federal, state, and/or local. Then give one example, not listed among the following, of a federal, a state, and a local law.

a. No parking on the east side of Main Street between 4:00 P.M. and 6:00 P.M.

b. All persons between the ages of 6 and 16 must attend school.

c. Whoever enters a bank for purposes of taking by force or violence the property or money in custody of such bank shall be fined not more than $5,000 or imprisoned not more than 20 years or both.

d. In order to sell any product on public streets, the seller must first apply for and receive a vendor's permit.

e. No employer of more than 15 persons may discriminate on the basis of race, color, religion, sex, or national origin.

f. All persons traveling on interstate airline carriers are subject to search before entering the airplane departure area.

Where You Live

What legislatures exist in your state and local area? What are some types of laws that each of these legislatures has enacted?

Legislatures and other lawmaking bodies try to respond to the needs of the citizens they represent by introducing legislation in the form of **bills.** Bills are used to enact new laws or amend or repeal old laws. Ideas for bills can come from legislators, the executive branch, individual citizens, citizens' groups, businesses, or lobbyists representing various groups. The courts also sometimes identify problems that legislatures need to address. A bill passed by the legislature and not vetoed by the executive branch becomes a law.

After a bill becomes a law, the people must obey it. Sometimes, though, the language of a law is open to differing interpretations. It is not always easy to know exactly what a law prohibits or allows. Disputes over what a law means frequently end up in court. A judge who interprets what the legislature means is determining **legislative intent.**

The Unclear Law

The city of Beautifica has established a lovely park in the city. The city council wishes to preserve some elements of nature, undisturbed by the city noise, traffic, pollution, and crowding. The park is a place where citizens can go and find grass, trees, flowers, and quiet. In addition, there are playgrounds and picnic areas, and at one time a road ran through the park. Now the road is closed. The city council has enacted a law requiring that at all the entrances to the park the following sign is to be posted: NO VEHICLES IN THE PARK.

Park rules should be clear to everyone.

Problem 2.2

The law seems clear, but some disputes have arisen over its interpretation. Interpret the law in the following cases, keeping in mind what the law says (the letter of the law) as well as the legislative intent. Examine each situation and decide whether or not the vehicle described should be allowed in the park. Write down the reasons for your choices. When you finish analyzing all of the situations, rewrite the law to make it clearer.

a. Tony lives on one side of the city and works on the other. He will save ten minutes if he drives through the park.

b. To keep the park clean, trash barrels are located throughout the area. The sanitation department wants to drive a truck into the park to collect the trash from the barrels.

c. Two police cars are chasing a suspected bank robber. If one police car cuts through the park, it can get in front of the suspect's car and trap it between the patrol cars.

d. An ambulance is racing to the hospital with a dying patient. The shortest route is through the park.

e. Elena wants to take her baby to the park in a stroller.

f. A monument is being erected to the city's citizens who died in the Vietnam War. A tank, donated by the government, is to be placed beside the monument.

g. Amul had both legs amputated and uses an electric wheelchair. He wants to visit the park.

Drafting a Bill

No matter where the idea for a bill originates, eventually there must come a time when the bill is drafted—that is, when actual language is written. As you can see from The Case of the Unclear Law, sometimes even the simplest language is not clear enough for people to understand what is expected. Legislation is often drafted and redrafted before being introduced and discussed by a legislative body. Despite these efforts, many laws are difficult to read and understand. When misunderstandings occur, one of the basic purposes of law—letting people know what conduct is expected of them, or what conduct is prohibited—is lost. When drafting laws or other types of rules, it is useful to ask the following questions to evaluate whether problems are likely to result.

- Is the law written in clear language?
- Is the law understandable?
- When does the law go into effect?
- Does the law contradict any other laws?
- Is the law enforceable? If so, by whom?
- Are the penalties for breaking the law clear and reasonable?

In deciding what a statute means, judges must follow certain rules. One rule is that courts will not enforce laws that are so vague that it is unclear exactly what conduct is prohibited. For example, a law that stated "it shall be illegal to gather on a street corner without a good reason" would be determined as being too vague. Another rule says that if there is doubt as to the meaning of a word in a criminal statute, the word must be strictly interpreted against the government.

Law in *Action*

Drafting a Law Simulation

Over the past year, traffic congestion in your town has worsened. One result has been an increase in accidents involving bicycles. Last year, there were nine accidents with serious injuries involving bicycles and cars or bicycles and pedestrians. A citizens' group asks the town council to draft some bicycle safety legislation. After examining the town ordinances, the council realizes that there is no existing law explaining where and how people should ride bicycles.

Problem 2.3

The town's legislative drafting commission—of which you are a member—has been asked to draft a new ordinance.

a. What problem does the town council need to address with the proposed ordinance?

b. What is the legislative intent of the town council in drafting the ordinance?

c. List all the details you think should be included in the proposed ordinance.

d. Create a draft of the proposed ordinance to deal with the problem. The draft should contain no more than 6 sentences.

e. After the law is drafted, use the guidelines for drafting laws listed above to analyze possible problems with the law. Are there any? If so, what are they? How can they be solved?

This usually means that words are given their ordinary meaning by the court. These rules are meant to ensure that people are not punished for failing to obey an unclear law.

Clarity in legal language is important. For that reason, some legislatures now attempt to write in simple, clear English rather than traditional legal language. Those who favor this practice argue that laws have been written in language that is too complex and should instead be written so that a person of ordinary intelligence and education can understand what is expected. However, many laws are still written in language that is difficult to understand.

Agencies

Many of the laws that affect you are made by government agencies. Legislative bodies usually deal with problems in only a general way. They authorize administrative agencies to develop rules and regulations to make laws more specific. These regulations influence almost every aspect of our daily lives and have the force of law. For example, Congress passed a law requiring safe working conditions in places of employment. To implement the law, Congress established the Occupational Safety and Health Administration (OSHA). This agency develops specific regulations governing health and safety on the job. These regulations dictate specifics, such as the height of guardrails in factories, the number of fire exits, and the type of safety equipment to be worn by employees in various occupations.

Another example of a government agency is the Environmental Protection Agency (EPA). It works with other federal agencies, state and local government, and Native American groups to develop and enforce regulations under existing environmental laws passed by Congress. The EPA sets national standards that help protect human health and safeguard the national environment with enforcement delegated to state governments. The agency also works with industry and government at various levels on pollution prevention and energy conservation.

In response to the attacks of September 11, 2001, the federal government created new agencies, and reorganized existing ones, to protect homeland security. For example, in November 2002 President Bush signed a bill creating a new federal Department of Homeland Security. The department's primary mission is to help

Specific rules and regulations are made by agencies, such as the Occupational Safety and Health Administration (OSHA). *Why do you think this agency is needed?*

Former Pennsylvania governor Tom Ridge was named as the first secretary of the new Department of Homeland Security in January 2003. *Why did the U.S. government create a new agency after the September 11, 2001, terrorist attacks?*

prevent, protect against, and respond to acts of terrorism on U.S soil. An existing agency, the Department of Transportation (DOT), was also reorganized when the Transportation Security Administration (TSA) was created within DOT to protect the nation's transportation system. When you travel by air, TSA employees screen you and your luggage to ensure the safety of your flight.

The administrative agencies with the greatest impact on your daily life are those at the state and local levels. For example, a zoning commission and other local agencies where you live may have developed a plan that determines what kind of buildings can be located in specific parts of your town. A local agency may hold public hearings to determine whether a new restaurant can serve alcohol and feature live music. And your state or local school board may have taken some administrative action that allows your school to offer this Street Law course!

Administrative agencies, then, are really hidden lawmakers, making numerous rules and regulations that affect business and industry, as well as individuals. For example, regulations govern the amount of pesticide that can be used on produce, the number of animals that can be killed by hunters, the ingredients that can be used in canned food, the costs of phone calls and electricity, the hours of operation for bars and restaurants, the qualifications of people employed in various professions, and hundreds of other issues. In addition to their lawmaking functions, agencies also administer government programs and provide many services.

Regulations issued by these agencies become law without being voted upon. However, agencies usually hold **public hearings** before issuing proposed regulations. These hearings give individuals or businesses an opportunity to express their views on the proposals. In addition, regulations proposed by the federal government must be published in a special newspaper called the *Federal Register*. This allows people to learn about and comment on proposed rules.

Where You Live

❶ Visit the EPA online at www.epa.gov to find environmental information about your local community. Information about environmental agencies and laws in your state is also available from the EPA online.

❷ What are the major departments or agencies of your state government? How are they organized and what do they do?

In recent years, there has been much criticism about the number of rules and regulations affecting businesses and individuals. Some groups have called for a limit on new regulations or the repeal of regulations they consider too costly and burdensome. Others say administrative regulations are an essential part of modern life.

Problem 2.4

Complete one of the following exercises as a research project.

a. Find an article in your local newspaper about an administrative agency. Then answer the following questions about the agency: What is its name? What does it do? Is the agency part of the federal, state, or local government? What does the article say about the agency?

b. Find evidence of an agency at work on a street in your community. What agency is acting? What action is the agency taking? Is there any way for the public to have an impact on the agency? If so, how? Is the agency part of the federal, state, or local government?

c. Choose an occupation or profession (such as an electrician, physician, lawyer, schoolteacher, or hair stylist). Interview someone in that occupation to get answers to the following questions: What agency or organization regulates the profession? What are the qualifications for the profession? Are any licenses or tests required? How does the agency decide who gets a license? Is the agency part of the federal, state, or local government?

Courts

Law is also made by courts. Later in this unit you will learn much more about how the court system is organized. But for now, think about courtroom scenes you have watched on television. These courts were conducting **trials.** The person who loses a trial can sometimes ask a higher court to review and change the result of the trial. These higher courts are called **appeals** or **appellate courts.** When an appeals court decides a case, it issues a written opinion that sets a **precedent** for similar cases in the future. All lower courts in the jurisdiction where the precedent was issued must follow it. For example, if a state's supreme court ruled that the state's constitution required that school funding be equalized throughout the state—richer and poorer school districts would each have to spend the same amount per student—then all lower courts in that state would have to follow that precedent.

International Lawmaking

International law is usually defined as the law that applies to the conduct of countries. It is most often made when national governments make treaties with each other or with a group of countries. A **treaty** is an agreement or contract between countries. These treaties are sometimes created by the joint action of countries or by actions taken by the United Nations. Various international laws, usually made by treaty, regulate commerce among countries, refugees crossing national borders, ownership of property including copyrights and patents, the environment, and many other areas. The U.S. Constitution provides that treaties are the supreme law of the land if they are signed by the president and then ratified by two-thirds of the U.S. Senate.

Important international law has been made by a series of treaties, signed since 1950 by various European countries, which formed the European Union (EU). These treaties established a European Parliament, which has the power to make laws that promote political and economic cooperation in Europe. A very visible example of this has been the EU's agreement to have a new common currency called the euro. In 2003 fifteen countries belonged to the European Union, and 13 others—mostly former member countries of the Soviet Union—were awaiting entry into the EU. Countries that join do not give up most of their sovereign power to make laws that are binding within their borders. However, in order to benefit all member countries they do give up power in selected areas by delegating some lawmaking authority to a European-wide organization.

The process of European integration has resulted in the creation of the European Parliament, the body that passes the majority of European laws. *Why are so many countries eager to join the EU?*

The United Nations (UN), formed in 1945 and headquartered in New York City, has nearly 200 member countries as well as many affiliated organizations such as the Commission on Human Rights, United Nations Educational, Scientific and Cultural Organization (UNESCO), International Monetary Fund (IMF), World Trade Organization (WTO), World Health Organization (WHO), and the World Bank. The UN also maintains a system of international courts and has become the most important institution in the area of international law. Countries that join the United Nations agree to abide by the provisions of its charter.

The United States was one of the founding members of the UN, and over the years it has been its biggest financial supporter. But many in the United States have criticized the UN for being a bloated bureaucracy that is slow to act, often wasting time and money. Others criticize the United States for not fully supporting UN actions, especially in instances when most UN member countries do not agree with U.S. policy.

Problem 2.5

The government of an African country has been very corrupt for many years and has violated the human rights of many of its citizens by jailing and executing opposition leaders who are all from one ethnic group. The United States and most other countries have been critical of this government for its actions. The opposition groups in the country want to overthrow the government. The government reacts by rounding up and executing hundreds of members of the ethnic group leading the opposition.

The United States and many other governments around the world speak out against this. The United Nations is considering a resolution authorizing sending UN troops into the country to stop what some are calling genocide, the systematic killing of an ethnic or racial group. The U.S. government is reluctant to get involved militarily in the internal affairs of another country.

The UN Charter (Article 55) states: With a view to the creation of conditions of stability and well-being which are necessary for peaceful and friendly relations among nations based on respect for the principle of equal rights and self-determination of peoples, the United Nations shall promote . . . universal respect for, and observance of, human rights and fundamental freedoms for all without distinction as to race, sex, language, or religion.

Article 56 states that all members pledge themselves to take joint and separate action in cooperation with the organization for the achievement of the purposes set forth in Article 55.

a. If you were the president of the United States, would you instruct our UN delegate to support the authorization to send troops into this African country? Explain.

b. Assume the U.S. government does not think sending troops is the best way to solve this problem, but more than two-thirds of the countries in the UN vote in favor of the resolution. Should the United States contribute troops to the UN effort? Explain.

c. After a presidential election and change of administrations in the United States, assume the U.S. government believes that forceful action must be taken against this African government, but most other governments come to believe that the UN should not take joint action in this case. Should the United States take action alone?

The United Nations building in New York City is the center of the organization's activities, which support global cooperation and world peace. *How does the UN influence international law?*

Advocacy

In the first two chapters of this unit, you were introduced to law and lawmaking. Now you will move on to learn about advocacy. Chapter 3 addresses one of the most important goals of *Street Law*—promoting positive involvement in public affairs. This chapter will teach you how citizen involvement can influence the lawmaking process.

In our democracy, the people are responsible for making the law, usually through their elected representatives. While voting is, of course, an important obligation of citizenship, an individual's lawmaking role is much broader than voting. Citizens are responsible for working to change laws that are not helping to solve problems. They are also responsible for working for new laws and policies that address problems in their communities, cities, states, or countries.

The Art of Advocacy

Advocacy is the active support of a cause. It also involves the art of persuading others to support the same cause. Advocacy is based on the careful gathering of facts, the development of excellent communication skills, and the creation of an effective plan and timeline. In order to advocate effectively, you must determine what level or levels of government are responsible for addressing the problem.

"Never doubt that a small group of thoughtful citizens can change the world. Indeed, it is the only thing that ever has."

— Margaret Mead

Street Law
online
Visit the *Street Law* Web site at streetlaw.glencoe.com for chapter-based information and resources.

Community members advocate their cause by publicly expressing their opinions.

29

High school students all over the country have become effective advocates for a variety of important issues ranging from national issues like violence prevention and homelessness to local concerns such as school attendance and school uniform policies. In some instances students have advocated change with their local schools and town (or city) councils; in other instances they have communicated with state representatives or with their representatives in Congress.

For example, high school students concerned about smoking in student bathrooms lobbied to get themselves on their school's safety committee. Once on the committee, they worked with the school resource officer, building principal, and assistant principal to convince their county board of education to give them funds to purchase smoke detectors. Then they lobbied their state representative, who was so impressed with the students' solution that he introduced a bill in the next legislative session to make smoke detectors mandatory in public school bathrooms across the entire state.

Law in *Action*

Changing the Law: Research and Role-Play

Divide the class into four groups. Each group should research one of the following proposed laws and answer the questions that follow. The proposed laws would:

- Require everyone under 18 years of age to wear a helmet while riding a bicycle on public property.

- Require a one-week waiting period and a background check for anyone who buys a handgun.

- Require that any teenage driver with less than one year of experience as a licensed driver drive only during daylight hours and never with more than one other teenage passenger (except siblings).

- Establish a curfew requiring that people under 18 years of age be off the streets by 12:00 A.M. Sunday through Thursday, and by 1:00 A.M. on Friday and Saturday unless commuting to and from work or traveling with a parent or guardian.

Problem 3.1

a. What arguments could be presented for and against the proposed law?

b. What groups, organizations, or businesses are likely to lobby for or against the proposed law? What techniques could they use to influence legislators?

c. Predict the outcome if your community held a voter referendum on the proposed law.

d. Role-play a meeting between legislators and groups of students who favor and oppose the proposed law. Discuss which lobbyists were effective, which were not, and why.

Lobbying

Lobbying is a way to influence the law-making process by convincing lawmakers to vote as you want them to. The word *lobbying* comes from the seventeenth century, when interested persons would corner legislators in the outer waiting room of the legislature—the lobby. While lobbying often has a negative connotation, it is actually a basic right protected by the U.S. Constitution. Lobbying involves the right of free speech and often other rights such as assembly, association, and freedom of the press.

A lobbyist is someone who tries to convince a lawmaker to vote for or against a particular issue. Anyone can be a lobbyist. As a private individual, you can lobby elected officials on issues you care about. You can influence elected officials by expressing your opinions individually or as part of a group, either in person or by letter, phone, or e-mail. Lobbyists also use political contributions, ads, favors, letter-writing campaigns, and other techniques to influence legislation.

Texas teens meet with Representative Terry Keel. *What techniques do lobbyists use to influence legislation?*

Steps to Take

Writing a Public Official

- **Write in your own words.** Personal letters are far more effective than form letters or petitions. Tell how the issue will affect you and your friends, family, or job.

- **Keep your letter short and to the point.** Deal with only one issue per letter. If you are writing about some proposed bill or legislation, identify it by name (for example, the National Consumer Protection Act) and by number if you know it (for example, H.R. 343 or S. 675).

- **Begin by telling the official why you are writing.** Ask the official to state his or her own position on the issue. Always request a reply, and ask the official to take some kind of definite action (for example, vote for or against the bill).

- **Always put your return address on the letter, sign and date it, and keep a copy, if possible.** Your letter doesn't have to be typed, but it should be legible. Perhaps most importantly, it should reach the official before the issue is voted on.

- **Consider using e-mail to contact public officials.**

Today, special interest groups and organizations lobby on behalf of every imaginable cause and issue. Businesses and organizations hire professional lobbyists to influence federal, state, and local legislators. For example, the National Rifle Association employs lobbyists to oppose restrictions on gun ownership and use, while Handgun Control, Inc., lobbies for gun control. Literally thousands of professional lobbyists work in Washington, D.C., and in state capitals throughout the country. Those who lobby the federal government must register with Congress and file reports four times a year. In these reports, they must identify their clients and the specific bills on which they are working. They must also indicate how much money they have been paid for their lobbying work and how much they have spent lobbying (for example, the costs of organizing grassroots letter-writing campaigns).

Professional lobbyists often have an advantage over grassroots lobbyists because they have more money behind them and they know legislators and their staffs personally. But grassroots lobbyists can be very effective, particularly when they join with others. Demonstration of grassroots support by large numbers of people is a very effective lobbying technique because legislators care about what voters think.

Many critics of the lobbying system in the United States say it enables some people and businesses to "buy legislation." It is true that contributors to political campaigns may have greater access to legislators and greater influence over how they vote on certain issues. However, others argue that lobbying is an integral part of American democracy. They claim that the use of money and influence is a legitimate way for groups to make their views heard.

Problem 3.2

a. Select a current issue that concerns you. Search the Internet to find sites that deal with this issue. What information is available at each site? Does the information seem reliable? How can you tell? Do any of the sites suggest strategies one could use to lobby for the issue?

b. Select a current issue that concerns you. Draft a letter about it to a public official. Use the guidelines listed in the Steps to Take box on page 31. For example, you may write to your mayor, city council member, state legislator, or federal representative or senator. Send your letter to the elected official and then analyze your letter and any reply you receive. Did the official acknowledge your concern for the issue? Did he or she answer your questions or provide additional information?

c. Do persons with more money have greater influence over legislators than those with less money? If so, is this unavoidable in a society like ours, or should steps be taken to reform the lobbying system? Conduct a class debate in which opposing groups discuss this issue.

Where You Live

What special interest, pressure, or lobbying groups exist in your state or community? On behalf of what issues or causes do these groups lobby? What techniques do they use?

Guidelines for Advocates

Before you begin to advocate, think through these steps for success:

1. **Identify the issue.** Think about your school or neighborhood. Is there a problem that needs to be addressed? How do you know it is a problem? Is it causing harm or preventing good? Can a new policy or rule address this issue?

2. **Set a goal.** Visualize a better tomorrow by answering the following questions:
   - What is the public policy solution you are proposing?
   - How will your community be improved if your policy is implemented?

3. **Become an expert on the issue.** Know the facts. Collect information to support your position. Monitor the media, search the Internet, go to the library, and interview community members. Learn both sides of the issue.

4. **Recruit allies. Identify roadblocks.** Identify coalitions already working on your issue. Recruit people harmed by the problem and others who may benefit from the policy change to act as allies. Identify your opponents. Why would they be against your proposed policy? What strategies might they use to resist your efforts? Who will be their allies?

5. **Identify your strategies.** To advocate effectively, you will likely use a variety of Take Action Strategies. Consider the following:
   - start a letter-writing campaign;
   - send out e-mail action alerts;
   - conduct a survey;
   - circulate a petition;
   - post your advocacy message on a community bulletin board;
   - coordinate a public rally, march, or vigil;
   - lead a protest or speak-out;
   - testify at a public hearing on your issue;
   - lobby in person; or
   - attend a community meeting.

6. **Plan for success.** What needs to be done first, second, etc.? Who will be responsible for what? How will you know you have been successful?

7. **Work the media.** The media is the best tool to get your solution out to a large audience. Seek to explain your issue in a convincing 15-second sound bite. Incorporate your "sound bite" into the following strategies:
   - write a letter to the editor;
   - hold a press conference;
   - create a public service announcement;
   - appear on a community cable television program or radio talk show; and
   - circulate posters, flyers, and brochures.

8. **Create a resource pool.** Money is only one resource that may be useful in your effort. Identify resources that exist within your group. What talents and skills do you and your team have to offer? Do you know a business or organization that may be willing to donate space, food, or other items to advance your cause?

Three Golden Rules for Advocacy

1. **Clarity:** create a single message and stick to it.
2. **Quantity:** create as large a network as possible to support your cause.
3. **Frequency:** get your message out to as many people as possible as frequently as possible.

Voting

Voting is a basic constitutional right. Eligible voters may vote for president, vice president, two U.S. senators, and one U.S. representative. They may also vote for governor, state legislators, and numerous other state, tribal, and local officials.

Initiative and Referendum

In a representative democracy, laws are usually made by elected legislators acting on the voters' behalf. However, in some situations, the people can vote directly on proposed laws. Initiatives and referenda allow citizens to circulate petitions and put proposed laws on the ballot. An initiative is a procedure that enables a specified number of voters to propose a law by petition. The proposed law is then submitted to either the electorate or the legislature for approval. A referendum occurs when a legislative act is referred to voters for final approval or rejection. Recent state referenda have been held on issues such as gun control, gay rights, abortion, environmental protection, and funding for schools, parks, roads, and other government programs. Many states also permit recall elections, which allow voters to remove elected officials from office.

Some argue that allowing voters to express their opinions directly through initiatives or referenda, rather than indirectly through representatives, is a more democratic system of lawmaking. Rather than being a true democracy, the United States is technically a republic, because the people elect representatives to vote on laws instead of voting on them directly. Supporters of the initiative and referendum processes point out that they promote direct involvement in lawmaking and reflect the true will of the people. Others argue that allowing direct voting on laws will sometimes result in the majority voting to take away rights from minorities.

Some form of direct voting exists in 24 states. In 1897 South Dakota became the first state to adopt statewide initiative and popular referendum. Most of the states that now have this system adopted it during the first two decades of the twentieth century. Through the initiative process many laws have been proposed including the right to vote for women, the eight-hour workday for government employees, term limits for elected officials, campaign finance reform, and environmental protection. This system has also been used to pass laws and establish public policy related to affirmative action.

Where You Live

Does your state allow referenda or initiatives? What issues have been on referenda in your state or local elections?

People go door-to-door encouraging voter registration. *What other ways can citizens register to vote?*

Who Can Vote?

To register to vote, you must be a U.S. citizen by birth or naturalization, at least 18 years old by the date of the election, and a resident of the community in which you register. It is a violation of federal law to falsely claim U.S. citizenship in order to register to vote. You cannot register to vote in more than one place at a time.

Registering to vote is easy. Applicants usually register by completing an application form in person or by mail. The National Voter Registration Act, also known as the Motor Voter Act, requires states to make registration forms available not only at motor vehicle departments, but also at numerous state offices, welfare offices, and agencies that serve the disabled. In addition, some organizations make voter registration forms available on the Internet.

A fair election requires that voters have access to information about the candidates, the issues, and the details of the voting process. Many organizations—some partisan and some non-partisan—provide election information on the Internet. The League of Women Voters (www.lwv.org) provides online information about federal, state and local elections and candidates. The League of Women Voters also sponsors DemocracyNet (www.dnet.org), an interactive Web site on which candidates address a wide range of topics by speaking directly to the voting public. On this site, candidates enter their own statements without any outside editing.

Information about federal elections, including past statistical data, is available from the Federal Election Commission (www.fec.gov). The FEC also provides online access to the National Mail Voter Registration Form, which has been translated into Spanish, Chinese, Pilipino, Japanese, Korean, Vietnamese, and Tagalog to encourage registration by language minority groups.

Registering to vote was not always as easy as it is today. African Americans did not receive the right to vote until 1870, with the passage of the Fifteenth Amendment. Until then, most states allowed only white males with property to vote. Women gained the right

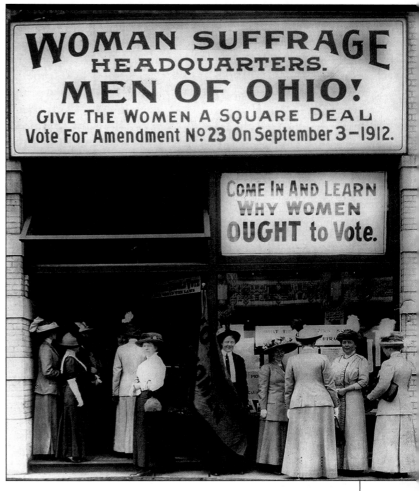

Women were effective in lobbying—their defeat of local candidates was especially persuasive in convincing Congress to pass the Nineteenth Amendment. *Why do some people believe that voting is the most important political right?*

to vote in 1920. Congress did not grant citizenship and therefore the right to vote to all Native Americans until 1924, although some Native Americans had been granted citizenship by special federal legislation before then (for example, veterans of World War I). Until 1965, some states had barriers such as poll taxes, literacy tests, and character exams that kept millions of people from voting. In 1971, the Twenty-sixth Amendment gave 18-year-olds the right to vote. Persons convicted of serious crimes usually lose the right to vote. In some states, however, these persons may regain the right to vote five years after their sentence is completed.

According to the Federal Election Commission, 76 percent of the voting age population was registered to vote in 2000, and 67.5 percent of those registered did in fact vote in the presidential election. This means that 51 percent of the voting age population voted in that election. During the past few decades, turnout in national elections has generally fallen from about 62 percent for the 1964 presidential election to 51 percent in 2000. Turnout for congressional elections in non-presidential election years is even lower. Voter turnout in Mexico and Canada are approximately the same as in the United States. However, many countries—including some of the world's newest democracies—have much higher voter turnout for national elections.

Problem 3.3

a. Make two lists: one of all the reasons given for voting, and another of all the reasons given for not voting.

b. Are you eligible to vote? If so, have you registered and voted? Why or why not?

c. The following proposals have been made to encourage more people to vote. Do you favor or oppose each proposal? Explain your answers.

- Levying a $20 fine on a person who is eligible to vote but does not do so and has no good excuse.
- Allowing people to register and vote on the same day.
- Lowering the voting age to 16 so students in high school could vote.
- Keeping the polls open for a week instead of one day.
- Holding all elections on weekends.
- Reducing people's taxes by $10 each if they vote.
- Allowing people to vote not just for representatives, but directly for or against issues on the ballot that they care about.
- Prohibiting the media from reporting poll results or projections until all polls are closed.
- Automatically registering everyone with a driver's license.

Where You Live

Where and how does one register to vote in your area? Is there a residency requirement? If so, what is it? What can people vote for in your area? When and where does one go to vote?

FIGURE 3.1 National Voter Turnout in Federal Elections: 1964–2000

Year	Voting Age Population	Registration	Turnout	% T/O of VAP
1964	114,090,000	73,715,818	70,644,592	61.92%
1966	116,132,000	76,288,283*	56,188,046	48.39%
1968	120,328,186	81,658,180	73,211,875	60.84%
1970	124,498,000	82,496,747**	58,014,338	46.60%
1972	140,776,000	97,328,541	77,718,554	55.21%
1974	146,336,000	96,199,020***	55,943,834	38.23%
1976	152,309,000	105,037,986	81,555,789	53.55%
1978	158,373,000	103,291,265	58,917,938	37.21%
1980	164,597,000	113,043,734	86,515,221	52.56%
1982	169,938,000	110,671,225	67,615,576	39.79%
1984	174,466,000	124,150,614	92,652,680	53.11%
1986	178,566,000	118,399,984	64,991,128	36.40%
1988	182,778,000	126,379,628	91,594,693	50.11%
1990	185,812,000	121,105,630	67,859,189	36.52%
1992	189,529,000	133,821,178	104,405,155	55.09%
1994	193,650,000	130,292,822	75,105,860	38.78%
1996	196,511,000	146,211,960	96,456,345	49.08%
1998	200,929,000	141,850,558	73,117,022	36.39%
2000	205,815,000	156,421,311	105,586,274	51.30%

*   Registrations from IA, KS, MS, MO, NE, and WY not included. Washington, D.C., did not have independent status.
**   Registrations from IA and MO not included.
*** Registrations from IA not included.

Problem 3.4

Study the table above showing voter turnout in federal elections from 1964 to 2000.

a. What voting trends do you notice when you compare voter turnout in the years when there was a presidential election to the years where there was no presidential election?

b. What voting trends do you notice over time when you look at the voter turnout in presidential elections?

c. Have registration figures, as a percentage of the voting age population, changed from 1976 to 2000? If so, how?

d. What conclusions can you draw from your analysis of this information?

• •

Sources: Data drawn from Congressional Research Service reports, Election Data Services Inc., and State Election Offices

Street Law online update Visit streetlaw.glencoe.com and click on **Textbook Update—Chapter 3** for an update of the data.

Campaign Finance Reform

Our 200-year tradition of privately financed elections has been accompanied by 200 years of campaign finance reform. However, efforts to counteract the influence of money on politics have usually been unsuccessful. Politicians have been quick to condemn fundraising scandals but slow to agree on campaign finance reform legislation.

According to the League of Women Voters, those who support campaign finance reform want to improve methods of financing political campaigns in order to ensure the public's right to know, combat corruption and undue influence, enable candidates to compete more equitably for public office, and promote citizen participation in the political process. Some groups argue for complete public funding of certain elections.

In recent years, federal elections have become extraordinarily expensive. To win, candidates have to be rich, be skillful fundraisers, or both. In fact, the candidate who raises the most money seldom loses the election.

Critics of the current system argue that (1) people of low or middle income cannot run for office successfully because they cannot raise huge sums of money; (2) special interests receive favors in exchange for substantial campaign contributions; and (3) elected officials spend too much time raising money and not enough time doing their jobs. Others argue that political contributions are a form of political speech and should be protected by the First Amendment to the

Senator John McCain (left) and Senator Russ Feingold (far right) hold a news conference after the approval of legislation to reduce the influence of big money in political campaigns. *Describe the arguments in support of campaign finance reform. Describe the arguments against it.*

U.S. Constitution. From their perspective it violates a voter's or a candidate's rights to limit the amount of money that can be contributed to a campaign.

Campaign finance laws are complex. During the 1990s large amounts of money were contributed by corporations and labor unions to political parties for the purpose of "party building." Laws during that time already prohibited corporations and labor unions from contributing directly to candidates, and individuals were limited in terms of how much they could contribute. The funds given to political parties were called "soft money." While the original idea behind these funds was to strengthen political parties through voter registration and get-out-the-vote drives, much of the soft money was used to pay for negative ads against candidates of the other party. These negative ads actually discouraged voters and reduced turnout, although they were often effective in terms of the outcome of the election.

Other significant funding outside of existing campaign finance rules occurred through ads that advocated issues such as a clean environment, gun control, and stiffer penalties for criminals rather than specifically for candidates. As long as these ads did not say "vote for," "elect," or "Jones for Congress," the courts viewed them as "issue ads." Unlike express campaign ads, the Federal Election Commission did not regulate the funding for these ads.

After years of discussion, Congress passed and President Bush signed the *Bipartisan Campaign Reform Act of 2002*. Many have referred to this as the McCain-Feingold law because those senators were the primary sponsors of the law in the U.S. Senate. This law was designed to ban the use of soft money in federal campaigns, prohibit certain types of broadcast political ads, and outlaw the solicitation of campaign contributions on federal property. Within a month of the passage of the bill, 84 plaintiffs filed 11 separate lawsuits challenging every provision of the act.

Problem 3.5

Read each of the statements that follow. Which is closest to your view in terms of campaign finance? Explain your reasoning.

a. The only way to take money out of politics is to have full federal funding of presidential and congressional elections.

b. In a free country it makes no sense to try to limit how much voters and candidates can give to elections. If people have the money and want to spend it on campaigns (either their own or for the candidate of their choice), they should be able to.

c. We have to balance the rights of those that want to contribute money to campaigns against the need to fight corruption and undue influence. The best way to do this is through disclosure laws—let everyone see who is giving money to candidates. If the candidates vote for the special interests that fund them, the voters can then vote that candidate out of office.

Settling Disputes

Effective community advocates work to solve community problems by proposing and lobbying for better laws and public policies. In doing so, they often use the legislative process to handle conflict. Conflict—sometimes called controversy in the public arena—creates an important opportunity to learn about issues that are of public concern in a democracy. The ability to collect the facts about an issue, formulate an opinion, listen to competing ideas, and discuss and debate the best course of action are all valuable civic skills in settling conflict. As you will learn later in this unit, courts can also help resolve conflicts, but most conflict is settled before it ever gets to court.

Since conflict is a natural part of everyday life, it is important to consider how to handle it. When we say we are in conflict with someone, we usually mean that we have had some type of unfriendly encounter. We frequently think of conflict as a problem, but it can also be productive. When conflict is managed responsibly, it can provide a great opportunity to learn. So the most important question is not whether there is going to be conflict in your life, but how you will handle it.

There are sometimes disadvantages in going to court to resolve conflict. The court process can be time-consuming and expensive. Going to court can even make some problems worse. For example, in divorces and child custody disputes, going to court often causes extreme anger and bitterness. Some people feel that by going to court, they will lose even if they win!

> *"Our task is not to fix the blame for the past . . . but to fix the course for the future."*
>
> — John F. Kennedy

Street Law online

Visit the *Street Law* Web site at streetlaw.glencoe.com for chapter-based information and resources.

Conflict is part of everyday life.

Methods for Solving Disputes

Among the most common methods for solving disputes out of court are negotiation, arbitration, and mediation. As you will learn, negotiation is the most informal of these methods. Arbitration is more formal, and in some ways, it resembles going to court. Mediation is also more formal than negotiation.

Negotiation is the process by which people involved in a dispute discuss their problem and try to reach a solution acceptable to all. It is important to learn to negotiate because the skills involved in handling conflict responsibly are used everyday by people in all aspects of life. You negotiate when you have a disagreement with your parents, your friends, or your teacher and you work out an agreement. The informality of negotiation makes it ideal for many types of problems. Sometimes people hire attorneys to negotiate for them. For example, people involved in auto accidents sometimes hire attorneys to negotiate with the insurance company over payments for injuries or damages to their cars. However, even if you use an attorney to negotiate, you must approve any agreement before it becomes final. Attorneys sometimes file a case in court and then still attempt to work out a settlement, or agreement, before the case goes to trial. A large number of civil cases are settled this way, saving both time and money.

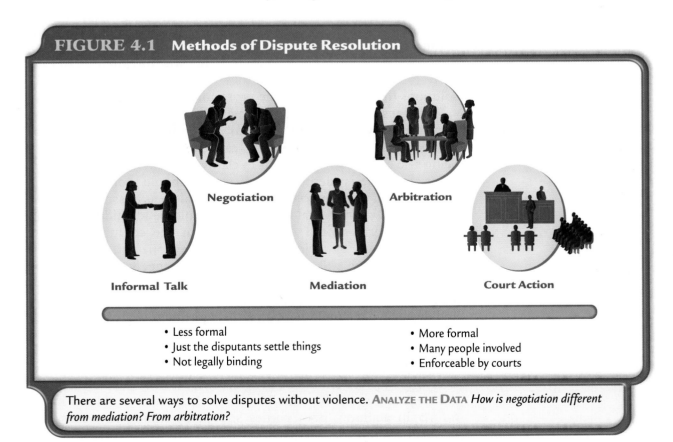

FIGURE 4.1   Methods of Dispute Resolution

Negotiation

Arbitration

Informal Talk

Mediation

Court Action

- Less formal
- Just the disputants settle things
- Not legally binding

- More formal
- Many people involved
- Enforceable by courts

There are several ways to solve disputes without violence. ANALYZE THE DATA *How is negotiation different from mediation? From arbitration?*

Divorce negotiations often become heated as both parties try to agree upon the best possible solutions to their problems. *Why is it important to separate the demands (positions) from what the parties really want (interests) during the negotiation process?*

It is helpful to think of negotiation in three phases—preparation for negotiation, negotiation, and post-negotiation. Each phase contains a set of steps that encourage a fair negotiation process. Each party in the dispute should follow all of the steps in each phase to make sure the process helps to resolve the problem.

The steps in the first phase help both parties prepare to negotiate. First, all involved should come to the discussion with a sincere interest in settling the problem. Then the issue that is causing the conflict must be identified as clearly as possible. Everyone should think about the issue that is really causing the problem, and try to separate the demands (positions) from what the parties really want (interests). In the third step, each party should consider the issue from the perspective of the other in order to help them understand the concerns and feelings on the other side of the conflict. Finally, each party should sort out his or her feelings about the problem so they both can understand how the interests of each party differ. From this, both parties should identify two workable solutions that might resolve the problem.

The steps in the second phase focus on the negotiation itself. Both parties must work together to identify the real issue that needs to be resolved. This involves listening carefully, understanding what is being said, and asking questions to clarify and gain more information. Once the issue is identified, both parties should work together to create a list of as many solutions to the problem as possible. Then the two or three most workable solutions should be identified from this list. Each party should be realistic about the solutions that are chosen, perhaps by giving examples so everyone can see how the potential solution will work. To conclude the negotiation, the main points of the agreement should be repeated to be sure that both parties understand them. It is also a good idea to write down the agreement and decide what should happen if the agreement is broken.

In the third phase of the negotiation process both parties to the dispute should make a few final decisions. For example, they should decide what to tell others about how the problem was handled. Everyone involved should be in agreement on what people outside of the negotiation will be told. This could help deter problems in the future. In addition, both parties should be willing to discuss the problem again if the agreement does not seem to be working.

In **arbitration,** both parties to a dispute agree to have one or more persons listen to their arguments and make a decision for them. The arbitrator is like a judge, but the process is less formal than a trial. Arbitrators, like judges, have the authority to make the final decision, and the parties must follow it (except in nonbinding arbitration). Arbitration is common in contract and labor-management disputes and in some international law cases. Agreements between labor unions and employers include arbitration clauses. This means that the union and the employer agree in advance to submit certain disputes to arbitration and to be bound by the arbitrator's decision.

Mediation is another method of alternative dispute resolution. It takes place when a third person helps the disputing parties talk about their problem and settle their differences. Unlike arbitrators, mediators cannot impose a decision on the parties. The agreement is the result of the parties' willingness to listen carefully to each other and

For Your Information . . .

Steps in a Typical Mediation Session

Step 1. Introduction
The mediator helps the people involved in the dispute feel at ease and explains the ground rules for behavior during the mediation. These ground rules can include such things as agreeing to remain seated and agreeing that any party may request a break during the mediation.

Step 2. Telling the Story
Each person tells what happened. The person who brings up the problem usually tells his or her side of the story first. No interruptions are allowed. Then the other person explains his or her side. These people are the disputants.

Step 3. Identifying Positions and Interests
The mediator tries to make certain that each disputant is clearly understood by listening carefully to each side, summarizing each person's view, and asking questions. Sometimes the mediator will encourage the disputants to ask questions and summarize each other's point of view in order to check for understanding.

Step 4. Identifying Alternative Solutions
The disputants think of possible solutions to the problem. The mediator makes a list and then asks each disputant to explain his or her feelings about each possible solution. Sometimes in a difficult situation, the mediator might also meet with each disputant separately.

Step 5. Revising and Discussing Solutions
Based on the feelings of the disputants involved, the mediator may help the disputants change some of the possible solutions and identify a better solution to which the disputants can agree.

Step 6. Reaching an Agreement
The mediator helps the disputants reach an agreement that both can accept. The agreement is written down. The disputants also discuss what will happen if they find out the agreement isn't working for them.

come up with a reasonable settlement. The mediator acts as a neutral third party by listening carefully to both sides. He or she also tries to help the parties understand each other's positions and find ways to resolve the dispute. Mediation is voluntary; the disputants themselves must reach a decision about the problem. Mediation allows the disputants to air their feelings, avoids placing blame, and concentrates on the future relationship between the parties. The key issue is how the disputants will work or live together after the mediation.

Mediation is used to solve a variety of disputes. Community mediation programs help settle disputes between husbands and wives, landlords and tenants, and consumers and businesses. For example, the Better Business Bureau (BBB) often mediates disputes between shoppers and store owners. In other places, neighborhood justice centers help settle disputes between community residents. Government agencies and some universities have **ombudspersons** who investigate complaints and then help the parties reach some agreement. Some schools train students to mediate conflicts and settle disputes that occur at school. To locate a mediation program in your community, contact your local court, district attorney's office, or social services agency.

The key to the success of both negotiation and mediation is that the ideas for resolving the conflict come from the people who have the conflict. The disputants take responsibility for their actions and work out the problem. Unlike court cases, both of these processes result in an agreement that is focused on the future relationship between the disputing parties. Because the solution comes from the parties, they are more interested in making the solution work.

Problem 4.1

Examine the following situations and decide the best method for solving each problem. Consider informal discussion, negotiation, arbitration, mediation, going to court (including small claims court), a government agency, and other methods. Discuss the reasons for your answers.

a. Two sisters share a room. However, they disagree over how the room should be arranged and decorated.

b. A new stereo breaks after two weeks, and the salesperson refuses to fix it.

c. A landlord will not make needed repairs because he believes the tenant caused the damage.

d. A labor union and an employer disagree over the wages and conditions of employment.

e. A married couple wants a divorce.

f. The Internal Revenue Service sends you a letter claiming that you owe another $200 in taxes. You disagree.

g. Carl invites Raquel to the prom, and she agrees to go with him. Then Miguel invites her to the prom. Raquel really wants to go with Miguel and accepts his invitation. Carl finds out about her decision after he has purchased flowers and paid for a limousine to take them to the prom.

Where You Live

Are there any programs in your community that could be used by people who would like to find an alternative to going to court? What types of disputes do these programs handle? How successful are the alternative procedures? Is there a peer mediation program in your school?

Law in *Action*

Problems at the Mall

Magda, David, and Rashida have been friends since the sixth grade. One of their favorite activities is to go to the mall and look around in the stores. Sometimes they make purchases and sometimes they are just window-shopping. There are lots of young people who do this, and it is fun to see people and hang out.

Recently, a number of stores in the mall have experienced an increase in shoplifting and vandalism. As a result, the stores have made a policy that no one under 16 years of age can enter without a parent or guardian. The new rules also state that if you are between the ages of 16 and 18 you cannot enter the store in groups larger than two. Other teens have to wait outside until each pair leaves. Store owners have threatened to call the police if the young people give them any trouble about the new policies.

This policy makes Magda, David, and Rashida angry. They feel it is unfair. After all, they are paying customers and spend money in these stores. Why is the rule directed only at young people? They do not want to get into trouble with the police, but they don't understand why they have to be treated as problems when they have not done anything wrong.

The manager of the shopping mall along with one of the store owners has agreed to meet with two of the teens and a mediator to try to find some workable solutions.

Teens at the mall

Problem 4.2

In preparation for the mediation session, the disputants should consider the following issues:

1. What are your concerns? How would you state the issue in the dispute?

2. What is your starting position (demand)? What are your underlying interests (what do you really want)?

3. What is the best conceivable outcome from your perspective?

4. What do you think the starting position and underlying interests of the other side will be?

5. Identify two workable solutions that would solve the conflict.

Use the Steps in a Typical Mediation Session on page 43 to walk through the process and develop a reasonable solution for the disputants.

The Court System

The United States has many court systems. Each state has its own court system, and there is also a system of federal courts. Each of these systems has trial and appeals courts. There are also a number of tribal justice systems. The highest court in the land is the Supreme Court of the United States. The Supreme Court hears appeals from the other court systems.

Trial Courts

Trial courts listen to testimony, consider evidence, and decide the facts in disputed situations. Evidence is provided by witnesses who are called to testify in the case. In a trial there are two parties, or sides, to each case. In a civil trial, the party bringing the legal action is called the plaintiff. In a criminal trial, the government (state or federal) initiates the case and serves as the prosecutor. In both civil and criminal trials, the party responding to the plaintiff (civil) or prosecution (criminal) is called the defendant. Once a trial court has made a decision, the losing party may be able to appeal the decision to an appellate, or appeals, court.

"Three features mark the Anglo-American system as different from all others. One is the extent to which our law is formed in litigation. Another feature is the way we conduct these cases: we pit antagonists against each other, to cast up from their struggles the material of decisions. A third—and largest in the public consciousness—is the trial by jury."

— Charles Rembar,
The Law of the Land

Street Law *online*

Visit the *Street Law* Web site at streetlaw.glencoe.com for chapter-based information and resources.

The use of juries builds the values of democracy into the court system.

Judges play a more active role under the inquisitional system than they do in the adversarial system. *In what ways are judges more involved in the court proceedings of an inquisitional system?*

The trial system in the United States is an **adversarial system.** This means it is a contest between opposing sides, or adversaries. The theory is that the trier of fact (the judge or jury) will be able to determine the truth if the opposing parties present their best arguments and show the weaknesses in the other side's case.

The adversarial process is not the only method for handling legal disputes. Many countries have different trial systems. Some European countries use the **inquisitional system,** in which the judge is active in questioning witnesses and controlling the court process, including the gathering and presenting of evidence. These judges can order witnesses to appear, conduct searches, present and comment on evidence, and, in general, take the lead role in trying to uncover the truth. This differs from the adversarial process, in which these matters are left to the competing parties, with a decision being made by the judge or jury based on the arguments and evidence presented.

The adversarial process is often criticized. Critics say that it is not the best method for discovering the truth with respect to the facts of a specific case. They compare the adversarial process to a battle in which lawyers act as enemies, making every effort *not* to present *all* the evidence. According to this view, the goal of trial is "victory, not truth or justice." Despite its drawbacks, the adversarial process is the cornerstone of the American legal system. Most attorneys believe that approaching the same set of facts from totally different perspectives will uncover more truth than would other methods.

Problem 5.1

a. Do you think the adversarial system is the best method for solving disputes? Why or why not?

b. Indicate whether you agree or disagree with the following statement: "It is better that ten guilty persons go free than that one innocent person suffer conviction." Explain your answer.

c. In a criminal case, should a lawyer defend a client he or she knows is guilty? Would you defend someone you knew was guilty? Explain.

Judges and juries are essential parts of our legal system. The judge presides over the trial and has the duty of protecting the rights of those involved. Judges also make sure that attorneys follow the rules of evidence and trial procedure. In nonjury trials, the judge determines the facts of the case and renders a judgment. In jury trials, the judge is required to instruct the jury as to the law involved in the case. Finally, in criminal trials in most states, judges sentence individuals convicted of committing crimes.

The Sixth Amendment to the U.S. Constitution guarantees the right to trial by jury in criminal cases. This right applies in both federal and state courts. The Seventh Amendment guarantees a right to trial by jury in civil cases in federal courts. This right has not been extended to state courts, but many state constitutions confer a right to jury trial in civil cases. However, the fact that a constitution protects the right to trial by jury does not mean that a jury is required in every case. Juries are not used as often as one might think. In civil cases, either the plaintiff or the defendant may request a jury trial. In criminal cases, the defendant decides whether there will be a jury. Most civil cases result in out-of-court settlements or trials by a judge. Most criminal cases are never brought to trial. Instead they are disposed of by a plea bargain, or pretrial agreement, between the government (prosecutor) and the defendant.

If a jury trial is requested, a jury is selected and charged with the task of determining the facts and applying the law in a particular case. To serve on a jury, you must be a U.S. citizen, at least 18 years old, able to speak and understand English, and a resident of the state. As citizens we have a duty to serve on juries when called upon. At one time, people from certain occupations were exempt from jury service. These included members of the clergy, attorneys, physicians, police officers, firefighters, and persons unable to undertake juror tasks because of mental or physical disability. In some places, these persons are no longer excluded. Convicted felons are usually ineligible for jury service unless their civil rights have been restored. People who are not exempt and are called for jury duty are sometimes excused if they can show "undue hardship or extreme inconvenience."

"We have a jury system which is superior to any in the world. Its efficiency is only marred by the difficulty of finding twelve men every day who don't know anything and can't read."

— Mark Twain

For Your Information . . .

Steps in a Trial

The following is a short explanation of the steps in either a civil or a criminal trial.

Step 1. Opening Statement by Plaintiff or Prosecutor

Plaintiff's attorney (in civil cases) or the prosecutor (in criminal cases) explains to the trier of fact (the judge or jury) the evidence to be presented as proof of the allegations (unproven statements) in the written papers filed with the court.

Step 2. Opening Statement by Defense

Defendant's attorney explains evidence to be presented to disprove the allegations made by the plaintiff or prosecutor.

Step 3. Direct Examination by Plaintiff or Prosecutor

Each witness for the plaintiff or prosecution is questioned. Other evidence (such as documents and physical evidence) in favor of the plaintiff or prosecution is presented.

Step 4. Cross-Examination by Defense

The defense has the opportunity to question each witness. Questioning is designed to break down the story or to discredit the witness.

Step 5. Motions

If the prosecution's or plaintiff's basic case has not been established from the evidence introduced, the judge can end the case by granting a motion (oral request) made by the defendant's attorney.

Step 6. Direct Examination by Defense

Each defense witness is questioned.

Step 7. Cross-Examination by Plaintiff or Prosecutor

Each defense witness is cross-examined.

Step 8. Closing Statement by Plaintiff or Prosecutor

Prosecutor or plaintiff's attorney reviews

Cross-examination

all the evidence presented (noting uncontradicted facts), and asks for a finding of guilty (in criminal cases) or a finding for the plaintiff (in civil cases).

Step 9. Closing Statement by Defense

Same as closing statement by prosecution/ plaintiff. The defense asks for a finding of not guilty (in criminal cases) or for a finding for the defendant (in civil cases).

Step 10. Rebuttal Argument

Prosecutor or plaintiff has the right to make additional closing arguments that respond to points made by the defense.

Step 11. Jury Instructions

Judge instructs jury as to the law that applies in the case.

Step 12. Verdict

In most states, a unanimous decision is required for a verdict. If the jury cannot reach a unanimous decision, it is a hung jury, and the case may be tried again.

Jury service is a very important civic duty. It is necessary to preserve the constitutional right to trial by jury. To determine who is called for jury duty, the clerk of the court uses a list with names of registered voters, licensed drivers, or some combination of the two. Usually a questionnaire is sent out to potential jurors to determine whether they are eligible to serve. Employers are required to let their employees take time off for jury service. Most courts pay jurors a small daily stipend, and some courts also provide a transportation fee. Some employers pay their employees during their jury service, but they are not required to do so. To reduce the burden of jury service, many courts have instituted a one-day, one-trial plan. A juror must show up on the day called. A juror selected for a trial on that day must then return for the duration of the trial. If not selected, the juror will not be called again for some period of time, usually at least a year.

> Attorneys for both the defense and the prosecution screen prospective jurors through the process of voir dire examination. *Why might a prospective juror be dismissed?*

Once selected, jurors are assigned to specific cases after being screened through a process known as **voir dire** examination. In this process, opposing lawyers question each prospective juror to discover any prejudices or preconceived opinions concerning the case. After questioning each juror, the opposing attorneys may request the removal of any juror who appears incapable of rendering a fair and impartial verdict. This is called **removal for cause.** In addition, each attorney is allowed a limited number of **peremptory challenges.** This means the attorneys can have prospective jurors removed without stating a cause.

Problem 5.2

a. Has anyone in your family ever served on a jury? What type of case was involved?

b. Why would someone choose not to have a jury trial in a civil case? In a criminal case?

c. What reasons can you give for excluding from jury service members of the clergy, attorneys, physicians, police officers, and convicted felons? Should everyone be required to serve on juries? Give your reasons.

d. If you were a defense attorney questioning jurors at the voir dire in a murder trial, what questions would you ask potential jurors to determine whether they could render a fair and impartial verdict?

e. For what reasons might an attorney use a peremptory challenge?

"A jury consists of twelve persons chosen to decide who has the better lawyer."

— Robert Frost

Appeals Courts

In an **appeals court,** one party presents arguments asking the court to review the decision of the trial court. The other party presents arguments supporting the decision of the trial court. There are no juries or witnesses, and no new evidence is presented. Only lawyers appear before the judges to make legal arguments.

Not everyone who loses a trial can appeal. Usually, an appeal is possible only when there is a claim that the trial court has committed an **error of law.** An **error of law** occurs when the judge makes a mistake as to the law applicable in the case. For example, a judge might give the wrong instructions to the jury or permit evidence that should not be allowed. A judge's error is considered minor as long as it does not affect the outcome of the trial. In cases involving minor errors of law, the trial court decision will not be reversed.

When an appeals court decides a case, it issues a written opinion or ruling. This opinion sets a **precedent** for similar cases in the future. All lower courts in the area where the decision was made must follow the precedent set in the opinion. This is what is meant by courts "making law." However, a higher court has the power to reverse or change the precedent. Courts in other parts of the country are not required to follow the precedent. A court in another jurisdiction or state can disagree with this precedent.

Typically, a panel of judges—or justices, as appellate judges are sometimes called—decides such cases. The panel may consist of three or more judges. Nine justices hear cases argued before the Supreme Court of the United States.

When these judges disagree on a decision, two or more written opinions may be issued in the same case. The majority opinion states the decision of the court. Judges who disagree with the majority opinion may issue a separate document called a **dissenting opinion,** which states the reasons for the disagreement. In some instances, judges who agree with the majority opinion, but for reasons different from those used to support the majority opinion, may write a **concurring opinion.**

Dissenting opinions are important because their reasoning may become the basis of future majority opinions. As society and the views of judges on appellate courts change, so can legal opinion. An example is the 1896 case of *Plessy* v. *Ferguson*, which upheld racial segregation in railroad cars as long as facilities for whites and African Americans were "separate but equal."

Where You Live

How are jurors selected by the courts in your community? How many persons are on the jury in a civil trial? In a criminal trial? Is a unanimous verdict required in a civil trial? In a criminal trial?

Only lawyers appear to make legal arguments before judges in an appellate court. *When is an appeal possible?*

Taking a Car by Mistake

Joe Harper left the key in his 2002 blue sports utility vehicle while he ran an errand. When he came back an hour later, he got into someone else's blue SUV by mistake. This car also had the key in the ignition. Harper, who did not notice it was a different car, started it and drove away. He was arrested for auto theft as a result of his mistake.

At the trial, the judge told the jury it was not necessary for them to consider whether Harper intended to steal the car. Instead, the judge instructed the jury that to find Harper guilty of auto theft, they only had to decide whether he was caught driving a car that was not his. Using these guidelines, the jury found Joe Harper guilty.

This case illustrates an error of law that could be appealed. Auto theft law requires that the accused person must have intended to steal the car. Since Harper did not intend to steal the car, the guilty verdict could be reversed by an appellate court.

Justice John Marshall Harlan dissented from the majority opinion because it allowed a state to pass regulations solely based on race, which he believed violated the U.S. Constitution. In the 1954 precedent-setting case of *Brown* v. *Board of Education,* some of the reasoning expressed in Justice Harlan's dissent in *Plessy* was accepted by the Supreme Court, and the "separate but equal" doctrine was declared unconstitutional.

State and Federal Court Systems

Figure 5.1 illustrates the two separate court systems in the United States—state and federal. State courts are courts of general jurisdiction. They can hear cases that deal with state law as well as many areas of federal law. The federal courts are courts of limited jurisdiction. Their power is limited to deciding certain types of cases. Federal courts hear criminal and civil cases involving federal law. They also hear some civil cases involving parties from different states when the amount in dispute is more than $75,000. Federal trial courts are known as U.S. District Courts. If you lose a trial in the U.S. District Court, you may be able to appeal to the U.S. Circuit Court of Appeals in your region. The United States has 94 district courts and 13 circuit courts. The court of final appeal is the U.S. Supreme Court.

State Courts

Most state court systems resemble the federal courts in structure and procedure. All states have trial courts. These are called superior, county, district, or municipal courts, depending on the state. State

Landmark Supreme Court Cases

Visit the Landmark Supreme Court Cases Web site at landmarkcases.org for information and activities about *Plessy* v. *Ferguson* and *Brown* v. *Board of Education.*

trial courts are often specialized to deal with specific legal areas. Examples include family, traffic, criminal, probate, and small claims courts.

Family or domestic relations courts hear actions involving divorce, separation, and child custody. Cases involving juveniles and intrafamily offenses (fights within families) may also be heard. Sometimes, cases involving juveniles are heard in a special juvenile court. Traffic courts hear actions involving violations committed by persons driving motor vehicles. Criminal courts hear cases involving violations of laws for which the violators could go to jail. Frequently, criminal court is divided between felony and misdemeanor cases. Probate courts handle cases involving wills and claims against the estates of persons who die with or without a will. Small claims courts hear cases involving small amounts of money (maximums of $500, $750, $1,000, or more, depending on the state). Individuals may bring cases to small claims court without lawyers—though it is sometimes advised that lawyers be present—and the court fees are low.

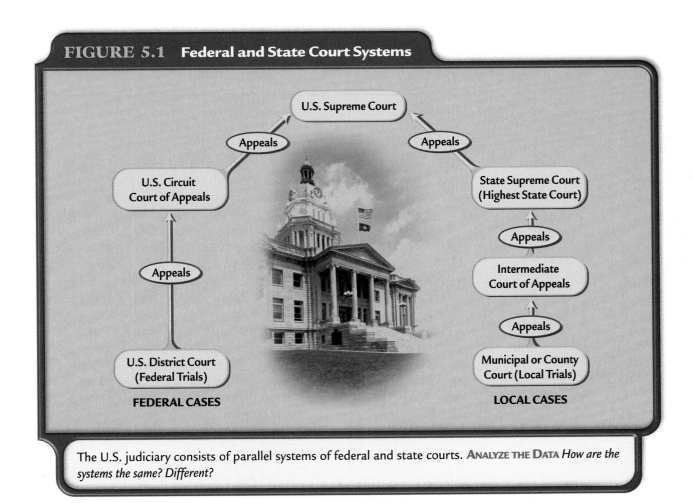

FIGURE 5.1   Federal and State Court Systems

U.S. Supreme Court

Appeals

Appeals

U.S. Circuit Court of Appeals

State Supreme Court (Highest State Court)

Appeals

Appeals

Intermediate Court of Appeals

Appeals

U.S. District Court (Federal Trials)

Municipal or County Court (Local Trials)

FEDERAL CASES

LOCAL CASES

The U.S. judiciary consists of parallel systems of federal and state courts. ANALYZE THE DATA *How are the systems the same? Different?*

If you lose your case in the trial court, you may be able to appeal to an intermediate court of appeals or, in some states, directly to the state supreme court. If a state supreme court decision involves only state law, it can be appealed no further. Each state's highest court has the final say on interpretation of state laws and the state constitution. If a state supreme court decision involves federal law or a federal constitutional issue, it can then be appealed to the U.S. Supreme Court.

Problem 5.3

Consider the following cases. For each, decide whether the case will be tried in a federal or state court. To what court could each case be appealed? Explain your answer. Then give an example, different from those listed, of a case that could be heard in a state court and a case that could be heard in a federal court.

a. A state sues a neighboring state for dumping waste in a river that borders both states.

b. A wife sues her husband for divorce.

c. A person is prosecuted for assaulting a neighbor.

d. Two cars collide. One driver sues the other for hospital bills and auto repairs.

e. A group of parents sues the local school board, asking that their children's school be desegregated.

Federal Courts

Article III of the U.S. Constitution creates a Supreme Court and gives Congress the power to create lower courts. Congress has divided the country into 94 federal judicial districts, with each having a district court known as a federal trial court. Within each district is a U.S. bankruptcy court that administers the federal bankruptcy laws. Approximately 70 percent of the cases filed in federal court each year are bankruptcy cases. (Bankruptcy is discussed in Chapter 25 on pages 307–308.) As Figure 5.2 shows, some federal judicial districts cover an entire state, while other states have several districts within their boundaries.

Congress placed the 94 districts in 12 regional circuits, each of which has a court of appeals. Court of appeals judges handle appeals of trial court decisions to determine whether district court judges applied the law correctly. There is also a U.S. Court of Appeals for the Federal Circuit, whose jurisdiction is defined by subject matter rather than by geography. This court, which meets in Washington, D.C., hears appeals from the U.S. Court of International Trade (which hears cases that deal with international trade and customs), the U.S. Court of Federal Claims (which hears claims for money damages against the federal government), and the U.S. Patent and Trademark Office

FIGURE 5.2 The Federal Judicial Circuits

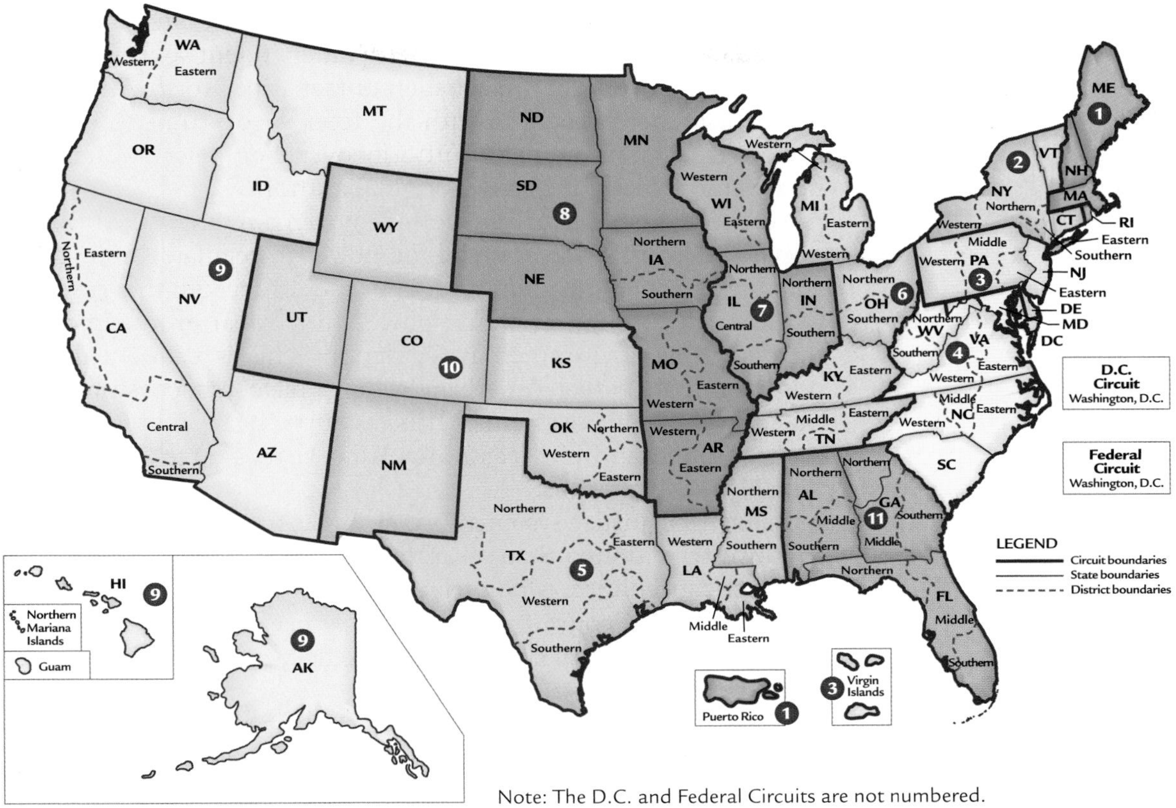

LEGEND
— Circuit boundaries
— State boundaries
- - - District boundaries

Note: The D.C. and Federal Circuits are not numbered.

Congress created district courts to serve as trial courts for federal cases. **ANALYZE THE DATA** *Which federal judicial circuit hears cases from the state where you live?*

(which hears administrative matters related to patents and trademarks). The Federal Circuit also hears appeals from the U.S. Tax Court and from the Court of Veterans Appeals. The Federal Circuit hears cases from all over the country, but only those that deal with specific types of issues. In creating this court, Congress believed that its judges would develop special expertise in these cases.

Overall, the federal courts handle about 1,000,000 cases per year and the state court systems handle about 30,000,000 cases per year. About 1,700 federal judges and about 30,000 state court judges decide these cases.

Tribal Courts

Many people, especially those who live in states with small Native American populations, do not realize that several hundred Indian tribal groups govern reservations in the United States today. Native American tribal groups are no longer independent sovereigns, as they were when Europeans first made contact with North America. As a result of their relationship with the federal government, the groups no longer possess complete authority over their reservations; they do, however, retain some of their original authority.

Sometimes the tribal powers that remain are called **inherent powers.** These powers include the power to regulate family relationships, tribal membership, and law and order on the reservation. Occasionally Congress grants power to a tribal group in a certain area, such as environmental regulation. This is called a **delegated power.** Most Native American groups have justice systems often called tribal court systems. Tribal courts hear a broad range of both criminal and civil cases involving both Native Americans and non-Native Americans.

Some tribal justice systems—for example, those of the Pueblos in the southwestern United States—are traditional and show little influence of American culture. Many tribal justice systems, however, resemble Anglo-American court systems, primarily because of federal influence. Still, the work of tribal courts strongly reflects the culture of the people who work in them.

Some confusion and a great deal of controversy surround the power of tribal governments and tribal courts. Both federal law and tribal law determine the jurisdiction of tribal courts. In the criminal area, for example, federal law gives federal courts jurisdiction over many felonies committed by Native Americans on the reservation. The criminal sentencing authority of tribal courts is limited to imprisonment for no longer than one year and a fine of no more than $5,000. Therefore, some tribal groups have chosen to criminalize only minor offenses, while others also criminalize more serious offenses. The United States Supreme Court has ruled that inherent tribal authority over the reservation no longer includes the authority to prosecute non-Native Americans for crimes committed on the reservation.

The power of a tribal court to hear civil matters on the reservation appears to be very broad. In recent years, the United States Supreme

Navajo Supreme Court Associate Justices Lorene Ferguson and Marcella King-Ben question counsel during oral arguments. *Why are many tribal court systems similar to Anglo-American court systems?*

Court has issued several decisions supporting tribal court authority and recognizing tribal courts as essential to the preservation of contemporary tribal self-government.

The Supreme Court of the United States

The most important legal precedents are established by the U.S. Supreme Court, where nine justices hear each case and a majority rules. All courts in the United States must follow U.S. Supreme Court decisions. Many laws have been changed by the Supreme Court. For example, the Supreme Court has upheld all-male draft registration and ended racial segregation in public schools.

The Supreme Court does not accept all appeals that are brought to it. Each year, about 8,000 cases are appealed to the Court. The justices issue complete written opinions on about 80 cases each year.

More than half of the cases appealed to the Court each year come from inmates in prison. Very few of these petitions for certiorari—a request of a lower court to send up its records—are granted by the Supreme Court. In fact, nearly 99 percent of all such requests for petitions for certiorari are denied by the Court. With few exceptions (such as federal voting rights cases), the Supreme Court does not have to hear a case appealed to it. With so many cases to choose from, it is able to set its own agenda. Most often the Court decides to grant a petition for certiorari when there is a difference of opinion among lower courts on the issue presented. The Court also takes cases that it believes deal with critical national policy issues.

The party who appeals to the Supreme Court is generally the losing party in an appellate case that was argued in a federal circuit court of appeals or a state supreme court. This party's first step is to request in writing that the Court hear the case. The written legal briefs, or legal arguments, initially submitted to the Court emphasize *why* the case should be heard rather than how it should be decided. The party that has won the case in the lower court submits a brief arguing why the case should not be heard. If the party appealing gets four of the nine justices to agree to hear the case, then the petition for certiorari is granted. This is the one exception to majority rule at the Court.

If the Court decides to hear the case, the parties then write briefs arguing to the Court *how* the case should be decided, and an oral argument is scheduled at the Court. During this hour-long argument, which is open to the public, each side has 30 minutes to present its case to the justices. The justices, who have already read the briefs and studied the case, ask many questions of the lawyers. Once the case has been argued, the justices meet in a private conference to discuss the case, and the process of drafting an opinion begins. While the media tend to emphasize the disagreements among the justices, nearly half of the cases are decided by a unanimous vote of 9 to 0.

Independent Courts

A key element of a democracy is that courts must act impartially and make fair decisions without being influenced by outside forces.

In the state courts, many judges are elected through popular elections. These elections are either nonpartisan—without endorsement by political parties—or partisan, with candidates endorsed by a political party.

One method of trying to ensure an independent judiciary is to appoint judges for a life term. This is done in the federal system and in a few states. Judges appointed for a life term can make decisions in cases without concern about how it might affect their reelection. Some believe that the need to raise funds for elections can result in a judge's not being impartial when deciding a particular case.

Another method of trying to preserve judges' independence is known as merit selection. In this approach, a judicial commission made up of lawyers, judges, and sometimes laypeople either decides who will be a judge or sends names of judicial candidates to the governor, who then chooses judges from that list.

Independent courts are an integral part of the U.S. system of government. Under the system of checks and balances, courts have the power of judicial review and can decide whether actions by a coequal branch violate the Constitution. For example, sometimes the U.S. Supreme Court has ruled that the president or Congress has violated the Constitution.

In many other countries, judges and courts are not independent. They are influenced or in some cases completely controlled by the legislature or the president of a country.

Problem 5.4

Do these actions violate judicial independence? Explain your reasons.

a. Judge Eric Donovan's decision in an abortion case is criticized in a local newspaper editorial.

b. Marsha Monroe is running for election to be a judge on her state's supreme court. She visits the offices of George Sanchez, the president of a large corporation, and asks for a donation of $1,000 to help in her campaign.

c. Some U.S. senators are unhappy about decisions of U.S. District Court Judge Marion Jones, who has ruled that the death penalty can never be used again in her jurisdiction because she believes that the U.S. Supreme Court decisions in this area are wrong. The senators call for Judge Jones to resign or be impeached by the Senate.

d. Judge Max Kaufman presides over a case involving a corporation. A distant cousin of his is employed by that corporation and is a witness for the corporation at the trial. Judge Kaufman rules for the corporation in the case.

e. Judge Maureen Kim is running for reelection and knows that crime is a big issue with the voters in her state. In the months just before the election, she hands down some unusually long sentences for drug offenses.

f. Arnold Swartz is running for election as county judge. He campaigns that he will never make a ruling in a case that takes money away from the education of children in the county.

The federal government participates in a significant number of the cases before the Court. Sometimes the United States is a party to the case. More often, it is involved through the Office of the Solicitor General of the United States. The solicitor general's office represents the United States in court. When a party files a petition for certiorari and the solicitor general's office also asks the Court to take the case, the Court is much more likely to grant review. In these cases a lawyer from the solicitor general's office may also participate in the oral argument, presenting the federal government's views—and answering the justices' questions—during 10 of the 30 minutes allotted to the party whose side the United States supports.

The Court's term begins on the first Monday of each October, and final decisions on cases argued during that term are handed down by the end of June of the following calendar year. In a typical year, about 75 percent of the cases the Court hears come from the federal courts, with the remaining cases coming from the state court system. In more than half of the cases argued before the Court, the lower court opinion is reversed.

The nine U.S. Supreme Court justices are nominated by the president and confirmed by the Senate. They have the authority to interpret the meaning of the U.S. Constitution and federal laws. All lower courts must follow these interpretations and other rules of law established by the Supreme Court. The Court's opinions are released in written form and later published in law books. They are also widely available on the Internet.

In recent years, many of society's most controversial issues have ended up before the Court. These include the death penalty, abortion, civil rights, and other issues. Because these issues are so significant, the views of persons nominated to become justices have become very important. This is especially true because justices are appointed for life.

Some individuals criticize the practice of appointing justices on the basis of their personal or political viewpoints. These critics say court appointees should be above politics because they sit for life and the Court makes its decisions in private. They say that other criteria should be used to select justices, such as demonstrated experience and expertise as a lawyer or a judge, as well as intelligence, integrity, and good moral character. Others say that the president should be able to appoint whomever he or she wishes. This includes people with political views similar to those of the president.

In 2003, the justices of the U.S. Supreme Court included (from left to right) Antonin Scalia, Ruth Bader Ginsburg, John Paul Stevens, David Souter, Chief Justice William Rehnquist, Clarence Thomas, Sandra Day O'Connor, Stephen Breyer, and Anthony Kennedy. *How does the Court determine which cases it will hear?*

The Case of . . .

Gideon v. *Wainwright*

In 1963, a case called *Gideon* v. *Wainwright* came before the U.S. Supreme Court. In this case, a Florida man named Clarence Gideon was charged with unlawful breaking and entering into a poolroom. Gideon asked the trial court to provide him with a free lawyer because he was too poor to hire one himself. The state court refused to provide him with an attorney. It said that state law provided free attorneys only to defendants charged with capital offenses (those crimes that carry a penalty of death or life imprisonment).

The Fourteenth Amendment to the U.S. Constitution says that no state may deprive a person of life, liberty, or property without **due process of law.** Due process means fair treatment. Gideon argued that to try someone for a felony without providing him with a lawyer violated the person's right to due process of law. The Supreme Court agreed with Gideon.

Problem 5.5

a. In the case of *Gideon* v. *Wainwright*, what was the precedent that the Supreme Court set? Who has to follow this precedent?

b. Who would have had to follow the precedent if the case had been decided by a judge in a state appeals court?

c. Does the *Gideon* case apply if you are charged with a misdemeanor? Does it apply if you are sued in a civil case?

d. Do you know of other precedents established by the U.S. Supreme Court? What are they?

Landmark Supreme Court Cases

Visit the Landmark Supreme Court Cases Web site at landmarkcases.org for information and activities about *Gideon* v. *Wainwright*.

- -

The Supreme Court has the power to reverse rules of law established in prior cases if the same issue comes before it again in a new case. This sometimes occurs when society's prevailing views change and the justices want the law to reflect these changes. It also occurs when one or more justices who voted a certain way in an earlier case leave the Court and new justices are appointed who disagree with the prior decision. If this happens, the justices may reverse the precedent by deciding a new case differently. This took place in the 1980s and early 1990s when Presidents Ronald Reagan and George Bush appointed a number of conservative justices. Many court decisions of the 1960s and 1970s—which were themselves often reversals of precedents from the 1930s and 1940s—had been viewed by some people as too liberal because they expanded the rights of individuals. The Court limited or reversed some of the earlier precedents involving the rights of accused criminals, and shifted some power back to the states. This occurred as the more conservative justices formed a new majority on the Court.

Law in *Action*

Who Should Be on the Supreme Court?

The president of the United States selects nominees for all federal judgeships—including the U.S. Supreme Court justices—"with the advice and consent of the Senate." The Senate must approve all nominees before they are appointed. Once appointed, justices serve for life unless they resign or are impeached. When the Senate receives a nominee from the president, it sends the nomination to the Senate Judiciary Committee for consideration. The committee schedules a hearing on the nomination. After the hearing, the committee votes. If a majority votes in favor of the nominee, the nomination is sent to the full Senate for consideration. If the majority of the Senate also votes for the nominee, the nominee is confirmed.

Problem 5.6

a. You are legal counsel to the president. One of the justices has just announced his resignation. Many groups and individuals are suggesting names of people they think should be nominated by the president. Write a memo to the president describing the type of person who should be nominated to the U.S. Supreme Court.

b. As legal counsel to the president, look at the following characteristics of potential Supreme Court nominees. Rank them from most important to least important. Be prepared to give your reasons.

- 45 years old
- Hispanic American
- female
- graduated first in class from a top law school

U.S. Supreme Court building

- respected trial court judge
- smoked marijuana while a law professor 20 years ago
- believes that affirmative action is unconstitutional
- believes in a woman's right to an abortion
- lives in California (assume there are no current justices from the West Coast)
- practicing Catholic (assume there are no Catholics at present on the Court)

International Courts

A number of international courts have been set up by the United Nations (UN) and other international organizations to apply and enforce international law. The first and most important one is the International Court of Justice, the principal judicial organ of the UN. It is located at The Hague in the Netherlands. This court may settle any dispute based on international law that a country submits to it. Some well-known cases submitted to this court in recent years included the case against Libya for support of the people who planted a bomb on an airplane that blew up over Lockerbie, Scotland, killing hundreds of passengers and crew members. In another case Iran is suing the United States over oil drilling rights. As of 2002, this court had rendered decisions in over 75 cases and advisory opinions in over 30 situations. In the 1990s, the UN also set up special courts, called tribunals, to try people for acts of genocide in Bosnia and Rwanda.

The International Criminal Court, created by the UN in 1998, began operating in 2003. This court has jurisdiction to try individuals for crimes such as genocide, crimes against humanity, war crimes and crimes of aggression. Initially, more than 80 UN member countries ratified the treaty setting up the International Criminal Court, but the United States opposed ratification. Opposition in this country is based on the belief that this court might put American citizens, including U.S. military personnel, on trial for political reasons. For example, a member of the U.S. military might be tried because some countries oppose U.S. military policy in some part of the world.

The International Court of Justice, also known as the World Court, is located in the Peace Palace in The Hague, the Netherlands. *What kind of disputes does the International Court of Justice settle?*

Problem 5.7

a. Why has the United States opposed having an International Criminal Court? Do you think the United States should be part of the new International Criminal Court? Give your reasons.

b. Can you give an example of when a U.S. citizen can be tried by a criminal court in another country? Is this different than having an international court try U.S. citizens for crimes for which the new International Criminal Court can try them? Explain.

Lawyers

There are more than one million lawyers, also referred to as attorneys, in the United States. About 65 percent of them are in private practice. Around 15 percent are government lawyers who work for federal, state, or local agencies. Another 15 percent work for corporations, unions, or trade associations. A small number of lawyers work for public interest or legal aid organizations. An even smaller number are law professors, judges, or elected officials.

Contrary to popular belief, most lawyers rarely go to court. Most law practice involves giving advice, drafting legal opinions, negotiating settlements, or otherwise providing out-of-court legal assistance.

Some lawyers do, however, go to court. Such lawyers are called trial attorneys or litigators. In civil cases, lawyers act as advocates for their clients' positions. Likewise, in a criminal case, the lawyer for the defendant has a duty to do everything possible—without violating a code of professional ethics—to secure the release and acquittal of his or her client.

"Discourage litigation. Persuade your neighbors to compromise whenever you can. Point out to them how the nominal winner is often a real loser—in fees, expenses, and waste of time. As a peacemaker, the lawyer has a superior opportunity of being a good man. There will be business enough."

— Abraham Lincoln

Street Law
online
Visit the *Street Law* Web site at streetlaw.glencoe.com for chapter-based information and resources.

The 16th president of the United States, Abraham Lincoln was also a lawyer.

When Do You Need a Lawyer?

It is important to know when to see a lawyer. Many people think of seeing an attorney only after they get into trouble, but perhaps the best time to consult an attorney is before the problem arises. Preventive advice is an important service that lawyers provide.

You should consider consulting an attorney about a number of common situations. These include:

- buying or selling a home or other real estate.
- organizing a business.
- changing your family status (for example, by divorce or adoption).
- making a will or planning an estate.
- signing a large or important contract.
- handling accidents involving personal injury or property damage.
- defending a criminal charge or bringing a civil suit.

How do you decide when you need a lawyer? If a question of law is involved, if a legal document needs to be drawn up or analyzed, or if you are involved in a court case, you will probably need legal help. However, if your problem is minor, you may be able to handle it on your own or with the help of someone other than a lawyer. For example, you can usually sue someone in a small claims court without a lawyer. Likewise, an argument with a spouse may be better handled through a marriage counselor or mediator. Relatives, friends, teachers, members of the clergy, doctors, or accountants may be more appropriate sources of advice in certain situations.

If you are not sure whether you need a lawyer, it may be advisable to see one to help you decide. Many **bar associations**—organizations that license lawyers—and other groups have services to help you decide if you need a lawyer. These are often provided free of charge or for a small fee.

Opening a new business may require you to seek the advice of a lawyer. *How would a lawyer's services help a new business owner?*

Problem 6.1

For each of the following situations, discuss the reasons why you may or may not need an attorney.

a. You hit another car in a parking lot. Your insurance agent indicates that the company will pay for bodily injury and property damage.

b. You borrow a friend's car without his knowledge, and he reports it to the police as stolen.

c. You buy a new stereo for $500. One month later, the receiver and speakers blow out. You return to the store, and the salesperson tells you he is sorry but his stereos have only a two-week guarantee.

d. You decide to trade in your old car and buy a new one.

e. Two friends are caught robbing the cashier at a local store, and they name you as one who helped plan the robbery.

f. The principal suspends you from school for two days because of an article you wrote for the student paper criticizing the school dress code.

g. You are turned down when you apply for a job. You think you were rejected because you are deaf.

h. You do not want your family to inherit the $10,000 you have saved. Told you will die within a year, you want the money to be used for cancer research.

i. You and your spouse find you can no longer get along. You want a divorce.

j. You earn $5,000 working in a restaurant during the year. You want to file your federal income tax return.

How Do You Find a Lawyer?

If you need a lawyer, how do you find one who is right for you and your particular problem? Perhaps the best way to find an experienced lawyer is through the recommendation of someone who had a similar legal problem that was resolved to his or her satisfaction. You might also ask your employer, members of the clergy, businesspeople, or other professionals for the name of a lawyer they know and trust.

You can always find a lawyer by looking under "Attorneys" or "Lawyers" in the Yellow Pages of your phone book. In addition, the *Martindale-Hubbell Law Directory*, available in your public library, lists most lawyers in the United States. It provides some general information about education, professional honors, and the types of cases each lawyer handles. Lawyers sometimes advertise their services. In many places, advertisements for lawyers appear in newspapers and magazines or on radio and television. In addition, a variety of Web sites also provide referrals to lawyers.

Lawyers have not always been allowed to advertise. For many years, it was considered improper and was forbidden by bar associations and

Where You Live

How do people find lawyers in your area? Does the bar association have a lawyer referral service? Do lawyers advertise? Are there lawyers or legal organizations that will represent you for free if you cannot afford a lawyer or are involved in certain types of cases?

Lawyers specializing in certain legal services, such as bankruptcy and personal injury, often advertise on large billboards. *What is the best way to find an experienced lawyer?*

courts. In 1977, the U.S. Supreme Court ruled that advertising by lawyers was protected by the First Amendment's freedom of speech clause. Those in favor of allowing lawyers to advertise think that it helps consumers decide which lawyer to hire. They add that statistics show advertising lowers legal fees through competition. Those against advertising by lawyers think that it encourages lawyers to be salespersons who are likely to make exaggerated claims. They think that lawyers should be hired based on competence and skill, qualities difficult to ascertain through advertising.

Many lawyers now advertise through various means, including telephone directories, newspapers, radio, television, and the Internet. Advertising has enabled large, lower-cost law firms, often called legal clinics, to develop—some of which have spread nationwide. However, many attorneys and others still consider advertising improper.

Problem 6.2

a. A television advertisement shows a lawyer in a bathing suit coming out of a lake. He says, "If you're in over your head because of bad debts, let us bail you out. We're the best firm in the state." Should there be any restrictions on ads like this? If so, what? Should there be other restrictions on ads? If so, what should they be?

b. A lawyer hears that many people have been injured as a result of accidents in a particular type of car. He runs a newspaper ad showing a car crash. The ad reads, "If this happens to you, I may be able to help you recover your losses." Should the lawyer be able to do this?

c. Many people in an area have lost their jobs and are about to lose their homes because they cannot make their monthly mortgage payments. Jane, a lawyer, writes to all of these people saying she is willing to represent them to prevent the loss of their homes. Should she be allowed to do this?

Another way to find a lawyer is to contact a local lawyer referral service. Most communities have bar associations that maintain lists of lawyers who specialize in certain kinds of cases. Many lawyers offer an initial meeting with clients at a special rate. If you call the referral service, you will be told the amount of the initial consultation fee and will be given a lawyer's name and phone number. If additional legal service is needed, the fee is subject to agreement between the lawyer and the client.

If you are unable to afford the services of a lawyer, you may be eligible for free legal assistance at a legal aid, legal service, or public defender's office. These offices are usually listed in the Yellow Pages of the phone book under "Legal Services." You may also contact the Legal Services Corporation or a local bar association or law school for the address of the legal aid office nearest you.

What to Ask Your Lawyer

Once you have found a lawyer who seems interested in your problem, you should get answers to the following questions:

- **What is the lawyer's fee?** Is the client required to pay a flat fee or by the hour? Is a retainer required? What about a contingency fee, in which the lawyer gets paid only if he or she wins your case?

- **Will there be a written fee agreement?** What will it say? How often will you be billed? Will the lawyer tell you when the fee is going to exceed a certain limit?

- **Has the lawyer ever handled cases like this before?** If so, with what results?

Working with a lawyer

- **Will the lawyer provide you with copies of all correspondence and documents prepared on your behalf?**

- **Will the lawyer keep you informed of any new developments in your case and talk to you in "plain English"?**

If you are not satisfied with the answers you get, do not hesitate to shop around.

The Car Crash

On April 1, Al and his friend Marie were driving along Sixth Street, returning home from a party. Al had stopped at a red light at the corner of Sixth Street and Florida Avenue when a 1999 Buick hit his car from behind.

Al's 2002 Volvo was smashed in as far as the back seat. Al suffered a severe neck injury, four broken ribs, and many cuts and bruises. As a result, he spent three weeks in the hospital. Al's passenger, Marie, was also severely injured. She suffered a fractured skull, facial and numerous other cuts, a broken right arm and hip, and internal bleeding. Marie, an accountant making $45,000 a year, spent six weeks in the hospital and returned to work after twelve weeks.

Fred, the driver of the Buick, suffered minor cuts on his face and arm and was released from the hospital after 24 hours. As a result of the accident, Fred was given a ticket for speeding and reckless driving.

Fred's insurance company has called Marie and offered her a $4,500 settlement. Marie is uncertain whether she should accept and decides to consult an attorney. After checking with a lawyer referral service, she is referred to a local attorney.

Problem 6.3

Role-play the initial attorney-client interview between Marie and the attorney. Persons role-playing the attorney should attempt to ask all the questions an attorney should ask at this point. Persons role-playing the client should provide the attorney with all necessary information and ask all those questions that are relevant to Marie's case and that relate to whether she should retain the attorney.

Whenever possible, it is wise to interview more than one lawyer before making a selection. Use these meetings to judge the differences between lawyers' fees, their experience in the type of case in which you are involved, and how you think you will be able to work with each one.

To avoid misunderstandings about legal fees, ask for an up-front estimate of the total charge. You should also find out who else will be working on the case, what each person charges per hour, and how often you will be billed. Lawyers often require a **retainer**—a down payment on the total fee. In addition, attorneys may charge clients for court costs, filing fees, or other expenses.

Attorneys sometimes take cases on a **contingency fee** basis instead of charging an hourly fee or a lump sum. A contingency fee is a percentage of whatever amount the client wins or settles for in the case. However, the client pays nothing except expenses if the case is lost. This fee arrangement is most common in personal injury cases in which money damages are being sought.

A typical contingency fee is one-third of the amount awarded to the client. However, it could be 40 percent or higher in some cases. If a client wins or settles for $300,000 in an auto accident case, the lawyer hired on a one-third contingency fee basis would take $100,000, and the client would receive $200,000 minus court costs.

"If you out-smart your lawyer, you've got the wrong lawyer."

— John T. Nolan, Esquire

The attorney-client relationship is often based on oral agreements. However, bar associations frequently recommend and sometimes require written fee agreements—which can cover flat fee or contingency fee agreements—signed by both the attorney and the client. This can help prevent disagreements later.

Another thing to consider before choosing a lawyer is whether your problem is one that may be of interest to the American Civil Liberties Union (ACLU), Institute for Justice (IJ), Environmental Defense Fund (EDF), National Association for the Advancement of Colored People Legal Defense Fund (LDF), American Conservative Union (ACU), or some other public interest group. These organizations are usually listed in the phone book and may provide free representation.

"The ethical practices of lawyers are probably no worse than those of other professions. Lawyers bring some of the trouble on by claiming . . . that they are interested only in justice, not power or wealth. They also suffer guilt by association. Their clients are often people in trouble. Saints need no lawyers: gangsters do."

— Lawrence M. Friedman, *American Law*

Working With Your Lawyer

Trust is the foundation of the attorney-client relationship—you must be able to trust your attorney. In order to help you, your attorney needs to know everything about your problem. To encourage clients to speak freely to their lawyers, the law grants an attorney-client privilege. This means that whatever you tell your attorney about your case is private and confidential. Such information cannot be disclosed to anyone without your permission.

Trust is an important factor between an attorney and his or her client. *What is the attorney-client privilege? Why is it important?*

FIGURE 6.1 Code of Professional Responsibility

The Code of Professional Responsibility consists of the following nine canons, or principles, which are broken down into ethical considerations and disciplinary rules.

Canon 1. A lawyer should assist in maintaining the integrity and competence of the legal profession.

Canon 2. A lawyer should assist the legal profession in fulfilling its duty to make legal counsel available.

Canon 3. A lawyer should assist in preventing the unauthorized practice of law.

Canon 4. A lawyer should preserve the confidences and secrets of a client.

Canon 5. A lawyer should exercise independent professional judgment on behalf of a client.

Canon 6. A lawyer should represent a client completely.

Canon 7. A lawyer should represent a client zealously within the bounds of the law.

Canon 8. A lawyer should assist in improving the legal system.

Canon 9. A lawyer should avoid the appearance of professional impropriety.

Source: Adapted from the American Bar Association

Problem 6.4

The following situations present ethical dilemmas faced by attorneys. Read the Code of Professional Responsibility, examine each case, and then decide whether the attorney acted ethically or unethically. Explain your answers.

a. Marta, an attorney for the family of a man killed in an auto accident, visits a bar and runs into a juror in the case. She has a drink with the juror.

b. Nicholas, a criminal defense attorney, puts his client on the stand to testify to her innocence, even though Nicholas knows she is lying.

c. Gene, a corporate lawyer, is asked by a wealthy client to recommend her son for admission to the state bar. Gene says yes.

d. Rosa represents a man injured by a defective lawn mower. The manufacturer's insurance company offers a $100,000 settlement. She accepts the settlement without consulting her client.

e. Nang, an attorney, has a trial next week before Judge DeSilva. Nang sees the judge in a grocery store and asks her if the trial can be postponed one week.

Working with an attorney also means making decisions. A good attorney will give you advice, but you must make the final decision. For example, you must decide whether to sue or not to sue, or to accept or reject a settlement. The attorney's job is to help you understand what is going on so that you can make informed decisions. You, in turn, should ask the questions needed to clarify things. However, you may discharge your lawyer if you are not satisfied. Once the case is in court, a judge will permit this change only for a very good reason.

Lawyers must follow certain standards of conduct. These standards are set out in a Code of Professional Responsibility (listed in Figure 6.1) and are enforced by state bar associations. In almost every state, a lawyer must pass an examination to become a member of the state bar. Lawyers who violate standards of conduct may be reprimanded, suspended, or **disbarred.** Once disbarred, a lawyer no longer has a license to practice law.

In recent years, there has been a great deal of concern about the conduct of lawyers. A client who has serious complaints that cannot be worked out with his or her attorney can report the problem to the local or state bar association. Like other professionals, lawyers can be sued by clients for serious errors that result in injury or loss. This type of case is known as a **legal malpractice** case. Additional information on malpractice can be found in Unit 3.

To handle attorney-client disputes, some bar associations have arbitration systems in which panels of lawyers—and sometimes nonlawyers—hold hearings and issue opinions. Some disputes deal with the amount charged for the lawyer's services. Panels may order the attorney to return a client's money if they decide the fee was improper.

For Your Information . . .

Becoming a Lawyer

More than 120,000 students are enrolled in over 200 law schools that operate in the United States. Law students typically attend class for three years, although students who attend classes at night may attend for four years. More than half of all law students enrolled today are female. As recently as 1980, only 30 percent of law students were women. Candidates must first complete a four-year college program, demonstrate good grades, and take the Law School Admission Test (LSAT).

To obtain a license to practice law, almost all law school graduates must apply to take a state bar examination. The rules for eligibility to take the bar and to qualify for bar admission are set by each state. However, to receive a license to practice law, one must be a graduate of a law school that meets certain standards and must achieve a passing score on the bar examination. In addition, the state's board of bar examiners checks the character and fitness of each applicant for a law license. Each year more than 50,000 people are admitted to practice law in the United States. Salaries and working conditions for lawyers vary widely.

UNIT
2

Criminal Law
and
Juvenile Justice

Visit the *Street Law* Web site at streetlaw.glencoe.com for unit-based activities.

Crime is a serious problem in the United States. According to the FBI, in 2001 a property crime occurred every 3 seconds and a violent crime occurred every 22 seconds. Public opinion polls show that citizens are very concerned about crime and about certain factors—such as illegal drug use and the availability of firearms—that can lead to criminal activity. While most measures of crime showed overall decreases throughout the 1990s and into 2001, data showed an increase in the proportion of young people involved as both perpetrators and victims of serious, violent crimes.

The first chapter of this unit—Chapter 7—provides an overview of crime in the United States, describing the nature and causes of crime and looking at the relationship between gangs, guns, alcohol, drugs, and crime. Chapter 8 introduces you to the study of criminal law. Chapters 9 and 10 contain information on crimes against persons and crimes against property. Defenses used in criminal cases are covered in Chapter 11.

Crimes committed by both adults and juveniles are a major problem in the United States.

Chapters 12 through 15 deal with the criminal justice process—from the rules that police must follow when conducting arrests, searches, or interrogations (Chapter 12), through the proceedings that occur before trial (Chapter 13) and the Bill of Rights protections that shape the trial itself (Chapter 14), to issues dealing with sentencing and corrections (Chapter 15). Chapter 16 looks at the operation of the juvenile justice system and the special challenges it faces in dealing with young people who commit serious and violent offenses. Chapter 17, the last chapter in this unit, discusses law as it applies to terrorism.

Both the criminal and juvenile justice systems continue to be a focus of intense public scrutiny. We look to these systems not only to control antisocial behavior, but also to protect individuals from having their freedoms taken away by the government. This unit should help you better understand your role as a citizen by discouraging you from committing crimes, teaching you effective crime prevention strategies, and encouraging you to work to improve the justice system.

Crime in America

Crime wears many faces. It may be the teenager snatching a woman's purse or the career criminal planning a kidnapping. It may be the youth who steals a car for a joyride or the car theft ring that takes it for later sale. It may be the professional criminal who profits from organized gambling, extortion, or narcotics traffic, or the politician who takes a bribe. Crime may be committed by the professional person who cheats on tax returns, the businessperson who secretly agrees to fix prices, the burglar who ransacks homes while the owners are at work, or the terrorist who acts under the claim of a greater cause.

The Nature of Crimes

A **crime** is something one does or fails to do that is in violation of a law. It can also be defined as behavior for which a government has set a penalty. Criminal law designates certain conduct "criminal" and other conduct "noncriminal." Decisions as to what constitutes a crime are made by legislatures, which try to protect the public based on what most people believe is right and necessary for the orderly conduct of society. Certain acts are prohibited or required to protect life and property, preserve individual freedoms, maintain the system

"Time is a great legalizer, even in the field of morals."

—H. L. Mencken

Street Law
online

Visit the *Street Law* Web site at streetlaw.glencoe.com for chapter-based information and resources.

Police duties range from writing simple parking tickets to investigating violent crimes.

of government, and uphold the morality of society. Ideally, the goals of law are to protect human rights for all and to regulate human conduct so that people can live in harmony.

Many people do not realize that crime victims are also victims of human rights violations. For example, people have a human right to ownership of their own property (Universal Declaration of Human Rights [UDHR], Article 17). Theft crimes violate this right. People also have a human right to protection of their personal security (UDHR, Article 3). Violent crimes such as murder, rape, and assault violate this human right.

Problem 7.1

Assume you are a member of a commission established to evaluate laws. Consider the following acts. In each case decide whether the act should be treated as a crime. Then rank the acts from most serious to least serious using the following scale: VS (very serious), S (serious), U (undecided), LS (less serious), and NS (not serious). Also note if you think an act should not be a crime (NAC). Give reasons for your decisions.

a. Robert sells crack cocaine and uses the proceeds to support his mother, who is on welfare.

b. Marley is a passenger in a car she knows is stolen, although she did not participate in the theft of the car.

c. A corporate executive gives a million dollars to a candidate for the U.S. Senate.

d. A wife finds out her husband is having an affair and runs over him with her car.

e. Paulina is caught with a pound of marijuana.

f. Ted robs a liquor store at gunpoint.

g. Ellen leaves a store with change for a $10 bill, knowing that she gave the cashier a $5 bill.

h. Lily approaches a man for purposes of prostitution.

i. The president of the United States lies under oath.

j. Ming refuses to wear a helmet while riding a motorcycle.

k. A company pollutes a river with waste from its automobile factory.

l. Pat gets drunk and hits a child while speeding through a school zone.

m. Dakota observes his best friend shoplifting but does not turn him in.

Crime has long been a major problem in the United States. Preventing crime is not an easy task. In 2001, U.S. residents over the age of 12 experienced nearly 24.2 million crimes, about 24 percent of which were violent in nature. Following a trend that began in 1994, the rate of violent crime declined 10 percent between 2000 and 2001. The rate of property crimes fell 6 percent during the same period, the lowest crime rate recorded in the United States since 1973.

FIGURE 7.1 Crimes Reported and Arrests Made (2001)

Type of Crime	Number Reported	Percent Arrested		Total Number Reported	Percent Arrested
Larceny/Theft	5,329,949	17.6	Total		
Burglary	1,585,074	12.7	Property	7,860,198	16.2
Motor Vehicle Theft	945,175	13.6	Crime		
Aggravated Assault	640,168	56.1			
Robbery	304,077	24.9	Total		
Forcible Rape	67,907	44.3	Violent	1,024,134	46.2
Murder and		62.4	Crime		
Non-negligent					
Manslaughter	11,982				
			Crime Index Total*	8,884,332	19.6

*The crime index is the sum of violent crimes and property crimes.
Source: FBI, 2001.

Problem 7.2

a. According to the information above, what was the most commonly reported crime in 2001?

b. What percentage of the total reported crimes resulted in arrest?

c. Of the crimes reported, for which crimes were people most likely to be arrested? Least likely to be arrested? Why do you think this is so?

d. How can citizens act to help police improve arrest rates?

Street Law online update

Visit streetlaw.glencoe.com and click on **Textbook Update—Chapter 7** for an update of the data.

According to surveys of victims, about 50 percent reported crimes against themselves to the police. Less than 40 percent reported property crimes to the police. Surveys of law enforcement records indicate that of the cases reported, about 20 percent led to an arrest. However, the arrest rate is considerably higher for violent crimes reported to police.

Crime rates are influenced by many factors, such as your location, age, and gender. Based on 2001 statistics, crime rates are higher in urban areas than in suburban areas. Similarly, crime rates are generally higher in suburban areas than in rural areas. Crime is not confined to any particular group, but people between the ages of 15 and 24 commit more violent crimes than any other group. Males commit almost four times as many crimes as females, but the rate for female offenses has increased in recent years. In 2001, 68 percent of female victims knew their offenders, whereas only 45 percent of males knew their offenders. About 35 percent of victims report that the offender had been using alcohol. Violent crimes are more likely to occur during the day, but two-thirds of rapes occur at night.

One way in which crime affects us all is that it costs everyone money. Aside from the very significant cost of lost or damaged lives or of fear and suffering, the total amount of government expenditures on crime is approximately $150 billion per year! A family of four pays an average of more than $1,500 per year in taxes relating to crime, even if they are not victims of crime.

Although authorities agree that crime is a major problem, much disagreement exists over the causes of crime and what can be done about it. Among the reasons suggested for the high crime rate in the United States are poverty, permissive courts, unemployment, lack of education, abuse of alcohol and drugs, inadequate police protection, rising population, lack of parental guidance, a breakdown in morals, an ineffective correctional system, little chance of being caught or punished, and the influence of television and films. This lack of agreement indicates that the causes of crime are many and complex.

Let's examine some suggested causes of crime more closely. Some people point to the economic system in the United States, with its wide disparity between rich and poor, as a major influence on the rate of crime. In the 1990s, with a generally strong economy and low unemployment, the crime rate did tend to go down. Between 2001 and 2002, the United States experienced a weaker economy and a rise in crime rates. At other times in American history a strong economy has not reduced crime, and a weak economy has not caused crime to increase. Further, there are other countries around the world where the poverty level is high, but the crime rate is low.

Researchers have also looked at data from high-crime urban areas. They have found that poverty by itself is not a good predictor of crime; a more important factor is the stability of the family. For example, many families with few financial resources raise children who are responsible, law-abiding citizens. However, it is also true that poverty and lack of educational and economic opportunities make it more difficult for families to achieve the stability that would help reduce crime.

Many communities organize neighborhood crime watch groups to help monitor suspicious activities. *What approaches has your community taken to prevent crime?*

Would tougher penalties curb crime? Many people think so, but the United States already has some of the toughest criminal laws—as well as the highest incarceration rate—of any industrialized nation. Tough penalties may deter some people from committing crimes, but compared with the number of crimes committed, only a small number of people ever go to prison. Thus, some experts say that longer prison terms are not the answer. They say the certainty of punishment is more important than the length of the sentence.

Adequate police protection obviously has something to do with the crime rate, but studies show that simply increasing the number of police officers does not necessarily reduce the overall crime rate.

FIGURE 7.2 U.S. Crime Clock

Crime	2001 Data	1996 Data
PROPERTY CRIME	One every **3 seconds**	One every **3 seconds**
Larceny/Theft	One every **4.5 seconds**	One every **4 seconds**
Burglary	One every **14.9 seconds**	One every **13 seconds**
Motor Vehicle Theft	One every **25.7 seconds**	One every **23 seconds**
VIOLENT CRIME	One every **22 seconds**	One every **19 seconds**
Burglary	One every **14.9 seconds**	One every **13 seconds**
Aggravated Assault	One every **34.8 seconds**	One every **31 seconds**
Forcible Rape	One every **5.8 minutes**	One every **6 minutes**
Robbery	One every **1.2 minutes**	One every **59 seconds**
Murder	One every **32.9 minutes**	One every **27 minutes**
TOTAL CRIME INDEX OFFENSE	One every **2.7 seconds**	One every **2 seconds**

Source: Uniform Crime Reports, 1996 and 2001.

Problem 7.3

Consider the frequency of crimes listed above and answer the questions that follow.

a. Did crimes occur less or more frequently in 2001 than they did in 1996? Do you think these changes are significant in any single category of crime? Among all the categories?

b. What are the possible explanations for these changes? Are there any crimes that people might be reluctant to report to police? Explain.

c. Based on what you read in the newspaper or watch on television news, do you think the data above accurately reflects the crime problem in your community?

Street Law online update

Visit streetlaw.glencoe.com and click on **Textbook Update—Chapter 7** for an update of the data.

Many communities have embraced the idea of **community policing**. This strategy builds closer connections between police and the communities they serve. Police officers who have more direct contact with residents in neighborhoods can more effectively participate in community crime prevention activities, understand the nature and extent of local crime problems, and gather information about criminal activity.

Crime on Campus

Crime on high school and college campuses has been a source of increasing concern in recent years. According to the U.S. Department of Education and the Department of Justice, in 2000, students 12 to 18 years old experienced nearly two million incidents of violent and property crime while at school. Of these, about 128,000 were serious violent crimes, including rape, sexual assault, robbery, and aggravated assault. In 2001, approximately 10 percent of male students surveyed in grades 9 through 12 reported carrying a gun to school at least once in a 30-day period (compared to about 3 percent of female students in the same grades). During 2001, nearly one-third of students reported that drugs were available to them at school, an increase of 20 percent from 1993. Although the total nonfatal crime rates for students generally declined between 1992 and 2001, there was an increase in incidents of bullying at school during that same period. The overwhelming majority of these incidents occurred among middle school students in grades 6 through 8.

College campus crime includes violent assaults, hate crimes, and property crimes. Many of these crimes involve alcohol. In 2000, 20 murders were reported on college campuses, along with 1,858 forcible sex offenses, 1,933 robberies, 3,644 aggravated assaults, 26,543 burglaries, and 5,792 motor vehicle thefts. The incidence of crimes involving college students that occur off campus is considerably higher. Unfortunately, these statistics may not reflect the extent of the crime problem, as some colleges and universities may not fully report crime out of concern that this information would reduce student applications.

Thinking about crime requires us to go beyond slogans and stereotypes. We should carefully consider each of the suggested causes and the possible solutions to the problem. Perhaps the most that can be said is that disagreement exists over the causes of crime and that solutions to the crime problem are not simple.

At some schools, "security dads" volunteer to provide an adult presence at after-school activities and in the halls. *How else might a school attempt to reduce crime on campus?*

Where You Live

What is the major crime problem in your school? In your community? Have most crimes increased or decreased over the last three years where you live? Where can you get this information?

After-school programs give kids a place to go instead of hanging out on the street. *How might the presence of after-school programs help reduce crime?*

> *It takes a village to raise a child.*
>
> — African Proverb

The National Council on Crime and Delinquency (NCCD) has been studying criminal justice in the United States since 1907, and recommends the following strategies for reducing crime:

- Build safer communities with special attention to safe schools, after-school programs, community policing, and prevention of domestic violence and child abuse.
- Reduce the costs and improve the fairness of the criminal justice system.
- Develop cost-effective alternatives to incarceration, reserving prison sentences for those who cannot be treated safely in the community.
- Create effective drug-control policies. Reduce funds spent on catching drug sellers and users; expand funding for drug treatment and job training; and repeal laws requiring mandatory prison sentences for drug possession.

Problem 7.4

a. Not everyone agrees with the NCCD's recommendations. Do you agree or disagree with their recommendations for reducing crime in the United States? Explain your answer.

b. List the causes of crime described on page 77. Then rank them from most important to least important. Discuss your ranking.

c. Are there other possible causes of crime not mentioned in the text? If so, what are they?

d. What steps should the federal government take to reduce crime? What steps should your state government take? What steps should be taken by your local government?

Weapons at School

Sunshine City is a suburb of Metropolis, the largest city in the state. Sunshine High School (SHS), the only high school in Sunshine City, has 1,500 students. SHS's student population is racially and economically mixed. The school has many student organizations, as well as girls' and boys' sports teams. There are college and personal counselors on staff.

Sunshine High School has its share of problems with underage drinking and drugs. Except for an occasional fist fight, however, until recently it has not had a problem with school violence. The school board is aware of the problem of weapons being brought into Metropolis schools. It is committed to SHS student safety and recently discussed installing metal detectors at the school. However, although security guards are on duty at SHS, no detectors have been installed.

Samuel is a 16-year-old junior at SHS. He moved to Sunshine City from another state with his family four months ago and started school in the middle of last term. Samuel is a loner, has few friends, and spends most of his time surfing the Internet and playing violent video games. He has not had any disciplinary problems at school, but has been caught shoplifting.

Samuel has had a difficult transition to SHS. His grades are poor, and his general demeanor is dark. He is picked on by the popular guys. He skips school and is not allowed to enter school if he is late. Samuel's parents have noticed that lately he has been more withdrawn than usual and have been concerned about him. They contacted the school counselor, who promised to talk to him. Samuel did not go to the two appointments the counselor scheduled with him.

One Wednesday morning, Samuel left for school early, telling his mother good-bye and that he loved her. Although this struck his mother as odd—usually, he was late and did not say anything as he left—she hoped it meant he was feeling better about things.

Because of the rain that day, the students congregated in the cafeteria to wait for the bell. Before going inside, Samuel saw Eddie, a quiet kid who sat next to him in algebra. Before reaching the front door, Samuel told Eddie that he "had to take care of something," but that he did not want Eddie to be around when "it all went down."

Eddie had the sense that something was wrong and went to the school resource officer. Officer Lee found Samuel just as he was about to enter the cafeteria. When the officer questioned Samuel and received a mumbled response, he decided to frisk him for weapons. Under Samuel's jacket was a semiautomatic gun. The actions that Eddie and Officer Lee took helped avoid a major tragedy at SHS.

The police and school administrators investigated. One student, Trisha, told a school counselor that Samuel advised her not to come to school that day. He wanted to keep her safe from danger, as she was always nice to him. The police discovered that Samuel had purchased the gun illegally from someone on the street and also found a disturbing note in Samuel's jacket pocket. In it, he outlined his plan to shoot people and remarked "after today, no one will push me around again!"

Problem 7.5

a. What conditions might have led up to Samuel's decision to commit this crime?

b. What, if anything, could have been done to help Samuel? Were there signs at school or home that he was at risk?

c. Are there measures in place at your school to prevent acts of violence from occurring? Are additional measures needed? If so, what are they?

Gangs and Crime

At one time, violent gangs were thought to operate only in the largest cities in the United States. Evidence indicates, however, that gangs are now active in towns and cities of all sizes throughout the country. Nearly all cities with populations of more than 200,000 now report having gang problems. In 2001, 20 percent of all students aged 12 to 18 reported that street gangs were present at school. One reason gangs have spread is the lure of profits from the sale of illegal drugs, an activity in which many gangs participate. Many gang members also buy, sell, and steal firearms. The combination of drugs and guns has led to increased gang violence.

Estimates of the numbers of gangs and gang members vary greatly. However, most experts believe that there are several thousand youth gangs and several hundred thousand gang members, indicating the magnitude of the problem.

What Are Gangs?

In this discussion, gangs refer to people who form groups closed to the general public, for certain common business or nonprofit purposes that may include violent criminal activity. While the media have featured gang activity a great deal in recent years, gangs are not new in the United States. In the nineteenth century, gangs existed in many American neighborhoods. They were primarily composed of adults and were usually organized along ethnic lines. Even then gangs had names, rules, emblems, initiation rituals, and distinctive ways of dressing. Early gangs were interested in protecting turf, reputation, and cultural heritage. But not all of these gangs engaged in criminal activity; neither do all gangs today. In fact, some gangs perform community work and operate job-training and other government-funded programs. Generally, however, these are not the gangs that contribute to the crime problem.

Today's gang members range in age from young children to middle-aged adults. While traditional youth gangs are still concerned with issues of status and turf, many gangs now operate with much more sophisticated organizational structures. Many focus on drug trafficking, firearm sales, auto theft, prostitution, and other criminal activity. Others use group-oriented violence or other criminal behavior to defend certain beliefs, which may be racist or sexist.

Many gangs identify themselves with colors. *How are today's gangs different from those of the nineteenth century?*

Gangs often associate themselves with one of several major gang "nations" and choose particular symbols, emblems, colors, phrases, and clothing with which to identify themselves. Gangs often use graffiti to mark, or "tag," particular territory as theirs, to intimidate rival gangs, or to instill fear in citizens of a neighborhood. People who join gangs usually have to endure some initiation ritual or test, such as committing a crime, being beaten, or for female initiates, having sex with multiple members of the gang. Many gangs, however, are more concerned with prospective members' abilities to sell drugs and make a profit. They may require new recruits to successfully complete a robbery or drug deal, or to commit an act of violence such as a drive-by shooting. It is not uncommon to have to endure a similar rite to get out of a gang, if getting out is an option at all. Violence, the use of deadly weapons, the use of drugs and alcohol, constant danger to themselves and their families, and criminal records are strongly associated with the lives of most gang members.

People join gangs for many reasons. *What are the factors that put young people at risk for gang involvement?*

Who Joins Gangs and Why?

While female gang membership is increasing, the overwhelming majority of gang members are male. In many cases, members' relatives or friends are also involved with gangs. Many gang members live under poor conditions at home, where their basic needs are often unmet, and they lack success in school. They are frequently very pessimistic about their job prospects and other opportunities for the future.

While the media and entertainment industry may portray gang membership as appealing only to inner-city minority youth, there is no shortage of white gang members in urban, suburban, and rural areas. In addition, the idea that gang members can become financially prosperous as the result of gang membership is just an urban legend. In reality, very few gang members ever find either financial or social success.

Researchers have identified a number of factors that put young people at risk for gang involvement: poverty, school failure, substance abuse, family dysfunction, and domestic and community violence. Many gang recruits have poor self-esteem and little adult participation in their lives. However, there is no magic formula for predicting whether a young person will or will not join a gang. Millions of young people face the conditions described above, yet never join gangs.

Some young people join gangs to receive attention and to feel a sense of belonging that is missing in their lives. Others are the children of gang members and are choosing a similar lifestyle. Still others join because they feel pressure from friends, possibly in the form of threats, or because they believe that once they join they will be protected from police or members of other gangs. To people who see a future without job or financial opportunities, gang membership may appear to be their only alternative. This may explain why many older members, still lacking opportunities, are not "maturing out" of gangs.

How Can the Gang Problem Be Solved?

Most experts agree that the best way to handle the problem of gangs is to prevent young people from getting involved with gangs. Communities that are successful in dealing with gangs take the following actions:

- Operate outreach and intervention programs in which social workers and trained counselors encourage gang members to become involved in positive, non-gang activities.
- Provide greater opportunities for young people, including athletics, clubs, school tutoring, community service work, and job training.
- Mobilize government agencies, schools, parents, community groups, religious organizations, and other youths to increase awareness of the problem and develop opportunities for young people.
- Organize prevention strategies in which police and probation officers identify gang members (and wanna-bes) and place them in anti-gang membership programs.
- Prosecute gang members for illegal activity.
- Organize neighborhood watch groups that regularly remove graffiti and make it difficult for gangs to establish a presence or intimidate the community.

Problem 7.6

a. Is there a gang problem in your community? If not, what steps should be taken now to prevent such a problem? If there already is a problem, how do you know it exists? What steps should be taken to deal with it? Should police be able to place gang members (and wanna-bes) in special programs without charging them with specific crimes? Explain.

b. Why do you think gangs are such a serious problem in the United States today? How do gangs resemble families? Why do you think people join gangs? What steps, if any, should be taken on the national level to deal with the problem?

c. Do you think gang membership appeals only to those from lower socioeconomic groups? Is a group of middle-class or rich kids that hangs out, vandalizes, and sells drugs a gang?

d. Do you think the nightly news and other television shows, certain cartoons and movies, and the lyrics of some popular music encourage violence? What, if anything, should be done about this?

Guns and the Law

Most Americans who own firearms own them legally and use them lawfully. However, guns are frequently used in violent crimes. Efforts (or lack of efforts) by the government to control firearms are very controversial among U.S. citizens, millions of whom believe passionately that their liberty and perhaps their safety will be at risk if gun ownership is restricted. Others believe that the relatively easy availability of firearms to young persons has aggravated the crime problem. Still others argue that it is not guns, but gun users, who cause violence and that law-abiding citizens have a right to own firearms.

Gun control is an extremely controversial issue. Some groups look to the Second Amendment as protection against government attempts to ban or regulate firearms. Other groups argue that the language of the Second Amendment protects a state's right to maintain a militia, or armed forces, but does not protect citizens against government efforts to legislate in this area.

The U.S. Supreme Court has interpreted the Second Amendment on several occasions, and so have many lower courts. All courts have ruled that the amendment guarantees a state's right to maintain a militia. However, the U.S. Supreme Court has not used the Second Amendment to strike down federal, state, or local legislation that controls guns.

The Million Mom March is a national organization advocating responsible limits to gun access and use. *How is the Second Amendment used as protection against government attempts to ban or regulate guns?*

Where You Live

What laws, if any, control gun possession in your area? Are they effective?

The primary federal gun-control law is the *Gun Control Act of 1968,* passed after the murders of Dr. Martin Luther King, Jr., and Senator Robert Kennedy. This law prohibits certain categories of persons—such as convicted felons, minors, and illegal aliens—from buying or possessing weapons. The act requires serial numbers on all guns and establishes a licensing-fee schedule for firearms manufacturers, importers, and dealers. It prohibits the mail-order sale of all firearms and ammunition, and it also prohibits the interstate sale of handguns. The passage of the *Gun Control Act* set penalties for carrying and using firearms in crimes of violence or drug trafficking, and it set age guidelines for firearms purchased through dealers (handgun purchasers must be at least 21; long-gun purchasers must be at least 18). A more recent federal law bans the importation of certain semiautomatic weapons.

In 1993 Congress amended the *Gun Control Act* by enacting the *Brady Act.* The *Brady Act* is named for former White House press secretary James Brady, who was shot and paralyzed by a bullet an assassin intended for President Ronald Reagan. The act required the attorney general to create a national system to instantly check the background of persons who want to buy guns. Gun dealers must check the instant background service before completing the proposed sale. Until the national background check system could be set up,

For Your Information . . .

Guns In America

- Although it is difficult to state with certainty how many guns there are in the United States (because of illegal guns), it is estimated that between 40 and 45 percent of households have a gun in their home. (U.S. Bureau of the Census)
- In 2000, firearms claimed the lives of 28,663 people in the United States. Of those, 10,801 were homicides, 16,586 were suicides, and 776 were accidental shootings. Another 270 were the result of legal intervention, and the causes of the other 230 were undetermined. (National Center for Health Statistics, 2002)
- Firearms are the second leading cause of injury-related death in the United States for people 19 and younger, second only to automobile fatalities. (National Center for Health Statistics, 2002)
- In 2001, guns were used in 63 percent of all homicides. Young people aged 20–24 were the most common victims. (Uniform Crime Reports, 2002)

Where You Live

Are there any restrictions in your state on who can purchase a handgun? Does your state allow citizens who have permits to carry concealed guns?

an interim provision required local law enforcement officers to conduct the background check and required gun dealers to wait five days for the results before selling guns. This interim provision, however, was declared unconstitutional by the U.S. Supreme Court in 1997, which said Congress does not have the constitutional authority to force states to conduct such background checks. Even so, many states have enacted their own legislation requiring background checks, fingerprinting, firearm training, and other application requirements to purchase a gun. In 2001, 8 million applications for guns were processed in the United States; 151,000 were rejected.

A wide range of gun laws have been enacted at the state and local levels. Some states require a person to take a training course or test before purchasing a gun. State laws permitting citizens to carry a concealed weapon became a trend during the 1990s. Proponents of these laws often justify them on the grounds that individuals have a right to carry a weapon for purposes of self-defense. By 2002, 30 states had passed laws making it relatively easy to get a permit to carry a concealed weapon. Thirteen states make this permit process more difficult by requiring a specific need, such as working in a security job. Six states and the District of Columbia do not allow citizens to carry a concealed weapon. Vermont is the only state that does not regulate the carrying of weapons (concealed or openly) in any way. While many states are making it easier to get permits, polling data show that a majority of Americans favor stricter gun control laws.

James Brady became concerned about gun control after he was shot during an assassination attempt on President Reagan in 1981. *How does the* Brady Act *control gun possession?*

Problem 7.7

a. Which is a better way to reduce crime—more gun control or less gun control? Give your reasons.

b. What restrictions, if any, should the government place on the manufacture of firearms? The sale of firearms? The possession of firearms? Explain.

Law in Action

Child Access Prevention (CAP) Laws

In 1989 Florida became the first state to pass a so-called child access prevention law. The purpose of the law is to limit children's access to guns owned by adults. Florida's law makes it a crime to store or leave a loaded firearm within the reach or easy access of a minor. For this law, a minor is a person under the age of 16. The law applies only if the minor gains access to the gun. The law does not apply if the gun is stored in a locked box or secured with a trigger lock. The gun owner's offense is a misdemeanor if the minor gains access to the gun, but a felony if the minor uses the weapon to harm himself or others. Fourteen additional states and some cities have passed similar laws.

After a series of tragic shootings on school grounds by young people in 1997 and 1998, Congress passed a similar federal law.

Problem 7.8

a. Do you think a child access prevention law is effective? Give your reasons.

b. Is it appropriate that there is a similar federal criminal law? Explain.

c. Suppose you wanted a similar law passed in your state. What steps might you take to get such a law enacted? What organizations might help you? What organizations might oppose such a law?

Substance Abuse and Crime

The term substance abuse has come into general use in recent years. The word *substance* is used to describe all the different kinds of chemicals that people abuse, including alcohol and drugs. This type of abuse has always plagued American society. Substance abuse contributes to many social problems, including the breakup of families, decreased productivity, injuries in the workplace, and automobile crashes. Criminal activity often results from substance abuse or the desire for money to purchase drugs.

Alcohol

Alcohol is the most widely abused substance in the United States today. One reason for this is that drinking alcohol is generally socially acceptable in our society. Alcohol use has been legal for adults over 21 years of age since the birth of the country—with the exception of a 14-year period from 1920 to 1933 known as Prohibition. Not all countries, however, believe alcohol use is acceptable. For example, it is a criminal offense to drink alcohol in Saudi Arabia.

Alcohol abuse is detrimental to society. Alcoholism contributes to the poor functioning of some families, and many people commit spouse and child abuse and other crimes while under the influence of alcohol. The annual cost of alcohol abuse to American society is estimated at nearly $150 billion.

When considering alcohol and crime, most people focus on the tragic loss of life resulting from drinking and driving accidents. This topic will be covered below. However, many people do not connect alcohol to other forms of violence. According to the U.S. Department of Justice, alcohol abuse was a factor in 35 percent of violent crimes committed in the United States in 2001. And two-thirds of the victims who suffered violence by a spouse, former spouse, boyfriend, or girlfriend report that alcohol had been a factor.

The term **drunk driving** is used in a general sense to refer to the legal terms *driving while intoxicated* (DWI) and *driving under the influence* (DUI). Legally, these terms have meanings more precise than their meanings in everyday usage. The legal definition of DWI/DUI refers to a person's blood alcohol concentration (BAC). The BAC indicates the grams per deciliter (g/dl) of alcohol in the blood. A person's BAC can be determined through breath, urine, or blood samples. Alcohol is a mind-altering drug, and tests have shown that thinking and reaction time are affected in varying degrees by the level of alcohol in the blood system. Although the legal levels on BAC vary from state to state, an individual generally is considered *impaired* when the BAC is between 0.01g/dl and 0.09g/dl, and *intoxicated* when the BAC is 0.10g/dl or greater.

Every state in the country has a DWI/DUI law. In 1999 nearly 1.5 million people were arrested for driving under the influence of alcohol. Use of drugs, legal or illegal, that impair driving ability is also a violation of DWI/DUI laws. People can receive a variety of penalties for driving under the influence:

- monetary fine
- enrollment in a DWI school
- community service
- license suspended (taken away for a period of time)
- license revoked (permanently taken away)
- jail sentence (some laws require a minimum term)

Any combination of these penalties may be imposed on a convicted drunk driver. A repeat offender is likely to receive stiffer penalties, and many states now automatically suspend

Tasks such as walking a straight line help police determine if a person is driving while intoxicated. *How does an implied consent law work?*

Where You Live

How does your court system handle drunk drivers? Does it treat adults and juveniles differently? Are there programs in your community designed to help teens and adults with alcohol problems?

drivers' licenses for DWI/DUI. In most states, repeat offenders end up in jail. In some states, even a first-time offender must serve a brief jail sentence.

A driver who has been stopped may choose not to take an alcohol test. However, most states have an **implied consent** law under which the driver agrees to submit to a BAC test in exchange for the privilege of driving. In those states, refusal to take the test could result in immediate and automatic suspension of the driver's license for a certain period, even if the driver is not found guilty of DWI.

As drivers or passengers, young people are at a greater risk of being injured or killed in alcohol-related accidents than are people of any other age group. This is because teens are affected by alcohol faster and to a greater extent than adults and because teens tend to be less-experienced drivers. Approximately 40 percent of all highway deaths involved alcohol in 2001, and thousands of teens are injured each year in alcohol-related car crashes.

National and local organizations exist to help reduce drunk driving and provide assistance to those who are victims of drunk-driving crashes. Such organizations include Mothers Against Drunk Driving, Students Against Destructive Decisions (formerly Students Against Drunk Driving), Remove Intoxicated Drivers, the National Commission Against Drunk Driving, and the National Coalition to Prevent Impaired Driving. The work of these groups and others has resulted in greater public awareness of the dangers of drinking and driving.

Arrests for driving under the influence (DUI) peaked in the early 1980s, and started to decline by the early 1990s. Although total arrests for DUI declined by over 20 percent from 1991 to 2000, underage drinking continues to be a significant problem. Even though the arrest rate for drivers under age 18 decreased after all states adopted a uniform drinking age of 21 in the 1980s, the arrest rates for persons under age 18 who are caught driving under the influence rose nearly 14 percent from 1991 to 2000.

Organizations such as MADD have focused public awareness on drunk driving in recent years. *Which of these organizations are active where you live?*

Problem 7.9

Assume your state has recently had a series of automobile crashes, including a number of deaths, caused by people driving under the influence of alcohol. A high percentage of these crashes have been caused by drivers aged 17 to 25. Others have been caused by older drivers who have had drinking problems for years. These drivers have been arrested before for DWI and were either fined or given probation.

a. You are a member of the state legislature, which has the power to change the law to try to solve this problem. Draft such a law.

b. Analyze the law that you drafted. Will it create any new problems? What can be done to resolve them?

c. What else could be done to reduce alcohol-related crashes? Would these measures work better than the law you proposed? Explain.

Drugs

While illegal drug use is not new, it has become increasingly widespread, and its effects have touched nearly everyone in American society. Illegal drug use costs society billions of dollars a year. The flourishing illegal-drug industry has led to a dramatic increase in criminal activity, ranging from murder to high-level government corruption. This has placed an overwhelming burden on the criminal justice system because so many people are arrested for selling or possessing drugs. Between 50 and 75 percent of persons taken into the criminal justice system test positive for one or more drugs at the time of their arrest. The trends in this area are difficult to determine: some cities have outbreaks of crack cocaine, while other cities experience increases in the use of marijuana, heroin, or methamphetamines. Some reports have shown a particularly close relationship between the increased use of crack cocaine and increases in the rate of violent crime in a community.

Earlier in this chapter you studied statistics that showed an overall reduction in crime in the 1990s. Various groups take credit for this reduction: economists cite the healthy economy, law enforcement credits community policing, and some politicians suggest that credit should go to get-tough-on-crime policies. While it is difficult to determine a certain cause-and-effect relationship, drug abuse arrests, prosecutions, and convictions rose during the 1990s. But increasing peer pressure *against* crack cocaine use may be the one factor that contributed most to reduced crime in specific communities. In fact, many teens have worked hard to show friends that using crack is a disastrous choice.

Possession, distribution, or sale of certain drugs is a crime that may violate federal law, state law, or both. Some drugs, such as heroin, are particularly addictive and can severely disrupt the personal life of the user. The federal drug law, known as the *Controlled Substances Act,* classifies drugs into five groups, depending on medical use (if any),

Where You Live

Many states have passed laws that deal with drug offenses. What state and local laws deal with drugs where you live?

potential for abuse, and capability to create physical or psychological addiction. The penalties and criminal sanctions are different for each of the five groups.

Federal laws and most state laws now carry harsher penalties for drug offenders than they once did. Those who sell drugs or possess large amounts with intent to sell often face mandatory jail terms even for their first offense. Under federal law and in some states, those found guilty of being major drug traffickers may face a sentence of "life without parole." Some states treat simple possession of even small amounts of certain types of drugs as felonies. In addition to the federal government, some states have also enacted special drug forfeiture laws, which allow the government to seize property such as bank accounts, airplanes, automobiles, and even houses that were used for, or were acquired through the proceeds of, drug crimes.

Partly in an effort to combat drug-related crime, more than 40 states have some type of repeat offender or recidivist law. These laws, passed primarily in the 1990s, require long sentences—including sentences of life in prison without parole—for persons who are repeatedly convicted of the same crime, even relatively minor ones. Some of these laws have been highly criticized as being unduly harsh. In 2003, however, the U.S. Supreme Court ruled that California's recidivist law (called the Three Strikes Law) did not violate the Eighth Amendment protection against cruel and unusual punishment.

Law in *Action*

Drug Courts

In 1989 the federal government began promoting the use of drug courts. Drug courts embody a humane philosophy of treating drug offenders in that they offer treatment in place of punishment. These specialized courts give nonviolent offenders a simple deal: submit to drug testing on a regular basis, enroll in court-supervised drug treatment, stay off drugs, and you can stay out of jail. Failure to meet any of these conditions results in prosecution. Drug courts also work with offenders, helping them obtain education, training, and employment. By the end of 2000, there were over 600 drug courts, with plans to add several hundred more.

Problem 7.10

a. Are drug courts a good idea? Explain.

b. Do you have a drug court where you live? If so, is it effective?

c. Why might some places not want a drug court?

As a result of escalating drug use and drug-related violence, some people, including a few politicians, have proposed that perhaps American society should consider legalizing certain drugs, such as marijuana. These people point to the failure of the "war on drugs" and say that as long as some drugs are illegal, we are creating a market for their illegal sale. They believe the United States would be better able to control the sale and use of drugs if the laws changed from drug prohibition to drug regulation. Proponents of the legalization of drugs suggest that the United States treat drugs as a health problem. It is hypocritical, they claim, to restrict the use of drugs while allowing the legal sale of alcohol and tobacco, which studies show are very harmful to people's health and cause many more deaths than drugs.

Drug courts require offenders to submit to regular drug testing. *What other conditions set by the drug court must an offender meet?*

Some people favor legalizing certain drugs that can be used for medical purposes. Several states have passed ballot initiatives in favor of removing state criminal penalties for marijuana possession because of its potential medical use. While not striking down these state laws, in 2002 the Supreme Court ruled that federal drug laws do not contain any "medical use" exception. For this reason, criminal penalties remain in place for those prosecuted under federal laws.

Many others are opposed to any sort of drug legalization. They believe that legalizing drugs and making them easier to get would lead to greater drug use, cause more deaths, and increase other drug-related problems. These people feel that criminal laws deter drug use and that reducing penalties would deliver a message of acceptance. Legalizing drugs, they say, would result in what some people call "the addicting of America" and would endanger our society as a whole.

Problem 7.11

a. Are there any controlled substances that should be legalized (which still might allow some form of government regulation and even fines)? If so, which controlled substances should be legalized?

b. What are the most convincing arguments in favor of legalizing some controlled substances?

c. What are the most convincing arguments against legalizing any controlled substances?

d. How would society change if some controlled substances were legalized? Would these changes be good or bad? Explain.

Drugs in the City

The city of Southland has been plagued by a growing drug epidemic. City officials and citizens are especially outraged that adults are using teenagers to sell drugs for them. This happens because teens often receive lighter sentences than adults do for drug-related offenses. Southland is also facing an influx of drugs and drug dealers from other cities. The mayor has called a special council meeting to address the problem. Six experts have been asked to testify and present six different approaches to address the problem.

Police Chief Anderson (Law Enforcement Approach): "We cannot be everywhere at once. The department needs 100 more officers. The best way to combat the drug epidemic is to put more officers on the street and arm them with the newest and best weapons. Let's show the dealers and their customers that we mean business."

District Attorney Fisher (Restrict Civil Liberties Approach): "I think the city should declare an emergency and clamp down on drug sales on the street. Because of the epidemic, the civil liberties of the citizens of Southland must be temporarily limited. Since teenagers are selling drugs late at night, we need to institute a 9 P.M. curfew for anyone under the age of 18. I also advocate conducting random searches of students at school and establishing checkpoints where all cars will be stopped and searched in areas where drug trafficking is high."

Terry Blade (Drug Treatment Approach): "I am an ex-drug addict who was cured because I was arrested and sent to a good treatment program. I see drug treatment as the best way to cut the demand for drugs, thereby driving the drug dealers out of business. Many addicts are turned away because treatment spaces are limited in this community. I want the city to devote more resources to treating people addicted to drugs."

School Superintendent Lee (Preventive Education Approach): "Preventive education is the real answer to the drug problem. We must address the issue of values and the choices every student has—obey the law, or use or sell drugs. I want innovative drug education for every student, starting in the first grade."

Judge Horton (Penalties Approach): "Stiffer penalties are needed. The city council should recommend to the state legislature tougher mandatory sentences for drug offenders. Anyone aged 15 or older who is convicted of selling drugs should be given a mandatory two-year sentence and be treated as an adult."

Alana Fuentes (Legalization Approach): "We should push for the legalization of drugs. If drugs are made legal, the government can regulate the price and quality of the product, and thereby reduce or eliminate the black market for drugs. Drug addicts won't need to commit other crimes in order to obtain money to buy drugs at outrageously high street prices. Finally, our tax dollars won't be wasted chasing drug traffickers and international cartels. Some of the money saved should be used to fund preventive education programs and treatment programs."

Problem 7.12

a. After listening to the experts, decide which of the approaches will most help the city of Southland. List the six approaches in order of your preference and give reasons for your rankings.

b. What are the costs and benefits of each approach? What are the problems of each?

c. Could more than one of the approaches be tried at the same time? If so, which ones go together most easily?

d. Which approach will you vote for? Explain.

Victims of Crime

Crime affects us all, but victims suffer most. Victims of crime are found among all segments of society: young, old, rich, poor, and among people of all racial and ethnic groups. Each year, more than 24 million Americans aged 12 and older are victims of crime.

Teens and young adults are more likely to be victims of crime than people in any other age group. In 2001, persons 12 to 24 years old were victims of violent crime at rates higher than any other age group. Among persons aged 12 to 15, 55 of every 1,000 were victims of violent crime, compared to 3 of every 1,000 persons over age 65.

Gender, socioeconomic status, race, and location are also factors that influence a person's likelihood of becoming a victim of crime. Except for rape and sexual assault, males are more frequently the victims of violent crime. Persons from lower-income households are more likely to be victims of crime than those with higher incomes. Members of minority groups, urban dwellers, and those who rent their homes are more likely to be victims of crime than persons who are white, nonurban and property owners. For example, in 2000, 49 percent of all murder victims were African American, even though only 12 percent of the U.S. population were African American.

In recent years, public interest in aiding victims of crime has grown. Most states now have victim assistance programs. These programs provide victims with counseling, medical care, and other services and benefits. Most states also have victim compensation laws. These laws provide financial help for victims—paying medical bills, making up lost salary, and, in some cases, paying funeral costs and death benefits to victims' families. In recent years some states have begun to allow prosecutors to submit victim impact statements to the court when a person is sentenced for a crime. These impact statements show the effect of the defendant's crime on the victim's physical and psychological well-being. In addition, courts sometimes order **restitution**—requiring criminals to pay back or otherwise compensate the victims of their crimes.

Today, victim advocacy groups are playing a more significant role in the criminal justice system. Their primary function is to help victims through their trauma and also to protect the rights of victims. Most of these groups deal with specific crimes, like rape, spouse abuse, drunk driving, and child abuse. One highly successful victim advocacy group is Mothers Against Drunk Driving (MADD). In recent years, MADD has been instrumental in calling attention to the problem of drunk driving and in lobbying for and winning stricter punishment for people caught driving while intoxicated.

Where You Live

Contact your police or prosecutor's office to learn whether there is a victim's assistance program in your community. If there is one, how does it operate? Is there a victim compensation law? If so, how does it operate?

Urban dwellers are more likely to become victims of crime. *What other factors influence a person's likelihood of becoming a victim of crime?*

FIGURE 7.3 Violent Crime Rates

Year	Age of Victim (Adjusted victimization rates per 1,000 persons aged 12 and over)						
	12–15	16–19	20–24	25–34	35–49	50–64	65+
1990	101.1	99.1	86.1	55.2	34.4	9.9	3.7
1991	94.5	122.6	103.6	54.3	37.2	12.5	4.0
1992	111.0	103.7	95.2	56.8	38.1	13.2	5.2
1993	115.5	114.2	91.6	56.9	42.5	15.2	5.9
1994	118.6	123.9	100.4	59.1	41.3	17.6	4.6
1995	113.1	106.6	85.8	58.5	35.7	12.9	6.4
1996	95.0	102.8	74.5	51.2	32.9	15.7	4.9
1997	87.9	96.3	68.0	47.0	32.3	14.6	4.4
1998	82.5	91.3	67.5	41.6	29.9	15.4	2.9
1999	74.5	77.6	68.7	36.4	25.2	14.4	3.9
2000	60.1	64.4	49.5	34.9	21.8	13.7	3.7
2001	55.1	55.9	44.9	29.4	23.0	9.5	3.2

Race and Gender of Victim
(Adjusted victimization rates per 1,000 persons aged 12 and over)

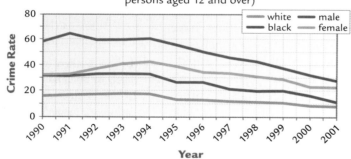

Sources: Rape, robbery, and assault data are from the *National Crime Victimization Survey (NCVS)*. The homicide data are collected by the *FBI's Uniform Crime Reports (UCR)* Supplementary Homicide Reports from reports from law enforcement agencies. Homicide estimates for 2001 are based on 2001 Preliminary Annual Release data.

Problem 7.13

Study the victimization data above. Then answer the following questions.

a. Which age group is most frequently the victim of crime? Least frequently?

b. What trend do you see in the data on victimization by age? Explain this trend.

c. What trend do you see in the data on victimization by gender? How would you explain this trend?

d. What trend do you see in the data on victimization by racial group? How might you explain this trend?

Visit streetlaw.glencoe.com and click on **Textbook Update—Chapter 7** for an update of the data.

Law in Action

Victims' Rights: Megan's Law as Advocacy

Victims' groups can often be successful in helping to pass legislation that provides protection for particularly vulnerable members of society. For example, in the early 1990s, seven-year-old Megan Kanka was abducted, sexually molested, and murdered by a neighbor who, unknown to her parents, was a convicted sex offender. Following this tragedy, through the advocacy of parent groups and communities, voters across the country began enacting local legislation that would help protect children from sex offenders. Within two years of Megan's abduction and murder, all 50 states and the District of Columbia had passed their own versions of Megan's Law, requiring the registration of all convicted sex offenders in the community. Ex-offenders have challenged these laws in several states, claiming they are being punished twice for the same offense—once by a term in jail and then again by being listed on these registries. In 2003 the U.S. Supreme Court upheld the Alaska and

Signing Megan's Law

Connecticut versions of these laws based on the states' interest in maintaining public safety and because the goal of an offender registry is to inform, not to judge an offender as currently dangerous to society.

Preventing and Reporting Crime

Crime is something that almost everyone worries about. As an effective citizen, you can help fight crime by learning how to protect yourself. This means knowing both how to prevent crime and what to do if you are ever a victim of crime. Remember that reporting crime helps to prevent others from becoming victims in the future. To reduce the risk of crime, be sure to take the following steps:

- Report suspicious activity to the police. The police cannot help you if you do not call them.

- Always lock doors and windows. You can prevent many burglaries by locking up! Also, when at home, do not open the door unless you know who is outside. Cancel newspapers and the mail when on vacation. Do not enter your home if you think someone has broken in. Instead, call police from a neighbor's house.

- Be alert when in high-crime areas such as dark, deserted streets and parking lots.
- Use the "buddy system." Criminals are less likely to target pairs or groups of people.
- Do not flash money in public.
- If you witness a crime or have been victimized, stay calm and call the police.
- Try to provide police with as much information as possible. If you can, write down the details of the situation as well as a description of the suspect.
- You may be asked to file a complaint or to testify in court. Helping the police will assist them in preventing the criminal from committing additional crimes in the future.

Crimes of identity theft and consumer fraud are also significant and growing problems. You can learn more about protecting yourself from these crimes in Chapter 10, Crimes Against Property. You will also learn about identity theft and consumer fraud in Unit 4, Consumer and Housing Law.

If You Become a Victim

There are two different views on what to do if you believe you are about to become the victim of a crime. The first theory is that you should not fight back. For property crimes, for example, many believe you should give up the property without objection to reduce your risk of injury. The second theory is that you should resist the assailant. Many advocate learning self-defense techniques to protect yourself in the event of a personal crime. Which course should you follow? Every situation is unique, but your safety should always come first.

If you choose to fight back against the assailant, be prepared to risk injury. Know your own limitations. Not everyone has the strength or size to be able to fight back successfully. If the assailant has a weapon, you should assume it is going to be used.

As a general rule, criminals do not want an audience. If you are able to scream or blow a whistle, do so if you know you will be heard. If you cannot run away, sit down so you will not get knocked down. Finally, call the police as soon as you can. Do not wait! The longer you wait, the more likely it is that the criminal will get away.

Survivors of crime can turn to governments and private organizations for assistance. *In what ways can a rape crisis center help a rape victim?*

Law in *Action*

Good Samaritan Laws

Are witnesses to crimes under any obligation to come to the aid of victims? Until recently, the legal answer, as opposed to the moral answer, was no. Most states have had Good Samaritan laws that relieve bystanders from most civil liability when they help people in danger, but they have not required bystanders to help. Now, however, several new state laws require witnesses to offer whatever help they can reasonably provide without endangering themselves. In the case of a violent crime, this simply means reporting the crime to the police. Does your state require witnesses to report violent crimes to police? If not, should it?

Problem 7.14

a. Do you know anyone who has been the victim of a crime? What was the crime? How did it affect the person? The person's family?

b. List and discuss at least four things you can do to protect yourself from becoming a victim of crime.

c. Have you ever witnessed a crime? What happened? What did you do? If it happened again, would you do the same thing?

Getting Help for Survivors of Crime

Many federal, state, and local governments, as well as private organizations, have established programs to assist survivors of crimes. These programs range from counseling and support groups to advocacy initiatives to funds established to lend financial assistance to families of and survivors of crime. Two such groups are the National Center for Victims of Crime and the Office for Victims of Crime.

The National Center for Victims of Crime is a nongovernmental organization that provides local services, crisis intervention, and practical information related to navigating through the criminal justice system. The organization also provides counseling services. Additional information about the National Center for Victims of Crime and its services can be found online at www.ncvc.org.

The Office for Victims of Crime is a federally administered program that was established by the *Victims of Crime Act of 1984*. It provides a vehicle for policy and legislative initiatives, as well as providing services to victims and families. The Office for Victims of Crime provides information online at www.ojp.usdoj.gov/ovc.

Introduction to Criminal Law

> "Criminal law has to do with relations between the misbehaving individual and his government . . . . Criminal law establishes rules of conduct; their breach, if prosecuted and conviction follows, results in punishment."
>
> — Lawrence M. Friedman, *American Law*

Street Law *online*

Visit the *Street Law* Web site at streetlaw.glencoe.com for chapter-based information and resources.

Almost all crimes require an act, accompanied by a guilty **state of mind.** A guilty state of mind usually means that the prohibited act was done intentionally, knowingly, or willfully. In most cases, mere carelessness is not considered a guilty state of mind. For example, if Meredith accidentally forgot to turn the stove off before leaving for work and the whole apartment building caught fire as a result, she would not be guilty of arson, which is the intentional burning of a person's property. She committed the act (burning a person's property) but did not have the guilty state of mind (intent).

State of mind is different from **motive.** While state of mind deals with the level of awareness of performing some act—whether it was done purposely, intentionally, or recklessly—motive is the reason for performing the act. For example, in murder, the motive is the reason a person kills someone (for revenge, to obtain money, etc.). Robin Hood may have had a good motive for stealing from the rich: to give to the poor. However, his state of mind in committing the theft was still intentional and knowing and, therefore, he would be guilty of a crime.

Police officers secure a crime scene to ensure that evidence is not lost.

A few crimes are **strict liability** offenses. These crimes do not require a guilty state of mind. The act itself is criminal, regardless of the knowledge or intent of the person committing the act. For example, the law makes it a strict liability crime to sell alcoholic beverages to minors. This is true regardless of whether or not the seller knew the buyer was underage. Just because a crime does not specify a state of mind, however, does not mean it is a strict liability offense. Courts will usually assume that some guilty state of mind is required unless the legislature specifically intended to pass a strict liability law. Most often, strict liability statutes are limited to crimes that do not carry severe penalties or to crimes that are part of a larger attempt to regulate some area of conduct.

General Considerations

Every crime is defined by certain **elements,** each of which must be proven at trial in order to convict the offender. Thus, in addition to proving any required guilty mental state, the prosecutor must prove beyond a reasonable doubt that every element of the crime was committed. For example, robbery is defined as the unlawful taking and carrying away of goods or money from someone's person by force or intimidation. Thus, the elements of robbery are (1) the taking and carrying away of goods or money, (2) the taking from someone's person, and (3) use of force or intimidation.

Problem 8.1

Anton is a bully. One night while eating at a local diner, he notices Derek selecting a tune on the jukebox. Anton does not like the song Derek picks, so to show his pals who is in charge, Anton orders Derek to change the song. When Derek refuses, Anton punches him in the face, breaking Derek's jaw. As a result of the injury, Derek misses several weeks of work and has to pay both medical and dental bills.

a. Has Anton violated civil laws, criminal laws, or both?

b. Who decides whether Anton should be charged criminally? Sued in a civil action?

c. If Anton is charged with a crime and sued in a civil action, would the civil and criminal cases be tried together? Why or why not?

d. Would procedures in a criminal trial be the same as those in a civil trial? Why or why not?

e. Is going to court the only way to handle this problem? What alternatives are there and which do you think would work best?

If someone breaks into your house when you are not home and takes your property, the person cannot be convicted of robbery. The person did not take the property from a person (no one was home) and did not use force or intimidation. However, the person could be guilty of burglary—breaking and entering into a home with intent to commit a felony—because the elements of that crime do not require the taking from a person or the use of force.

A single act can be both a crime and a civil wrong. For example, if Clay purposely sets fire to Tamika's store, the state may file criminal charges against Clay for arson. Tamika may also bring a separate civil action (lawsuit) against Clay to recover for the damage to her store. You will learn more about civil cases (torts) in Unit 3.

State and Federal Crimes

Criminal laws exist at both the state and federal levels. Some acts, such as simple assault, disorderly conduct, drunk driving, and shoplifting, can be prosecuted only in a state court unless they occur on federal property, such as a national park. Other acts, such as failure to pay federal taxes, mail fraud, espionage, and international smuggling, can be prosecuted only in a federal court. Certain crimes, such as illegal possession of drugs and bank robbery, can violate both state and federal law and can be prosecuted in either state or federal court.

Classes of Crimes

Crimes are classified as either felonies or misdemeanors. A felony is a crime for which the potential penalty is imprisonment for more than one year. Felonies are usually more serious crimes. A misdemeanor is any crime for which the potential penalty is imprisonment for one year or less. Minor traffic violations are not considered crimes, although they are punishable by law. This chapter deals primarily with felonies and major misdemeanors.

Parties to Crimes

The person who commits a crime is called the principal. For example, the person who fires the gun in a murder is the principal. An accomplice is someone who helps the principal commit a crime. For example, the person who drives the getaway car during a bank robbery is an accomplice. An accomplice may be charged with and convicted of the same crime as the principal. A person who orders a crime or helps the principal commit the crime but who is not present during the crime—for example, the mob leader who hires a professional killer—is known as an accessory before the fact. This person can usually be charged with the same crime and can receive the same punishment as the principal. An accessory after the fact is a person who, knowing a crime has been committed, helps the principal or an accomplice avoid capture or helps them escape. This person is not charged with the original crime but may be charged with harbor-

ing a fugitive, aiding the escape, or obstructing justice. Being an accessory after the fact has been made a separate crime by statute in many jurisdictions.

> An accomplice can be charged with the same crime as the person who commits the crime. *Describe the difference between an accessory before the fact and an accessory after the fact.*

Problem 8.2

Jeb and Marci decide to burglarize Superior Jewelers. Their friend Carl, an employee at Superior, helps by telling them the location of the store vault. Marci drives a van to the store and keeps a lookout while Jeb goes inside and cracks the safe. After Jeb and Marci make their getaway, Jeb meets a friend, Shawn, who was not involved in the actual burglary. Jeb tells Shawn about the burglary, and Shawn helps Jeb get a train out of town. David, a former classmate of Jeb and Marci, witnesses the crime but does not tell the police, even though he recognizes both Jeb and Marci. How will each person be charged?

Crimes of Omission

Most crimes occur when a person does something or performs some act in violation of a law. In a few cases, however, failing to act—called an omission—may be a crime if the person had a legal duty to act. For example, it is a crime for a taxpayer to fail to file a tax return or for a motorist to fail to stop after being involved in an automobile accident. A person is guilty of a **crime of omission** when he or she fails to perform an act required by a criminal law, if he or she is physically able to perform the required act.

Preliminary Crimes

Certain types of behavior take place before, and often in preparation for, the commission of a crime. However, these preliminary crimes are nevertheless complete crimes in themselves. These offenses—solicitation, attempt, and conspiracy—give the police the opportunity to prevent the intended crime. Each offense can be punished even if the harm intended never occurred. For example, when two people agree to rob a bank, they commit the offense of conspiracy—whether or not they actually commit the robbery.

Solicitation

A number of states make it a crime for a person to solicit—or ask, command, urge, or advise—another person to commit a crime. The offense is committed at the time the solicitation is made. It does not require that the person solicited, or asked, actually commits the crime. For example, Dennis wishes to kill his wife, Carmella. Lacking the nerve to do the job himself, he asks William to kill her. Even if William refuses, Dennis has committed the crime of solicitation.

Attempt

In most states, an attempt to commit a crime is itself a crime. To be guilty of an attempted crime, the accused must have both intended to commit a crime and taken some "substantial step" toward committing the crime. Mere preparation to commit a crime is not enough.

When someone performs all of the elements of a crime but fails to achieve the criminal result, an attempt has occurred. For example, when a person intends to shoot and kill someone but misses or merely wounds the intended victim, the person is guilty of attempted murder. Sometimes, the crime is foiled before all of the necessary steps are completed, such as when a person purchases a gun, intends to shoot another person, but is arrested on the way to the intended victim's house. Courts must then determine whether the actions of the accused constituted a "substantial step" toward the actual commission of the crime or were mere acts of preparation.

The Case of . . .

The Drowning Girl

Abe, Kristi, Chin, and Hannah see Jill drowning in a lake, but none of them takes steps to save her. Abe is the girl's father. Kristi deliberately pushed Jill into the lake by shoving Chin against her. Hannah, a medal-winning swimmer, just stands and watches. Would any of the four be criminally liable for Jill's drowning? Should any of them be liable? Explain your answer.

Problem 8.3

Examine the following situations and decide whether any of the individuals involved would be guilty of the crime of attempt.

a. Martin, a bank teller, figures out a foolproof method of stealing money from the bank. It takes him some time to get up the nerve to steal any money. Finally, he makes up his mind and tells his girlfriend, Yuka, that tomorrow he will steal the money. Yuka goes to the police, and Martin is arrested an hour later.

b. Gilbert, an accomplished thief, is caught while trying to pick Lewis's pocket. He pleads not guilty and says he cannot possibly be convicted, because Lewis did not have a penny on him.

c. Rita and Anwar decide to rob a liquor store. They meet at a pub and talk over their plans. Rita leaves to buy a revolver, and Anwar leaves to steal a car for use in their getaway. Rita is arrested as she walks out of the gun shop with her new revolver. Anwar is arrested while trying to hot-wire a car.

d. Amy decides to burn down her store to collect the insurance money. She spreads gasoline around the building. She is arrested while leaving the store to get a book of matches.

Conspiracy

A **conspiracy** is an agreement between two or more persons to commit a crime. The designation of conspiracy as a crime is meant to prevent other crimes and to strike against criminal activity by groups. It also allows police to arrest conspirators before they come dangerously close to completing the crime. For example, the federal government aggressively pursued anyone believed to have conspired with the

The U.S. government took into custody people, such as Zacarias Moussaoui, believed to have conspired against the United States in the September 11, 2001 terrorist attacks. *Why is the designation of conspiracy as a crime sometimes criticized as a threat to First Amendment freedoms?*

al-Qaeda network in the terrorist attacks of September 11, 2001. The goal is to punish those involved in the attacks and to prevent any future terrorist activities from being carried out against U.S. interests. However, the designation of conspiracy as a crime is sometimes criticized as a threat to freedom of speech and association. For example, during the Vietnam War, the government charged several people with conspiracy for speaking publicly to young men on how to avoid the draft. Many critics of criminal conspiracy said the accused were being denied the freedom of speech.

An example of criminal conspiracy is the situation in which Nick, a drug dealer, asks Lyle, his associate, to help him kill another dealer. If Lyle agrees to Nick's request and then takes some step toward committing the crime, both are guilty of conspiracy to commit murder, even if the murder is never attempted or accomplished.

In most states and under federal law, an *overt* act—an act that is open to view—is required for conviction on a conspiracy charge. For example, a young man named John Walker Lindh was charged and pled guilty to several counts of conspiring against the United States in the wake of the 2001 terrorist attacks. The fact that he failed to warn the U.S. government about his knowledge of planned attacks against the country constituted overt acts upon which the conspiracy charges were based.

Law in *Action*

Conspiracy and the Oklahoma City Bombing

On April 19, 1995, there was a tragic bombing of a large federal building in Oklahoma City, Oklahoma. Many employees, as well as children in a day-care center located in the building, were killed.

In addition to federal and state prosecutions of the individuals who allegedly committed the bombing, the federal government also prosecuted an individual who did not actually take part that day in the bombing. He was convicted of conspiracy to transport explosives across state lines and of failing to inform authorities about this illegal activity.

A federal law called **misprision of felony** makes it a felony, punishable by up to three years in prison, for a person with knowledge of the actual commission of a felony that violates federal law to actively conceal this information (i.e., that he knew about the planned bombing) from law enforcement or judicial officers. What are the benefits of having a law that punishes actively concealing information about the commission of a felony that violates federal law? What obstacles might the government face in prosecuting the violation of such a law? Do you think such a law should exist? Explain.

Crimes Against the Person

Crimes against the person include homicide, assault, battery, and rape. All of these crimes are serious offenses. A defendant found guilty of any one of them may receive a harsh sentence. The law also protects the defendant from overly harsh penalties by defining various levels of these crimes and by considering the circumstances of each offense.

Homicide

Homicide—the killing of one human being by another—is the most serious of all acts. Homicides may be either criminal or noncriminal. Criminal homicide is committed with intent, or a plan. It is also considered criminal homicide if a person's reckless actions, without regard for human life, result in the killing of another person. Noncriminal homicide can be classified as either "excusable" or "justifiable," and is not subject to criminal charges.

Street Law *online*

Visit the *Street Law* Web site at streetlaw.glencoe.com for chapter-based information and resources.

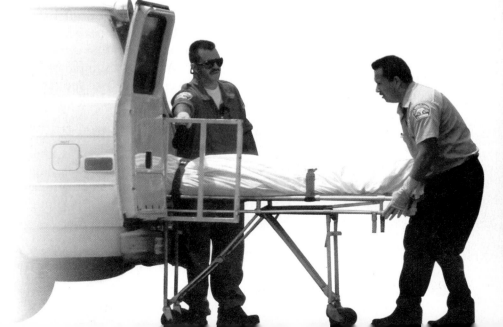

Coroners remove a body from the scene of a homicide.

Where You Live

What forms of homicide exist under your state's criminal statutes? What is the range of punishments for each level of the crime?

Criminal Homicide

Murder, the most serious form of criminal homicide, is killing that is done with **malice**. Malice means having the intent to kill or seriously harm another person or acting in an extremely reckless manner which shows a lack of regard for human life. At one time, there were no degrees of murder. Any homicide done with malice was considered to be murder and was punishable by death. To reduce the punishment for less-grievous homicides, most states now have statutes that classify murder according to the killer's state of mind or the circumstances surrounding the crime.

First-degree murder is usually defined as killing that is premeditated (thought about beforehand), deliberate, and done with malice. It is an action with an intent to kill or cause severe bodily injury or with a depraved indifference to human life. Courts have often found that the premeditation and deliberation can occur very close to the time of the homicide.

Felony murder is any killing that takes place during the commission of certain felonies, such as arson, rape, robbery, or burglary. It is not necessary to prove intent; malice is presumed because the homicide occurred during the felony, even if the killing was accidental. Most states consider felony murder to be first-degree murder regardless of whether malice, premeditation, and deliberation exist.

Second-degree murder is killing that is done with malice, but without premeditation or deliberation. That is, the intent to kill did not exist until the moment of the murder. Second-degree murder includes intentional but spontaneous killings that are unplanned.

Voluntary manslaughter is killing that would otherwise be murder, but that occurs after the victim has done something to the killer that would cause a reasonable person to lose self-control or act rashly. A person who kills someone in a violent argument or quarrel without first planning to do so is guilty of voluntary manslaughter. Words alone, no matter how offensive, do not reduce the severity of a murder to voluntary manslaughter. Also, the killing must occur just after the provocation so that the killer did not have an opportunity to "cool down." A typical example of voluntary manslaughter is when a person discovers his or her spouse with someone else and that person kills the spouse's lover in a jealous rage. Voluntary manslaughter is punished somewhat less severely than murder as a concession to the frailty of human character.

Involuntary manslaughter is a killing in which there is no intent to kill at all. It is unintentional killing resulting from conduct so reckless that it causes extreme danger of death or bodily injury. An example of involuntary manslaughter is killing that results from playing with a gun known to be loaded.

Negligent homicide means causing death through criminal negligence. **Negligence** is the failure to exercise a reasonable or ordinary amount of care in a situation, thereby causing harm to someone. Some states classify death by gross, or extreme, negligence as involuntary manslaughter. The most common form of negligent homicide is vehicular homicide. This is killing that results from operating a motor vehicle in a reckless and grossly negligent manner. Any death that results from careless driving may lead to a civil suit for damages, but it is usually not considered a crime unless the death results from gross negligence.

YOU BE THE JUDGE

Homicide Cases

Read each of the following situations carefully. For each one, determine who can be charged with homicide and the degree of homicide for which they should be charged. Give your reasons.

a. Walt decides to shoot Yolanda, whom he blames for all his troubles. As he is driving to her home to carry out the murder, he accidentally hits a jogger who darted out from behind a tree. Stopping immediately, Walt rushes to help the jogger, who is already dead. Assume that Walt was driving at a safe speed and that the collision was unavoidable.

b. Belva is cheated when she buys a car from Fast Eddie's Car Mart. She attempts to return the car, but Eddie just laughs and tells her to go away. Every time Belva has to make a repair on the car, she gets angry. Finally, she decides to wreck Eddie's car to get even with him. Following him home from work one evening, Belva tries to ram his car, hoping to bend the axle or frame. Instead of bending the frame, the collision smashes Eddie's gas tank, causes an explosion, and kills him.

The car explosion

c. Alison and Brad decide to rob a bank. Brad drives the getaway car. Alison goes into the bank and pulls out her gun, announcing, "This is a stickup. Don't move!" The bank guard, Gordon, shoots at Alison but misses, killing Dawn, a customer.

Noncriminal Homicide

Some homicides are not considered crimes at all. Noncriminal homicide is killing that is justifiable or excusable and for which the killer is deemed faultless. Examples of noncriminal homicide include the killing of an enemy soldier in wartime, the killing of a condemned criminal by an executioner, the killing by a police officer of a person who is committing a serious crime and who poses a threat of death or serious harm, and a killing performed in self-defense or in defense of another person.

Suicide

Suicide, the deliberate taking of one's own life, was once considered a crime. States that regard it as a crime today, however, prohibit only *attempted* suicide. Courts often treat suicide as a plea for help, requiring the person who attempted it to undergo a psychological examination and receive treatment, often in the form of counseling. Someone who helps another person commit suicide can, however, be found guilty of the crime of murder or manslaughter.

Suicide is one of the leading causes of death among teenagers. The Centers for Disease Control and Prevention (CDC) reported that in 2001, 19 percent of teens in grades 9 through 12 reported seriously considering suicide, 15 percent made a plan to commit suicide, and 9 percent attempted suicide. The CDC also reported that, on average, a high school student succeeds in killing himself or herself every 15 minutes.

Although many people have suicidal thoughts at some point in their lives, most never attempt suicide. Many can be helped by suicide hotlines, medication, counseling, and other programs for those who may be considering suicide. Despairing individuals may need someone else to talk to who can help them see positive alternatives to ending their life.

There are many national hotlines that may be helpful for teens considering suicide, a few of which are described here. The National Crisis Helpline assists by locating the nearest crisis service in the United States, and can be reached by calling toll-free 1-800-999-9999.

Hotlines and other services are available for people who are considering suicide. *How can hotlines help such individuals?*

The Dying Cancer Patient

Wilfred, age 75, has been suffering from cancer for 10 years. The pain associated with the cancer is severe and has become worse over time. Wilfred's doctors say there is no treatment to either slow down the cancer's growth or substantially reduce the pain. Wilfred asks Martha, his wife of 50 years, to relieve him of the terrible pain. He asks her to bring him a bottle of pills that would help him end his own life. Martha, who cannot stand watching Wilfred suffer anymore, gives him the pills. He swallows them all, slowly fades off to sleep, and dies.

Problem 9.1

a. Was Wilfred's request related to suicide? Explain.

b. If you were the district attorney in the state where Martha lives, would you file criminal charges against her? Explain.

c. If manslaughter charges were filed and you were on the jury, would you vote to convict Martha? Give your reasons. If Martha were convicted, what sentence should she receive? Why?

d. If the bottle of pills had been given to Wilfred by a physician instead of by his wife, would your answers have been different? Give your reasons.

e. If you were a state legislator, would you advocate a law allowing assisted suicide? Explain.

The National Youth Crisis Hotline provides guidance and support to teens in crisis. Volunteers discuss issues and provide referrals in such areas as suicide prevention, pregnancy, gangs, runaway services, eating disorders, physical abuse, and substance abuse. The National Youth Crisis Hotline can be reached by calling toll-free 1-800-HIT-HOME (448-4663) or 1-800-442-HOPE (4673). It also offers information online at www.1800hithome.com.

You can also use the phone book or Internet to find suicide hotlines and prevention programs located in your community. A directory of suicide hotlines for every state can be found online at www.suicidehotlines.com. There may also be programs especially for teenagers or the elderly.

Assault and Battery

Assault is any attempt or threat to carry out a physical attack upon another person. **Battery** is any unlawful physical contact inflicted by one person upon another person without consent. Actual injury is not necessary. The only requirement is that the person must have intended to do bodily harm. Today, there is often not much difference in law or practice between the uses of the words *assault* and *battery*.

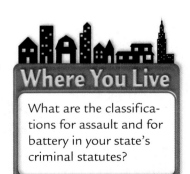

Where You Live

What are the classifications for assault and for battery in your state's criminal statutes?

Anti-stalking laws protect people from harassment and threats. *Does your state have anti-stalking laws?*

Just as there are degrees of murder, there are also different classifications for assault and battery. Many states now have separate statutes for assault with intent to rob or assault with intent to murder. Aggravated battery is often defined by the harm inflicted: an unarmed assault that results in a serious physical injury is an aggravated battery rather than a simple assault.

Assaults typically result from arguments between people who know each other. In such arguments, rage—often stimulated by alcohol or jealousy—leads to violence. Whether the violence leads to serious injury or death often depends on the presence of a weapon.

Stalking occurs when a person repeatedly follows or harasses another person and makes threats, causing the victim to fear death or bodily injury. Women are the targets of most of the cases of stalking that occur each year. To deal with the growing problem of harassment, most states now have anti-stalking laws.

Sexual assault is a specific kind of assault that can include rape or attempted rape. Sexual assault includes a wide range of victimizations from verbal threats of a sexual nature to unwanted sexual contact between the victim and the offender. Like assault and battery, sexual assault can be an attack that is either completed or attempted. The unwanted contact might include grabbing or fondling and may, but does not have to, involve force. Contrary to traditional views of male and female roles, both men and women are capable of committing and being victims of sexual assault.

Rape

Traditionally, the law has recognized the separate crimes of rape and statutory rape. **Rape** is sexual intercourse without consent. An aggravated form of rape occurs when the perpetrator uses a weapon or some other form of force to compel the victim to have intercourse. **Statutory rape** is intercourse between an adult and a minor.

This area of law is in transition as many states are replacing their rape laws with criminal sexual assault laws. Rape is a serious form of criminal sexual assault. As noted, the crime requires a lack of consent on the part of the victim. There is no consent if the victim is unconscious or mentally incompetent or if drugs or alcohol impair the victim's judgment. The perpetrator and the victim can be of either sex. These laws, therefore, can be used to prosecute women as well as men and can be used to prosecute same-sex criminal sexual assault.

Statutory rape—sexual intercourse between an adult and a minor child—has traditionally been used to punish males for having sexual relations with underage females (generally females under the age of 12 or under the age of 16, depending on the state's law). Statutory rape differs from rape in a very important way: lack of consent is not an element of the crime. This crime is based on the notion that a minor is incapable of giving legal consent. A male can be prosecuted for statutory rape with a minor even if the female lied about her age. Statutory rape goes to the crime when the victim is younger than the specific age and "consents." Statutory rape laws are also changing. The tendency is to recognize that either males or females can commit or be victims of statutory rape. There is also a trend in many states not to charge a person with statutory rape unless the perpetrator is several years older than the victim, although this age difference requirement is never used to define rape.

There is a range of ways that states define forcible or statutory rape. States also tend to have specific sentencing laws that require more severe punishments for certain forms of sexual assault. When the victim is under a certain age, over a certain age, disabled, or threatened with a weapon, punishment may be more severe.

In the past, defendants in rape cases were allowed to present evidence to the jury about the victim's past sexual behavior and reputation in order to show that she had probably consented to the act. Most states and the federal system have passed "rape shield" laws, which now prohibit introducing such evidence. To convict a person

Authorities must confirm the rape victim's story in order to proceed with the case. *What are "rape shield" laws?*

of rape, some states require independent proof that the act took place. This means confirmation or support for the story of the victim, including testimony of a witness, a doctor's report that sexual intercourse took place, or a prompt report to the police.

The trend has been to be more protective of victims—that is, to make sure the defendant and not the victim is put on trial. Yet it is also true that the sometimes unclear nature of male-female relationships, as well as same-sex relationships, presents challenges for the criminal justice system. While criminal sexual assault is a serious crime and should be punished as such, the criminal justice system must also protect against punishing an accused person unless the victim clearly expresses a lack of consent.

In recent years, the term acquaintance rape (also known as date rape) has been used to describe a sexual assault by someone known to the victim—a date, steady boyfriend, neighbor, or friend. Many victims of acquaintance rape do not report the assault. This may be because they do not realize an attack that occurs on a date can in fact constitute a rape.

Where You Live

How do the sexual assault or rape laws work in your state? Have they changed in recent years? Do they need to be changed? If so, how?

Problem 9.2

For each case below, assume that the two people have sexual intercourse. Assume that the police find out about the sexual activity in each instance. How should each situation be handled?

a. At midnight, a man breaks into the home of a woman he does not know. He goes to her bedroom, awakens her, pulls out a knife, and threatens to stab her unless she has sex with him. She tells him that she does not want to have sex. But then she says, "If you are going to do this, you'd better use a condom." He agrees.

b. A famous boxer serves as a judge at a beauty contest. After the contest, he invites an 18-year-old contestant to his hotel room. She meets him there. Later, she says he forced her to have sex.

c. A male high school student, aged 17, and a female high school student, aged 14, go out on a date. After attending a party, they agree to have intercourse in his car. The next day, he brags about this at school, and she goes to the police. There is some evidence that he is part of an informal organization of high school seniors who are involved in a competition to have sex with as many girls as possible.

d. Leo and Nina are college juniors who have had three dates. On these dates, they have never engaged in any sexual activity beyond a brief good-night kiss. On their fourth date, he invites her to an all-night drinking party at his fraternity house. She drinks too much, goes up to his room alone around 1:00 A.M., and falls asleep. In the morning, she wakes up to discover that she and Leo had intercourse during the night.

e. Lori, a 25-year-old high school teacher, becomes a good friend of Jim, a 17-year-old student in one of her classes. On a senior class trip to the state capital, Jim knocks on her hotel room door late at night. Lori lets him in, and they have sexual intercourse.

Crimes Against Property

> *"The more laws, the more offenders."*
>
> — Anonymous

The category of crimes against property includes two groups. Crimes in which property is destroyed include such acts as arson and vandalism. Crimes in which property is stolen or otherwise taken against the will of the owner include those acts such as robbery and embezzlement.

In recent years the number of property crimes has fallen, in part at least because Americans have developed better crime prevention behaviors. These behaviors include security lighting, home and automobile alarm systems, steering wheel locks, greater attention to locking doors and windows, and a tendency to carry less cash due to the greater use of credit cards.

Street Law *online*

Visit the *Street Law* Web site at streetlaw.glencoe.com for chapter-based information and resources.

Crimes against property include arson, the deliberate burning of property.

Arson

Arson is the willful and malicious burning of a person's property. In most states, it is a crime to burn any building or structure, even if the person who burns the structure owns it. Moreover, burning property with the intent to defraud an insurance company is usually a separate crime, regardless of the type of property burned or who owned the property.

At various times arson has also been a form of racial violence. To help federal prosecutors deal with a rash of racially motivated church arsons, Congress passed the *Church Arson Prevention Act of 1996*. This act helps oversee the investigation and prosecution of arson at places of worship across the United States. The act also seeks to increase the penalties for such crimes.

Vandalism

Vandalism, also known as malicious mischief, is willful destruction of, or damage to, the property of another. Vandalism is responsible for millions of dollars in damage each year. It includes such things as breaking windows, ripping down fences, writing graffiti, and breaking off car hood ornaments. Depending on the extent of the damage, vandalism can be either a felony or a misdemeanor.

Problem 10.1

a. Why do young people sometimes commit acts of vandalism?

b. What, if anything, can be done to reduce vandalism?

c. Should parents be criminally responsible for willful damage caused by their children? Why or why not?

d. If you saw two youths throwing rocks through the windows of a school at night, would you report the youths to the police? Why or why not? Suppose you saw two friends throwing rocks through the windows of a neighbor's home. Would you report your friends to the police? Why or why not? Did you answer both questions the same way? If not, explain why.

Larceny

Larceny is the unlawful taking and carrying away of the property of another person with intent to permanently deprive the owner of it. In most states, larceny is divided into two classes, grand and petty, depending on the value of the stolen item. Grand larceny involves the theft of anything above a certain value, often $100 or more, and is a felony. Petty larceny is the theft of anything of small value, usually less than $100, and is a misdemeanor.

There are several ways store owners can reduce shoplifting. *How do sensor tags on clothing reduce shoplifting?*

The crime of larceny also includes keeping lost property when a reasonable method exists for finding the owner. For example, if you find a wallet that contains the identification of its owner but nevertheless decide to keep it, you have committed larceny. Likewise, you may be guilty of larceny if you keep property delivered to you by mistake.

Shoplifting is a form of larceny. It is the crime of taking items from a store without paying or intending to pay for them. Some states have a separate crime called concealment. This is the crime of attempted shoplifting.

Shoplifting results in businesses' losing billions of dollars each year. The costs are usually passed on to consumers in the form of higher prices. Consequently, everyone ends up paying for shoplifting.

Problem 10.2

a. Why do you think people shoplift? List the reasons.

b. What could be done to address each of the reasons for shoplifting you listed? Which would be most effective? Why?

c. If you saw a stranger shoplifting in a store, what would you do? Would your answer be different if you knew the person? If the person were a good friend of yours?

d. A famous movie star is caught shoplifting thousands of dollars worth of merchandise from an upscale women's clothing store. It is her first offense. What penalty should she receive? Would the penalty you recommend be different if she were not famous?

Human Rights USA

Discussions of human rights often refer to the importance of every person treating every other person with dignity. Closely related to this are the human rights to equality and for people not to be subjected to degrading treatment or discrimination (Universal Declaration of Human Rights, [UDHR] Articles 1, 2, 5, and 7).

There is also a human right to own property and to not be deprived arbitrarily of it (UDHR, Article 17).

Examine the case below from a human rights perspective.

The Case of the Teenagers and the Store Owner

Mr. Zimmerman, who is white, has owned Smart Clothing, a clothing store in an urban area, for over twenty years. The city's population used to be about 80 percent white, and most of Smart Clothing's customers were also white. Crime—and in particular, shoplifting—used to be very low, but the rate has risen in recent years. During this time more African Americans and Hispanics have moved into the city, and they have become the store's principal customers.

Over the past year, Mr. Zimmerman increased security in the store and even began to search some suspicious-looking customers. He put up a highly visible sign for people to see as they entered the store:

"Due to an increase in shoplifting, all customers must agree to be subject to random searches as requested by the security guard. We apologize for the inconvenience, but reducing the incidence of shoplifting will result in lower prices for our law-abiding customers and enable us to stay in business."

During the past year, over 200 customers have been searched because they were viewed as suspicious. In 50 cases, unpaid-for goods were discovered. In 40 of these 50 cases, the arrested shoplifters were teenagers, and 90 percent of them were either African American or Hispanic. Because of the high percentage of teen and minority shoplifters, Mr. Zimmerman has instructed his security guards to "pay particular attention to these types of people." Consequently, the guards watch minority teens very closely, walking behind them while they are in the store, and search them more often than white teens or adults.

These events have upset many African American and Hispanic teens and some of their parents. The parents believe the teens' human rights have been violated. Mr. Zimmerman says he is just trying to protect his own human rights and those of his other customers. He says the increase in shoplifting has reduced his profits and that he may have to close the store if shoplifting continues at the same rate.

Problem 10.3

a. What human rights might the teenagers claim are being violated by the searches?

b. What human rights might Mr. Zimmerman claim are being violated by the shoplifting?

c. Whose human rights are more important in this situation? Explain.

d. Role-play a meeting between Mr. Zimmerman, his security guards, and the teens. What other options might Mr. Zimmerman have for addressing the problem of shoplifting in his store? Were these or any other options discussed in the role play?

Embezzlement

Embezzlement is the unlawful taking of property by someone to whom it was entrusted. For example, the bank teller who takes money from the cash drawer or the stockbroker who takes money that should have been invested are both guilty of embezzlement. In recent years, a number of states have merged the crimes of embezzlement, larceny, and obtaining property by false pretenses (intentional misstatements of fact) into the statutory crime of theft.

Robbery

Robbery is the unlawful taking of property from a person's immediate possession by force or intimidation. Though included here as a crime against property, robbery, unlike other theft offenses, involves two harms: theft of property and actual or potential physical harm to the victim. In most states, the difference between robbery and larceny is the use of force. Hence, a pickpocket who takes your wallet unnoticed is guilty of the crime of larceny. A mugger who knocks you down and takes your wallet by force is guilty of the crime of robbery. Robbery is almost always a felony, but many states impose stricter penalties for armed robberies—thefts committed with a gun or other weapon.

After being charged with illegal business practices, Enron corporation laid off many employees. *How are larceny and embezzlement different? How are they similar?*

Extortion

Extortion, popularly called blackmail, is the use of threats to obtain the property of another. Extortion statutes generally cover threats to do future physical harm, destroy property, or injure someone's character or reputation. For example, a person who threatens to injure you or your property unless you give him your car is guilty of extortion.

Burglary

Burglary was originally defined as breaking and entering the dwelling of another person during the night with intent to commit a felony therein. Modern laws have broadened the definition to include the unauthorized entry into any structure with the intent to commit a crime, regardless of the time of day. Many states have stiffer penalties for burglaries committed at night, burglaries of inhabited dwellings, and burglaries committed with weapons.

Identity Theft

Despite the great benefits our society has gained from technological developments, technology has also spawned the development of a new kind of crook: the identity thief. This thief steals a piece of personal information like your Social Security number, your bank account number or a credit card number and uses it to commit a fraud or further theft. Everyday actions like throwing out your garbage, sending a rent check to your landlord, or ordering a book online put you at risk for identity theft. If someone steals and uses your personal information illegally, it can cost you hundreds or thousands of dollars. Identity theft can also cost you your credit rating and good name, not to mention the significant time and emotional expense of trying to clean up the mess. While it might not be possible to prevent identity theft altogether, there are steps you can take to minimize your exposure to this crime.

- **Check your credit report.** Order your credit report from each of the three main credit bureaus in the United States (www.equifax.com, www.transunion.com, www.experian.com), and check each for accuracy.

- **Protect your personal information in your own home.** This is especially important if you have roommates or other people who have access to your home.

- **Place passwords that are not easy to guess on your bank, credit card, and phone accounts.**

- **If you work, ask about security procedures in place to protect your personal**

A secure Web site

records and hiring information. Do not leave your purse or wallet unattended at your desk.

- **Do not give out personal information unless you know who you are dealing with and are satisfied that your information will be handled in a secure manner.** This applies to transactions over the phone, through the mail, or on the Internet.

- **Guard your mail and trash from theft.** Ask a friend to pick up your mail while you are away from home. Tear up or shred mail containing your personal or financial information.

- **Do not carry your Social Security card with you, and avoid giving out your Social Security number when possible.** Instead, ask for a unique identification number to be assigned to you.

- **Pay attention to your bank statements and statements and billing cycles for any credit and charge cards you have. Report any inconsistencies you discover.**

You will learn more about protecting yourself as a consumer in the marketplace, including the electronic marketplace of the Internet, in Unit 4, Consumer and Housing Law.

Forgery

Forgery is a crime in which a person falsely makes or alters a writing or document with intent to defraud. This usually means signing the name of another person to a check or some other document without permission. It can also mean changing or erasing part of a previously signed document. Uttering, which in many states is a separate crime, is offering to someone as genuine a document (such as a check) known to be a fake.

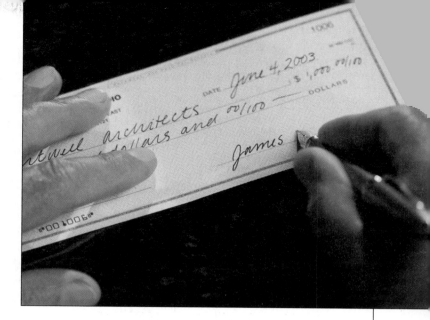

Forgery is a serious crime. *Why is it dangerous to give someone a signed check without filling out the rest of the check?*

Receiving Stolen Property

If you receive or buy property that you know or have reason to believe is stolen, you have committed the crime of receiving stolen property. Knowledge that the property is stolen may be implied by the circumstances, for example, buying goods out of the trunk of an automobile or for a price that is unreasonably low. In most states, receiving stolen property is a felony if the value of the property received is more than $100 and a misdemeanor if the value is $100 or less.

Problem 10.4

Ivan met his friend Anthony, who was driving a flashy new red convertible. Ivan knew that neither Anthony nor his family owned this car, but it looked good, so he got in and let Anthony take him for a ride. Ivan also knew Anthony used drugs and sometimes took other people's things and sold them to get money to buy cocaine. Anthony offered to sell Ivan a Discman he had in the back seat of the car for $20. Ivan agreed to pay him the money.

a. Have any crimes been committed? If so, which crimes and by whom?

b. Why does society make receiving stolen property a crime? Do you think it should be a crime?

c. Would you ever buy something for an extremely low price from a friend? How would you know for sure it was not stolen?

Unauthorized Use of a Vehicle

Several crimes may occur when a person unlawfully takes a motor vehicle without the owner's consent. The crime of unauthorized use of a vehicle (UUV) is committed if the person only intends to take the vehicle temporarily. This crime includes joyriding. However, if the person intends to take the car permanently, then the crime may be larceny or auto theft. These crimes usually have stiffer penalties than UUV. The crime of **carjacking** occurs if a person uses force or intimidation to steal a car from a driver. Carjacking is a federal crime and is punishable by a sentence of up to life in prison.

Computer Crime

Computer crime has been defined broadly to include any violation of criminal law that involves the use of computer technology to commit the prohibited act. Computer crime includes traditional crimes that now may be committed through use of a computer, such as using an art program to create fake identification or making fraudulent credit card purchases with someone else's credit card number that has been intercepted over the Internet. Computer crime also involves crimes that are relatively new and specific to computers, such as spreading a harmful virus to other computer systems or using programs to steal passwords and gain free access to computer services.

Computer crime has become more of a problem with the rapid expansion of the Internet, which had more than 500 million users worldwide by the end of 2002. The Internet is a vast network of interconnected computers over which users may send and receive e-mail, download and upload files, access chat rooms, access World Wide Web pages, read and post to newsgroups, play games, and buy goods and services. Just as in the "real" world, a wide variety of crimes occur on the Internet.

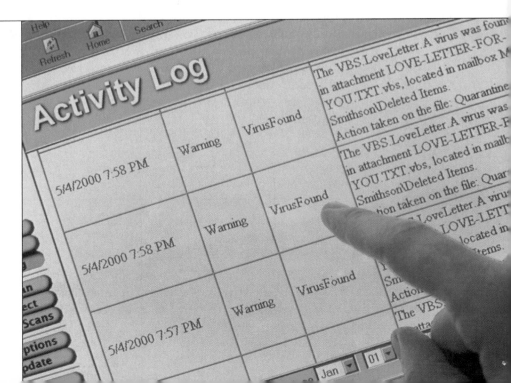

Computer viruses can delete information and damage your computer. *How has the U.S. government attempted to deal with computer crime?*

Filtering software is used to protect children from adult content available on the Internet. *What is the* Children's Internet Protection Act?

Computer crime is committed for several different reasons. Some computer crime is committed by employees who are angry with their company for some reason. Youthful **hackers** sometimes gain illegal access to government or corporate computer systems. There is disagreement over how hackers should be punished. Many feel that hackers are dangerous and should receive jail terms and pay large fines like other white-collar criminals. Others argue that hackers break into systems as a hobby, do not intend any harm, and can be rehabilitated. A distinction has been drawn between hackers—who are relatively harmless and tend to break into sites for fun, for a challenge, or to point out security flaws—and "crackers," or criminal hackers, who seek to make money from breaking into computers. However, breaking into a corporate or government system to which one does not have access is a federal crime regardless of motive (as long as one has the guilty state of mind of intending to break into the site). In the wake of the terrorist attacks of 2001, several provisions related to using computers and the Internet in the commission of terrorist activities were included in the *USA Patriot Act of 2001*.

One common Internet crime is the transmission of obscene images, movies, and sounds. Concerned that children may be harmed by their access to this material on the Internet available at public libraries, in 2000 Congress enacted the *Children's Internet Protection Act*.

This act requires that all public libraries purchase and install filtering software on all of their computers or risk losing federal technology funding. In 2003, the Supreme Court decided that this law did not violate the First Amendment (freedom of speech) rights of those sending and receiving information on the Internet. For further information on computer crime and the First Amendment, see the information on freedom of speech in Chapter 37.

Some hackers release viruses, which are programs capable of automatically copying themselves and attaching themselves to other programs. Viruses may be designed to play practical jokes, slow down computers, erase or damage data, or act in a variety of other harmful ways. Logic bombs are also frequently employed. These are programs that are set to activate upon the occurrence of some event, such as the arrival of a particular date or time. Hackers may also use "sniffers" to gather passwords to systems, or password-cracking programs that use dictionary files to try different combinations of letters until they come across valid passwords.

Throughout the 1980s, federal legislation related to computer crime, as well as traditional criminal statutes, was used to prosecute computer criminals. However, the laws proved to be vague and ineffective. In response, Congress passed the *Computer Fraud and Abuse Act of 1986,* which provided the government with a specific law to prosecute hackers. The law made it a crime to modify, destroy, or disclose information gained from unauthorized entry into a computer. The *National Information Infrastructure Act of 1996* makes it illegal to threaten to cause damage to a computer system unless the owner gives something of value, such as when someone threatens to crash a system unless they are given system privileges. Another part of the act makes it illegal to intentionally give or receive passwords that would permit unauthorized access to systems. The law is jointly enforced by the United States Secret Service and the FBI. By 2003, all 50 states had also enacted laws specifically dealing with computer crime.

Copyright laws apply to users of computer software. *How are copyright laws broken by software users?*

Despite the attention given to computer crimes, most probably go unreported. Many companies are reluctant to publicize their vulnerability to computer criminals. Also, many are discouraged by the resources and time needed to prosecute individuals.

The federal government has also been carefully watching computer bulletin board systems. Bulletin boards allow users to exchange computer files and messages using computers and modems. Some of these bulletin boards make commercial software programs available to users. However, making the programs available without the publisher's permission is illegal. Many bulletin board operators claim that users upload these programs without the operators' knowledge. Nevertheless, many states hold the operator responsible for making sure that no illegal copies appear. Furthermore, the person downloading the program is in possession of illegal software.

Another type of computer crime occurs when someone illegally copies software he or she has purchased. Software companies lose over $2 billion each year to illegal copying. A person who opens a software package is agreeing to use the software on one computer only. This person is allowed to make copies of the software only to use as a backup. Placing software on more than one computer without the publisher's permission is illegal and violates federal copyright laws. The violator is subject to a possible jail term and a fine of up to $250,000. Violators can include individuals, businesses, and schools.

Computers have become a way of life for most people. Courts, Congress, and state legislatures will continue to deal with new criminal law problems as computer technology evolves.

Problem 10.5

Jamahl and Nigel are college freshmen who run a computer bulletin board system. They decide to hack into the computer system of the local telephone company. They enter the system without being asked for a password. While looking through computer files, Jamahl finds a confidential memo written by the company president admitting that the telephone rates are too high. Jamahl copies the file and posts it on the bulletin board for users to read. To get even with the telephone company, Nigel inserts a worm to slow its computer system down and sends the company president the message "You are a crook." However, because of a mistake Nigel made in creating the worm, the system crashes, and telephone service is out for eight hours. Many office buildings and government services are disrupted. The police chief shuts down Jamahl and Nigel's bulletin board, and the prosecutor charges both young men with trespassing, theft, and the intentional destruction of property.

a. Should Jamahl and Nigel be prosecuted? What purpose would be served?

b. Are Jamahl and Nigel guilty of the charges? Explain your answer.

c. If they are convicted, how should they be punished?

Defenses

For a conviction to occur in a criminal case, the prosecutor must establish beyond a reasonable doubt that the defendant committed the act in question with the required intent. The defendant is not required to present a defense but can instead simply force the government to prove its case. However, a number of possible defenses are available to defendants in criminal cases.

"Necessity has no law."

— Oliver Cromwell

Visit the *Street Law* Web site at streetlaw.glencoe.com for chapter-based information and resources.

No Crime Has Been Committed

The defendant may present evidence to show that (1) no crime was committed or (2) no criminal intent was involved. In the first case, a defendant might attempt to show that she was carrying a gun but had a valid license, or a defendant might attempt to show that he did not commit rape because the woman was of legal age and consented. In the second case, the defendant might attempt to show that he mistakenly took another person's coat when leaving a restaurant. The defendant is innocent of a charge of larceny if it was an honest and reasonable mistake.

A jury reaches consensus on a verdict.

Defendant Did Not Commit the Crime

Often, no doubt exists that a crime has been committed. In such cases, the question is, who committed it? In this situation, the defendant may present evidence of a mistake in identity or may offer an **alibi,** which is evidence that the defendant was somewhere else at the time the crime was committed. Developments in science and technology have made it possible to use biological evidence, called **DNA evidence,** to connect an offender conclusively to a crime. Even if an offender does not leave fingerprints at a crime scene, he or she may leave biological evidence— a single hair, for example—at the scene without knowing it. It is possible through a blood test to then conduct a test to determine whether that hair or other piece of evidence belongs to the defendant. Although it is possible for the state to prove through DNA evidence that the defendant was at the scene or committed the crime, a defendant may also use DNA evidence to prove that he or she *did not* commit the crime. Additionally, many people who have been convicted of crimes have used DNA evidence, which may not have been available at the time of the trial, to exonerate themselves and be set free.

Scientific developments allow the use of DNA evidence to connect an offender to a crime. *How else may DNA evidence be used?*

Defendant Committed a Criminal Act, but the Act Was Excusable or Justifiable

Sometimes, a criminal act may be considered excusable or justifiable. Defenses in this category include self-defense, defense of property, and defense of others.

The law recognizes the right of a person who is unlawfully attacked to use reasonable force in self-defense. It also recognizes the right of one person to use reasonable force to defend another person from an attack that is about to occur. There are, however, a number of limitations to these defenses.

A person who reasonably believes there is imminent danger of bodily harm can use a reasonable amount of force in self-defense. However, a person cannot use more force than appears to be necessary.

Where You Live

Does your state allow convicted felons to introduce new DNA evidence in an appeal that follows conviction when that evidence was neither available nor introduced at the trial?

If, after stopping an attacker, the defender continues to use force, the roles reverse, and the defender can no longer claim self-defense. Deadly force can usually be used only by a person who reasonably believes that there is imminent danger of death or serious bodily harm. A person is also allowed to use deadly or nondeadly force to defend a third person if the person defended can claim self-defense.

Reasonable nondeadly force may be used to protect property. Some states have enacted controversial Make My Day laws, which give persons the right to use deadly force to defend their property against unwarranted intrusion. See page 241 in Chapter 19 for more information on these laws.

Problem 11.1

a. Ms. Urbanski kept a pistol in her home as protection against intruders. One evening, she heard a noise in the den and went to investigate. Upon entering the room, she saw a man stealing her television. The burglar, seeing the gun, ran for the window, but Ms. Urbanski fired and killed him before he could escape. In a trial for manslaughter, Ms. Urbanski pleaded self-defense. Would you find her guilty? Why or why not?

b. Mr. Peters has a legal handgun to protect his home against intruders and against the increasing crime in his neighborhood. One night, Takeshi, a 16-year-old Japanese exchange student, walks up Mr. Peters's driveway looking for a party. Takeshi thinks Mr. Peters is hosting the party and begins yelling and waving his arms. Mr. Peters gets scared, retrieves his handgun, and points it at Takeshi while yelling "Freeze!" Takeshi does not understand English and keeps walking toward Mr. Peters. Thinking he is an intruder, Mr. Peters shoots and kills Takeshi at the front steps of his house. Mr. Peters is charged with first-degree murder. Does he have a defense?

c. Would your answers to **a.** and **b.** above be any different if your state had a Make My Day law?

d. The owner of a jewelry store spots a shoplifter stealing an expensive necklace. Can the owner use force to prevent the crime? If so, how much?

Defendant Committed a Criminal Act but Is Not Criminally Responsible for His or Her Actions

Some defenses rest on the defendant's lack of criminal responsibility even though it is acknowledged that he or she committed the criminal act. In this category are the defenses of infancy, intoxication, insanity, entrapment, duress, and necessity.

Infancy

Traditionally, children of a young age, usually under age 7, were considered legally incapable of committing a crime. Children between the ages of 7 and 14 were generally presumed incapable of committing a crime, but this presumption could be shown to be wrong. Under modern laws, many states follow some version of this common-law approach. Other states simply provide that children under a specified age shall not be tried for their crimes but shall be turned over to the juvenile court. Children under the specified age have the defense of infancy.

It is argued that those states that either do not have a defense of infancy or allow prosecutors to decide whether to try a child as an adult have more discretion to deal with juvenile delinquency on a case-by-case basis. However, these policies sometimes lead to the controversial result of trying a child for heinous crimes as an adult, and allowing sentencing of up to life in prison. In Florida, for instance, a 12-year-old boy was tried as an adult for the death of a 6-year-old girl that resulted from the boy using a wrestling move on her that he saw on television. He received a mandatory life sentence under a "tough on crime" law that was passed in the mid-1990s.

The defense of infancy rests on the defendant's lack of criminal responsibility. *How does this defense vary among states?*

Intoxication

Defendants sometimes claim intoxication as a defense—that is, they claim that at the time of a crime, they were so drunk on alcohol or high on drugs that they did not know what they were doing. As a general rule, voluntary intoxication is not a defense to a crime. However, it may sometimes be a valid defense if the crime requires proof of a specific mental state. For example, Grady is charged with assault with intent to kill. He claims he was drunk. If he can prove that he was so drunk that he could not have formed the intent to kill, his intoxication may be a valid defense. Grady can still be convicted of the crime of assault, because specific intent is not required to prove that crime. However, if Grady had decided to kill the victim before he got drunk or if he got drunk to get up enough nerve to commit the crime, then intoxication would not be a defense. This is because the required mental state (the intent to kill) existed before the drunkenness.

Where You Live

Under what age in your state are children presumed incapable of committing a crime?

After an assassination attempt on President Ronald Reagan, John Hinckley, Jr., pled insanity. *How should a person who successfully pleads insanity be punished?*

Insanity

Over the centuries, the insanity defense has evolved as an important legal concept. Ancient Greeks and Romans believed that insane people were not responsible for their actions and should not be punished like ordinary criminals. Since the fourteenth century, English courts have excused offenders who were mentally unable to control their conduct. The modern standard grew out of an 1843 case involving the attempted murder of the British prime minister.

The basic idea is that people who have a mental disease or disorder should not be convicted if they do not know what they are doing or if they do not know the difference between right and wrong. About half the states and the federal government use this standard. The other states hold that accused persons must be acquitted if they lack the *substantial capacity* to appreciate the nature of the act or to conform their conduct to the requirements of the law.

During criminal proceedings, the accused's mental state can be an issue in determining whether (1) the defendant is competent to stand trial, (2) the defendant was sane at the time of the criminal act, and (3) the defendant is sane after the trial. The insanity defense applies only if the accused was insane at the time of the crime. Insanity at the time of the trial may delay the proceedings until the accused is competent to stand trial or can understand what is taking place. However, insanity during or after the trial does not affect the defendant's criminal liability.

In most states, there are three possible verdicts: guilty, innocent, or not guilty by reason of insanity. In some states, the last verdict results in automatic commitment to a mental institution. In others, the judge or jury exercises discretion, sometimes in a separate hearing, to determine commitment of the accused. In recent years, a number of states have come up with a new verdict: guilty but mentally ill. About one-third of the states have this verdict. Defendants found guilty but mentally ill can be sent to a hospital and later transferred to a prison once they are judged sane.

To prove insanity, the defense must produce evidence of a mental disease or disorder. Psychiatrists usually give testimony in these cases. Both the defense and the prosecution may have psychiatrists examine the defendant, and the testimonies are often in conflict. The decision as to whether insanity is a valid defense rests with whoever—judge or jury—decides the facts of the case.

There is a great deal of controversy about the insanity defense. Three states—Montana, Idaho, and Utah—have abolished it entirely in their state courts. According to polling information, Americans believe that this defense has been successfully used by many heinous criminals. In reality, however, this defense is seldom used. Virtually all studies conclude that it is used in about one percent of criminal cases. When it is used, it is seldom successful.

Problem 11.2

a. What is the insanity defense? How does it work?

b. Should the insanity defense be kept as is, changed in some way, or abolished? Explain your answer.

Where You Live

How does the insanity defense work in your state? Is it difficult or easy for a defendant to plead the insanity defense and win in your state? Have there been recent changes? Are changes needed? If so, what are they?

Entrapment

The entrapment defense applies when the defendant admits committing a criminal act but claims that he or she was induced, or persuaded, to commit the crime by a law enforcement officer. There is no entrapment when a police officer merely provides the defendant

Entrapment is difficult to prove. *Could the situation in this photograph be considered entrapment?*

with an opportunity to commit a crime; rather, it must be shown that the defendant would not have committed the crime but for the inducement of the police officer. Entrapment is difficult to prove and cannot be claimed as a defense to crimes involving serious physical injury, such as rape or murder.

Problem 11.3

Can entrapment be claimed as a valid defense in any of the following cases? Explain your answer.

a. Mary, an undercover police officer masquerading as a prostitute, approaches Edward and tells him that she'll have sex with him in exchange for $50. Edward hands over the money and is arrested.

b. Jan, a drug dealer, offers to sell drugs to Emilio, an undercover police officer disguised as a drug addict. Emilio buys the drugs, and Jan is arrested.

c. Rashid, an undercover FBI agent, repeatedly offers Sammy a chance to get in on an illegal gambling ring, with the promise that he will win big. After refusing several offers, Sammy, who has no history of gambling and who just lost his job, finally gives Rashid $200 as a bet. Rashid immediately arrests Sammy.

Duress

A person acts under duress when he or she does something as a result of coercion or a threat of immediate danger to life or personal safety. Under duress, an individual lacks the ability to exercise free will. For example, suppose someone points a gun at your head and demands that you steal money or be killed. You steal the money. Duress would be a good defense in this case if you were prosecuted for theft. Duress is not a defense to homicide.

Necessity

An individual acts under necessity when he or she is compelled to react to a situation that is unavoidable in order to protect life. Suppose, for example, that a group of people is left adrift in a lifeboat and the lifeboat is so heavy with cargo that it is in danger of sinking. The group throws the cargo overboard to make the lifeboat lighter and more manageable. In this case, necessity would be a good defense to a charge of destruction of property. Necessity is not a defense to homicide.

Problem 11.4

Reread The Case of the Shipwrecked Sailors on page 6. Would any of the defenses discussed in this section be available to the sailors who survived and were prosecuted? Should they be? Explain your answers.

Criminal Justice Process: The Investigation

Street Law *online*

Visit the *Street Law* Web site at streetlaw.glencoe.com for chapter-based information and resources.

The criminal justice process includes everything that happens to a person from arrest through prosecution and conviction to release from the control of the state. The vast majority of crimes that occur are investigated and are adjudicated, or judged, under state laws. There are, however, many federal crimes that are handled in the federal criminal justice system. The federal and state systems are similar in many ways. However, the significant differences that do exist between these systems are noted throughout this chapter.

Freedom is sometimes gained almost immediately at the police station or after time has been served in a correctional institution. Freedom may also come at any stage in between. At various points in the process, the prosecutor may drop a case for lack of evidence. A judge can also declare a mistrial if the jury is unable to reach a verdict. The criminal justice process is illustrated in Figure 12.1.

This chapter deals with the investigation phase of this process, including how the U.S. Constitution limits what police can do. The

Arrests must be based on probable cause.

next three chapters cover proceedings before trial, the trial itself, and sentencing and corrections. The juvenile justice process is somewhat different from the adult criminal justice system and is discussed in Chapter 16. The final chapter of this unit examines some of the legal issues that have arisen in the criminal justice system as the United States tries to protect itself against terrorism.

Arrest

An **arrest** takes place when a person suspected of a crime is taken into custody. An arrest is considered a seizure under the Fourth Amendment, which requires that seizures be reasonable. A person can be taken into custody by a police officer in one of two ways: with an arrest warrant issued by a judge or without a warrant if there is probable cause. Someone who is taken into custody under circumstances in which a reasonable person would not feel free to leave is considered to be under arrest, whether or not he or she is told that.

An **arrest warrant** is a court order commanding that the person named in it be taken into custody. A warrant is obtained by filing a complaint before a judge or magistrate. The person filing the complaint is generally a police officer but may be a victim or a witness. The person making the complaint must also describe and swear to the facts and circumstances of the alleged crime. If, on the basis of the information provided, the judge finds probable cause to believe that an offense has been committed and that the accused committed it, a warrant will be issued. On many occasions, police do not have time to get a warrant. In certain felony cases and in misdemeanor cases, they may make a warrantless arrest in public based on probable cause.

Probable cause to arrest means having a reasonable belief that a specific person has committed a crime. This reasonable belief may be based on much less evidence than is necessary to prove a person guilty at trial. For example, suppose the police receive a radio report of a bank robbery. An officer sees a man matching the description of the bank robber waving a gun and running away from the bank. The officer would have probable cause to stop and arrest the man, but that evidence alone would likely not be enough to convict him of the crime.

There is no exact formula for determining probable cause. When arresting without a warrant, police must use their own judgment as to what is reasonable under the circumstances of each case. In all cases, probable cause requires more than mere suspicion or a hunch. Some facts must be present that indicate that the person arrested has committed a crime.

In recent years, the courts have allowed drug enforcement officials to use what is known as a **drug courier profile.** This profile is used to provide a basis to stop and question a person or to help establish probable cause for arrest. Drug courier profiles are often based on commonly held notions concerning the typical age, race, personal appearance, behavior, and mannerisms of drug couriers.

Where You Live

Make a chart showing the steps in your state's criminal justice system. Who could help you get the information needed to make this chart?

Some argue that it is unfair to use such factors in determining probable cause. These critics argue that individualized suspicion—as opposed to the generalized characteristics of drug couriers—should be required to establish probable cause. Others believe that drug interdiction presents unique law enforcement problems and that the use of the profiles is necessary in order to stop drug trafficking.

Police may establish probable cause from information provided by citizens in the community. Information from victims or witnesses can be used to obtain an arrest warrant. Police also use information from informants to establish probable cause if they can convince a judge that the information is reliable. In determining the reliability of an

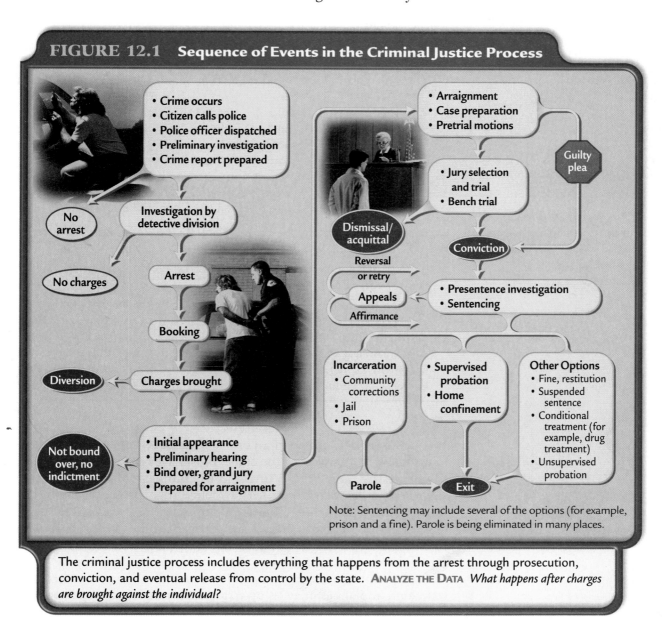

FIGURE 12.1   Sequence of Events in the Criminal Justice Process

Note: Sentencing may include several of the options (for example, prison and a fine). Parole is being eliminated in many places.

The criminal justice process includes everything that happens from the arrest through prosecution, conviction, and eventual release from control by the state. **ANALYZE THE DATA** *What happens after charges are brought against the individual?*

An officer pats down a suspect's outer clothing. *When can an officer stop and frisk a person?*

informant's tip, a judge will consider all the circumstances. These include whether the informant has provided accurate information in the past, how the informant obtained the information, and whether the police can corroborate, or confirm, the informant's tip with other information.

Problem 12.1

The police receive a tip that a drug pusher named Richie will be flying from New York City to Washington, D.C., sometime on the morning of September 8. The informant describes Richie as a tall man with reddish hair and a beard. He also tells police that Richie has a habit of walking fast and that he will be carrying illegal drugs in a brown leather bag. The police have received reliable information from this informant in the past. On the morning of September 8, the police watch all passengers arriving from New York City. When they see a man who fits the description—carrying a brown leather bag and walking fast—they arrest him. A search of the bag reveals a large quantity of cocaine.

a. Based on what you know, do you think the police had probable cause to arrest Richie? Why or why not?

b. Should the police have obtained a warrant before arresting Richie? Why or why not?

c. Assume the police have not received a specific tip but they know that crack cocaine is being brought regularly on trains from one city to another by teenagers hired by older drug dealers. They see a 16-year-old African American male arriving by train. He is alone, and is carrying a small canvas bag. Should the police be able to stop and question him? Under what circumstances should they be able to search or arrest him?

A police officer does not need probable cause to stop and question an individual on the street, but the officer must have reasonable suspicion to believe the individual is involved in criminal activity. Reasonable suspicion is based on even less evidence than probable cause, but must be more than a mere hunch. If the officer has reasonable suspicion that the person is armed and dangerous, he or she may do a limited pat-down of the person's outer clothing—called a stop and frisk—to remove any weapons the person may be carrying.

Even if a police officer does not have probable cause or reasonable suspicion, the officer may go up to any individual and ask to speak to him or her. The person may decline and continue his or her activity, and the officer is not legally permitted to take the person's silence or departure into account in determining probable cause or reasonable suspicion. In all states, however, if the person runs from the police upon being asked for identification, that flight may give the officer reasonable suspicion to stop the person again, at which point the person is not free to walk away. This is especially true with stops in high crime areas.

The most common kind of arrest occurs when people do not realize they are being arrested at all. When a police officer stops a person driving a car for violating traffic laws, the driver is technically under arrest because the driver is not free to leave, but must stay until the officer releases him or her. Further, in 1997, the U.S. Supreme Court ruled that police can order all passengers out of a car when making a lawful traffic stop. The detention in this common situation is brief, usually lasting only as long as it takes the officer to check identification and registration, and typically ends when a citation (ticket) is issued for the violation.

The Case of . . .

The Unlucky Couple

After an evening at the movies, Lonnie Howard and his girlfriend, Melissa, decide to park in the empty lot behind Briarwood Elementary School. They begin talking and start drinking the beer they brought with them. After several beers, the couple is startled by the sound of breaking glass and voices from the rear of the school.

Unnoticed in their darkened car, Lonnie and Melissa observe two men loading office furniture and electronics equipment from the school into the back of a van. Quickly concluding that the men must be burglars, Lonnie decides he should leave the parking lot. He revs up his engine and roars out of the parking lot onto Main Street.

Meanwhile, unknown to Lonnie and Melissa, a silent security alarm has also alerted the local police to the break-in at the school. Responding to the alarm, Officer Vicki Ramos heads for the school. She turns onto Main Street just in time to see one vehicle—Lonnie's car—speeding away from the school.

Problem 12.2

a. If you were Officer Ramos, what would you do in this situation? If you were Lonnie, what would you do?

b. If Officer Ramos chases Lonnie, will she have probable cause to stop and arrest him?

c. How do you think Officer Ramos would act after stopping Lonnie? How do you think Lonnie and Melissa would act?

d. Role-play this situation. As Officer Ramos, decide what you would say and how you would act toward the occupants of the car. As Lonnie and Melissa, decide what you would say and how you would act toward the police officer.

e. What could Lonnie and Melissa do if they were mistakenly arrested for the burglary? What could they do if they were abused or mistreated by Officer Ramos?

f. Assume Lonnie takes a baseball bat from the back of the car and begins to wave it after being stopped by Officer Ramos. Would it be legal for Officer Ramos to use deadly force?

What To Do If You Are Arrested

Cooperating with the police

- **Do not struggle with the police.** Be polite. Avoid fighting or swearing, even if you think the police have made a mistake. Resisting arrest and assaulting a police officer are usually separate crimes that you can be charged with even if you have done nothing else wrong. If you believe you have been assaulted by the police, be sure to write down the officer's name and badge number. If possible, also write down the names and phone numbers of any witnesses.

  Give your name, address, and phone number to the police. Otherwise, keep quiet until you have spoken to a lawyer. Do not discuss your case with anyone at this point, and don't sign any statements about your case.

  You may be searched, photographed, and fingerprinted. Notice carefully what is done but do not resist. If any personal property is taken from you, ask for a written receipt.

  As soon as possible after you get to the police station, call a trusted relative or friend. Tell this person where you are, what you have been charged with, and what your bail or bond is. See Chapter 13 for information about bail.

  Please note that this information applies to adults who are arrested. When juveniles are taken into custody, parents must be notified and there is no right to bail. There may also be other differences between juvenile and adult arrest procedures and the steps you should take. See Chapter 16 for information about the juvenile justice system.

- **When you are arrested for a minor offense, you may, in some places, be released without having to put up any money.** This is called an unsecured bond or citation release. If you do not qualify for a citation release, you may have to put up some money before release. This is called posting a cash bond or collateral. Ask for a receipt for the money.

- **When you are arrested for a serious misdemeanor or felony, you will not be released immediately.** Ask the friend or relative you have called to get a lawyer for you. If you cannot afford a lawyer, one will be appointed by the judge when you are first brought to court.

  Before you leave the police station, be sure to find out when you are due in court. *Never be late or miss a court appearance.* If you do not show up in court at the assigned time, a warrant will be issued for your rearrest.

- **Do not talk about your case with anyone except your lawyer.** Be honest with your lawyer, or he or she will have trouble helping you. Ask that your lawyer be present at all lineups and interrogation sessions. Most criminal defense lawyers recommend that you not talk to police about the crime until you speak with a lawyer.

A police officer may use as much physical force as is reasonably necessary to make an arrest. However, most police departments limit the use of deadly force to incidents involving dangerous or threatening suspects. In 1985, the U.S. Supreme Court was asked to decide whether it was lawful for police to shoot an "unarmed fleeing felony suspect." In deciding the case, the Court ruled that deadly force "may not be used unless it is necessary to prevent escape, and the officer has probable cause to believe the suspect poses a significant threat of death or serious physical harm to the officer or others."

If a police officer uses too much force or makes an unlawful arrest, the accused may bring a civil action for a violation of the federal *Civil Rights Act*. The government could also file a criminal action against the police. In addition, many local governments have processes for handling citizen complaints about police misconduct. You should know, however, that a police officer is never liable for false arrest simply because the person arrested did not commit the crime. Rather, it must be shown that the officer acted maliciously or had no

The Case of . . .

The Arrest for Seat Belt Violations

Gail Atwater was driving through the streets of her small town in Texas when Officer Turek stopped her. Her three-year-old son and five-year-old daughter were with her in the front seat of her pickup truck. None of them were wearing seat belts. Texas law allows police to make a warrantless arrest for seat belt violations or allows them to give out a citation (ticket) to the offender. The penalty under Texas law for this offense is a fine of no less than $25 and no more than $50.

The officer asked Ms. Atwater for her license and registration. She was unable to produce them, telling Officer Turek they had been stolen the day before. Turek told her she was "going to jail." Her two small children began to cry. Fortunately, a neighbor saw the incident and took the children into her home. Once the children left, Officer Turek handcuffed Ms. Atwater and took her to the police station. After an hour in jail she was taken to a magistrate who released her on bond. She eventually paid a small fine but brought a lawsuit against the town and the police department for violating her rights.

The lower federal courts found for the town. The U.S. Supreme Court agreed to review the case to determine whether or not a warrantless arrest could be made by police for a misdemeanor that did not involve a breach of the peace and that is punishable only by a fine.

Problem 12.3

a. Did Officer Turek have probable cause to believe that Gail Atwater had violated the Texas seat belt laws?

b. Do you agree or disagree with the way the officer handled the case? Would it make a difference to you if he had stopped her for a seat belt violation with her children in the past? Explain.

c. Given the circumstances of the case, was the seizure reasonable?

d. How should the Court decide this case? Give your reasons.

reasonable grounds for suspicion of guilt. Also, if an arrest is later ruled unlawful, the evidence obtained as a result of the arrest may not be used against the accused. (See Pretrial Motions: The Exclusionary Rule, on pages 161–163 in Chapter 13.)

Search and Seizure

Americans have always valued their privacy. They expect to be left alone, to be free from unwarranted snooping or spying, and to be secure in their own homes. While there is no explicit right to privacy in the U.S. Constitution, the Fourth Amendment sets out the right to be free from "unreasonable searches and seizures" and establishes conditions under which search warrants may be issued. This right, like others in the Bill of Rights, limits the power of government; it does not apply to limit actions by private citizens. If an individual violates your privacy, however, you may be able to make a claim under tort law, discussed in Unit 3.

Balanced against the individual's reasonable expectation of privacy is the government's need to gather information. In the case of the police, this is the need to collect evidence against criminals and to protect society against crime.

The Fourth Amendment does not give citizens an absolute right to privacy, and it does not prohibit all searches—only those that are unreasonable. In deciding if a search is reasonable, the courts consider the facts and circumstances of each case. Traditionally, courts have found searches and seizures of private homes to be reasonable when authorized by a valid warrant. In practice today, warrantless searches are very common (except for searches of homes) because courts have carved out many exceptions to the warrant requirement as long as the search is reasonable. These exceptions to the warrant requirement are discussed on pages 144–146.

The U.S. Supreme Court has considered many cases involving the reasonableness of warrantless searches. For example, it used the concept of "reasonable expectation of privacy" to help determine whether a search was reasonable or unreasonable. In one such case, the Court found that a person did not have a reasonable expectation of privacy in garbage left in a plastic bag for pickup on his front curb. The police were allowed to search this person's garbage without first obtaining a warrant.

Police officers search a house to collect evidence against criminals. *What is the exclusionary rule?*

Although the language of the Fourth Amendment is relatively simple, search and seizure law is complex. There are many exceptions to the basic rules. Once an individual is arrested, it may be up to the courts to decide whether any evidence found in a search was legally obtained. If a court finds that the search was unreasonable, then evidence found in the search cannot be used at the trial against the defendant. This principle—the exclusionary rule—does not mean that the defendant cannot be tried or convicted, but it does mean that evidence seized in an unlawful search cannot be used at trial.

Problem 12.4

Examine each of the following situations. Decide whether the search violates the Fourth Amendment and whether the evidence seized can be used in court. Explain your decisions.

a. The police see Dell standing at a bus stop on a downtown street, in an area where there is extensive drug dealing. They stop and search him and find drugs in his pocket.

b. After Brandon checks out of a hotel, the police ask the hotel manager to turn over the contents of the wastebasket, where they find notes planning a murder.

c. Jill's former boyfriend breaks into her apartment and looks through her desk for love letters. Instead he finds drugs, which he turns over to the police.

d. Terry is on a bus traveling from Miami to New York City. Three police officers board the bus wearing "RAID" jackets, and Terry can see that at least one is carrying a gun. One officer stands in the front of the bus partially blocking the aisle, while the other two officers eye the passengers, pick out Terry, and ask him for identification and his ticket. After returning both to him without comment, they then ask Terry for permission to search his luggage. He gives his permission. The officers open his bag and find cocaine.

e. Pamela is observed shoplifting items in a store. Police chase Pamela into her apartment building and arrest her outside the closed door of her apartment. A search of the apartment reveals a large quantity of stolen merchandise.

f. Sandi is suspected of receiving stolen goods. The police go to her apartment and ask Claire, her roommate, if they can search the apartment. Claire gives the police permission, and they find stolen items in Sandi's dresser.

Searches With a Warrant

A search warrant is a court order. It is obtained from a judge who is convinced that there is a bona fide need to search a person or place. Before a judge issues a warrant, someone, usually a police officer, must file an affidavit—a sworn statement of facts and circumstances—that

Law in Action

Police and the Problem of Excessive Force

While most well-trained police officers respect the rights of the citizens they protect, there is a persistent issue of police abuse in the United States. In 2001, more than 12,000 civil rights complaints were filed with the U.S. Department of Justice. The majority of these alleged abuses involved law enforcement officers. The problem appears to be more serious in urban areas. In 1998, the group Human Rights Watch issued a report based on a two-year study conducted in 14 cities. The report noted that police brutality exists because of a failure to establish effective accountability systems.

Where data are available, members of minority groups report cases of police brutality far in excess of their representation in the population. According to the report, civilian review boards in these cities—established to deal with complaints about police—lack the funding needed to monitor police adequately. The report also found that police department internal affairs units tend to operate under a cloak of secrecy, seldom releasing results of investigations to the public. In addition, the report criticizes the U.S. Department of Justice's Civil Rights Division for its lack of zeal in prosecuting police misconduct cases.

In 2000, a bill designed to curb law enforcement and police abuses was introduced in Congress. The *Law Enforcement Trust and Integrity Act* garnered strong support from police organizations and civil rights organizations, but failed to become law. It provided for many of the same recommendations made by Human Rights Watch in its 1998 report, including:

- creating national standards for training, management, and oversight of officers;

Using excessive force

- mandatory data collection on racial, ethnic, and gender profiling in law enforcement;
- protections for due process rights of all those accused of abuses;
- new protections from abuses by the Immigration and Naturalization Service and the U.S. Customs Service; and
- whistleblower protection for officers who break the "blue code of silence" covering abuses.

Problem 12.5

a. How are citizen complaints about the police handled in your community?

b. Do you have a problem with police brutality in your community?

c. What do you think about the recommendations made in the 2000 congressional bill? What steps would work best to improve local police-citizen relations?

provides the probable cause to believe that a search is justified. If a judge issues a search warrant, the warrant must specifically describe the person or place to be searched and the particular things to be seized.

Once the search warrant is issued, the search must be conducted within a certain number of days specified in the warrant. Also, in many states the search must be conducted only in the daytime, unless the warrant expressly states otherwise. Finally, a search warrant does not usually authorize a general search of everything in the specified place. For example, if the police have a warrant to search a house for stolen 20-inch televisions, it would be unreasonable for the police to look in desk drawers, envelopes, or other small places where such televisions could not possibly be hidden. However, the police can seize evidence related to the case and any other illegal items that are in their plain view when they are properly searching the house for the televisions.

When the police have a warrant to search a house, the Fourth Amendment's reasonableness requirement usually means that they must knock, announce their purpose and authority (i.e., that they are police officers), and request admission. Police generally cannot enter a house forcibly—even with a warrant—unless they have met this "knock and announce" test. However, the U.S. Supreme Court has allowed for "no-knock" entries when circumstances present a threat to the officers or where evidence would likely be destroyed if advance notice were given (e.g., in drug cases). But the Court also ruled that a state law authorizing no-knock warrants in all felony drug dealing cases violates the Fourth Amendment, reiterating the requirement to consider the circumstances of each particular case.

> *The right of the people to be secure in their persons, houses, papers, and effects, against unreasonable searches and seizures, shall not be violated, and no Warrants shall issue, but upon probable cause, supported by Oath or affirmation, and particularly describing the place to be searched, and the persons or things to be seized.*
>
> **— Fourth Amendment to the U.S. Constitution**

Search warrants must state the specific place to be searched and the particular items to be seized. *What other requirements must police follow with a search warrant?*

Searches Without a Warrant

According to the law, searches of private homes usually require a warrant. However, because of the number of exceptions to the Fourth Amendment warrant requirement, most searches are warrantless. These searches, however, must still be reasonable. The courts have recognized a number of situations in which searches are reasonable and may be legally conducted without a warrant.

- **Search incident to a lawful arrest.** A search that is part of, or incident to, a lawful arrest is the most common exception to the warrant requirement. This exception allows the police to search a lawfully arrested person and the area immediately around that person for hidden weapons or for evidence that might be destroyed. This is called a "grab area" search. If the arrest occurs next to the accused's car, police may also search the passenger compartment of the car, but usually not the trunk. The Supreme Court also allowed a "protective sweep" through an arrested person's home in search of other potentially armed persons.

- **Stop and frisk.** A police officer who reasonably thinks a person is behaving suspiciously and is likely to be armed may stop and frisk the suspect for weapons. This exception to the warrant requirement was created to protect the safety of officers and bystanders who might be injured by a person carrying a concealed weapon. Such a search may only be for weapons. In 1993, however, the Supreme Court said that seizing an illegal substance (such as drugs) during a valid frisk is reasonable if the officer's sense of touch makes it immediately clear that the object felt is an illegal one. This is known as the "plain feel" exception.

- **Consent.** When a person voluntarily agrees, the police may conduct a search without a warrant and without probable cause. Normally, a person may grant permission to search only his or her own belongings or property. In some situations, however, one person may legally allow the police to conduct a search of another person's property. For example, a parent may usually allow officers to search a child's property.

- **Plain view.** If an object connected with a crime is in plain view and can be seen from a place where an officer has a right to be, it can be seized without a warrant. For example, if an officer legally stops a car for a traffic violation and sees

These agents are authorized to search without a warrant. *Is it reasonable to search all airline passengers using a metal detector even when there is no probable cause?*

The Case of . . .

Fingers McGee

While on duty, Officer Michelle Yomoto and Officer Liam Jones received a radio report of a robbery at the Dixie Liquor Store. The report indicates only that the suspect is male, about six feet tall, and wearing old clothes. Meanwhile, Fingers McGee is finishing up some shopping at a nearby store and has just seen the owner of the Dixie Liquor Store chasing a man. The man was carrying a paper sack and what appeared to be a knife as he ran down the street. Fingers McGee thinks the man looks like Mark Johnson, a drug addict, and he thinks the man was running toward Johnson's house located at 22 Elm Street. Officers Yomoto and Jones encounter Fingers McGee on a street corner and begin to ask him questions.

Problem 12.6

a. Role-play this encounter. As the officers, decide what questions to ask McGee. As McGee, decide what to tell the officers.

b. Assume McGee tells the police what he knows. What should the police do then?

c. Should the police get a search warrant before going to Johnson's house? If they go without a warrant, do they have probable cause to arrest him? Why or why not?

d. If the police decide to enter Johnson's house, what should they do? Should they knock and announce themselves, or should they break in unannounced?

e. If the police enter the house, can they arrest Johnson? Where can they search, and what, if anything, can be seized? Role-play the scene at the house.

. . . .

a gun lying on the car seat next to the driver, he may seize it without a warrant. Likewise, if an officer has gained legal entrance into a suspect's house and sees drug paraphernalia on a coffee table, the officer does not need a warrant to seize the contraband (illegal items).

- **Hot pursuit.** Police in hot pursuit of a suspect are not required to get a search warrant before entering a building that they have seen the suspect enter. It is also lawful to seize evidence found in plain view during hot pursuit of a suspected felon.

- **Vehicle searches.** A police officer who has probable cause to believe that a vehicle contains contraband may conduct a search of the entire vehicle, as well as any containers in the vehicle that might contain the contraband, without a warrant. This does not mean that the police have a right to stop and search any vehicle on the streets. The right to stop and search must be based on probable cause.

- **Emergency situations.** In certain emergencies, the police are not required to get a search warrant. These situations include searching a building after a telephoned bomb threat, entering a house after smelling smoke or hearing screams, and other situations in which the police do not have time to get a warrant. The

U.S. Supreme Court has also allowed warrantless entries of a person's home where the police have probable cause to believe that failure to enter immediately (i.e., before getting a warrant) will result in destruction of evidence, escape of the suspect, or harm to the police or another individual inside or outside the building. This exception has been limited by the Supreme Court to serious crimes.

- **Border and airport searches.** Customs agents are authorized to search without warrants and without probable cause. They may examine the baggage, vehicles, purses, wallets, and similar belongings of people entering the country. Body searches or searches conducted away from the border by customs agents are allowed only where there is reasonable suspicion of criminal activity. In view of the danger of terrorist activities, security personnel and airlines are permitted to search all carry-on luggage and to search all passengers by means of fixed and hand-held metal detectors. Since the September 11, 2001 terrorist attacks, these searches can take place several times from the time a passenger enters the airport until he or she boards the flight.

Public School Searches

As you have learned, the Fourth Amendment does not protect citizens against all government searches and seizures, but only *unreasonable* searches and seizures. In its consideration of the extent to which students at public schools enjoy Fourth Amendment rights while they are at school, the U.S. Supreme Court has granted school authorities broad discretion to search students and their possessions in several situations.

The touchstone of the Court's analysis under the Fourth Amendment in criminal searches is the reasonableness, considering all the circumstances, of the particular government invasion of an individual's personal security. In the context of public schools, however, the main concern is whether a search is reasonable in the context of the school's legitimate interests. In *New Jersey* v. *TLO* (1985), an assistant principal suspected a student of violating the public high school's rule against smoking. The principal searched the student's purse, and found evidence of marijuana use. Although the Court recognized that a

Although the Fourth Amendment protects students at school, the Supreme Court has given school administrators broader power than the police to search students and their possessions. *How has the Court helped schools combat the issue of drugs?*

Student Drug Testing

Tecumseh High School offers a variety of extracurricular activities for its students. These activities include choir, band, color guard, Future Farmers of America (FFA), Future Homemakers of America (FHA), and the academic team, as well as athletics and the cheerleading squad. The majority of the school's 500 students participate in one or more of these activities.

At the start of the 1998 school year, the school district adopted the Student Activities Drug Testing Policy. While the school acknowledged only a minimal problem with drugs, they adopted this policy to prevent a bigger problem from developing. The policy required drug testing of all students who participated in any school-sanctioned extracurricular activity. Specifically, in order to participate in an activity, each student had to sign a written consent agreeing to be tested for drug use on several occasions: prior to participating in the activity, randomly during the year while participating in the activity, and at any time while participating in the activity upon reasonable suspicion.

According to the policy, students to be tested at random are called out of class in groups of two or three. The students are directed to a restroom, where a faculty member serves as a monitor. The monitor waits outside the closed restroom stall for the student to produce the sample. The monitor pours the contents of the vial into two bottles. Together the faculty monitor and the student seal the bottles. The student signs a form, which the monitor places with the filled bottles into a mailing pouch in the presence of the student. The bottles are then sent to be tested at a designated laboratory. Random drug testing was conducted in this manner on approximately eight occasions during the 1998 and 1999 school years.

There are no academic penalties for refusing to take the test or for a negative result, and results of the tests are not shared with law enforcement authorities. Students who refuse to submit to the policy simply cannot participate in the extracurricular activity. In two school years, a total of 484 students were tested as part of this policy. Four students tested positive.

Two students—neither a student athlete—challenged this policy in federal court as a violation of their right to privacy. The trial court sided with the school, but the federal court of appeals reversed the decision. The school board has appealed to the U.S. Supreme Court, which has agreed to hear the case.

Several years earlier, the U.S. Supreme Court upheld the policy of an Oregon high school to conduct random, suspicionless searches of student athletes at a high school with a serious drug problem. In that case, school officials had determined that the student athletes were among the leaders of the "drug culture" at the school.

Problem 12.7

a. How is this case like the Oregon case? How is it different? How is this case similar to and different from the *New Jersey* v. *TLO* case discussed on page 146?

b. What are the most convincing arguments for the students?

c. What are the most convincing arguments for the school?

d. How should this case be decided? Explain.

e. Assume the case is decided in favor of the school. Will this mean that schools can test all students? Faculty and staff? Should schools be able to test everyone for drugs? Explain.

student does have a reasonable expectation of privacy while at school, it nevertheless upheld the search. Instead of requiring that the school have probable cause to suspect a student of criminal activity (as in a traditional criminal search), the school authority only needs to have reasonable suspicion to believe that a search will turn up evidence that the student is violating either school rules or the law.

Because drug use is a serious issue in schools today, courts have given schools great discretion in devising ways to combat the problem. For example, the courts allow schools to search student lockers on the theory that lockers belong to the school and that students do not have a reasonable expectation of privacy in property owned by the school. Most courts have also allowed drug-sniffing dogs to enter schools to search for drugs. However, the courts have usually been reluctant to allow strip searches of students suspected of drug use, finding such searches to be unreasonable.

Suspicionless Searches

Searches and seizures are usually unreasonable if there is no individual suspicion of wrongdoing. For example, the police could not search all the people gathered at a street corner if they suspected that only one of the individuals possessed evidence of a crime. They could search only the person upon whom their individual suspicion is focused so that the privacy rights of the others are protected.

However, the U.S. Supreme Court has recognized some limited circumstances in which this requirement of individualized suspicion need not be met. For example, the court has upheld suspicionless searches conducted in the context of a program designed to meet special needs beyond the goals of routine law enforcement. These special circumstances include fixed-point searches at or near borders to detect illegal aliens, and mandatory drug and alcohol tests for railroad employees who have been involved in accidents. The Court found these searches to be reasonable and in support of a special need beyond ordinary law enforcement. These searches continue to be controversial because they seem to depart from the Fourth Amendment's explicit requirement that searches be based on probable cause.

Racial Profiling in Police Investigations

Racial profiling, sometimes called racially biased policing, can be defined as the inappropriate use of race as a factor in identifying people who may break or have broken the law. Racial profiling occurs when, for example, a police officer stops a car solely because an African American is driving it, or an airport security guard selects an "Arab-looking" person to be searched because of his or her appearance. Critics of racial profiling, including civil rights advocates and some police professional organizations, say that it

Landmark Supreme Court Cases

Visit the Landmark Supreme Court Cases Web site at landmarkcases.org for information and activities about *New Jersey* v. *TLO*.

"Race relations between police and the community is one of the fundamental things that we must work through and 'get right' if we are to have any hope of significant and lasting progress on stopping illegal drugs, reducing youth crime and improving public safety."

— **Chief Charles Ramsey, Metropolitan Police Department, Washington, D.C.**

YOU BE THE JUDGE

Police Searches Without Individualized Suspicion

Each of the cases below deals with the policy of allowing the government to conduct searches that are not based on individualized suspicion of criminal wrongdoing. Analyze the facts carefully. Balance the individual's interest in privacy against the government's justification for conducting the searches. Then decide whether or not the U.S. Supreme Court should allow each search.

A sobriety checkpoint

a. In early 1986, the Michigan Department of State Police established a sobriety checkpoint pilot program. All vehicles passing through a checkpoint would be stopped and their drivers briefly examined for signs of intoxication. If an officer detected any signs of intoxication, the driver would have his or her driver's license and car registration checked. If warranted, the officer could decide to conduct further sobriety tests. Should the field tests and the officer's observations suggest that the driver was intoxicated, an arrest would be made. All other drivers would be permitted to resume their journey immediately. The program was carried out on only one night. During the hour-and-fifteen-minute duration of the checkpoint's operation, 126 vehicles passed through the checkpoint, with an average delay of approximately 25 seconds per vehicle. Two drivers were detained for field sobriety testing, and one of the two was arrested for driving under the influence of alcohol. A third driver who drove through without stopping was pulled over by an officer in an observation vehicle and arrested for driving under the influence. Before any further checkpoints could be carried out, several drivers filed a lawsuit claiming that the checkpoints created an unreasonable seizure of their vehicles in violation of their Fourth Amendment rights.

b. In August 1998, Indianapolis began to operate checkpoints in an effort to catch drug traffickers. Between August and November, the city conducted six checkpoints and stopped a total of 1,161 vehicles. At the checkpoint, police would stop a group of cars at random and inform the drivers that they were being detained briefly. One officer would ask the driver for license and registration information and check for evidence of the driver's impairment. Another officer would conduct a plain view search of the inside of the vehicle from outside, while a trained dog would sniff around the outside of the car for drugs. Unless this procedure produced evidence of probable cause, the drivers were able to leave, typically within five minutes. These stops resulted in 104 arrests, about half of which were for drug offenses. Several drivers who were detained sued the city for violation of their Fourth Amendment rights.

Racial profiling is a controversial issue. *When is it appropriate for a police officer to use race in deciding whom to stop?*

violates people's constitutional right to equal protection before the law and presumption of innocence. They also say it is an ineffective law enforcement tactic, it reinforces racial stereotypes in society, and it creates negative relations between police and citizens.

The general rule is that it is inappropriate for an officer to stop a person solely because of his or her race. However, in some situations officers may appropriately use race as one factor among others in deciding whom to stop. For example, if an eyewitness to a robbery describes the robber as an African American man, a police officer may use race as a factor in deciding to stop an African American man that she sees running from the immediate vicinity.

Problem 12.8

Determine if race was appropriately or inappropriately used as a factor in making each of the following decisions. Give your reasons.

a. After a terrorist attack, the government decides to use more telephone wiretaps to gather information in communities that have mosques.

b. In a neighborhood where several African Americans have been arrested for recent burglaries, a police officer searches an African American youth who is walking down the street.

c. A man reports overhearing two Spanish-speaking men in a coffee shop planning to rob a specific jewelry store the next day. The witness could not see the men's faces and does not know their names. The next day the police go to the store and question two "Latino-looking" men who are sitting in a car outside.

d. A woman entering the United States holds a passport from a country with which the United States was recently at war. A customs agent detains her for questioning.

What Should Be Done About Racial Profiling?

A committee of state legislators is meeting to discuss solutions to the problem of racial profiling. A study by the state government shows that African American drivers are 35 percent more likely to be stopped and searched by police than drivers of other races. A survey of people who have been pulled over in the state shows that an overall majority of people felt that they were stopped for legitimate reasons. However, one in three African Americans and one in four Latinos felt they had been unfairly stopped. Many complained of abusive treatment by police.

Assume you are a state legislator on the committee trying to solve these problems. Read the following excerpts from proposals offered by committee members.

Gomez: The problem is that police are not used to dealing with people from other cultures and have stereotypes of people from other races. All police should receive training on diversity and how to be culturally sensitive.

Wu: This practice has gone on so long because people are not aware of their rights. When people are stopped, they should immediately be told why and be given a card that lists their rights and a business card listing the name and contact information for the officer.

Letaliano: Police officers are not being disciplined for their inappropriate behavior because the police chiefs are unaware of what is going on. We need to collect data regularly to make police officers more aware of why they are really stopping people and to keep them accountable to the public. Each time a driver is stopped, the officer should be required to fill out a form detailing the time and date, driver's age, probable race, gender, and the reason for stopping the person.

Reynolds: The U.S. Constitution and state laws already prohibit searches not based on probable cause. The police department already has internal complaint procedures people can follow if they feel they were stopped because of their race. This is enough to protect citizens. To do more may make the police reluctant to stop people who may be criminals.

Al-Aziz: It's too hard for citizens to prove that they were stopped illegally. All stops by police should be videotaped so we can see how the police treat the suspect and then take disciplinary action against officers who act improperly.

Debouche: We can't rely only on laws or the police department to solve the problem. The answer is to have a board made up of citizens that hears complaints and has the power to require disciplinary action against officers who act inappropriately.

Problem 12.9

a. Which of these proposals seems most likely to help address the problem as you see it? Give your reasons.

b. Invite members of your community to participate in this activity. Be sure that representatives from both law enforcement and a group concerned about racial profiling are invited. Is there evidence that racial profiling is a problem in your community? If so, what is the evidence? What can be done to deal with the problem? If it is not a problem where you live, are there measures that can be taken to keep it from becoming a problem?

Interrogations and Confessions

After an arrest is made, it is standard police practice to question, or **interrogate,** the accused. These interrogations often result in confessions or admissions. The accused's confessions or admissions are later used as evidence at trial.

Balanced against the police's need to question suspects are the constitutional rights of people accused of a crime. The Fifth Amendment to the U.S. Constitution provides citizens with a privilege against **self-incrimination.** This means that a suspect has a right to remain silent and cannot be forced to testify against himself or herself. This protection rests on a basic legal principle: the government bears the burden of proof. Suspects are not obliged to help the government prove they committed a crime or to testify at their own trial. Under the Sixth Amendment, a person accused of a crime has the right to the assistance of an attorney.

The U.S. Supreme Court has held that a confession is not admissible as evidence if it is not voluntary and trustworthy. This means that using physical force, torture, threats, or other techniques that could force an innocent person to confess is prohibited. In the case of *Escobedo* v. *Illinois*, the Supreme Court said that even a voluntary confession is inadmissible as evidence if it is obtained after the defendant's request to talk with an attorney has been denied. The Court reasoned that the presence of Escobedo's attorney could have helped him avoid self-incrimination.

Miranda warnings are read to suspects in custody if the police want to interrogate them. *How has the* Miranda *rule changed in recent years?*

MIRANDA WARNING

1. YOU HAVE THE RIGHT TO REMAIN SILENT.
2. ANYTHING YOU SAY CAN AND WILL BE USED AGAINST YOU IN A COURT OF LAW.
3. YOU HAVE THE RIGHT TO TALK TO A LAWYER AND TO HAVE HIM PRESENT WITH YOU WHILE YOU ARE BEING QUESTIONED.
4. IF YOU CANNOT AFFORD TO HIRE A LAWYER, ONE WILL BE APPOINTED TO REPRESENT YOU BEFORE ANY QUESTIONING IF YOU WISH.
5. YOU CAN DECIDE AT ANY TIME TO EXERCISE THESE RIGHTS AND NOT ANSWER ANY QUESTIONS OR MAKE ANY STATEMENTS.

WAIVER

DO YOU UNDERSTAND EACH OF THESE RIGHTS I HAVE EXPLAINED TO YOU?
HAVING THESE RIGHTS IN MIND, DO YOU WISH TO TALK TO US NOW?

Miranda v. Arizona

Ernesto Miranda was accused of kidnapping and raping an 18-year-old girl near Phoenix, Arizona. The girl claimed she was on her way home from work when a man grabbed her, threw her into the back seat of a car, and raped her. Ten days later, Miranda was arrested, placed in a lineup, and identified by the girl as her attacker. The police then took Miranda into an interrogation room and questioned him for two hours. At the end of the two hours, the officers emerged with a written and signed confession. This confession was used as evidence at trial, and Miranda was found guilty.

Miranda later appealed his case to the U.S. Supreme Court, arguing that he had not been told of his right to remain silent or of his right to counsel. Miranda did not suggest that his confession was false or brought about by coercion but rather that he would not have confessed if he had been advised of these rights.

Problem 12.10

a. Summarize the facts in the *Miranda* case. On what grounds did Miranda appeal his conviction?

b. Do you think Miranda's confession should have been used as evidence against him at trial? Why or why not?

c. Do you think police should be required to tell suspects their rights before questioning them?

d. Do you think suspects would confess after being warned of their rights?

Landmark Supreme Court Cases

Visit the Landmark Supreme Court Cases Web site at landmarkcases.org for information and activities about *Miranda* v. *Arizona*.

Although some defendants might ask for an attorney, others might not be aware of or understand their right to remain silent or their right to have a lawyer present during questioning. In 1966, the Supreme Court was presented with such a situation in the case of *Miranda* v. *Arizona*. In its decision, the Supreme Court ruled that Ernesto Miranda's confession could not be used at trial because officers had obtained it without informing Miranda of his right to a lawyer and his right to remain silent. As a result of this case, police are now required to inform people taken into custody of the so-called *Miranda* rights before questioning begins.

Suspects sometimes complain that they were not read their *Miranda* rights and that the entire case should therefore be dropped and charges dismissed. Failure to give *Miranda* warnings, however, does not affect the validity of an arrest. The police have to give *Miranda* warnings only if they want to use statements from the accused at the trial. In fact, in his second trial, even though the court could not use his confession as evidence against him, Miranda was convicted based on other evidence.

Where You Live

What is the practice regarding *Miranda* warnings in your area? How do the police provide warnings to people who are deaf, are mentally impaired, or speak a language other than English?

The Parolee and the Detective

Local police were investigating a burglary in a large city. They believed that the burglary had been committed by Blaine, a person who had served a prison term but was now out on parole. A detective went to Blaine's home and left him a note asking him to come down to the police station. Blaine read the note and went to the station to speak to the detective. Upon entering the detective's office, he was told that he was not under arrest. Then he was told that police were investigating a burglary at a specific address and that his fingerprints had been found at this location. At this point, Blaine confessed to the crime. The detective never read him his *Miranda* warnings, and the detective knew that Blaine's fingerprints had not been found at the scene. Before Blaine's trial on the burglary charge, he and his attorney asked the court to throw out the confession because he had not been given his *Miranda* warnings. The judge refused and, after a trial, Blaine was convicted.

Problem 12.11

a. State the issue the appeals court will have to decide.

b. What arguments can be made for Blaine? For the state?

c. Was Blaine in custodial interrogation at the time of his confession?

d. What is the purpose of *Miranda* warnings?

e. How should this case be decided?

No person . . . shall be compelled in any criminal case to be a witness against himself, nor be deprived of life, liberty, or property, without due process of law.

— Fifth Amendment to the U.S. Constitution

In all criminal prosecutions, the accused shall . . . have the Assistance of Counsel for his defence.

— Sixth Amendment to the U.S. Constitution

The *Miranda* case has been controversial. It illustrates the delicate balance between the protection guaranteed to the accused and the protection from crime provided to society. This balance is constantly changing, and the effect of the *Miranda* case has been somewhat altered by more recent cases. In one case, the Supreme Court created a public safety exception to the *Miranda* rule. In this case, a police officer who was arresting a rape suspect in a grocery store asked the suspect where his gun was before advising him of his rights. The suspect then pointed to a nearby grocery counter, where the gun was found. The Court held that police may ask questions related to public safety before advising suspects of their rights. The Court has also limited the impact of the *Miranda* rule by strictly requiring that the person be in a condition of *custodial interrogation* before the warnings are needed. Custodial interrogation means that the person is in custody (not free to leave) and is being interrogated (questioned) by the police.

Remember that defense counsel will ask the judge before trial to exclude the results of an illegal search. Similarly, defense counsel will ask the judge at a pretrial hearing to exclude any statement given by the defendant in violation of the *Miranda* rule.

Criminal Justice Process: Proceedings Before Trial

"Unless this right to bail before trial is preserved, the presumption of innocence, secured only after centuries of struggle, would lose its meaning."

— *Stack v. Boyle* (1951)

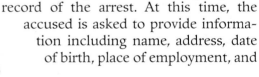

Visit the *Street Law* Web site at streetlaw.glencoe.com for chapter-based information and resources.

Police use fingerprints to investigate the crime.

Before a criminal case reaches the courtroom, several preliminary proceedings take place. Most of these proceedings are standard for every case. Depending on the circumstances and the result of preliminary proceedings, charges may be dropped or the defendant may plead guilty. If charges are dropped or the accused pleads guilty, there will be no trial.

Booking and Initial Appearance

After an arrest, the accused is normally taken to a police station for booking. Booking is the formal process of making a police record of the arrest. At this time, the accused is asked to provide information including name, address, date of birth, place of employment, and

details about any previous arrests. Then the accused is usually finger-printed and photographed. In certain circumstances, the police are allowed to take fingernail clippings, handwriting specimens, or blood samples. Urine tests to ascertain drug use have also become a common booking requirement.

Within a limited period following arrest and booking, the accused must appear before a judicial officer (a judge or magistrate). At this initial appearance, the judge explains the defendant's rights and advises him or her of the exact nature of the charges. The defendant has an attorney appointed or is given the opportunity to obtain one. The judge may also set bail.

In a misdemeanor case, the defendant is asked at the initial appearance to enter a plea of guilty or not guilty. In a felony case, the procedure is somewhat different. The defendant is informed of the charges and advised of his or her rights, as in a misdemeanor case, but does not enter a plea until a later stage in the criminal process, known as the felony arraignment. In addition, in some jurisdictions, the defendant may be entitled to a preliminary hearing to determine if there is probable cause to believe that a crime was committed and that the defendant committed it. The arraignment and the preliminary hearing are discussed later in this chapter. The most important part of the initial appearance is deciding whether the defendant will be released from custody and, if so, under what conditions.

Bail bond companies have gone out of business in some places. *Why might this be?*

Bail and Pretrial Release

An arrested person can usually be released after putting up an amount of money known as **bail.** The purpose of bail is to assure the court that the defendant will return for trial. A constitutional right to bail is recognized in all but the most serious cases, such as murder.

Bail may be paid directly to the court. The entire amount may be required, or in some places, the defendant may be released after paying just a portion of the total amount (for example, 10 percent). If a person released on bail fails to return, the court will keep the money. If the defendant does not have the money, a bond company may put up a bail bond in exchange for a fee. For example, a defendant with bail set at $2,000 might be released after paying $200 (10 percent of the total) to the bond company. If a bond is posted, the bond company will be required to pay the amount of the bond to the court if the defendant does not report for trial.

There are several pretrial release programs that do not require a defendant to post bail. *What factors should a judge consider when determining whether a defendant will return for trial?*

The Eighth Amendment to the U.S. Constitution states that "excessive bail shall not be required." However, a poor person unable to raise any money could be detained in jail before trial or conviction. Many people consider this unfair, and some courts and legislatures have developed programs to release defendants without requiring any money.

To be eligible for release on **personal recognizance,** or personal bond, the defendant must promise to return and must be considered a low risk of failing to show up for trial. In determining the likelihood of the defendant's return, judges consider factors such as the nature and circumstances of the offense and the accused's family and community ties, financial resources, employment background, and prior criminal record.

In addition to personal recognizance programs, courts may set a variety of nonmonetary conditions designed to ensure the return of the defendant. These conditions include placing the defendant in the custody of a third party or requiring the defendant to maintain or get a job, to reside at a certain address, or to report his or her whereabouts on a regular basis.

Despite the advantages of these programs, releasing defendants may involve problems even though they have not yet been found guilty of a crime. Statistics indicate that a large number of defendants

Where You Live

How does the bail system work in your locality? How difficult is it for a defendant to remain free before trial in your area?

commit crimes while out on bail. As a result, some people argue that it should be made more difficult to get out on bail. In 1984, Congress passed the *Bail Reform Act*, which can prevent someone from being freed on bail if he or she is charged with a federal felony offense and believed to be dangerous. In order for this to occur, there must be a hearing, and the person being denied bail must have been charged with a violent crime or a drug offense. In addition, the individual must already have been convicted of a felony more than once. While the U.S. Supreme Court has upheld the *Bail Reform Act* as constitutional, most states have not adopted similar legislation.

Supporters of pretrial release say that it prevents punishment prior to conviction and gives defendants the freedom to help prepare their cases. Supporters also claim that the U.S. justice system rests on the presumption that defendants are innocent until proven guilty and that setting high bail or holding a person in jail before trial goes against that presumption.

Problem 13.1

a. What is the purpose of the constitutional right not to be subjected to excessive bail? Should it apply to all people who are arrested?

b. Can you think of any circumstances in which a person should be released without any bail requirements? Explain.

c. Can you think of any circumstances under which a person should not be released on bail of any kind? Explain.

d. Do you think the bail system in the United States needs reform? If so, how?

Prosecutors conduct preliminary investigations to determine whether the defendant committed the crime. *What is included in the prosecutor's information?*

Information

In most states, a defendant will proceed to trial for a misdemeanor based on a prosecutor's information, which details the nature and circumstances of the charge. The information is a formal criminal charge filed with the court by the prosecutor without the aid of a preliminary hearing or a grand jury. It is based on the evidence a prosecutor collects during his or her preliminary investigation that suggests that the defendant in custody committed the crime in

YOU BE THE JUDGE

Bail Hearing

The following people have been arrested and charged with a variety of crimes. For each, decide whether the person should be released and, if so, under what conditions: (1) bail (release after a certain amount of money is paid; set an amount), (2) personal recognizance (release with no money), (3) conditional release (release under certain conditions; set the conditions), (4) pretrial detention (no release).

Case 1

Name: Marta Garcia   Age: 26
Charge: Possession of crack cocaine
Residence: 619 30th Street; lives alone;
no family or references
Employment: Unemployed
Education: 11th grade
Criminal record: As a juvenile, five arrests, mostly misdemeanors. As an adult, two arrests for petty larceny and a conviction for possession of dangerous drugs. Probation was successfully completed.
Comment: Arrested while leaving a train station with a large quantity of crack cocaine. Urine test indicates use of narcotics.

Case 2

Name: Gloria Hardy   Age: 23
Charge: Prostitution
Residence: 130 Riverside Drive, Apt. 10;
lives with female roommates
Employment: Call girl; earns $2,500 per week.
Education: Completed high school.
Criminal record: Five arrests for prostitution, two convictions. Currently on probation.
Comment: Allegedly involved in prostitution catering to wealthy clients.

Case 3

Name: Stanley A. Wexler   Age: 42
Charge: Possession and sale of crack cocaine
Residence: 3814 Sunset Drive; lives with wife and two children

Employment: Self-employed owner of a drug-store chain; annual salary $400,000.
Education: Completed college; holds degrees in pharmacology and business administration.
Criminal record: None
Comment: Arrested at his store by undercover police after attempting to sell a large quantity of heroin. Alleged to be a big-time dealer. No indication of drug usage.

Case 4

Name: Michael D. McKenna   Age: 19
Charge: Assault
Residence: 412 Pine Street; lives alone;
parents are in prison
Employment: Waiter; earns $400 per week.
Education: 10th grade
Criminal record: Six juvenile arrests (possession of marijuana, illegal possession of firearms, and four burglaries); convicted of firearms charge and two burglaries; spent two years in juvenile facility.
Comment: Arrested after being identified as assailant in a street fight. Alleged leader of a street gang. Police consider him dangerous. No indication of drug usage.

Case 5

Name: Chow Yang   Age: 34
Charge: Possession of stolen mail and forgery
Residence: 5361 Texas Street; lives with common-law wife and two children by a prior marriage
Employment: Works 30 hours per week at a service station; earns minimum wage.
Education: Quit school after 8th grade.
Criminal record: Nine arrests, mostly vagrancy and drunk and disorderly conduct. Two convictions: (1) driving while intoxicated (fined and lost license) and (2) forgery (completed two years' probation)
Comment: Arrested attempting to cash a stolen Social Security check. Has a drinking problem.

question. Defendants charged with a misdemeanor are not entitled to a preliminary hearing or a subsequent grand jury review. A few states use the information system in felony prosecutions as well.

Preliminary Hearing

A **preliminary hearing** is a screening device used in more than half of the states. It is used in felony cases to determine if there is enough evidence to require the defendant to stand trial. At a preliminary hearing, the prosecutor is required to establish that a crime probably has been committed and that the defendant probably did it.

In most states, the defendant has the right to be represented by an attorney, to cross-examine prosecution witnesses, and to call favorable witnesses. If enough evidence supports the prosecutor's case, the defendant will proceed to trial. If the judge finds no probable cause to believe that a crime was committed or that the defendant committed it, the case may be dismissed. However, dismissal of a case at the preliminary hearing does not always mean that the case is over. The prosecution may still submit the case to a grand jury for further review of the charges.

Grand Jury

A **grand jury** is a group of 16 to 23 people charged with determining whether there is sufficient cause to believe that a person has committed a crime and should be made to stand trial. The Fifth Amendment to the U.S. Constitution requires that before anyone can be tried for a serious crime in federal court, there must be a grand jury **indictment,** or formal charge of criminal action. Only about 20 states regularly use grand juries instead of a preliminary hearing to determine the probability that a particular defendant committed the alleged crime. Some states utilize both procedures.

To secure an indictment, a prosecutor presents evidence designed to convince members of the grand jury that a crime has been committed and that there is probable cause to believe the defendant committed it. Neither the defendant nor his or her attorney has a right to appear before a grand jury. A judge is not present and rules of evidence do not apply. The prosecutor is not required to present all the evidence or call all the witnesses as long as the grand jury is satisfied that the evidence presented amounts to at least probable cause.

Historically, the grand jury—standing between the accuser and the accused—was seen as a guardian of the rights of the innocent. If a majority of the grand jurors do not believe that sufficient evidence has been presented by the prosecutor, there will not be an indictment, and the complaint against the defendant will be dismissed. In some instances, the grand jury system has protected citizens from being unreasonably harassed by the government.

Where You Live

What pretrial proceeding is used in your state for felony prosecutions? For misdemeanors? Can a prosecutor utilize more than one proceeding to bring a suspect to trial? Is this system fair?

One common pretrial motion is a request to change the location of the trial. *How might media attention influence a trial and its outcome?*

Felony Arraignment and Pleas

After an indictment or information is issued, the defendant is required to appear in court to enter a plea. If the defendant pleads guilty, the judge will set a date for sentencing. If the defendant pleads not guilty, the judge will set a date for trial and ask whether the defendant wants a jury trial or a trial before a judge alone (called a "bench trial").

Nolo contendere is a plea in which the defendant does not admit guilt but also does not contest the charges. It is equivalent to pleading guilty. The only advantage of this plea to the defendant is that it cannot be used as evidence in a later civil trial for damages based on the same set of facts. After such a plea, there is no trial. Instead, the defendant proceeds directly to the sentencing phase.

Pretrial Motions: The Exclusionary Rule

An important preliminary proceeding is the pretrial motion. A motion is a formal request that a court make a ruling or take some other action. Prior to trial, a defendant may file motions seeking to have the case dismissed or to obtain some advantage or assistance in preparing the case. Common pretrial motions include the following:

- **Motion for discovery of evidence.** This is a request by the defendant to examine, before trial, certain evidence in the possession of the prosecutor.

- **Motion for a continuance.** This request seeks more time to prepare the case.
- **Motion for change of venue.** This is a request to change the location of the trial to avoid community hostility, for the convenience of witnesses, or for other reasons.
- **Motion to suppress evidence.** This is perhaps the most important and controversial pretrial motion. It is a request that certain evidence not be allowed to be presented.

As you learned in Chapter 12, the Fourth Amendment protects citizens against "unreasonable searches and seizures" by the government. But it does not say what happens if the police violate the amendment. To give teeth to the amendment, the U.S. Supreme Court interpreted the amendment as requiring an exclusionary rule. This rule states that any evidence illegally seized by law enforcement officials cannot be used to convict the accused at trial. It also applies to evidence obtained from illegal questioning of the accused.

The exclusionary rule is used by criminal defense lawyers when they file a motion to suppress evidence. This motion asks the court to exclude any evidence that was illegally obtained. If the judge agrees that the evidence was obtained in violation of the accused's constitutional rights, it will be suppressed. However, this does not mean the evidence is returned to the defendant. For example, if the police illegally seize contraband, such as marijuana, that information cannot be used at trial, but the marijuana does not have to be given back to the defendant.

The exclusionary rule has been used in federal courts since 1914. However, the rule was not extended to state courts until the 1961 Supreme Court case *Mapp v. Ohio*. This famous case made the exclusionary rule binding on the states. Over the years since the *Mapp* decision, courts have modified and reevaluated the exclusionary rule, but the basic premise remains.

The exclusionary rule does not prevent the arrest or trial of a suspect. However, in some cases, it does mean that people who committed a crime might go free. This could happen because when an important piece of evidence is excluded from the trial, the prosecutor may not have other evidence sufficient to obtain a conviction. As a result, such a case is often dismissed or the defendant is acquitted.

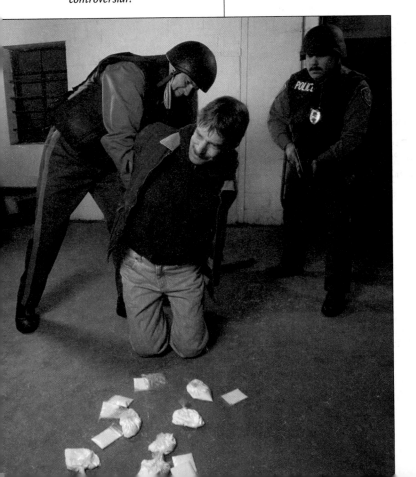

Police often make arrests to seize contraband or to disrupt criminal activity. *Why is the exclusionary rule controversial?*

The exclusionary rule is very controversial. Many people claim that it is a legal loophole that allows dangerous criminals to go free. They also point out that many other countries have no such rule; instead, those countries punish the police for violating citizens' rights. Others say the rule is necessary to safeguard our rights and to prevent police misconduct. The two major arguments in support of the rule are judicial integrity and deterrence. **Judicial integrity** is the idea that courts should not be parties to lawbreaking by the police. **Deterrence** means that police will be less likely to violate a citizen's rights if they know that illegally seized evidence will be thrown out of court.

As a practical matter, police are sometimes more concerned with arrests than with convictions. They may make arrests primarily to seize contraband, gather information, or disrupt criminal activity, regardless of whether a suspect can be convicted of the crime. Even when they are seeking a conviction, they sometimes make mistakes.

In recent years, the U.S. Supreme Court has established a "good faith" exception to the exclusionary rule. In one of the cases the Court used to establish this rule, police were seeking evidence related to a homicide. However, the magistrate who approved the search warrant signed a warrant normally used to conduct searches for drugs. The officers did not look at the warrant after it was signed by the magistrate. Technically, this warrant did not meet the requirement of describing "with particularity" the items to be seized. The Supreme Court held that the "exclusionary rule should not apply to bar evidence obtained by police acting in reasonable reliance on a search warrant, issued by a detached and neutral magistrate, that is later found to be invalid."

Landmark Supreme Court Cases

Visit the Landmark Supreme Court Cases Web site at landmarkcases.org for information and activities about *Mapp v. Ohio*.

Problem 13.2

a. What is the exclusionary rule? How does it work?

b. Why do you think the Supreme Court adopted the exclusionary rule? What are some arguments in favor of the rule? Against the rule? Do you favor or oppose the rule? Explain your answer.

c. What is the good faith exception to the exclusionary rule? What are some arguments in favor of the good faith exception? Should it be extended to warrantless searches?

Plea Bargaining

Contrary to popular belief, most criminal cases never go to trial. Rather, most defendants who are convicted plead guilty before trial. In minor cases, such as traffic violations, the procedure for pleading guilty is simple. The defendant signs a form waiving the right to appear and mails the court a check for the amount of the fine. In major cases, guilty pleas result from a process of negotiation among

Where You Live

Do your local courts use plea bargaining? Are there proposals to change the system? Are changes needed?

the accused, the defense attorney, and the prosecutor. This process is known as **plea bargaining.** It involves granting certain concessions to the defendant in exchange for a plea of guilty. Typically, the prosecution will allow the defendant to plead guilty to a less serious charge or recommend a lighter sentence on the original charge in exchange for a guilty plea. When accepting a guilty plea, the judge must decide if the plea was made freely, voluntarily, and with knowledge of all the facts. Thus, once a defendant pleads guilty, withdrawing the guilty plea and appealing the subsequent conviction are very difficult.

Plea bargaining allows the government to avoid the time and expense of a public trial. It may also benefit the defendant, who often receives a lighter sentence than if the case had resulted in a conviction at trial. Plea bargaining is controversial, however. Critics charge that plea bargaining allows dangerous criminals to get off with light sentences. Others, more concerned with the plight of the defendant, argue that the government should be forced to prove guilt beyond a reasonable doubt at trial. They say a prosecutor with a weak case can use the plea bargaining system to unfairly influence a defendant to accept a lower charge in lieu of risking a longer sentence as the result of a guilty conviction at trial. Finally, victims of crime argue that their rights are completely overlooked in the plea bargaining process.

Some places have abolished or limited plea bargaining. Without plea bargaining, some argue that the criminal justice system will be overwhelmed by the increase in cases coming to trial. Others say that eliminating plea bargaining will provide greater justice because the government will drop (not prosecute) weak cases and defendants will still plead guilty when the government's case is very strong.

Many cases conclude with a plea bargain and never go to trial. *How does the process of plea bargaining work?*

Law in Action

The Power of Plea Bargaining

Prosecutors play a significant role in the criminal justice system and, therefore, have an awesome responsibility to the community. They are responsible for charging wrongdoers with crimes and suggesting appropriate sentences for those who are convicted of those crimes. Prosecutors are often burdened with heavy caseloads, so they may choose to offer plea bargains to defendants in order to avoid the cost of a lengthy trial.

The ability to plea bargain places a great deal of power in a prosecutor's hands, which raises many concerns in the community on both sides of the issue. Some feel that defendants—especially those who are poor or uneducated—are taken advantage of and denied certain constitutional trial rights. People are concerned that the plea bargaining system places these defendants in an unfair and powerless position where they feel that taking a plea is their only choice to avoid a costly conviction.

Others believe that the plea bargaining system allows the government to provide for lighter sentences and to direct defendants to rehabilitation programs. It also includes the defendant in deciding the most appropriate sentence, and helps to relieve the significant burden on the state of bringing all criminals to trial.

Problem 13.3

a. Should plea bargaining be allowed? Do you think plea bargaining offers greater advantages to the prosecutor or to the defendant? Explain your answer.

b. Do you think prosecutors have a disproportionate amount of power in the plea bargaining process, forcing the defendant to accept a plea that might not be in his or her best interest?

c. Assume that a defendant who is charged with a serious felony declines a plea bargain offer but then receives a much harsher sentence upon being convicted at trial. Is he or she being unfairly punished for exercising his or her constitutional right to a trial?

d. Do you think that poor or uneducated defendants could be forced to accept plea bargains because they cannot afford to finance a costly trial?

e. What role do you think defense counsel should play in the plea bargaining process?

f. Consider the following scenario: Marty, who is 22 years old, is arrested and charged with burglarizing a warehouse. He has a criminal record, including a previous conviction for shoplifting and two arrests for auto theft. The prosecutor has evidence placing him at the scene of the crime but no other physical evidence linking him to the crime. Because of his record, if Marty is convicted, he could face up to 10 years in prison. Marty's defense attorney tells him that the prosecutor will reduce the charge to petty larceny, carrying a one-year suspended sentence and community service, in exchange for a guilty plea.

- If you were Marty, would you plead guilty to the lesser charge? Why or why not?

- Suppose Marty pleads guilty after being promised the more lenient sentence by the prosecutor, but the judge overrules the plea and assigns a longer prison term. Is there anything Marty can do about it?

g. Do you think anyone accused of a crime would plead guilty if he or she were really innocent? Explain your answer.

Criminal Justice Process: The Trial

Due process of law (fair procedures) means little to the average citizen unless and until he or she is arrested and charged with a crime. This is because many of the basic rights set out in the U.S. Constitution apply to people accused of crime. Accused people are entitled to have a jury trial in public and without undue delay, to be informed of their rights and of the charges against them, to confront and cross-examine witnesses, to compel witnesses to testify on their behalf, to refuse to testify against themselves, and to be represented by an attorney. These rights are the essence of due process of law. Taken together, they make up the overall right to a fair trial.

Right to Trial by Jury

The right to a jury trial in criminal cases is guaranteed by the Sixth Amendment to the U.S. Constitution. It is applicable in all federal and state courts. However, a jury is not required in every case. In fact, juries are not used very often.

In all criminal prosecutions, the accused shall enjoy the right to a speedy and public trial, by an impartial jury . . . , and to be informed of the nature and cause of the accusation; to be confronted with the witnesses against him; to have . . . witnesses in his favor, and to have the Assistance of Counsel for his defence.

— Sixth Amendment to the U.S. Constitution

Street Law online

Visit the *Street Law* Web site at streetlaw.glencoe.com for chapter-based information and resources.

Persons accused of a crime have a right to a trial.

Most criminal cases are resolved by guilty pleas before ever reaching trial. Jury trials are also not required for certain minor offenses—generally, those punishable by less than six months in prison. Furthermore, defendants can **waive**, or give up, their right to a jury trial and instead have their case heard by a judge (a bench trial). In some states, waivers occur in the majority of cases.

Jury panels are selected from voter registration or tax lists and are supposed to be generally representative of the community. In some communities potential jurors are also selected from drivers' license rolls. In federal courts, juries consist of 12 persons who must reach a unanimous verdict before finding a person guilty. While many states also use 12-person juries, they are not required to do this by the U.S. Constitution. The U.S. Supreme Court only requires at least 6 jurors. Similarly, most states require unanimous verdicts in criminal cases, but the Supreme Court, in interpreting the Constitution, has not required unanimous verdicts in state courts.

The Supreme Court has ruled in a number of cases that attorneys may not exclude or try to exclude prospective jurors from serving on a jury solely because of their race or gender. Racial discrimination in the selection of jurors has been especially problematic in the nation's courts, and the Supreme Court has struck down attempts by attorneys to exclude both white and African American jurors from jury panels.

Of particular concern is an attorney's use of **peremptory challenges**—a device an attorney can use a limited number of times in asking the court to exclude a particular juror without giving a reason. Under the current law, if a defendant can make a plausible case of racial bias by a prosecutor, the prosecutor must prove that he or she had a race-neutral reason for each peremptory exclusion. Once the defendant gives a counterargument, it is then up to a judge to decide whether the prosecutor's reasons are valid.

Those in favor of the system believe that it gives both sides an opportunity to be heard. They stress that appellate courts should usually defer in these matters to the decisions of trial court judges because they were able to witness the actual proceeding from start to finish. Critics argue that the system is flawed because local trial judges are often reluctant to question the motives of prosecutors in their community. Critics also claim that the deference given to trial court judges may further disadvantage defendants, especially in communities whose court systems have histories of alleged discrimination.

Problem 14.1

a. Why is the right to a jury trial guaranteed by the Bill of Rights? Why might someone choose not to have a jury trial?

b. Do you think jury verdicts should be unanimous? Why or why not?

c. Do you think juries should deliberate and come to a conclusion in private, or should this proceeding be televised and made public? Explain.

Right to a Speedy and Public Trial

The Sixth Amendment to the U.S. Constitution provides a right to a speedy trial in all criminal cases. The Constitution does not define speedy, and courts have had trouble deciding what this term means. To remedy this problem, the federal government and some states have set specific time limits within which a case must be brought to trial. Without the right to a speedy trial as an element of due process, an innocent person could await trial—possibly in jail—for years.

If a person does not receive a speedy trial, the case may be dismissed. However, defendants often waive their right to a speedy trial. They may do this because of the unavailability or illness of an important witness or because they need more time to prepare their cases. Before dismissing a case, courts will consider the cause and reasons for the delay and whether the defendant was free on bail or in jail during the pretrial period.

Where You Live

Does your state have a speedy trial law? If so, how does it work? If not, should your state enact one? Explain.

Law in Action

Jury Nullification

Jurors and juries have a great deal of power in the U.S. legal system. Some people see the jury box, like the ballot box, as an essential element of democracy and as a potential check on the government.

Juries determine the facts provided at trial and apply the law based on instructions given by the judge. However, there is a long history in the United States of juries sometimes disregarding the law and the judges' instructions when they believe they must do so in the interest of justice. This is called jury nullification. For example, during the nineteenth century, some juries refused to convict people who hid runaway slaves, even though it was illegal to do so at that time. Today, juries sometimes refuse to convict when they believe a law is unfair or is being enforced unfairly. One example of this might be a refusal to convict for marijuana possession when the defendant uses the drug for strictly medicinal purposes.

While legal scholars acknowledge the history of jury nullification in the United States, some experts believe that expanded use of this extraordinary power could lead to anarchy or an undermining of the rule of law. Others argue that it is an effective way for citizens (jurors) in a democracy to check abuse of power.

Problem 14.2

a. Are there laws where you live that jurors might find so unfair (or so unfairly enforced) that they would refuse to convict a defendant, even with proof beyond a reasonable doubt of guilt? If so, which laws?

b. Should juries be told by judges that they have the power to ignore the law? Why or why not?

Problem 14.3

a. Why is the right to a speedy trial important?

b. How soon after arrest should a person be brought to trial? What are some reasons for and against bringing a defendant to trial within a short time after arrest?

c. Do you think that televising criminal trials is a good idea? Explain.

Right to Compulsory Process and to Confront Witnesses

Defendants in a criminal case have a right to compulsory process for obtaining witnesses. This means that the defendant can get a subpoena—a court order—requiring a witness to appear in court to testify. Without this basic right, defendants would have great difficulty establishing a defense.

The Sixth Amendment provides people accused of a crime with the right to confront (be face-to-face with) the witnesses against them and to ask them questions by way of cross-examination. Although a defendant has the right to be present in the courtroom during all stages of the trial, the U.S. Supreme Court has said that this right may be restricted if the defendant becomes disorderly or disruptive. In such instances, judges have the power to remove the defendant from the courtroom, to cite him or her for contempt of court, or, in extreme circumstances, to have the defendant bound and gagged.

The right to confrontation is sometimes modified for child witnesses, especially in abuse cases. Many courts in these cases install closed-circuit television cameras. This practice enables the child to testify on camera in a room separate from the one in which the defendant is located.

Problem 14.4

a. What are the arguments for and against closed-circuit television in child abuse cases?

b. Should it be allowed in cases involving rape or any other violent crime?

Freedom From Self-Incrimination

Freedom from self-incrimination means that you cannot be forced to testify against yourself in a criminal trial. This right comes from the Fifth Amendment and can be exercised in all criminal cases. In addition, the prosecutor is forbidden to make any statement drawing the jury's attention to the defendant's refusal to testify. While defendants in a criminal case have a right not to testify, they also have a right to

Where You Live

How is representation provided to poor criminal defendants where you live? Is there a public defender? Does the system work?

take the stand and testify if they wish. (In other countries, defendants in criminal cases are *required* to testify.) Defense attorneys often counsel their clients not to take the stand for their own protection. For example, a defendant does not have to answer an inappropriate question if her attorney objects to it and the judge sustains, or agrees with, that objection. This is true for all witnesses, but once a defendant takes the stand, the prosecutor can use anything she says to elicit contradictory and harmful statements that can be used against her.

Related to the right against self-incrimination is the concept of **immunity**. Being granted immunity means that a witness cannot be prosecuted based on any information provided in a testimony. However, a person with immunity must answer all questions—even those that are incriminating. Prosecutors often use these laws to force people to testify against codefendants or others involved in the crime.

Problem 14.5

a. Suppose you are a defense attorney. What are the advantages and disadvantages of having a criminal defendant testify at trial?

b. If you were a member of the jury in a criminal trial, what would you think if the defendant refused to testify? Would you be affected by the judge's instruction not to draw any conclusion from this?

c. If a defendant is forced to stand in a lineup, give a handwriting sample, or take an alcohol breath or urine test, does this violate the privilege against self-incrimination?

d. Do you think that U.S. law should be changed so that defendants are required to testify in criminal cases? Explain.

Right to an Attorney

The Sixth Amendment provides that "In all criminal prosecutions, the accused shall enjoy the right to . . . have the Assistance of Counsel for his defence." At one time, this meant that, except in capital cases—those involving the death penalty or life imprisonment—a defendant had the right to an attorney only if he or she could afford one. However, in 1938, the U.S. Supreme Court required the federal courts to appoint attorneys for indigent defendants—those without financial means—in all federal felony cases. Twenty-five years later, in the case of *Gideon* v. *Wainwright* (1963), the Supreme Court extended the right to counsel to all felony defendants, whether in state or federal court. In 1972, the Supreme Court further extended this ruling by requiring that no imprisonment may occur, even in misdemeanor cases, unless the accused is given an opportunity to be represented by an attorney.

The right to the assistance of counsel is basic to the idea of a fair trial. In a criminal trial, the state (the people) is represented by a prosecutor who is a lawyer. In addition, the prosecutor's office has other resources, including investigators, to help prepare the case against the accused.

Landmark Supreme Court Cases

Visit the Landmark Supreme Court Case Web site at landmarkcases.org for information and activities about *Gideon* v. *Wainwright*.

At a minimum, the defendant needs a skillful lawyer to ensure a fair trial.

As a result of these Supreme Court decisions, criminal defendants who cannot afford an attorney have one appointed to them free of charge by the government. These attorneys may be either public defenders or private attorneys. The public defender's office is supported by the government. The job of the public defender's office is to represent poor people in criminal cases. Lawyers appointed by the court to handle criminal cases for indigent defendants are typically paid less than a private lawyer hired directly by a defendant. Some people criticize the overall quality of representation that poor criminal defendants receive in this country. These critics say that criminal defendants with money to hire their own lawyer have a much better chance of being found not guilty than economically disadvantaged defendants do.

It is important for a criminal defendant to have a skillful defense attorney. *In what ways can an attorney help a defendant prepare for trial?*

Problem 14.6

a. Are court-appointed attorneys as good as privately paid ones?

b. Assume a defendant wants to handle his or her own defense. Should this be allowed? Do you think this is a good idea?

c. Assume a lawyer knows that his or her client is guilty. Is it right for the lawyer to try to convince the jury the person is not guilty? Explain.

Criminal Appeals

If the jury returns with a "not guilty" verdict, this is normally the end of the case. The state (prosecution) cannot appeal once the defendant has been acquitted of the offenses for which he or she was tried. If the verdict is "guilty" then the sentencing will follow.

Defendants who think they have been wrongly convicted have several options once the trial judge has entered the final judgment in the case. The defendant can ask the judge to overturn the jury's verdict and enter a verdict of not guilty or ask the judge to set aside the jury's verdict, declare a **mistrial,** and ask for a new trial. These strategies are seldom successful. The defendant can also appeal to a higher court. An appeal requests that a higher court review and change the decision of the trial court. In the appeal, the defendant can challenge the conviction or the sentencing decision.

Sometimes the defendant will want to hire a different lawyer for the appeal. This happens because lawyers who do trial work may not specialize in appellate work. It may also happen because the defendant's

Where You Live

❶ How is representation provided to poor criminal defendants where you live? Is there a public defender? Does the system work?

• • • • • • • • • •

❷ How does the criminal appeals process work in your state? Do appellate courts schedule oral arguments on criminal appeals, or do the judges make their decisions based on the briefs submitted by the parties?

appeal may be based on an alleged violation of the Sixth Amendment, which guarantees the right to effective assistance of counsel. Depending on the resources available, the public defender's office may be available to provide assistance to indigent defendants who wish to appeal.

Generally, the defendant must file a notice of appeal shortly after the final judgment is entered. This notice lets the prosecution and the court know that there will be an appeal. The appellate court then sets a schedule, which involves the preparation of legal briefs—short statements of each lawyer's side of the case. In some instances, an oral argument is presented before a panel of appellate court judges. The defendant's brief sets out the alleged errors of law at the trial that led to the conviction. The state's reply brief provides a response to those arguments. Among the possible errors are: ineffective assistance of counsel, improperly admitting evidence, giving the jury the wrong instructions, improper use of a sentencing guideline, and others.

In addition to the briefs, the appellate court receives the official trial record, which includes a transcript (what was said at the trial) and the documents and exhibits admitted into evidence by the judge. New information is not presented at the appeal. It can be expensive for the defendant to have the transcript prepared, which limits appeals. An indigent defendant, however, may be able to have a transcript prepared for free or for a small fee, depending on the state.

Remember from Chapter 5 that trial courts determine questions of fact (e.g., guilty or not guilty in a criminal case) and that appellate courts determine questions of law. In order to win an appeal, the defendant—now called the petitioner or appellant depending on the state's terminology—must convince the appeals court that there were serious errors of law made at the trial. Appeals courts tend to defer to trial judges and are not usually eager to overturn the result of the trial. If there are legal errors of a minor nature, then the outcome of the trial will not be changed.

In an appeal, the defendant claims that legal errors were made in his or her trial. *How does the appeals process work?*

In addition to appeals, the defendant may apply to a court for help by seeking a writ, which is an order from a higher court to either a lower court or to a government official, such as the warden of a jail or prison. The writ of habeas corpus—which literally means "to produce the body"—claims that a defendant is being held illegally and requests release. The writ can sometimes be used when an appeal could not be. For example, a defendant might use a writ to argue for his innocence based on DNA testing that occurred after the trial, a point that could not be made using an appeal.

The writ of habeas corpus can be filed with a state court for alleged state law violations or with a federal court for alleged violations of federal law. The writ of habeas corpus gives criminal defendants the right to ask for relief from confinement, but of course filing this writ does not necessarily mean that the court will grant the relief.

Criminal Justice Process: Sentencing and Corrections

"It is insufficient to restrain the wicked by punishment unless you render them virtuous by corrective discipline."

— Inscription over the door of the Hospice of San Michele in Rome, Italy, 1704

The final phase of the criminal justice process begins with sentencing. Once found guilty, the defendant will be sentenced by the judge or, in a few states, by the jury. The sentence is perhaps the most critical decision in the criminal justice process. It can determine a defendant's fate for years or, in some cases, for life.

Street Law *online*

Visit the *Street Law* Web site at streetlaw.glencoe.com for chapter-based information and resources.

Imprisonment is just one of several sentencing options.

Sentencing Options

Most criminal statutes set out a basic sentencing structure, but judges generally have considerable freedom in determining the actual type, length, and conditions of the sentence. Depending on the state, judges may choose from one or a combination of the following options:

- **Suspended sentence.** The sentence is given but does not have to be served at the time it is imposed. However, the defendant may have to serve the time later if he or she is rearrested on another charge or violates a condition of probation.

- **Probation.** The defendant is released to the supervision of a probation officer after agreeing to follow certain conditions, such as getting a job, staying drug-free, and not traveling outside of the area during the probation period.

- **Home confinement.** The defendant is sentenced to serve the term at home. Normally, the only time this defendant can leave the home is for essential purposes such as work, school, or a doctor's appointment. The defendant is sometimes required to wear an electronic monitoring device so that his or her activities can be monitored by the probation officer.

- **Fine.** The defendant must pay the government an amount of money set by the court.

- **Restitution.** The defendant is required to pay back or make up for whatever loss or injury was caused to the victim of the crime.

- **Work release.** The defendant is allowed to work in the community but must return to prison at night or on weekends.

- **Imprisonment.** The defendant is sentenced to a term in jail or prison. Some states require that a definite sentence be given, in which case the judge specifies the exact amount of time to be served (for example, two years). Some states provide for an indeterminate term, in which case the sentence is stated not as a specific number of years but as a minimum and maximum term (for example, not less than three years nor more than ten years). Some judges allow defendants in misdemeanor cases to serve short jail sentences on weekends.

- **Death.** The defendant is sentenced to die for his or her crime. In many states and in the federal court system, judges have the option of handing down the death penalty for the most heinous offenses. This controversial issue is discussed in more depth later in this chapter.

Electronic monitoring devices are often used for home confinement. *What are the advantages and disadvantages of such a sentence?*

The Three Strikes Law

California lawmakers passed the "Three Strikes" Law in March 1994, following the high-profile kidnapping and murder of 12-year-old Polly Klaas. Her abductor was a violent offender out on parole, living in the Klaas family's community. Outraged by this awful crime and eager for the legislature to get tougher on crime, California voters overwhelmingly approved Proposition 184. This law was designed to deter offenders from committing new crimes and to give longer prison terms to criminals who have been convicted of felonies in the past. By the late 1990s about 40 states had some form of recidivist statute, a law designed specifically to punish serious, repeat offenders.

Under California's Three Strikes Law, a strike is a conviction for a serious or violent felony. Once a defendant has one strike, conviction for the second strike results in the usual sentence for that crime being doubled. If a defendant is convicted of a third felony, the law requires that he or she receive a sentence of at least 25 years to life, with no possibility of parole before 25 years.

While strikes one and two must be for serious or violent felonies, *any felony conviction* will qualify as the third strike, whether or not the felony was serious or violent. In addition, certain offenses (called "wobblers") can be prosecuted as either misdemeanors or felonies, at the discretion of the prosecutor or the judge. Finally, the Three Strikes Law is retroactive and is not limited to crimes committed in California. Therefore, convictions from before the law was passed (1994) or in other states can count as strikes.

In November 1995, Leandro Andrade attempted to steal five G-rated videotapes from a Kmart, but was arrested upon leaving the store. Two weeks later, Andrade was arrested outside of another Kmart for attempting to steal more videotapes. The total value of all the tapes was approximately $150. Andrade, a longtime heroin addict, had a 15-year criminal history with five felonies and two misdemeanors on his record. None of the previous convictions were for violent offenses. Prosecutors determined that he already had two strikes under the California law when the prosecution for the Kmart thefts commenced. Under California law, petty theft with a prior conviction is one of the so-called wobblers, misdemeanors that can be prosecuted as felonies. Andrade, then 37, was convicted and sentenced to 25 years to life for *each* of the two petty theft counts (strikes three and four). According to the Three Strikes Law, those sentences must be served consecutively, not concurrently, so Andrade will not become eligible for parole for 50 years.

A federal appeals court found his sentence "grossly disproportionate" to the crime and a violation of the Eighth Amendment's prohibition against cruel and unusual punishment. Prosecutors for the state of California appealed to the U.S. Supreme Court.

Problem 15.1

a. Why did California pass the Three Strikes Law? Why do you think these laws have become so popular in the United States?

b. What are the most convincing arguments for upholding Andrade's sentence?

c. What are the most convincing arguments for reversing the sentence?

d. How should the Court decide the Andrade case? What arguments might the dissenting justices make?

e. As a matter of public policy, do you support or oppose laws like the Three Strikes Law? What information would you need to come to a decision on this matter?

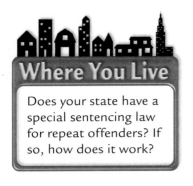

Where You Live

Does your state have a special sentencing law for repeat offenders? If so, how does it work?

Many considerations must be made in the sentencing process. The most critical of these are whether or not the state has fixed, or mandatory, sentencing statutes, and if so, whether or not the judge can exercise any discretion in assigning that statutory sentence. A judge who can exercise discretion may consider many factors. These include the judge's theory of corrections and what he or she thinks is in the best interest of society and the individual. In addition, most states authorize a **presentence report.** This report is prepared by the probation department, and contains a description of the offense and the circumstances surrounding it. The report also sets out the defendant's past criminal record, data on the defendant's social, medical, educational, and employment background, as well as a recommended sentence. After studying the report and listening to recommendations from the defense attorney and the prosecutor, the judge will impose sentence.

Many people criticize the system of sentencing because they think it gives too much discretion to the court. Two people who commit the same crime may receive very different sentences, which some view as an injustice. To combat the problem of inconsistency in sentencing, in 1988 Congress passed federal sentencing guidelines that listed more specifically the sentences judges should impose for certain federal crimes. These guidelines included mandatory sentences without the opportunity for parole. Many states have similar statutes that limit a judge's discretion and that impose mandatory sentences, especially for repeat offenders. In some cases, these statutes have resulted in harsh sentences for seemingly minor offenses.

Critics of these federal and state guidelines argue that it is a mistake to take away a judge's discretion because many outside factors, such as poverty, lack of education, abuse, and drug addiction, contribute to criminal behavior. They believe judges should be able to consider these factors in deciding an appropriate sentence for each individual defendant. However, the U.S. Supreme Court has upheld the constitutionality of the federal sentencing guidelines. And, although the Eighth Amendment provides protection from cruel and unusual punishment, appellate courts are reluctant to overturn sentencing decisions of trial courts or sentencing guidelines established by state legislatures.

Purposes of Punishment

Over the years, the criminal sentence has served a number of different purposes, including retribution, deterrence, rehabilitation, and incapacitation. At one time, the primary reason for punishing a criminal was **retribution.** This is the idea behind the saying "an eye for an eye and a tooth for a tooth." Instead of individuals seeking revenge, society, through the criminal justice system, takes on the role of punishing those who violate its laws.

Another reason for punishing criminals is **deterrence.** Many people believe that punishment discourages the offender from committing another crime in the future. In addition, the punishment is meant to serve as an example to deter other people from committing crimes.

A third goal of punishment is **rehabilitation.** Rehabilitation means helping convicted persons change their behavior so that they can lead useful and productive lives after release. Rehabilitation is based on the idea that criminals can overcome the social, educational, or psychological problems that caused them to commit a crime and that they can be helped to become responsible members of society. Educational, vocational, and counseling programs in prisons and jails are designed to rehabilitate inmates.

A fourth reason for punishment is **incapacitation.** This means that the criminal is physically separated from the community and the community is protected as a result of this incapacitation. While confined in prison, the offender does not pose a threat to the safety of the community.

Rehabilitation programs help inmates change their behavior so they can lead productive lives after release. *What kind of education and training should an inmate receive?*

Parole

In most states, the actual length of time a person serves in prison depends on whether **parole** is granted. Parole is the release of a convicted person from prison before his or her entire sentence has been served. Depending on the state, a person might become eligible for parole after serving a minimum sentence specified by the judge or law. In other states, people automatically become eligible after serving a portion of the total sentence (for example, one-third).

Eligibility for parole is not a right but, rather, a privilege. Inmates may go before a parole board that makes the decision. Some inmates are never paroled and serve their full sentences in prison. The federal system and some states do not have a system of parole, and critics of parole say this is better, because it gives certainty to the sentence and is more likely to have a deterrent effect. Others believe inmates should be evaluated periodically and released early if there is evidence they have been rehabilitated.

At the end of 2001, nearly 6.6 million people were on probation, in jail or prison, or out on parole. This figure represents 3.1 percent of all U.S. adult residents.

Where You Live

Does your state have a parole system, or has it been abolished? Do you think the parole system is a good thing? Explain.

Problem 15.2

Review the information on the five defendants described in the bail hearing on page 159. Assume that each is convicted of the crime charged. Study the sentencing options on page 174 and prepare a presentence report for each of these defendants. Recommend a sentence and explain what purposes would be served by each sentence you recommend. Explain why and when each should be eligible for parole, if they should be eligible at all.

Capital Punishment

Capital punishment, also known as the death penalty, is the most controversial sentence given to defendants. It has a long history in America. The first person executed for murder among settlers in America was hanged in 1630. In colonial years, the death penalty was imposed for a number of different crimes. Gradually, however, capital punishment was restricted to the most serious crimes—usually murder and rape. In 1977, however, the U.S. Supreme Court held that the death penalty was an unconstitutional punishment for the crime of rape.

People have debated the issue of capital punishment for many years. Public protest against the death penalty gradually reduced the number of executions from a peak of 199 in 1935 to only one in 1967. For the next 10 years, executions were halted while the courts studied the legality of capital punishment.

In the 1972 case of *Furman* v. *Georgia,* the U.S. Supreme Court held that the death penalty as then applied was unconstitutional because juries were given too much discretion in assigning this sentence. States then rewrote their capital punishment laws. In 1978, the Court ruled that the new laws were constitutional as long as aggravating and mitigating circumstances were considered in sentencing. Executions soon resumed. According to the U.S. Department of Justice, at the end of 2001, there were 3,581 prisoners sentenced to death. Among them:

- 1,969 were Caucasian
- 358 were Hispanic
- 1,538 were African American
- 28 were Native American
- 33 were Asian
- 13 were classified as "other race"
- 51 were women
- 2 in 3 had prior felony convictions
- 1 in 13 had prior homicide convictions
- the average education attained was 11th grade
- the average age at the time of arrest was 28 (about 13 percent were 19 years old or younger at the time of their arrest)
- the youngest person on death row was 19, and the oldest was 86

Law in Action

DNA and the Death Penalty

Opponents of the death penalty point out that some people sentenced to death were found to be innocent after their executions. Much of the proof of wrongful convictions has been based on DNA evidence—precise technology that has been widely available only since the 1990s. These findings have cast doubt on the guilt of many death row inmates who were sentenced prior to the availability of this conclusive evidence. In recent years, policy makers have considered how to deal with this problem in light of the possibility—even if remote—that someone might be waiting to be executed for a crime he or she did not commit.

In a stark demonstration of concern about the capital punishment system, in early 2003, Illinois governor George Ryan commuted the death sentences of all 156 inmates on Illinois's death row. This came after more than a dozen inmates were exonerated through an investigation initiated by journalism students at Northwestern University. Governor Ryan's decision followed his discovery that four other death row inmates had been tortured into confessing to crimes they did not commit. Although many of these commutations have been appealed and most have been converted to life sentences, Governor Ryan believed his decision was appropriate in light of the error-ridden system in his state, and a necessary challenge to what he believed to be "one of the great civil rights struggles of our time."

Problem 15.3

a. Do you think Governor Ryan was justified in commuting the death sentences of all death row inmates based on investigations of only a fraction of individual cases?

b. What systematic problems do you think may have led to the incarceration and sentence of those and other innocent defendants?

c. Do you favor or oppose the use of the death penalty? Explain your answer. If you favor it, to what crimes should it apply?

d. If you oppose the death penalty, what do you think is the strongest argument in favor of it? If you favor the death penalty, what do you think is the strongest argument against it?

e. How do you think states should deal with the possibility that new evidence (such as conclusive DNA evidence) could prove the innocence of someone on death row?

Illinois governor George Ryan

Many states use lethal injection as the method of execution in execution chambers such as this. *Does capital punishment deter crime?*

Where You Live

Does your state have capital punishment? If so, has it been an effective deterrent to crime in your state? If your state does not have capital punishment, how does it punish those convicted of the most severe crimes?

As of 2003, 38 states had death penalty statutes. States use various methods to carry out the death penalty, and some states use more than one method. Thirty-seven states use lethal injection, ten states use electrocution, five states use lethal gas, three states use hanging, and three states use firing squads. State-by-state death penalty information can be found on pages 619–621.

Most capital punishment laws call for a two-part trial. In part one, the jury decides guilt or innocence. The defendant usually knows if he or she may face the death penalty if convicted. If the defendant is found guilty, in part two of the trial process, the jury decides whether the defendant should receive the death penalty. The laws set forth guidelines for determining whether death or life imprisonment is appropriate. Judges and juries are required to consider both aggravating and mitigating circumstances. **Aggravating circumstances** are factors that suggest a more severe punishment is appropriate, such as a particularly gruesome murder, crimes involving children, or previous convictions of the accused. **Mitigating circumstances** are factors that suggest a less severe punishment is appropriate. Examples include a history showing that the victim had previously abused the defendant, the defendant's age, or the defendant's having no prior criminal record.

More than half of the countries in the world have abolished the death penalty either in law or in practice. Although many countries still use the death penalty, the controversy over capital punishment continues. The debate involves legal, political, and moral issues: Is the death penalty constitutional? If so, for what crimes? Is it a moral punishment for murder? Does it deter crime? Is it applied fairly?

Opponents of capital punishment claim that no one who values life can approve of the death penalty, saying "thou shalt not kill" also applies to those who carry out the death penalty. They further argue that the death penalty does not deter murder, citing statistics showing that murder rates are the same in states with the death penalty as in those without it. Opponents also argue that the death penalty is applied in an unfair manner, that members of minority groups are more likely to receive it, and that it violates the Eighth Amendment's ban against "cruel and unusual punishment."

Opponents of the death penalty agree that communities must be protected from dangerous criminals, but many feel that a sentence of life without parole is a better way to accomplish this goal. Life without parole is still a very severe punishment, communities are protected, and yet the sentence can be reconsidered if evidence of innocence is discovered after conviction.

The Death Penalty for Mentally Disabled Defendants

Daryl Atkins and an accomplice abducted Eric Nesbitt, robbed him, and drove him to an ATM where cameras recorded them forcing him to withdraw more cash. They then took him to an isolated location and shot him eight times. Atkins, who had a history of felony convictions, and his accomplice were convicted of the killing in a Virginia state court.

At the penalty phase of the trial, Atkins's lawyer presented evidence from a psychologist showing that Atkins was mildly mentally disabled. The jury imposed the death penalty and the Virginia Supreme Court upheld the sentence. The case was appealed to the U.S. Supreme Court. At issue was whether it is a violation of the Eighth Amendment's cruel and unusual punishment clause to impose the death penalty on a mentally disabled person.

Opinion A

Mentally disabled persons who meet the law's requirements for criminal responsibility should be tried and punished when they commit crimes. However, because of their disabilities in reasoning, judgment, and impulse control, they do not act with the same level of culpability as other serious adult criminals. In 1988, when Congress enacted a federal death penalty law, it excluded persons who are mentally disabled from receiving that sentence. Since then, 18 states with death penalty laws have decided not to apply them to mentally disabled persons. Combined with the 14 states that completely reject the death penalty, this indicates a national consensus against imposing the death penalty on mentally disabled defendants. Because the Eighth Amendment prohibits punishments that are excessive, we hold that a state cannot impose the death penalty on a mentally disabled offender.

Opinion B

While it is true that 18 states have passed laws exempting mentally disabled defendants from the death penalty's application, 19 other states (including Virginia) continue to leave the question of the proper punishment of individual defendants to judges or juries familiar with the particular offender and with his or her crime. Surely a national consensus does not exist against applying the death penalty to all defendants who are mentally disabled. In determining what is cruel and unusual punishment under the Eighth Amendment, we look to state legislatures for objective evidence of contemporary values. Under our system of shared power (federalism), the best way to determine whether Atkins received an acceptable punishment is to look at the jury's decision and Virginia state laws. Neither national opinion polls nor the laws of other states should result in our reversing the opinion of the Virginia Supreme Court.

Problem 15.4

a. What happened in this case? Why was Atkins given the death penalty?

b. Based on the opinions, what are the strongest arguments for upholding the state supreme court decision? For reversing it?

c. How should this case be decided? Explain.

d. Assume the U.S. Supreme Court decides to overturn the Virginia Supreme Court decision. Now assume the Court is presented with a case where a 15-year-old is convicted and sentenced to death in a state that allows such sentences for juveniles. If that case is appealed to the U.S. Supreme Court, how might the justices analyze it?

Advocates of the death penalty say that killers get what they deserve. They argue that the threat of death does deter crime. They concede that studies on deterrence are inconclusive, but maintain that people fear death more than any other punishment. Advocates also point to opinion polls showing that most Americans favor capital punishment. They argue that execution protects society, saves the government money, and that the death penalty is fairly applied (the Supreme Court has upheld this view). Finally, in light of evidence that there may be innocent people on death row, many proponents are willing to consider post-conviction relief measures. These measures include an automatic appeal in the event that conclusive evidence of innocence becomes available. However, these same proponents are not willing to abolish the death penalty altogether.

For Your Information . . .

Jails and Prisons: What's the Difference?

- Jails are operated by cities and counties. They are used to detain people awaiting trial and to hold mental patients, drug addicts, alcoholics, juvenile offenders, and felons on a temporary basis as they await transfer to other facilities. Jails also hold people convicted of minor crimes for which the sentence is one year or less.
- Jails in the United States vary in size from big-city facilities holding over 1,000 inmates a day to small rural jails consisting of an office and a few cells.
- Prisons are operated by federal or state governments. They are used to incarcerate people convicted of more serious crimes, usually felonies, for which the sentence is more than one year.
- As of 2000, the federal government operated 84 prisons, state governments operated 1,558 prisons, and 26 facilities were privately run (housing mainly federal inmates).
- U.S. prisons range in size from small facilities to huge, maximum-security penitentiaries sprawling over thousands of acres.
- Some U.S. prisons are so big that they resemble small cities. For example, both Louisiana's State Prison at Angola and Michigan's State Penitentiary at Jackson house over 4,000 inmates and employ thousands of staff members.

Inmates' lives are controlled by many rules. *Should inmates lose all rights once they are sent to prison? If not, which rights should they keep?*

Corrections

When a person is convicted of a crime, state and federal governments have the right to place the offender in the corrections system. There are several treatment and punishment options available to the government. These include community corrections, halfway houses, jails, and prisons.

Life Behind Bars

A prison or jail inmate's life is controlled by many rules. Inmates are told when to get up and when to go to sleep. Mail and phone calls are screened. Access to radio, television, and books is controlled. Visitors are limited, and inmates are subject to constant surveillance and searches. Some inmates work at prison jobs, which usually pay very little. Others spend all day locked in their cells.

Until the 1960s, courts had a hands-off policy toward prisons. Inmates had few, if any, rights. Prison officials could make almost any rules they wanted. As a result, harsh treatment, solitary confinement, and beatings were all fairly common.

Over the years courts established and enforced some prisoners' rights. However, in recent years the U.S. Supreme Court has said that people who enter prison must give up certain rights. Inmates retain limited versions of some rights after entering prison. These include the right to be free from cruel and unusual punishment, the right to freedom of religion, the right to due process, the right to medical treatment, and the right of access to law libraries and the courts.

Prison Overcrowding

During the 1990s and into the twenty-first century, there was a significant increase in the number of people incarcerated in the United States. From 1995 to 2001, there was a 23 percent increase in the number of people under some form of correctional supervision (see Figure 15.1). By the middle of 2002, there were more than 1.4 million adults in U.S. prisons, with nearly 700,000 awaiting trials or serving shorter sentences in jails.

According to the U.S. Department of Justice Bureau of Justice Statistics, in the 12 months that ended June 30, 2002, the jail population went up by 34,235 inmates, a 5.4 percent increase—the largest since 1997. State prisons added 12,440 inmates, a 1 percent increase, while the federal prison system grew by 8,042 inmates, a 5.7 percent increase. The current rate of incarceration in the United States is six to ten times higher than that of most industrial nations.

This increase was caused by a get-tough-on-crime policy that resulted in more criminal defendants going to prison for longer periods. There was increasing use of mandatory sentences, a lengthening of some prison terms, and decreasing use of parole and other early-release options. As the crime rate fell into the twenty-first century, prison populations remained high because of longer sentences and a greater willingness to revoke probation and parole.

With more defendants entering the correctional system, there was a need to expand jail and prison capacity. In 2000 alone, there were 27 new state and 4 new federal institutions built, increasing the capacity of the system by more than 23,000 beds. In addition, expansions and renovations at 58 institutions increased capacity by nearly

FIGURE 15.1 Changes in the Criminal Justice System Population*

Year	Probation	Jail	Prison	Parole	Total
1990	2,670,234	405,320	743,382	531,407	4,350,300
1995	3,077,861	507,044	1,078,542	679,421	5,342,900
2001	3,932,751	631,240	1,330,980	731,147	6,592,800

*Federal and state figures combined
Source: U.S. Department of Justice, Bureau of Justice Statistics

The number of offenders in the criminal justice system increased throughout the last decade of the twentieth century. **ANALYZE THE DATA** *By how much did the number of people in prison increase between 1990 and 2001?*

Visit streetlaw.glencoe.com and click on **Textbook Update—Chapter 15** for an update of the data.

14,000 beds. The average construction cost per bed in 1996 was just over $40,000, while the average cost of maintaining a person in prison was about $20,000 per year (about $56.00 per day). Today, the cost of maintaining a person in prison ranges from $15,000 to more than $50,000 per year.

Some critics of the prison-building boom argue that funds could be better spent on prevention and treatment programs. Much of the increase in the federal inmate population, for example, resulted from more aggressive prosecution in drug cases. Some argue that community-based corrections programs with drug treatment opportunities would be a more effective and less expensive way to deal with these offenders. Others contend that longer, more certain punishment has been an effective deterrent to crime and has increased public safety, as dangerous criminals have been taken off the streets and placed in secure facilities.

The growing prison population has created many problems. Overcrowding sparks fights and riots. Drug use, sexual assault, and violence are all common occurrences. Life behind bars is often dangerous and unpleasant. Many prisoners live in tiny cells under uncomfortable conditions.

In recent years, the overcrowding problems have led some states to contract with other states or the federal government to send their prisoners elsewhere. Others have looked to private corporations to run their prisons for them, claiming that private prisons can save millions of dollars and lead to better and more efficiently run institutions. Critics worry that private corporations may violate inmates' rights more often, lobby for longer sentences, and be less concerned about rehabilitation. The courts have consistently held, however, that private prison and jail operators must protect the rights of prisoners to the same extent as public correctional agencies.

Where You Live

Does your community have any prisons, jails, or halfway houses? Who is sent to these facilities? What are living conditions like in these institutions? Where do people from your community serve jail or prison time when they are convicted of a crime? Are there programs available in your community to help ex-convicts reenter society?

Problem 15.5

a. Should prisoners have rights? If so, what rights should they have? Make a list of these rights.

b. If you were a prison warden, what rules would you make to control the prisoners? List these rules.

c. What, if anything, should be done to reduce prison overcrowding? Should more and bigger prisons be built, or should the criminal justice system be more selective about who is locked up?

d. Should private corporations be allowed to run jails and prisons for profit? Role-play the following scenario: As the head of a corporation that runs private homes for the elderly, explain to a county sheriff why the county should hire your corporation to build and operate a new jail to replace the old, overcrowded one. Would you support the idea if you were the sheriff? Would you support the idea if you were a prisoner? A defense attorney? Explain.

Reentry programs provide counseling and long-term support. *What challenges do ex-offenders face in reentering society?*

Reentering Society

While tougher sentencing laws have put greater numbers of people behind bars, state corrections budgets stretched by this larger prison population have had to reduce some of the programs designed to help offenders reenter society once they have served their sentences. Of special concern is the need to help offenders avoid becoming repeat offenders. More than 630,000 adult offenders leave prison every year and return to their communities. More than 100,000 juveniles leave residential facilities and return to their communities. Within three years more than half of both groups typically become repeat offenders.

The U.S. Department of Justice, in collaboration with other federal agencies, has developed a comprehensive initiative to enhance community safety and reduce serious crime committed by ex-offenders. This initiative targets both adult and juvenile offenders. It is called *reentry* and has three phases. Phase one programs begin in correctional institutions and are focused on providing education, mental health services, substance abuse treatment, job training, and mentoring to convicts to psychologically prepare them to reenter society. Phase two programs focus on the actual transition from the institution back into the community, including making logistical decisions about where to live, how to find a job, and ways to reestablish ties with members of the community. This phase also provides mental health and substance abuse treatment. The final phase helps link individuals who have left the supervision of the justice system with a network of social services agencies and community-based organizations. These groups can provide long-term support and mentoring relationships between convicts and counselors.

Planning for successful reentry begins when the defendant enters the correctional system. While reentry is not an "anti-punishment" philosophy, it does recognize that the overwhelming majority of inmates will at some point return to their communities. Adequate preparation of inmates—and of the community—for reentry can reduce recidivism.

Juvenile Justice

In the United States, juveniles in trouble with the law are treated differently from adults. However, this has not always been the case. In earlier times, children were thrown into jails along with adults. Long prison terms and corporal punishment (involving striking the juvenile's body) were common. Some children were even sentenced to death for crimes that seem relatively minor by today's standards.

History and Overview of Juvenile Courts

In the mid-nineteenth century, reformers began to argue that the failure of the family was the cause of delinquent behavior. In other words, parents had failed to teach their children proper values and respect for authority. The solution that evolved was for a separate juvenile court to assume the responsibility that had been the parents' job. Instead of punishing young people through the adult system, a separate juvenile court would seek to rehabilitate them by taking a moralistic approach and trying to help them learn community values.

"Better build schoolrooms for the boy than prison cells for the man."

— Eliza Cook
(1817–1889)

Street Law
online

Visit the *Street Law* Web site at streetlaw.glencoe.com for chapter-based information and resources.

Juvenile offenders may be put to work as part of their punishment.

Truancy, or skipping school, is a status offense. *What other acts are considered status offenses?*

Under this philosophy, the first juvenile court was set up in Cook County, Illinois, in 1899. Juvenile courts were designed to be informal, allowing the court to act as a parent or guardian for the child. The right of the state to intervene in the life of a child is based on the concept of *parens patriae,* a Latin term meaning "parent of the country." Using this concept, the court assumed the role of a parent and was permitted to do whatever it thought was necessary to help the child. Hearings were closed to the public so the youth's identity would remain private. In addition, the juvenile court used terms different from those used in the adult court. (See the FYI feature on page 195 for a comparison of terms used in the juvenile and adult justice systems.)

Today, juvenile courts generally handle three groups of juveniles: delinquent offenders, status offenders, and neglected and abused children. **Delinquent offenders** are youths who have committed acts that would be crimes if committed by adults under federal, state, or local law. **Status offenders** are youths who have committed acts that would not be crimes if committed by adults. Status offenses include running away from home, skipping school, violating curfew, refusing to obey parents, or engaging in certain behaviors such as underage consumption of alcohol. Status offenders are considered to be unruly or beyond the control of their parents or legal guardians; they are persons or children in need of supervision (PINS or CHINS).

Neglected and **abused children** need the court's protection from a parent or guardian. A neglect case occurs when the parent or guardian is charged with failing to provide adequate food, clothing, shelter, or medical care for the child. An abuse case occurs when a child has been sexually, physically, or emotionally abused. In either case, a judge must decide whether the child needs the protection of the court. The next step is to determine whether the child should remain with the family while under court protection. The judge has several options to choose from and works closely with social services agencies. Such agencies can provide a range of services, including counseling and treatment. The judge usually sets certain conditions for the child to remain with his or her family, such as participation by the parents in a counseling program or a later hearing to monitor the progress of the case. The judge may also decide to place a child with relatives or in foster care.

Some people believe parents should be held responsible for crimes committed by their children. Those in favor of these **parental responsibility laws** believe they are particularly appropriate in cases in which parents know or should know that their children are using or selling drugs or belong to juvenile gangs. In some states, parents may also be charged with **contributing to the delinquency of a minor.**

Since 1899, the juvenile justice system has continued to be defined in part by the tension between a "humanitarian" philosophy (rehabilitate the offender) and a "control" philosophy (punish the offender). This tension has played a major role in determining the current system's practices.

Problem 16.1

a. Why did reformers want to change the way children were treated?

b. What is *parens patriae*? Do you agree with this idea?

c. What is the difference between a status offender and a delinquent offender?

d. Do you favor or oppose parental responsibility laws? Explain. If you believe parents should be held criminally responsible, give three examples of situations in which this should apply.

e. Which philosophy—humanitarian or control—is more appropriate for juveniles who have been found delinquent? Should there be a balance between the two? Explain.

Who Is a Juvenile?

Before the establishment of juvenile courts, children under the age of 7 were never held responsible for criminal acts. The law considered them incapable of forming the necessary criminal intent. The law at that time also assumed that children between the ages of 7 and 14 were incapable of committing a criminal act. However, this belief could be disproved if it was shown that the child knew that the act was a crime or that it would cause harm to another and committed it anyway. Children over the age of 14 could be charged with a crime and handled in the same manner as an adult.

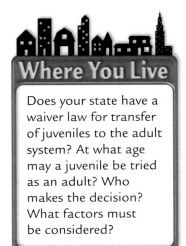

Where You Live

Does your state have a waiver law for transfer of juveniles to the adult system? At what age may a juvenile be tried as an adult? Who makes the decision? What factors must be considered?

YOU BE THE JUDGE

Determining Juvenile Status

In each of the following situations, decide whether the person should be tried as a juvenile or transferred to criminal court and tried as an adult. Describe the factors you considered and the reasons for your decisions.

a. Marshall, 15, is accused of robbing an 86-year-old woman at gunpoint. He has a long juvenile record, including acts of burglary, and has bragged about the robbery.

b. Leigh, 17, is accused of killing a pedestrian while driving a stolen car. She has never been in trouble before, is remorseful about the killing, and claims that she planned to return the car after a short joyride.

c. Carter, 14, is accused of selling drugs for his older brother. According to the police, one day a customer stole the money Carter had collected for his older brother. The police claim that Carter then stabbed the customer with a knife. He has been arrested twice before for selling drugs, but the charges were dropped.

d. Angela, 15, is taken into custody by police for carrying a handgun without a license. This is the second time she has been taken into custody for a weapons violation. Her brother was killed in a drug deal one year earlier. Angela says she carries a gun because she does not feel safe at school or in her neighborhood.

Today, almost all states set age limits to determine whether a person accused of a crime will be handled in adult or juvenile court. In most states, young people are considered juveniles until age 18. However, some states set the age limit at 16 or 17.

In most states, a juvenile charged with a serious felony such as robbery, assault, rape, or murder can be tried as an adult. Some states have laws that automatically transfer a youth to adult court under certain conditions. In other states, judges have the authority to waive certain cases to adult criminal court. Still other states allow the prosecutor to make the decision, while some states require a hearing before a youth may be transferred.

At the **transfer hearing** (or **waiver hearing**), a judge usually considers: (1) the juvenile's age and past record, (2) the seriousness of the crime, and (3) the likelihood that the juvenile may be rehabilitated before the **age of majority.**

As a result of a "get-tough" attitude involving juvenile crime, many states have revised their juvenile codes to make it easier to transfer juveniles to adult court. Today, most states give juvenile courts discretionary power to designate appropriate cases for adult prosecution. Several states have provisions mandating the waiver of cases that meet certain age and offense requirements, while others designate a category of cases in which the waiver to adult court is presumed to be appropriate, but may be challenged by the juvenile offender. Gang members who are involved in violent crime are often transferred to adult court under these provisions.

Problem 16.2

The Office of Juvenile Justice and Delinquency Prevention (OJJDP), a part of the U.S. Department of Justice, is a federal agency responsible for addressing the public safety issues of juvenile crime and youth victimization in the United States. It is guided by the *Juvenile Justice and Delinquency Act*, which was reauthorized in 2002 and designed to promote greater accountability in the juvenile justice system. Federal funds are available to state and local governments to combat juvenile crime through education and evaluation programs.

The OJJDP has determined that an effective juvenile justice system should do three main things. First, it must hold the juvenile offender account-able for delinquent acts. Second, it must enable the juvenile to become a capable, productive, and responsible citizen. Third, it must ensure the safety of the community.

Many status offenders are runaways. *Where can runaways find help on the streets?*

a. Will carrying out these three elements make the juvenile justice system effective? Why or why not? Would you change this list in any way? If so, how?

b. Does your state's juvenile justice system perform each of these elements? Could any of them be done better? Explain.

c. Do any of these three elements conflict with each other? Which ones? Is it possible to do all three at once? Why or why not?

d. Do you think it should be mandatory that all juveniles who commit a serious violent crime be tried in adult criminal court? Why or why not? Should it be automatic, or should the decision be left to a judge? A prosecutor? Someone else? Explain.

Status Offenses

When a juvenile court is confronted with a status offender, special problems arise. Juveniles who fall into this category are charged with being "beyond control," "habitually disobedi-ent," truant from school, or other acts that would not be crimes if committed by an adult.

Status offenders may be emotionally troubled juveniles who need help. Many status offenders are runaways or young people with drinking and drug problems. Some are trying to escape from abusive or other difficult home situations. It is estimated that 13 million youths are on the street each day, and that 1 in 7 minors will run away each year. Nearly 70 percent of these youths are between the ages of 14 and 17, and more than 75 percent of runaways are girls. Although most runaways return home of their own accord, others are picked up by the police and referred to the juvenile court.

In recent years, a number of programs have been set up to help runaways. The primary service provider for runaway and homeless youths is a national network of runaway shelters. These include counseling centers, shelters, and a nationwide toll-free phone number that runaways can call for assistance. For example, the National Runaway Switchboard (1-800-621-4000 or www.nrscrisisline.org) provides information you can pass on to a young person living on the street. Many of these young people need to earn money. Your local runaway shelter may be able to help you and your family structure a job to fit the needs of a young person on the street. You and your family can also help by making a donation to a shelter or volunteering your time.

As a general rule, a single act of unruly behavior is not enough to support a finding that a juvenile is in need of court supervision. Rather, most states require proof that the young person is habitually disobedient or has repeatedly run away, skipped school, or been out of control.

Because of problems at home, parents sometimes ask the court to file a PINS (person in need of supervision) petition against their child. Children charged with status offenses may defend their conduct by showing that it was justified or that the parents were unreasonable and at fault. In such cases, the PINS petition might be withdrawn by the court and replaced by a neglect petition against the parents.

Problem 16.3

a. Do you think courts should interfere in disputes between parents and children? If not, why not? If so, why and under what circumstances?

b. Should attendance at school be mandatory? Why or why not? What should be done about students who are chronically absent from school?

Juvenile Justice Today

In the 1960s, many people argued that the juvenile court system was providing harsher treatment than the adult system without the procedural safeguards and constitutional rights that defendants would have in adult courts. Beginning in 1966, this movement found support in the U.S. Supreme Court, and several decisions were later made that began to change the theory and operation of the juvenile justice system.

Where You Live

What programs or resources are available for runaways in your area?

Law in *Action*

Hearing on a Curfew for Teens

As communities have become concerned about violence by and against young people, teen curfew laws have become popular. Some people welcome the idea of such curfews. Others feel they violate the rights of teens and are unfairly enforced.

Problem 16.4

Read the proposed curfew law:

IT WILL BE AN OFFENSE FOR PERSONS UNDER THE AGE OF 18 TO BE OUT OF THEIR HOMES FROM 11:00 P.M. TO 6:00 A.M. SUNDAY THROUGH THURSDAY NIGHTS. ON FRIDAY AND SATURDAY NIGHTS THE CURFEW SHALL BEGIN AT MIDNIGHT. VIOLATORS WILL BE FINED $100. EXCEPTIONS ARE YOUNG PEOPLE CHAPERONED BY ADULTS, ATTENDING A PLANNED COMMUNITY ACTIVITY, OR TRAVELING TO OR FROM WORK.

After reading the law, identify who in the community is likely to oppose the law. Who is likely to support the law? Then divide into five groups:

- **Group one is the city council.** You will conduct a hearing and decide whether to enact the law, change it, or not act on it, based on the testimony you hear from the community.

- **Group two is the police department.** Your group opposes the law and will testify against it. You believe the curfew will require too much time and energy to enforce and that existing laws are sufficient to combat drug abuse and violence.

- **Group three is "Families Against Violence."** Your group supports the law and will testify in favor of it. Parents and students in your group believe the curfew will reduce drug sales and use, help parents with out-of-control children, and promote family communication about following rules.

A curfew reminder

- **Group four is the local merchants association.** Your group opposes the law and will testify against it. Teens are important customers—and employees—at local stores and movie theaters, and the merchants believe the curfew will harm business.

- **Group five is the school board.** Your group supports the law and will testify in favor of it. The board members believe that students should be home doing their homework and preparing for the next school day.

Group one should meet to decide how to run the hearing and to discuss questions it will ask the other groups. The other groups should meet to further develop their testimony. Additional groups can be added to the hearing.

After the hearing, the city council should deliberate and decide whether to pass, not to pass, or to amend this law.

Gerald Gault

Gerald Gault, 15, was taken into custody and accused of making an obscene phone call to a neighbor. At the time he was taken into custody, his parents were at work and the police did not notify them of what had happened to their son. Gault was placed in a detention center. When his parents finally learned that he was in custody, they were told that there would be a hearing the next day, but they were not told the nature of the complaint against him.

Mrs. Cook, the woman who had complained about the phone call, did not show up at the hearing. Instead, a police officer testified to what he had been told by Mrs. Cook. Gault blamed the call on a friend and denied making the obscene remarks. No lawyers were present, and no record was made of what was said at the hearing.

Since juries are not allowed in juvenile court, the hearing was held before a judge, who found by a preponderance of the evidence that Gault was delinquent and ordered him sent to a state reform school until age 21. An adult found guilty of the same crime could have been sent to a county jail for no longer than 60 days.

Problem 16.5

a. Make lists of the fair and unfair things that happened to Gerald Gault. Explain your reasoning for each item.

b. How would you change the unfair things on your list to make the proceedings fairer for Gerald Gault? Why is it important to change these things?

c. What rights that adults have were not granted to juveniles in the *Gault* case?

d. Do you agree with the *Gault* decision? Why or why not? Should adults and minors have the same legal rights? Why or why not?

e. Do you think Gerald Gault's hearing would have turned out differently if he had initially been given the rights the U.S. Supreme Court later ruled that he was entitled to?

In the *Gault* case discussed above, the U.S. Supreme Court held that juveniles should receive many of the same due process rights as adults. Specifically, the Court ruled that juveniles charged with delinquent acts are entitled to four rights: (1) the right to notification of the charges against them, (2) the right to an attorney, (3) the right to confront and cross-examine witnesses, and (4) the right to remain silent.

The *Gault* decision gave young people accused of a crime many of the same rights as adults, but it also left some unanswered questions. In the case of *In re Winship* (1970), the U.S. Supreme Court decided that juveniles charged with a criminal act must be found "delinquent by proof beyond a reasonable doubt." This is the same standard required in adult criminal court. However, in *McKeiver* v. *Pennsylvania* (1971), the Supreme Court decided that jury trials were not required in juvenile cases. In reaching this decision, the Court expressed concern that jury trials could hurt juveniles by destroying the privacy of juvenile hearings.

More recently, a series of court decisions and legislative actions have changed the informality of juvenile court proceedings somewhat. Some courts even grant spectators and newspaper reporters access to juvenile court proceedings. In general, however, although juveniles now possess many of the same rights as adults, the Supreme Court has made it clear that not all of the procedures used in an adult court apply in a juvenile court proceeding.

The federal government has also played a major role in guiding the juvenile courts. The *Juvenile Justice and Delinquency Prevention Act of 1974* requires the Department of Justice to oversee changes ordered by Congress. The act required the juvenile court system to change the way in which it treated status offenders and delinquent offenders. For example, status offenders were removed from institutions, or "deinstitutionalized." Juvenile offenders remaining in institutions were separated from incarcerated adults. In addition, each state took responsibility for developing community alternatives to incarceration and for improving the juvenile justice system.

In the 1980s and 1990s, communities became concerned with both the rise in crime and a juvenile court system that was seen as being too soft on crime. The public demanded law and order and harsher penalties for juveniles as well as adults. Many proposed sending youthful offenders to military-style "boot camps" in which offenders enter the program in groups referred to as platoons or squads. Those who support such boot camps claim that the structured atmosphere is conducive to growth and change. Some critics even called for abolishing the juvenile court system altogether.

Where You Live

How does the juvenile justice system operate where you live? Are certain types of offenses transferred to adult court?

For Your Information . . .

Juvenile Law Terms
Compared with Adult Law Terms

Juvenile Law Term	Corresponding Adult Law Term
Offense	Crime
Take into Custody	Arrest
Petition	File Charges
Denial	Not Guilty Plea
Admission	Guilty Plea
Adjudicatory Hearing	Trial
Found Delinquent	Found Guilty
Disposition	Sentencing
Detention	Jail
Aftercare	Parole

Instead, many states changed their laws to make it easier to prosecute juveniles in adult criminal court. As these laws changed, there was an increasing trend in the early 1990s to waive juvenile cases to adult criminal courts, reflecting the preference toward harsher punishment for juveniles. As the twenty-first century approached, however, this trend began to decline. Perhaps the combination of these state laws and federal initiatives illustrates that a new balance is being struck between accountability, community safety, and programs to rehabilitate young people, with greater weight being given to accountability and community safety. It is interesting to note that much of this trend toward harsher treatment of juveniles occurred during the 1990s—when juvenile crime rates were decreasing.

Procedures in Juvenile Court

Suppose a young person is accused of a delinquent act. What happens to this person from the time he or she is taken into custody until release from the juvenile justice system? The exact procedures vary from state to state, but the general process is similar throughout the country.

Juveniles taken into custody can be detained and referred to juvenile court. *Describe the instances in which a juvenile offender may be released.*

Taking into Custody On the whole, young people may be taken into custody for the same reasons the police might arrest an adult. However, juveniles also can be taken into custody for status offenses. These offenses include running away from home, truancy, promiscuity, disobeying one's parents, and other actions suggesting the need for court supervision.

After taking a juvenile into custody, the police have broad authority to release or detain the juvenile. If the offense is minor, the police may give the juvenile a warning, release the juvenile to his or her parents, or refer the case to a social services agency. If the offense is serious or if the young person has a prior record, the police may detain the youth and refer him or her to juvenile court.

Intake is the informal process by which court officials or social workers decide if a complaint against a juvenile should be referred to juvenile court. This decision is usually made after interviewing the youth and considering the seriousness of the offense, the youth's past record, family situation, and other factors.

Figure 16.1   The Juvenile Justice Process

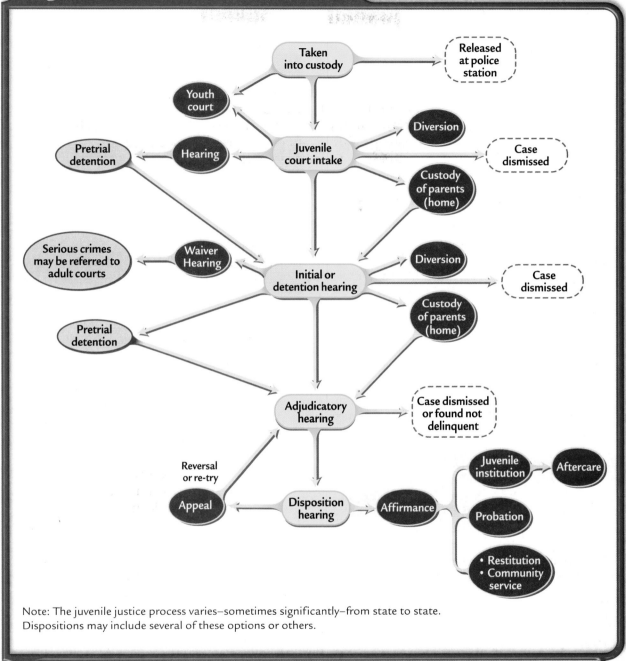

Note: The juvenile justice process varies—sometimes significantly—from state to state. Dispositions may include several of these options or others.

There are several different outcomes for an offender in the juvenile justice process.
ANALYZE THE DATA *What may happen to a juvenile after he or she is taken into custody?*

For Your Information . . .

Alternative Programs—
Youth Courts

Alternative programs that focus on prevention and treatment, rather than punishment, have developed within the juvenile justice system. Some of these programs divert young people out of the juvenile justice system and into services that deal with problem behaviors or difficult family or community challenges. Some diversion programs provide counseling, while others focus on education or job training. Still others provide more comprehensive services to help young people deal with their family, school, and community.

The fastest-growing alternative program is called **youth court.** As of 2003, there were more than 900 youth courts in the country. About half of the youth courts operate in the juvenile justice system, while others are situated in school or community-based settings. Although there are several different program models, the basic idea behind all youth courts is that young people sentence their peers.

In almost all youth court programs, the young person charged with an offense must admit to having committed the offense before being accepted into youth court. Typical offenses dealt with by youth courts include theft, assault, vandalism, disorderly conduct, and alcohol and marijuana use. The sentences imposed by the peer juries include community service, essays, written and oral apologies to victims, and educational workshops. Also, most youth courts require offenders to serve on juries to sentence other youth offenders.

Youth courts are based on a philosophy called **restorative justice.** The idea behind restorative justice is that problem behavior harms victims and communities and that steps should be taken to involve offenders in repairing harm and restoring broken relationships.

A youth court in progress

Problem 16.6

a. Evaluations of youth court programs show that the rate of re-offending is very low. Why do you think these programs are so successful?

b. What benefits do youth courts offer to juvenile offenders, their families, and the community? Are there disadvantages to youth courts?

c. What do you think of the idea of restorative justice? Is this the best approach in dealing with all juvenile offenders? Explain your answers.

d. In general, do you favor treatment or punishment for juvenile offenders? Does it depend on the seriousness of the crime? Give reasons for your answer.

e. Consider how federal sentencing guidelines (certain offenses require certain sentences) operate to limit the discretion of judges. Would you favor or oppose a state law like this for juveniles? Be sure to explain the reasons for your answer.

It is estimated that as many as one-third of all complaints in the juvenile system are disposed of during the intake process by dismissal, diversion, or transfer. Most of the cases disposed of are dismissed. Some youths are diverted, which means that they receive educational services—including, in some places, "Street Law" classes—and treatment services without going through juvenile court. In addition, a prosecutor may decide to charge a juvenile as an adult and request a waiver hearing. (Waiver hearings are discussed on page 190.)

Initial or Detention Hearing   Young people who are taken into custody and formally referred to juvenile court are entitled to an **initial hearing** on the validity of their arrest and detention. At this initial hearing, the state must generally prove two things: that an offense was committed and that there is reasonable cause to believe that the accused committed it. If the state wants to further detain the juvenile, it must prove that the juvenile is a danger to himself or herself or others, is likely to run away if released, or has a past record that warrants detention. If the juvenile does not have an attorney, the court will usually assign one at this time and set a date for a hearing on the facts.

The U.S. Supreme Court has held that juveniles do not have a constitutional right to bail. No money bond is set, and the juvenile court may decide either to release juveniles to their parents or other adults or to detain them until trial. The Supreme Court justified what is referred to as **preventive detention** of juveniles on the grounds that it serves the legitimate purpose of protecting the community and the juveniles themselves from the consequences of future crime. It is based on a judge's decision that a juvenile is better off in detention than in his or her own home. Federal law requires juveniles who are detained to be held separately from adults who have been accused of crimes. However, this is still not enforced in a number of places around the country.

Problem 16.7

a. Should juveniles have the same right to bail as adults? Why or why not? When should they be detained?

b. Should juveniles be detained separately from adults in all cases? What if a small town only has one jail or the juvenile detention center is full?

Adjudicatory Hearing   A juvenile charged with a delinquent act is given a hearing. Generally known as an **adjudicatory hearing,** its purpose is the same as that of an adult trial—to determine the facts of the case. Unlike an adult trial, however, a juvenile hearing is generally closed to the public, and the names of the accused and the details of the offense are withheld from the press. Although juveniles do not have a constitutional right to a jury trial, some states do provide for juries in juvenile cases.

Where You Live

Where are juvenile offenders placed in your state and community? What is the maximum length of time for which a juvenile can be committed to a juvenile institution? What happens to status offenders in your community?

Juveniles on probation must follow a set of conditions, including regular meetings with a probation officer. *What are other examples of conditions of probation?*

At the adjudicatory hearing, the juvenile, like the adult defendant, is entitled to be represented by an attorney. The attorney can examine and cross-examine witnesses, and force the prosecution to prove its case beyond a reasonable doubt. If the judge finds the juvenile nondelinquent (not guilty), he or she is free to go. If the judge decides that the facts, as set out in the petition, are true, the court will enter a finding of delinquent. This is similar to a conviction in adult proceedings.

Dispositional Hearing The dispositional hearing is perhaps the most important stage in the system for juveniles who are found delinquent. At this hearing, the judge decides what sentence, or disposition, the juvenile offender should receive. The judge's sentence is usually based primarily on the presentence report prepared by the probation department. This report is the result of an investigation of the juvenile's social, psychological, family, and school background.

In theory, in making their disposition, courts are supposed to provide for individualized treatment geared toward rehabilitating the juvenile offender. However, in practice, courts often balance the needs of the offender against the obligation to protect the community. Alternatives usually include probation, placement in a group home or community treatment program, or commitment to a state institution.

Probation is the most common disposition. The judge can impose a number of conditions on the juvenile on probation. For example, the juvenile might be ordered to attend school regularly, hold a steady job, attend counseling sessions at a treatment center, take weekly drug tests, be home by 8:00 P.M., or stay away from certain people. A juvenile on probation usually has to meet with a probation officer on a regular basis. If the conditions of probation are not met, the youth can be sent back to court for another hearing. At that time, the judge can decide to send the juvenile to a group home or a state institution.

For serious offenses, the juvenile can be committed to a juvenile institution. Most courts have the power to place a juvenile in such an institution for an indeterminate length of time. This means that no matter what the offense, the juvenile offender can be locked up for the maximum period allowed by state law. This generally varies from one to three years. In certain cases, it lasts until the young person reaches the age of majority, and it can continue in some states until age 21. Most juveniles, however, do not serve the maximum sentence. The exact time of release is usually up to the agency that operates the institution.

Although the stated goal of any juvenile correctional institution is rehabilitation, many corrections officials say this is seldom achieved. One of the main problems is overcrowding in juvenile facilities. Up to one-half of the nation's juvenile facilities have more residents than they were designed to hold. In addition, the overrepresentation of

The Case of . . .

The 15-Year-Old Murderer

William Wayne Thompson was found by an Oklahoma jury to have actively participated at the age of 15 in the brutal murder of his former brother-in-law, Charles Keane. There was evidence that Keane had in the past physically abused Thompson and his sister. Thompson and three others kidnapped Keane, beat him, kicked him, cut his throat and chest, shot him in the head, and dumped his body into the river. Photographs of the body were described by the court as "ghastly."

It was determined at a hearing that Thompson, who had been arrested previously for a number of serious assaults, had "no reasonable prospects for rehabilitation within the juvenile justice system." He was then tried as an adult and convicted. The law of Oklahoma did not specify that any minimum age was required before the death penalty could be ordered. The judge, following the jury's recommendation, ordered the death penalty for Thompson. The sentence was appealed and upheld by the Oklahoma Supreme Court. Thompson's appeal ended up before the U.S. Supreme Court.

Problem 16.8

a. Should William Wayne Thompson have been transferred and tried as an adult? Give your reasons.

b. Are you for or against capital punishment as a possible penalty for those under the age of 16 who commit murder? Write down the two strongest reasons in support of your position. What are the two strongest arguments in support of the other position?

c. If you were on the U.S. Supreme Court, would you find imposing the death penalty on William Wayne Thompson to be "cruel and unusual punishment"? Give reasons for your position.

d. If this crime had occurred in a state without the death penalty, what would be an appropriated punishment? Explain.

minorities has been increasing. Some critics claim that this is a result of discrimination. They say that more whites than minorities seem to be placed by juvenile courts in private programs to meet their special needs, while more minorities are placed in government-run juvenile facilities. Other concerns include the safety and security of the facilities, due process, and health care. The courts have also seen an increase in claims of abuse of children in training schools and detention centers.

Some juvenile justice reformers call for a new philosophy in which violent offenders would be housed in small facilities offering many services. Most other offenders, especially status offenders, would be placed in well-structured, community-based programs. Some states have already moved in this direction, and supporters say it works. Critics counter that the approach will not work, and call for tougher measures. Today, many practitioners seek a balanced approach to juvenile corrections. They consider the individual in light of community protection, offender accountability, and the development of life skills that will enable the offender to experience success once he or she is released from the juvenile justice system.

Dealing with status offenders presents special problems. Should they be taken out of the home? Should they be committed to institutions? Should they be mixed with delinquents or adult offenders? In response to these concerns, many states have removed status offenders from large institutions and placed them in foster homes, halfway houses, or other community facilities.

Postdisposition Most states give young people the right to appeal decisions of a juvenile court. However, because the U.S. Supreme Court has never ruled on this issue, the provisions for appeal vary greatly from state to state.

Once released from an institution, a juvenile may be placed in aftercare. This is the equivalent of parole in the adult system. Aftercare usually involves supervision by a parole officer who counsels the juvenile on education, jobs, vocational training, or other issues.

Although the goal of juvenile correctional facilities is rehabilitation, many claim that this is seldom achieved. *What problems limit the goal of rehabilitation?*

Some employers have access to juvenile records, which may cause problems for an adult seeking a job. *What do most states require in order to expunge a person's juvenile record?*

Having a Record A juvenile who is found delinquent does not have a criminal record, as would someone who is tried as an adult. This means that, if asked, a juvenile may legally say that he or she has not been convicted of a *crime*—a legal term that refers only to the adult system. In general, juveniles who are adjudicated do not lose any civil rights and can still register to vote upon reaching adulthood. Unfortunately, juvenile records can cause problems later. Most states restrict access to juvenile court proceedings. In many states, however, some or all information on juvenile cases becomes public record. This means that individuals, agencies, and employers may be able to access it. A juvenile record also is often considered in sentencing adults, so that defendants with no criminal record may still receive a harsher sentence if they have a juvenile record.

In a few states, juvenile records are automatically sealed or expunged (destroyed) when the juvenile reaches the age of 18 or 21, giving the individual a "clean slate." In most states, however, the record continues to exist unless the person officially requests that his or her record be expunged. To be eligible for such a request, most states require that several years have passed since the offense and that the person not have committed any further offenses during that time. If the person with the juvenile record meets these conditions, he or she can go before a judge to request that the record be expunged. If the judge approves the request, there will no longer be a public record of the person's involvement in the juvenile justice system.

Where You Live

In your community, are juvenile records sealed or are they destroyed? What is the procedure? Can juveniles in your state appeal decisions of the juvenile court?

Law and Terrorism

The rise of the problem of terrorism at the end of the twentieth and the beginning of the twenty-first century led President George W. Bush, Congress, state legislatures, and mayors to institute many new laws and policies. Law enforcement officials from the U.S. attorney general and the directors of the FBI and CIA to local police have all become involved in what is sometimes called "the war on terrorism."

Civil liberties groups and others have challenged many of these laws and executive actions, saying they go too far in restricting individual rights at a time when the country is not officially at war. Proponents of antiterrorism measures say that these measures are warranted. They claim the danger from terrorism to the United States is even worse than during a declared war because the enemy is hidden and so must be uncovered and arrested.

"The laws will thus not be silent in time of war, but they will speak with a somewhat different voice."

— Chief Justice William Rehnquist, U.S. Supreme Court

Street Law
online
Visit the *Street Law* Web site at streetlaw.glencoe.com for chapter-based information and resources.

The Pentagon was one target of the terrorist attacks of September 11, 2001.

The Law in Times of War

The horrific events of September 11, 2001, shook U.S. society and its people to their core. These were the largest attacks on U.S. soil since World War II. The fact that the attacks were the result of terrorism made people feel especially vulnerable. As a result of the attacks, Congress passed many new federal laws and made changes to existing laws.

President George W. Bush declared a "war on terrorism." He requested a number of new powers to enable the executive branch to find those who committed these acts of terrorism and to prevent future attacks. At the urging of President Bush, Congress passed a law called the *USA Patriot Act* in 2001. The act was intended to combat terrorism by tracing the sources of money that fund terrorist acts, finding and detaining terrorists who entered the country as immigrants, and intercepting communications among terrorist groups. The act expanded the powers of certain law enforcement and intelligence agencies such as the Department of Justice, the Federal Bureau of Investigation (FBI), and the Central Intelligence Agency (CIA). The act enabled these groups to share information among themselves, track communications on the Internet, install telephone and computer wiretaps, obtain search warrants for voice mail and e-mail messages, and access personal, educational, medical, and financial information. In 2002, Congress created the Department of Homeland Security to better coordinate antiterrorism activities across the government.

The expanded powers allowed by the *USA Patriot Act* raised key questions for U.S. society: Do these measures infringe on the rights of citizens? How much freedom and privacy are we willing to give up so that we may be more secure?

In past times of crisis, the U.S. government has taken away some of the rights of citizens, and courts have upheld some of these measures. During the Civil War, for example, President Lincoln suspended the right of prisoners to seek a *habeas corpus* petition, a legal means by which prisoners may challenge the constitutionality of their imprisonment in court. During World War I, the federal government restricted citizens' rights to criticize U.S. involvement in the war, either verbally or in writing. During World War II, the government removed more than 100,000 people of Japanese heritage, most of whom were U.S. citizens, from their homes and detained them in camps. Much of their personal property, including homes and businesses, was never returned to them. However, in 1988 the U.S. government formally apologized for the detention of Japanese Americans, and Congress approved a reparations payment for surviving detainees.

As wartime hysteria mounted, the U.S. government rounded up thousands of people of Japanese ancestry, most of whom were U.S. citizens, and forced them into internment camps during World War II. *Does the government have the right today to relocate or keep a group such as noncitizens in detention?*

Problem 17.1

a. Is the war on terrorism similar to other wars when rights have been restricted? How is it the same? How is it different?

b. Assume you were the president after the September 11, 2001 attacks. What special powers would you want?

c. Assume you were the leader of a civil liberties organization. What civil rights would you fight hardest to protect?

Surveillance and Searches

Since September 11, 2001, the government has had more power to conduct surveillance against ordinary people, much of which is provided for in the *USA Patriot Act*. Passengers in airports, for example, often have to open all of their luggage or submit to searches of their clothes, shoes, and persons. The act gives the government broader powers to intercept Internet or telephone communications of people it believes to be engaged in terrorist-related crimes.

The Case of . . .

The Sneak and Peek Search

U.S. law usually requires that a search warrant, based on probable cause, be obtained before a person's home is searched. A law enforcement officer is supposed to give the person whose premises are searched a receipt for any items that are taken as part of the search.

Maria Ramirez is originally from a country where there has been some terrorist activity against U.S. citizens. Federal officers see her at a restaurant in Chicago talking to people who are suspected of terrorism, though they have not been arrested. Federal agents come to her apartment when she is not there and look though all her letters and computer files. They make copies of some documents. The government agents do not inform her that they searched her apartment or copied documents until two weeks later.

A sneak and peek search

Problem 17.2

a. What reasons might the federal agents give for not obtaining a warrant and presenting it to Maria?

b. What arguments might Maria give that she should have been informed of the search?

c. If you were writing the law, would you allow sneak and peek searches like this in cases of suspected terrorism, or make them illegal?

The act enables law enforcement officials to call on a special court called the Foreign Intelligence Surveillance Act Court—whose records and rulings are kept completely secret—to authorize wiretaps to help gather evidence to prosecute terrorists. This court was originally set up in 1978 to authorize surveillance to gather foreign intelligence, not evidence for domestic criminal trials. For that reason, this court is not required by law to obey the rules that ordinary courts must observe to protect the rights of alleged criminals. For example, the Foreign Intelligence Surveillance Act Court can approve wiretaps to monitor an individual's communications even if the government has not proven that there is probable cause to believe the individual is involved in criminal activity.

Before the *USA Patriot Act*, evidence gathered using such wiretaps could not be used in criminal trials. In 2003, the U.S. Supreme Court let stand a lower-court ruling allowing evidence authorized secretly by the Foreign Intelligence Surveillance Act Court to be used in criminal trials. In addition, in some cases under the *USA Patriot Act*, the government can delay notifying people whose premises have been searched until after the search has taken place.

Problem 17.3

a. On a scale from one to five, with one meaning that you strongly agree and five meaning that you strongly disagree, indicate where you stand on the following statement:

"In a time of heightened concern about domestic terrorism and national security, the government should be allowed to do whatever it believes is necessary to uncover and arrest terrorists."

b. Using the same scale, take a stand on each of the following statements. In each case, assume that Congress has proposed laws giving the federal government the power to take the following actions:

- Look at everyone's e-mail at work.
- Look at everyone's e-mail at home.
- Install surveillance cameras on all public streets.
- Plant small cameras in the homes of suspected terrorists.
- Monitor everyone's video rental records.
- Check the travel records of people coming into the country.

Detention and Interrogation

As a result of the September 11, 2001 attacks, many people suspected of terrorism have been detained inside the United States. Most have been noncitizens. Under most federal laws, noncitizens can be detained for only 24 hours without being formally charged with a crime. However, the *USA Patriot Act* allows noncitizens suspected of terrorist

The U.S. government held people suspected of being involved in terrorist activities at a U.S. military base in Cuba. *What information do you think the U.S. government wanted from the prisoners?*

activity to be detained without being formally charged with an offense for as long as it takes to either prove that the detainees are not involved in terrorism or to gather enough evidence to press charges. Many of the detained are Arab or Muslim people who were called in for questioning after the September 11 attacks.

Problem 17.4

Achmed, 26, is a university student from a country in the Middle East. He is in the United States on a student visa. He goes to his state's motor vehicle administration office to renew his driver's license. Since the September 11, 2001 attacks, federal law enforcement officials have been stationed around this facility to help gather information on possible terrorists. Achmed is pulled out of line and questioned about when and why he entered the United States. His answers sound suspicious to the officers, and they decide to detain him while they investigate his background further. He is not allowed to talk to anyone outside the detention facility, including his family or a lawyer. He is held for four months and then is released without having been charged with a crime.

a. If you were a government official charged with locating possible terrorists, what reasons would you give for detaining Achmed?

b. Should the government be allowed to detain people for these reasons?

c. Were Achmed's rights violated? If so, how?

Unlawful Combatants

A number of people who were detained and interrogated after the September 11, 2001 attacks were called "unlawful combatants" by the U.S. government. This term refers to people who have fought against the United States but not in the context of a conflict between two internationally recognized governments. Some of these people were from a number of foreign countries and were suspected of being involved in terrorist activities in the United States and abroad. Others were believed to have direct ties to al-Qaeda, the terrorist group based in Afghanistan and responsible for the September 11, 2001 attacks. They were rounded up by the U.S. forces who entered Afghanistan to bring down al-Qaeda and its operations.

These unlawful combatants were brought to a U.S. military base in Guantánamo Bay, Cuba. The government argued that because this base was not on U.S. soil, the prisoners there need not be accorded the same rights as people in the United States who have been arrested for committing a crime. In addition, the government said it did not have to guarantee the detainees' rights under international treaties such as the Geneva Convention because the United States had not formally declared war on Afghanistan, and because the detainees were terrorists and not soldiers fighting under a legitimate foreign government. The people detained in Guantánamo Bay were questioned extensively and held in cells that critics called "small cages." During their detention, they were not allowed to see lawyers. The U.S. government said that it held these detainees under humane conditions and that torture was not used to get information from the prisoners. Torture is illegal under both U.S. law and international law through the U.N. Convention Against Torture, which the United States signed and ratified.

Rights at Trial

A person charged with terrorism could be tried in a U.S. court, where he or she would be guaranteed the full rights provided to other criminal defendants, including the right to a jury, right to a lawyer, and right to a public trial. However, various groups have voiced a number of arguments against trying terrorists in a regular criminal court. The U.S. government has argued that trying a suspected terrorist in a regular criminal court allows the defendant to use the trial as a political platform to attack the government publicly. Some defendants' rights groups say that it is impossible to guarantee a defendant in a terrorist case a fair trial in the United States because public opinion is so strong against alleged terrorists. The government also worries that such public trials might help terrorist groups learn what information the government has about them.

The U.S. government has proposed trying suspected terrorists, including unlawful combatants, in a military tribunal rather than a criminal court. Under rules issued in 2002, these tribunals—unlike criminal courts—can meet in secret and can allow hearsay as evidence. These tribunals, which consist of three or more judges, can convict defendants and authorize the death penalty if two-thirds of the judges vote that the defendant is guilty. There is no procedure to appeal a decision by a military tribunal.

Problem 17.5

In 2002, the U.S. military in Afghanistan captured Jackson, a U.S. citizen, as he was fighting there against the United States. Along with others designated as unlawful combatants, he was brought to Guantánamo Bay, Cuba. His request for a lawyer was denied. After three months in detention, he was told he will have to stand trial for terrorism. Should he be tried in a U.S. criminal court or in a military tribunal? Which would the U.S. government prefer? Which would Jackson prefer? Give your reasons.

UNIT 3

Torts

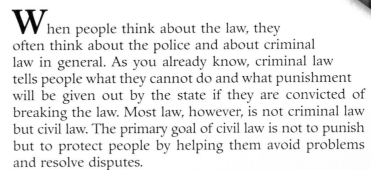

Street Law online

Visit the *Street Law* Web site at streetlaw.glencoe.com for unit-based activities.

When people think about the law, they often think about the police and about criminal law in general. As you already know, criminal law tells people what they cannot do and what punishment will be given out by the state if they are convicted of breaking the law. Most law, however, is not criminal law but civil law. The primary goal of civil law is not to punish but to protect people by helping them avoid problems and resolve disputes.

In this unit, you will study torts—the largest area of civil law. Tort law encourages people to act responsibly by awarding money or damages to victims who are harmed by wrongdoers. While tort law cases can be resolved by lawsuits, far more are settled without going to court. The mediation, negotiation, and arbitration skills you learned in Chapter 4 are frequently used to settle tort cases. Studies have consistently found that more than 90 percent of tort cases are settled without going to trial.

The primary goal of civil law is to protect people by helping them avoid problems and resolve disputes.

Tort law will help you learn about:

- your obligations as a babysitter;
- whether your younger brother or sister can be sued for pulling a chair out from under a friend and causing injury;
- what kind of insurance you need;
- your rights if you are injured on the job;
- whether you can recover money damages if you fall into a neighbor's unfenced swimming pool and are hurt;
- what steps you can take to protect your rights regarding an invention;
- whether you can recover money damages if you are bitten by a neighbor's dog; and
- your rights if you are injured by a consumer product.

Tort law also deals with some of society's most controversial issues. For example, should cigarette manufacturers who place a warning on cigarette packages be required to pay damages to a smoker who develops lung cancer as a result of smoking? Should gun manufacturers be required to pay damages to a youngster injured by a gun that did not have a safety lock?

211

Torts:
A Civil Wrong

In criminal law, when someone commits a wrong, we call it a crime. In civil law, when a person commits a wrong, it is called a **tort.**

A crime is considered a wrong against all of society, even though there is usually a specific victim. The criminal is prosecuted and punished by the state. By contrast, civil law deals with wrongs against individuals. A harmed individual becomes the **plaintiff** in a civil lawsuit. The plaintiff seeks to win a **judgment** against the **defendant,** or accused wrong-doer. A defendant who loses the judgment in a civil case will not be punished with jail or other penalties associated with criminal law. Instead he or she will be ordered to compensate the plaintiff for injuries, usually by paying monetary **damages.**

Although a tort and a crime are two different legal issues, the same illegal activity can be both a crime and a tort. For example, a person who breaks into a house has committed a crime and can be prosecuted by the state. If the same person causes damage to the house or steals property, a tort has also been committed, and the victim may sue to recover monetary damages.

Street Law
online

Visit the *Street Law* Web site at streetlaw.glencoe.com for chapter-based information and resources.

Automobile crashes may result in civil lawsuits.

The Idea of Liability

The rules that govern civil wrongs are called tort law. Tort law deals with basic questions such as (1) who should be responsible, or **liable,** for harm caused by human activities, and (2) how much should the responsible person have to pay. Almost any activity—driving a car, operating a business, speaking, writing, or using property—can be a source of harm and therefore of tort liability. Knowledge of torts can help people resolve their conflicts, often without going to court.

For practical purposes, a tort occurs when one person causes injury to another person or to another's property or reputation. The injured party, the plaintiff, can take the alleged wrongdoer, the defendant, to court. Tort law provides the injured party with a **remedy,** something to make up for the harm done. This usually takes the form of monetary damages. For example, a person injured in an auto crash might receive $5,000 for physical injuries and damage to his or her vehicle. So, one purpose of tort law is to compensate people for what was lost. However, not all injuries result in compensation. A person may be injured in an accident through no fault of another person. In such cases, tort law generally provides no remedy.

The question of liability is not always clear when athletes are injured during participation in a sports event. *Why does tort law provide no remedy for this type of situation?*

Tort law also establishes standards of care that society expects from people. Simply put, the law requires us to act with reasonable care toward people and their property. Failure to exercise reasonable care may result in legal liability. The person harmed may sue the person who acted unreasonably for damages. Requiring payment of damages is intended to prevent future injuries and losses and to encourage more reasonable behavior.

Whenever a person is injured, *someone* will bear the cost of the harm. Broken bones will create medical bills that must be paid. A hospitalized person will miss work and lose earnings. Damaged property will cost money to repair. Less tangible costs, such as emotional suffering, may also be a cost of an injury. Tort law is concerned with determining who will pay. When a person either purposely or through carelessness causes injury to another, society usually thinks that the wrongdoer, rather than the victim, should bear the cost of the harm. However, sometimes an injury is partially or entirely the fault of the victim or nobody is at fault, as in the case of true accidents. In such cases, the victim will usually have to bear the costs of the injury.

Problem 18.1

Read the following descriptions. Each case involves an injury. Assume that a civil suit is brought by the injured person. For each case (1) identify the plaintiff and the defendant or defendants, and (2) determine whether the defendant should pay for the plaintiff's damages. Explain your answers.

a. Sixteen-year-old Carrie is babysitting for four-year-old Jill. Carrie leaves Jill in the living room and goes into the kitchen to call her boyfriend. From the kitchen she can hear but not see Jill. While Carrie is away, Jill falls off a chair and is hurt.

b. Ben, a high school football player, tackles a teammate in practice. When the teammate hits the ground, his shoulder is dislocated.

c. Mr. Ghosh owns a large apartment building. When his janitors wax the lobby floor, they place near the front door a 12-inch-square sign that reads: "Caution. Wet Floors." Mrs. Gonzalez is hurrying home from shopping carrying two large bags of groceries. She does not see the sign and slips and falls on the freshly waxed floor, injuring her knee and arm.

d. Corina leaves a sharp knife on the kitchen table after making a sandwich. A three-year-old neighbor who has been invited over to play with Corina's daughter climbs up on a chair, grabs the knife, and seriously cuts his finger.

e. Jamal, a school bus driver, has a heart attack while driving the bus. The bus slams into a wall, injuring several students. One month earlier Jamal's doctor had warned him of his heart condition.

f. Matt and Emily are sitting in the upper deck behind first base at a major league baseball game. A foul ball hit by their team's star player bounces off a railing, smacking Matt in the head and giving him a concussion.

g. Jess, an expert auto mechanic, continues to drive her car even though she knows that the brake linings are badly worn. Driving on a rain-slick road at night, she skids into a bicyclist who is riding one foot away from the right curb.

Liability—legal responsibility for harm—is not the same as moral responsibility. A person may be morally at fault for harming someone, but not civilly liable for the injuries. For example, assume you lie to a friend about the correct time, causing her to miss a job interview. As a result, she does not get the job. The lie would be morally wrong and would cause harm, but would not usually result in civil liability. In contrast, someone may be civilly liable for injuries to another without being morally at fault. For example, in strict liability cases the law makes certain parties bear the cost of injuries even though there is no proof of fault. (Strict liability is discussed in detail in Chapter 21.) However, moral fault is one of the many considerations that courts often look at in developing the law of torts and drawing up the rules of who will pay for injuries people suffer.

Tort law provides a legal process for injured persons to recover monetary damages from wrongdoers who cause them harm. The two parties can simply meet and discuss how to compensate the injured person. The agreement they reach is called a **settlement.** If, however, they cannot agree on compensation, or if the wrongdoer insists that he or she was acting reasonably when the injury occurred, then the injured party may decide to sue. In such instances, a trial may be conducted to decide the rights and liabilities of both parties.

Settlements are much more common than trials. Approximately 90 percent of tort cases filed in court are settled without a trial. For cases that do go to trial, there can be delays of a year or more between the time the case is filed in court and the trial.

The following example illustrates the tort law process. Evan claims that Martha shoved him, causing him to fall down a flight of stairs and break his leg. Evan wants $5,000 from Martha to compensate for his injury. This dispute can be resolved in at least three different ways.

First, Martha could acknowledge that she acted unreasonably and agree to pay a settlement of $5,000. However, a settlement does not have to be for the full amount demanded, and usually the amount is a result of a compromise between the two parties. Besides negotiating a settlement, other forms of dispute resolution could allow Martha and Evan to avoid a civil trial. (Methods for settling disputes are discussed in Chapter 4.)

Second, Martha could argue that she did not act unreasonably—that Evan ran past her, bumped into her, and then tripped down the stairs—and refuse to pay any monetary damages. If Evan wanted to recover the money, he would have to sue Martha in court.

In a third scenario, Martha might admit nudging Evan a bit but claim that she should only have to pay $4,000, because the $5,000 Evan wants includes money for a subscription to cable television, a DVD player, and three DVDs that Evan bought when he was home in bed for two weeks. Here, the dispute is not about liability, but about the amount of damages. In this situation, Evan might accept Martha's $4,000 offer, or he might sue Martha for $5,000. However, there is risk in not accepting the $4,000. If a court decides that Martha did not act unreasonably, then Evan might recover no damages at all!

Injured persons can be compensated by negotiating a settlement with the wrongdoer. *What other methods could help the parties involved avoid a civil trial?*

The Idea of Torts: Yesterday, Today, and Tomorrow

The concept of a tort is not new. Judges in England were deciding tort cases as far back as the fifteenth century. Tort law has always tried to weigh the usefulness of certain conduct against the harm that conduct might cause.

Tort law is generally based on **common law.** This is law made by judges through court decisions, generally in state appellate courts. These decisions are written down, and appellate decisions become precedents used to decide future cases. Tort law may also be based on **statutes,** or written laws. For example, in some states there is a law specifically providing that a person who is injured as a result of someone furnishing alcohol to a minor may be awarded damages in civil court. The damages are paid by the person who served the alcohol to the minor. In other states, this same law exists as a result of an appellate court decision, rather than the passage of a statute.

There are a number of specific torts, which are described later in this chapter. There is also a saying that "for every interference with a recognized legal right, the law will provide a remedy." If you can convince a judge that you deserve compensation for some injury, you may occasionally be able to recover damages without fitting your case into an existing category of tort protection.

Tort law balances usefulness and harm. For example, how safe must a drug be before the manufacturer is not considered legally responsible if the drug harms somebody? If a drug is discovered that saves the lives of many cancer patients but causes the deaths of others, should the drug manufacturer be liable for the deaths?

Tort law balances usefulness and individual choice with harm. *Should cigarette companies and drug manufacturers be held liable for side effects or illness sustained by people who use their products?*

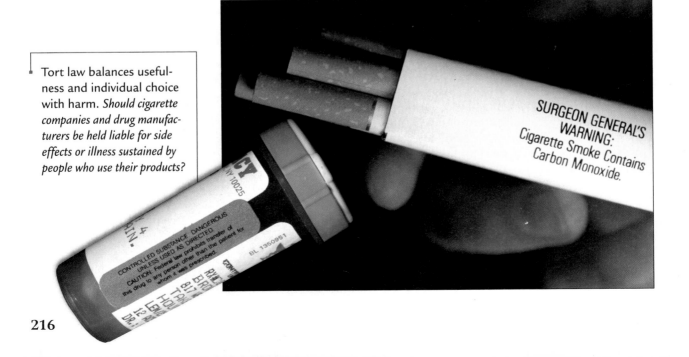

The Lung Cancer Death

Mrs. Garrett dies of lung cancer at the age of 42. Her family brings a civil suit against ABC Tobacco Company, the manufacturer of the cigarettes she had smoked daily for the previous 20 years. Her doctors say that cigarette smoking was the major factor leading to her death.

Problem 18.2

a. If you were the Garrett family's attorney, what arguments would you make at the trial? What evidence would you want to introduce?

b. If you were the attorney for the ABC Tobacco Company, what arguments would you make for the company? What evidence would you want to introduce to support your arguments?

c. If you were the Garrett family's attorney, would you want a judge or a jury to decide this case? Why?

d. Assume that each package of ABC cigarettes carries the following warning: "Caution: Cigarette smoking can be harmful to your health." How should this case be decided? Give reasons for your decision.

. . . .

Tort law also tries to preserve individual choice. When the mandatory government warning about the dangers of smoking is prominently displayed on the package, adults are permitted to purchase cigarettes. This product may be more harmful than useful. However, some people argue that letting adults purchase cigarettes preserves their individual choice and that the warning allows the individual to make an informed choice. Others criticize this government decision and argue that the sale of cigarettes should be restricted or banned.

Tort law is often at the forefront of public controversy in the United States. It is closely related to economic and political policy decisions, as well as legal policy decisions. As you will see throughout this unit, tort cases often involve a clash of values and interests. Arriving at fair solutions is rarely easy.

Types of Torts

Tort liability exists for three major categories of conduct: intentional wrongs, acts of negligence, and activities for which strict liability is imposed. An **intentional wrong** occurs when a person acts with the intent of injuring a person, his or her property, or both. For example, Ali is angry at Tom, so he intentionally smashes the windshield of Tom's car. Tom may sue Ali to recover the cost of the damage to his windshield. In another example, Lucy writes a letter telling her friends that Andrew is an alcoholic and a drug addict, even though she knows this is not true. Andrew may recover damages from Lucy for harm to his reputation caused by her intentional lie.

Intentional torts may also be crimes. In these cases, the defendant can be prosecuted by the state as well as sued by the plaintiff. However, punishing a criminal does not usually make up for the harm to the victim. A civil tort action is used to recover monetary damages.

The most common tort is negligence. **Negligence** is an unintentional tort. It occurs when a person's failure to use reasonable care causes harm. If a drunk driver accidentally hits a pedestrian, the driver is negligent. Although the driver did not intend to hurt the pedestrian, he acted unreasonably in driving drunk and will be liable for the harm caused to the pedestrian.

Strict liability differs from both negligence and intentional wrongs. It applies when the defendant is engaged in an activity so dangerous that there is a serious risk of harm even if he or she acts with utmost care. In a strict liability case, a plaintiff is not required to prove that the defendant was either negligent or intended to cause harm in order to recover damages. For example, suppose you are hit by a brick falling from a building being demolished. In this case, you do not have to prove that the contractor was careless in order to recover damages. Demolishing buildings is so dangerous that contractors are automatically responsible if a passerby is injured. Three groups of people face strict liability: (1) owners of dangerous animals, (2) people who engage in highly dangerous activities, and (3) manufacturers and sellers of defective consumer products.

Not all injuries to you or your property will lead to a recovery under tort law. In some instances, harmful behavior may not be a tort. In other cases, the person causing the harm may have a legal defense to a tort action. In still other cases, the defendant may be liable, but may simply be unable to pay for the harm caused to the plaintiff.

Problem 18.3

Carefully examine each of the following situations and determine whether a tort has been committed. If there is a tort, do you think it is an intentional wrong, an act of negligence, or an activity for which strict liability should be imposed? Give your reasons.

a. José trips over his untied shoelace while running to catch a bus, breaking his ankle.

b. Mr. Slifko buys a strong painkiller at the drugstore and takes the capsules according to the directions on the package. He has an extremely bad reaction to the drug and has to be taken to the hospital.

c. Chen drinks too much alcohol at the office Christmas party. His supervisor, Ruth, advises him to take a taxi home, but he thinks he will be okay if he drives slowly. Not noticing a stop sign, he strikes and kills a pedestrian crossing the street.

Raking and burning leaves are common chores during the autumn months. *Suppose a gust of wind blows flaming leaves onto a neighbor's garage and sets it on fire. Has a tort been committed? Explain.*

Taking Your Case to Court

Tort law is civil law. Civil law deals with disputes between individuals or groups of individuals. In a civil case, the injured party may sue the party who caused the damage. This differs from criminal law, in which the state brings charges against the accused. Criminal law deals with actions that are defined as crimes against the general public, even if there is an individual victim.

In some situations, an act can be both a tort and a crime. This may lead to two separate actions—civil and criminal—against the defendant. For example, Chen (Problem 18.3 on the previous page) may be sued for driving while intoxicated and killing a pedestrian. Chen may also be charged with the crime of negligent homicide or manslaughter for his actions.

The criminal case will be brought by the state, which must prove beyond a reasonable doubt that Chen was guilty. This is called the standard of proof. It is the amount of evidence the prosecutor must present in order to win the case.

The victim's family may also sue Chen in civil court. In the civil case, the victim's family will attempt to recover damages for the wrongful death. The civil court will use preponderance of the evidence as the standard of proof. This standard requires that to win, more than 50 percent of the weight of the evidence be in the plaintiff's favor. The civil standard is easier to meet than the criminal standard. This is appropriate, because the penalties for those found liable in a civil action are less severe than the penalties for those found guilty of a crime. A person does not go to jail for committing a tort, but instead pays damages to those injured.

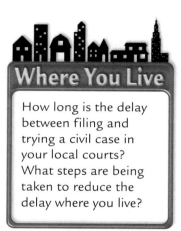

Where You Live

How long is the delay between filing and trying a civil case in your local courts? What steps are being taken to reduce the delay where you live?

Who Can Be Sued?

Almost anyone can be sued, including individuals, groups of individuals, organizations, businesses, and even units of government. Plaintiffs sometimes sue several different defendants at once. Typically, plaintiffs try to sue a defendant who has enough money to pay for the damages. This is called looking for a defendant with "deep pockets." For example, suppose you slip on a wet rag that the janitor left on the floor of a local restaurant. You break your leg as a result of the fall. You will probably sue the restaurant owner rather than the janitor because the owner will usually have deeper pockets—more money—from which to pay monetary damages.

People can sue employers for torts committed by employees in the course of their employment. The reason for this rule is that the employer is usually in a better position than the employee to handle the cost of the suit. The employer may purchase liability insurance or raise prices, for example. In addition, imposing financial responsibility on the employer encourages employers to be very careful when hiring, training, and supervising employees.

Children who commit torts may also be sued for damages. To recover damages from a minor, you have to prove that the child acted unreasonably for a person of that age and experience. Because most children do not have very deep pockets, plaintiffs also often sue the

Where You Live

Are parents responsible for torts committed by their children in your state? Should they be?

The Case of . . .

The Spilled Peanut Butter

Mr. Grant is in Foodland Supermarket doing the weekly grocery shopping. His four-year-old daughter Jenny is seated in the shopping cart. As they pass a large peanut butter display, Jenny reaches out and pulls a jar off the shelf. The display collapses, and a dozen jars come tumbling down. Some of the jars break, spreading peanut butter and glass all over the floor. Mr. Grant scolds Jenny severely as he wheels her down the aisle.

Ten minutes later, Mrs. Hightower slips and falls on the peanut butter. She breaks her hip in the fall and suffers several deep cuts from the broken glass. Because she is elderly, the hip injury develops complications and may never heal properly.

Problem 18.4

a. Whom should Mrs. Hightower sue for damages? Why?

b. Which possible defendant is likely to have the deepest pockets?

c. Who, if anyone, was at fault in this case? Give your reasons.

d. What methods other than a civil trial could the plaintiff use to deal with this situation? How would these methods work? (Refer to Chapter 4 and the information on settling disputes.)

child's parents. For example, assume a child leaves toys on the front step, injuring a visitor who trips on them. The visitor may sue the parents and try to prove that they were negligent in failing to supervise their child.

Certain defendants are immune, or protected, from some kinds of tort suits. In some situations, society has decided that for public policy reasons certain groups of people should not be sued, even though their conduct may have been improper. These immunities involve suits within families and against governments and certain government officials. Generally, courts do not allow children to sue their parents or vice versa. Historically, courts have also refused to allow husbands and wives to sue each other in tort actions. This was because of the traditional idea that the husband and wife were one legal entity! Times change and so do tort laws. Today many states allow husbands and wives to sue each other for certain torts. Even where these intrafamily immunities remain, brothers and sisters may be able to sue each other in civil actions.

The federal and state governments are also immune from tort liability unless they waive, or give up, this immunity. The notion of government immunity comes from England, where there was a tradition that "the king can do no wrong." Today the federal government, through the *Federal Tort Claims Act,* has agreed to be held liable in civil actions for negligent acts or omissions by government employees. While the *Federal Tort Claims Act* does not allow citizens to sue the federal government for most intentional torts, other laws may allow citizens to recover damages from the federal government for intentional violations of their rights.

The president, federal judges, and members of Congress are completely immune from tort liability for acts carried out within the scope of their duties. However, in the 1997 case of *Clinton* v. *Jones,* the U.S. Supreme Court found that the president was not immune from being sued while in office for a tort he allegedly committed before he was president. Other high-ranking officials, including members of the cabinet and presidential aides, have qualified immunity, meaning that they can be sued only if they knew or should have known that their acts were violating the legal rights of another person.

Sometimes there can be more than one plaintiff or injured party. In some cases, hundreds of people may be injured by one action. When this happens, the injured parties may be able to

Where You Live

Can a minor child sue a parent in your state? Can spouses sue each other for torts? Should any of these laws be changed in your state? If so, how?

Children who commit torts may be sued for damages. *How are parents often involved when their child commits a tort?*

form a "class" and bring their lawsuit together. This is called a **class action.** For example, if an entire town gets its drinking water from the same source and a company pollutes the water, the townspeople may get together and file a class action suit against the company. The settlement or damage award will be divided among the townspeople who bring the suit.

A class action lawsuit can also be filed to recover damages from an economic injury. For instance, in 2003 music CD distributors and retailers settled a lawsuit in which they were accused of agreeing to inflate and fix the price of CDs above what was fair to consumers. Consumers who paid too much for music CDs were entitled to collect a rebate for the amount they overpaid.

Individuals wishing to file a tort action should hire an attorney to file the legal papers, negotiate with the other side, and, if necessary, represent them at the trial. Some plaintiffs' lawyers will work for a **contingency fee.** This means the lawyer does not charge the client an hourly fee. Rather, the lawyer receives a portion of the recovery—typically between 30 and 40 percent—if the plaintiff wins. If the plaintiff loses, the attorney does not receive a fee. This arrangement allows a person who might otherwise be unable to afford an attorney to be represented by counsel in a tort action. The contingency fee is, of course, something of a gamble for the attorney. Lawyers rarely agree to this arrangement unless the plaintiff has a very strong case.

The Case of . . .

The Airline Explosion

On December 21, 1988, a bomb was smuggled onto an international flight from Frankfurt, Germany, to New York City. The flight carried 259 passengers, many of them students returning from a European trip, along with a crew of 11. The bomb exploded over Lockerbie, Scotland, killing everyone on board.

Surveying the wreckage

Problem 18.5

a. Could the families of those who died bring a class action? Explain.

b. Who are the possible defendants in this case?

c. Which defendant, if any, should be held liable for the deaths?

d. How much should a family receive in damages for the wrongful death of a loved one? Explain your answer.

The Steering Wheel Failure

Sarah buys a new car at Town and Country Motors. Just before her first scheduled maintenance visit (at 3,000 miles), she hears an odd noise coming from her steering wheel. She tells the service manager about the sound, and he notes it on the work order. After picking up the car the next day, she has a serious accident when the steering suddenly fails. The car is totaled, and her medical bills from the accident come to more than $30,000.

Problem 18.6

a. Could Sarah bring a civil action? Who are the potential defendants in this case?

b. Who do you think would win? Why?

c. Should Sarah hire a lawyer on a contingency-fee, hourly, or fixed-fee basis? Explain your reasoning.

d. What methods other than a civil trial could the plaintiff use to deal with this situation? How would these methods work? (Refer to Chapter 4 and the information on settling disputes.)

The contingency fee may not always be a good arrangement for the plaintiff. For example, a lawyer may be able to negotiate a large settlement with an insurance company without even filing a case in court. In such a case, it may be better for the plaintiff to hire a lawyer on an hourly basis or for an agreed-upon, overall fixed fee.

Insurance

Americans buy billions of dollars of liability insurance every year so that when an accident occurs, the injured party can recover money from the wrongdoer's insurance company, not from the wrongdoer. While insured persons must sometimes go to court, most tort cases between insurance companies and injured persons are settled without resorting to a trial.

Liability insurance is a contract, or agreement. The insured person agrees to make payments—known as premiums—to the insurance company, and the company agrees to pay for damages caused by the insured persons for the length of the contract. Insurance companies set a limit on how much they will pay. Usually the contract also requires the insurance company to provide an attorney to defend the insured person in court.

Most doctors, lawyers, and other professionals carry liability insurance to protect themselves against malpractice suits. These are lawsuits brought by clients or patients who claim that a professional person provided services in a negligent manner. Plaintiffs in malpractice cases sometimes win verdicts or settle for large sums of money—sometimes millions of dollars. Without liability insurance, doctors and lawyers would be personally liable for these verdicts.

Manufacturers often carry liability insurance to protect against lawsuits brought by customers injured when using the manufacturers' products. For manufacturers and professionals alike, the cost of insurance is usually added into the price of their products or services. This allows them to spread the costs of insurance among all of their customers or clients.

Home owners and renters may also carry liability insurance. These policies typically provide coverage for loss and damage to the insured person's property. For example, if your property is taken during a burglary, you can ask the insurance company for money to replace the stolen items. This is usually more practical than trying to sue the burglar for the value of the items.

While many different types of liability insurance exist, very few insurance policies cover intentional harm caused by the insured person. Therefore, a home owner's insurance policy will not pay damages if the home owner assaults a guest.

Insuring a Car

Auto insurance is the most important liability insurance for young people. In 2001, approximately 6.3 million automobile accidents resulted in more than 42,000 deaths—41 percent of which involved alcohol—and over 3 million injuries. These accidents caused more than $230 billion in losses. So it is not surprising that most states require drivers to carry insurance and that many drivers purchase more insurance than their state requires.

Auto insurance protects you by promising to pay for certain possible losses. Insurance can pay for the cost of repairing your car, medical bills, lost wages, and pain and suffering arising from injury.

Health insurance is an important financial issue for some people. *Why do people purchase insurance?*

The Case of . . .

The Expensive Insurance Premium

Dr. Sam Akiba, a surgeon, complains that he must pay $100,000 each year in premiums for adequate malpractice insurance. This insurance protects him against having to pay claims made by a patient or a patient's family in the event that the patient suffers injury or death due to a medical error during surgery.

Problem 18.7

a. What might happen to Dr. Akiba if he did not carry malpractice insurance?

b. Why do you think Dr. Akiba's insurance premium is so high?

c. Who pays the cost of Dr. Akiba's insurance?

d. What action or actions can be taken to lower these premiums?

A doctor at work

When you buy insurance, you can choose various coverage combinations. Coverage depends on the kind of protection you want and how much you can afford to pay. Common kinds of coverage include liability, medical, collision, comprehensive, uninsured motorist, and no-fault.

Your liability insurance pays for injuries to other people and property if you are responsible for the accident. It may also include representation in court by the insurance company's attorneys or payment of your legal fees. Liability coverage pays for damages up to, but not more than, the limits listed in your policy. If injuries and property damage are greater than the policy limits, you will have to pay the difference.

Liability policies generally have three limits on how much a person can collect: (1) a limit on injuries per person, (2) a limit on total injuries to all persons involved in the accident, and (3) a limit on property damage per accident. For example, a "100/300/50" policy would pay up to $100,000 per person for personal injury, $300,000 per accident for all personal injuries, and $50,000 per accident for property damage. Sometimes an injured person brings a lawsuit against the driver or car owner responsible for the injuries. Because the damages in these cases can be very high, you should give careful consideration to how much insurance you want to carry. For example, a $50,000 limit on injuries per person might be far less than the damage incurred in a serious accident. If you were negligent, you would be liable for the amount in excess of your insurance policy limit.

Your **medical coverage** pays for your own medical expenses resulting from accidents involving your car or the car you are driving. It also pays for the medical expenses of any passengers in your car, no matter who is at fault. The amount of medical benefits and the kind of medical costs covered, such as hospital bills and office visits, are limited in the policy. For example, medical coverage may be limited to $100,000 per person injured. This amount is usually in addition to the coverage you receive through your health insurance.

Your **collision coverage** pays for damage to your own car, even if the accident was your fault. Collision coverage usually pays up to the actual value of the car, but not for its replacement with a new car. You can lower the cost of collision insurance by including a **deductible.** This is an amount that you agree to pay toward repairs before the insurance company pays anything. For example, a $100 deductible means that if your car has $250 in damages, you will pay $100 and the insurance company will pay the remaining $150. The higher the amount of the deductible, the less expensive the collision insurance.

Problem 18.8

You have an eight-year-old car with a market value of only $4,000. The annual cost of collision insurance is $500. If your state does not require collision insurance, should you continue to purchase it? Give your reasons. Should you carry liability insurance? Explain.

The Case of . . .

The Nonstop Car

Pulling left into the outside lane to pass a slow-moving truck, Terrell saw the traffic light ahead turn yellow. "If I step on it, I'll make this light," he thought. He speeded up, exceeding the limit slightly. Just then an oncoming car made a left turn in front of him. Terrell hit the brakes, but it was too late. A few seconds later, pinned against the steering wheel, he saw the other driver, Candace, stagger out of the car, bleeding and holding her shoulder in pain.

Problem 18.9

a. Who should be responsible for the medical and car repair bills resulting from this accident?

b. In most cases, who pays for repairs resulting from auto accidents?

Some auto insurance companies have a preferred list of authorized repair shops they want their policyholders to use. *What is a deductible? How does it work?*

Your comprehensive coverage protects you against damage or loss to your car from causes other than collisions. For example, comprehensive coverage includes damages due to vandalism, fire, or theft. Read your policy carefully to determine whether valuables in your car, such as a CD player, are covered in case of theft. Insurance policies sometimes include—usually at an extra charge—coverage for towing or car rental costs.

Your uninsured motorist coverage protects you from other drivers who do not have insurance or do not have enough insurance. It does this by paying you for the personal injuries or damage they cause. Be sure to find out how much your policy pays for personal injuries caused by uninsured motorists and whether it pays for damages to your car. Uninsured motorist coverage is usually an inexpensive and worthwhile addition to your policy.

Only a few states have no-fault insurance. If you have no-fault insurance, your own insurance company will pay up to a certain amount for injuries you receive in an accident, regardless of who is at fault. In exchange for this payment, you typically have to waive your right to sue the other party to recover any damages. Notice the difference between no-fault and liability insurance. With liability insurance, your company pays the other driver only if you were at fault, whereas no-fault laws may allow settlement of such claims without the delay and expense of determining fault in a court case. Some people criticize no-fault benefits because they are limited to a certain amount of money and usually cover only personal injuries but not damages to your car. However, when damages are higher than the no-fault limits, the injured person may be able to sue the other party.

Where You Live

❶ What type and amount of auto insurance does your state require? Is there a law dealing with uninsured motorists? What does it provide? How much does auto insurance cost for high-school-age drivers in your state? Is there a discount for taking driver's education? Does the rate differ depending on the driver's age, the driver's gender, and the type and home location of the car? Are there criminal penalties in your state for failing to have insurance?

❷ Is there a no-fault insurance law in your state? If so, how does it work?

Problem 18.10

Reread The Case of the Nonstop Car on page 226. Assume that the accident happened in a state without no-fault insurance and that both Terrell and Candace had insurance coverage. Each had a policy covering all types of losses and including a $250 deductible for collision insurance. Also assume that Terrell was at fault.

a. Whose insurance company would pay for Candace's hospital and car repair bills?

b. Whose insurance company would pay for Terrell's hospital and car repair bills?

c. What do you think would happen if the damages to Candace and her car were greater than the limits of Terrell's policy?

d. If the damages were less than the policy's limits, would Terrell have to pay any money to get his car fixed?

Workers' compensation systems can restrict the recovery of damages if the accident is the result of an employee's refusal to follow safety rules. *Should workers' compensation pay for the injury if the worker without the hard hat is injured?*

Workers' Compensation

Every state has a workers' compensation system that operates to automatically compensate, or pay, employees who are injured on the job. Employers make regular contributions to a state fund or buy insurance for this purpose. Workers are compensated for injuries that occur in the course of their employment. However, they do not have to go to court to prove that their employer was at fault. Workers also receive a portion of their salary while they are recovering and unable to work. Many states provide employees with two-thirds of their regular salary. In exchange, the injured employee usually gives up the right to sue his or her employer. Accidents that occur while the employee is commuting to or from work are rarely covered.

NOTICE
HARD HATS
MUST BE WORN
IN THIS AREA

Unlike the plaintiffs in typical tort cases, workers can usually recover monetary damages for their injuries even if they were negligent. However, workers' compensation statutes generally deny recovery when the accident was caused by the employee's intoxication. In addition, nearly half of the states either reduce or prohibit recovery when a worker's refusal to follow safety rules caused the accident. For example, a welder who is blinded on the job after ignoring repeated warnings to wear safety goggles would not be able to recover money under workers' compensation statutes in some states.

The amount of money awarded for a specific injury is limited according to a schedule the state determines. The schedule sets the amount a worker can recover based on the seriousness of the injury, the amount of time the worker is expected to be out of work, and the worker's average weekly wage. Workers cannot usually recover additional damages from the employer through a civil tort action. This means that workers' compensation is the **exclusive remedy** for on-the-job injuries.

A worker who is injured on the job must notify the employer. Often the employer will ask a doctor to certify the injury. Then either the employer or the injured employee will file a claim. Once the claim is filed, the injured employee will regularly receive a workers' compensation payment, just like a paycheck. The payments will continue until the employee can return to work or recovers from the injury.

Many states have a workers' compensation commission that hears claims and decides how much money will be given to injured workers. If the commission decides that little or no money should be given, the injured person may appeal to a court.

Where You Live

Are all jobs covered by your state's workers' compensation system? What are the principal provisions of your state's law? How effectively and fairly does the system work?

The Case of . . .

The School Slip and Fall

Mrs. Braun is the art teacher at Central High School. Dale is a tenth-grade student. One afternoon the maintenance staff forgot to display a warning notice that the floors had been mopped and were wet. The stairway leading to the art studio was so slippery that Dale fell down the stairs, breaking his arm. Mrs. Braun was teaching an art class at the time. When she heard the noise of his fall, she ran out to see what was wrong. She, too, slipped on the wet floor and broke her ankle.

Problem 18.11

a. Who is responsible for Dale's injury? For Mrs. Braun's injury?

b. From whom can Dale recover damages? Is there a limit to the amount he can recover?

c. From whom can Mrs. Braun recover damages? How will she recover these damages? Is there a limit to the amount she can recover?

d. Why does the law treat these two injured people differently? Is this fair? Explain.

Intentional Torts

Small children have a natural understanding of what it means to act **intentionally.** When a mother scolds her child for breaking something, the child may plead, "But it was an accident. I didn't do it on purpose!"

A person who plans to perform a certain act, and then does so, is said to have acted with intent. For example, a child who knocks a glass off the table on purpose does it intentionally. This is true even if the child genuinely hoped the glass would land softly on the rug unharmed, rather than shattering into many pieces.

Actions taken to deliberately harm another person or their property are called **intentional torts.** There are two general types of intentional torts: those causing injury to persons and those causing harm to property. In the law of torts, the required intent is to *do* the forbidden act—knocking the glass off the table—not a bad motive or a desire to cause harm.

Street Law *online*

Visit the *Street Law* Web site at streetlaw.glencoe.com for chapter-based information and resources.

Intentional torts are deliberate acts.

Types of Damages

A person who proves that someone else committed an intentional tort against him or her can recover damages to make up for the harm caused. These are called compensatory damages because the award compensates for harm caused by the defendant. For example, when Gus is punched and hit by Seth, he receives damages of $6,000 to cover his hospital bills.

Compensatory damages can also include lost wages and pain and suffering. The plaintiff has to prove any future losses—such as medical bills, reduced or lost wages, and pain and suffering—with reasonable certainty. Juries decide how much money will fully compensate the injured person for pain and suffering.

In some cases, the plaintiff recovers only nominal damages, or a token amount of money awarded by the court to show that the claim was justified. These are symbolic awards of money that are paid even if the plaintiff is unable to prove economic harm. Nominal damages are awarded to recognize that the defendant acted wrongfully even though he or she did not cause substantial injury or loss. For example, suppose Juan slapped Matthew in a heated argument. In court, it is shown that even though Juan wrongfully slapped Matthew, Matthew suffered no serious injury. The court might award $1 in nominal damages to Matthew.

The Case of . . .

The Mischievous Child

Jeremy, a five-year-old child, was playing in the backyard when his neighbor, an elderly woman named Helen, went outside to sit down. Jeremy pulled the lawn chair away just before Helen sat down. Helen was unable to catch herself and fell to the ground. As a result, she fractured her hip.

Although Jeremy did not intend to hurt Helen and did not believe she would be hurt, the child was aware that if he pulled the chair away as Helen was sitting down she would almost certainly land on the ground.

Problem 19.1

a. Did Jeremy act intentionally? Is a five-year-old too young to act intentionally or to understand the significance of his actions?

b. Did Jeremy cause Helen's fall? Explain your answer.

c. Can Helen sue Jeremy and force him to pay for her injuries? Can she sue Jeremy's parents?

d. Should it matter that Jeremy did not mean to hurt the woman?

e. Would the legal outcome be different if the child had been running in the yard and tripped over the chair just as Helen was sitting down, resulting in the same injury to her? Explain your answer.

Punitive damages are amounts of money awarded to the plaintiff to punish the defendant for malicious, willful, or outrageous acts. Punitive damages serve as a warning to others not to engage in such conduct.

It is possible for both nominal and punitive damages to be awarded even where there is little or no actual harm that would justify compensatory damages. Suppose that Kate shoots a gun at Mark and misses him. This is an intentional tort. The court could award nominal damages (because there was no actual harm inflicted) and punitive damages (because Kate's act was so outrageous).

Sometimes people sued for intentional torts do not have to pay any damages at all, even though they did exactly what the plaintiff claims. In these instances, the defendant may have a legal defense.

Torts That Injure Persons

There are several acts that are classified as intentional torts causing injury to a person or persons. The following sections explain the five most common types of these intentional torts.

Battery

A **battery** occurs when a person intentionally causes a harmful or offensive contact with another person. The perpetrator is liable for all resulting damages, regardless of whether he or she wanted or expected the contact to cause injury. For example, Elaine became angry at Ravi and shoved him toward an open window. Although the shove was not hard, he fell backward through the window and suffered serious injuries. While Elaine did not want him to suffer such serious injury, she will be liable for damages if Ravi sues her for battery.

What is a harmful or offensive contact? Certainly a punch in the nose or a gunshot through the chest are harmful and offensive contacts. But what about an unwanted kiss on the cheek? The law considers offensive to be whatever would offend an average person in society. For example, most people would not be offended by a light tap on the shoulder accompanied by a pleasant "Excuse me, sir, do you have the time?" Such a touch would not be considered a battery, even if it somehow led to an injury.

Battery is one of the most common intentional torts. *In what ways does the definition of battery help protect people's dignity from being violated?*

Assault

The tort of **assault** occurs when a person goes beyond mere words and intentionally makes someone fear an immediate harmful or offensive contact. An assault can be an intentional threat, show of force, or movement that causes a reasonable fear. For example, if Jeb throws a rotten tomato at Colin's head, Jeb has committed the tort of assault, even if Colin ducks at the last instant and does not get hit. If Colin fails to duck and the tomato hits him, there has been both an assault and a battery. While battery requires a harmful or offensive contact, assault merely requires *fear* that a harmful or offensive contact is about to occur.

For assault to occur, the fear of harmful or offensive contact must be reasonable or well-founded. For example, assume Simon is sitting at a traffic light and Monica is crossing the street in the intersection in front of Simon's car. Monica suddenly becomes overwhelmed by a terrible feeling that Simon is going to step on the gas and run her over. As a result of this fear, she has a heart attack. There is no assault in this case, because Monica's fear was not reasonable. Also, Simon did not intend to make her fear an immediate harmful or offensive contact.

As the result of an assault, the plaintiff can recover compensation for mental disturbance, such as fright or embarrassment, along with any physical injury that directly results from the assault.

Problem 19.2

a. Lenny is a successful—and very rich—bank robber. He is also careful not to harm bank tellers. In fact, he always uses weapons without bullets. Unfortunately for Lenny, he holds up one bank too many, and the police catch him. The day before he is caught he sticks an unloaded gun into the face of Cynthia, the teller at the Last National Bank. Cynthia wants to bring a civil suit against Lenny for assault. Will she be successful?

b. The tort of battery can be committed against someone who is asleep or unconscious, but the tort of assault cannot. Explain.

Infliction of Emotional Distress

A relatively new tort is known as intentional **infliction of emotional distress;** courts have only recognized it since about 1940. A person commits this tort by intentionally using words or actions that are meant to scare someone or cause them extreme anxiety or emotional distress. Actual physical injury is not required for the plaintiff to recover damages. However, courts do require that the defendant's conduct be quite outrageous and that the plaintiff prove extreme distress. Mere insults are not enough to form the basis of a lawsuit for emotional distress.

Bullying: When Do You Cross the Line?

Read the following cases. Can a successful claim of infliction of emotional distress be brought against any of these defendants? If so, decide on a fair remedy. Remember that remedies are not always monetary damages. Have other torts been committed? Consider whether you think it is a good policy to allow students who are picked on at school to sue their bullies.

a. Evan's family just moved from Metropolis, where he attended a large urban school, to Smallville, which has just one high school of 500 students. Evan is a quiet, wiry boy with braces and purple spiked hair. He obviously stands out from the crowd at his new school. There is a group of students, led by Shawn and Jason, who constantly make fun of Evan by calling him names like "freak boy" and "grape head." Four times in the last month, these two boys have waited for him after school and thrown him into the garbage dumpster. The last time this happened, Evan broke his arm. He has become withdrawn from his family and is scared to go to school, for fear of what might happen next.

b. Tiana is a very shy high school sophomore who always wears black. She is not performing well in her classes, does not have many friends, and has thought a lot about dropping out of school. Some of her classmates have started calling her "witch" and "ghoul girl." Tiana wants to be a poet and spends her free time writing in her journal, which she keeps in her locker when she is at school. Most of her entries are her private thoughts and poems about how lonely the world seems and how mean the others at school can be. One morning when Tiana checks her e-mail, she finds an anonymous broadcast message that has been sent to the entire student body. The subject is

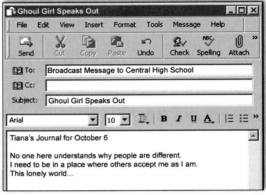

The anonymous e-mail

"Ghoul Girl Speaks Out" and the message contains an entry from her journal and several of her most private poems. Not willing to endure any more teasing, Tiana leaves school before her classes begin and never comes back.

c. Ramon is a senior on his high school's varsity football team. He suffers from a speech impediment that causes him to stutter when he is upset or nervous. Although several years of speech therapy have taught him how to keep it under control, he is still very sensitive about his condition.

The football team had a chance to advance to the state finals. In the remaining seconds of their last game, Ramon fumbled the ball and the team lost the game, ending their hopes of advancing to the finals. Two of his teammates, Diego and Kyle, took the loss especially hard. For the past three days, they have been harassing Ramon by booing, taunting, and stuttering insults. Ramon tries to defend himself, but in his nervousness, he stutters severely, causing Diego and Kyle to taunt him even more. Despite all of his hard work in therapy, his stuttering has gotten worse.

When the actions of bill collectors, insurance adjusters, and landlords have been truly outrageous and excessive, courts have sometimes allowed plaintiffs to recover damages. For example, in one case a young man owed a store money. The store tried to collect the debt from the youth's father by falsely accusing him of guaranteeing the son's debt, making late-night calls to the father, and sending letters telling the father that his credit had been revoked. In this case, the court found that the store had intentionally caused the father severe emotional distress.

Extremely outrageous conduct by restaurants, hotels, or transportation companies can also sometimes form the basis for the tort of emotional distress. These businesses, and certain others, have a special obligation to deal with the public in a courteous manner.

Recovery for this tort is sharply limited in order to keep the legal system from being flooded with lawsuits brought by persons suffering from unkind, inconsiderate acts. In addition, there is some value for a free society in letting angry people express their anger without fear of being sued. Among the legal defenses that can be used are that the defendant's conduct was not outrageous, that the plaintiff is overly sensitive, and that a reasonable person would not suffer extreme distress as a result of the defendant's conduct.

Problem 19.3

Give a specific example of a situation in which you believe someone should be able to recover damages for infliction of emotional distress. Write the dialogue, showing exactly what each party said and did. Determine the amount of damages that should be awarded.

False Imprisonment

Being able to sue for false imprisonment protects a person's right to be free from unreasonable restraint. False imprisonment does not mean being kept in jail or even arrested by police. It occurs when someone intentionally and wrongfully confines another person against his or her will.

For example, assume that a restaurant manager tells an employee to get out of the walk-in refrigerator so she can lock up and go home. When the employee takes too long, the manager shuts the refrigerator door with the employee still inside and leaves for the night. The restaurant manager has committed the tort of false imprisonment.

Suspected shoplifters sometimes sue shopkeepers who detain them. In balancing an individual's right to be free from confinement and a shopkeeper's right to protect his or her property from theft, the law recognizes a shopkeeper's privilege to temporarily detain a person suspected of shoplifting. However, shopkeepers must act reasonably, using no more restraint than is necessary to protect their property.

Shelter for Street People

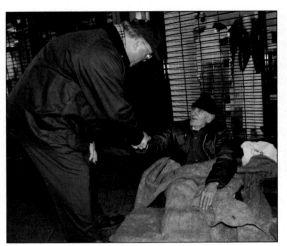

Social services worker talks with homeless man.

In order to prevent homeless citizens from freezing during the winter, Big Town passes an ordinance. It requires its social services workers to pick up homeless street people whenever the nighttime temperature is predicted to fall below 32° F (0° C). The homeless people are then taken to a city shelter and provided with food, clothing, and a bed. They are not allowed to leave until the next morning.

Mr. Stobbs, a homeless person, believes the shelter is dangerous and unsanitary. He also believes he has a right to live on the street. One night, he is taken to the shelter against his will. He later convinces a public-interest law firm in Big Town to help him sue the city for false imprisonment.

Problem 19.4

a. What arguments can Mr. Stobbs make?

b. What arguments can Big Town make?

c. How would you decide this case? Explain how your decision best serves the public interest.

d. Would your answer be different if Mr. Stobbs were mentally disturbed? What should happen then?

Torts Related to Defamation

A person's reputation is protected by laws prohibiting defamation. Defamation includes acts that harm a person's reputation and can be classified as oral or written. Oral statements that harm reputation are called slander; written defamation is called libel. Damages are often more difficult to prove for slander than for libel.

Defamation occurs when someone makes a false statement about another person that is communicated to a third party, causing harm to the person's reputation. If a patient yells, "You're a drunken butcher!" to his surgeon, it is not slander if no one else hears the statement. However, if the patient yells this false statement in the hospital hallway where others can hear it and the doctor's reputation is harmed, a tort has been committed.

Proving that the offensive statement is *true* is a complete defense in a defamation lawsuit. For example, Sid brings his car to a garage and yells at the mechanic, "You ruined my transmission!" in front of other customers. This statement might be harmful to the mechanic and his business. But if Sid can prove that the mechanic did ruin his transmission, he has a good defense to slander charges.

The law also protects opinion. Assume a movie critic watches a new movie and, in her review, is particularly critical of one actor's performance. The review may harm the actor's reputation and economic interests, but such statements are usually protected as opinion.

In the United States, freedom of speech and freedom of the press are very important. Therefore, courts balance a person's right to protect his or her reputation against the public's interest in receiving a wide range of information. For this reason, the U.S. Supreme Court has established rules making it difficult for public figures to win damage awards against the media. To win a defamation suit against the media, a public figure must prove not only that a statement was false and caused harm, but also that the statement was made with actual malice. This means that the statement was made with knowledge of its falsity or with a reckless disregard for whether the statement was true. These rules make it difficult for famous people to sue the media and win. In a sense, famous people sacrifice some protection of their reputations.

The Case of . . .

The Captured Shoplifter

Kathleen, 17, is in a music store. As she passes a rack of CDs, she slips one under her jacket. Thinking that no one has noticed, she turns to leave the store. The store manager, however, has been watching her on a closed-circuit television. As she passes the cash register, he stops her before she leaves the store.

Problem 19.5

a. The store manager has several options. Rank the following in order of most reasonable to least reasonable:

1. The manager calls the police and keeps Kathleen in his office until they come.

2. The manager tells an assistant manager to keep Kathleen in the back room until the police arrive. The assistant manager is called away on another task, and he ties Kathleen's hands and feet together so she cannot run away.

3. The manager yells, "Stop, you thief!" as he runs after Kathleen in the store. He also shouts at her as he walks her back to his office. Then he calls her parents and tells them he is taking her to the police station immediately.

4. The manager locks Kathleen in the storage room for seven hours, until he is ready to close the shop. Then he takes her to the police station.

5. The store manager tells his security guard to arrest Kathleen. The guard pulls a gun, takes her to the back of the store, and calls the police.

b. Would any of these alternatives qualify as false imprisonment? If so, which ones and why? What should a shopkeeper do if he or she catches a shoplifter?

Torts That Harm Property

Tort law protects your property in two ways: (1) it protects against interference with the owner's exclusive use of the property, and (2) it protects against the property being taken or damaged. Three kinds of property are protected: **real property** (land and the items attached to it, such as houses, crops, and fences), **personal property** (property that can be moved, such as cars, clothing, and appliances), and **intellectual property** (the ownership interest in creations of a person's mind). The U.S. legal system is very protective of private property rights.

Real Property

Everyone has seen signs that read "Private Property—Keep Out" or "No Trespassing." The tort of **trespass** occurs when a person enters another person's property without permission. The owner can recover damages from the trespasser even if there is no harm to the property because the law protects the owner's *exclusive* right to the property.

In a technical sense, a trespass occurs every time you cut across a neighbor's lawn on the way to the store. Obviously, landowners rarely sue people who merely walk across their property. But what would you do if someone committed a continuing trespass by going onto your property without permission and erecting a sign advertising a nearby restaurant?

Tort law protects you when others damage your property. In some instances, tort law also requires that you use reasonable care to protect other persons from harm when they are on your property. In general, though, you are not liable if a trespasser is injured on your property. For example, if a trespasser walks across your lawn, trips on a sprinkler, and sprains her ankle, she will not be able to recover damages from you.

An exception to the general rule occurs when the trespasser is a child too young to appreciate a dangerous condition on your property. The law requires landowners to use reasonable care to eliminate a dangerous condition on their land, or to otherwise protect children when the condition presents an unreasonable risk of serious injury where children are likely to trespass. Because of this law, sometimes called the **attractive nuisance** doctrine, construction companies generally fence in excavation sites.

Posting "No Trespassing" signs can help protect property. *In what other ways does tort law protect property?*

YOU BE THE JUDGE

Real Property and Reasonable Interference

Read each case carefully. Decide whether a nuisance exists. Does an unreasonable interference exist? If a nuisance does exist, decide on a fair remedy. Explain the reasons for your answers.

a. Mr. Iwamoto works the 11 P.M. to 7 A.M. shift at the factory and then comes home to sleep. On his way to school, Darrell walks by Mr. Iwamoto's house every weekday at about 8 A.M. with his boom box blaring heavy metal music. The loud music awakens Mr. Iwamoto.

b. A passenger on a commuter train uses his cell phone to make and receive business and personal calls each day during his one-hour ride to work.

c. Morgan owns a restaurant next to High Penn's oil refinery. The refinery occasionally emits gases and odors that make people feel sick. Morgan, believing that this hurts her restaurant business, brings a suit against the oil refinery. High Penn argues that (1) the refinery was properly constructed, (2) there is no way to operate the refinery without these occasional odors, and (3) the refinery was in operation before Morgan opened her restaurant.

d. Commercial advertisements constantly appear in the inbox of your personal e-mail account. The ads are for products that do not interest you. You did not request information about these products.

e. In order to earn the extra money they need to send their two children to college, Larry and Meg operate a small auto repair and body shop in their garage. After returning from their day jobs, they work on cars until about 10 P.M. The noise produced when they rev up car engines disturbs their neighbors.

f. Adriana Stein is a successful musician who travels extensively to give concerts. To enjoy some peace and relaxation when she is not traveling, she buys a house in the countryside only five miles from the nearest airport. As the surrounding metropolitan area grows, air traffic at the airport increases. Eventually, the airport needs to build another runway to accommodate the increased traffic. Experts report that the runway can be built in only one location at the airport. Airplanes using this runway would descend directly over Adriana's house, creating loud noise and disrupting the quiet of the countryside. In response to the airport's plan to build the runway, Adriana organizes her neighbors into a citizen action group called RAMP (Residents Against More Planes). The group sues the airport, seeking an injunction to stop the planning and construction of the new runway.

A jet approaches the airport.

The Unfenced Swimming Pool

The Garcia family built a large swimming pool in their backyard. The pool was two feet deep in the shallow end and nine feet deep near the diving board. They placed lights around the pool that turned on automatically at dusk. They also placed four large "Danger—Deep Water" signs around all sides of the pool.

One day, a four-year-old who lived a block away wandered onto their property, entered the pool, and drowned. The child's parents sued the Garcia family for not fencing in the pool.

Problem 19.6

a. How should this case be decided?

b. Suppose the Garcias had fenced in the pool and the child had climbed the fence and drowned. Should the child's parents be able to recover damages in that situation?

Most people who enter your property are probably not trespassers. Generally, they are either guests in your home, or businesspeople and customers visiting your workplace. In most states, you have a legal duty to warn guests of any known danger on your property. For example, if your front porch is being repaired, you have a duty to warn your guests to avoid this dangerous situation.

If you own a store or other business establishment and the public enters your property for a business purpose, the law imposes an even higher duty. Business owners have a duty to use reasonable care to inspect their property to make it safe for business visitors. For this reason, a restaurant owner is not merely required to warn customers of a slippery sidewalk on a snowy day, but is obligated to use reasonable care to make the sidewalk safe. This may be done by shoveling the snow or spreading salt or sand.

In some cases, tort law protects against harm caused by someone who never *physically* enters your property. A nuisance occurs when there is an unreasonable interference with your ability to use and enjoy your property. Courts will balance the usefulness of the activity complained of against the harm caused.

You do not have a right to be free from all interference with your property, only unreasonable interference. For example, Ari and Brenda are neighbors. One Sunday, Ari has a large barbecue in his backyard, and Brenda is unable to listen to the baseball game on the radio while lying on her hammock. This one-time event is not a nuisance. If Ari were to cut his lawn at six o'clock every Sunday morning, however, that would probably be a nuisance.

You can recover damages if you win a nuisance suit. In some cases, you may also be able to get a court order requiring the defendant to stop the activity. This court order is called an injunction. An injunction requires that a person do, or not do, a specific act.

Personal Property

Tort law also provides compensation to someone whose personal property is taken, damaged, or interfered with. Suppose a burglar breaks into Laura's house and steals her television set and DVD player. If the person is arrested, there will be a criminal prosecution for burglary. Laura could also sue the thief in civil court for a tort called **conversion.** Conversion occurs when someone unlawfully exercises control over the personal property of another person.

A series of privileges has developed for protecting property. You can always use nonviolent means to protect real property ("Please get off my land . . . you are trespassing") or to recover personal property. However, you must use careful judgment in these cases. Telling your locker mate that she has taken the wrong lunch bag may work well; yelling at a fleeing thief to put down your possessions is likely to fail!

Law in Action

Make My Day Laws

Some states have passed Make My Day laws. These laws allow the occupant of a dwelling to use any degree of force, including deadly force, if the occupant reasonably believes that an intruder might use any force at all against any occupant of the dwelling. These state laws protect the occupant using the force against both criminal prosecutions as well as civil suits for damages filed by an injured intruder.

Problem 19.7

a. Why do you think a state would pass a Make My Day law?

b. What are the possible benefits of such a law? The possible costs?

c. Does your state have such a law?

d. Do you support or oppose Make My Day laws? Explain your reasons.

Make My Day laws are controversial.

The Burglar Who Was Bitten

The Kings own a small store in a crime-ridden section of town. They have been the victims of break-ins in the past. To protect their family and store, they purchase a guard dog. The dog is trained to attack on command. The dog also stays in the store from 11 P.M. to 7 A.M., while the store is closed. One night, a person breaks into the store and is attacked by the dog. The police catch the person, and he is convicted of burglary. After the judge gives him a suspended sentence, the burglar sues the Kings for the injuries caused by the guard dog. How would you decide this case? Give your reasons.

. . . .

Reasonable force can also be used to protect property. Precisely how much force is reasonable depends on the circumstances. Generally, deadly force cannot be used to protect property, although the rules of self-defense allow the use of deadly force to protect a person if serious bodily harm is threatened.

Intellectual Property

Imagine that you have created a brilliant, action-packed computer game with dazzling 3-D graphics. You are sure that everybody will love it, so you begin to sell copies of your program to people over the Internet. A large software company buys your program and begins to market your game on a much larger scale and for a much cheaper price. The company makes millions of dollars by taking credit for and selling the game that you created. Unable to compete with the large company, you have to discontinue your business.

Or perhaps you are a musician and you perform original songs at your school's dances. What if one day you saw a celebrity musician on television performing a song that you wrote? What if this musician falsely took credit for writing the song, performed it on a hit CD, and made a fortune from it without giving you a cent?

If people knew that they could not protect their work from being stolen, there would be little reason or incentive to create anything, or to show new creations to others. This is why the law protects the creations of people's minds as a form of property that can be owned, and thus may not be stolen. Another word for the mind is intellect, so property in the form of creations of the mind is called intellectual property.

If the intellectual property is something you have invented, a **patent** recognizes your ownership of the invention. If the intellectual property is in some form of creative expression such as a book, movie, computer program, or song, a **copyright** recognizes ownership of the expression. When a person has a patent or a copyright indicating ownership over some invention or expression, any other person who uses the patented or copyrighted work commits a tort called **infringement.**

Intellectual property law promotes progress because it provides an incentive, or a reward, for engaging in creative pursuits. Also, most people think it is fair that creators profit from their creations. However, advancements are often made by building on the work of others. If people cannot use the work of others, it might hinder technology and progress, so intellectual property rights (especially patents) are kept somewhat limited.

Patents

Patents protect useful inventions such as processes, machines, and new products. However, patents are only given to inventors who have thought of something that has never been invented before. That is, the idea must truly be new or *novel.* For example, notebooks are usually sold with space for either three or five subjects. You would not be able to get a patent for a four-subject notebook, however, because there is nothing truly new or novel about the idea. It is an obvious extension of an existing idea. On the other hand, if you invented a notebook with a clipping mechanism that allowed it to be attached to the desk to prevent it from slipping, you would have a better chance of getting a patent for your novel idea.

Dr. Gertrude Elion and Dr. George Hitchings invented and received patents for several drugs, including a leukemia-fighting drug. *What characteristic must an idea have before it can receive a patent?*

Getting a patent requires a lengthy—and sometimes expensive—legal process. An inventor who gets a patent has a complete monopoly over the product for 20 years. If anyone else tries to sell the product or profit from the idea, the patent-holder can sue for infringement. After 20 years the patent expires, and the invention becomes public domain. Anyone may then use or profit from the invention.

Copyrights

Copyrights protect any expression that is somehow fixed (written down, recorded on tape, stored on a computer disk, painted on a canvas, etc.). Unlike a patent, you do not have to go through any legal process in order to obtain a copyright. As soon as you make your expression permanent (for example, by writing it down), you automatically have a legal copyright without doing anything else. If you keep a diary or take notes during class, then you hold copyrights.

In 1998, Congress provided further protection for creative endeavors, extending the life of a copyright to the lifetime of the holder plus 70 years. The existing law had protected copyrights for the lifetime of the holder plus 50 years. In 2003, the U.S. Supreme Court agreed that Congress had the power to make such an extension, thus providing significant protection to those who want to safeguard their expressions. The Court's decision was based on an analysis of Article 1, Section 8, of the Constitution that gave Congress the power to promote progress in science and the arts by "securing for limited times to authors and inventors the exclusive right to their writings and discoveries." In fact, copyright protections were extended numerous times during the twentieth century. However, the policy debate about this case dealt with whether it was in the public's interest to allow people to copy and distribute old movies, music, or

For Your Information . . .

Protecting Your Creations

The federal government makes information available online to help you protect your intellectual property and creations. Visit the U.S. Copyright Office online at www.copyright.gov and learn how to search copyright records, register a work, and record a document. Then follow the links to visit the U.S. Patent and Trademark Office—www.uspto.gov—to check the status of patents and trademarks. You can also learn how to search and apply for patents. This site also has an award-winning kid's page as well as a link to the online National Inventors' Hall of Fame.

books on the Internet rather than continue protecting the interests of those in the entertainment industry for an additional period of years. At some point old works enter the public domain; the question is, when?

Although copyrights exist as soon as expression is fixed, there are legal benefits to registering the copyright and putting a copyright notice on your work. Registering is easy and does not require a lawyer. You merely fill out a simple form and send it to the U.S. Copyright Office. You should also submit two copies of the work to the Library of Congress. Placing the copyright notice on your work serves to warn others that a work is copyrighted. Notice consists of the © symbol, the year the work was created, and the author's name.

Unlike patents, copyrights do not require novelty. Copyrightable expression need only have some slight "spark of creativity." For example, the arrangement of legal cases in a textbook and the written label on a shampoo bottle have been held to be creative enough for a copyright. While copyrights protect the form of expression, they do not protect ideas or facts. A network news anchorperson who writes a script for the evening news owns the copyright for that expression, and nobody else may report the news in the same way. But anybody may report the same facts (the news) using his or her own expression. Anyone may create a mischievous son and a father who love to eat (ideas), but copying Bart and Homer Simpson (expression) would infringe on the author's copyright.

Copyrights give the owner the exclusive right to copy the work, to make **derivative works** (works very similar to a copyrighted work), to sell copies of the work, to display copies of the work in public, and to perform the work. To prove infringement, the infringing work must be "substantially similar" to the copyrighted work. If you copy your next report from the encyclopedia but change a few words around, you are infringing on a copyright!

Exceptions to the exclusive rights of a copyright holder include first sale and fair use. **First sale** means that once the copyright owner sells a copy of the work, the lawful owner of the particular copy may resell that particular copy. First sale does *not* mean the owner of a copy can make further copies and sell them. If you purchase a copy of a popular video, you are free to sell that tape to your friend without infringing on the copyright (under first sale). You may not, however, make fifty copies of it and open up your own video store.

Downloading music files from the Internet raises ethical and legal issues. *How might downloading files or copying songs from a CD be a copyright infringement?*

The **fair use** clause of the copyright statute allows limited legal reproduction of copyrighted works for certain noncommercial purposes, such as for criticism, news reporting, scholarship, or research. For example, if you copy a video clip of the movie *Titanic* to show during an oral presentation for your history class, this would be fair use and not a copyright infringement. This is because the material is being used to help educate your classmates, you are not showing the entire three-hour movie, and you are not charging your friends to watch the clip. These are all relevant factors in determining whether your use of the copied video is fair to the creator of the movie.

In recent years technology, principally computers and the ability to download materials from the Internet, has raised ethical and legal issues. For example, one software company used the slogan "Rip, mix and burn" to describe how a buyer could produce his or her own music CDs by "ripping" songs from other CDs they owned, mixing them in the order they liked, and burning them onto another CD which they might give to a friend. The question arose: If people copy songs or other materials from CDs, are they infringing on copyrights?

The general rule is that copying songs from CDs is a copyright violation, as is making additional copies of music, movies, books, or computer software that you buy. However, you may legally copy free over-the-air broadcast television shows to watch later.

The courts have also ruled that the copyright law prohibits the copying of copyrighted music using the digital technology known as MP3, which stores songs on computers or personal MP3 players. In the famous Napster case, a court shut down the Napster Web site because it enabled users to download MP3 files without the permission of the copyright owner. The court found that the sharing of music files among Napster users was really unauthorized copying and distribution of the music, which directly violated federal copyright laws.

What is the bottom line? There are some general rules of thumb to use when deciding whether the law would consider your copying "fair use." However, as technology advances, these questions become more difficult. The most reliable guide may be to imagine that you are a songwriter, a movie director, an author, or a computer programmer. Then ask yourself whether it would be fair for people to copy your work without paying you or getting your permission.

Consent can be implied based on the situation. *Can a child be charged with battery if he knocks another child down during play?*

Problem 19.8

Gloria has a computer at home that she uses for schoolwork and entertainment. In some situations, she must decide what to do with certain content she finds on the Internet. Consider the law and ethics involved and advise her on what she should do in each of the following situations:

a. She sees a Web site that advertises unlimited downloading of top 50 songs for $9.95 a month.

b. Gloria's friend Janet sends her a copy of a DVD of a new movie on which Janet worked.

c. Gloria's friend Alex wants her to help him start a business in which the two would buy music CDs, copy them, and sell the copies for $5.

d. Gloria is doing a homework assignment and wishes to download a photograph from a television network's Web site to use in her report.

> *The rules of unauthorized copying and distribution should be enforced on the Internet in much the same way as they are enforced in stores that sell physical goods that have intellectual property: books, DVDs, CDs. I don't think anyone advocates the right to shoplift these. Even if you think they are overpriced, you've got to buy them.*
>
> — **David Kendall, Partner, Williams & Connolly Attorney for Recording Industry Association of America**

Defenses to Intentional Torts

Even if a plaintiff proves that the defendant has committed a tort, the defendant can still escape liability if the plaintiff has a valid defense. Consent is the most common defense to intentional torts. This defense means that the plaintiff consented, or agreed, to the harmful conduct and thus gave up the right to sue later. In boxing, punches are thrown that in almost any other situation would be serious batteries. However, boxers sign a contract consenting to be punched during a match. Of course, if one boxer tries to stab another with a knife, this would be an assault, as the consent was limited to punches.

Consent can be written, spoken, or simply assumed based on the situation. For example, children often knock each other down while playing, but this conduct does not constitute a battery. In another example, suppose you were seriously injured in an auto accident and taken to the hospital for emergency surgery. Ordinarily, you would sign a consent form before the operation, but in an emergency, when it is impossible to sign a form, the law assumes that you consent to lifesaving surgery.

Privilege is another defense to intentional torts. Privilege justifies conduct that would otherwise be a tort, because the defendant's interests (or those of the public) require it. Privilege also often justifies conduct that would otherwise be a tort because public policy is best served by permitting such behavior.

Legal authority is one such privilege. For example, a police officer has legal authority to restrain a person's liberty while carrying out an arrest warrant, and therefore has a valid defense to a false imprisonment suit. Parents have legal authority to use reasonable force to discipline their children. Owners have legal authority over their property and may use reasonable force to recover their property from a thief, even though they would otherwise be committing false imprisonment, battery, or assault.

Perhaps the best-known privilege is **self-defense.** If Julie attacks Amanda, then Amanda can use reasonable force to protect or defend herself. If Julie later sues Amanda for battery, Amanda will be able to use self-defense to justify her actions, as long as the force she used was not excessive. Deadly force—force that may cause life-threatening harm—would be considered excessive unless Amanda's life was in danger. Also, defenders who take control of a situation and become aggressors commit battery and have no self-defense claim. For example, while self-defense allows Amanda to defend herself against Julie, it does not allow her to teach Julie a lesson or seek revenge. Self-defense also allows someone to come to the rescue of another person and to use the same amount of force the victim could have used to repel the attacker.

Defense of property is another privilege that allows people to use reasonable force to defend their homes or property. Except in states with Make My Day laws (see page 241), deadly force is not considered reasonable when defending property.

YOU BE THE JUDGE

Intellectual Torts and Legal Defenses

Determine whether any intentional torts have been committed. Is there a legal defense in each situation? Give reasons for your answer.

a. A pitcher in a high-school baseball game loses control of an inside pitch. The ball hits the batter, shattering a bone in his arm.

b. Josh arranges to have an oral surgeon remove a tooth that has been causing him discomfort. While Josh is under anesthesia, the surgeon notices that two other teeth are emerging in a crooked position. She believes the crooked teeth are likely to cause Josh pain in the future, so she removes them as well.

c. Sandy, 17, throws a snowball at a friend on a crowded street corner. The snowball misses the friend but hits an elderly man, who falls to the ground and is injured.

d. Maya, a prison guard, is attacked by an inmate. The inmate knocks Maya down and kicks her in the head and ribs. Maya responds to the inmate in a similar fashion.

e. Wendy breaks into the first floor of Amy's house and begins to steal valuable property. Hearing the intruder, Amy comes downstairs wielding a baseball bat. Seeing this, Wendy drops the property and runs toward the front door of the house. Amy runs after her and hits her on the head with the bat, knocking her unconscious. She then calls the police.

f. Kemal borrows money from the bank to purchase a car. After he fails to make the required payments, the bank sends somebody to Kemal's house. This person drives Kemal's car away while he is not at home.

Human Rights USA

The essence of human rights involves the responsibility of all human beings to treat each other with dignity. When people commit intentional torts, such as assault or battery, they are not treating each other with dignity. They are also violating internationally accepted human rights, such as those listed in the following articles of the Universal Declaration of Human Rights:

Article 3: Everyone has the right to life, liberty and personal security.

Article 17: (1) Everyone has the right to own property, alone as well as in association with others. (2) No one shall be arbitrarily deprived of his (or her) property.

Consider how these human rights may relate to the facts in the following case study:

The Case of the Fraternity Hazing

Wade is a first-year student at Everett College. The social life at Everett primarily revolves around fraternities, so Wade is very interested in joining a fraternity. He visits the Sigma Tau house and decides this is the best place for him. He must go through a two-week pledge period to join. He has heard it is pretty difficult, but is willing to endure it to be initiated. If he does not fulfill all of the requirements during the pledge period, Wade will not be allowed to join the fraternity.

During the pledge period he is required and agrees to do the following things:

- Bow to all fraternity members when they enter the room.
- Stand outside the sorority house and yell out a rating of each woman based on her looks as she leaves for class.
- Make breakfast to order for the 70 fraternity members every morning.
- Streak naked across campus at midnight on a designated night.
- Allow any fraternity member to enter his room and use his computer and stereo, and listen to his CDs whenever they want.
- Sleep only from the hours of 3:00 A.M. to 5:00 A.M. each night for a week, and then only on an individual step in the stairwell of the fraternity house.
- Run through a line of fraternity members as they hit him with the traditional fraternity paddles.

Problem 19.9

a. Are any of the pledge requirements described above violations of human rights? If so, which ones and why? Do any of the requirements violate the rights of anyone besides Wade? Why or why not?

b. Do any of the requirements involve intentional torts? If so, which ones and why?

c. Should Wade be able to sue anyone for any injuries he might sustain from the hazing activities? Why or why not?

d. If Wade does file a suit, who should be held liable and why? Should the fraternity or its individual members be held liable for his injuries? What about the college? Explain your reasons.

e. Are there defenses that can be successfully raised against these tort claims?

f. Why do people join fraternities? Do you think that all fraternities engage in activities such as those listed here? Suggest some possible requirements and activities that neither violate human rights nor constitute torts.

Negligence

Street Law *online*

Visit the *Street Law* Web site at streetlaw.glencoe.com for chapter-based information and resources.

Public works projects can create risks of harm through negligence.

We have already examined intentional torts and their defenses. Now we move on to another type of tort called **negligence.** Tort law establishes standards of care that society expects from people. Negligence is conduct that falls below the standard established by law for protecting others against unreasonable risks of harm. But what does this mean?

The word *negligence* comes from the root word *neglect.* This may lead us to think of negligence as forgetfulness, inattentiveness, or lack of care about others. But tort law requires us to analyze negligence as it relates to a person's conduct. Even a person who cares a great deal about the welfare of others may be negligent if his or her conduct creates an unreasonable risk of harm. On the other hand, a person who is totally unconcerned about the safety of others may not be negligent if his or her conduct does not subject another person to an unreasonable risk of harm.

These are some examples of negligent conduct:

- Dr. D'Angelo, a surgeon, forgets to remove a clamp from a patient's body while operating and stitches the patient up.
- Monica leaves a loaded rifle on the floor where her younger brothers and sisters usually play. A child is shot.
- A city employee working in a manhole forgets to replace the cover when he goes to lunch and a pedestrian falls in and is injured.
- A drug company markets a birth control device for women without conducting adequate medical testing. It assumes the device is safe because people have used similar devices for years. A woman develops a serious illness from using the device.

Elements of Negligence

Unlike intentional torts—many of which have specific names—negligence is a very broad term that deals with many kinds of wrongful conduct. While the different types of wrongful conduct may not have separate names, they do have something in common. For a plaintiff to win a negligence action against the defendant, each of the following elements must be proven by a preponderance of the evidence:

1. **Duty:** The defendant, or accused wrongdoer, owed a duty of care to the plaintiff, or injured person.
2. **Breach of duty:** The defendant's conduct breached or violated that duty.
3. **Causation:** The defendant's conduct caused the plaintiff's harm.
4. **Damages:** The plaintiff suffered actual injuries or losses.

All of these elements must be proven or the plaintiff will not prevail. For example, in the case of the drug company described on the previous page, the woman bringing the lawsuit would have to prove each of the elements of negligence by a preponderance of the evidence against the company. Specifically, she would have to prove that the company had a duty of care to its customers to adequately test any new birth control product before selling it, that the company breached this duty through its failure to adequately test the device, and that this breach resulted in a defective product that caused actual damage (ill health, hospital bills, and so on) to her.

As in intentional torts, defendants in negligence cases sometimes have legal defenses. These defenses, which are explained below, are different from those used in intentional torts.

Duty and Breach

Everyone has a general duty, or legal obligation, to exercise reasonable care toward other persons and their property. Negligence law is primarily concerned with compensating victims who are harmed by a wrongdoer's action or inaction that breaches, or violates, this standard of reasonable care. If a mechanic fixes the brakes on your car without using reasonable care and skill, and this faulty repair causes you to have an accident, you can recover damages from the mechanic as the result of his or her negligence.

What if someone is harmed by another person's inaction? For example, Brian is drowning in a lake and Jennifer, an expert swimmer, passes by in a boat. Does she have a legal duty to rescue Brian? While she may have a moral obligation to help, she generally does not have a legal duty to act unless there is some special relationship between them. For example, Jennifer is a lifeguard and Brian is drowning in an area she is supervising.

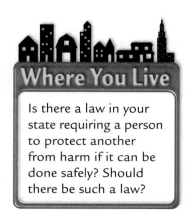

Where You Live

Is there a law in your state requiring a person to protect another from harm if it can be done safely? Should there be such a law?

The Spilled Coffee

In 1994, 79-year-old Stella Liebeck bought a cup of coffee from the drive-thru window at a fast-food restaurant. While the car in which she was a passenger was stopped to allow her to put cream and sugar in her coffee, she balanced the cup between her knees and attempted to remove the lid. The coffee spilled, causing third-degree burns to over six percent of Liebeck's body and causing her to spend eight days in the hospital and undergo skin graft operations. Liebeck sued the restaurant for damages.

The restaurant was part of a large national chain that served its coffee at approximately 180°F (82°C), despite the fact that coffee at such a high temperature is too hot to drink. At the trial, the chain's quality control manager testified that the sale of any food over 140°F (60°C) would create a burn hazard.

The restaurant argued that, according to its surveys, many of its customers take coffee back home or to work with them and consume it there, so the higher temperature is necessary to assure that it will still be hot when consumed. They also claimed that many customers choose this particular chain specifically because they do serve their coffee so hot. However, the chain was also aware that, between 1982 and 1992, approximately 700 claims had been filed by people burned by their coffee.

The jury awarded Liebeck $160,000 in compensatory damages (finding her 20 percent at fault for her own negligence) and $2.7 million in punitive damages (the equivalent of two days of the chain's coffee sales). The trial judge reduced the amount of punitive damages to $480,000, and the parties eventually came to a secret settlement agreement for an undisclosed amount.

The case launched a public debate about the appropriateness of lawsuits with high damage awards in situations such as this one.

Problem 20.1

a. Who is the plaintiff in this case? Who is the defendant?

b. What, if anything, did the defendant do wrong? What, if anything, did the plaintiff do wrong?

c. Did the defendant cause the plaintiff harm on purpose? Did the defendant's conduct in some way cause the harm suffered by the plaintiff?

d. What duty, if any, did the defendant have toward its customers? Did the defendant uphold or breach that duty?

e. Do you agree or disagree with the outcome of this trial? Give your reasons.

f. What are the arguments for and against the award of punitive damages in a case like this one?

Buying coffee from a drive-thru window

The Reasonable Person Standard

Everyone has a duty toward everyone else in society: the duty to act reasonably. If you act unreasonably, then you have breached this duty. If the breach causes damage, then you will be liable for damages.

To help judge whether certain conduct is negligent, the law has developed an imaginary creature—"the reasonable person of ordinary prudence or carefulness." The reasonably prudent person does not represent the typical, average individual. Rather, this is an idealized version of such a person. This person acts the way a community expects its members to act, not exactly as they do in fact act.

How does the reasonable person behave? The reasonable person considers how likely a certain harm is to occur, how serious the harm would be if it did occur, and the burden involved in avoiding the harm. The likelihood and seriousness of the harm are balanced against the burden of avoiding the harm.

For example, assume a pedestrian is about to cross a road where there is very little automobile traffic. The harm to be avoided, of course, is being hit by a vehicle. Our imaginary person asks: How likely is it that such an accident will occur? Not very likely. How serious would the harm be if it did occur? Very serious. How difficult would it be to avoid this harm? Not difficult at all; simply look both ways before crossing. Our reasonably prudent person looks both ways before crossing such a street.

In a second example, the walkway to a secluded home in the woods has a crack in it. The crack is large enough to cause a person to trip and fall. This is the harm the homeowner needs to avoid. In this instance, the likelihood of the harm is small, the harm would probably not be very serious, and the cost of avoiding it (fixing the walkway) may be substantial. Even our reasonably prudent person may decide not to fix this crack in the walk. However, it may be reasonable to post a sign warning of the danger, because the burden (cost) of the sign would be less than the burden of making the repair.

The law assumes that reasonable people do not break the law. Therefore, if somebody violates a law, then they are automatically considered to have breached the duty to act reasonably. If the breach causes injury, then the wrongdoer is negligent. For example, most states have laws prohibiting you from leaving your vehicle running while unattended. Such laws were established because of the risk that cars in this situation can easily be stolen. What would happen if you borrow your friend's car to run an errand, leave it running while you run into a gas station to buy a soda, and it is stolen? Have you breached your duty to act responsibly? Can your friend sue you for the value of the car?

Certain professionals, such as doctors, plumbers, and pilots, are considered to have the abilities of reasonably skilled persons qualified to be members of their professions. For this reason, a plumber who repairs a kitchen sink that later leaks and damages the floor cannot defend against a tort action by claiming that he completed the job as skillfully as the ordinarily prudent person. The work must be at the level of the ordinarily prudent plumber.

As you know, minors are liable for torts they commit. However, the standard used in negligence cases involving minors is not the same as it is for adults. Instead, the law compares the minor's conduct with reasonable conduct for others of the same age, intelligence, and experience. When a minor reaches the age of majority, the adult standard of care applies. There is one important exception to this rule: when minors engage in what is ordinarily considered an adult activity, such as driving a car, they are held to the adult standard of care.

The Case of . . .

Bartender Liability

Lance is a 16-year-old high school junior. He gathers the alcohol left over from his parents' New Year's party and decides to throw a party at his house on a Saturday night when his parents are out of town. He knows that some of his friends have driven to his house, but doesn't pay much attention to whether or not they are drinking. He sees his friend Abby finish a beer, grab her car keys, and walk out the door to go home. Stefan, another friend, leaves with Abby to get a ride home. Lance does not know whether Stefan has been drinking, but watches as Abby drives the car away with Stefan in the passenger seat. As Abby pulls her car onto the highway, she swerves and hits another car head-on. Stefan and the driver of the other car are seriously injured.

Police investigate a party.

Problem 20.2

a. Who can sue whom in this situation?

b. What duty did Lance have in this situation? Did he violate that duty?

c. What duty, if any, do Lance's parents have in this situation? Did they violate that duty? Would it make a difference if his parents had been at home?

d. Now assume that Lance is a 25-year-old bartender who serves Abby and Stefan, who are both over 21, although he knows that they are intoxicated. The rest of the facts remain the same. Answer questions **a.** and **b.** using this scenario.

e. Is it fair to hold Lance responsible in either situation? Give your reasons.

f. If you were at the underage drinking party described, what would you do? What if you were at the bar in the second scenario?

g. Some bars have "designated driver" programs. Why have they done this? Should people who hold private parties in their homes do anything special to protect their guests from drinking and driving? What, if anything, could be done?

AIDS Liability

Tyler is infected with HIV, the virus that causes AIDS. He is new in town and wants to meet people and make friends. So he does not want anyone to know about his HIV status. He meets and becomes romantically involved with Audrey. He has unprotected sex with her, but he does not disclose his HIV status to her. Audrey contracts the virus as a result of her relationship with Tyler.

Problem 20.3

a. Did Tyler have a duty to tell Audrey about his condition? Explain.

b. Would it make a difference if AIDS were curable?

c. What, if anything, should Audrey be able to recover in damages from Tyler? Explain.

d. Could Audrey sue Tyler if she did not contract the virus but was very upset when she learned that he had not told her about it?

Causation

Once a plaintiff proves that the defendant owes him or her a duty and that this duty was violated, there must be proof that the defendant's acts caused the harm to the plaintiff. While it seems like common sense to require a causal connection between the act complained of and the plaintiff's injury, the concept is sometimes troublesome to apply. See The Case of the Great Chicago Fire on page 256 for an example.

When you think about the element of causation, you must consider two separate issues: cause in fact and proximate cause. Cause in fact is easy to understand. If the harm would not have occurred without the wrongful act, the act is the cause in fact. If Mrs. O'Leary had not placed the lantern too close to the cow, it would not have been kicked over, and the Great Chicago Fire would not have occurred. Her act was the cause in fact of the fire.

It is often hard to draw the line in proximate cause situations. The basic idea behind proximate cause is that there must be a close connection between the wrongful act and the harm caused. The harm caused must have been a foreseeable result of the act or acts. Negligence law does not hold people responsible for harm that was completely unforeseeable.

The more difficult part of causation is establishing proximate cause. Would it have been fair to make Mrs. O'Leary pay for all the damage caused in the Chicago fire? A certain amount of damage from her wrongful act was foreseeable harm. At some point, however, the damage to the city of Chicago was greater than what could have been foreseen when she negligently placed the lantern near the cow.

Assume, for example, that your car wrongfully crosses the center line and collides with a truck. It turns out that the truck is carrying dynamite, which explodes and kills a person two blocks away. Your negligent crossing of the yellow line is the cause in fact of the harm to the person two blocks away. However, most courts would say that your negligence was not the proximate cause of this death. Crossing a yellow line does not usually result in harm two blocks away. That harm was not foreseeable. This case would be decided differently, though, if the person who died was a pedestrian on the sidewalk close to the collision.

Sometimes the negligence of more than one person harms someone. For example, suppose two cars, each negligently driven, collide and injure a pedestrian on a nearby sidewalk. Each driver is responsible for the pedestrian's injuries. If one driver is unable to pay, the other driver may have to pay the entire amount of the damages.

Damages

A plaintiff who proves duty, breach, and both forms of causation still must prove actual **damages** to recover in a negligence action. The basic idea behind damages is that the plaintiff should be restored to his or her pre-injury condition, to the extent that this can be achieved with money.

Courts allow plaintiffs to recover for hospital bills, lost wages, damage to property, reduced future earnings, and other economic harm. Plaintiffs may also recover for noneconomic harm such as pain

The Case of . . .

The Great Chicago Fire

In 1871, a major fire destroyed much of the city of Chicago. After a thorough investigation, the cause of the fire was determined. It began in Mrs. O'Leary's shed when a cow she had been milking kicked over a kerosene lantern she had placed too close to the cow's rear leg.

Problem 20.4

a. Was Mrs. O'Leary negligent in placing the lantern so close to the cow's leg?

b. Should she have had to pay for all the damage caused by the fire? Give reasons for your answer.

Aftermath of the fire

and suffering, emotional distress, and permanent physical losses (for example, loss of a limb or blindness). However, in some states, a plaintiff must first prove economic harm—even if only one dollar—before a judge or jury can make an award for noneconomic harm like pain and suffering.

Problem 20.5

As a freshman college prank, Carolyn decides to remove a stop sign from an intersection and put it in her dormitory room. To avoid being noticed, she chooses a stop sign at the intersection of a little-used country road and a two-lane state highway several miles out of town. The night after her prank, a motorist from out of state drives through this intersection and is struck by a car traveling at 50 miles per hour along the state highway. Both motorists are seriously injured, and their cars are totally demolished. They recover from their injuries after several months. The police suspect a college prank, and after some investigating, are able to find out who removed the sign. The injured motorists bring a civil action against Carolyn, claiming extensive damages.

a. Can the injured motorists prove that Carolyn's act caused their harm? Explain your answer.

b. Assume that the plaintiffs can prove duty, breach, and causation. List all the types of damages each plaintiff might have suffered. Could they recover all of these damages? Explain your answer.

Defenses to Negligence Suits

People can recover for injuries when they are able to prove each of the elements of negligence by a preponderance of the evidence. However, even when all the elements can be proven, the defendant may be able to raise a valid legal defense. One group of legal defenses in negligence cases is based on the plaintiff's conduct.

One traditional legal defense is **contributory negligence.** This means that as a plaintiff, you cannot recover damages from the defendant if your own negligence contributed in any way to the harm suffered. For example, suppose a train station attendant warns a passenger not to walk in an area where ice has formed on the platform. The passenger walks there anyway, falls, and is hurt. The passenger might sue the railroad for allowing ice to remain on the platform. However, by ignoring the warning and stepping on the ice, the passenger breached the duty to act reasonably. The breach was the cause—both cause in fact and proximate cause—of her injury. The passenger and the railroad were negligent, so the passenger cannot recover damages.

When both parties are equally at fault, the contributory negligence rule perhaps provides a fair result. Neither party can recover damages from the other. However, the contributory negligence defense also allows for a very slight amount of negligence on the part of the plaintiff

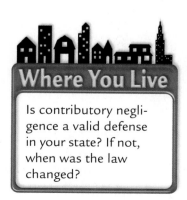

Where You Live

Is contributory negligence a valid defense in your state? If not, when was the law changed?

Law in *Action*

Cigarettes and the Law

Prior to the mid-1990s, tobacco companies were usually able to defend against lawsuits brought by smokers harmed from cigarettes. They did so by claiming that the smokers had assumed the risks—based on the warning printed on cigarette packages—related to smoking. In 1994, despite testimony earlier that year before Congress that smoking was not addictive, documents surfaced showing that tobacco company executives actually had a great deal of information about the addictiveness of nicotine and the harm caused by smoking. Not surprisingly, in the next few years, many class action lawsuits were filed in state courts to recover damages from cigarette companies.

In 1998, the leading cigarette manufacturers settled these lawsuits. Not only did they promise to pay an estimated $246 billion to the states over 25 years, but they also agreed to restrict the way they market cigarettes and make them available to the public. The cigarette companies also agreed to pay special attention to restricting young people's access to cigarettes. Some of these restrictions include not advertising on billboards or within public transportation systems, not using cartoon characters to sell tobacco products, and not sponsoring concerts or other events at which young people will be present. In addition, the cigarette companies agreed to dedicate $300 million toward public education efforts to reduce underage tobacco use and to educate consumers about causes and prevention of diseases associated with the use of tobacco products.

Problem 20.6

a. Is it fair to the cigarette companies to subject them to liability when they had been manufacturing a legal product that contained a health notice printed on cigarette packages?

b. Should it make a difference that the product, although legal, caused great harm?

c. Should the federal government regulate such a product?

d. Should it make a difference that the companies withheld information about the harmful effects of their products?

e. A bartender who never smoked develops lung cancer as a result of inhaling secondhand smoke during her many years of work at the bar. Should the bartender be able to recover damages against cigarette manufacturers? Explain.

to give the defendant a complete legal defense. This is true even when the damage to the plaintiff is great and the defendant has been very negligent. Many people think this produces an unfair result. Therefore, this defense has been eliminated in most states by either state law or judicial decision.

Most states now allow a defense called **comparative negligence.** This means dividing the loss according to the degree to which each person is at fault. For example, Paul and Javier are in a car crash and Paul sues Javier for the $20,000 in damages that he suffers. If the jury finds that Paul was somewhat negligent himself—

Signs are often posted to give notice of a certain danger. *If someone is injured or drowns at this beach, can the property owner be held liable?*

for example, by not wearing his seat belt—the damages will be reduced. If Paul was 10 percent at fault and Javier was 90 percent at fault, Paul will receive $18,000 ($20,000 reduced by 10 percent, the amount that was Paul's fault). If Paul was 30 percent at fault, he will receive only $14,000. But if he was more than 50 percent at fault, he will receive no damages in many states, and Javier might be able to sue Paul for some damages. Javier's action against Paul is called a **counterclaim.**

Sometimes several people commit a negligent act against a third person. If Paul and Javier in the example above had negligently collided and injured Charles, who was in another car and was not at fault, Charles could recover damages from both Paul and Javier. Paul and Javier might be able to divide their liability to Charles between themselves, according to each one's degree of fault. However, if one of the defendants was unable to pay because he had no money, the other defendant might have to pay all the damages awarded to Charles.

Another legal defense in negligence cases is **assumption of risk.** This defense is used when a person voluntarily encounters a known danger and decides to accept the risk of that danger. For example, a hockey fan knows that on rare occasions a hockey puck can be deflected off a player's stick, over the glass that surrounds the rink, and into the seats. A fan who buys a seat knows the risk and agrees to accept the danger. If a fan is hit by the puck, assumption of risk will be a complete defense for the team or the players involved should the injured fan try to sue.

This defense is also used when a warning is posted that gives notice of a certain danger. For example, many hotels operate swimming pools without hiring lifeguards. The hotels post large "Swim at Your Own Risk" signs near the pools.

Even without a warning notice, everyone knows that knives are sharp and may cause injury. When someone accidentally slices off a finger while cutting cucumbers, the knife manufacturer will not be held liable. The injured party assumed the risk by picking up the knife.

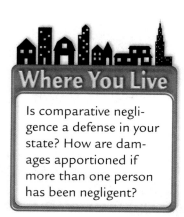

Where You Live

Is comparative negligence a defense in your state? How are damages apportioned if more than one person has been negligent?

Roller coasters are equipped with safety bars to prevent injury. *What questions would you have to answer to determine liability if a rider is hurt on this ride?*

Problem 20.7

Analyze each case below. Identify the plaintiff and defendant and decide whether the defendant has a legal defense. Assume the state has a comparative negligence law.

a. Olivia and her friends go to an amusement park, and she decides to ride the scariest roller coaster. After each rider is seated, the attendant secures that rider with a safety bar. Olivia tells her friends that she does not need the safety bar. After the first large hill, she detaches it. Later in the ride, Olivia is thrown from the roller coaster and is badly hurt.

b. A large sign posted at the foot of the lifeguard station warns of a very dangerous undertow beyond the first sandbar. There are buoys floating around the sandbar. Howard swims out beyond the sandbar and drowns before the lifeguard is able to reach him.

c. Joel's car runs out of gas on a railway crossing in a rural area. He puts on his flashers to warn approaching cars and begins walking to the nearest gas station, which is a mile away. A freight train approaches, and the engineer sounds his horn several times, thinking the driver will move off the tracks. By the time the engineer realizes that the car is abandoned, it is too late to stop the train. The car is totally demolished.

For Your Information . . .

Waivers

You may have been asked to sign a waiver, or a release from liability, before participating in certain potentially dangerous activities. A waiver is designed to release the person sponsoring the activity from liability if you are injured through his or her negligence. In most states such waivers, or releases, are enforceable as long as they are clear and understandable to a layperson. However, if the conduct of the party asking you to sign the waiver is worse than negligent and this causes you damage, then the waiver will not protect them from liability. In addition, in some states certain other businesses—typically those regulated by government and those providing essential services—may not use waivers to protect themselves from liability for their negligence.

Where You Live

Are waivers, or releases from liability, enforceable where you live? Does the law in your state prohibit some businesses from being protected by waivers? If so, which ones?

Strict Liability

Until now we have examined tort cases in which the defendant was, to some degree, at fault and therefore liable to the plaintiff. In tort law, one exception to this requirement of fault is strict liability, also known as liability without fault.

Strict liability means that the defendant is liable to the plaintiff regardless of fault. In some situations, even if the defendant acted in a reasonable and prudent manner and took all the precautions necessary, liability is imposed without proof of fault. Strict liability is applied to ultrahazardous activities such as storing or transporting dangerous substances, or using explosives. It is also applied to harm caused by dangerous animals and to harm caused by the manufacture and sale of defective products.

Remember that proving negligence involves establishing four elements: duty, breach, causation, and damages. To prove strict liability, you must only prove causation and damages. However, you must also convince the court that the activity that caused the harm is the type of unreasonably dangerous activity to which strict liability is applied. Public policy and common sense require people who conduct dangerous activities to accept responsibility for any harm caused, even if they were not negligent. The alternative would be to place the burden of harm on a totally innocent victim.

> "Law is experience developed by reason and applied continually to further experience."
>
> — Roscoe Pound, Dean Emeritus, Harvard Law School

Street Law *online*

Visit the *Street Law* Web site at streetlaw.glencoe.com for chapter-based information and resources.

The company in charge of this demolition is liable without fault if a bystander is injured.

Dangerous Activities

Strict liability applies to activities that are unreasonably dangerous. Activities are considered unreasonably dangerous when they involve a risk of harm that cannot be eliminated even by reasonable care. These activities may be socially useful or necessary, but because of their potential for harm, those who conduct them are held to the strict liability standard. For example, assume that a demolition company has been hired to dynamite an old downtown building. While demolition may be necessary, it is dangerous to use dynamite in a populated area. No amount of care by the demolition team can totally eliminate the risk. Therefore, the law imposes strict liability. This means that the demolition company must assume the risk of any foreseeable harm caused, even if the company is careful and not negligent.

Companies conducting dangerous activities know that they are strictly liable for any harm they cause. Therefore, they include this cost in the price they charge for the work. In the example above, the company using the dynamite has a financial incentive to be as careful as possible because of strict liability.

The concept of toxic torts was developed in response to companies guilty of industrial pollution. *What must the injured parties do before they can recover damages from an industrial polluter?*

Problem 21.1

In which of the following situations should the plaintiff be able to recover damages based on strict liability? Explain your reasons.

a. Anytown's waste treatment plant develops a leak, and harmful bacteria are released into the water supply. Hundreds of families become sick.

b. Anita takes her car to a mechanic for repairs. As she enters the garage, she slips on spilled motor oil and breaks her ankle.

c. Donna drives by a construction site in a downtown shopping district. Following a sudden blast from the site, a piece of cement crashes through her windshield and injures her.

d. Kyung Lee is eating lunch at a cafeteria. A waiter races by and knocks a pot of coffee on Kyung Lee's arm, badly burning him.

In recent years, a concept called **toxic torts** has been introduced to address harm resulting from the use of toxic chemicals and other hazardous materials. Historically, some industrial manufacturers disposed of their wastes by dumping them into the nearest river or other convenient location. It was not until the 1960s that the public began to understand that prolonged exposure to toxic chemicals could cause illness and even death.

The toxic torts concept was developed to allow injured parties to recover damages from industrial polluters if the injured parties could establish causation—that is, if they could establish that the harm resulted from the manufacture or disposal of hazardous materials. For example, when a Massachusetts mother found that her son and a dozen other neighborhood children had leukemia, she successfully sued a chemical company that had contaminated local drinking water by dumping its waste products into a nearby stream.

Problem 21.2

Mr. Mattingly, a well-to-do farmer, has a legal right to apply pesticides to his fruit trees. One year, he decided to hire a crop-dusting airplane to spread a pesticide on his orchard. An unexpected gust of wind blew the chemical onto a neighbor's beehives, killing all the bees. The neighbor sued Mattingly for the value of the 60 beehives. Mattingly argued that a good fruit farmer has to apply pesticides and that the crop duster had exercised extreme caution in applying the chemicals.

a. Was Mr. Mattingly negligent? Should strict liability apply to this case? Give your reasons.

b. How should Mr. Mattingly defend this case?

c. How would you decide this case? Explain your answer.

Animals

The law has traditionally held owners strictly liable for any harm caused by their untamed animals. Even the owner of a tamed wild animal such as a lion may be held strictly liable for any harm it causes because of the nature of the animal itself. The situation differs, however, for household pets. In most states, an owner of a pet is strictly liable only if he or she knew, or should have known, that the pet was dangerous or destructive. There is a saying that "Every dog is entitled to one free bite." However, an owner who knows his dog is vicious may be liable for the first bite. There may also be liability if "near misses" have put the owner on notice of the dog's viciousness.

Even the first bite by a pet with no history of violent behavior can result in liability if the owner is negligent. For example, some states and localities have leash laws requiring that pets be kept under the owner's control and on a leash in public places. If you violate the duty to keep your pet under control, you can be sued based on your negligence. In extreme situations, a pet owner might even be held criminally responsible for the harm caused by a pet if the owner knows that the pet is dangerous or cannot be controlled.

Leash laws require pet owners to keep their pets restrained and under control. *Would a dog owner be liable if his or her dog attacked and injured someone in a public place?*

The Case of . . .

The Dangerous Dog

Five-year-old Matthew opens a gate and walks into his neighbors' yard to play with their dog, a pit bull terrier. The dog—which had never attacked anyone before—attacks Matthew, badly mauling his hand. Matthew's parents sue the dog's owners for not keeping the animal inside or in a pen in the yard. The owners defend themselves by saying that even though there have been reports of attacks by other pit bull terriers, their dog had been affectionate with family members and had never shown any dangerous or destructive tendencies.

Problem 21.3

a. What arguments can you make for Matthew's parents?

b. What arguments can you make for the dog's owners?

c. How should this case be decided? Explain your answer.

d. Would you have decided this case differently if Matthew had been 15? What if he had been 35? What arguments could you make for each situation? How would they differ?

Defective Products

Harm caused by defective products is a significant social problem. Product liability—the legal responsibility of manufacturers for injuries caused by defective products—is an important legal issue. In fact, some lawyers specialize in product liability law. In a typical year, more than one million consumers suffer product-related injuries and nearly half of them sue to recover damages. In many cases, the manufacturer is held strictly liable for harm caused by the defective product. In some instances, injured consumers bring cases together as a class action against a manufacturer.

The U.S. Consumer Product Safety Commission (CPSC), created in 1972, is the federal agency that deals with consumer product safety. It protects the public by issuing and enforcing mandatory product standards or banning consumer products. The commission has the power to force many dangerous products off the market and advises consumers on product safety.

As a matter of public policy, manufacturers and sellers are frequently held strictly liable for harm caused by their products. Strict liability is meant to create a strong incentive for companies to design safe products, test products thoroughly before placing them on the market, and include clear directions and warnings on products. Strict liability causes companies to spend more money on research and development, safety features, and insurance. This increase in spending usually results in higher prices for consumers. Some people criticize these higher prices, while others say that safer products are worth the extra cost.

Where You Live

Does your state have strict liability laws covering harm caused by defective products? Can the consumer use strict liability to sue everyone from the manufacturer to the seller of the product? Is this fair?

Problem 21.4

a. Make a list of five items that are or can be dangerous to use.

b. For each item, decide whether the government should ban it, regulate it (for example, require warnings), or take no action at all.

c. Explain why you treated each item as you did. Consider in your explanation both the danger(s) and the benefit(s) of each item.

An unsafe product that causes many injuries and subsequent lawsuits may become too expensive to compete successfully with safer products in the marketplace. For example, in the 1990s, more than 5.8 million Americans began taking weight loss drugs, including a product called fen-phen. About 20 percent of those taking fen-phen developed serious heart problems, and some of them lost normal heart function. In a successful class action, several people recovered damages from the pharmaceutical company. As a result, fen-phen is no longer on the market in the United States.

The fear of expensive lawsuits may also discourage the production of new and useful—but unavoidably dangerous—products such as vaccines. Some people argue that this is a reasonable restraint on development. Others argue that the government should provide some type of insurance or immunity from lawsuits as an incentive for companies to develop new products in the spirit of progress.

The Case of . . .

The First Responders

Gabriella, a doctor, is a member of the team her city established to be the first to respond in case of a bioterrorist attack. As part of her preparation for such an event, Gabriella and her colleagues are each required to be vaccinated for smallpox, a highly infectious and deadly disease that kills 30 percent of those who contract it. The government believes that the smallpox virus could be used in a terrorist attack. Even though Gabriella does not want to receive the vaccination because she knows there is a minor risk (1 in 1,000,000) that she could contract smallpox, she is forced to do so in order to keep her job.

Problem 21.5

a. If Gabriella becomes sick after having the vaccination, should the drug company that manufactures the vaccine be held strictly liable for Gabriella's injury?

b. Is the risk of getting sick from the vaccine unreasonable? Do the benefits outweigh the dangers?

c. What arguments can the drug company make to defend itself? Identify the public policy issues that the company might use in its defense.

d. Should Gabriella be able to sue the government for forcing her to take a drug she doesn't want to take? Why or why not?

Law in Action

Should Gun Manufacturers Be Held Liable?

After a particularly horrible shooting spree that killed eight and wounded six others in California, a bill was introduced in the state legislature that would have removed (for future cases) the state's existing law (passed in 1983) that protected gun manufacturers from liability. In the shooting spree case, the shooter used a semiautomatic weapon produced by a company that listed the following statements in its advertising literature: "Excellent resistance to fingerprints" and "Tough as your toughest customers."

In the floor debate on the bill, the author of the 1983 law argued that the new law would not be effective. He stated, "A crazy person who wants to commit murder won't have any problem getting a weapon [after gun makers are no longer immune from suit]." Another state senator argued, "It's the nut behind the trigger, not the gun, that does the damage." Yet another said, "Automobiles are as dangerous as a gun, yet automakers are not held liable on the basis that their product is inherently harmful."

Problem 21.6

a. If you were a lawmaker, would you vote for a law that allowed gun makers to be held liable for damages, or would you support a law that protected gun makers from tort suits? Explain your answer and your reasoning.

b. Are gun manufacturers able to be sued in your state? Is this a current legislative issue where you live? Should it be?

A controversial issue

Courts have been reluctant to apply strict liability to unavoidably unsafe products whose benefits outweigh the dangers. Certain vaccines are unavoidably risky to use. For example, even if the rabies vaccine is properly tested, prepared, and labeled, some people who receive it may become sick. However, if untreated, rabies leads to death. Because the benefits of the vaccine outweigh the danger, strict liability does not apply. This does not mean that drug manufacturers are automatically protected from any liability. If a drug that causes harm has not been properly tested, prepared, or labeled, the plaintiff may be able to recover damages based on negligence (rather than on strict liability).

Defenses to Strict Liability

There are very few defenses in strict liability cases. The defendant's best strategy may be to argue that the plaintiff should have to prove negligence in a particular case and that sound public policy does not require the use of a strict liability standard. It is almost always more difficult for the plaintiff to win a negligence suit, because there must be proof of the defendant's fault, or breach of duty.

While you do not have to prove fault in a strict liability case, you do have to prove both causation and damages. Therefore, a defendant could try to show that there is no causation or that there are no damages. For example, assume that a person has a heart attack and dies instantly while driving a car with faulty brakes. That person's family might argue that the car manufacturer is strictly liable. However, if the defect (the faulty brakes) did not cause the damage (the heart attack), the manufacturer would not be liable for the driver's death.

In product liability cases, manufacturers or sellers may have a defense if the consumer misuses a product or ignores clear safety warnings. Many courts, however, require manufacturers to anticipate some misuse and to make products safe against any foreseeable misuse. For example, a manufacturer should assume that a stool meant for seating at a kitchen counter might also be used as a step ladder. The stool should be built to hold a person whether seated or standing.

Problem 21.7

In each of the following cases, the injured person sues the manufacturer for damages based on strict liability. Does the defendant have a good defense? Give your reasons.

a. Hannah's parents give her a teddy bear on her sixth birthday. While playing with the teddy bear, she pulls out one of the toy's eyes. The sharp pin that held the eye in place punctures her skin, causing an injury.

b. Marilyn is rushing to complete her housework so she can go out on a date with Andy. To speed up the defrosting of the freezer, she uses a hair dryer. A melting piece of ice hits the hair dryer, and Marilyn receives a serious electric shock. The warning on the dryer says, "Electrocution possible if used or dropped in bathtub. Unplug after using."

Torts and Public Policy

As a matter of public policy, the tort law system should serve to (1) compensate harmed persons in a prompt and efficient way, (2) fairly allocate benefits to victims and costs to wrongdoers, and (3) deter conduct that is unreasonably risky or dangerous. However, some argue that our tort law system does not always meet these goals. Critics generally claim that:

- The amount of money awarded to plaintiffs is sometimes unreasonably high.
- Going to court has become much too expensive with lawyers getting too much of the money awarded.
- Civil courts take too long to resolve disputes.
- Tort law is so complicated that it can be difficult to determine who is at fault.
- The injured party should sometimes receive compensation for a loss, regardless of whether the other party was at fault.

> *"Law reform is far too serious a matter to be left to the legal profession."*
>
> — Leslie Scarman (speech to NYC Bar Association)

Street Law *online*

Visit the *Street Law* Web site at streetlaw.glencoe.com for chapter-based information and resources.

Tort reform has many supporters in the community.

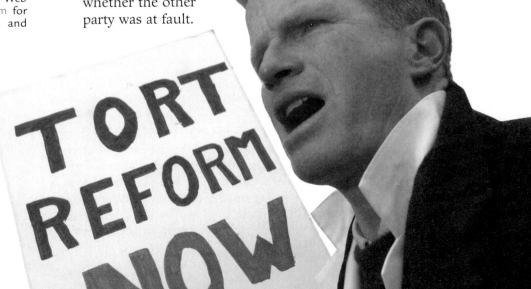

TORT REFORM NOW

Tort Reform

As a result of the concerns listed on the previous page, a movement called **tort reform** has developed. Some efforts at reform target the *process* of settling tort claims. These efforts may require participants to try to settle a tort case before beginning a trial. In some civil courts, for example, the judge is required to ask the parties if they have tried to settle the case outside of court before a trial starts. For some cases, a judge will send the parties to a mediation service in an attempt to settle the case without a trial. Some states have laws—such as no-fault auto insurance—that eliminate the need for civil suits in certain auto accident cases. States are also reducing the amount of time after an injury is suffered that a plaintiff has to bring a case to court.

Other tort reform efforts focus on placing a limit on how much a plaintiff can recover for noneconomic damages. These laws may limit recovery for pain and suffering to a particular amount, such as $250,000. They may also make it more difficult for plaintiffs to win punitive damages, and limit punitive damages in cases where they are awarded.

Some interesting research has been done on tort reform issues. For example, a researcher reviewed court records in one state and also conducted a phone survey of almost 800 residents of that state. The survey examined the residents' views of personal injury litigation.

The residents surveyed estimated that 40 percent of the civil suits filed in their state were personal injury claims. Court records examined over a four-year period showed that fewer than 5 percent of civil suits were tort claims. Over 70 percent of the civil suits filed involved such family law issues as divorce and child custody. While residents thought that the number of cases involving personal injury was on the increase, court records showed that the number of suits filed had remained stable over a four-year period.

From time to time there are news reports of very large damage awards made by juries in tort cases. Not surprisingly, the residents surveyed in the study above estimated that the average damage award in tort cases exceeded $200,000. An examination of court records showed that plaintiffs won only half the time, and when they won, the average award was just under $30,000.

Finally, residents thought that 43 percent of tort cases were settled out of court but believed that 65 percent should be. In reality, 93 percent of the disputes were resolved without going to trial. A national study of tort cases in 75 large urban counties provided similar results. However, the debate over tort reform continues in legislatures.

One hotly debated issue is the handling of medical malpractice cases. Various advocates regularly urge state legislatures and Congress to reform medical liability laws, primarily by limiting the amount of monetary damages a plaintiff can recover in a civil tort suit. As the size of awards increases, the insurance premiums paid by doctors and hospitals rise in an effort to make up for money paid out in lawsuits. At least part of the increased cost of medical malpractice insurance is

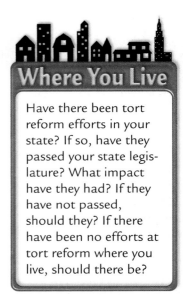

Where You Live

Have there been tort reform efforts in your state? If so, have they passed your state legislature? What impact have they had? If they have not passed, should they? If there have been no efforts at tort reform where you live, should there be?

passed along to patients, who pay these higher costs either directly through higher fees or indirectly through higher health insurance premiums. As medical costs skyrocket, some people cannot afford needed care. In addition, patients with inadequate health insurance are sometimes turned away from hospitals. Doctors who cannot afford malpractice insurance premiums have stopped practicing medicine. Some hospitals have closed their doors.

Some people believe that the present system works well and that high damage awards against doctors and hospitals fairly compensate patients for their injuries. They maintain that medical malpractice can result in permanent injuries or even death to patients. Moreover, they argue that relatively few doctors are responsible for a significant number of the malpractice claims and that the medical profession can and should do much more to identify and discipline these doctors. Those who support the present system also believe that doctors, hospitals, and insurance companies should have to live by the same rules as other defendants in tort cases.

Others contend that the system is out of control because juries sometimes award damages out of proportion to the harm suffered. For example, awards can exceed $1 million. In addition, a large proportion of this money is awarded for punitive damages as opposed to compensating a victim for pain, suffering, and out-of-pocket costs.

Reformers believe that opportunistic patients and greedy lawyers sometimes drag competent doctors through the legal system, hoping to make money from a sympathetic jury. This group argues that in those states that have passed tort reform laws, there has been a decrease in the number of claims filed. Reformers also note a reduction in the dollar amount of jury awards made in those states.

Crash testing has resulted in cars that are both safer and more expensive. *Is greater safety worth a higher price?*

The Cost of Safety

They say that the best things in life are free, but safety is not! There is nearly always some monetary cost involved in making the world a safer place. For instance, people can be injured at concerts. Hiring a security force to monitor people's actions can reduce the chance of injury. But the cost of hiring these people will be passed on to concert-goers in the form of higher ticket prices. Some people who could have gone to the concert at the lower price will not be able to afford a ticket to the more expensive, but safer, concert. However, even a security force cannot guarantee complete safety. So, the best way to ensure injury-free concerts is to cancel them altogether, but many people would say that this is going too far.

The Case of the Pyrotechnics Nightclub Fire

Nightclubs have been the scenes of a number of fire tragedies in U.S. history. When these catastrophes occur, local, state, or federal governments take steps to try to prevent them in the future. Officials examine how laws or regulations were being enforced and, if necessary, propose changes to them. When there is a fire, the issue of who or what caused it and who should be held responsible is important.

As a gift, Shannon bought her boyfriend Philip tickets for a concert by the rock band Extortion, which sometimes uses special effects such as pyrotechnics, or fireworks.

For this concert at Heaven's Gate, a local nightclub, the band brought a pyrotechnic device known as a gerb. A gerb is a paper tube packed with ground aluminum and set on a base. When activated, the base heats up, igniting the aluminum and causing flames to shoot into the air.

A band member set off this device during the first song. The flames set fire to the sound-proofing foam on the walls and ceiling. Panic ensued and about 100 people died. Many others, including a band member, were injured.

Heaven's Gate had four exit doors, but two were locked to keep people from entering without paying. The club's approved capacity is 300; however, 350 people attended the concert. Philip and Shannon first ran for the two exits that were locked. They died trying to reach the other doors.

The club had recently been inspected and met all safety standards, though at the time of the inspection all four exit doors were unlocked.

The band's leader, Bill Black, claims that he asked for and received permission from the club's owner, Will Jones, to use pyrotechnics.

Jones denies that claim. There is nothing in the contract between Heaven's Gate and Extortion that refers to pyrotechnics. State law requires that anyone in the state using fireworks must obtain a permit, but neither the band nor the club had obtained one. Black says that Extortion always asks permission before using pyrotechnics and when club owners say not to use them, they don't. Some club owners where Extortion has played before say the band has used fireworks without asking for permission. Other bands that have played at Heaven's Gate say Will Jones has given them permission to use pyrotechnics.

An expert says the gerb should never have been used in this club, which has low ceilings and no sprinkler system. A sprinkler system could have prevented this tragedy, but state law only requires such systems in buildings constructed after 1972. Heaven's Gate was built in 1957.

Problem 22.1

a. Do you think the club owner is responsible for the deaths and injuries? What should he have done differently? Explain.

b. Do you think Extortion is responsible for the deaths and injuries? What should they have done differently? Explain.

c. What responsibility does the state bear?

d. Do Philip and Shannon bear any responsibility for their own deaths?

e. Assume you are a member of the legislature in the state where this happened. How would you change any of the laws or regulations involving clubs or bands? Draft your proposed changes and give reasons for them.

Sometimes a business does not pay in advance for safety costs, and instead creates a product or performs a service that injures people. When this happens, plaintiffs may sue the business to recover monetary damages. The business may then have to raise its prices to pay these judgments. Whether preventing injuries by paying safety costs, or compensating for injuries by paying for damages, costs are spread to consumers through higher prices at the cash register. In some instances, the cost of lawsuits forces companies to go out of business, depriving consumers of the goods and services the business provided.It is easy to see that all of us pay for additional safety. A more difficult question is, how *much* should we pay for safety?

Generally, tort law requires that a reasonable amount of money be spent on safety. To determine how much is reasonable in a particular instance, one could calculate the benefits of adding a safety precaution (e.g., before air bags were required in automobiles, one could have calculated the savings that would be generated by injury prevention through air bag use). These benefits could be compared to the costs of adding a safety precaution (e.g., how much it would cost to design, manufacture, and install air bags in automobiles). If the benefits exceeded the costs, then it is reasonable to require this safety precaution. If the costs exceeded the benefits, it is unreasonable.

Problem 22.2

Identify three items in your school, home, or community that have the potential to be dangerous. How could each be made safer? Would it be worth the cost in any of these instances? Explain your reasoning.

Like Brooklyn, Ohio, several cities and towns in the United States have passed laws banning the use of cell phones while driving. *Why has this issue become such an important concern for tort reform?*

Law in *Action*

Driving While Yapping (DWY): Should There Be a Law?

Assume that you live in a state without a law regulating the use of cell phones in automobiles. In your state, as elsewhere, more than half of the residents own a cell phone. National surveys show that about half of all drivers have cell phones in their vehicles, and 80 percent of cell phone owners keep their cell phones on at least some of the time when they are driving.

You also know the following facts:

- "Driver distraction" (eating in the car, adjusting the radio, etc.) is the cause of 20 to 30 percent of all car crashes.
- Most states do not collect data on whether cell phones are in use when investigating auto accidents.
- While many states have considered and rejected bans on cell phone use in cars, several municipalities have passed laws. These include prohibiting school bus drivers and taxi drivers from using cell phones. In addition, some municipalities have passed laws that prohibit the use of handheld cell phones only within their city limits.
- Police have been able to catch drunk drivers faster and emergency vehicles have been able to save lives because of calls from cell phone users.

A group of concerned citizens is asking its state legislature to pass a bill that would increase highway safety by limiting or even prohibiting the use of cell phones while driving.

The following groups will testify before a panel of state legislators responsible for deciding whether to have such a law.

Law enforcement groups: They realize that cell phone users help catch unsafe drivers but also believe that cell phone use has caused accidents.

Messengers: They believe they cannot do their job unless they can use cell phones in cars and on bicycles.

Wireless companies: They believe that cell phones can be made safe for use in cars if drivers use devices such as headsets.

Highway safety group: This group believes that cell phones should be used in cars only when the car is not in motion.

Libertarians: They believe that there may be a problem but that the answer is using common sense, not passing more laws. For example, they argue that there are no laws against changing radio stations or eating while driving—activities which may be just as dangerous.

Problem 22.3

a. Assume the role of either the panel of legislators or of one of the interest groups that will testify. Then research the issue to see what other states have done or are in the process of doing.

b. Conduct a hearing in which each interest group makes a brief statement and then answers questions from the panel of legislators. Those testifying should make specific recommendations and also be as responsive as possible to the questions from the legislators.

c. The legislators should draft a law and circulate it to the interest groups for comment. Invite lobbyists, legislators, or other interested citizens from the community to discuss it with the entire class.

d. Share your recommendations with real-world decision makers where you live.

UNIT
4

Consumer
and
Housing
Law

Visit the *Street Law* Web site at streetlaw.glencoe.com for unit-based activities.

Have you ever bought a meal in a restaurant, had your car repaired at a service station, or purchased a product over the Internet? If you did any of these things, you were a consumer. A consumer is a person who buys goods or services from a seller.

For many years, the legal expression caveat emptor, a Latin phrase meaning "let the buyer beware," characterized consumer law. In other words, consumers had to look out for unfair and misleading sales practices before buying, or be prepared to suffer the consequences. Today the law is more balanced. Consumers have the right to be correctly informed of important information such as quality, price, and credit terms. Consumers also have the responsibility of being fair and honest to sellers. A consumer who buys an article of clothing, wears it once to a dance, and then returns it is not being fair and honest. Consumer law establishes a variety of rights and responsibilities to make the marketplace fair for both buyers and sellers.

The Federal Trade Commission is the federal government's primary consumer protection agency.

While most sellers are honest, consumers may sometimes run across a merchant whose practices are not fair, or a product or service that is not of acceptable quality. When this happens, consumer law can help you solve the problem either on your own or, if this fails, with the help of an agency or the court system.

Unit 4 covers many aspects of consumer law, beginning with a study of contracts. You will learn how the law enforces agreements, including those that are implied as well as those that are spoken or written down. Throughout this unit you will learn about specific laws passed and enforced at the federal, state, and local levels to help make the marketplace fair. Some of the most important consumer protection laws you will study provide consumers with warranties, prohibit deceptive sales practices, and forbid unfair credit and collection practices. This unit on consumer and housing law concludes with a focus on two of the most significant consumer transactions young people face: buying a car and obtaining a place to live.

275

Contracts

A **contract** is an agreement between two or more persons to exchange something of value. A contract legally binds parties to do what they promise. A party who fails to live up to such a promise has **breached** the contract. When you agree to buy something, you usually form a legal contract. If you pay to ride a bus to a friend's house or buy a cold drink in the school cafeteria, then you form legally binding contracts because you promise to pay money in exchange for either the bus ride or the cold drink.

The law of contracts reaches into many aspects of our daily lives. For example, when you buy lunch at a restaurant and tickets to see your favorite movie, you are entering into contracts. To protect yourself as a consumer, you need to understand how contracts are formed and how they affect your rights and responsibilities.

"The whole duty of government is to prevent crime and to preserve contracts."

— William Lamb Melbourne, British statesman

Street Law *online*

Visit the *Street Law* Web site at streetlaw.glencoe.com for chapter-based information and resources.

Elements of a Contract

A legally binding contract has certain elements. There must be an **offer** by one party and an **acceptance** by another. An offer must be directed to a specific person. For example, the menu over the counter

A contract is a legally binding agreement.

at a fast-food restaurant listing their prices is not an offer, because it is not directed at anyone in particular. When you place your order, *you* make an offer. When they begin cooking your food, the restaurant has accepted your offer, and a contract has been formed. The law infers acceptance from certain actions, such as signing a contract or beginning to carry out the terms of a bargain.

For a contract to be valid, there must also be an exchange of **consideration.** This means something of value is given for something else of value. For example, when you buy a new shirt at a store, your consideration is the money you pay, and the merchant's consideration is the item you are buying. The items being exchanged do not have to be of the same value. The law allows consumers and merchants to make both good deals and bad deals.

People entering into a contract must be legally competent to make contracts. For example, they cannot be mentally ill or intoxicated. Also, agreements to do something illegal or against public policy are not enforceable.

If Lorenzo says to Christine, "I will sell you my cell phone for $50," this is an offer. If Christine says, "OK" and if she pays the $50 to Lorenzo or if she signs an agreement to pay $50, then there is an acceptance. The exchange of the cell phone for the money is the exchange of consideration. Both parties are competent, and the agreement is not to do something illegal or against public policy. Therefore, a contract has been made.

You should not be too quick to enter into a contract. Be sure you understand and agree with all the terms before you accept them; otherwise, it may be too late to back out of the deal.

Problem 23.1

For each of the following situations, decide whether a contract has been made. Give your reasons.

a. An auctioneer says, "Do I hear a bid for this antique sofa?" Someone in the crowd says, "$300."

b. Yukiko says to Basil, "I'm going to sell my car for $500." Basil replies, "All right, here is the money. I'll take it."

c. The citizens of a small town collect $1,000 and offer it as a reward for the capture of a suspected criminal. The sheriff captures the suspect and seeks the reward.

d. Megan's father promises to pay her $1,000 when she turns 18. On her eighteenth birthday, she seeks the money.

e. Standing at one end of a long bridge, Shelly says to Lynn, "I'll give you $5 if you walk across the bridge." Lynn says nothing but starts walking across the bridge.

f. Liz offers Sharon $100 to steal four hubcaps for her new sports car. Sharon steals the hubcaps from a car dealership, brings them to Liz, and asks for the money.

Minors and Contracts

A minor is a person under the age of legal majority, which is 18 in most states. Minors may make contracts. However, as a general rule, they cannot be forced to carry out their promises and may cancel or refuse to honor their contracts. Minors who cancel contracts usually must return any goods or consideration still in their possession. This rule is designed to protect minors from being taken advantage of because of their age and lack of experience. As a result of this rule, minors may have a tough time getting credit. Many stores require minors to have a parent or other adult cosign any major contract. The adult cosigner is responsible for making payments if the minor does not honor the deal.

Minors may, however, be held to contracts that involve necessities, such as food, clothing, shelter, or medical aid. Minors can be required to pay for the reasonable value of such goods and services.

In most states, a minor who continues making payments on a contract after reaching the age of majority is considered to have ratified the contract. Once the contract has been ratified, it can no longer be canceled without some type of penalty.

Minors often want to buy big-ticket items, such as computers and stereos. *Can minors be held responsible for any contracts they enter into?*

Problem 23.2

Kara, 17, wants a computer of her own. She goes to a local electronics store to purchase a new computer system. The computer costs $950. She offers to put down $150 and make monthly payments on the remaining amount. Because Kara is only 17, the manager of the store refuses to sell her the computer.

a. Is this fair?

b. Is this legal?

c. What concerns might the manager have about selling a computer to a minor?

Written and Oral Contracts

Most contracts may be either written or oral (spoken). However, certain kinds of contracts must be in writing to be enforceable. These include contracts for the sale of land or real estate, contracts for the sale of goods priced at $500 or more, agreements to pay another person's debt, and agreements for services that will not be performed within one year from the date of the agreement.

The law favors written contracts. For your protection, it is always better to have a written contract. Otherwise, it can be difficult to prove that a party promised to do something. If there is a written contract, a court will not consider evidence of promises made before the signing of the contract, except when the written contract is unclear or one party was tricked into entering the contract.

Problem 23.3

Ruth made an oral agreement to sell her used racing bicycle to Mike for $400. A few days later, she got an offer of $600 from Paul and orally accepted this higher offer. Prior to delivering the bicycle, Ruth decided she did not want to sell it anymore. Both Mike and Paul sued her for breach of contract.

a. What will the court do?

b. Is this decision fair?

c. How would the case be different if the agreement with Paul were in writing?

Illegal contracts, such as an agreement to commit a crime, are not enforceable in court. *Describe some other situations in which the court would not enforce a contract.*

Illegal Contracts

Some contracts are unenforceable in court because they are illegal or against public policy. For example, an agreement between two persons for the sale of illegal drugs could never be enforced in court.

In addition, courts sometimes find that a contract is so unfair, harsh, and oppressive that it should not be enforced. Such a contract is considered to be **unconscionable.** Courts will usually not refuse to enforce a contract simply because it requires someone to pay a very high price for something. As noted earlier, the law allows freedom of contract, and consumers are allowed to make bad deals as well as good ones. On rare occasions, though, a court may not enforce an extremely unfair contract (or an unfair clause in a contract).

A court is more likely to find an extremely unfair contract unconscionable when (1) the consumer is presented with a contract on a take-it-or-leave-it basis, and (2) there is very uneven bargaining power between the parties (as when an experienced seller is dealing with an inexperienced consumer). Remember that many contracts that consumers make are based on uneven bargaining power and on a

The Unfair Contract

A furniture store required an unemployed woman on public assistance to sign its standard contract for credit every time she made a purchase at the store. One of the terms of the contract stated that the store would own every item the woman purchased until all the items were fully paid for. The woman made several purchases at the store, signing this same standard contract each time.

After several years of making all her payments, she purchased a stereo and missed two payments. The store believed it had the right, under the contract, to take back all the items the woman had ever purchased there.

A court of appeals found a portion of the contract to be unconscionable and did not enforce this unfair term in the agreement. The woman had to return the stereo, but was able to keep all the items she had already paid for.

Reading a contract carefully

Problem 23.4

a. Why did the court refuse to enforce the entire agreement in this case?

b. Was the court's decision fair to the owner of the furniture store?

c. What should the contract have said to make it fair to both parties?

take-it-or-leave-it basis. Imagine, for example, trying to bargain with the utility company over the price of your electricity. Despite the uneven bargaining power and take-it-or-leave-it basis, the utility company can require you to pay your bill.

Fraud and misrepresentation are also grounds for invalidating a contract. Fraud is a false statement about an important fact that is made to induce, or persuade, a person to agree to a contract. For example, if a sports memorabilia salesperson fakes a famous baseball player's signature on a baseball card and sells it, the unsuspecting buyer can cancel the contract and may win damages in court after uncovering the fraud. Although salespersons may not lie about a product's features, they are usually not required to volunteer information about the negative aspects of a product unless they are asked. Only in rare instances, when a special relationship of trust exists between buyer and seller, will courts require the disclosure of negative information. Therefore, it is important for consumers to examine products carefully and ask a lot of questions before buying.

Warranties

"Those that are most slow in making a promise are the most faithful in the performance of it."

— **Jean-Jacques Rousseau**

A warranty is a promise or guarantee made by a seller about the quality or performance of goods for sale. A warranty may also contain a statement of what the seller will do to remedy the problem if the product does not perform as promised. If the seller does not live up to the promises made in the warranty, the contract has been breached.

Warranties give consumers very important rights. You should always be aware of the warranties that exist when you make a purchase. However, not all warranties are the same, so it is worthwhile to compare warranties when shopping. When you look at a warranty, consider the duration (how long does it last?), the scope (what parts or problems are covered or excluded?), and the remedy (what do you get under the warranty and what must you do to get the remedy?). You should also check your own state's warranty laws. They may give you other rights that are not in the warranty.

Street Law *online*

Visit the *Street Law* Web site at streetlaw.glencoe.com for chapter-based information and resources.

Express Warranties

An express warranty is a statement—written, oral, or by demonstration—concerning the quality or performance of goods offered for sale that becomes a part of the

Smart consumers comparison shop for warranty protection.

bargain between the parties. For example, if a salesperson tells you, "This TV will not need any repairs for five years," the salesperson has created an express warranty. Similarly, an express warranty is created if you purchase a vacuum cleaner from an appliance store after seeing a demonstration of the vacuum picking up small particles from a deep-pile rug. Because oral warranties and warranties by demonstration are difficult to prove, it is always best to get a written warranty.

Express warranties are created by statements of fact. Not everything a seller says is a warranty. If the seller's statement is merely an opinion or an obvious exaggeration, it is considered puffing, or sales talk, and cannot be relied on. For example, a used-car dealer advertising "Fantastic Used Cars" is engaged in puffing. No warranty is created, and no customer should rely on such a statement.

What happens if your TV quits working or your watch won't keep time? The first thing to do is check the warranty. One TV may be guaranteed for 90 days, while another may be covered for a full year. Your warranty may provide a remedy when things go wrong. You may be able to return the item for a refund, exchange it for a replacement, or have it repaired.

Sellers do not have to give written warranties. However, if they do, the *Magnuson-Moss Warranty Act* requires that the written warranties (1) disclose all the essential terms and conditions in a single document, (2) be stated in simple and easy-to-read language, and (3) be made available to the consumer before a sale. Written warranties must also tell you exactly what is included and what is not included. For example, the warranty must explain what repairs are covered and who will make them. The act does not apply to products that cost $15 or less.

Under the *Magnuson-Moss Warranty Act,* warranties are labeled as either full or limited. Under a full warranty:

- A defective product will be fixed or replaced at no cost, including removal and reinstallation, if necessary.
- The consumer will not have to do anything unreasonable (such as shipping a piano to a factory) to get the warranty service.
- The product will be fixed within a reasonable time after the consumer complains.
- If the product cannot be fixed after a reasonable number of attempts, the consumer can get a refund or a replacement.
- The warranty applies to anyone who owns the product during the warranty period (not just the first purchaser).

Any protection less than this is called a limited warranty. Such a warranty usually covers some defects or problems but not others. For example, the limited warranty on a video recorder might cover the cost of new parts but not the labor involved in installing the new parts. Or it might cover only certain parts. To learn what is covered, read the entire warranty carefully.

FIGURE 24.1   One-Year Limited Warranty

Your Excellent Digital Camera Warranty

Excellent Digital Cameras fully guarantees this entire product to owner against defects in material or workmanship for one year from purchase date.

Defective product may be brought or mailed, freight pre-paid, to purchase place, authorized service center, or Service Department, Excellent Digital Cameras, Inc., 3rd & Maple Streets, Arlington, PA 15616, for free repair or replacement at our option.

Warranty does not include cost of inconvenience, damage due to product failure, transportation damages, misuse, abuse, accident, or commercial use.

For information, write Consumer Claims Manager at previously listed Arlington address. Send owner's name, address, name of store or service center involved, model, serial number, purchase date, and description of problem.

This warranty gives specific legal rights. You may have other rights that vary from state to state.

This warranty becomes effective upon purchase. Mailing the enclosed registration card is one way of providing purchase date but is not required for warranty coverage.

Problem 24.1

Read and evaluate the one-year limited warranty for the digital camera above and answer the following questions.

a. Who is making the warranty? Who will make any repairs—dealer, service center, manufacturer, or independent repairer?

b. How long is the warranty in effect? Does the buyer have to do anything to make the warranty effective?

c. What is covered—the entire product or only certain parts? What is promised—repair, replacement, labor, postage? Is this a full or a limited warranty? Why?

Implied Warranties

Many consumers believe they have no protection if a new product without an express warranty does not work. In many cases, however, consumers are protected—even though they may not realize it—by an implied warranty. An implied warranty is an unwritten promise, created by law, that a product will do what it is supposed to do. In other words, the law requires products to meet certain minimum standards of quality and performance, even if no express promise is made. Implied warranties apply only to products sold by bona fide, or authentic, dealers of that product. They do not apply to goods sold by casual sellers. For example, if a friend sells you her bike, no implied warranties are involved. The three types of implied warranties are (1) warranty of merchantability, (2) warranty of fitness for a particular purpose, and (3) warranty of title.

A **warranty of merchantability** is an unwritten promise that the item sold is of at least average quality for that type of item. For example, a radio must play, a saw must cut, and a freezer must keep food frozen. This warranty is always implied unless the seller expressly disclaims it. Be especially wary of goods marked with disclaimers such as "as is" or "final sale." Using a disclaimer, a seller can legally avoid responsibility for the quality of the product.

A **warranty of fitness for a particular purpose** exists when a consumer tells a seller before buying an item that it is needed for a specific purpose or will be used in a certain way. A salesperson who sells an item with this knowledge makes an implied promise that the item will fulfill the stated purpose. For example, suppose you tell a salesperson you want a waterproof watch and the salesperson recommends a watch, which you then buy. An implied warranty of fitness has been created. If you go swimming and water leaks into the watch, the warranty has been breached.

A **warranty of title** is a seller's promise that he or she owns the item being offered for sale. Sellers must own the goods in order to transfer title or ownership to the buyer. If a person sells stolen goods, the warranty of title has been broken.

Consumers who are harmed by products may be able to sue for damages because the manufacturer or seller has breached the warranty. Consumers may also be able to recover damages based either on the negligence of the manufacturer or seller or on a legal theory called **strict liability**. The topic of harm caused by dangerous products is explained more fully in Chapter 21.

You should remember that if you fully examine goods—or have the opportunity to do so—before making a purchase, the implied warranty may not apply to those defects you should have discovered

Car dealers often advertise "certified used cars" to show that they have been inspected and approved by a mechanic. *What warranty protection is typically available when you purchase a used car?*

during the inspection. Therefore, *carefully inspect any goods you buy for defects.* Be especially careful with used cars. It is wise to have a mechanic you trust examine the car before you purchase it.

Problem 24.2

Is a warranty created in any of the following situations? If so, what type of warranty? Has the warranty been broken?

a. Juan sells Terri his used car. As Terri drives home, the car breaks down. The cost of fixing the car is greater than the sale price.

b. Deidre buys a dress after telling the sales clerk that she plans to wash it in a washing machine. The clerk replies, "That's fine. This material is washable." Deidre washes the dress in her washing machine and the dress shrinks.

c. A salesperson tells Neva, "This is the finest digital camera on the market. It will last for years." Eight months later, the button that advances the photos stops working.

d. Scott steals a diamond ring from a jewelry store and sells it to Maria after telling her his mother gave it to him.

e. Trina orders a book from a bookstore's Web site. The Web site says "Hardcover Edition, $12.95," and includes a picture of the book's cover. Five days later, Trina receives the paperback edition of the book in the mail.

f. Ned buys a new sofa from a furniture store. One of the legs falls off two weeks after delivery.

Be sure to carefully read all instructions that come with a product. If you fail to use the product properly, or if you use it for an improper purpose, you may invalidate the warranty.

Disclaimers

A disclaimer is an attempt to limit the seller's responsibilities should anything go wrong with a product. The clause quoted in The Case of the Guitar That Quit (page 286) is a disclaimer. It is an attempt by the store to avoid responsibility for anything that goes wrong with the guitar. The quoted clause makes it clear that an express warranty is not being offered. But does the clause disclaim the implied warranty?

Sellers can usually disclaim the implied warranty of merchantability by using such expressions as "with all faults" or "as is." Unless these or other easily understood words are used, the seller must actually use the word *merchantability* in disclaiming the implied warranty of merchantability. In addition, to be effective, the disclaimer must be written and placed so as to be easily seen by the consumer. Because the sales receipt for the guitar did not say "as is," "with all faults," or

The Guitar That Quit

Shari wants to buy a new guitar. She shops around to compare prices at a few different music stores. City Music offers the best price at $300, so Shari buys the guitar there. On the sales receipt is a clause that reads: "This constitutes the exclusive statement of the terms of agreement between the parties. Seller makes no warranties either express or implied with respect to this product." The third time Shari plays the guitar, the neck breaks.

Problem 24.3

a. What should Shari do? What should the store do?

b. Assume there is a large sign by the cash register that reads: **All Guitars Sold "AS IS."** How would you react to such a sign?

Guitars for sale

"merchantability," it is probably not effective as a disclaimer of the implied warranty of merchantability. Shari should be protected if she returns the guitar.

Under the *Magnuson-Moss Warranty Act,* sellers offering a written warranty may not disclaim or modify any implied warranty during the effective period of the written warranty. No matter how broad the written warranty is, the customer will always receive the basic protection of the implied warranty of merchantability. A warranty of merchantability is a promise that the product does what it is intened to do.

Sellers sometimes use disclaimers to limit the consumer's remedy. For example, a contract may read, "It is expressly understood and agreed that the buyer's only remedy shall be repair or replacement of defective parts. The seller is not liable in damages for injury to persons or property." Suppose the warranty limits the remedy to "repair or replacement of defective parts" and this remedy is not sufficient. That is, after repeated attempts at repair, the product still does not work. In such cases, the buyer can usually seek other remedies, for example, getting a refund. However, courts will usually require that the buyer give the seller a reasonable opportunity to repair the product.

Credit and Other Financial Services

"Creditors have better memories than debtors."

— Benjamin Franklin

Consumers have three primary sources from which to pay for goods and services in the marketplace: cash, bank accounts (including checking and savings), and **credit.** Everyone knows what cash is, and virtually all sellers accept it. But it is not always convenient to use cash as a method of payment in today's global marketplace. Bank accounts and credit offer consumers convenient alternatives to paying cash for goods and services. However, the largely electronic nature of bank accounts and credit sometimes presents more complex problems for consumers. In addition, when using a bank account or credit—unlike times that you use cash— there is no physical reminder of how many dollars and cents you have rattling around in your pocket to spend. There are also special risks associated with these financial arrangements. This chapter will focus on the use of bank accounts and the payment devices associated with them as well as the use of credit to pay for goods and services.

Street Law online

Visit the *Street Law* Web site at streetlaw.glencoe.com for chapter-based information and resources.

Credit cards offer consumers a convenient alternative to cash.

The Basics About Bank Accounts

Checking and savings accounts are the primary types of bank accounts that people use to manage their money on a daily basis. Banks offer checking accounts to consumers as convenient places to deposit cash and checks for safekeeping, and from which the consumer can easily withdraw money to pay bills and make purchases. To withdraw money, an account holder can write checks to vendors and creditors, use an automatic teller machine (ATM) card to withdraw cash directly from the account, or make purchases using debit cards (another type of ATM card). Many smart consumers also open savings accounts into which they deposit a certain amount of money each month. Although an account holder can link an ATM or debit card to a savings account, many believe it is better to limit daily access to savings accounts so that money is available in case of an emergency. Smart consumers also use savings accounts as a way to save up for a special purchase or vacation.

The key to maintaining a checking account is to record all deposits and withdrawals in the check register so that you do not spend more than what is in the account. Many banks offer overdraft protection, which assures the account holder that checks written on and debits made from the account up to the limit of the overdraft protection will be honored. This service is like a line of credit and is typically offered only to customers with a good credit history and for a certain amount—up to $1,000, for example. Interest is charged, usually on a daily basis, until the line of credit is repaid.

Smart consumers should review monthly bank statements and accounts for all checks written. *What is overdraft protection? How does it work?*

Banks are required by law to provide account holders with periodic information regarding their bank accounts. For a checking account, this often includes the canceled checks you have written on your account (meaning they have been paid and returned to your bank), and a monthly statement detailing the status and activity on your account during that period, including all deposits and withdrawals of any kind. It is important that you review these statements to ensure that there has been no unauthorized activity on your account.

If you encounter a problem with an electronic funds transfer (EFT) or debit card transaction on your monthly statement, the *Electronic Fund Transfer Act* provides you with protection if the errors are of a computational nature. Two examples are withdrawals of the wrong amount or unauthorized withdrawals. You must file a written complaint within 60 days of the date the statement was mailed. The bank must investigate the error within 10 business days, but it can take up to 45 days in most situations if the bank credits the amount in dispute to your account during the investigation. If no error is found at the end of the investigation, the bank can take back the money it credited to you provided that it sends you a written explanation. If you do not notify your bank within 60 days after your statement with the error is sent to you, you could lose the total amount in question in your account and more.

Banking Fees

Banks usually charge fees for having a checking account, so it is important for consumers to shop around for the best deal. Some accounts are free and some carry a monthly service charge. Standard charges often include fees for ordering checks, writing too many checks (over a minimum decided upon at the time you open the account), failing to keep a minimum average amount in the checking account throughout the month, and for bouncing checks because there was not enough money in the account. You may also be charged a small fee by your bank to use ATMs that it does not operate, as well as a "guest" fee by the bank that does.

Transactions with an ATM card are deducted from your checking account. *What are the advantages to using an ATM card?*

ATM and Debit Cards

In recent years, many banks have offered their customers electronic funds transfer cards—more commonly known as automatic teller machine (ATM) cards—as an alternative to writing checks or having to go into a bank to withdraw money from an account. These embossed plastic cards look like a credit card, but are connected to a bank account designated by the holder of the card. They allow you to withdraw money from your bank account by using an automatic teller machine. They may also allow you to make "point-of-sale" purchases for food, gasoline, clothing or other items at stores, using your personal identification number (PIN). The amount of your purchase is instantly deducted from your bank account. For example, when you purchase gasoline using your ATM card, the amount of the purchase is transferred immediately from your bank account to the gas station's bank account.

Banks also regularly issue debit cards, commonly called "check cards," to their customers as a convenient way to make purchases without the added costs associated with credit cards. Debit cards look like credit cards, complete with your name, the credit card company symbol, a unique 16-digit account number, and an expiration date. However, debit cards are not credit cards and do not have the same legal protections as credit cards. Debit cards may be used anywhere that major credit cards are accepted, and are used to make purchases in exactly the same way as a credit card. The difference is instead of borrowing the money and paying interest on a balance as you would on a line of credit, the amount of the purchase is deducted directly from your bank account, and the total amount you can spend is limited to your account balance. As with a credit card transaction, you will be required to sign a receipt when making a purchase with your debit card. The amount of the purchase will be deducted from your bank account, usually within a couple of days.

Lost and Stolen Checkbooks and Bank Cards

Carrying a checkbook is safer than carrying cash because only the authorized signers on the account are allowed to use checks to withdraw funds from the account. If you lose a checkbook or it is stolen, you must notify your bank and ask them to cancel all of the checks in the book. This is called stop payment. By law, the bank may charge you a small fee to stop payment on a check, but it cannot charge you to stop payment on each of the checks in your checkbook if it is lost or stolen.

Although carrying bank cards is typically safer than carrying cash, there are significant risks to consumers if an ATM or debit card is stolen or lost. Because ATM cards generally require the use of a PIN

For Your Information . . .

Personal Identification Numbers

ATM cards and some debit and credit cards require you to choose a personal identification number (PIN) in order to retrieve cash from cash machines. To avoid fraudulent withdrawals from your account, you should never give out your PIN. Do not write your PIN on your card or carry it in the same purse or wallet that you carry your card in. Your PIN should be easy for you to remember, but not something too simple like sequential numbers or your birth date that others could easily figure out. Some customers prefer to use cards that have a PIN, as these cards are harder to use if stolen.

The Case of . . .

The Lost Wallet

Bridget went to the beach on a sunny Saturday afternoon, where her wallet fell out of her beach bag. On Monday morning, she realized that her wallet was gone when she reached into her bag for bus fare. Worried that someone might be using her cards, she looked up her checking account balance online, but learned that no unauthorized purchases had been made using her debit card.

Unfortunately, when she called her credit card company, she discovered that $500 had already been charged to her account. Bridget was so upset about the purchases on her credit card that she forgot to call her bank to notify them of the lost debit card.

Problem 25.1

a. What amount, if any, is Bridget liable for on her credit card?

b. Suppose she goes to make a withdrawal from her bank account on Thursday, and finds that all of the money—$755—in her account is gone. What if she immediately notifies the bank about the problem? Would she have been better off to notify the bank on Monday when she discovered that her debit card was gone?

c. Do you think a consumer's liability should be different for lost credit cards than for lost debit cards? Why or why not?

d. Why might a bank agree to provide better protection to its customers than what is required by law?

. . . .

to access cash from an account, it is more difficult for someone to make unauthorized withdrawals using your card if you keep your PIN secret. On the other hand, a debit card is used like a credit card and does not require the use of a special code. Thus, anyone can use your debit card as they would a credit card and can potentially drain all of the money out of your bank account.

With lost or stolen credit cards, your liability is limited to $50 no matter when you discover the loss. By contrast, your liability for lost or stolen ATM or debit cards depends on how quickly you notify your bank. If you notify the bank within two business days of discovering a lost or stolen ATM card, you cannot be charged more than $50. As with errors in your bank statement, if you discover unauthorized use of your card and notify your bank within 60 calendar days of the date your statement was mailed, your liability is limited to $500. If, however, you fail to notify your bank within this 60-day period, your potential loss is unlimited. Although banks are prohibited from imposing greater liability on a consumer than what is provided for under the law, a bank may voluntarily provide greater protection by reducing a consumer's potential loss in the event of a stolen ATM or debit card. Make certain you understand your bank's rules regarding your potential liability for your ATM and debit cards. You should also read your monthly bank statement carefully to monitor your account for unauthorized activity.

An Introduction to Credit

Using credit means buying goods or services now in exchange for a promise to pay in the future. It also means borrowing money now in exchange for a promise to repay it in the future. People who lend money or provide credit are called **creditors**. People who borrow money or buy on credit are called **debtors**. Debtors usually pay creditors additional money over the amount borrowed for the privilege of using the credit. This additional money owed to the creditor is called the **finance charge**. It is based on the **interest** charged plus other fees.

The two general types of credit are unsecured and secured. **Unsecured credit** is credit extended in exchange for a promise to repay in the future. The consumer is not required to pledge property in order to obtain the credit. Most credit cards and store charge accounts are examples of unsecured credit.

Secured credit is credit for which the consumer must put up some property of value—called **collateral**—as protection in the event the debt is not repaid. A borrower who does not make the required payments is said to default on the loan. If a borrower defaults on a secured loan, the lender can take the collateral.

For example, a person who buys an automobile may be required by the lender (often a bank) to post the car as collateral until the debt is paid off. If the buyer fails to pay off the loan, the lender can repossess and sell the car, using the proceeds of this sale to pay off the debt.

How Credit Works

Today, many stores and companies (including banks) issue credit cards and allow their customers to maintain charge accounts. Consumers can use credit cards to buy gasoline, go out to dinner, buy clothing, pay bills, and many other things. Some of these cards can also be used to obtain cash advances from banks and bank machines.

Credit cards are embossed with the account holder's name and identification number. They entitle the holder to buy goods or services on credit. Some companies provide these cards free of charge, while others charge a yearly fee, typically between $15 and $75. All lenders charge interest on unpaid balances. Consumers are usually given a credit limit and can make purchases up to that limit. If you exceed that limit, the creditor may or may not permit the charge

Some consumers use credit cards for everyday things such as food and gasoline, while others use credit cards for big-ticket items only. *What is an annual percentage rate?*

to go through; even if they do, they may impose an over-limit fee. You should be aware of your credit limit and be sure to stay within that amount. Exceeding your credit limit could lead to a negative credit report and/or termination of your credit account.

Companies issuing credit cards send out monthly statements indicating how much you owe. Most credit card and charge accounts allow you to pay bills over time, making a minimum monthly payment. You then pay interest on the unpaid portion of the bill. The interest rate can be as high as 18 to 21 percent on unpaid balances. Often, if you pay the entire amount on or before the due date indicated on the bill, there is no extra charge. However, some companies impose interest charges from the date of the transaction. A few require full payment of money owed each month.

Companies use different methods to compute interest. However, you may be able to estimate the monthly interest charge by multiplying the balance owed by the monthly rate. For example, if the monthly interest rate is 1.5 percent, you will multiply by .015. Suppose you owe a balance of $500. The monthly interest charge will be about $7.50 ($500 × .015), and the total amount owed for the month will be approximately $507.50 ($500 + $7.50 interest). It is important to remember that different companies use various methods of calculating the balance on which interest is charged. The interest you estimate that you owe may differ considerably from the amount your credit card company calculates that you actually owe.

To more easily compare the rates charged by different companies, you can ask what **annual percentage rate (APR)** is charged. This rate is calculated the same way by all lenders. The APR is the percentage cost of credit on a yearly basis. Federal law requires creditors to give the APR when consumers ask about the cost of credit.

Choosing a Credit Card Wisely

When deciding which credit cards or charge accounts to maintain, you should find out the annual fee, if any; the percentage rate charged on money owed; and whether interest is charged from the date of the transaction or only on balances unpaid at the end of the billing period. Providers of credit compete with each other to get new customers. Some offer credit without a fee or at very low interest for a certain period of time. Some have agreements with airlines through which frequent flyer miles can be earned and redeemed for airline tickets or other merchandise. Others provide cash rebates, insurance benefits, logos of popular sports teams, or the status of a particular card color (e.g., silver, gold or platinum). Annual interest rates may vary by 10 percentage points or more, so it pays to shop very carefully for credit. Once you establish yourself as a creditworthy customer, you can try to negotiate a lower interest rate. Some companies will significantly reduce their interest rate as a show of goodwill to their long-term customers.

Credit cards are in such wide use today that certain goods and services may be difficult to obtain without one. For example, some car rental companies will not rent to people without a major credit card. While credit cards are an important convenience for many consumers, others may use their cards repeatedly to obtain "instant loans." They may regularly purchase goods and services with credit cards, but then be unable to pay the balance at the end of the month or for some time. The interest rate on unpaid credit card balances is almost always higher than the interest on a bank loan, so using credit cards is not a smart way to borrow money on a regular basis.

Credit card companies compete for your business by offering low interest rates, no annual fees, or low APR. *How might you be able to negotiate a lower interest rate on a credit card?*

Lost and Stolen Credit Cards

If your credit card is lost or stolen, you should report it immediately to the credit card company. For protection, any person with credit cards should keep a list of the following information for each card: (1) the name of the company issuing the card, (2) the account number on the card, and (3) the number to call if the card is lost or stolen. Some people recommend photocopying both sides of all credit cards and keeping these records in a safe spot.

If your credit card is lost or stolen, you are not responsible for any unauthorized charges made after you have notified the issuer that the card is missing. Although federal law limits your liability for charges made before notification to $50 per card, many card issuers waive this fee as a way of competing for business. If your card itself was not used but the thief obtained your credit card number and made unauthorized charges, you are not responsible for any of those charges.

Billing Errors

Billing errors can be a real problem. It takes time and energy to sort them out, and they can cost you money if you do not discover them right away. To avoid billing problems, check all sales slips, save receipts and canceled checks, and go over each bill or monthly statement carefully.

If you do encounter a problem, the *Fair Credit Billing Act* provides you with a measure of protection. This law requires that if you complain *in writing* about your erroneous monthly statement within 60 days of the date the statement was mailed, creditors must acknowledge and respond to your complaint within 90 days. Phone calls do not protect your rights under this act. The written complaint must include your name, address, account number, and the nature and amount of the error. You may withhold payment of the disputed amount pending the investigation; however, undisputed amounts must be paid as normally required. Until your complaint is settled, the law forbids the creditor from reporting the matter to a credit bureau.

If it is determined that the bill is correct, you may have to pay a finance charge on the unpaid amount in dispute. However, a creditor who does not follow the requirements of the law may not collect the first $50 of the disputed amount, even if the bill turns out to be accurate. A consumer can sue such a creditor for damages and can also recover attorney's fees.

When Should You Use Credit?

To make an informed decision about a credit purchase, you must first answer this question: Is it worth having a car, television, vacation, or other item before you have saved enough money to pay the entire purchase price, even though you will pay more for the item in the long run?

Most American families answer yes to this question. In fact, many American families are seldom debt free. More than 75 percent of American families carry some kind of debt. In 2001, more than 44 percent of credit card holders carried a balance, and for those families the average monthly unpaid balance was $1,900.

Extensive use of credit is here to stay, but consumers should know that credit purchases usually cost more than cash purchases. In addition, studies show that consumers who use credit spend more and buy more often. This is the reason many merchants offer "easy credit." Furthermore, consumers who buy on credit risk losing their products, and their previous payments, if they fail to make the required payments.

As a general rule, consumers who spend more than 20 percent of their take-home salary to pay off debts (excluding mortgages) are using too much credit. Consumers who skip payments to cover living expenses or who take out new loans to cover old loans are also using too much credit.

Paying for College

In the 1999–2000 academic year, 16.5 million students were enrolled in colleges and universities in the United States. More than half of them received some kind of financial aid, including one-third who relied on student loans to pay the cost of attending school. Those

The responsibility of paying for college provides some young people with their first experience of credit and debt. *What are important issues to consider when borrowing money for school?*

FIGURE 25.1 A Billing Statement

PAYMENTS SHOULD BE ADDRESSED TO
UNITED VIRGINIA BANK CARD CENTER
7818 PARHAM RD. P.O. BOX 27182
RICHMOND, VIRGINIA 23270

ACCOUNT NUMBER
4366-040-878-000

CREDIT LIMIT	CREDIT AVAILABLE
2,500	1,831.28

CUSTOMER REPRESENTATIVE TELEPHONE NUMBER

(804) 270-8474

INQUIRIES SHOULD BE ADDRESSED TO
UNITED VIRGINIA BANK CARD CENTER
7818 PARHAM RD P.O. BOX 27172
RICHMOND, VIRGINIA 23261

UNITED VIRGINIA BANK CARD
STATEMENT

STATEMENT CLOSING DATE
02/12/05

JOHN Q. CONSUMER
1000 MAIN STREET
ANYWHERE, USA

POSTING DATE	REFERENCE NUMBER	TRANSACTION DATE	TRANSACTION DESCRIPTION			AMOUNT	
01 18	*76145324	01 07	DODGE STATE PARK	FT WAYNE	IN	30	03
01 25	*81983773	01 03	ECONOMY HOTEL, INC.	ASHVILLE	NC	69	71
02 08	21575724	01 27	THRIFTY MOTEL	SOUTH HILL	VA	56	51
02 09	22161982	02 05	SNAP SHOT CAMERA	WASHINGTON	DC	125	67
02 09	56672234	02 04	THE PASTA HOUSE	CHERRY HILL	NJ	46	92
			FINANCE CHARGE – LATE PAYMENT FEE			10	00

Your account is past due.
Please pay the minimum amount due to avoid further finance charges and possible harm to your credit record. If your payment has already been mailed, please accept our thanks.

VISA. **VISA.**

TYPE OF CREDIT	PREVIOUS BALANCE		CREDITS		PAYMENTS		NEW TRANSACTIONS		PERIODIC RATES	CORRESPONDING ANNUAL PERCENTAGE RATES	BALANCE ON WHICH COMPUTED		FINANCE CHARGE		NEW BALANCE	
ADVANCES		00		00		00		00	1.66%	19.99%		00		00		00
OTHER EXTENSIONS OF CREDIT	425	00		00	100	00	338	84	1.50%	18.0%	325	00	4	88	668	72
TOTALS	425	00		00	100	00	338	84	ANNUAL PERCENTAGE RATE	18.0%	325	00	4	88	668	72

PAST DUE	20	00
CURRENT DUE	20	00
MINIMUM PAYMENT DUE	40	00

171870
TO PAY IN INSTALLMENTS
PAY THIS AMOUNT
BY THE PAYMENT
DUE DATE

DUE DATE
03/12/05

To avoid additional
FINANCE CHARGES on
other extensions of
credit, pay this amount
by the payment due
date.

<u>NOTICE:</u> SEE REVERSE SIDE FOR IMPORTANT INFORMATION

Problem 25.2

Examine the billing statement above and answer the following questions.

a. Who is the creditor? Who is the debtor?

b. What is the new balance? How did the creditor arrive at the new balance?

c. How much credit is available? How did the creditor determine the available credit?

d. Assume the debtor had a store receipt from the camera shop for $77.67. Draft a letter to the creditor about this billing error.

borrowers who graduated from four-year universities left school with an average of $17,000 in student loan debt.

Student loans are often a young person's first exposure to the world of credit and debt. Both private and government-sponsored student loan programs often provide the only means for students to attend college, thus providing a great public benefit. Student loans, however, create debt that must be managed and paid back, just like a credit card bill or a car loan. Borrowers default on student loans just as they do on other commercial loans. While lenders make it relatively easy for students to obtain loans to pay for college, it is important for students and their parents to minimize the amount of loans they take out. Because borrowers who do not finish school are more likely to default on student loans than those who do finish school, it is also very important to decide how committed you are to attending and graduating from college. In deciding whether and how much to borrow for school, you should carefully consider the following:

Student loan programs are available from private lenders as well as the federal government. *What are the advantages of federal student loans?*

- What is the total owed for tuition, fees, and books?
- How much will living expenses be? Will you be living at home? On campus? In an apartment alone or with roommates? How will you pay for your meals?
- Are there other sources of income that will help pay your expenses? Can your parents contribute anything? Will you have a job during school? Do you have any money in savings? How much can you save from working over the summer?
- How will you pay back your loans once you finish school?

The good news is that student loan programs are quite borrower-friendly. Various loan programs exist, including those where either a parent or the student is the borrower. Others allow the student to be the primary borrower, but require a co-borrower as added assurance that the loan will be paid back. A co-borrower is someone who promises to pay the debt in the event the student defaults on the loan. Many banks and universities offer private loans to pay for education expenses. However, the vast majority of students—97 percent in 1999–2000—take out federal student loans, which have very low interest rates ranging between 3.5 and 8.25 percent and offer other significant advantages. For example, repayment of student loans can be deferred while you are in school, and many lenders offer grace periods, forbearance periods (if you encounter a difficult financial situation during the repayment period), consolidation programs, and graduated payment programs that allow your payments to start out low and increase as your income increases.

You can get more information about student loan programs from any college or university, as well as online from private lenders, loan servicing companies, and the federal government. The following government Web sites are a good starting place to learn about student loan programs:

- Visit FAFSA (Free Application for Federal Student Aid) online at www.fafsa.ed.gov.
- The U.S. Department of Education also provides online information at www.ed.gov.

You may also want to use an Internet search engine to find the Web sites for colleges and universities, private lenders, and loan servicing companies.

For Your Information . . .

Students and Credit Cards

More students have credit cards than ever before. Companies aggressively market credit cards to college students, often setting up booths on campuses and offering free gifts for applying. They may also mail preapproved application forms and offer discounts on items students are particularly interested in. Some students get credit cards just for the free gifts offered.

While students may plan to destroy the cards, they sometimes keep them, accumulating multiple cards and unrealistically high credit limits. Initially attractive interest rates often may last for only a limited time. While having one credit card may be useful, carrying many cards can be an invitation to trouble.

Students can quickly accumulate thousands of dollars in debt by:
- paying only the minimum on each card,
- paying off one credit card debt by using another credit card (and never lowering the total amount owed), and
- failing to exercise restraint.

With most college students already taking out loans to finance their education, additional credit card debt can put students in a very deep financial hole.

Failure to make timely payments can also contribute to a negative credit rating, which has the potential to harm you in the future. For example, some employers will not hire job applicants with a bad credit history.

Problem 25.3

a. What are the advantages of taking out student loans rather than using credit cards to pay for college expenses?

b. How might a person determine whether it is worth incurring debt in order to attend college?

The Cost of Credit

As mentioned earlier, you should shop for credit just as you shop for products and services, by comparing costs and the terms of the agreement. The cost of credit includes interest and other finance charges. Because there are different methods for calculating interest rates, always ask for the annual percentage rate (APR). This number is calculated the same way by all lenders, so you can use it to compare rates.

Interest Rates

Each state sets limits on the amount of interest that can be charged for various types of credit. Charging any amount above the legal limit is called usury. Lenders who charge interest rates above the legal maximum may be liable for both civil and criminal penalties.

Interest rate ceilings vary from state to state. Generally, however, loans from banks or finance companies carry interest rates of 10 to 30 percent per year. Department stores often charge about 1.5 percent per month, or about 18 percent per year, but these rates can vary widely depending on the lender and the economic conditions at the time. Installment contracts for consumer goods such as new cars or furniture also vary widely.

Many major credit card companies now offer variable interest rates. With a variable rate, the amount of interest you are charged changes slightly from time to time. Your rate is computed based on conditions in the economy and can go up or down with the changing economy.

Typical variable interest rates for new credit card holders range from 19.9 to 23.9 percent. These rates may be lowered over time if your credit is good, but the rates can also go up if your bank thinks you are a credit risk. Borrowers should carefully review the information provided by the lender to determine how often the rate can change and how much it can change at each adjustment, as well as over the entire term of the loan. When the rate changes, your minimum required payments will also change. While your payments may start out low, they could increase over time if the rate goes up.

Other Charges

In addition to the interest paid on a credit sale, other charges sometimes may be added onto the basic price. Some of these services are offered as options by credit card companies, but others are unavoidable costs of having credit. These costs include:

- **Credit property insurance**—Insures the purchased item against theft or damage.
- **Credit life/disability insurance**—Guarantees payment of some or all of the balance due if the buyer should die or become disabled during the term of the contract.
- **Service charge**—Covers the seller's cost of bookkeeping, billing, and so on.
- **Penalty charge**—Covers the seller's inconvenience in case of late payments. May include court costs, repossession expenses, and attorney's fees. In addition, many credit card companies increase your interest rate if you fail to make timely payments.

Problem 25.4

Choose an item you would like to have but could purchase only by using credit.

a. Name at least two institutions where you could shop for this credit.

b. What is the APR for each creditor? What other finance charges are required? Are there any optional changes?

Costly Credit Arrangements

Consumers may fall prey to loan sharking. Loan sharks are people who lend money at high, often usurious (illegal) rates of interest. They promise "easy credit" and appeal to people who have problems

The Case of . . .

The 50/50 Credit Plan

Linda wants to buy a new washing machine. The sales clerk at The Washer Mart tells Linda, "This washing machine is a good buy—only $500. But don't worry if you don't have the cash. I can arrange easy credit for you; only $50 down and $50 a month for 12 months. Just sign here." Linda signs the paperwork and pays $50.

Problem 25.5

a. What is the total price Linda will pay for this washing machine if the contract calls for 12 monthly payments of $50 each? How much of this is interest? What is the annual interest rate? Is this a fair price?

b. What might happen if Linda misses a payment to The Washer Mart?

c. Would it be better for Linda to buy the washing machine on her credit card, which charges monthly interest of 1.5 percent (18 percent annually)?

obtaining and keeping a good credit standing. Usurious loans are illegal under state laws. There are, however, a variety of legal but costly credit arrangements that consumers may want to avoid.

Some creditors call for **balloon payments** in their agreements. In such agreements, the last payment is much larger than the monthly payments. Consumers may find it difficult to make the final payment. You should carefully consider any agreement that calls for a large final payment. Be sure you can save up enough to make this payment. If you cannot make this payment, you may have to return the item to the seller even though you have made all of the other required payments.

When shopping for credit, you should compare the costs and the terms of the agreement. *What charges are included in the cost of credit?*

Another feature to watch for in financing agreements is the **acceleration clause.** This clause permits the creditor to accelerate the loan, making all future payments due immediately in the event a consumer misses a single payment. Most auto sales finance agreements have acceleration clauses. If you miss a payment, you may suddenly owe the creditor the entire amount of the loan. Many cars are repossessed by lenders for this reason.

You should also beware of **bill consolidation.** This means combining all your debts into a single one. Lenders sometimes claim you can wipe out all your bills by making one easy monthly payment to them, which they will distribute to your creditors. However, the consolidation loan may require payments over a longer period of time and at a higher rate of interest. Some lenders also charge a substantial fee for these loans. They may subtract the fee from your monthly payment to them before paying off your creditors, so you wind up falling deeper in debt.

Credit unions may offer the best terms to borrowers who want to consolidate debts, as they may lend you an amount sufficient to pay off all your bills. Then the credit union becomes your only creditor. Depending on your creditworthiness, they may also offer you a better interest rate than other lenders. Investigate any loan consolidation plan carefully, analyzing the terms of such a loan.

Truth in Lending

To prevent credit abuses, Congress passed the *Truth in Lending Act.* This law requires creditors to give you certain basic information about the cost of buying on credit. The creditor must tell you— *in writing and before you sign a contract*—the finance charge and the annual percentage rate. The finance charge is the total amount you pay to use the credit, including interest charges and any other fees. The APR is the percentage cost of credit on a yearly basis.

The law also requires creditors to give you special information about variable-rate loans if you are being offered this type of plan. Remember that with such a plan, your payments may increase over time.

Additionally, the law requires that consumers be given a copy of the disclosure form containing the credit information. Consumers must also be told the rules and charges for any late payments. Violators can be subject to both civil and criminal penalties, and consumers who sue creditors under this act may recover damages, court costs, and attorney's fees.

What Lenders Want to Know Before Extending Credit

Any store, bank, or credit card company that lends money or extends credit to consumers wants to know that the money will be repaid. Before making a loan, the lender will want to know several things about the consumer:

- Is the consumer a reliable person? For example, a person who moves or changes jobs frequently might not be considered reliable.
- Does the consumer have a steady income that is likely to continue into the future?
- Is the consumer's income high enough to enable him or her to pay for the items to be purchased?
- Does the consumer have a good record (credit rating) in paying off other loans and bills?

Lenders are in business to make money; thus, it is understandable that they would ask questions such as these. However, lenders have sometimes unfairly denied credit and loans for reasons such as the applicant's race, gender, or source of income (such as public assistance or alimony). A federal law, the *Equal Credit Opportunity Act,* protects consumers against credit discrimination based on sex, marital status, race, color, religion, national origin, age, or source of income. The Federal Trade Commission handles credit discrimination complaints against finance companies, retail stores, oil companies, and travel and entertainment credit card companies. Bank regulatory agencies, such as the Federal Reserve Board, the Comptroller of the Currency, and others handle complaints against banks and bank credit cards. If you think you have been discriminated

Lenders make credit decisions based on information provided on loan applications. *Describe the things a lender may want to know before extending credit to a consumer.*

against, you may complain to one of these agencies or sue the creditor in court.

Many states also have their own laws that forbid credit discrimination. Complaints should be directed to the state or local consumer affairs office or human rights commission.

What to Do If You Are Denied Credit

If you ever apply for credit, the lender or creditor will evaluate your application according to certain standards. They may investigate you personally or may pay a credit bureau to check your credit record. Many do both. Credit bureaus operate nationwide, and often share financial and personal information about consumers. The Internet has resulted in an increased amount of information about consumers available to lenders and creditors. Information in a credit bureau's files can be a key factor in determining whether you get loans, credit cards, or other forms of credit in the future.

If a credit report indicates that you are a high credit risk, the creditor will probably deny credit or offer credit on less favorable terms. Also, if you are trying to get credit for the first time and have no credit record at all, the lender may deny credit. Sometimes lenders deny credit or a loan based solely on information in the application, without taking the time to order a credit report.

Problem 25.6

You are a loan officer at a local bank. Each of the following people is seeking a loan. Based on the information provided, evaluate each applicant and make a decision regarding each loan request. Discuss your reasons for granting or denying credit.

a. Erika Campbell is the mother of four children. Her only income consists of public assistance payments of $1,020 per month and $100 per month from the pension of her deceased husband. She wishes to buy a new oven and refrigerator totaling $1,100. She lives in a public housing development where her rent and other expenses usually total about $950 a month.

b. Jerry Levitt is a carpenter seeking work wherever he can find it. Depending on the weather and other factors, he is subject to seasonal unemployment. He currently brings home about $1,200 per month, but has no money in the bank. His monthly expenses include car and insurance payments of $350, minimum credit card payments of $50, and rent of $500. He would like to borrow $7,500 to buy a motorcycle.

c. Barbara Griego, 20, is in her second year of college. She has excellent grades and plans to attend medical school after graduation. Until recently, her parents paid her bills, but she is now on her own. She is seeking $4,000 for her college tuition and expenses. She has never borrowed money before, but she plans to repay all loans after finishing medical school.

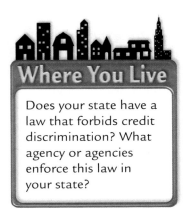

Where You Live

Does your state have a law that forbids credit discrimination? What agency or agencies enforce this law in your state?

The *Equal Credit Opportunity Act* says that creditors and lenders must tell consumers why they were turned down. The reasons given must be specific. For example, "applicant does not meet our standards" is not specific enough. On the other hand, "insufficient income" is a specific reason. It tells you how your circumstances must change to qualify for credit.

Another federal law protects you from inaccurate credit bureau reporting. The *Fair Credit Reporting Act* requires creditors who deny credit based on information received from a credit bureau to tell you that fact. The creditor must also give you the name and address of the credit bureau that supplied the report.

Every consumer has the right to learn what is in his or her credit file. Although credit bureaus are not required to disclose any credit ratings or risk score they assign to a consumer, they must disclose the nature and substance of the information contained in the report. A consumer must submit a request for his or her credit report *in writing*. A small fee is often required by the bureau.

If you discover false, misleading, incomplete, or out-of-date information in your file, you can request *in writing* that the credit bureau recheck its information and correct the errors. The credit bureau is required by law to make such corrections. If the credit bureau does not cooperate in correcting your credit file, you may complain to the Federal Trade Commission or sue the bureau in court. If after reinvestigating the information the bureau still believes that it is correct, you have the right to have your version of the dispute inserted in the file. If the information being reported about you is accurate, the credit bureau can report it for seven years. After this period of time the consumer can usually have this information removed from the file.

Default and Collection Practices

Consumers who use credit sometimes have difficulty making all their payments. Problems can arise because the consumer is overextended or too deeply in debt. Problems can also arise because of unexpected unemployment, family illness, or a variety of other reasons. A consumer who is unable or unwilling to pay a debt is said to be in default.

What a Consumer Can Do in Case of Default

If you have problems paying your bills, you should consider the following options:

- Reassess your financial lifestyle to determine how the problem arose. If you are not already on a budget, consider starting one.
- Notify each creditor of the problem and ask to have the term of debt extended (resulting in smaller monthly payments) or to have the amount of the debt reduced or refinanced. Keep in mind that refinancing over a longer period usually results in increased finance charges.

Where You Live

What agencies and organizations in your community provide financial counseling services? Do they charge a fee for their services?

- Contact a consumer credit counseling service or a family service agency that offers free or low-cost financial counseling.
- Seek assistance from friends or relatives to reduce the debt to a manageable level.

Bankruptcy   If taking the steps listed above does not resolve your problem, you may have to declare bankruptcy. This is a procedure through which a person places assets under the control of a federal court in order to be relieved of debt. In recent years, an enormous number of bankruptcies have been filed in the United States. In fact, the majority of civil cases filed in federal courts are bankruptcies. In 2002, more than 1,000,000 consumers filed for bankruptcy. This represented 98 percent of bankruptcy petitions filed that year.

Under Chapter 13 of the federal bankruptcy law, a wage earner can make an arrangement, supervised by a federal court, to pay off some or all of what is owed to creditors over an extended period of time. A more severe form of bankruptcy is called a Chapter 7 bankruptcy. Under Chapter 7, the federal court takes control of most of the debtor's assets (some states allow the debtor to keep certain items), sells them, and pays off as much debt as possible. Generally, the money received from the sale of the assets is not enough to fully pay all creditors.

A declaration of bankruptcy has serious long-term consequences for the debtor. Records of personal bankruptcy remain in credit reports for 10 years. Even after that time, it may be very difficult to obtain credit or borrow money. In addition, some debts are not wiped out through bankruptcy. Taxes, alimony, child support, and student loans must still be repaid.

Bankruptcy is just one of the options people have when they cannot pay their bills. *How does bankruptcy work?*

Creditor Collection Practices

Creditors have many ways of collecting money from consumers who are unwilling or unable to pay their debts. It is understandable that creditors will take action to recover money or property owed them. However, in the past, some bill collectors engaged in unsavory practices. As a result, some debtors suffered family problems, lost their jobs, and had their privacy invaded.

These practices prompted Congress to pass the *Fair Debt Collection Practices Act* in 1978. This act protects consumers from abusive and unfair collection practices by professional debt collectors. It does not apply to creditors collecting their own bills. Under the act, the debt collector's communications are limited to reasonable times and places. False or misleading statements, as well as acts of harassment or abuse, are strictly prohibited.

Calls and Letters   If you receive unreasonable or harassing phone calls or letters from a debt collector, you should report the collection practice to the Federal Trade Commission or to your local consumer protection agency. Under federal law, you can send bill collectors a notice demanding that all collection contacts cease. You might still owe the money, but the collection contacts would have to stop. You should also consider contacting the phone company, which has the power to discontinue telephone service to anyone using the telephone for harassment.

Repossession   As mentioned earlier, consumers sometimes post collateral when they take out a loan or sign credit sales contracts. The creditor can usually **repossess,** or take back, the collateral if the borrower defaults on the loan or obligation. Most states do not permit creditors to repossess collateral if doing so would involve violence or disturbing the peace. Usually the creditor will hire a repossession company to take back the collateral. This may happen at very late or very early hours of the day to ensure that the collateral can be found.

After repossessing the collateral, the creditor can sell it and then apply the proceeds of the sale to the amount owed. Debtors are also charged for any costs incurred in the repossession and sale. After the sale, the debtor is entitled to get back any amount received by the seller that is in excess of the amount owed (plus expenses). However, if the sale brings in less than the amount owed (plus expenses), the debtor must still pay the difference.

Court Action   As a last resort, creditors may sue debtors in court for the exact amount owed on the debt. At times, the trouble and expense of suing in court make creditors avoid this method. However, creditors often sue debtors in small claims court. You will learn more about small claims court in Chapter 27.

Just because you are sued does not mean the creditor is entitled to collect the disputed amount. Consumers may have legitimate defenses, such as the fact that the goods were defective. For this reason, *if you ever receive a summons to go to court, don't ignore it.* If you cannot appear in court on the date set in the summons, contact the court clerk in advance to arrange for a postponement of the trial. In addition, contact a lawyer immediately. If you are unable to afford one, you may call the local legal services or legal aid office.

The main thing to avoid when being sued is a **default judgment.** This is a judgment entered for the plaintiff (creditor) against the defendant (debtor). Most default judgments occur simply because the

Vehicles can be repossessed when the borrower defaults on the loan. *Are there any instances in which a creditor cannot repossess collateral?*

The Case of . . .

The Missed Payment

Orlando buys a used car from Top Value Cars for $1,200 and signs a contract agreeing to monthly payments for three years. After paying $800, he misses two payments because of unexpected medical bills.

Top Value needs to determine which debt collection method to use. Read each option and consider whether the action is legal and fair to Orlando. What arguments could creditors make in support of each option? What arguments could debtors make against them?

Problem 25.7

a. Top Value could hire someone to repossess the car. If Top Value takes this route, incurring expenses of $200, and is able to sell the car for $500, will Orlando get any money back? Will he still owe money to Top Value even though he no longer has the car?

b. Top Value has contracted previously with a collection agency that has an impressive record of getting consumers to pay their debts. The collector sends a letter every day to both the consumer's home and place of business demanding payment under the threat of contacting their employer about the debt. The collector also calls the debtor at home and at work, leaving messages every hour, beginning at 6 A.M. until 11 P.M. Is this contact reasonable, or does it amount to harassment? Would it be any different if one of Top Value's employees conducted the debt collection activities? Is it proper for a debt collector or a creditor to threaten to contact a debtor's employer?

c. Top Value could file a suit in small claims court against Orlando to sue him for the unpaid amount on the contract. Is this a reasonable first step in the collection process? Is there something else they could do before resorting to a court action?

. . . .

defendant fails to show up in court. If the debtor fails to show up, a default judgment could be entered for the creditor even if the debtor had a good reason for failing to make a required payment.

Garnishment and Attachment   A creditor who wins a judgment against a consumer may still have trouble collecting if the consumer does not pay voluntarily. It was once common practice to put people in prison for not paying their debts. This is no longer allowed, except in some cases of failure to pay court-ordered child support.

One solution creditors use is to get a court order that forces the debtor's employer to withhold part of the debtor's wages and pay it directly to the creditor. This is called garnishment. The federal *Wage Garnishment Act* limits the amount that can be garnished to 25 percent of the debtor's take-home pay (pay after taxes and Social Security deductions). The act also prohibits employers from firing employees who have their wages garnished for a single debt. State laws may further limit and sometimes completely prohibit garnishment.

Creditors can also get possession of a debtor's money or property by attachment. This is a court order that forces a bank to pay the creditor out of a consumer's bank account or that allows the court to seize the consumer's property and sell it to satisfy the debt.

Deceptive Sales Practices

Although most sellers are honest, some are not. Dishonest sellers may use deceptive or unfair sales techniques. In order to protect themselves, consumers should learn to recognize and avoid deceptive sales practices. This chapter introduces you to such sales practices, tells how sellers may use them to deceive buyers, and teaches you how to recognize these deceptive techniques.

Door-to-Door and Telephone Sales

Most door-to-door salespeople are honest. They offer products and services many consumers may need or want. Some, however, use high-pressure tactics and smooth talk to get you to buy things that you otherwise would not buy. Once in the door, this type of salesperson will not take no for an answer and will do almost anything to make the sale.

"Whenever a political body passes legislation on behalf of the consumer, the consumer will wait longer and pay more for the same product or service."

— Richard W. Trace

Street Law
online
Visit the *Street Law* Web site at streetlaw.glencoe.com for chapter-based information and resources.

Many companies use telemarketing to reach consumers.

Some state laws and a Federal Trade Commission (FTC) rule give consumers a "cooling-off" period of three business days after they have signed any contract for more than $25 with a door-to-door salesperson. During this period, consumers can notify door-to-door sellers in writing that they wish to cancel the contract. It is best to send this letter by registered mail and keep a copy. The FTC rule also requires door-to-door salespeople to tell their customers about the right to cancel, and to put this notice in writing. If the seller does not do this, the consumer may be able to cancel the contract at any time by sending a letter to the seller.

Consumers should be cautious about sales offers made by telephone. Many fraudulent schemes are conducted this way. Be particularly careful if a telephone salesperson, or telemarketer, asks for your credit card number. This person may not only fail to send what you order but may also make additional purchases using your credit card number. See the materials on identity theft on page 120.

The Federal Trade Commission (FTC) and the Federal Communications Commission (FCC) have many regulations to help protect consumers from telemarketers. Some of these regulations restrict when and how a telemarketer can contact you:

- Telemarketers are restricted to calling you between the hours of 8 A.M. and 9 P.M.

- Once you ask a telemarketer not to call you, it is illegal for them to call you again.

- Computerized voice or prerecorded voice calls to your home are prohibited.

- The FCC prohibits the practice of "slamming," or switching your long distance carrier without your knowledge or consent.

For Your Information . . .

Telemarketing Scams

According to the Federal Trade Commission, telemarketing fraud robs people in the United States of more than $40 billion a year. The FTC lists the following as the most common telemarketing scams:

- prize offers in which you must buy something or give a credit card number to collect the prize
- "free" travel packages (with hidden costs)
- vitamin and health product scams
- investments, business opportunities, and other "get-rich-quick" schemes
- fake charities

Other rules regulate the information a telemarketer must provide to you:

- They must tell you who is calling and that it is a sales call.
- Telemarketers must tell you the total cost of products or services offered and any restrictions—such as all sales being final and nonrefundable—before you pay.
- For prize promotions, they must tell you the odds of winning, that no purchase or payment is necessary to win (Remember, free is free!), and any conditions for receiving the prize.
- Advertisements that induce you to dial pay-per-call phone numbers (such as 900 numbers) must disclose the cost of the call.
- It is illegal for telemarketers to lie or misrepresent any information.

In 2003, the FTC established the National Do Not Call Registry, which allows consumers to place their phone numbers on a list to reduce the number of calls from telemarketers. You can register your home and cell phone numbers for free at www.donotcall.gov. Your registration is effective for five years. Once your phone number is registered, you may also file consumer complaints through the Web site.

The Case of . . .

Easy Money

Mr. and Mrs. Johnson were struggling to make ends meet and to feed their family of five. They decided that they needed to borrow money to pay their expenses for the month. They considered going to a bank for a loan, but they knew they each had poor credit histories, and they did not want to be paying off interest over a long period of time.

They were very interested when they read the following ad in the newspaper:

EASY MONEY: Having trouble making ends meet? Need a short-term loan just to get you through a rough time? We offer quick loans to anyone regardless of credit background. No interest payments. Just a nominal processing fee. Call today!! 1-555-EZ-MONEY.

The offer sounded too good to be true. The Johnsons were skeptical, but they called anyway. The operator said she would be happy to offer them a no-interest loan of $2,000, repayable in six easy monthly installments. All the

Johnsons had to do was pay a one-time fee of $200 to process the paperwork.

The Johnsons did not have to meet anybody from the loan company, and nobody bothered them at their home. They scraped together the $200 and sent Easy Money, Inc., a money order.

When they had not received their money in three weeks, they began to worry. They again called the number listed in the paper, but the line had been disconnected. Finally, after two more weeks, they realized they were not going to get their loan and would never see the "processing fee" again.

Problem 26.1

a. Did any unfair or deceptive practices take place in the Johnsons' story? Explain.

b. What could the Johnsons have done to prevent their loss?

c. What can they do now? Can any state or federal agencies help them?

Consumers encounter ads hundreds of times each day. *In what unusual places have you seen advertising?*

Referral Sales

A seller may convince consumers that they can save money by referring the seller to other customers. The consumer then enters into a sales contract assuming that the price will be reduced if he or she gives a list of other potential purchasers of the product to the seller. However, the agreement usually provides savings to the consumer only if the potential customers actually buy the product. This selling technique is called a **referral sale.** Unless the seller uses deceptive means to induce a customer to provide this information, referral sales are generally legal.

Advertising and the Consumer

Advertising is everywhere. Each day, American consumers are bombarded by ads on radio, television, and Internet sites, in newspapers and magazines, on billboards, bus shelters, and park benches, before movies, and at sports arenas.

The United States has always been a commercial society, but in recent years advertising has become more widespread. The advertising industry reported that more than $225 billion was spent on advertising in the mass media in 2000. Advertising has also become more persistent and intrusive. As a result, people sometimes try to avoid advertising by changing the channel during TV commercials or tossing unopened junk mail into the trash can. There are even devices available that block incoming telemarketing phone calls.

The First Amendment to the U.S. Constitution protects advertising as an expression of free speech. Courts have ruled, however, that the federal and state governments have some authority to regulate, and even prohibit, certain types of advertising. You will learn more about protections for commercial speech in Unit 6 on individual rights.

The Guaranteed Jeep

Janine Gomez received a letter addressed to her with the word *URGENT* in bold letters across the front. The letter said she was a guaranteed prizewinner. The two prizes listed in large, bold letters were a brand new Jeep and a big-screen television. In much smaller print, the letter said that there were other valuable prizes that she could win instead. No matter what, she was preselected as a certain winner.

All she had to do to claim her prize was call a direct number: 1-900-NEW-JEEP. In even smaller print, the letter informed her that the call would cost $5 for the first minute, $3 for each additional minute, and that it would take from three to five minutes to adequately discuss her prize. Although this was an expensive call, Janine decided that the prize she would get would be worth the cost of the call.

Problem 26.2

a. Assume that the prize Janine is offered is a kitchen utensil available in grocery stores for less than $2. What should she do?

b. What mistake, if any, did Janine make in deciding to respond to the letter?

c. Have you or has anyone in your family ever received notice of a guaranteed prize in the mail? How did you respond?

d. What, if anything, was deceptive about the letter?

e. In what way, if any, should the law regulate situations such as the one encountered by Janine?

. . . .

One of the most controversial types of advertising involves tobacco. Tobacco advertising is controversial because smoking is the nation's leading preventable cause of death. More people die from smoking each year than from AIDS, accidents, fires, homicides, suicides, and drunk driving combined. As a result, there have been efforts to eliminate or restrict tobacco advertising. For example, Congress adopted the *Federal Cigarette Labeling and Advertising Act* in 1965 and the *Public Health Cigarette Smoking Act* in 1969. Together, these laws required a health warning from the surgeon general on cigarette packages, banned cigarette advertising on radio and television, and called for an annual report on the health consequences of smoking. While the courts have upheld some regulation of tobacco advertising, other government efforts to restrict certain commercial speech have been found to violate the First Amendment rights of advertisers and consumers unless the advertising was deceptive or misleading.

When the government cannot bring about changes in the private sector through regulation, however, sometimes such restrictions can be agreed upon by the industry itself as the result of pressure from consumers. For example, in 1998, the tobacco industry settled a massive lawsuit brought against it by many states on behalf of their citizens to recover health care costs associated with tobacco-related illnesses. A primary concern in the litigation was the impact that tobacco advertisements had on kids. As part of that settlement, the various tobacco companies agreed to restrict the way that they advertise, including banning advertisements on billboards and in transit systems. Further, tobacco companies agreed not to use cartoon characters to sell their products, or to distribute tobacco products at any event to which minors are admitted. Although tobacco advertising is still allowed in magazines, newspapers, direct mail, and on the Internet, all advertisements, no matter where or in what form they appear, must include the surgeon general's warning about the harmful effects of tobacco.

Problem 26.3

To determine the impact of one form of advertising on you and your community, conduct a study of outdoor advertising in your neighborhood and around your school. Next time you travel from home to school, note the following:

a. How many billboards do you see? If you do not see any, do you see any other forms of outdoor advertising? Explain.

b. How many advertisements do you see for alcoholic beverages and cigarettes? How many for other products? What percentage of the outdoor ads you see are for alcohol and tobacco?

c. How many billboards are located in inappropriate locations, such as near schools, churches, homes, or parks?

d. What is the character of the neighborhood around your school and home? Are most residents African Americans? Latinos? Asian Americans? Whites? Is the neighborhood racially mixed?

e. Examine the outdoor ads. Describe the models used in the ads and images created by the ads. To which emotions, needs, and desires do the ads appeal?

f. Compare your answers with those of other students. Are there any differences in the number of outdoor ads among different types of neighborhoods? (Note: If you do not see any outdoor advertising at all, it is probably because your city or town has an ordinance prohibiting this form of advertising.)

Advertising can, of course, be beneficial. For example, merchants use advertising to tell potential customers about their products. Ads can also help consumers by telling them about new goods and services and by providing other useful information.

Although ads can be helpful, they can also mislead, deceive, and confuse. The federal and state governments have laws that prohibit false or deceptive advertising. However, these laws are difficult to enforce, and deception can take many forms.

When the public is widely exposed to a misleading ad, the FTC can order the seller to stop the false advertising. It can also order **corrective advertising.** This means that the advertiser must admit to the deception in all future ads for a specified period of time. For

example, a well-known mouthwash company once advertised that its product cured sore throats and colds. When an investigation proved this claim false, the FTC ordered that all new ads state that the previous claims were untrue.

Although false or misleading ads are generally illegal, one type of ad is an exception to this rule. Ads based on the seller's opinion, personal taste, or obvious exaggeration are called **puffing**. While perhaps not literally true, ads that puff are not illegal. For example, a used-car dealer that advertises the "World's Best Used Cars" is engaged in puffing. A reasonable person should know better than to rely on the truthfulness of such a statement. Similarly, announcing a sale at a furniture store, an ad reads: "2,750 items of furniture have to go *tonight*!" This ad is not literally true; but again, a reasonable consumer should understand that it is just "seller's talk."

In contrast, consider an ad that reads: "Giant Sale—Top-Quality CD Players, formerly $300, now just $225." If the compact disc players were never sold at $300 and could have been purchased at anytime for $225, this ad is deceptive and therefore illegal. The ad is not puffing, because it is not based on the seller's opinion, personal taste, or an obvious exaggeration. Rather, it misleads consumers about an important fact concerning the product.

The difference between illegal advertising and puffing may be slight, so consumers should be on guard. If an ad misleads consumers about an important fact concerning the product, it is probably illegal. If the ad is merely an exaggeration or a nonspecific opinion, it is probably puffing and therefore legal.

Problem 26.4

Study ads that appear in your local newspaper, or write down the text of ads you see on television or storefront signs. Bring to class three examples of puffing. For each, explain why the ad is not illegal, even though it may not be literally true.

Bait and Switch

The bait and switch sales technique involves an insincere offer to sell a product on terms that sound almost too good to be true. The seller does not really want to sell the product, or "bait," being offered. The bait is simply used to get the buyer into the store. Once the consumer is in the store, he or she finds that the product is much less appealing than expected. Furthermore, on some occasions, the store may have a very limited quantity of the "bait," or the product may not be available at all. The seller then tries to "switch" the consumer to a more expensive item. Salespersons who use the bait and switch technique are told to "talk down," or disparage, the advertised product and then encourage the consumer to buy a higher-priced item. As an incentive, sales people may receive a higher commission if they sell the higher-priced item.

The Federal Trade Commission has rules against use of the bait and switch selling technique and will take appropriate action when it receives complaints from consumers. Many state and local agencies also handle such complaints. If state law prohibits bait and switch, a consumer may be able to cancel a contract with a seller who has used this technique.

Sellers can legally advertise specials at very low prices to get customers into their stores without violating the bait and switch law. The items offered in these specials are sometimes referred to as *loss leaders*, because the seller may lose money or make very little money on them. It is not illegal to advertise a loss leader, so long as the seller has an adequate supply of the item in stock and does not disparage the item in order to switch the buyer to a more expensive product.

Problem 26.5

Kara and her brother Aaron are shopping for a new motorcycle. They see an ad in the Friday newspaper that says, "Come to Big Wheel for the Best Deals on the Slickest Wheels in Town! This weekend only, a 250 cc street bike, only $1,395!"

When they arrive at Big Wheel, the salesperson tells them that the street bike is not very powerful, tends to vibrate above 40 miles per hour, and is uncomfortable for long trips. He suggests that they test ride a 500 cc, four-cylinder motorcycle on sale this weekend for $2,795.

a. Role-play this encounter.

b. What is the best way for a customer to handle an aggressive seller?

c. Has the salesperson used the bait and switch technique, or was the advertised product a loss leader for Big Wheel? Would it matter if Kara and Aaron arrived at the store on Saturday at noon and were told that all the 250 cc cycles have already been sold? Do they have a right to buy one at the advertised price? Give reasons for your answer.

d. Assume that Kara and Aaron purchase the larger bike for $2,795 but later find out that a store across town is selling the same bike for $2,400. What, if anything, can they do?

Mail-Order Sales

Millions of consumers shop by mail. Mail-order shopping is convenient, items may cost less, and some items may be available that are not available in local stores. However, mail-order shopping can also cause problems. For example, mail-order packages can arrive late, broken, or not at all. In addition, shipping and handling costs can sometimes exceed any savings the customer might be expecting.

According to federal law, you have a right to know when you can expect merchandise to be shipped. Sellers must comply with the promises in their ads, such as "Will be rushed to you within a week." If no shipping date is stated, the merchandise must be shipped within 30 days of the seller's receipt of your order. If the seller does not ship within 30 days, you have the right to cancel the order.

There are several things you can do to protect yourself when shopping by mail or the Internet:

- Carefully read the product description.
- Be sure to fill out the order form correctly and provide all required information.
- Pay by check or money order. Never send cash in the mail.

Many consumers like the convenience of mail-order and online shopping. *What special laws protect consumers who shop by mail?*

- Keep a copy of the order form, the seller's name and address, and the date you mailed the order or submitted it online.
- Note the promised delivery time.
- Carefully inspect all mail-order packages upon receipt to be sure that nothing is missing or broken.
- Do not provide credit card information unless you are dealing with a company you trust.
- Look for online verification from the Internet seller that your personal information is in a secure environment.

The Federal Trade Commission monitors compliance with the mail-order rules. These rules also apply to online sales and to telephone sales, such as orders for merchandise on home shopping channels or in infomercials.

Consumers should watch out for ads sent through the mail offering "free" items in exchange for subscriptions or memberships. Offers of free items almost always require a commitment to purchase other items in the future. Consider, for example, "Four free books now if you purchase four more during the next year at the members' price." However, under federal law, all unordered merchandise received by mail may be kept as a gift. Sending unordered merchandise is unlawful, and such activity should be reported to the U.S. Postal Service or the Federal Trade Commission. It is lawful for companies to send free samples and to ask for charitable contributions, but the receiver of the goods cannot be forced to pay for them.

Book and music clubs often mail catalogs to members on a monthly basis. The clubs preselect the item that will be sent to you unless you take some action—usually within 10 days—to make another selection or to reject all selections. These plans are legal, but they can be inconvenient. If you are not careful, they can also be expensive.

Problem 26.6

Britt receives a mailing announcing a special introductory offer for persons who join a popular music club. As part of the promotion, she can get six CDs for only $1, plus shipping. In smaller print, the offer says that she will also be required to purchase at least three CDs per year for two years. The additional CDs are sold at the club's regular members' price, plus shipping.

The club publishes a catalog of new releases every other month. The catalog is mailed to each member with one preselected CD identified. A member who does not want that CD must return a card to the company within two weeks of receiving the catalog. Otherwise the CD will automatically be sent, along with a bill for the price of the CD plus shipping.

a. Is this type of mailing legal?

b. If Britt takes advantage of this introductory offer, how many CDs will she have to purchase?

c. What are the advantages and disadvantages of membership in this club?

Many people purchase daily necessities such as food and groceries over the Internet. *How can consumers protect themselves when making purchases online?*

Internet Commerce

The Internet is a rapidly expanding area of commercial activity, known as *e-commerce*. Almost anything can be purchased on the Internet, from clothes to exercise equipment to CDs. In its infancy it was unsafe to submit credit card information and other personal information over the Internet because this information could easily be intercepted and used illegally. Recent technology such as encryption techniques has made such transactions safer, but it is still important to make sure that any personal information you send is secure.

The Internet can be a dangerous place for consumers. It is cheap and easy for anyone to distribute massive amounts of information by computer, and it is nearly impossible for such information to be effectively monitored. Phony contests, pyramid schemes, fake companies, and other rip-offs that are found in the real world may be even more prevalent on the Internet due to the low cost of advertising. In general, if it seems too good to be true, it probably is not true! Before making a purchase online, get the company's permanent, real-world location and address (not just a post office box).

Consumers can do more than make purchases on the Internet. For instance, Internet auction sites are some of the most popular sites on the Web. Here, consumers can buy and sell goods in a massive marketplace. These auction sites give buyers a virtual international flea market through which to browse for nearly anything they can imagine, and they give sellers a storefront from which to display virtually anything they want to sell.

While Internet auction sites provide a great service for consumers and those looking to make money, buyers should take precautions to protect themselves. The federal laws prohibiting fraud and deceptive practices in other types of sales apply to Internet auctions as well. Among the chief concerns with purchasing goods from an online auction is making sure that buyers understand what they are purchasing and that they receive the goods they pay for in a timely manner.

As a buyer, you can take several steps to protect yourself in an online auction:

- Research any product before you bid on it so you know what is a fair price.
- Understand the rules of the auction site, including the terms and conditions of the sale and who pays shipping costs.
- Establish a top bid and stick to it.
- Identify the seller and read any feedback from other customers regarding the seller.
- Evaluate the methods of payment available to you and decide on one that is most secure, such as a credit card or using a third-party escrow service which will hold your money until you receive and approve the merchandise. This service usually charges a small fee, which the buyer is responsible for paying.
- You may also want to inquire whether the product you are buying is still covered under the manufacturer's warranty. Otherwise, products sold in an Internet auction do not generally come with a warranty unless the seller is an authorized dealer of that product.

The courts have found that the First Amendment does not prevent Internet service providers, online services, or individuals from using programs to screen and delete unsolicited "junk mail" advertisements before they reach the user's mailbox. However, sellers often find ways of evading such screening software, and unwanted commercial e-mail may be difficult to avoid. In addition to unsolicited e-mail, or *spam*, products can be cheaply promoted through advertisements on news groups, company Web pages, and the placement of commercial banners on other Web pages.

Problem 26.7

Search the Internet to find Web sites about safe online shopping. Read the information available to consumers. Then write an article for students who are not in your law class that will help them avoid problems with online purchases.

Repairs and Estimates

Even the highest-quality products sometimes require repair. So it is always a good idea to find out ahead of time how much the repairs will cost. Sometimes service mechanics will give an oral estimate of the cost of the repair, but then have you sign a repair agreement that says—usually in small print—that you authorize all repairs deemed necessary. You should always get a written estimate and insist that any repairs not listed on the repair agreement be made only after you give your specific approval.

Where You Live

Is there a repair and estimate law in your community? If so, how does it work?

Where You Live

Is home repair fraud a problem in your community? If so, have laws been passed to deal with this problem?

Some communities have laws that require repair shops to give written estimates. Frequently, these laws limit the percentage difference allowed between the estimate and the final bill.

You should also watch out for "free estimates." Sometimes the estimate is free only if you agree to have the shop make the repairs.

Another way to protect yourself when having repairs made on your car or appliance is to ask the repair shop to save and return all used and replaced parts. This identifies you as a careful consumer. Also, if you suspect fraud, you will have the old parts as evidence to make it easier to prove your case.

Being careful ahead of time is particularly important, because if you refuse to pay for repairs after they have been made, the repair shop or garage may be able to place a lien on the repaired item. This means the repair shop can keep the item until you pay the bill.

To protect yourself and your property when having repairs done, remember the following steps:

- Become generally familiar with how cars and major appliances operate.
- Get estimates from several repair shops. Find out if there is a charge for each estimate.
- Demand and keep an itemized written estimate.
- Insist that any repairs not listed on the estimate be made only after you give your approval.
- Request that replaced parts be saved and returned to you.

The Case of . . .

The Costly Estimate

Nicole takes her car to City Repair Shop. The mechanic tells her the car needs a tune-up and estimates the cost at $75. Nicole tells the mechanic to go ahead with the tune-up, but when she returns to pick up the car, the bill amounts to $125. Did Nicole do something wrong? Did the repair shop do something wrong? What can happen if she refuses to pay?

Getting an estimate

Becoming a Smart Consumer

Becoming a smart consumer involves learning about several issues related to buying and selling. The first part of this chapter will help you think more critically about advertising and other factors that influence your purchases. Next, you will look at how laws at the federal, state, and local levels protect consumers. Finally, you will study practical steps that you can take before and after making a purchase to either avoid or remedy consumer problems. These steps include comparison shopping, gathering information about products and services, negotiating with sellers, writing effective complaint letters, working with government agencies and organizations, and using the court system (especially small claims court).

"The buyer needs a hundred eyes; the seller but one."

— Italian proverb

Street Law *online*

Visit the *Street Law* Web site at streetlaw.glencoe.com for chapter-based information and resources.

Influences on Consumers

While smart consumers understand contracts, warranties, deceptive sales practices, credit arrangements, and collection practices, they also understand the factors that influence

Many factors influence consumers' decisions.

their shopping habits. They think about whether they need a product, whether they can afford it, and how they can purchase it carefully. Smart consumers also know the difference between *wanting* and *needing* a product. Of course, all consumers sometimes splurge and buy things they really do not need. But smart shoppers don't spend so much on things they want that they cannot afford what they really need.

Problem 27.1

Select an item costing more than $250 that you or your family would like to purchase. Use the library or the Internet to find answers to the following questions:

a. What specific information is provided about the product?

b. How can this information help you be a smart consumer?

c. Which source—the library or the Internet—is better for researching products? Give your reasons.

Consumers often buy things in response to advertising. A great deal of television, radio, newspaper, magazine, and Internet advertising is geared toward specific groups of people. For example, sellers know that teenagers are an extremely important market for their goods and services, so they develop specific ads for this audience. Advertising to teens has increased as studies have shown that today's parents make fewer buying decisions for their children. The ads, often purchased for television shows, movies, or publications that particularly appeal to teens, are designed to increase sales of the products advertised. Many ads provide useful information about products or announce the start of a sale. However, ads may also attempt to influence you to purchase a product that you do not need or want or that you cannot afford.

Ads That Appeal to Our Emotions

Advertisers try to connect with consumers on a personal level by creating ads that appeal to our emotions. There are several techniques, examples of which can be found in television, radio, newspaper, and online ads every day. Smart consumers learn to identify each of these techniques so they can separate the product from the characters and images in the ads.

Some ads *associate* products with popular ideas or symbols, such as family, motherhood, wealth, or sex appeal. These ads try to convince you that purchasing the advertised products will associate you with the same ideas or symbols. Nearly all perfume ads in magazines, for example, include photos of beautiful women. The message to consumers is: Use this perfume and you will be as beautiful as the woman in our ad.

The *bandwagon approach* is a technique that promotes the idea that everyone is using the product. Automotive manufacturers sometimes claim, for example, that their car, truck, or minivan is "best selling in its class in America . . . three years running." The message to consumers is: Because others have bought our product, you should too.

Related to the bandwagon approach is *celebrity appeal*. This technique uses famous athletes or movie stars to advertise the product. The best-known celebrity ads show professional athletes promoting sports equipment. Some products even bear the name of their celebrity spokesperson. These people bring glamour and style to ads, but this does not necessarily mean the products are of high quality.

Still other ads try to convince consumers by resorting to the *claims of authorities*, such as doctors, or by citing test results or studies that appear scientific. Ads for certain medicines include the phrase, "recommended by doctors." Of course, smart consumers would want to know which doctors recommend it, and for what symptoms.

A common television ad technique is based on the notion that *seeing is believing*. A 30-minute "infomercial" for a psychic telephone line may show typical people amazed at the accuracy of their psychic readings. Ads that use the seeing-is-believing technique often rely on the testimonials of people who have bought and used the product.

Some ads simply try to make us laugh or feel good. One popular TV ad campaign features a cute white duck quacking the name of the product. Another has a group of frogs in a pond vocalizing the name of the product.

Other ads use music to appeal to our emotions and individuality. One popular clothing chain uses well-known musicians to sing and dance in its ads. Consumers remember both the music and the product.

Smart consumers learn to separate the product from the characters and images in its ads. *Why do some companies use celebrities to advertise their products?*

Problem 27.2

Identify an ad for a product you would consider buying. If the ad appeared in a newspaper or magazine, cut it out and bring it to class. If it appeared online, print it out. If it was aired on the radio or television, either tape the ad or write a description of it and bring it to class. Answer the following questions about your ad:

a. What product or service does the ad promote?

b. Who is the target audience for this product or service?

c. If the ad appeared on radio or television, at what time and during what program did it appear? If it appeared in print or online, in what publication or Web site did it appear? Why do you think the advertiser chose to run the ad at this time, place, and manner?

d. What information do you need to make a wise choice about this purchase? How much of this information does the ad provide? What information does the ad not provide? Where could you get this information?

e. How does the ad try to get you to buy the item? What makes the ad effective?

f. Create an ad that would encourage a teenager to buy one of the following products: jeans, a portable DVD player, perfume, new basketball shoes, a meal at a fast-food restaurant, or a scooter. What ideas did you use to appeal to your audience as you designed your ad? Do professional advertising people use these ideas?

Consumer Protection

The federal, state, and local governments all have ways to protect the consumer. These may range from consumer protection agencies to laws. As you read this section, and whenever you think about consumer protection problems, ask yourself: What are my rights under federal law? Under state law? Under local law?

Federal Consumer Protection

The U.S. Congress has passed many laws that protect consumers in several ways. First, they prohibit unfair or misleading trade practices, such as false advertising, unfair pricing, and mislabeling. The Federal Trade Commission (FTC) is the federal agency primarily concerned with unfair or deceptive trade practices.

Second, federal laws set standards for the quality, safety, and reliability of many goods and services. Failure to meet these standards can result in legal action against the seller. For example, the *Consumer Product Safety Act* allows the government to ban, seize, or prevent the sale of harmful products. This law also allows the federal government to create standards that help make dangerous products safer.

Nutrition Facts
Serving Size 15 crackers (30g)
Servings Per Container 8

Amount Per Serving	
Calories 130	Calories from Fat 25

	% Daily Value*
Total Fat 3g	
Saturated Fat 0g	5%
Cholesterol 0mg	0%
Sodium 190mg	0%
Total Carbohydrate 22g	8%
Dietary Fiber 2g	7%
Sugars 5g	8%
Protein 3g	

Vitamin A 0% • Vitamin C 0%
Calcium 2% • Iron 2%

* Percent Daily Values are based on a 2,000 calorie diet. Your daily values may be higher or lower depending on your calorie needs:

	Calories:	2,000	2,500
Total Fat	Less than	65g	80g
Sat Fat	Less than	20g	25g
Cholesterol	Less than	300mg	300mg
Sodium	Less than	2,400mg	2,400mg
Total Carbohydrate		300g	375g
Dietary Fiber		25g	30g

Calories per gram:
Fat 9 • Carbohydrate 4 • Protein 4

Third, the federal government has established many agencies that enforce consumer laws and help consumers. For example, the FTC has the power to prohibit unfair or deceptive trade practices—such as false advertising—and can take legal action to stop such practices. The Consumer Product Safety Commission (CPSC) helps protect the public from unreasonable risks of injury associated with consumer products. The CPSC also provides safety information about products consumers might want to buy.

Fourth, Congress passes laws and agencies issue rules to improve the operation of the marketplace. In many instances, these laws and rules are designed to give consumers better information about products. For example, in 1992, Congress passed the *Nutrition Labeling and Education Act*. This law requires that all food product labels list ingredients and nutritional information in a form that most people will be able to understand. Such information allows consumers to make smarter dietary choices.

Fifth, the *Americans with Disabilities Act* (*ADA*) protects individuals against discrimination on the basis of disability. Under the *ADA*, consumers who are disabled must have equal access to goods and services. Consumers who are disabled include, but are not limited to, persons who are blind, deaf, or have a physical disability requiring them to use a wheelchair. The *ADA* applies to all establishments that are open to the public. These include grocery, clothing, and hardware stores, as well as laundromats, hair salons, and gas stations.

What does it mean to state that consumers with disabilities must have equal access? It means that businesses must make reasonable accommodations to ensure that their goods and services are available

Federal law requires that all food labels contain the list of ingredients and nutritional information. *How does this help protect consumers?*

to persons who are disabled. One accommodation you may have noticed is a ramp that allows persons using wheelchairs to enter a restaurant with several steps leading to the entrance. The *ADA* requires businesses to accommodate the needs of persons with disabilities as long as the accommodation is commercially reasonable. This means that business owners must provide any accommodations that are easy to do and not prohibitively expensive.

Assume that a group of teens, some of whom are disabled, want to attend a professional baseball game. In order for the teens who are disabled to have equal access to this form of entertainment, the *ADA* requires that the baseball club make reasonable accommodations at the ballpark. These accommodations can include ramps for wheelchair use, areas in various parts of the park where fans in wheelchairs can sit, messages in print on the scoreboard that would provide a person who is deaf with the information that others hear over the public address system, and Braille menus allowing persons who are blind to order food at the concession stands.

Consumer protection extends to people with disabilities. *How does the Americans with Disabilities Act help disabled consumers?*

Where You Live

Has your city or county passed any consumer protection laws giving you greater protection than you already had under state and federal laws? If so, what do these laws cover? How are they enforced?

State and Local Consumer Protection

States also have their own consumer protection laws and agencies. Many of these laws prohibit unfair and deceptive trade practices. State laws allow consumers to file complaints in state court and with state agencies. They also enable agencies, such as the state attorney general's office or the state office of consumer affairs, to sue on behalf of consumers in order to halt illegal practices. In some cases, consumers can join together to bring class action lawsuits, which allow one or more persons to seek redress on behalf of an entire group.

Like federal consumer protection laws, state laws give the government power not only to stop unfair and deceptive practices, but also to provide consumers with a variety of remedies. A remedy makes up for harm that has been done. Remedies include cease and desist orders, by which an agency can require a business to stop a forbidden practice; consent decrees, which are voluntary agreements to end a practice that is claimed to be illegal; and restitution, in which a business refunds or repays any money illegally obtained.

Cities and counties may also have consumer protection laws. These laws are usually passed to deal with specific consumer issues that arise at a local level. For example, some cities have "truth-in-menus" laws. Under these laws, if the menu reads "fresh salmon," the restaurant cannot serve salmon that has been frozen.

Protecting Your Rights as a Consumer

Consumers can encounter a wide variety of problems. This section will help you avoid some of these problems and will explain how to deal with any difficulties that may arise.

Problem 27.3

You and a friend are planning a summer bicycle trip across your state. You own a very old one-speed bicycle and have decided to shop for a new one to use on this trip. List at least five ways you would gather information before making this purchase.

What to Do Before Buying

Generally, making large purchases on impulse is not wise. When shopping for products or services, learn as much as possible about them before buying. Careful consumers always compare prices and products before purchasing "big-ticket" items. This is called *comparison shopping*. They purchase the product only after considering other products that could also meet their needs.

The Case of . . .

The Cheap Vacation Home

David and Michele Cole were reading the newspaper after dinner one night when the phone rang. A pleasant-sounding person on the other end of the line told them that people in their community had a chance to purchase brand-new vacation homes for only $40,000. The homes were located in a beautiful, wooded setting just two hours by car from where the Cole family lived. In order to take advantage of this low price, the seller said that the Coles had to make a 20 percent down payment immediately. The rest of the money could be paid over the next 10 years with no interest.

The Coles had been thinking about buying a little place away from the city for weekend escapes, and this deal seemed too good to be true. They gave the seller their credit card number for the down payment of $8,000. The seller promised to send literature about the dream home. Unfortunately, the literature never arrived. When the Coles complained to their state's office of consumer affairs, they found that others in their community had also been tricked. Fortunately, a thorough investigation enabled authorities to locate the persons responsible for this fraudulent sales scheme.

Problem 27.4

a. What steps could the Cole family have taken initially to avoid this problem?

b. What remedies could the office of consumer affairs ask for?

c. Draft a law that would reduce the chances that this situation would happen again.

For major purchases, careful shoppers use the library or the Internet to research consumer reports about competing brands. You should also consult your friends for product recommendations.

Once you have determined what product you need, you may discover that it is available at more than one store in your community. It makes good sense to buy from a store with a good reputation, especially for important purchases. Your local Better Business Bureau (BBB), listed in your telephone directory, can tell you if there have been complaints about a particular store.

Policies regarding products and services may differ among stores. For some products, there may be additional charges for delivery, installation, and service. A price that seems lower at one store may really be higher once extra charges have been added on. Also check the store's return policy. A very low price at a store where all sales are final may not turn out to be such a good deal if you decide that you are unhappy with the product after you have purchased it. Sometimes a shopper may even spend a little more money to purchase an item from a store with an outstanding reputation for service or the ability to deliver the item quickly and install it free of charge.

Before making a purchase, consumers should read the warranty carefully. Different manufacturers and stores may provide different warranty coverage on very similar products. When studying the warranty, be sure to find out what you must do and what the store or manufacturer must do if you have a problem with the product. A warranty that requires you to ship a broken product to a faraway place for repair at your expense may not be of much value to you.

If you are required to sign a contract as part of the purchase, be sure that you read and understand the entire contract and that all blanks have been filled in before you sign. If you have trouble

Many teens now buy big-ticket items with their own money. *What should a smart consumer do before buying a cell phone?*

For Your Information . . .

Things to Consider Before Making a Purchase

- Determine exactly what product or service you need.
- Compare brands. Read about various brands in consumer magazines and on the Internet. Ask friends for recommendations.
- Compare stores. Check out a store's reputation. Find out if there are extra charges. Learn about the store's policy regarding exchanges or refunds.
- Read and compare warranties.
- Read and understand the contract (or get someone else to help you do this).
- Determine the total purchase price (including interest).

understanding the contract, ask the store for permission to take the contract to someone who can help you understand it before you sign it. You may not want to deal with a store that will not let you do this.

Finally, do not believe everything you hear from the seller. In Chapter 26, you learned about puffing, or seller's talk. Just because a seller says "This is a real bargain!" does not make it true. You have to determine for yourself whether it is a bargain through careful shopping.

What to Do After Buying

Sometimes even careful shoppers have problems. When this happens, it is important to remain calm and be persistent. Often, smart consumers can solve their own problems. When they cannot, it is very likely that an agency or organization in their community will be able to provide the needed help.

The first thing to do after buying a product is to inspect it. If you do not receive the exact product you purchased or if it has a defect, take it back to the seller and ask for a replacement or refund.

In addition, you should always read and follow the instructions provided and use the product only as recommended by the manufacturer. If the instructions are unclear or seem incomplete, contact the seller. Misuse of a product may be dangerous and may also cause you to forfeit your legal rights! Be sure to report any problem with a product as soon as possible. Trying to fix the product yourself could make the warranty void. If you believe the product is dangerous, or if you have been injured by the product, consider reporting the information to a government agency such as the Consumer Product Safety Commission.

If you experience a problem with a product, you should always try to contact the seller first. Reputable businesspeople are interested in a customer's future business, and most problems and misunderstandings can be cleared up with a face-to-face discussion or a telephone call. If you are not successful, then all future contacts should be in writing or documented in a log or journal.

Provide the seller with all the necessary information—identify the item (including model and serial number), give the date and location of purchase, describe when and how the problem arose, and explain how you would like the problem resolved. Be sure to bring along your sales receipt, warranty, or other pertinent information. Be polite but firm. If the seller refuses to help or gives you "the runaround," send a written complaint to the store owner or store manager. Mention that you will take other measures if you do not receive satisfaction within a reasonable amount of time. Be sure to date the letter and include your name, address, and a phone number where you can be reached during regular working hours. Keep a copy of the letter, along with any response, for your records. To complete your records, make notes about any conversations you had with the seller. Include promises made, if any, and the date of the conversation.

If the seller still refuses to help you, consider contacting the product's manufacturer. If you do not know the name of the manufacturer, ask your librarian for the *Thomas Registry of American Manufacturers*, a volume listing thousands of products and their manufacturers. If the seller is part of a chain store, consider writing to the corporate headquarters of the store. If you do not know the address of the manufacturer or the corporate headquarters, go to your local library and look it up in *Standard and Poor's Register of Corporations*, or look it up on the Internet.

Although they have been careful, some shoppers still experience problems. *What information should a consumer present when returning an item?*

Many companies have consumer affairs departments, but you may get faster action by writing directly to the company president. Review the following list of suggestions for writing a consumer letter of complaint:

- Include your name, address, phone number(s), and account number, if appropriate.
- Be brief and to the point. Do not be sarcastic or angry.
- Include all important facts, such as date and place of purchase, and information identifying the product, such as model and serial number.
- Explain the problem, what you have done about it, and what you want to have done.
- Include copies of documents relating to your problem. Do not send originals.
- Type the letter if possible. If this is not possible, print it neatly.
- Keep a copy of whatever you send.
- Before you mail the letter from your post office, ask for a return receipt, which will cost extra. This receipt will be signed by the company when it receives your letter and then returned to you. If you wind up in court with your problem, the receipt is your proof that the company was aware of the problem.

Consider sending copies of your letter to local and state consumer protection organizations and to your local Better Business Bureau. If you still are not satisfied, it may be time to seek outside help. Many agencies and organizations may be able to help you. For example, you could take your complaint to a consumer protection agency, a media "action line," or a small claims court. You may also wish to contact an attorney at this point.

Problem 27.5

Jeff and Kristin Burt saw a newspaper ad for major-brand color TV sets on sale at Tally's Electronics Shop. They rushed down to Tally's, where they bought a new 32-inch model for $435. Several weeks later, the TV completely lost its picture. A TV service mechanic who came to their home told them that the picture tube had blown and that repairs would cost $200. The next morning, Jeff and Kristin returned to the store and asked to speak to Mr. Foxx, the salesperson who had sold them the TV.

a. Role-play the meeting between the Burts and Mr. Foxx. What should the Burts say, and what should Mr. Foxx say?

b. If Mr. Foxx refuses to help, what should the Burts do? If they decide to write a letter of complaint, to whom should they send it? Make a checklist of information needed in the letter. Write a letter for the Burts.

c. What should the Burts do if they get no response to their letter within a reasonable amount of time?

Published by
Consumers Union

Consumer Protection Agencies and Organizations

Your telephone directory can save you hours in dealing with consumer protection agencies and organizations. Check the beginning of the white pages of your directory for information about local community resources. Many directories also have a section that provides a comprehensive listing of government agencies. Look in that section under "Consumer and Regulatory Agencies" to find the phone numbers of organizations that can help you with a consumer problem. You can also use the Internet to search for consumer protection agencies and organizations.

Some communities have arbitration programs to help with consumer complaints. These programs arbitrate disputes between buyers and sellers who have not been able to settle a problem. If you choose to use such a service, be sure to ask for and read a copy of the rules before you file your case. In some instances, the decision of the arbitrators is binding on both the business and the consumer; in others, only on the business; and in still others, on neither party. The party bound by the decision usually agrees not to pursue any other remedy, such as going to court.

Consumer Groups   Many private organizations help consumers. National organizations such as the Consumer Federation of America, the Consumers Union, and the National Safe Kids Campaign educate consumers and lobby for passage of consumer protection legislation.

The Consumer Federation of America (www.consumerfed.org) is primarily an advocacy organization that works to promote policies that help protect consumers on the federal and the state level. It also works to educate the public about consumer issues and developments in consumer law.

The Consumers Union (www.consumersunion.org) is a nonprofit, independent testing organization that provides unbiased reports to consumers about products and services, personal finance, health and nutrition and other consumer concerns. CU publishes the well-known *Consumer Reports,* which many people refer to when making decisions to purchase goods and services in the marketplace.

The National Safe Kids Campaign (www.safekids.org) is the only national nonprofit organization that is dedicated solely to the prevention of unintentional injury to children. This advocacy group works for the production of safer products and lobbies for laws and regulations aimed at protecting the safety of children. Safe Kids also educates the public about harmful goods and services.

Private state and local consumer groups may give advice, investigate complaints, contact sellers, try to arrange settlements, and make legal referrals. To find similar organizations in your community, contact a local university, your state attorney general's office, or a member of your city council. You should also check the phone book under both "Consumer" and "Public Interest Organizations."

Business and Trade Associations   One of the best-known consumer help organizations is the Better Business Bureau (BBB). Better Business Bureaus are supported by private businesses; they are not government agencies. While BBBs have no law-enforcement power, they do monitor business activity and try to promote high standards of business ethics. In many places, the BBB investigates consumer complaints, contacts the company involved, and tries to mediate a settlement. Reasonable complaints can often be settled with the BBB's help, but BBBs usually act only as mediators and do not force a business to settle. In communities that do not have a BBB, you can contact the local chamber of commerce.

Media   Many local newspapers as well as radio and television stations have special "action line" or "consumer affairs" services that help consumers. Publicity is a powerful weapon, and many consumers find that they can settle problems simply by contacting, or even threatening to contact, the media. To use these services, check with your local newspaper, radio and television stations, or library.

Professional Associations   Many business and professional people belong to associations that act on behalf of the entire profession or occupation. While such an association may have no legal enforcement powers over its members, a consumer complaint may result in pressure on, or dismissal of, the offending member. For example, if you have a complaint against an attorney, you can contact the American Bar Association or the bar association for your city or state.

State and Local Government   All states, as well as many local governments, have consumer protection groups. These groups deal with everything from regulating public utilities to making sure you get

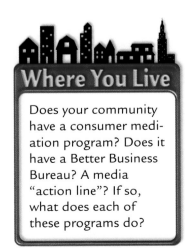

Where You Live

Does your community have a consumer mediation program? Does it have a Better Business Bureau? A media "action line"? If so, what does each of these programs do?

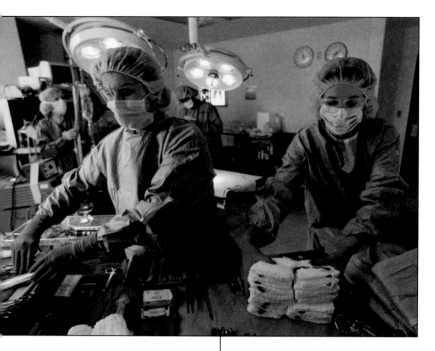

State licensing boards, such as those for nurses and doctors, help protect consumers. *What kind of issues do state boards address?*

a fair deal when you have your car repaired. Consumer protection groups are often located within the state attorney general's office, consumer affairs bureau, consumer protection agency, public advocate's office, or public utilities commission. To learn more about what the attorneys general in all of the states are doing to advance local and national consumer protection issues, you can visit the Web site of the National Association of Attorneys General at www.naag.org.

In addition, states and cities have boards or agencies that set minimum standards for health and safety. For example, local public health inspectors routinely inspect restaurants to ensure that they are clean and free of health hazards.

There are also over 1,500 state boards that license or register members of more than 550 professions and service industries. Commonly regulated under these boards are accountants, architects, attorneys, barbers, bill collectors, doctors, electricians, engineers, funeral directors, teachers, nurses, plumbers, and real estate agents. Professional and occupational licensing was started by state legislatures to protect the public's health, safety, and welfare. These state boards set rules and standards for the occupation, prepare and give exams, issue or deny licenses, and handle complaints from consumers. State boards have the power to **revoke** (take away) or suspend licenses for violations of established standards.

Finally, many places now have mediation centers to help consumers solve problems without going to court. Some of these centers are operated by local governments, while others are sponsored by Better Business Bureaus or other private organizations.

Problem 27.6

Choose a service that you or your family has used, such as medical care, legal aid, or auto repair.

a. Is there a professional association, licensing board, or other agency that could assist you if you had a problem with this service? Conduct research using your phone book and/or the Internet to locate sources of help.

b. What steps must a consumer take to register a complaint with this agency or association?

c. What power does this agency have?

Federal Government It is usually best to try to solve your problem on a local level. For certain problems, though, the federal government may provide the only remedy. Even if a federal agency cannot help, it may suggest a way to solve your problem. Some of the major federal consumer protection agencies are described below:

- **Federal Trade Commission (FTC)**—As the federal government's main consumer protection agency, the FTC acts to prevent unfair or deceptive trade practices as well as problems with bills, credit, and warranties. Consumers can file a complaint online at www.ftc.gov or by calling 1-877-FTC-HELP.

- **Food and Drug Administration (FDA)**—The FDA regulates the safety of food, drugs, cosmetics, and medical devices through a testing program, and can order unsafe products off the market. Consumers can file complaints regarding FDA-regulated products either directly with the FDA or with regional consumer complaint coordinators in each state. Contact information can be found online at www.fda.gov.

- **Consumer Product Safety Commission (CPSC)**—The CPSC makes and enforces safety standards for many consumer products. It can ban, seize, or require warnings for unsafe products. You can file a complaint regarding an unsafe product online at www.cpsc.gov.

- **U.S. Postal Service (USPS)**—The USPS investigates mail fraud and other mail problems. Consumers can contact the USPS regarding services or problems with their mail online at www.usps.com or by calling 1-800-ASK-USPS.

For Your Information . . .

Government Consumer Publications

The Federal Citizen Information Center (FCIC) provides answers to questions about consumer issues and government services. Consumers can get the information they need through printed publications. The federal government has hundreds of consumer publications, many of them free. Subjects include automobiles, budgets, children, clothing, consumer education, food, health, housing, insurance, landscaping, recreation, and senior citizens.

A free list of publications is available in both English and Spanish. Consumer information is also available through the mail. Write to: Federal Citizen Information Center, Pueblo, CO 81009. Or visit the FCIC online at www.pueblo.gsa.gov.

- **Federal Communications Commission (FCC)**—The FCC regulates consumer practices and interactions that take place over communications devices such as the radio, television, and telephone. The FCC receives consumer complaints online at www.fcc.gov/cgb/complaints.html.
- **Department of Transportation (DOT)**—Various consumer protection offices within the department set standards for safe air, rail, bus, and auto travel and handle complaints from passengers. Passenger and consumer complaints must be filed with the agency governing the type of travel in which you are engaged:
  - For defects related to automobile performance and products, contact the National Highway Traffic Safety Administration online at www.nhtsa.dot.gov/hotline.
  - For mass transit-related issues (buses and subways), visit the Federal Transit Administration Safety and Security online at www.transit-safety.volpe.dot.gov.
  - For issues related to travel on the nation's railroad system, contact the Federal Railroad Administration's Office of Safety Analysis online at http://safetydata.fra.dot.gov/officeofsafety.
  - To report safety issues related to air travel, visit the Federal Aviation Administration online at www.faa.gov.

The United States Postal Service is just one of the many federal consumer protection agencies. *How does the USPS help consumers?*

Problem 27.7

What federal agency described on pages 335–336 could help with each of these problems? Could a local or state agency be helpful with any of the problems? If so, which agency?

a. Your parents are considering buying an exercise bicycle and are concerned that your younger brother may be injured if he plays with or uses the bike incorrectly.

b. You buy an airline ticket to visit a college campus for an interview. When you arrive at the airport, you find that the plane is already full. You miss your interview.

c. A friend has lost an arm in a serious accident. Her doctor is planning surgery that will result in the use of a new type of artificial limb. You want to learn more about the safety of this product.

d. A vocational school in your community runs an advertisement that promises job placement for every graduate. You are suspicious about this claim.

Direct Action by Consumers

Sometimes consumers who have concerns with an organization's business practices take **direct action** to make their voices heard. Direct action refers to actions that consumers take to make an impact on a business' or other organization's operations or profits. These steps can include letter-writing campaigns, boycotts of certain goods, press conferences, and picketing or other types of demonstrations. In recent years, for example, some college students have organized direct action campaigns to protest the treatment of the workers in developing countries who make clothing sold on their campuses.

Taking Your Case to Court

Suppose you cannot settle your complaint and a consumer agency has been unable to help. Sometimes your complaint may form the basis for a criminal action against the seller. Whether or not a crime is involved, you may wish to take your case to civil court. Anyone can go to court. Minors can sue through their parents or guardians.

Sweatshops are often the target of direct action by consumers. *Why might consumers be concerned about this issue?*

Criminal Court

In some cases, a seller's action may be a crime. Such acts can be prosecuted as criminal **fraud.** Criminal fraud occurs when a salesperson knowingly misstates or misrepresents some important fact with the intent to defraud you, resulting in harm.

For example, assume you contract with a builder to construct a deck on your home. You pay the builder several thousand dollars to purchase the necessary materials. However, the builder does not intend to build the deck. He simply uses the scheme to take your money. In such a case, you are the victim of a crime. You should contact the police or your local prosecutor. Cases like this can be prosecuted by the government in criminal court. State laws not only provide a fine or jail term (or both) for a convicted defendant, but may also require that the defendant pay back the defrauded consumer.

Civil Court

If a civil dispute involves a large amount of money, the case will be brought in the local civil trial court. Taking a case to court can be costly and time-consuming. In some places, though, free or low-cost legal services may be available to consumers who cannot afford an attorney.

No Sweats From Sweatshops

Much of the apparel sold on Aragon State University's (ASU) campus comes from factories in developing countries or countries in the process of becoming industrialized. Factory owners in these developing countries sign contracts with U.S companies to produce clothing.

A local newspaper has reported that workers in factories that make ASU's clothing are paid very low wages, beaten by factory guards, and forced to work many hours of overtime. A group of students feels that these conditions violate the Universal Declaration of Human Rights, particularly Article 25, which guarantees every person "the right to a standard of living adequate for the health and well being of himself and his family." These students form an organization called No Sweats from Sweatshops (NSFS) whose goal is to stop the university from selling clothing made in exploitative factories. NSFS organizes a boycott of ASU clothing until the university president agrees to listen to the group's concerns.

At the meeting with President William Arnoz, NSFS president Katie LeFevre states the students' position: "NSFS does not want our university to make money on the backs of factory workers who are paid wages below even what their own country's government calls a 'living wage.' We demand that the university join the Universities for Fair Wages Association. All the schools in the association have pledged to sell only clothing from U.S. companies that guarantee the factories they use meet the association's code of humane conduct."

President Arnoz states the university's position: "The university has no control over working conditions in these factories. In fact, many of these workers are paid better wages than most other people in their countries. If the U.S. companies pulled out of these countries, thousands of workers would be unemployed. Joining the Universities for Fair Wages Association costs a lot of money, which we would have to pass on to students through higher tuition. We would also have to pay a lot more for clothing made by companies that guarantee certain labor conditions. That means customers would have to pay much more for the clothing in our shop. The state has entrusted me with the job of making decisions for all students and faculty. Tactics such as boycotts are an attempt to intimidate me into changing those decisions. A university is not a democracy, and I will not be bullied into changing my mind."

Problem 27.8

a. Why do the ASU students call themselves No Sweats from Sweatshops? What does the group's name mean?

b. What are the pros and cons of sweatshops to the American consumer? The sweatshop worker? The American worker?

c. Role-play a meeting between President Arnoz and Katie LeFevre. What demands did Katie make on the president? Did he agree to any of the demands? Should he have?

d. Should there be codes of conduct for the way workers are treated? Is it a university's responsibility to ensure that workers in other countries are treated decently?

In civil court, you can ask for a number of different remedies for breach of consumer contracts. First, you can sue for expectation damages. **Expectation damages** are the difference between the value that would be expected if the breaching party had fulfilled its promise and the value of what the injured party actually received. For example, assume you order ten compact discs through a mail-order catalog and pay $100. However, the company only sends you six compact discs. Assume that the market value of the six discs is $60. The expectation damages would be $40: the difference between the full value of what you were promised ($100) and the value of what you actually received ($60). You would not have to return the discs you received.

Another remedy is **rescission** and **restitution.** When you ask the court for this remedy, you ask it to cancel the contract (rescission) and order the person you are suing to give back any money you have already paid (restitution). This releases you from any further obligations under the contract, but you will have to return any benefit already received under the contract. Assume, for example, that you sign a contract to purchase a set of cookware and a pan melts the first time it is exposed to a direct flame. In such a case, you might seek rescission and restitution. You would get your money back and would have no further obligations under the contract. However, you would have to return the cookware set.

A third type of civil remedy is **specific performance.** Here, you ask the court to order the seller to carry out the specific terms of the agreement. For example, if you ordered goods that were never delivered, the court could order the company to deliver the goods. In this case, you would still have to pay for them.

A suit for expectation damages or for specific performance is designed to place you in approximately the same position you would have been in if the contract had been successfully completed. A suit for rescission and restitution is designed to return both the buyer and the seller to the positions they were in before the contract began.

The amount of damages awarded for breach of contract is often affected by the **duty to mitigate** damages. *Mitigate* means to make less severe. The law usually requires an injured party to take reasonable steps to mitigate damages. For example, suppose Martin got several offers of $100 for the used compact disc player he was selling. Then Gina agreed to buy the item for $150, but she later refused to follow through on the purchase. Martin would be required to

Remedies for breach of contract in mail-order and online transactions can be sought in civil court. *Describe the three types of civil remedies.*

mitigate his damages. If he could still sell the used compact disc player for $100, his damages for a breach of contract claim against Gina would be only $50.

Problem 27.9

Each of the following consumers has a problem. If the consumer has to go to court in each matter, what is the best remedy? Why? Could any of these situations result in a criminal prosecution? Explain.

a. Jeanine takes a floor-length dress that originally belonged to her mother to the dry cleaner. When she picks it up, she finds several holes in it. The store claims the holes were there when the garment was brought in. Jeanine is certain that they are the result of the cleaning.

b. The Zhou family hires the Weed Out Chemical Company to spray their lawn twice a month during May, June, July, and August. Weed Out sends a monthly bill. By June 10, Weed Out has not yet sprayed, although it sent a bill in May, which the Zhou family paid. Weed Out is behind schedule with its spraying because there is great demand for its product, which contains a successful new formula not yet available from other local companies.

Small Claims Court

In the early twentieth century, court reformers recognized that the typical civil court was too slow, expensive, and complicated for many minor cases. These reformers proposed a "people's court" designed to give citizens their day in court for small claims.

Today, every state has a small claims court system. There is often a small claims court in each region of every state, where you can sue for small amounts of money. Each state or local jurisdiction has a different monetary limit on the cases that qualify for small claims actions, ranging from a few hundred to several thousand dollars.

The small claims court system offers citizens many advantages over the traditional civil court system. Filing a suit in small claims court is very inexpensive, as attorneys are not required (in some states they are not allowed), and there are few time-consuming delays. There are no juries in small claims court; a judge decides all cases. This can be a significant advantage, as the judge will typically make a decision about your case immediately. However, not all decisions in small claims court may be appealed. Whether or not you can appeal the decision in a small claims action depends on your state. Some states allow only a defendant—not a plaintiff—to appeal an adverse ruling. Some states require an appeal to be filed within a certain time frame. Others allow an appeal only if the judge made a legal error, and still others do not allow appeals of any kind. To find the rule regarding small claims appeals in your state, you should contact the clerk of the court before filing a claim.

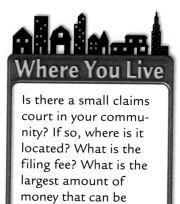

Where You Live

Is there a small claims court in your community? If so, where is it located? What is the filing fee? What is the largest amount of money that can be awarded? Are lawyers permitted in this court?

Steps to Take

Taking Your Complaint to Small Claims Court

Filing a suit in small claims court involves three general steps:

1. **File the Claim.**
   a. **Eligibility.** Discuss your case with the court clerk by calling or visiting the local courthouse. The clerk will be able to determine if the court can handle your claim. You may also be able to get this information on the Internet by visiting the Web site for your local court system.
   b. **Paperwork.** If you have a claim that is appropriate for small claims court, you will be required to fill out some forms and pay a filing fee. This fee varies among jurisdictions, but is usually no more than $30. To fill out the forms, known as a "Complaint" or "Statement of Claim," you will be asked for the name and address of the party you are suing, the reason for your complaint, and the amount you are asking for. The amount of the claim should be based on the loss you have incurred.

2. **Prepare for Your Day in Court.**
   a. **Notification.** In most states, the court will notify the defendant of the date and place of the hearing. You should confirm that your jurisdiction takes responsibility for notifying the defendant, because your case cannot proceed unless the other party receives notice of the lawsuit.
   b. **Evidence.** You should gather all of the evidence necessary to present your case. This includes receipts, letters, canceled checks, sales slips, and estimates of repair. If a defective product is involved, be sure to bring it along, if possible. Contact all witnesses to be sure they come to court. Uncooperative witnesses

Small claims court

can be subpoenaed. This means they can be ordered to appear in court. If you have time, visit the court before your hearing so you'll know what to expect. Also, practice presenting your case to a friend beforehand.

3. **Go to Court on Time with Confidence.**
   a. **Punctuality.** Be on time for court on the date scheduled for the hearing. If for any reason you cannot make it, call the court clerk to ask for a postponement, called a continuance.
   b. **Confidence.** Once your hearing begins, the judge will ask you to tell your story. Do this by presenting your facts, witnesses, and any evidence you may have. Do not get emotional. Be prepared for questions from the judge. After both sides have presented their stories, the judge will make a decision.

Law in *Action*

Mock Trial: *James Phillips v. The Radio Shop*

FACTS

James Phillips purchased an MP3 player from The Radio Shop and later tried to exchange it because it did not work. The date of the sale was November 14, and the return was 10 days later. The sales slip says: "Fully guaranteed for five days from the date of purchase. If defective, return it in the original box for store credit."

The store refused to make the exchange, and James brought this action in small claims court.

EVIDENCE

James has (1) the sales slip for $124.95 plus tax and (2) the broken MP3 player. He claims to have thrown away the original packaging.

WITNESSES

For the plaintiff:
1. James Phillips
2. Pam Phillips, James's sister

For the defendant:
1. Al Jackson, the salesperson
2. Hattie Babcock, the store manager

COURT

The judge should allow James to make his case and should give the store representatives a chance to tell the court why the money should not be returned. At the end, the judge should make a ruling and provide reasons for the decision.

WITNESS STATEMENT: James Phillips

"I went into The Radio Shop to buy a portable MP3 player. The salesperson talked me into buying the Super Mini X-15. I paid the $124.95 price, and he gave me the player in its original box. When I got home, it didn't work. I went back to the store to get my money back, but the salesperson wouldn't return it. He said I should have brought it back right away. I explained to him that my mother had been sick. Here are the broken MP3 player and the receipt as proof."

WITNESS STATEMENT: Pam Phillips

"When James got home that day he was excited and wanted to show me something. He called me into his room to show me his new MP3 player. He had downloaded 20 of his favorite tunes and I saw all of them on the song list. He pushed play, but nothing happened."

WITNESS STATEMENT: Al Jackson

"I sold the kid the MP3, but as far as I know it worked. All the display models worked well enough, so why shouldn't the boxed one straight from the factory? He probably dropped it on his way home. Or maybe he broke it because he didn't know how to use it correctly."

WITNESS STATEMENT: Hattie Babcock

"As Mr. Jackson said, all the other MP3s have worked fine. We've never had a single complaint. Our store policy is not to make refunds unless the merchandise is returned within five days in the original box. The guarantee even says this. That's why Mr. Jackson didn't give the kid his money back. Otherwise, we'd have been more than happy to give him credit toward a new purchase. Personally, I agree with Mr. Jackson. The kid probably didn't bring back the box because it was all messed up after he dropped it."

Problem 27.10

a. Role-play a small claims court hearing. Participants should be divided into groups of five, each with a judge and four witnesses. Witnesses should testify and answer questions from the judge. Once all testimony is complete, the judge should give his or her ruling to the entire class. Was the decision the same for each hearing?

b. Is this an effective way to resolve this type of problem? Explain.

Cars and the Consumer

An automobile might be one of the most important purchases you will ever make. Buying, leasing, maintaining, and selling an automobile involve many legal issues. Earlier in this unit, you learned how the law affects car owners in cases of repair fraud and repossession. Now you will apply some other concepts you have already studied—comparison shopping, contracts, warranties, and credit—to automobiles.

Buying a Car

When you shop for a new or used car, you should consider at least five general characteristics: (1) safety, (2) price, (3) quality, (4) warranty, and (5) fuel economy. Unfortunately, many consumers fail to compare safety features when shopping for a car. Safety features are important

Street Law online

Visit the *Street Law* Web site at streetlaw.glencoe.com for chapter-based information and resources.

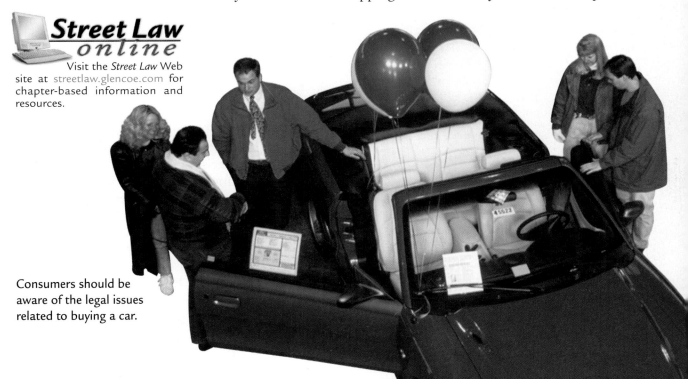

Consumers should be aware of the legal issues related to buying a car.

Where You Live

Are there laws in your state requiring that used cars be sold with some warranty protection?

because, in an average year, one out of every three motorists is involved in an automobile accident. Federal law requires car dealers to provide a pamphlet that details safety aspects of all new cars. This pamphlet includes information on acceleration and passing ability, stopping distance, and tire load. As well as obtaining this information, you should always check visibility from the driver's seat—check for blind spots, windshield glare in strong sunlight, and positioning of inside and outside mirrors. In addition, you should check whether you can reach all controls while sitting in the driver's seat with the seat belts fastened, and consider what protection is afforded by bumpers, safety belts, and air bags. If you have child safety seats, be sure they fit the car.

In considering price, remember that virtually no one pays the sticker price for a new or used car. Discounts are common. The size of the discount depends on the time of year, your negotiating ability, special sales, manufacturer's bonuses, rebates, and other factors.

You should compare fuel economy, warranties, and the dealer's capability to make repairs the same way you compare safety features and price. Many new cars have bumper-to-bumper warranties covering most parts—except batteries and tires—against defects for 36,000 miles or 36 months, whichever comes first. Some manufacturers warrant the engine and drivetrain for a longer period. Other manufacturers offer a warranty as part of the purchase price, but also make available an extended warranty (actually a service contract) for an additional cost. Warranties vary, so be certain that you read and fully understand exactly what protections the warranty provides.

In some instances, used cars come with warranties. The Federal Trade Commission now requires used-car dealers to place a large sticker—a "Buyer's Guide"—in the window of every vehicle offered for sale. The sticker must tell you whether the vehicle comes with an express warranty. If it does, the sticker must detail what the warranty includes. If the sticker says the car comes "as is," this means no warranty is provided. In some places, however, state law prohibits a car from being sold "as is." Finally, the sticker will advise you to get all promises in writing and to have the car inspected by a mechanic before you buy it. Keep in mind that a car's new-car warranty might still apply when you purchase it used.

Examine both the inside and outside of a car before you buy. *What information is available to consumers on the window sticker of a car for sale?*

For Your Information . . .

Internet Resources for Car Buyers

Car shoppers can get blue-book prices for used cars, pricing for new cars, quality reviews, and information on available financing at the Kelley Blue Book Web site (www.kbb.com). Begun in 1926, the Kelley Blue Book is the industry standard for evaluating cars. Much of the information is also available in Spanish.

Safety information is available from the U.S. Department of Transportation's National Highway Transportation Safety Administration (www.nhtsa.dot.gov), which has a special online feature that allows you to compare crash and rollover tests for various cars, light trucks, vans, and SUVs. Tire information is also available at this site.

Although car warranties are now easier to read and protections have been expanded, there are still time or mileage limits (or both) on warranties. Also, a warranty may become ineffective if you fail to perform scheduled maintenance or if you misuse the car. Always be sure the warranty and any additional promises are in writing. Keep these papers in a safe place.

Problem 28.1

In addition to the purchase price, what other costs should you consider when you are deciding to purchase a car? Where can you find information about each of these costs?

Financing a Car

Most new-car buyers and many used-car buyers make their purchases on credit. Buyers may select the length of the repayment period, which may be as long as five years. The longer the repayment period, the lower the monthly payments will be. However, longer repayment periods also result in a larger amount paid in interest. Figure 28.1 on page 347 shows the total interest charges on a $6,000 loan for a used car at a 10 percent interest rate over various repayment periods. Actual interest rates for car loans will vary depending upon a variety of factors, including whether the car you are purchasing is new or used. Interest rates are generally lower on new cars because of the higher price of the vehicle. Interest rates also vary based on your lender, your creditworthiness, and general economic conditions.

Automobile financing is usually available from the following sources: car dealers, banks, credit unions, and finance companies. When comparing finance charges among lenders, make certain that the same down payment and repayment periods are used for each loan. In comparing terms, you will mostly be concerned with the annual percentage rate (APR). However, you should also read all of the terms carefully so that you can answer the following questions:

- Will there be a refund of finance charges if the loan is repaid ahead of schedule?
- Will there be fair warning in the event of a repossession?
- Is there a penalty for late payments? If so, how much?
- Will all payments immediately become due if a payment is missed?

If you cannot answer all of these questions by reading the loan terms, have someone help you read and understand the agreement.

The Case of . . .

The Used-Car Purchase

Having saved $1,000 from her summer job, Sasha responded to an ad for "Like-New! One-Owner Used Cars." A salesperson for A-1 Used Cars watched Sasha wander around the lot until she was attracted to a bright-red compact car. Sasha told the salesperson that this car looked just right for her. He replied, "You've made a good choice. This is an excellent car. It will give you many years of good service."

Although the sticker price was $3,550, the salesperson thought that he might be able to get Sasha a $50 discount because she was "a nice young kid getting her first car." After conferring with the sales manager, he told Sasha that she could have the car for $3,500 and that the dealer could arrange to finance the car and sell her all necessary insurance.

Sasha knew that she would need a loan, and her parents had warned her that insurance was required by law. Her excitement increased as it appeared that all her needs could be met in one stop.

Sasha saw a sticker on the car's window indicating that this car came with a warranty. The salesperson told her that A-1 Used Cars would make any repairs to the engine for damage not caused by her misuse for 30 days or 10,000 miles, whichever came first. Now she felt confident about using all of her savings as a down payment. After all, what repair bills could she have with such a nice car accompanied by a terrific warranty?

Problem 28.2

a. Make a list of things Sasha should have done or thought about before going to A-1 Used Cars.

b. Make a list of things Sasha should have done at A-1 before agreeing to buy the car.

c. What promises, if any, did the seller make to her? Did he say anything that could be considered puffing? If so, what?

d. What are the advantages and disadvantages to Sasha of obtaining financing and insurance from the dealer?

e. Taking into account the lists you have made, role-play Sasha's encounter with the salesperson.

FIGURE 28.1 Interest on a $6,000 Loan

Amount Borrowed	APR (Annual Percentage Rate)	Term of Loan (in months)	Monthly Payment	Total Finance Charge
$6,000	10%	24	$276.87	$644.87
$6,000	10%	36	$193.60	$969.71
$6,000	10%	48	$152.18	$1,304.42

Problem 28.3

Nathan is buying a used car for $7,000. He can make a down payment of $1,000 and needs to borrow the remaining $6,000. Assume that credit is available only from the source listed above.

a. What is the total cost of the car if the term of the loan is 24 months? 36 months? 48 months?

b. If Nathan decides to borrow the money, which credit arrangement would be least expensive? Which would be most desirable? Explain your answers.

Leasing a Car Rather than buying, consumers are increasingly opting to lease automobiles. Under a lease agreement, the consumer does not own the car, but pays a monthly fee to drive the car for a certain time period (often two to four years). Sometimes, the consumer pays an agreed-upon amount to purchase the car—which amounts to the rest of the car's value—at the end of the term and then gets ownership of the car. More often, though, the consumer returns the car, pays any required end-of-lease charges, and "walks away" at the end of the term. The lease agreement usually includes restrictions on mileage and wear and tear, and imposes additional fees for exceeding the limits on those terms. The lease agreement also includes provisions for an initial down payment, security deposit, and other fees.

Typically, monthly lease payments are lower than monthly loan payments. However, you do not own the car after paying off the lease as you do after paying off an automobile loan. Under the federal *Consumer Leasing Act*, consumers have a right to information about the costs and terms of a vehicle lease. This information helps you compare lease offers and negotiate a lease that best fits your needs, budget, and driving patterns.

In considering how much you can afford for a car, you must also consider the cost of fuel, repairs, license, registration fees, taxes, and auto insurance. Insurance payments can be a major cost. The price will vary based on the type of car you buy, where you live, how much you plan to drive the car, your driving record, your age and gender, and the company that sells you the insurance. A discussion of the various types of insurance can be found in Chapter 18.

Where You Live

What procedures must you follow to register a car and obtain license plates in your community?

What to Do in the Event of an Auto Accident

- **Check for injuries.** Get medical help if needed.

- **Route traffic around the accident.** Set up road flares or another emergency signaling device to alert other drivers of the accident. Another motorist or bystander can also stand at the side of the road and caution motorists to slow down and drive around the accident. This keeps everyone safe.

- **Call the police, even if the accident is minor.** Some insurance companies may require the police report of the accident.

- **Exchange information with the other driver(s).** Include names, addresses, and phone numbers; license and registration numbers; makes, models, and years of cars; and names, addresses and phone numbers of insurance agents.

- **Look for witnesses to the accident.** Get the names, addresses, and phone numbers of any witnesses. This includes passengers in all vehicles involved in the accident. Doing so can prevent disagreement concerning how the accident actually happened.

- **Do not tell the other driver(s) the extent of your insurance.** Do not confess guilt, do not indicate that your insurance company will take care of everything, and do not sign any paper indicating you were not injured.

- **Note the name and badge number of the police officer who comes to the scene of the accident.** Your state law may require that you file an accident report with the police.

Exchanging information

- **Make careful notes about the accident while the information is fresh in your mind.** Be sure to describe the specific damages to all vehicles involved. Also note details such as the location of the accident, weather conditions, road conditions, and visibility.

- **Contact your insurance agent as soon as possible after the accident to file a claim.** Give your agent as much information as possible about the accident. Follow his or her instructions carefully to avoid problems later.

Housing and the Consumer

"Property has its duties as well as its rights."

— Thomas Drummond

Some families own their homes. To finance a home purchase, most people obtain a loan called a **mortgage** from a lender—a bank or other financial institution. With a mortgage, the lender pays the seller the purchase price, and the buyer makes regular payments to the lender over a long period of time, usually 15 or 30 years. The buyer pays interest to the lender for the ability to repay the loan over many years. Depending on interest rates and the **term,** or length, of the loan, a buyer might make payments of more than $200,000 in order to pay off a $100,000 mortgage. Because homes are so expensive to buy, most young people initially rent a place to live when they move out of their family's home.

This chapter deals primarily with renting a home. A renter **(tenant)** pays the owner **(landlord)** a certain amount of money in return for the right to live for a period of time in property owned by the landlord.

Choosing a place to live is very important to consumers.

Leases: A Special Kind of Contract

The landlord-tenant relationship is created by a type of contract called a lease, or rental agreement. A lease specifies the amount of rent that must be paid and the length of time for which the dwelling may be rented. It also states the rights and duties of both landlord and tenant.

Before you rent an apartment or a house, you should do at least two things to protect your interests. First, completely inspect the dwelling to ensure that it meets your needs and is in good condition. Second, because most leases are written to the advantage of the landlord, carefully read the lease. If you do not understand or cannot read the lease, get help from someone else before signing it. The following list includes issues you should consider before renting:

- In what kind of area do you wish to live?
- What are the costs, including rent, utilities, security deposit, and so on?
- What is the condition of the apartment or house? Will repairs be made by the landlord before you move in?
- How long will the lease last, and how can it be ended? Can you sublet this apartment to someone else or add other tenants to the lease?
- Will the landlord make or pay for repairs that occur after you move in?
- What services (storage, trash removal, maintenance of yard, appliances, and the like) will the tenant receive?
- Are there any special rules (for example, no pets or no parties)?
- Do you understand all the clauses in the lease? Are any of them illegal or difficult for you to accept?

Problem 29.1

Assume that you are looking for a new apartment. You are married and have a two-year-old child and a small dog.

a. What things should you look for when inspecting an apartment? Make a checklist.

b. What questions would you ask the landlord?

Once you have inspected a rental house or apartment, you will probably be asked to fill out a lease application. This is a form that the landlord uses to determine whether you qualify for the rental property. You will be asked for information such as your name, age, address, place of employment, source of income, and a list of previous residences. You will also be asked for credit references, including from

The Summer Rental

A college student moves to a resort town to work for the summer. After searching the classified ads in the local newspaper, she finds an apartment for rent. She phones the landlord and after seeing the apartment tells him she will rent it for three months. After a month, she moves to a cheaper apartment down the street. The landlord demands rent for the two remaining months, but the young woman claims she does not owe any money because the lease was not in writing.

Problem 29.2

a. Is the student obligated to pay the additional two months rent?

b. Would it make a difference if the landlord rented the apartment immediately after the student moved out?

c. What should the woman have done when she found the cheaper apartment?

d. Role-play a phone call between the woman and the landlord after she finds the cheaper apartment and wishes to get the landlord's permission to move.

previous landlords. Landlords use this information to determine your ability to pay the rent. If the landlord approves your lease application, you will then be asked to sign a lease.

A lease is a legal contract in which both the landlord and the tenant agree to certain things. A lease usually includes the date the tenant may move in, the amount of the rent, the dates on which the rent is to be paid, and the term or length of the lease. It also includes the amount of any security deposit, the conditions under which the rent may be raised, and information about whether the tenant can sublet the rental property to someone else. The lease also states the rules governing repairs, maintenance, and other conditions in the apartment or house.

Depending upon your particular situation, one type of lease may be better than another. For example, if you are planning to rent for only a short period of time, or if your job often requires you to move on short notice, you might prefer a **month-to-month lease.** While this type of lease usually enables you to leave after giving 30 days notice, it has the disadvantage of allowing the landlord to raise the rent or evict you with just 30 days notice as well. You should also keep in mind that renting an apartment on a month-to-month basis will usually be more expensive than entering into a long-term lease.

Another type of lease allows a tenant to move in with the understanding that the lease is for an indefinite period. This arrangement is called a **tenancy at will.** Tenants who remain in an apartment after their lease has expired are usually considered to be tenants at will. There is very little protection for either the landlord or the tenant in a tenancy at will, because the tenant may leave—or be asked to

Tenants should understand all parts of their lease agreement before they sign the paperwork. *Why might a tenant want to negotiate with the landlord before signing the lease?*

leave—at any time. Often, however, such a lease will have a provision requiring that the party who wants to end the lease give the other party fair notice, such as 30 days.

A lease for a fixed period of time—such as six months or a year—is called a **tenancy for years.** This type of lease generally prevents the landlord from raising the rent or evicting the tenant during the term of the lease. If you are planning to rent for a long period of time, this may be the best type of lease for you.

Written leases can be difficult to read and understand. To protect yourself, be sure to read all clauses in your lease carefully before signing it. Never sign a lease unless all blank spaces are filled in or crossed out. If you are unsure of anything in the lease, ask to take it home and consult with a representative of a tenant organization, legal aid office, private law firm, or others experienced with leases. Also make sure that any promises made by the landlord are written into the lease. For example, if the landlord promises to paint the apartment before you move in, get the promise in writing.

Leases with a term of one year or longer must be in writing to be enforceable in court. However, leases for less than one year may not have to be written to be legally effective, and an oral agreement may be binding. To avoid problems, you should always get a written lease that is signed and dated by both you and the landlord. If there is only an oral agreement and problems arise, one of you may remember the terms of the agreement differently than the other.

Landlord-Tenant Negotiations

In many places, housing is in great demand and short supply. In this kind of market, landlords generally have the upper hand and can often tell tenants to "take it or leave it." Negotiating with a landlord about rent and other lease terms can be difficult, but it is worth a try, particularly if you know your rights and know what you want in an apartment or house. If you do try negotiating with a landlord, it is best to be assertive, yet tactful and polite. Landlords want to know you will be a good tenant. But tenants expect something in return—namely, fair treatment and a clean, well-maintained place to live.

FIGURE 29.1 A Rental Agreement

RANDALL REAL ESTATE CO.
PROPERTY MANAGEMENT–INVESTMENT
PROPERTY–SALES–INSURANCE

THIS AGREEMENT, Made and executed this ____ day of _____A.D., 20___, by and between RANDALL REAL ESTATE COMPANY, hereinafter called the Landlord, and _____, hereinafter called the Tenant.

WITNESSETH, That Landlord does hereby let unto Tenant the premises known as Apartment No. 301, at 12 Marshall Street in Johnstown, for the term commencing on the ____day of _____, 20___, and fully ending at midnight on the ____ day of _____, 20___, at and for the total rental of _____ Dollars, the first installment payable on the execution of this agreement and the remaining installments payable in advance on the ____ day of each ensuing month, to and at the office of RANDALL REAL ESTATE COMPANY, 1000 Columbia Road, in Johnstown.

On the ____ day of _____, 20___, a sum of _____ shall become due and payable. This sum shall cover the period up to the ____ day of _____, 20___; thereafter, a sum of _____ shall be due and payable on the ____ day of each month.

AND TENANT does hereby agree as follows:
1. Tenant will pay the rent at the time specified.
2. Tenant will pay all utility bills as they become due.
3. Tenant will use the premises for a dwelling and for no other purpose.
4. Tenant will not use said premises for any unlawful purpose, or in any noisy or rowdy manner, or in a way offensive to any other occupant of the building.
5. Tenant will not transfer or sublet the premises without the written consent of the Landlord.
6. Landlord shall have access to the premises at any time for the purpose of inspection, to make repairs the Landlord considers necessary, or to show the apartment to tenant applicants.
7. Tenant will give Landlord prompt notice of any defects or breakage in the structure, equipment, or fixtures of said premises.
8. Tenant will not make any alterations or additions to the structure, equipment, or fixtures of said premises without the written consent of the Landlord.
9. Tenant will pay a security deposit in the amount of $_____, which will be held by Landlord until expiration of this lease and refunded on the condition that said premises is returned in good condition, normal wear and tear excepted.
10. Tenant will not keep any pets, live animals, or birds of any description in said premises.
11. Landlord shall be under no liability to Tenant for any discontinuance of heat, hot water, or elevator service, and shall not be liable for damage to property of Tenant caused by rodents, rain, snow, defective plumbing, or any other source.
12. Should Tenant continue in possession after the end of the term herein with permission of Landlord, it is agreed that the tenancy thus created can be terminated by either party giving to the other party not less than Thirty (30) days' Written Notice.
13. Tenant shall be required to give the Landlord at least thirty (30) days' notice, in writing, of his or her intention to vacate the premises at the expiration of this tenancy. If Tenant vacates the premises without first furnishing said notice, Tenant shall be liable to the Landlord for one month's rent.
14. Both Landlord and Tenant waive trial by jury in connection with any agreement contained in the rental agreement or any claim for damages arising out of the agreement or connected with this tenancy.
15. Landlord shall not be held liable for any injuries or damages to the Tenant or his or her guests, regardless of cause.
16. In the event of increases in real estate taxes, fuel charges, or sewer and water fees, Tenant agrees during the term of the lease to pay a proportionate share of such charges, fees, or increases.
17. Tenant confesses judgment and waives any and all rights to file a counterclaim, or a defense to any action filed by the Landlord against the Tenant and further agrees to pay attorney's fees and all other costs incurred by the Landlord in an action against the Tenant.
18. Tenant agrees to observe all such rules and regulations which the Landlord or his agents will make concerning the apartment building.

IN TESTIMONY WHEREOF, Landlord and Tenant have signed this Agreement the day and year first hereinbefore written.

Signed in the presence of

_____   _____

_____   _____

It may be possible to change parts of the lease. To strike a section from a lease, both the tenant and the landlord or rental agent should cross out the particular clause and put their initials next to the change. If anything is added to the lease, be sure the addition is written on all copies of the lease and is signed by both the landlord and the tenant.

Some landlords ask that you sign a standard form lease, because it is usually written to the landlord's advantage. It may even contain clauses that are unenforceable in court. The lease reprinted in Figure 29.1 contains many provisions found in standard form leases. Since landlord-tenant laws differ from state to state, a few of the clauses in this lease would be illegal in some states. You should learn about the landlord-tenant laws in your particular state.

Problem 29.3

a. What are the key provisions of the lease in Figure 29.1 on page 353? Who is the landlord? Who pays the utilities? Is the tenant allowed to have a pet?

b. As a tenant, would you object to any of the provisions in this lease? If so, which ones?

c. As a landlord, would you add any clauses to the lease? If so, draft them.

The following pages provide information on several of the clauses in the lease in Figure 29.1. This material is designed to help you read and understand a lease and avoid problems. After a person signs a lease and moves into a rental home, both the landlord and the tenant take on certain rights and duties. Most of these are spelled out in the lease, but others exist regardless of whether or not they are expressly stated in the lease.

If the tenant violates a provision of the lease—for example, does not pay the rent—the landlord can go to court and attempt to have the tenant evicted. The tenant may be able to defend against the landlord in court and prevent the eviction.

Paying the Rent

Tenant will pay the rent at the time specified. (Clause 1)

A tenant's most important duty is paying the rent. Leases generally state the amount of rent to be paid and the dates on which it is due. Most leases require payment on the first day of each month. If you and the landlord agree to a different day, be sure that it is written into the lease and that both parties have initialed the change.

Courts and legislatures in most states have decided that in situations in which a house or apartment is made unlivable by fire, landlord neglect, or other causes, the tenant cannot be forced to pay the rent. Keep in mind, however, that tenants have a duty to pay the rent and that landlords generally have a right to evict tenants who do not pay it. It is best not to assume that you are excused from paying rent.

Law in Action

Lease Negotiation

Read the following information, then work in groups of four. In each group two classmates should role-play the landlords (the Randalls), and two others should role-play the tenants (the Monicos). The Monicos should inspect the apartment and ask all the questions a tenant should ask before signing a lease. The Randalls should find out everything a landlord needs to know before renting to a tenant. The landlords should give a copy of the lease to the tenants. The tenants should discuss it and reach a decision on whether to sign it. Use a copy of the lease on page 353 for this activity.

Mr. and Mrs. Randall own an apartment building in the city of Johnstown. They have a two-bedroom apartment for rent. They require all their tenants to sign a two-year lease and pay a two-month security deposit. The rent is $900 per month plus utilities, which average about $75 a month. In addition, no pets are allowed in the building. The Randalls are eager to rent the apartment right away because it has been empty for two weeks.

Mr. and Mrs. Monico have just moved to Johnstown, where they have new jobs. Mrs. Monico's job may last only one year, and they may then have to move back to Williamsport, a city 100 miles away. They have a three-year-old son and a dog. Based on their salaries, the Monicos wish to pay only $750 a month in rent and utilities. They want a nice neighborhood and are a little worried about the crime in Johnstown. However, they need an apartment right away because Mrs. Monico starts work in three days. They see an ad for the Randalls' apartment. They do not know much about the neighborhood, but decide to look at the apartment.

The apartment has two bedrooms, a living room, a dining area, and one bathroom with a bathtub but no shower. It is on the second floor and has a small balcony overlooking a parking lot. The paint is peeling in the larger bedroom, and a small window is broken in the bathroom. The kitchen has a new refrigerator and sink, but the stove is old and worn and has a missing handle. The front door and the door to the balcony have locks that could easily be opened by an intruder.

Problem 29.4

After the role play, answer the following questions:

a. Did the Monicos ask any questions about the neighborhood or about the building as a whole? Should they have?

b. What was decided regarding the amount of rent and other costs of the apartment? In reality, can tenants ever convince landlords to take less than they are asking?

c. In discussing the condition of the apartment, did the tenants get the landlords to agree to any repairs?

d. Did the Monicos ask about such facilities as laundry, parking, and playgrounds? Should they have?

e. Are there any special rules in the lease that the Monicos did not like? Did they ask the landlords to discuss these rules? If so, what was decided? Could the Monicos have done a better job of negotiating these rules?

f. Is it worthwhile for tenants to try to negotiate with landlords? Can tenants be hurt by doing this?

Where You Live

Does rent control exist where you live? If so, how does it operate, and how successful has it been?

Raising the Rent

In the event of increases in real estate taxes, fuel charges, or sewer and water fees, Tenant agrees during the term of the lease to pay a proportionate share of such charges, fees, or increases. (Clause 16)

Generally, landlords cannot raise the rent during the term of a lease. When the term is over, the rent can normally be raised as much as the landlord wants. Some leases, however, include provisions (like Clause 16 in the sample lease) that allow for automatic increases during the term of the lease. Many landlords include such clauses to cover the rising costs of fuel and building maintenance. A lease with an escalation clause is usually not favorable to a tenant.

Another factor that can affect whether the landlord may raise the rent is **rent control.** Many communities—especially large cities—have rent-control laws, which put a limit on how much existing rents can be raised. Cities with rent-control laws use various standards to control the rise in rents. Some places limit rent increases to a certain percentage each year. In other places, rent increases are tied to the cost of living or improvements in the building or are allowed only when a new tenant moves in.

Rent-control laws slow down the rising cost of housing. However, there are many arguments for and against rent control. Wherever it has been tried, it has been controversial.

Landlords should keep the dwelling in a condition fit for living. *Is the landlord or the tenant responsibile for making these repairs?*

Upkeep and Repairs

Landlord shall be under no liability to Tenant for any discontinuance of heat, hot water, or elevator service, and shall not be liable for damage to property of Tenant caused by rodents, rain, snow, defective plumbing, or any other source. (Clause 11)

In the past, landlords did not have a duty to maintain the premises or make repairs to a rented house or apartment. In the few places where this is still true, tenants have to make all repairs that are needed to keep the property in its original condition. Clause 11 from the sample lease states that the tenant must continue to pay the rent whether or not the landlord provides a dwelling fit to live in. In some states, this provision is unenforceable. Today, most states require landlords to keep houses or apartments they own in a condition fit to live in. The landlord is also responsible for maintaining common areas such as hallways and lobbies.

Many state courts and legislatures say that a warranty of habitability is implied in every lease. This means that the landlord promises to provide a place fit for human habitation. The warranty of habitability exists whether or not it is written into the lease. Thus, if major repairs are needed—the furnace breaks down, the roof leaks, or the apartment is overrun by insects or rodents—the landlord has a duty to correct the problems.

Problem 29.5

a. If you were a landlord, what repairs and maintenance would you expect the tenant to perform? Make a list and explain each item.

b. If you were a tenant, what repairs and maintenance would you expect the landlord to perform? Make a list and explain each item.

c. Role-play the following situation, with one person playing the tenant and another the landlord.

A tenant's apartment is seriously infested with roaches and mice. The tenant also feels that the walls should be repainted because the children have made them dirty over the seven months that they have lived there. The tenant meets with the landlord to complain.

In performing the role play, consider the following questions:

- How should the tenant present his or her rights?
- How should the landlord respond when the tenant complains?
- Should the landlord agree to correct any or all of the problems?
- Would it be better for the tenant to complain by writing a letter to the landlord?

d. Would it make a difference to your role play if your state had a warranty of habitability? Explain.

Where You Live

❶ What is your state's law regarding repairs and the warranty of habitability? Is there a housing code in your community? If so, what does it cover? Who enforces it?

❷ Is there an agency in your community that handles complaints from tenants? Does it enforce a housing code? Is there a special landlord-tenant court where you live? If so, where is it located and what procedures does it follow? Can tenants with limited incomes in your community get legal assistance when they have problems with landlords?

In addition to the implied warranty of habitability, many communities also have housing codes. These codes set minimum standards for repairs and living conditions within rental houses or apartments. Landlords are required by law to meet the standards of the housing code, and they may lose their license to rent if the standards are not maintained. Housing codes differ from area to area, but in most places, tenants have the right to call in a government housing inspector to examine their apartment for code violations.

Although most places hold landlords responsible for major repairs, remember that the landlord's duty to make repairs differs from place to place and from lease to lease. It is always best to make sure the responsibility for repairs is spelled out in the lease. Also, remember that tenants have a duty to notify the landlord when repairs are needed. If someone is injured as a result of an unsafe or defective condition, the landlord cannot be held liable unless he or she knew or should have known that the condition existed.

For Your Information . . .

Sample Housing Code

The following are examples of provisions included in a typical housing code.

Maintenance and Repair
- Floors and walls shall be free of holes, cracks, splinters, or peeling paint.
- Windows and doors shall be weatherproof, easily operable, free of broken glass, and equipped with workable locks.
- Stairs and walkways shall be in good repair, clean, and free of safety hazards or loose railings.
- Roof shall be free of leaks.

Cleanliness and Sanitation
- Each unit shall be generally free of rodents and insects. Common areas shall be free of dirt, litter, trash, water, or other unsanitary matter.

Use and Occupancy
- Each unit shall have a minimum of 120 square feet of livable floor space per occupant.

- Each bedroom shall have a minimum of 50 square feet of floor space per occupant.
- Each unit shall have a private bathroom.
- Each common area shall be accessible without going through another apartment.

Facilities and Utilities
- Sinks, lavatories, and bathing facilities shall be in working order.
- Every room shall have a minimum of two electrical outlets and no exposed wiring.
- Water, electricity, gas, heating, and sewer services shall be in good operating condition.
- Halls, stairways, and common areas shall be adequately lighted.
- The building shall be free of fire hazards and secure from intruders or uninvited visitors.

Use of the Property

Tenant will use the premises for a dwelling and for no other purpose. (Clause 3)

Tenants pay for the right to use a landlord's property. As a general rule, tenants may use the property only for the purposes stated in the lease. For example, if you rented a house as a residence, you would not be allowed to use it as a restaurant or a dry cleaning business.

Most leases contain clauses that permit eviction if the landlord reasonably believes that the tenants have committed crimes or allowed the commission of crimes on the rented premises. Even if the lease does not contain a clause banning criminal activity, the landlord may still be able to have the tenants evicted. Judges frequently enforce such requests from landlords.

A lease may specify the names, ages, and number of people who will live on the premises. Although having occasional guests will not violate such a lease, there can be problems if the number of people permanently occupying the premises changes, as happens after the birth or adoption of a child or after getting married.

Although tenants have a right to use the rental property, they also have a duty to take care of the property and return it to the landlord in the same general condition in which it was rented. Tenants generally are responsible for the upkeep of the premises, including routine cleaning and minor repairs. Major repairs and upkeep of common areas, such as apartment hallways, normally are the responsibility of the landlord. However, the landlord and tenant may make different arrangements if they mutually agree to do so.

Where You Live

What is the law in your community regarding the steps a landlord must take to evict a tenant accused of committing a crime on the rental premises? What steps must be taken if the tenant lives in public housing?

The Case of . . .

The Unsavory Visitors

Mr. and Mrs. Larkin were excited about the birth of their first child. On the day they returned home with the new baby, the Larkins' friends gathered at their apartment to greet them. The Larkins did not notice that two of their friends had some marijuana, which they took into the back bedroom and smoked. However, their landlord, who was also present for the occasion, did notice. A week later, the Larkins received a notice that they were being evicted for allowing drug use in their apartment.

An eviction notice

Problem 29.6

a. Does the law allow the Larkins to be evicted for what their friends did in their apartment? Should the law allow this?

b. Does the Larkins' ignorance of their friends' possession and use of marijuana affect your answer to question **a**?

c. After the Larkins receive the landlord's notice of eviction, are there any steps they can take to prevent her from evicting them?

d. Should the government assist private landlords in identifying possible drug users and sellers and in evicting them? What are the arguments for and against doing this?

Where You Live

What is the law in your area regarding security deposits? Is there a limit on the amount that can be required? Does the landlord have to pay interest on the security deposit?

Tenants are not responsible for damages that result from normal wear and tear or ordinary use of the property. For example, tenants are not liable for worn spots in the carpet caused by everyday foot traffic. In contrast, damages caused by a tenant's misuse or neglect are known as **waste.** For example, a tenant whose dog has severely scratched the landlord's hardwood floors would be responsible for this damage. The landlord can force the tenant to pay for such repairs. Moreover, tenants have a duty to let the landlord know when major repairs are needed and to take reasonable steps to prevent unnecessary waste or damage.

Security Deposits

Tenant will pay a security deposit in the amount of $_____, which will be held by Landlord until expiration of this lease and refunded on the condition that said premises is returned in good condition, normal wear and tear excepted. (Clause 9)

In most places, landlords have the right to ask for a security deposit. This deposit is an amount of money—usually one month's rent, but sometimes more—that is held by the landlord to ensure that the tenant takes care of the apartment or house and abides by the terms of the lease. If the tenant damages the landlord's property, the landlord may keep the security deposit (or a part of it) to pay for the damage. Also, if the tenant does not pay all the rent, the landlord may be able to keep the security deposit to cover the portion of the rent still owed.

Some states put a limit on the amount of the security deposit. Some also require landlords to pay tenants interest on the money and to return it within a specified time after the end of the lease. When a

For Your Information . . .

Security Deposits

- Before signing the lease, inspect the apartment, and make a list of all existing defects or damages.
- Give a copy of the list to the landlord, and keep a copy for yourself.
- Always get a receipt.
- Ask to be paid interest on your money. In many places, you are entitled to this.

- Before moving out, inspect the apartment and make a list of all damages.
- Clean the apartment. Repair any damage for which you are responsible, and remove trash so you will not be charged for cleaning or repairs.
- Have a friend go through the apartment with you in case you later need a witness.

landlord requires a security deposit, the tenant should always get a receipt and should keep it until the deposit is returned. The tenant may also ask that the money be placed in an interest-paying bank account (whether or not this is required by state law).

Security deposits are frequently the subject of disputes between landlords and tenants. Whether damages to the landlord's property are determined to result from normal wear and tear or from tenant neglect depends on all the facts. To protect yourself, make a list of all defects and damages that exist at the time you move in. Keep a copy of the list, and give another copy to the landlord.

Problem 29.7

In each of the following situations, the tenant is moving out and the landlord wants to keep part of the tenant's security deposit. Decide who should pay for the damages involved in each case.

Inspect the apartment and make a list of all the damages before signing the lease. *Why is it important to inspect the apartment both before you move in and after you move out?*

a. The tenant moves without cleaning the apartment. The landlord is forced to remove trash, clean the walls and floors, wash the windows, and clean out the oven and refrigerator.

b. The toilet overflows in the apartment above that of the tenant moving out. The water leaks through the floor, ruining the ceiling and carpet in the tenant's apartment below.

c. The tenant's pet stains the carpet. The lease allowed the tenant to have a pet.

d. The stove stops working, and the repairer says that it has simply worn out. The tenant is a cookware salesperson who has held many cooking demonstrations in the apartment.

e. The walls are faded and need repainting.

f. The roof leaks, ruining the hardwood floors. The tenant has never told the landlord about the leak.

g. The tenants panel the recreation room of their apartment, build kitchen cabinets, and install drapes and two air-conditioning units. When they move, they remove all of their improvements and keep them.

When moving out, you should inspect the apartment or house again and make a list of any damages. Sometimes an inspection with both the landlord and the tenant present can help avoid any disagreements. Bringing a friend along as a witness and making careful notes at the

Where You Live

Can tenants sue landlords for injuries or damage to property in your state? Will courts enforce a waiver of tort liability clause in the lease?

time can also be helpful in case you have a dispute with the landlord. If there are no damages, the landlord should return your money within a reasonable period of time. When a lease expires, most states require the landlord to either return the full amount of the security deposit to the tenant or provide an itemized list of deductions. In some states, you can sue for punitive damages if the landlord fails to return the security deposit or give you the list of deductions. In every state, you have the right to sue the landlord in small claims court if you disagree with the reasons for not returning the security deposit.

Finally, tenants generally have no right to make any changes in the structure or character of the property without the permission of the landlord. Even if the landlord agrees to changes or improvements, the improvement becomes the property of the landlord if it cannot be removed without serious damage to the premises. For example, if you build new cabinets in the kitchen, they become a **fixture** of the property and cannot be removed at the end of the lease. Fixtures are items attached to the property in such a way that their removal would damage the property. As noted, fixtures belong to the owner of the property.

Responsibility for Injuries in the Building

Landlord shall not be held liable for any injuries or damages to the Tenant or his or her guests, regardless of cause. (Clause 15)

Many standard form leases contain clauses stating that the tenant cannot hold the landlord responsible for damages or personal injuries that result from the landlord's negligence. For example, the lease may say that the tenant cannot sue the landlord if the tenant is injured because of a broken guardrail that the landlord should have repaired.

This type of clause is known as a **waiver of tort liability.** Under this provision, the tenant agrees to **waive,** or give up, the usual right to hold the landlord responsible for personal injuries. Most courts will not uphold such a clause. Therefore, if you or your guest is injured as a result of a landlord's negligence, you can usually recover damages no matter what the lease says. However, you are always better off getting a lease without this type of clause so that you can avoid going to court if at all possible. A few courts still enforce waivers of tort liability.

Most courts will not uphold a waiver of tort liability included in a lease. *Why should landlords always be sure stairs and handrails are in good repair?*

Landlord Access and Inspection

Landlord shall have access to the premises at any time for the purpose of inspection, to make repairs the Landlord considers necessary, or to show the apartment to tenant applicants. (Clause 6)

Most leases give landlords and their agents the right to enter the premises to make repairs, collect the rent, or enforce other provisions of the lease. This provision is called a right of entry or access clause. Taken literally, this provision would allow the landlord to enter your apartment any time, day or night, without your permission.

The law in almost every state, however, requires that visits by the landlord be at a reasonable time and that reasonable notice of the visit be given to the tenant. Moreover, landlords do not have the right to enter your apartment or house without your permission simply to snoop around or check on your housekeeping.

Rules and Regulations

Tenant agrees to observe all such rules and regulations which the Landlord or his agents will make concerning the apartment building. (Clause 18)

Some leases require tenants to obey all present and future rules that landlords make concerning their property. In most cases these rules are reasonable, but not always. Typical examples include rules against having pets; rules against keeping bicycles or other items in the halls; and rules concerning visitors, cooking, storage, children, building security, and hanging pictures on the walls.

It is important to read and understand all the rules and regulations before you move into a building. Otherwise, you may lose your security deposit or be evicted for violating the apartment rules.

The Case of . . .

The Dormitory Rape

One Saturday night, Audrey was asleep in her college dormitory room. Her roommate was away for the weekend. There was a guard at the front door to the dormitory, and all the students were supposed to use that door to enter and leave the building after dark. Earlier in the evening, someone had gone out a side door and failed to shut it securely, but no guard ever checked it that night. Audrey was awakened after midnight by a strange man in her room, who then raped and beat her. Although she later notified the police, they never found the man.

Problem 29.8

a. Should the college have a responsibility to provide security for dormitory residents? If so, did the college provide adequate security in this instance?

b. What other measures might the college have taken to ensure the security of the dormitory residents?

If you are going to sign a lease that requires you to obey all rules—even those made in the future—it is best to have the lease state, "The tenant agrees to follow all *reasonable* rules and regulations."

Problem 29.9

a. Suppose you own a three-bedroom house that you wish to rent. Make a list of all the rules and regulations you would want for your house.

b. Suppose you are a tenant seeking to rent the house in question **a**. Which rules would you consider reasonable, and which would you consider unreasonable?

c. If tenants do not like some of the landlord's rules, what should they do?

Some leases include a list of rules and regulations about such things as pets, visitors, and hanging pictures on the walls. *Why is it important to read and understand the rules and regulations before you move in?*

Sublease of a House or Apartment

Tenant will not transfer or sublet the premises without the written consent of the Landlord. (Clause 5)

Clause 5 is a sublease clause. It requires you to obtain the landlord's permission before subleasing the apartment or house. A sublease takes place when the tenant allows someone else to live on the premises and pay all or part of the rent.

For example, suppose you sign a one-year lease on a small house. After six months, you find a larger house and want to move. If the landlord agrees, a sublease clause would allow you to rent the small house to someone else for the remainder of the lease. In a sublease situation, the original lease remains in effect. This means that if the new tenant fails to pay the rent, you are still responsible for paying.

To avoid continued responsibility under the lease, a tenant can seek a release. If the landlord gives a release, the tenant is excused from all duties related to the apartment or house and the lease.

Landlords do not have to agree to the tenants' requests to sublease. Therefore, you are better off with a lease that says, "The landlord agrees not to withhold consent unreasonably." Under such a lease, you would be able to sublease except when the landlord could give a good reason for refusing. Remember, even if your lease lets you sublet, you are still responsible for paying the rent if the person to whom you sublet does not pay.

Problem 29.10

a. Why do most leases require the tenant to get the landlord's permission before subleasing an apartment?

b. Assume the lease requires the tenant to get the landlord's permission before subletting. Bimal, the tenant, leaves town and lets his friend Daniel take over the lease, but Daniel never pays the rent. Does Bimal still owe the landlord the rent?

Quiet Enjoyment

One of a tenant's most basic rights is the **right to quiet enjoyment** of the property. This simply means that a tenant has a right to use and enjoy the property without being disturbed by the landlord or other tenants. Of course, there is always some noise involved in living in a building with other people. Nevertheless, each tenant should be able to live in relative peace.

Tenants have a right to quiet enjoyment even if it is not stated in the lease, and landlords have a duty to ensure that no tenant unreasonably disturbs the other people in the building. A tenant annoyed by noisy or otherwise bothersome neighbors should send a written complaint to the landlord and keep a copy of it.

Although it may not be stated in the lease, all tenants have a right to quiet enjoyment of the property. *Can a tenant play a musical instrument without violating the rights of other tenants?*

The Noisy Neighbor

Luis and Angelina Allende sign a one-year lease, and they are pleased when they move into a beautiful old apartment building in their favorite part of town. Soon after moving, however, they discover that the building is incredibly noisy and disorderly. During the first week, their next-door neighbor throws several wild parties, keeping the Allendes up all night. They also discover that when their neighbor isn't having parties, he is receiving visitors at all hours of the day. These visits are almost always accompanied by loud music, shouting, and constant coming and going. The partying often spills into the halls, and the Allendes are frequently hassled by the visitors.

The Allendes complain to the landlord on a dozen occasions, but the late-night parties and noisy visitors continue. Finally, the Allendes decide they have had enough, and they move out. The landlord then sues the Allendes, claiming they owe her eleven months' rent. Will the Allendes have to pay?

Homelessness: Is There a Right to Housing?

Homelessness means lack of a fixed residence. Homeless people live in public or private shelters, in emergency temporary housing, and in abandoned buildings, as well as on the street, in parks, in transportation terminals (bus and subway stations), and in automobiles. While the exact number of homeless people in America is not known, estimates suggest that there are several million.

Most housing experts agree that the leading cause of homelessness is the lack of affordable housing. Many people who need homes do not have enough money to pay for the housing that is available. Substance abuse and the policy of treating more people with mental problems in the community rather than in institutions have also contributed to the large number of homeless people in the United States.

Homelessness affects people of different ages and backgrounds. *What are the causes of homelessness in the United States?*

Human Rights USA

Though the U.S. Constitution does not include a right to housing or shelter, a few state constitutions and state laws have been interpreted to include that right. In addition, some international documents expressly include housing as a human right. For example, Article 25 of the Universal Declaration of Human Rights provides the following:

"Everyone has the right to a standard of living adequate for the health and well-being of himself and of his family, including food, clothing, housing and medical care and necessary social services, and the right of security in the event of unemployment, sickness, disability, widowhood, old age or other lack of livelihood in circumstances beyond his control."

In addition, Article 11 of the International Covenant on Economic, Social and Cultural Rights recognizes "the right of everyone to an adequate standard of living for himself and his family, including adequate food, clothing and housing and to continuous improvement of living conditions." This multilateral treaty has been signed but not yet ratified by the United States. Many other countries have ratified it.

The Case of the Homeless Family

Roman and Nora O'Reilly and their two children were evicted from their apartment when Roman, the primary wage earner, became ill and they were not able to pay the rent. After spending several nights sleeping at various friends' and relatives' homes, they went to the city's emergency shelter. Workers at the shelter told them that they had no room for a family, just space for single men. Following conversations with several government social workers, the O'Reillys received a voucher to pay for the rental of an apartment or hotel room. After several days of searching, however, they found that all the voucher would pay for was an unfurnished room. They did not own any chairs or a bed on which they or their children could sleep.

The O'Reillys and several other families in similar situations have sued the city with the help of a public-interest organization dedicated to assisting the homeless. They claim that under their state's constitution, they are entitled to adequate shelter.

Problem 29.11

a. Assume that their state constitution does not provide a specific right to housing or shelter. Are there any other arguments the O'Reillys or a lawyer can make as to why they should receive housing? What arguments are there against them receiving housing from the government? How should their case be decided?

b. Do you believe that there is a human right to shelter? Why or why not? If so, who should provide it to people like the O'Reillys?

c. Assume that a right-to-shelter amendment is proposed to your state constitution. Would you support or oppose it? Explain.

d. What other human rights are at issue in this case?

e. What do you think are the causes of homelessness in the United States? Can anything be done to solve this problem? If so, what steps should be taken?

UNIT
5

Family Law

Street Law
online

Visit the *Street Law* Web
site at streetlaw.glencoe.com for
unit-based activities.

In this unit you will consider the basic but
difficult question: what is a family? The family is
the basic unit of society. It is the most intimate and
important of all social groups. A strong family can help its
members when they have problems in their lives. In fact,
families are the strongest influence on what kind of person you turn out to be. Laws and government also have
an effect on individuals and families throughout their lives.

In many ways, family life is private and the law is kept
at a distance. For instance, if you argue with your parents
or a sibling, decide to marry and have many children, or
decide not to marry at all, the law will not interfere. At
the same time, the law is an important part of certain
aspects of family life.

Families in the United States increasingly take a variety of forms. Individuals make different decisions about
love, marriage, and with whom they will live. Mothers,
fathers, children, grandparents, stepparents, and many
others create intricate family relationships in today's
society. Not everyone spends life in a traditional family

Although family life is private, it is influenced by laws and government.

with a legally married mother and father. Some families consist of a single parent with children, while other families include a same-sex couple and children. The law in this area is changing rapidly to deal with both traditional and non-traditional families.

In this unit, you will learn the legal requirements for getting married. For those who are married, the law has a great deal to do with setting the rights and responsibilities of husbands and wives as well as of parents and children. The law also comes into play when marriages end and families face difficult choices about child custody, support, and division of property.

Even if parents separate or divorce, they still need to work together, especially if they have children. For this reason, many families use mediation to resolve conflicts.

Finally, there has been a spirited national debate in recent years about the nature and size of government programs for families. The last chapter in this unit gives you an opportunity to analyze government support for families and individuals.

369

Law and the American Family

The law is involved every time a birth, death, marriage, or divorce takes place. In fact, the law affects families in many different ways throughout the course of a person's life. The federal government, as well as every state, has laws affecting the family.

Law From Birth to Death

The law affects children beginning at their birth. When a child is born, a birth certificate is issued by the state, and the child receives a unique federal identification number called a Social Security number. All babies and young children are required by law to receive immunizations to protect them from certain diseases, such as polio. In addition, children between certain ages are required to attend school or provide proof of homeschooling.

> "This Court repeatedly has recognized that 'the whole subject of the domestic relations of husband and wife . . . belongs to the laws of the States and not to the laws of the United States.'"
>
> — Justice Blackmun in *McCarty v. McCarty*

Street Law online

Visit the *Street Law* Web site at streetlaw.glencoe.com for chapter-based information and resources.

The law affects every stage of an individual's life.

A different set of laws affects teens and young adults. As young people reach a certain age, they often take a test, given by the state, to get a driver's license. The age at which a person can drink alcoholic beverages is also regulated by law. Males are required by law to register for Selective Service when they turn 18. State laws set requirements that must be met before anyone can be married.

The law outlines the basic rights and responsibilities of parents. For example, parents are entitled to tax deductions for each dependent child. The *Family and Medical Leave Act* allows employees time off from work to care for new babies or sick relatives. Parents are responsible for providing basic necessities, such as food, clothing, shelter, and medical care for their children. If paternity is established, the father of a child may be forced by the courts to support that child until the child is 18.

States also have laws that specify limits in the relationships among family members. Chapter 32 examines the line between permissible parental discipline and child abuse. Other laws govern areas such as adoption, alimony, child care, custody, divorce, and support.

There are even laws that apply after a family member dies. A **will** is a document that explains how a person wants his or her property distributed after death. Everyone who has any money or property should consider making a will. Even if you do not presently have much money or property, this may not be the case when you die. For example, if you die in an auto or other type of accident, those you name in your life insurance policy could receive a great deal of money.

If you die without a will, state law determines who receives your property. State law usually requires that a portion of the property go to your spouse if you are married. The remainder may go to your children, parents, grandchildren, or brothers and sisters, depending on the state law where you live. Having a will ensures that your estate goes to whomever you wish in the amounts you choose.

In most states, persons cannot legally make wills until they reach the age of majority, usually 18 or 21. However, some states allow persons as young as age 14 to make wills if they are married, emancipated, near death, or in other special circumstances. When minors die without a will, their property, such as money and clothes, goes to their parents or legal guardians, who decide what to do with it.

Laws govern how a person's property is divided after he or she dies. *Why is it important to write a will?*

Problem 30.1

a. Jacob, age 60, owns a house, a car, and other property. He is married with two children, ages 28 and 25. He dies without a will. Who will inherit his property? In another case, who will inherit the property of Sabrina, who also dies without a will but is 18 years old, single, and has no children? She has beautiful clothes and a car she bought with money from her part-time job. Do you think Jacob's and Sabrina's property will be distributed in the best way? If not, how would you change the law governing distribution of property?

b. At what stage in your life would you consider writing a will? Explain. Would you hire a lawyer or try to write it on your own? Why?

What Is a Family?

If asked to identify a family, most of us would say we know one when we see one. We are surrounded by families wherever we go, and most of us live in family settings. However, families come in all shapes and sizes, and defining the term *family* is sometimes difficult.

Legally, the word *family* is used to describe many relationships: parents and children; people related by blood, marriage, or adoption; or a group of unrelated people living together in a single household, sharing living space and housekeeping. Because the word *family* does not have a precise meaning, many laws define the term when they use it. For example, zoning laws that set aside certain areas for single-family homes define family one way. Laws involving insurance, Social Security, or inheritance may define family in other ways.

The American family has undergone dramatic changes during the past 100 years. One of these changes has been a reduction in size. In 1900, the average family size was 5.7 persons. By 2000, the average family had shrunk to 2.59 persons. Today, some couples have fewer children or, in some cases, no children at all.

Families have also changed because women's roles have changed. During the early part of the twentieth century, most married women did not work outside their homes. Today, however, 73 percent of all married women hold jobs outside their homes.

Changes in marriage practices have changed the face of the U.S. family. Single-parent families and unmarried couples raising children have both become more common as the rate of divorce has increased and the rate of marriage has decreased. Blended families with stepparents and stepchildren are increasingly common.

Laws that fit old ways of understanding the family have been challenged as more and more families do not fit these models. New laws have been written and judges have adapted the decisions they make to help solve conflicts and challenges that families in today's society face.

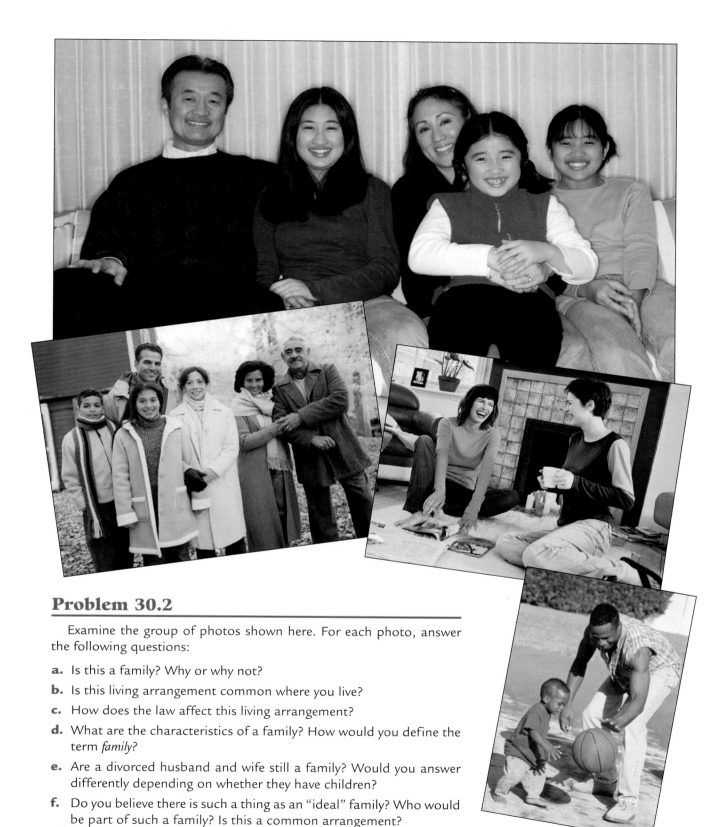

Problem 30.2

Examine the group of photos shown here. For each photo, answer the following questions:

a. Is this a family? Why or why not?

b. Is this living arrangement common where you live?

c. How does the law affect this living arrangement?

d. What are the characteristics of a family? How would you define the term *family*?

e. Are a divorced husband and wife still a family? Would you answer differently depending on whether they have children?

f. Do you believe there is such a thing as an "ideal" family? Who would be part of such a family? Is this a common arrangement?

FIGURE 30.1 Changes in American Families, 1980–2000

Year	1980	1990	2000
Marriages performed	2,390,300	2,243,000	2,384,000
Divorces granted	1,189,000	1,182,000	1,163,000
Married couples	49,112,000	52,317,000	54,493,232
Married couples with children	24,537,000	24,961,000	24,835,505
Average size of household	2.76	2.63	2.59
Families with both partners working	19,028,000	22,053,000	22,674,000
Unmarried couples living together	1,589,000	2,856,000	4,736,000
Unmarried couples with children	431,000	891,000	1,675,000
Same-sex couples living together	NA	1,678,000*	1,653,000

Source: U.S. Census Bureau
* 1994 data

Problem 30.3

a. Study the data above. What do you think are the most significant changes in American families since 1980? In your opinion, why have these changes occurred?

b. Identify any ways in which these patterns are reflected in your own family.

c. What do you think families will be like in the future?

In addition to families having fewer members living together in recent years, there has been a tendency to define family more inclusively over time. Some of these changes have met with strong opposition. Until the 1960s some states had laws that prohibited marriage between persons of different races. These laws were called **anti-miscegenation laws.** In 1967 the Supreme Court declared unconstitutional Virginia's law that prohibited interracial marriage in the case of *Loving* v. *Virginia*.

More recently, gay and lesbian couples have been asking the state for recognition of their relationships. Canada granted same-sex couples the right to marry in June 2003. In the United States, recognition of same-sex unions has been extremely controversial. The Vermont legislature passed a bill authorizing "civil unions" after the Vermont Supreme Court ruled in 1999 that denying gay and lesbian couples the right to marry violated the state's constitution. Civil unions, while not exactly the same as legal marriage, offer same-sex couples similar protections, responsibilities, and benefits. Some other states are considering legalizing same-sex marriage or civil unions. The U.S. Congress passed the *Defense of Marriage Act (DOMA)* in 1996, which declared that states do not have to recognize the same-sex unions created in other states, and as of 2003 at least 37 states had passed state versions of the *DOMA*. Many legal experts expect the issue to eventually come before the U.S. Supreme Court.

Problem 30.4

The law reflects the idea that marriage and the family are essential to the strength of society. As a result, the law affects families and family life. Below is a survey that asks for your ideas about law and the family. For each statement, decide whether you strongly agree (SA), agree (A), are undecided (U), disagree (D), or strongly disagree (SD). Discuss your answers.

a. The process for getting married should be more difficult.

b. A wife and a husband should have an equal say about all decisions in their marriage.

c. Adopted children should have the right to know the identity of their birth parents.

d. Mothers with small children should not work outside the home.

e. One parent should stay home with children until they reach school age.

f. All children should be required to go to school until age 18.

g. Parents should be able to discipline their children in any way they see fit.

h. Getting divorced should be made more difficult.

i. Spouse abuse should be a crime.

j. Grown children should be required to support elderly or disabled parents.

k. When a woman gets married, she should keep her own name.

l. Husbands and wives should own everything equally, regardless of who pays for it.

m. If parents get divorced, their children should live part-time with each parent.

n. Gay and lesbian couples should be able to marry under the law.

o. Unmarried persons should not be able to adopt children.

Family structure has changed in recent years. *Give specific examples that show how families have changed.*

Marriage

Marriage is a personal, social, economic, legal, and often religious relationship. More than 90 percent of all Americans will be married at some time during their lives. This chapter examines the legal aspects of marriage. It describes the steps that one must follow to get married, the requirements for a legal marriage, and the difference between formal and common-law marriage.

Getting Married

To get legally married, a couple must follow certain steps. These usually include the following:

- **Blood test.** Most states require a couple to have blood tests for sexually transmitted diseases (STDs), which may include a test for HIV/AIDS, before getting married. A few states also require a physical examination. These tests can make the couple aware of certain medical problems that may affect their marriage.

- **Marriage license.** All states require a marriage license. When they apply for a marriage license, the couple will be asked to provide certain information, such as proof of age and a copy of their blood test results. They then must swear to the truth of the information they provided and pay a small fee.

"Marriage is the only union that cannot be organized. Both sides think they are management."

— William J. Abley, British Columbia, Canada

Street Law *online*

Visit the *Street Law* Web site at streetlaw.glencoe.com for chapter-based information and resources.

Marriage is a legal relationship.

- **Waiting period.** After applying for a marriage license, the couple must often wait for a short period before they can pick it up. In some states, there is another waiting period between getting the license and participating in the marriage ceremony. Waiting periods help ensure that people are serious about marriage. For example, the waiting period gives people the time to think over their decision carefully.

- **Wedding ceremony.** A wedding ceremony can be either religious or civil. Weddings may be conducted by members of the clergy or by public officials such as judges or justices of the peace. The law does not require any set form for the wedding ceremony. However, to be legally married, each person must, in the presence of an official and a witness, state that he or she agrees to marry. After the ceremony, the couple will receive a marriage certificate. Some states recognize common-law marriage, which does not require a ceremony (see page 380).

Applying for a marriage license is one of the most important steps in getting married. *Why do states require couples to get a marriage license?*

Although no state requires premarital counseling as a prerequisite to obtaining a marriage license, many states have considered ways to encourage couples to participate in counseling or marriage education classes. Many feel that premarital counseling will encourage couples to enter marriage more carefully and, thus, help to reduce divorce rates.

Problem 31.1

a. Marriage involves many considerations. Rank the following considerations in order of importance: money, desire for children, sexual relations, religious beliefs, similar racial or ethnic backgrounds, common interests, relationships with in-laws, faithfulness, and age differences. Are there any other factors that you consider important to a successful marriage?

b. Make a list of all the questions you would ask yourself before deciding to get married. Make a separate list of questions you would ask your partner. Are any of the questions the same? Do any of these questions involve the law?

c. What social, religious, and legal arrangements would you have to make in order to get married?

Where You Live

Where does a person obtain a marriage license in your community? Is a physical exam or a blood test required? Is there a waiting period? If so, how long is it?

Loving v. Virginia

In 1958, Harvey Loving, a white man, and Diana Jeter, an African American woman, decided to get married. Legal residents of Virginia, they went to Washington, D.C., to get around a Virginia law forbidding marriage between white and nonwhite people. After their marriage, they returned to Virginia, where they were arrested and charged with violating the ban on interracial marriage. The Lovings pleaded guilty and were each sentenced to one year in jail. The judge agreed to suspend the sentence if the Lovings would leave Virginia for 25 years. The Lovings moved to Washington, D.C., but appealed their case to the U.S. Supreme Court. They asked that the state law against interracial marriages be declared unconstitutional.

Problem 31.2

a. What arguments do you think the state made in favor of the law? What arguments do you think the Lovings made against the law?

b. How would you decide this case? Explain.

c. Some marriage regulations are appropriate, and others are not. Should states regulate marriage based on age? Mental capacity? Physical disability? Health? Religious or racial differences? Sexual orientation? Explain.

Legal Aspects of Marriage

Marriage is a contract between two persons who agree to live together as husband and wife. It creates legal rights and duties for each party. To get married, a couple must meet certain legal requirements.

In the United States, marriage laws are set by the individual states. State laws vary, but most states have the following requirements:

- **Age.** A couple wishing to marry must meet certain age requirements. Usually, women must be 16 years old and men 18 years old. Some states allow younger couples to get married if their parents consent. Some states also allow a couple under the minimum age to marry if the female is pregnant.

- **Relationship.** Every state forbids marriage between close relatives. It is illegal for a person to marry his or her parent, child, grandparent, grandchild, brother, sister, uncle, aunt, niece, or nephew. Many states also prohibit marriages between first cousins. Most of these laws are based on bloodlines. Hence, although the law forbids marriage between half brothers and half sisters, marriage to an adopted brother or sister is often permitted. Marrying or having sexual relations with a close relative is a crime known as incest.

- **Two people.** Marriage is between two persons only. Marrying someone who is already married is illegal. Having more than one husband or wife is a crime known as bigamy.

- **Man and woman.** Marriages between two persons of the same sex have traditionally been considered legally invalid.

Where You Live

What is your state's law regarding who may legally marry? Are there any restrictions regarding people with disabilities?

- **Consent.** Both persons must agree to the marriage. No one can be forced to marry someone against his or her will. For example, no one can be forced to marry someone at gunpoint.

As a rule, if a marriage is legal in one state, it will be recognized as legal in all other states. However, if a couple goes through a wedding ceremony without meeting the requirements for a legal marriage, the marriage may be annulled. **Annulment** is a court order declaring that a marriage never existed. It is different from a **divorce,** which is a court order that ends a valid marriage. In other words, a divorce means that a man and a woman are no longer husband and wife. An annulment means that a man and a woman were never legally husband and wife.

The grounds for annulment vary from state to state, but common reasons for annulment include the following:

- **Age.** One or both spouses were too young to get married.
- **Bigamy.** One spouse was already married.
- **Fraud.** One spouse lied to the other about an important matter, such as the desire to have children.
- **Lack of consent.** One spouse was forced to marry against his or her will, was too drunk or incapacitated to understand that a wedding was taking place, or was insane.

Laws place many restrictions on marriage. They prescribe who can marry, some of the obligations created by marriage, and how marriage can be ended. However, states cannot prohibit marriage between consenting adults without a good reason.

Many U.S. marriages take place in a church, mosque, or synagogue. Customs and religious traditions play an important role in married life in the United States. These customs and traditions, however, may not be used as justification for ignoring established civil laws governing marriage.

In 1878, George Reynolds, a Mormon living in Utah, was arrested and charged with the crime of bigamy. At the time, many Mormons regarded plural marriages as a religious obligation. Some believed that refusal to practice **polygamy** when circumstances permitted would lead to "damnation in the life to come." Reynolds argued that the anti-bigamy law violated his constitutional right to freedom of religion. After his conviction, he appealed his case to the U.S. Supreme Court.

Some couples have civil wedding ceremonies, while other couples choose to have a religious wedding ceremony. *What legal requirements are common to marriage, regardless of ceremony?*

In the case of *Reynolds* v. *United States,* the Supreme Court upheld the anti-bigamy law. It ruled that a religious belief cannot justify an *illegal act.* Reynolds could believe anything he wanted, but he could not put into practice a belief that society condemned. Today, the Mormon Church condemns polygamy and excommunicates members who practice it.

Common-Law Marriage

Common-law marriage is a marriage without a blood test, a license, a wedding ceremony, or a certificate. It is created when two people agree to be married, hold themselves out to the public as husband and wife, and live together as if married. Only the District of Columbia and 13 states—Alabama, Colorado, Georgia, Idaho, Iowa, Kansas, Montana, Ohio, Oklahoma, Pennsylvania, Rhode Island, South Carolina, and Texas—recognize common-law marriage.

Some of these states require a couple to have lived together for a certain number of years before they are considered legally married. In others, there is no minimum waiting period if a couple actually agrees that they are married, lives together, and represents themselves as husband and wife. If a couple splits up after entering into a common-law marriage, they must divorce legally before either may remarry. If either one remarries without first getting a divorce, he or she can be charged with the crime of bigamy.

States that do not allow common-law marriages do recognize such a marriage if it originated in a state that recognizes common-law marriage. If a marriage is legal in the state where it begins, other states usually recognize it as legal.

The Case of . . .

The Common-Law Marriage

Rick Schwartz and his girlfriend, Sarah, live together in Montana. They talk about having a wedding but never do. They are in love and think it is simpler to tell people that they are married. They buy a house together, open a joint bank account, and are known everywhere as Mr. and Mrs. Schwartz. But one day Sarah gets bored and leaves. She soon finds a new boyfriend, Dylan. Coming from a traditional background, Dylan insists that they get married before living together.

Problem 31.3

a. What are the requirements of a common-law marriage?

b. Do Rick and Sarah have a valid common-law marriage? Why or why not?

c. If Rick and Sarah had lived together in Arizona instead of Montana, would they have a valid common-law marriage?

d. Can Sarah marry Dylan? Will she have to divorce Rick first? Why or why not?

e. Should all states allow common-law marriage? Explain.

In addition to the basic necessities, some courts require the husband to maintain the family in accordance with his economic position. In general, however, a woman cannot obligate her husband to pay for luxury items bought without his knowledge.

Property Ownership

Who owns property acquired during a marriage? At one time, the law considered a husband and wife as one person. This meant the wife had no property rights. Any money or property a woman owned before marriage or acquired during marriage became the property of her husband. In 1887, states began to pass married women's property rights acts that changed the law. These acts gave married women the right to own and control their own property.

Today, any property owned by either spouse before the marriage remains the property of that person throughout the marriage. This is called **separate property**. Although each spouse may still collect separate property by gift or inheritance, generally, all other property acquired during a marriage is called **marital property**. This includes joint bank accounts, real estate, automobiles, or other property in both names.

During marriage, couples may decide together whether to combine all of their property and earnings or keep them separate. The longer the marriage lasts, however, the more difficult it may be to track each spouse's separate property. The laws of the state in which the couple lives will determine what happens to that property in the event the marriage ends.

Nine states—Arizona, California, Idaho, Louisiana, Nevada, New Mexico, Texas, Washington, and Wisconsin—as well as Puerto Rico have **community property** systems. These systems, generally derived from French and Spanish law, usually provide that all property acquired during the marriage belongs equally to the husband and wife, no matter who earns or purchases it. Regardless of the duration of the marriage, if the couple breaks up, either by death or divorce, each spouse is entitled to any separate property brought into or acquired during the marriage, as well as one-half of all the community property acquired during the marriage.

Property ownership can become an issue if a marriage ends. *What is separate property? Marital property? Community property?*

Where You Live

Do you live in a community property state? What standard do the courts in your state apply in distributing marital property?

Most states follow a system of **equitable distribution** in dividing property at the end of a marriage. In these states, each spouse is entitled to his or her separate property brought into or acquired during the marriage. The marital property, however, is divided based on a variety of factors, including need, financial and nonfinancial contributions of each party to the acquisition of property, and length of marriage. The goals of equitable distribution are to balance ownership rights and equitable claims by each spouse and to consider obligations each spouse has to third parties, such as children.

Contrast the community property system with the equitable distribution system by considering a couple married for 18 months, in which one spouse has not worked outside of the home. In a community property state, by law this spouse is usually entitled to any separate property brought into or acquired during the marriage and half of everything the couple acquired during the marriage, including the income of the other spouse. In an equitable distribution state, this spouse is entitled to his or her separate property, but the court can exercise discretion. It considers what is an equitable distribution of the marital property, based on the spouse's needs and contributions to the marriage in light of the relatively short duration of the marriage.

Problem 31.6

a. Lloyd and Gloria were married four months ago. Before they were married, Gloria inherited some land from her grandfather. Now that they are married, to whom does the land belong?

b. Frances and Leon are married and have two children. Frances is an architect making $75,000 a year. Leon is an artist who earns very little money. Frances uses some of her income to buy a vacation home. If Frances and Leon divorce, who owns the vacation home in a community property state? In an equitable distribution state?

c. Which is fairer: an equitable distribution or a community property system? Why?

The issue of having and raising children is an important decision in a marriage. *What are some basic decisions a couple must make once they decide to have children?*

Decisions in a Marriage

Married life involves many decisions and responsibilities. Couples need to cooperate, share, and make decisions together about their lives. For instance, how will housework be divided? Who will handle the money? Will they have children? How will any children they have be brought up? Today, some couples use prenuptial agreements to put some of these issues in writing. A **prenuptial agreement** is a written document made before marriage that sets forth certain rights and responsibilities of the husband and wife (for example, whether any alimony will be paid in the event of a divorce).

In most matters, wives and husbands are free to make their own decisions and work out their own problems. Except in rare cases, the law does not interfere in everyday family life. There are, however, some issues you should be aware of:

Although tradition suggests that a woman take her husband's last name, it is not a legal rule. *What name change options do couples have once they are married?*

- **Name change.** Women have traditionally taken their husbands' last names as a matter of social custom. However, a woman is not legally required to do so. Legally, a woman can keep her maiden name, take her husband's name in combination with her own (for example, Smith-Larkin), or use her husband's name. Likewise, a man may take his wife's name or use one that is hyphenated. Some people have a professional name they use at work and a family name they use in their personal lives. Children may be given any surname the parents choose.

- **Support.** A husband used to have a legal duty to support his wife and children. However, these laws have changed in most states and spouses now have equal responsibility to support each other and their children. Spouses share equally the duty to pay for necessary family items bought by either of them. For more information about support, see page 396.

- **Privileged communications.** The law considers certain relationships private and confidential. Attorney-client, doctor-patient, and husband-wife relationships are all considered privileged. This means that neither person can be forced to disclose information received as part of the relationship. The only information that is covered by this privilege is confidential communications between spouses that occur during the marriage. Historically, a spouse who was a witness at a trial could not testify against his or her spouse unless the spouse consented, or agreed. However, in 1980, the U.S. Supreme Court decided that one spouse could testify against the other in federal criminal prosecutions without the spouse's consent. A person also can testify against a spouse under other circumstances, such as when one spouse is accused of abusing the other. Communications between parents and children are not considered privileged.

- **Inheritance.** If a husband or wife dies, the other spouse is automatically entitled to a share of the deceased's estate. This amount varies from one-third to one-half, depending on state law. One spouse may leave the other a different amount of money—either more or less—than the statutory share in a will. However, the surviving spouse usually has the option to give up the amount in the will and to take the statutory share instead. Even if a spouse is left out of a will, state laws usually give the survivor the right to receive a portion of the estate.

Problem 31.7

a. Raul is in an auto accident with a delivery truck. At the hospital, he tells his wife, Serena, that the accident was all his fault. Later, in a lawsuit for damages resulting from the accident, the delivery company subpoenas Serena to testify about Raul's statements at the hospital. Does Serena have to testify against her husband? What if Raul had made the statements to his daughter? Could she be forced to testify about those statements?

b. Brent has argued with his wife, Liza, for years. In a fit of anger, he rewrites his will, leaving his entire fortune to charity. If Brent dies, will Liza be left with nothing? Explain your answer.

c. James and his wife, Eleanor, both work for local companies. The company James works for, however, is experiencing financial difficulties. He is offered a better position with a company 400 miles away. Eleanor is doing very well in her job and would rather not move. How do they decide what to do? Who has the legal right to make the final decision? Who should have that right?

Spouse Abuse

Domestic abuse occurs across the entire spectrum of relationships. While this section specifically addresses the issue in the context of a traditional marriage, it is important to remember that the same trends, problems, and legal issues apply in all intimate relationships, including traditional and same-sex couples and teenage dating situations (see Chapter 9).

Spouse abuse occurs among families of all backgrounds, rich and poor; all ethnic groups; and in all settings, urban, suburban, and rural. Victims suffer injuries ranging from psychological abuse to severe battering and murder. In fact, spousal assaults are more likely to result in serious injuries than assaults committed by strangers. Approximately one-fourth of all murders in the United States involve people who are related, and many of these are husband-wife killings. Both women and men can be abusers, but women suffer 95 percent of the injuries inflicted by spouses. An estimated four million women are abused each year.

The *Violence Against Women Act* approves spending for counseling and education programs. *Why is it important for adults and children to learn about the cycle of abuse that can occur in families?*

Abuse is rarely a one-time incident. Batterers typically repeat the act, often with increasing severity. Spouse abuse, however, usually remains behind closed doors and often goes undetected or ignored by friends and neighbors.

Historically, the police and the courts have been reluctant to get involved in domestic disputes. In fact, until the late 1800s, it was legal in most states for a man to strike his wife. Even after spousal battering was outlawed, police officers often refused to respond to requests for assistance from battered women or to arrest battering husbands. In part, police officers hesitated to become involved in domestic disputes because they lacked training in safe, effective methods of intervention. In the past, most police officers were taught to either "counsel" the abuser and the victim or make the abuser leave the home for several hours.

These practices have changed. Most urban police departments now encourage officers to arrest spouses or domestic partners suspected of assault. Most states have enacted statutes that require the arrest of alleged batterers if there is any sign of abuse, even if their injured spouses refuse to sign complaints against them. Advocates of arrest point to studies that show that arrest is the most effective way to prevent repeated abuse.

Still, prosecutors sometimes do not bring charges against abusive spouses and are often more willing to reduce the charges than in cases of assault between two strangers. This may be because the battered spouse feels threatened by the perpetrator or because the evidence against the batterer is weak. Some judges merely dismiss spouse abuse cases or give warnings or probation to spouses found guilty. They cite the need to protect family privacy or to promote domestic harmony as the reason for their inaction. However, some court decisions recognize that there may be little family harmony to protect when one family member is assaulting another.

Women face economic, cultural, and personal barriers to leaving an abusive relationship. *How do these barriers make it difficult to find safety?*

The *Violence Against Women Act of 1994* addresses domestic violence, sexual assault, and stalking, and strengthens federal laws. This law includes protections against dating violence, establishes nationwide enforcement of protection orders, and expands stalking laws to include cyberstalking. The act also authorizes expenditures for a wide range of counseling and education programs, shelters and temporary housing, advocacy groups, protections for children and the elderly, and more.

Despite advances in the law and in society's recognition of the problem, spouse abuse continues to be very difficult to combat because of the intense emotional strain it places on women, its primary victims. Several factors contribute to the vicious cycle of violence that is spouse abuse, often including a woman's belief that the abuse is somehow her fault and that she can make the situation better. An abuser often apologizes, promises to change, and then provides gifts in an attempt to gain forgiveness.

Additionally, women face enormous barriers to leaving an abusive relationship. These barriers make it difficult to find safety or to successfully prosecute their abusers:

- Women fear retaliation from their abusers if they try to leave, go to the police, or press charges.
- Often, the woman is not the family's primary wage earner, and she faces economic hardship if she leaves or if her husband goes to jail, especially if she has children.
- A woman may face ethnic pressures to stay, including mistrust of the community, cultural pressures to stay, language barriers, and immigrant status.
- A woman may have a sense of duty to her family and feel that to leave would hurt the family by breaking up the marriage and taking the children away from their father.

While victims of abuse can receive help through counseling, spouse abusers usually need treatment to help them learn to change their pattern of behavior. Abusers are frequently addicted to alcohol or drugs and must deal with their addiction as well as their abusive behavior. Independent men's organizations, in addition to services started by battered women's programs, offer men counseling and support. Social services agencies, such as the Red Cross, and faith-based organizations, such as the YMCA, often can refer men to nearby programs. Some state statutes require counseling for spouse abusers as a condition of their probation. So, even though

Where You Live

What programs does your community have to help abused spouses? Are there facilities where abused spouses can go if they decide to leave home?

many women do not want their abusive husbands to go to jail, the most effective way to ensure that a batterer receives counseling is to prosecute him.

Until recently, men could not be criminally prosecuted for raping their wives. All 50 states and the District of Columbia now recognize marital rape as a crime. In addition, a battered wife can file a civil damage suit against her husband for rape.

Problem 31.8

a. Why do you think that in the past courts did not prosecute husbands for raping their wives?

b. Assume you are a prosecutor. A woman files a complaint against her husband, stating that he forced her at knifepoint to have sexual intercourse with him. She tells you that she and her husband have been arguing violently for years. Knowing that a rape conviction carries a penalty of 20 years in prison, would you file a rape charge against the husband? Explain your answer.

c. Assume that the facts are the same as in question **b**, except that the husband and wife are legally separated. Should it make any difference in proving rape that the couple is separated rather than living together?

The Case of . . .

Spouse Abuse

Late one night, you hear screams and the sounds of crashing furniture coming from the apartment next door. You look out in the hall and see your neighbor, Mrs. Darwin, being slapped and punched by her husband. Before she can get away, Mr. Darwin pulls her back in and slams the door. You hear breaking glass and more screams. You know that Mr. Darwin has a drinking problem. You also know that this is not the first time he has beaten his wife.

Problem 31.9

a. If you were the Darwins' neighbor, what would you do? Would you call the police? If so, what would you tell them? If you would not call the police, explain why not.

b. If you were a police officer, what would you do in this situation? Would you question the couple? Would you arrest the husband? Would you remove the wife from the house?

c. If you were the husband, how would you react to the police in this situation? If you were the wife, how would you react? Would you press charges against your husband? Would you stay in the home? Would you do something else?

d. Suppose you are a judge confronted with the Darwin case. Would you send Mr. Darwin to jail? Would you take some other action? What other information would you want to know?

e. Besides calling the police, what are some things Mrs. Darwin could do about the problem?

What to Do If Spouse Abuse Occurs

Both victims and their abusers need to seek help to end the cycle of spouse abuse. The first incident of domestic violence is rarely the last. Victims of abuse can take the following steps:

- **Call the police.** Assaulting anyone is a crime, and many consider arrest to be the most effective means of halting spouse abuse. Moreover, even if the police do not make an arrest, a police report can support later legal action. For instance, victims can later (1) file charges on their own and testify against their spouses, (2) request protective orders, or (3) file for divorce.

- **Consult a domestic violence advocate.** Various organizations can provide victims of domestic violence with assistance in the areas of economic independence and safe housing. They may also offer the opportunity to participate in a support group for battered persons.

- **Obtain a protective order.** Courts can order an abuser to (1) stop the abuse, (2) cease all contact with his or her spouse, (3) leave the home, (4) get counseling, or (5) do something else. Violating a court order is considered contempt of court, and a person found guilty of contempt can be jailed or fined.

- **Move out.** The law does not require an abuse victim to stay in the family home. Despite the significant barriers victims face in leaving the home, with help, it is possible for the victim to leave. For example, many communities have protective

Talking to police

shelters where a woman and her children can live temporarily. Either the police or crisis hotline personnel can help a victim locate a shelter. She should then notify a friend or relative of her reasons for leaving.

- **Obtain a divorce.** If a couple is legally separated, one spouse has no right to enter the other's home without permission. Local bar associations, legal aid offices, family courts, and women's organizations can give victims information about divorce.

Legal Issues for Single People in Nontraditional Relationships

There have been dramatic increases in recent years in the number of unmarried couples living together and in the number of unmarried couples with children. In the past, if a man and a woman lived together, shared household duties and expenses, and then split up, they could go their separate ways without legal obligation. On the other hand, if the couple had been married, numerous laws would have set out their legal rights and duties concerning divorce, division of marital property, child support, and other issues.

The situation is changing for single people in nontraditional relationships. Unmarried adults may think that their love lives are their own concern, but they should be aware that legal issues can arise when single people live together. Certain legal rights and duties may exist between the partners.

Palimony

Some unmarried couples develop a cohabitation agreement—a written or oral contract that outlines how they want to deal with their money, property, or responsibilities, both during and after their relationship. Until recently, courts would not enforce agreements between unwed couples with respect to support or property ownership. Courts would not require that one member of an unwed couple make payments, sometimes called palimony, to the other after the couple split up. Courts said that contracts could not be based on an immoral relationship or be used to enforce an agreement for sex. If an unwed couple split up, any property went to the person who had legal title to it. In relationships in which the man was the wage earner and the woman was the homemaker, this meant the man often got all the property. In these situations, the wage earner owned any property acquired with his wages.

The rules changed in 1976 with the California Supreme Court's decision in *Marvin* v. *Marvin*. Since then, some state courts have enforced cohabitation agreements between unwed couples, including same-sex couples. In *Marvin* v. *Marvin*, the court ruled that unmarried adults who voluntarily live together can make contracts regarding their earnings and property rights. For the first time, a court said that unmarried persons may be entitled to property

Legal issues can arise when unmarried people live together. *What do you think some of these legal issues may be?*

The Model v. The Football Player

After seeing a photograph in a magazine, a professional football player named Bill phoned a modeling agency to arrange a meeting with Heather, one of its models. Bill and Heather began dating. Later, Heather left her career and moved in with Bill. They never married. After three years, Bill left Heather and moved in with an actress. Heather filed a breach of contract and unjust enrichment suit against Bill. She claimed that she had worked without pay as Bill's homemaker, chauffeur, and business and public relations manager and that Bill had received financial benefits from these services. She said he had promised to pay her at least $2,000 per month but had never done so. Her suit demands that he pay her $680,000 plus attorney's fees.

Problem 31.10

a. Why did Heather sue Bill?

b. Assuming that an unwritten contract is enforceable in the state where they lived, should the court enforce the agreement described?

c. What effect do you think enforcing such unwritten agreements between unmarried couples will have on marriages? What effect will it have on relationships between unmarried couples?

d. Do you think Heather and Bill should have signed a cohabitation agreement? If so, what terms should they have included?

rights and certain survivor benefits similar to those of married couples. Nevertheless, the court said that for this to happen, there must have been some form of contract between the partners. Only Oregon's courts recognize such property rights without the existence of a contract, and some states do not do so under any circumstances.

Same-Sex Partners

The rights of gay and lesbian couples to marry has been a controversial issue for many years. In recent years, several same-sex couples have challenged this notion in state courts. Their theory is that they have the right to marry whomever they wish, and that it would be unconstitutional for the state to deny them a marriage license or a valid marriage certificate. These court challenges were successful in the states of Hawaii (1996) and Alaska (1998). Further, in 1999, the Vermont Supreme Court decided that the state is required under its constitution to extend the same privileges and benefits of traditional marriage to same-sex couples.

As you learned earlier in this chapter, traditional marriages are recognized in every state, and married couples have the same rights and responsibilities regardless of where the wedding ceremony took place. In response to the decision in Hawaii, and concerned that all states would be forced to recognize same-sex unions that took place in other jurisdictions, Congress enacted the *Defense of Marriage Act* in 1996. This federal law defines marriage as the union of a man and a woman and declares that no state is required to recognize a relationship between persons of the same sex that is treated as a marriage by another state, territory, or tribe. Despite the earlier state court rulings upholding rights of same-sex couples, in 1998, voters in Alaska and Hawaii voted not to recognize same-sex marriages.

The legislature of Vermont, however, had a different reaction. In 2001, Vermont became the only state in the country to adopt a law that allows same-sex couples to enter into a civil union. Careful not to define such a union as a marriage, the law allows two persons to establish a relationship that will be recognized by the law and must be dissolved by the law. The civil union law incorporates restrictions on incest and bigamy, protects spousal benefits that would apply to partners in a traditional marriage, and provides the same protections with respect to children as those that flow to a married couple.

Although treatment of same-sex unions varies from state to state, some states and localities have domestic partnership laws that protect couples from discrimination in seeking domestic-partner benefits. These laws require that employers who offer fringe benefits such as medical, dental, disability, and life insurance to their employees must include domestic partners in the same way the benefits would be available to an employee's spouse.

One area in which same-sex couples still face significant discrimination is in the adoption of children. Some states specifically prohibit same-sex couples from adopting children, regardless of their fitness as parents.

The rights of couples—especially to marry—in same-sex relationships has become an important issue. *How have some states approached this issue in an attempt to extend rights to same-sex partners?*

Problem 31.11

a. In your opinion, do same-sex partners constitute a family? Should the law treat the union of a same-sex couple as it does a traditional marriage? Explain your reasons.

b. Should employers treat same-sex partners as families? Give your reasons.

c. Should same-sex couples be able to adopt children without any barriers, in the same way a traditional married couple can?

Parents and Children

The relationship between parents and children is a special one. Being a parent involves many rewards and also many responsibilities. Parents have a legal obligation to care for, support, and control their children. When parents are unable or unwilling to fulfill their responsibilities, the law becomes involved. This chapter explores the legal rights and responsibilities of parents and children.

Responsibilities Between Parents and Children

Parents are legally responsible for their children in many ways. Most importantly, they must provide the necessities of life. They must also provide for their children's social and moral development, and must control and supervise their children's behavior.

Parents are responsible for their children's education.

DNA testing is used to determine paternity. *What does the* Family Support Act of 1988 *require of all states?*

Paternity

No one can be forced to marry someone against his or her will; such a marriage would be invalid and could be annulled. When children are involved, however, the law does force parents to support their children whether or not the parents are married or dating, and regardless of where the child lives. For example, if a man denies being a child's father, the mother may bring a paternity suit, or action in court to establish his fatherhood, and force him to pay pregnancy expenses and child support. If the mother is a minor, some states allow her parents to bring the suit. The *Family Support Act of 1988* requires all states to assist mothers and children in obtaining paternity testing and to allow paternity suits until the child is 18 years old. It is the job of state lawyers to assist in finding missing parents and to help mothers and fathers prove paternity.

Blood samples can be used to prove that a particular man is not a particular child's father. For example, if both the mother and the alleged father have blood type A and the child has blood type B, the man cannot be the child's father. A child cannot have type B blood unless either the father or the mother has that type.

Blood type alone, however, cannot prove that a man is a child's father. Recently, more courts are using DNA tests to prove paternity. This is a method of testing blood or tissue for genes that link a specific parent and child. Test results are 99.9 percent accurate and greatly reduce the uncertainties that once plagued paternity suits.

Problem 32.1

Martha, 15, becomes pregnant. She claims that Michael, 17, is the father, but Michael denies it and refuses to marry her or support the child. Does the law require Michael to marry Martha? Does the law require unmarried teenagers to provide support for their children?

Where You Live

How is paternity determined in your state? What agencies can a mother or child go to for help in determining paternity?

The Mentally Disabled Child

When Diem and Kim divorce, the court orders Diem to pay $250 per month in child support for their six-year-old daughter, Meena. Meena is mentally disabled and is not expected to ever function at a level higher than that of a second grader. She lives with her mother and will probably never be capable of living independently. When Meena reaches the age of 18, Diem files a motion seeking to end his child support payments.

Problem 32.2

a. How should the court rule in this case?

b. What is the general rule for how long parents must financially support their children? Should that rule be different if the child is mentally or physically disabled?

c. What other conditions might make it reasonable to require that a parent support a child who is no longer a minor?

A mentally disabled child

Where You Live

In your state, how long must a parent support a child? What if the child is disabled? Does your state have any programs to assist parents of children with disabilities? Does the law in your state require adult children to support their parents?

Support

The most basic responsibility of parents is to support their minor children. This means that parents must provide the basic necessities of life, including food, clothing, shelter, education, and medical care. These are things minor children cannot provide for themselves.

All parents—rich and poor, married and unmarried, teenagers and older parents—are expected to support their minor children. The amount of support a family can give, of course, depends on what it can afford. Poor parents, for example, would not be in a position to provide expensive clothes or fancy meals.

Increasingly, the law is making mothers and fathers equally responsible for child support. This does not mean that each parent pays the same amount of money but that each parent provides according to his or her ability. In the event of a divorce, there is usually a support agreement or court order that indicates how much each parent must pay.

Emancipation

Parents are not usually required to give financial support to an adult child. Parents' legal responsibility ends when their children become emancipated. Emancipation means that children are free from the legal control and custody of their parents. Emancipation normally takes place when the child reaches adulthood—age 18 in most states. It also can occur when a child gets married, joins the armed forces, or becomes self-supporting. Some states also provide for emancipation at a younger age if a child successfully petitions the court for this legal status.

Family Responsibility Laws

A long tradition of law and social custom has called upon adult children to support their parents when the parents are in need. In most states, children are not legally required to support their elderly or disabled parents. Some states, however, have family responsibility laws that require adult children to care for elderly parents. Other states have abolished these laws, and almost all states limit the support obligation to an amount the relative can reasonably afford.

Where You Live

What special services does your school provide to students with disabilities? To what extent are students with disabilities mainstreamed, or included, at your school? What happens to such a student in your community if the schools cannot provide these essential services to students with special needs?

Problem 32.3

Rose, 42, owns a successful business. Her mother, 65, will retire from her job at the end of the year. However, her meager savings and Social Security payments are not enough for her to continue paying rent where she lives. She can move to a publicly supported home for the elderly but would prefer to stay in her own apartment. Does Rose have a legal obligation to support her mother? Should the law require adult children to support their parents when they are in need? Do people have a moral obligation to support their needy parents?

Many adult children support their elderly or disabled parents. *What are family responsibility laws? Does your state have them?*

The School at Home

Homeschooling

Michelle and Larry Novitzki have four children. Two are of school age. Both parents are high school graduates, and Michelle has a college degree. They began educating their children at home because they disapproved of the public school's sex education classes, were concerned about violence in schools, and believed that the children would learn more in a less-structured environment. They designed lessons that related to activities around their house and community.

The Novitzkis use books and materials obtained in their state and have set aside one room to serve as a classroom. The children receive instruction six hours a day, year-round. Both children score above average on standardized tests and appear to psychologists to be healthy and normal. An educational official claims that the Novitzkis' program does not satisfy the state's compulsory education law.

Problem 32.4

a. Should the Novitzkis be allowed to instruct their children at home? Do you think their reasons for wanting to do so are valid?

b. What are the advantages and disadvantages of homeschooling?

c. What qualifications, if any, do you think a parent should have in order to teach his or her children at home?

d. Do you think homeschooled students should be able to participate on school sports teams? Why or why not?

Education

All children have a right to a free public school education through the twelfth grade. Each state sets standards for its public school system, but parents have a right to choose the kind of school to which they want to send their children—public, private, parochial, or homeschool. School attendance is generally required for children ages 7 to 16, although state laws vary. A child who misses school without justification is considered a truant. Because states generally hold parents responsible for their children's welfare and education, parents who fail to send their children to school may be fined or arrested.

Some parents decide that the traditional public or private school system is not adequate to meet the needs of their children, and that they would rather educate their children at home. Prior to the 1980s, many states did not permit children to be homeschooled. As of 2002, all 50 states and the District of Columbia allowed a child's formal education to take place at home under certain circumstances, such as having dedicated space for instruction to take place, meeting state curricular requirements, and participating in mandated achievement testing. In 2003, more than one million school-aged children were educated at home.

Parents are not legally required to pay for college tuition. However, many parents do, if they are financially able to. Some separation agreements require parental financial support through college for the couple's children.

Medical Care

Parents have a legal duty to protect and supervise their children's health. This means that they must provide proper medical and dental care. For example, children should be current on immunizations and should visit the dentist twice a year.

Children usually need their parents' permission to obtain medical treatment. For example, suppose a 14-year-old boy wants cosmetic surgery. Without his parents' permission, a doctor could not perform such surgery. Parents have a right to supervise medical care, but they can also be charged with neglect if they ignore their children's health. In very serious cases, a court may permit a doctor to treat a child without parental consent. Doctors may also act in life-threatening emergencies without permission from either parent or a court.

Where You Live

May teenagers receive health services without their parents' permission in your state? Can these services include birth control counseling? At what age may a person legally obtain contraceptives in your state?

For Your Information . . .

The *Individuals with Disabilities Education Act*

A federal law, the *Individuals with Disabilities Education Act (IDEA)*, provides for a public school education for children with disabilities. Under this law, children with physical, mental, and emotional disabilities who need special services in order to learn are entitled to an evaluation and an appropriate individual educational plan. Children who need services must be granted specialized instruction, as well as any related services necessary for the child to benefit from the program. Such services may include transportation, speech and language therapy, and psychological or psychiatric counseling. These services are all provided at no cost to the child or family.

The School Health Clinic

A study shows that many students in your school district do not receive proper medical care. In response, the school board decides to open a health clinic in your high school. The county Board of Health staffs the clinic with two full-time registered nurses. A doctor is in attendance two mornings and three afternoons each week.

The clinic offers all students emergency medical care, routine physical exams, and instruction in preventive health care and nutrition. Clinic doctors are authorized to prescribe and administer medication. Noting the rise in teen pregnancy, the county Board of Health also suggests that the clinic be authorized to counsel students regarding birth control and to dispense contraceptives.

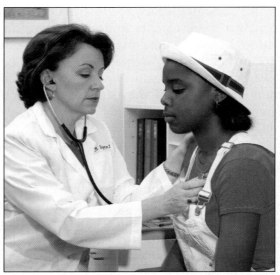

Receiving medical care

Problem 32.5

a. Should teenagers be able to obtain routine health care (as described above) at the school clinic without parental consent? Give your reasons.

b. Should teenagers be able to obtain contraceptives at school without parental consent? Give your reasons.

c. If the clinic does provide counseling about birth control and distributes contraceptives, what limitations (if any) should it place on students who may receive them? What legal issues should you consider?

d. Should high schools teach sex education? If so, should the classes be required or optional? If the classes are required and a parent has religious objections or does not want his or her child to take the class, should the student be exempt from the requirement?

Care and Supervision

Parents may decide what is best for their children as long as they do not abuse or neglect their children. There are no minimum requirements for the number of hours parents must spend with their children. Both parents may work, and their children may be left home alone after school or at other times. However, state laws govern the age at which a child may be left alone in the home, so parents must be sure that someone responsible is caring for their young children at all times. These laws concerning child care and supervision vary from state to state.

Discipline

Parents have a right and a duty to supervise their children. Likewise, children have a legal obligation to obey their parents and to follow reasonable rules. Parents can ask children to do chores around the house and yard. Parents may also decide where their children live, what school they attend, what religion they practice, and other aspects of their lives. However, parental authority is not absolute. Children do not have to obey parents who order them to do something dangerous or illegal. Parents who resort to unreasonable forms of treatment in order to discipline their children can be charged with child abuse or child neglect.

Children who *continually* disobey their parents or run away from home may be charged as status offenders. As explained in Chapter 16, status offenses are acts that are not illegal if committed by adults. Status offenses include running away from home, skipping school, refusing to obey parents, or engaging in immoral or dangerous behavior. A status offender may be placed under court supervision. When this happens, the child is known as a PINS, CHINS, or MINS—a person, child, or minor in need of supervision. Under these circumstances, courts may order counseling or special schooling or, in serious cases, may place the child in a juvenile facility or a foster home.

Problem 32.6

Consider the following situations. In each case, decide whether the parents have the legal authority to make the decision involved. What arguments can you make in support of the parents? In support of the children?

a. Mr. McBride disapproves of the lifestyle of his 19-year-old son, Larry, who regularly smokes marijuana. When Larry refuses to stop using the drug, Mr. McBride cuts off his financial support, including college tuition.

b. Monica, 17, has a birthmark on her cheek. On the advice of a friend, she decides to have plastic surgery to remove it. Her parents forbid it.

c. Hiroshi, a high school senior, does not want to move to a new city with his parents. He wants to finish high school with his friends. His parents insist that he live with them.

d. Mr. and Mrs. Parham think that their 16-year-old daughter is mentally ill and needs psychiatric treatment. The daughter objects, but her parents decide to commit her to a mental institution.

Parental Responsibility for Children's Acts

Parents who fail to exercise proper supervision and control over their children may be held legally responsible for their children's acts. This is especially true if they aid or encourage improper conduct. For example, a parent who allows an underage child to drink and drive may be held liable if the child has an accident.

Almost all states hold parents civilly liable for certain acts of their minor children, such as property damage, theft, or vandalism. Some states also recognize as a crime an action termed **contributing to the delinquency of a minor.** A parent who encourages a child to sell drugs could be charged with this crime. Some states are passing and trying to enforce laws that make parents criminally responsible for certain delinquent acts committed by their children. Other states see such laws as unworkable and believe they shift responsibility away from the children, who should be held accountable for their own actions.

Historically, parents were not held responsible for injuries caused by their children. This applied whether the injuries were accidental or intentional, unless the parents were somehow to blame. For example, if a parent gave a child a gun to play with, the parent could be liable for any injuries caused by the child.

Today, all states make parents legally responsible for harm caused by their children, up to a certain dollar amount. This amount varies from $200 to $50,000, depending on state law. A special rule known as the **family car doctrine** makes parents responsible for damages caused by any driver in the family. This means that if you cause an accident while driving your parents' car, your parents may have to pay for any damage.

Problem 32.7

Vanessa, 14, constantly stays out late at night and often misses school. She seems to have a lot of cash and nice clothes. When her parents ask where she gets the money, she says she earns it babysitting at night. Her parents suspect she's involved in drugs—maybe even selling them. One night Vanessa and her boyfriend break into a neighbor's house, steal a television, and sell it to get money for drugs. A neighbor sees them buying drugs, and Vanessa and her boyfriend are arrested.

a. Have Vanessa's parents adequately supervised their daughter? If not, what should they have done differently? Can parents' actions affect the actions of their children?

b. Should Vanessa's parents have to pay for the neighbor's television? Why or why not?

c. Should parents be held criminally responsible for the actions of their children? If so, under what circumstances?

Many children work after-school jobs to earn money. *What does the law allow parents to do with their children's earnings?*

Earnings and Employment

In many families, children who work can keep and spend their own money. Nevertheless, parents have the legal right to take the earnings of their minor children. Children may keep

FIGURE 32.1 Child Abuse Reported, 1962–2002

Year	Cases
1962 (prior to reporting laws)	662
1976 (first year data collected)	1.1 million
1984	1.7 million
1988	2.2 million
1992	2.9 million
1995	3.2 million
2002	3.5 million

Source: National Committee to Prevent Child Abuse

Reporting laws have resulted in an increased number of reported cases of child abuse. **ANALYZE THE DATA** *By how much did the number of reported cases change in the 10 years between 1992 and 2002?*

only the wages that their parents want them to keep. However, parents have no right to use other money that legally belongs to their children. For example, if a minor receives an inheritance or recovers damages in a lawsuit, he or she has the right to have this money set aside in a bank account until reaching adulthood.

Child Abuse and Neglect

Child abuse takes many forms. It occurs whenever any adult or older child inflicts or threatens to inflict intentional physical, emotional, or sexual harm on a child. Child neglect occurs more frequently than child abuse and involves the failure to properly feed, clothe, shelter, educate, supervise, or tend to the medical needs of a child. Abuse and neglect are among the leading causes of death of children in the United States.

Abuse and neglect of children have effects that go far beyond the obvious immediate dangers. Studies have shown that nearly 85 percent of all juveniles who break the law have themselves been victims of abuse. Truancy and suicide attempts often result from emotional abuse. Moreover, abused children frequently grow up to be abusive adults.

Not surprisingly, most youths who run away from home have suffered physical and emotional abuse and neglect. Nearly three-fourths of all female runaways have been sexually abused, and so have many male runaways. Older teenage runaways are sometimes termed "throwaways." These are children whose parents refuse to care for them.

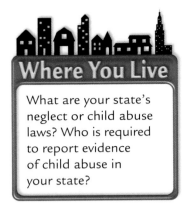

Where You Live

What are your state's neglect or child abuse laws? Who is required to report evidence of child abuse in your state?

Abused children often are not in a position to do anything about their abuse. Accordingly, every state has laws requiring doctors, nurses, teachers, social workers, and others to report suspected cases of abuse or neglect. At least 18 states require all citizens to report any reasonable suspicions. Accusing someone of child abuse without having any reason to suspect the person of abuse might provide the basis for a civil lawsuit. However, you will not be held legally liable for a mistaken report made in good faith. In fact, failure to report suspected abuse if you are obligated under state law to do so can lead to criminal or civil penalties, or both. If you suspect that someone is a victim of abuse, you should exercise your responsibility to report it.

Sexual Abuse

Reported cases of child sexual abuse have increased dramatically in recent years. Sexual fondling, using a child in pornography, and making a child view pornography all constitute sexual abuse, along with other forms of sexual contact. The sexual offender is often a person the child knows and trusts, such as a family member, a family friend, a child care worker, a school employee, or even a clergy member. The abuser can be an older child, an adult, or even a parent. Despite the benefits we enjoy from the Internet, growing use of the Internet by children and adults has provided child abusers with another way of preying on juveniles—through online forums such as chat rooms. Child sexual abusers prey on a child's obedience, trust, and embarrassment. In the online context, they often lie to a child about who they are, their age, and the basis of their interest in the child. In all contexts, abusers often use threats to prevent a child from reporting the abuse.

Problem 32.8

For each situation, decide whether or not the action of the parent or parents should be considered child abuse or neglect. Explain your answer. If you find abuse or neglect, what should be done to protect the child?

a. Sixteen-year-old Theresa returns home late one evening. As punishment, her parents ground her for a week.

b. Eighteen-year-old Shauna and her two-year-old son, Jeffrey, live with her mother. Shauna has to be at work at 9 P.M., but her mother does not get home until 10 P.M. Shauna feeds Jeffrey, puts him to bed, and leaves him asleep and alone for the hour or so until her mother returns home from work.

c. George's parents refuse to allow him to date or go anywhere without them, even though he is 16 years old.

Increasingly, parents are bringing civil suits against child abusers and their employers. The suits typically charge an employer, such as a day-care center, with negligence for not properly overseeing employees or screening job applicants for a history of child abuse. As a result, it is now common for organizations that employ adults who work with children to require job applicants to submit to fingerprinting. The fingerprints go to the FBI, which checks for any past child abuse violations by the applicant.

Some people say that children simply imagine episodes of sexual abuse. However, most psychologists stress that young children lack the sexual experience to make up stories of sexual abuse by themselves. Moreover, while it is possible for an older child to invent such a story, such instances are considered unusual. Therefore, anytime a minor reports sexual abuse, his or her story should be taken seriously and investigated.

If a child does report sexual abuse, the police should be notified immediately, and, if justified, charges should be brought against the abuser. An investigation will determine whether the child is in immediate, ongoing danger and whether the case should go to trial. If the alleged abuser is a parent, the child may be removed from the home. Most states currently allow child victims to testify in court through closed-circuit television or by means of videotaped questioning to save them from the trauma of having to face their attackers.

The Case of . . .

A Parent, Drug Use, and Neglect

Jenna is the mother of six-year-old Kimberly. The police recently searched their apartment for drugs and found it to be a "shooting gallery" for heroin. Numerous syringes and needles were found, and Jenna and others present were arrested. Kimberly sat on the living room couch during the raid.

There is no definite evidence that Jenna is using drugs, although she has a history of drug use and is currently in a drug rehabilitation program. She claims that her boyfriend comes into her apartment with his friends and that they use drugs without her permission. Jenna has a full-time job as a secretary, and Kimberly is doing well in school. She loves her mother and does not want to be taken from her home.

The state law regarding child neglect reads: "Neglect means the negligent treatment or the maltreatment of a child by a person responsible for the child's welfare under circumstances indicating harm or threatened harm to the child's health or welfare. The term includes both acts and omissions on the part of the responsible person."

Problem 32.9

a. Assume that the state brings a neglect petition against Jenna. What are the arguments for and against finding Kimberly to be a neglected child?

b. If you were the judge, would you find neglect in this case? Why or why not?

c. If Kimberly is found to be neglected, would you terminate parental rights and remove her from the home? What other orders might you issue?

d. Do you think a parent who uses drugs is committing neglect? Does it make a difference if the child is aware of the drug use? What other factors should be considered before neglect is found to exist?

How to Report Child Abuse and Neglect

- **To whom do I make a report?**

To make a child abuse or neglect report, call the National Child Abuse Hotline, 1-800-4-A-CHILD, or visit them online at www.childhelpusa.org. The hotline will tell you how to contact your local child protective services (CPS) agency. You also may want to talk to a teacher, counselor, medical person, or other trusted adult. If you believe the child is in immediate danger, contact the police.

- **Who must report suspected cases of child abuse?**

Usually, medical practitioners, teachers, child care professionals, school officials, and social workers report suspected cases of abuse.

- **Who may report?**

Suspected cases of child abuse can be reported by anyone suspecting that a child is being mistreated. This may include the child who is being abused.

- **What conditions should I report?**

You should report any situation that suggests abuse or neglect of a child. This may include unexplained bruises or burn marks; constant hunger or repeated inappropriate dress for the weather; major weight gain or loss; or chronic uncleanliness, exhaustion, or school absences. You may also want to talk to the child's teachers or another trusted adult. If a child is in immediate danger or if you witness a child being beaten, call the police for immediate response.

Receiving help from a CPS worker

- **What happens if I report someone?**

After you make the report, a CPS worker will ask for all the information you have. Then the CPS worker will visit the family to determine if the child in question is in immediate danger and whether it is necessary to call in the police or a doctor. Under extreme circumstances, the child may be removed from the home immediately. In such cases, the child is placed in foster care or with another family member who does not live in the same household. Otherwise, the CPS worker will interview the parents, observe the physical and emotional conditions of the household, and decide if there is a need for counseling or family support services.

- **Must I give my name when I make a report?**

No, although it might assist the CPS worker in gaining more information and enable the authorities to take legal action against the abuser.

Foster Care and Adoption

Children do not always remain with their biological families. Neglected or abused children may be removed from the family home, placed in foster care, and sometimes made available for adoption. Some parents decide for a variety of reasons to give their children up for adoption, usually at birth.

Foster Care

In some extreme cases of child abuse, neglect, or deaths in the family, courts may decide that parents are unable to care for their children. The state becomes the child's temporary legal guardian—making most decisions about that child's life while the child's parents retain limited legal rights. Judges and social workers then decide where and with whom the child will live. As of 2002, nearly 600,000 children were living in out-of-home care in the United States. Family foster care is a system of licensed families in each state who act as temporary parents for children who cannot live with their families. Foster parents have temporary

"There are no unwanted children, just unfound families."

— The National Adoption Center

Street Law
online
Visit the *Street Law* Web site at streetlaw.glencoe.com for chapter-based information and resources.

One goal shared by foster care and adoption is to place children in safe and healthy homes.

physical custody of children and care for them day to day. They do not have legal custody of the child. Children may also live in **group homes,** where several children in foster care live together. **Kinship care** refers to children being placed with relatives who are not their parents. If they are placed there by the state, the law requires that these relatives be licensed like any other foster family.

Foster care is meant to be only a temporary solution. Judges regularly review the case and are required to do everything they can to provide children with permanent homes. Courts first try to help the families from which the children came to make changes necessary to provide safe homes. This solution—*family reunification*—is the most common outcome for children in foster care. If the court finds that there is no way for the child to return home, then the judge may **terminate parental rights.** Once this happens, children may be adopted by their foster families, relatives, or others.

A permanent home cannot be found for every child. Each year, thousands of youths leave the foster care system because they have reached the age at which they become **emancipated.** This can be age 16, 18, or 21, depending on the state. These young people become legal adults, which means no one has custody of them. The *Foster Care Independence Act of 1999* requires that these youths be given "independent living services" until the age of 21, which may include temporary housing, job training, and help attaining further education.

Adoption

Adoption is the legal process by which an adult or adults become the legal parent(s) of another person. Though adults usually adopt children, most states permit adults to adopt another adult. The law places few restrictions on who can adopt another. Therefore, most people—regardless of marital status, race, religion, or age—are eligible to adopt anyone else. In practice, however, adoption agencies and courts try to make a child's new family as much like a traditional family as possible. Adoption agencies thus are sometimes reluctant to place children with a single parent or with parents of a different race or religion. Some states also prohibit gay and lesbian people from becoming foster or adoptive parents.

Most adoptions are arranged through public or private adoption agencies. People wishing to adopt apply to an agency and are investigated and evaluated to determine whether they would be suitable parents. While public agencies usually charge little or no fee for this service, private agencies often charge substantial fees for their

Some children are placed in the care of relatives rather than in the foster care system. *What are the advantages to kinship care?*

For Your Information . . .

Removing Children From the Family

When a child is removed from the family, court hearings are held. Both the child and the parents have a right to attend and to have lawyers represent them.

- **Preliminary protective hearings** are held either immediately before or immediately after a social services agency removes a child from the family and places the child in protective custody. If there is immediate danger to the child, social services may remove the child until a hearing is held, usually within two or three days. A judge decides whether there is a good reason for the child to stay in the care of the state until a full hearing can be held, and identifies the child's immediate needs.

- **Jurisdictional or adjudication hearings** are held to hear testimony from the social services agency, the parents, and the court-appointed guardian for the child (a *guardian ad litem* or Court-Appointed Special Advocate [CASA] worker). If the court finds clear evidence of abuse or neglect indicating that the child cannot

safely return home, the child is placed in the care of the state. If not, the child is returned to the home.

- **Disposition hearings** are held to determine where, and with whom, the child should live. This is sometimes combined with the jurisdictional hearing. Dispositional decisions must be reviewed regularly by the judge, with the goal of returning the child to the family from which they were removed.

- **Permanency hearings** are held to find a permanent, stable home for the child. All youths in foster care have a right to these hearings, and to have a say in where they want their permanent home to be. For most children, the goal is reunification with their family. For others, adoption, guardianship, or emancipation may be best.

- **Termination of parental rights hearings** are held when the court feels a parent cannot or will not be able to provide a safe home for a child. Once the parents' rights are terminated, the child may be adopted.

services. Some people work through agencies to adopt children living in foreign countries. Other people turn to "go-betweens," who arrange for pregnant women to turn their babies over to adoptive parents without going through an adoption agency. Some states allow this practice and license the go-betweens. Other states refer to the practice as "black-market adoption" and make it illegal.

People who wish to adopt must also apply to a court to have the adoption legally approved. An attorney often takes the legal steps to make the adoption final. An adoption agency will submit its report on the adopting parents and will seek written consent from the birth parents. In most states, consent is required, but in some cases, even if the birth parents refuse or cannot be found, courts may still grant adoptions that they decide are in the best interest of the child. Children over a certain age—often 12 or 14—must also consent to the adoption.

Interracial Adoptions

The U.S. Supreme Court first addressed the roles of race, ethnicity, and religion in court cases involving child custody and adoption in 1980. The Court ruled that a judge should not consider the race or races of a child's parents when deciding whether to take a child from a home. In 1994 Congress passed a law allowing the race of adoptive parents and the child to be used as a factor in deciding whether to allow adoptions. This was reversed in 1996 when Congress passed a law specifying that no adoption could be delayed or denied on the basis of race. This legislation, however, applies only to adoption agencies receiving federal funds. In many instances today, race *is* one of the factors considered by social workers, courts, and private-sector adoption agencies in determining the homes where children should be placed.

Read the proposed law and the arguments below. Then answer the questions.

Proposed Law: In making decisions regarding the adoption of a child, the race of the child and the adoptive parents shall *not* be considered as a factor.

Arguments in Favor of the Law: At any given time, there are often more white families wishing to adopt children than families of other races. There are several reasons for this disparity. Whites in this country tend to be wealthier overall than certain other races. If families can choose the race of the children they adopt, children of other races will wait longer periods for adoption than white children. Children's needs for safe and healthy homes should be given more weight than the adoptive parents' preference for a child of their own race. In

addition, allowing racial preference is a form of discrimination. The law should promote equality.

Arguments Against the Law: Several races and ethnicities in U.S. society have a history of being oppressed, especially African Americans. It is important to place children of historically oppressed races and ethnicities in homes that will practice and preserve the traditions of their cultural heritage, promote knowledge and pride in their cultural history, and equip children with the coping skills necessary to live in a society in which traces of oppression still exist. Even if they strive to promote cultural knowledge and self-respect, white parents who adopt African American children, for example, will find it difficult to foster such an environment. White parents tend to associate socially more with white people, practice traditions from a European background, and lack knowledge of African American history and culture. African American children raised by white parents, therefore, will be confused about their identities, unaware of the accomplishments and history of people of their race, and unprepared to function well in either culture.

Problem 33.1

a. Debate both sides of the proposed law. Should it be adopted? Explain.

b. Should the religion of the adoptive parents or the child be considered in making adoption decisions?

c. If the child to be adopted is a Native American, should the adoptive parents be required to be Native American?

In most states, when the court approves an adoption, it issues a temporary order. This means the agency or birth parents remain the legal guardians for a specified waiting period, such as six months or a year. After this waiting period, a new birth certificate is issued showing the adopting parents as the parents of the child. The child and the adoptive parents then assume the same rights and responsibilities as children and their birth parents.

Some couples who have had difficulty conceiving their own biological children turn to surrogate parenting. A **surrogate mother** is a woman, other than the wife, who agrees to be artificially inseminated with the husband's sperm. The surrogate and the couple typically sign a contract before the child is born in which the surrogate consents to the child's adoption by the couple and releases all parental rights. State laws vary widely on the legality of surrogacy contracts and the terms that may be included in them. Several states have passed laws regulating the enforcement of surrogacy contracts. These restrictions range from requiring advance judicial approval of the agreement, to barring the enforcement of an agreement if the surrogate is compensated beyond pregnancy expenses, to barring all such surrogate contracts completely.

Do you think adopted children should have a right to know who their birth parents are? Traditionally, adoption records were sealed, and adopted children were not allowed to find out the names or whereabouts of their birth parents. However, adoptive children are often interested in learning about and meeting their birth parents. Some adoptees spend a great deal of time seeking information on their family history. Today, a few states allow access to adoption records. Other states have laws that give adopted children who have reached the age of majority the right to obtain the names of their birth parents. Many people oppose these laws, believing that the birth parents have a right to privacy and a right not to see children they put up for adoption unless they desire to do so.

Where You Live

Does your state law allow adopted children to find out the identities of their birth parents? What does the law provide?

Sealing adoption records is a controversial issue. *Should adopted children be able to find out the names of their birth parents?*

Scarpetta v. The Adoption Agency

Olga Scarpetta, 32, comes from a wealthy California family. During an affair with a married man, she becomes pregnant. Olga thinks her pregnancy will embarrass her family, so she goes to New York to have the baby. The child is born May 18 and turned over to an adoption agency four days later. On June 1, Olga signs a document giving the agency full authority to find new parents for the child.

The agency places the infant with the DeMartino family on June 18. Dr. DeMartino and his wife have previously adopted a four-year-old boy from the same agency.

Within two months after the birth, Olga changes her mind and asks for her baby. The agency refuses and will not tell her who has adopted the child. After several weeks of arguing with the agency, Olga goes to court. She tells the judge that she was physically and emotionally distraught following childbirth. She is now sure that she wants to keep the child. Her family has learned of the birth and also wants Olga to get the baby back.

Problem 33.2

Read the following opinions and decide which one you agree most with. Give reasons for your choice. Note that the adoption agency is the defendant in this case because the DeMartinos have not yet received final legal custody of the child. The court must decide whether to return the child to the birth parent or leave the child with the adoptive parents.

Opinion A

There are many reasons this court believes it is in the best interest of the child to leave her with her adoptive parents, the DeMartinos.

First, Ms. Scarpetta waited six weeks after putting the child up for adoption before requesting the child's return. During this period, the DeMartinos formed a strong attachment to the child and made many sacrifices because they had every reason to believe the child would be their own.

Second, the DeMartinos' situation is much more secure than Ms. Scarpetta's. She is unmarried, and, from the evidence before us, appears emotionally unstable. As for the DeMartinos, the agency selected them because they had already adopted a four-year-old boy and proved themselves well able to provide for the child's moral and physical well-being. They can give the attention of two parents to the child. To take the baby away at this point would cause them a great deal of suffering.

Finally, Ms. Scarpetta freely gave up the child, and the agency acted in a proper manner in obtaining her consent.

Opinion B

There is a legal presumption that, unless proven to be unfit, the birth mother is best suited to provide support and care for her child. This court believes that Olga Scarpetta is a fit birth parent.

First, Ms. Scarpetta was under great pressure when she placed the child for adoption. She had just gone through an unplanned pregnancy, labor, and delivery. She was worried about the reaction of her highly religious family. Her decision could not have been freely made under these circumstances.

Second, she now clearly wants the child and is able to provide for the child's welfare. Her wealthy family also supports her in this decision and will no doubt help her if she needs financial assistance.

Finally, there is no evidence that she will be an unfit parent. Even though the DeMartinos may be good or even better parents, they should not be given rights ahead of those of the birth mother.

Law in *Action*

Adoption Records Hearing

Assume that your state proposes the following law: "All adopted persons over the age of 18 shall have the right to obtain copies of their original birth certificates and shall be given the names and last known addresses of their birth parents." At a hearing on the proposed law, two people testify.

Mrs. Margaret Jones: "When I was 16, I became pregnant. The father, a soldier at a nearby military base, was transferred and I never saw him again. My parents could not afford to support another child, and I didn't want to leave school. I was also embarrassed, so I went to stay with my aunt in another town. I had the baby and then placed him for adoption. I then returned home and finished school. I am now married and the mother of two children, ages 11 and 14. My husband does not know about the child I gave up. The adoption agency promised that it would never tell anyone my name. I do not wish to see the child I put up for adoption, and I believe it best that we live our own separate lives."

Michael Franklin: "I am 19 years old. Last year my parents told me that I was adopted at birth. I love my adoptive parents, but I need to find out who my birth parents are and meet them. I would like to know about important family medical issues. Besides, I want to know where I came from and more about why I am the way I am. Everyone needs to belong somewhere. It's inhuman not to let me know who my birth parents are."

Problem 33.3

a. If you were a member of the legislature and heard these testimonies, how would you vote on the adoption records law? Explain.

b. Would the law be better if it allowed adopted children to look at records only after the birth parents had given their consent?

c. Would fewer people place children for adoption if they knew the children could later find out their names?

d. Would opening adoption records result in more abortions and more black-market adoptions?

e. What problems do you think might arise if the proposed law is passed? How would you rewrite the law to improve it?

f. Should Michael's adoptive parents have told him sooner that he was adopted? If they know, should they tell him who his birth mother is and why he was placed for adoption?

A pregnant teen

CHAPTER
34

Separation, Divorce, and Custody

When problems arise in a marriage, they can often be resolved with help from friends, family members, or counselors. Sometimes, however, a husband and wife may consider ending their marriage. When this occurs, it involves difficult changes for the entire family. This chapter covers procedures for ending a valid marriage through separation or divorce, as well as the many legal issues raised by divorce, including child custody, alimony and child support, and property division. If parents remarry or find a new life partner, new relationships are created for stepparents and children. All of these changes involve the law.

Marriage Problems

A national survey identified the most common problems in a marriage. Some of the difficulties a couple may experience are conflicts with in-laws or relatives, job and career pressures, adultery, conflicts about children, sexual problems, and a breakdown in communication. Alcohol or drug abuse, money problems, and loss of shared goals or interests may also affect a couple's relationship.

"For a couple with young children, divorce seldom comes as a 'solution' to stress, only as a way to end one form of pain and accept another."

— Fred Rogers, U.S. television personality

Street Law online

Visit the *Street Law* Web site at streetlaw.glencoe.com for chapter-based information and resources.

Separation and divorce can be painful experiences for children.

414

Minor disagreements are usually settled by the couple themselves, or with the help of family members and friends. Major differences may require the couple to seek the help of a marriage counselor, psychologist, or social worker. A **marriage counselor**, for example, can help them explore the reasons for their problems and, ideally, work out a solution. The American Association for Marriage and Family Therapy can help couples find a local qualified marriage counselor. Couples can also ask for help from friends or members of the clergy.

A breakdown in communication is one of the most common problems in a marriage. *How are separation and divorce similar? How are they different?*

Separation and Divorce

If a married couple decides that their marriage has broken down and cannot be repaired, the partners have two legal options:

- **Separation.** The couple may decide to live apart. This may be for a short cooling-off period, or it may be permanent. In either case, the couple is still legally married and may reunite at any time.
- **Divorce.** A divorce is a court order that legally ends a valid marriage. Once a divorce is final, each partner may legally remarry.

Separation

Just as the process for beginning a marriage is governed by state law, so is the process of ending a marriage. Most states require a couple to enter into a separation period prior to obtaining a final divorce. This period can range from a few months to more than a year. During this time, both spouses have time to consider the consequences of ending the marriage and to get their affairs in order so that they can go on with their separate lives. A separation period can be especially helpful to couples who have children.

In addition, some couples will not consider divorce for religious or other reasons. Sometimes, however, a husband and wife need time apart to consider the future. In these situations, a separation rather than a divorce may be the best idea.

If a married couple separate, they still have legal and financial responsibilities to each other and their children. They remain husband and wife, and neither can remarry. For these reasons, having a **separation agreement** is a good idea. This is typically a written document that sets out the couple's agreed-upon terms for child custody and visitation, child and spousal support, division of property, and other issues. It is often the result of mediation between the husband and wife.

Where You Live

What marriage or family counseling agencies exist in your community? Are these privately or publicly operated? How much do they charge?

When a separation agreement has been signed by both the husband and the wife, it becomes a legally enforceable contract. For example, if one spouse refuses to pay promised support money or will not leave the home as agreed, he or she can be taken to court by the other.

A separation agreement can say anything the husband and wife want it to say. Separation agreements do not have to be approved by a court. Once the parties have agreed to the terms of the contract, each side must abide by it. However, in certain cases, the partners may choose to go to court to have a judge approve the agreement. In this case, after it is signed, the agreement cannot be changed unless the court changes it or both spouses agree to the change. If a couple later seek a divorce, the terms of the separation agreement usually form the basis for the final divorce decree (court order).

Divorce

Each year, more than one million couples are divorced in the United States. Today, about half of all marriages end in divorce. Divorce is the process by which a couple legally ends their marriage and divides their property. This does not mean, though, that the couple's legal relationship is ended. There may be continuing financial obligations and, if there are children, there will almost certainly be continuing rights and responsibilities that the parents must share.

Ending a marriage can be expensive. Legal fees, alimony, child support payments, and the cost of maintaining two households are likely to pose a financial challenge. Divorce can also be very hard on all of those involved—the spouses, children, friends, and extended family. This is why it is important that couples not rush into a divorce, which will have a long-term effect on their lives and the lives of their children.

Because of the difficulties that arise when marriages end, lawyers and judges often recommend that couples considering a divorce first go through the process of mediation. The presence of a neutral third party to assist couples in identifying, confronting, and solving the problems that divorce presents can make the process easier and may produce a more harmonious resolution.

Second or third marriages present additional difficulties. Each partner may bring in problems left over from a previous marriage. There may be alimony, child support payments, or debts to resolve. Children and parents from previous marriages often form a "blended family." Children gain stepparents, spouses acquire stepchildren, and all must learn to live with new persons in the household.

Blended families are formed when parents with children from previous relationships get married. *Describe the challenges a divorcing couple might face.*

For all these reasons, a couple should be aware that divorce is a serious step that will affect them and their children for the rest of their lives. A couple should not decide to seek a divorce in the heat of anger or without at least trying to work out their problems. This is why states recommend and some require a period of separation before they will grant a divorce.

When a couple has decided to seek a divorce, they can proceed in several ways. Until recently, most divorcing couples hired lawyers to prepare their cases. However, it is not always necessary to have attorneys involved in every aspect of a divorce. *Pro se* (or do-it-yourself) divorce kits and classes are available in many places. To learn more about this, check with your local court, library, bookstore, or legal aid office. If the divorce involves disagreements over children, large sums of money, property, or anything else substantial, then each spouse should have an attorney or consult a family mediation service.

A family mediator works with a couple, guiding them through a series of negotiations designed to achieve an agreement with which both can live. The agreement is usually then reviewed by the couple's lawyers before being filed in court. Mediators can help divorcing couples reach a settlement without the time, expense, or hard feelings of the traditional adversary process. Working with a mediator is also beneficial because the couple involved know the most about their own situation, and can therefore better devise a solution that will work.

There are several types of resources available for a couple who has decided to proceed with a divorce. *What are the advantages and disadvantages of using an attorney when divorcing?*

Problem 34.1

Bill and Rachel married when both were 19 years old. One year later, they had a baby. After two years of marriage, they fight constantly and are miserable. They are unsure about a divorce, but both think it might be better to live apart for awhile. Bill works as an auto mechanic, making $2,200 a month. Rachel works as a teller in a local bank, making $1,750 a month. Bill and Rachel rent an apartment for $850 a month and spend $600 a month on child care. They also have $2,000 of joint credit-card debt. They own the following assets: $750 in a savings account; a used, but paid for, car worth $6,000; and furniture and appliances.

a. Do Bill and Rachel have any choices besides divorce? Explain.

b. Do Bill and Rachel need a lawyer to help them? How could a mediator help them? Who else could help them?

c. List the things that Bill and Rachel must decide before agreeing to a separation.

Typical grounds for divorce include mental and physical cruelty. *Why have many states changed their laws to include no-fault divorce?*

At one time, most states allowed divorce only if one spouse could show that the other spouse had done something wrong or was at fault. Typical faults, or grounds for divorce, included the following:

- **Adultery.** Sexual intercourse between a married person and someone other than his or her spouse.
- **Desertion.** Leaving one's spouse with no intention of returning.
- **Mental cruelty.** Acts of emotional abuse against one's spouse.
- **Physical cruelty.** Acts of violence or physical abuse against one's spouse.
- **Insanity.** Mental illness.

Proving that one spouse was at fault was often hard, and divorce used to cause great embarrassment. In many cases, a finding that one spouse was at fault would preclude him or her from receiving any support after the marriage ended. Eventually, in part because of the personal nature and high levels of emotion inherent in marriage and divorce, courts decided that they were not always in the best position to decide when and under what circumstances a couple should stay married or get divorced.

In recent years, the laws have changed. Most states now also maintain a **no-fault divorce** system. To obtain a no-fault divorce, a spouse does not have to prove that the other spouse did something wrong. Instead, the husband or wife has to show only that there are **irreconcilable differences.** This means that the marriage has completely broken down and is beyond repair. Many states also allow divorce when a couple can show that they voluntarily lived apart for a certain period of time—several months to more than a year, depending on state law—whether or not it was a formal period of separation.

Many states still have laws allowing divorce based on the fault grounds listed above. Most couples who choose to divorce do not use these fault grounds; instead they obtain no-fault divorces. However, some argue that divorce has been made too easy and that divorce rates would go down if states required proof of fault before granting a divorce. Partially in response to this argument, some states have lengthened the time it takes to get a no-fault divorce.

In 1997, Louisiana passed a law enabling couples who are planning to marry to choose a covenant marriage instead of obtaining a regular license to marry. Couples choosing a covenant marriage agree in advance (in writing) to make no-fault divorce more difficult to obtain. Under traditional marriage laws in Louisiana, a couple must separate for six months before getting a no-fault divorce. To end a covenant marriage by no-fault divorce, the couple must separate and live apart for a period of two years.

Where You Live

What are the grounds for divorce in your state? Does your state allow no-fault divorce (also known as divorce by consent)? How long does it take to obtain a divorce in your state?

Covenant marriages try to encourage lifelong commitments by both partners, thereby aiming to reduce the divorce rate, by limiting access to relatively easy divorces. Couples who are already married also have the option to convert their existing marriage to a covenant marriage.

Problem 34.2

a. The divorce rate is now much higher than it was 30 years ago. Develop a hypothesis to explain why.

b. Explain the difference between a fault divorce and a no-fault divorce.

c. Do you think that couples should be allowed to obtain no-fault divorces? What are the arguments in favor of allowing no-fault divorce? Or should couples wanting to divorce be required to demonstrate fault by one party? What are the reasons to require demonstration of fault?

d. Do you think states should make it harder or easier to get a divorce? Why?

Child Custody

If a couple with children separate or divorce, important questions arise: Who will take care of the children? With whom will the children live? In legal terms, the question is: Who will have **custody** of the children? The importance of the custody issue is illustrated by the fact that in 2000, more than 25 percent of minor children in the United States were living with single parents. Many of these situations were the result of divorce.

Custody decisions are important because the parent with custody decides most aspects of the child's life, such as where the child will live and go to school. Custody may be temporary, or it may be permanently awarded to one parent. After it is awarded, unless circumstances change significantly, it is rarely changed. For example, if the custodial parent became addicted to drugs, the court could order a change of custody.

The noncustodial parent is usually given visitation rights. This means that he or she can visit with the child on certain days and at certain times of the year. Both parents are required to contribute to the support of a child. The parent who has custody makes these contributions in the day-to-day life of the child. The noncustodial parent makes these contributions in the form of a regular monetary payment to the parent who has custody of the child.

Sometimes courts award custody to both parents. This is known as **joint custody.** Both parents have full responsibility for the child's supervision, and both have an equal say in important issues, such as schooling and religion. The child may live part-time with each parent. However, the child need not spend the same amount of time with each parent. For example, a child who attends school near her father might spend school nights with him and weekends with her mother.

Joint custody is becoming more common, but courts are careful about awarding it. There is concern that parents who cannot cooperate during marriage may not be able to cooperate after a divorce. Therefore, most judges are reluctant to approve a joint custody arrangement unless the parents can demonstrate an ability to work well together. Furthermore, joint custody is successful only if both parents want responsibility for the child or children. A court cannot impose joint custody upon a parent who does not want it; the court must have both parents' agreement. Mediation is often helpful for couples trying to make joint custody work.

Problem 34.3

Wilma and Robert are getting divorced. They have a four-year-old child. Both are employed full-time, and they plan to live 10 miles apart after the divorce.

a. What are the advantages and disadvantages of a joint custody arrangement for Wilma and Robert?

b. What are the advantages and disadvantages of sole custody with visitation awarded to the noncustodial parent?

c. What other information would you want to know before deciding the best custody arrangement?

d. If they choose joint custody, will both Wilma and Robert have to agree to the arrangement? What will happen if they cannot agree?

If parents cannot agree on custody or the court does not approve their agreement, the decision is made by the court. Traditionally, the law presumed that young children were better off with their mothers. This presumption was called the **tender years doctrine.** Today, most states have laws that require courts to treat men and women equally in custody disputes. In reality, though, some judges still favor the mother, especially when the decision involves young children, regardless of the desire or ability of the father to care for his child. It is becoming more common, however, for some judges to favor fathers who show an interest in the custody of their children. Their reasons may range from promoting nondiscrimination, to wanting to encourage paternal interest, to punishing mothers who do not fit stereotypes of the "good mother" (for example, mothers who work rather than stay at home).

In determining custody, courts apply a standard of what is in the **best interests of the child.** This is often difficult to determine. Courts look at factors such as the youth's actions in the home, school, and community; the emotional and economic stability of the parents; which parent has stronger bonds with the child; and which parent has been the primary care provider. Courts often consider the children's desires, especially if they are old enough to understand the ramifications of their wishes or are over a certain age (in many states, age 12). To help with this decision, judges often assign a social services agency to study the parents and children. The results of this study are used as the basis for a custody recommendation.

Increases in substance abuse, divorce, incarceration, and other family and community crises have resulted in many grandparents and other relatives raising children whose parents cannot do so. This caregiving relationship is called **kinship care.** In 2000, more than 2.4 million grandparents reported they had primary responsibility for meeting their grandchildren's daily needs.

Many states have passed laws that allow grandparents to petition for visitation rights if the child's parents will not voluntarily grant visitation to them. However, challenges to these laws brought by parents have been upheld in many states. In 2000, in the case of *Troxel* v. *Granville,* the United States Supreme Court struck down a Washington state law that allowed visitation by any person who could show that such visitation would be in the best interests of the child. The Supreme Court was concerned that such a broad granting of visitation rights to third parties—even to family members, including grandparents—would undermine a parent's fundamental interest in the care, custody, and control of his or her children. The Court was concerned that this

The Case of . . .

The Two Fathers

Carole and Gerald were married and lived in California. While they were married, Carole became romantically involved with a neighbor, Michael. She remained married to Gerald, and when her daughter Victoria was born, Gerald was listed as the baby's father on the birth certificate. Carole told Michael, however, that she believed he was the biological father. Carole and Gerald later separated, and mother and daughter went to live with Michael, who acted as Victoria's father.

Later Carole reconciled with Gerald, and she and Victoria returned to live with him. A blood test showed that Michael was Victoria's biological father. He went to court and sued to be declared Victoria's legal father and for visitation rights. Gerald opposed this, claiming that he was Victoria's legal father since he was married to her mother and was currently living with her and acting as her father.

Problem 34.4

a. What are the strongest arguments for Gerald?

b. What are the strongest arguments for Michael?

c. How should this case be decided? Explain.

d. Do you think that a child should be allowed to have more than two legal parents? Give your reasons.

Some missing children may be the victims of parental abduction. *What laws have been passed to help address the issue of parental abduction?*

statute did not give proper deference to a parent's wishes, but instead placed a burden on the parent to prove that a third party's wish to see his or her child would not be in the child's best interest.

Some custody disputes are so bitter that one parent takes the children from the other parent and hides them. This may involve taking the children and moving permanently to another state. Or the parent and children may move constantly to avoid being found. Thousands of parents have resorted to this illegal means of opposing a court's custody decision. Such abductions may account for the majority of children reported missing each year. The *Federal Parental Kidnapping Prevention Act of 1980* prevents parents who abduct their children from getting new custody orders in a different state. It also provides resources to help custodial parents locate their missing children.

The *Uniform Child Custody Jurisdiction and Enforcement Act (UCCJEA)* has now been passed in all 50 states. Under this law, a custody decree entered in one state is valid in all states. Therefore, a parent without custody cannot remove his or her children from their home state and attempt to obtain a different custody order in another state. In addition, most states have statutes that make parental kidnapping—taking or hiding a child from a parent who has custody—a crime.

Alimony, Property Division, and Child Support

Since the development of no-fault divorce, most divorce disputes center on two issues: children and money. The major financial issues are alimony, child support, and property division. These issues are frequently negotiated between the parties on their own, through their attorneys, or in mediation. The parties then make a brief courtroom appearance to finalize the breakup.

U.S. Census Bureau statistics show that most women suffer financial hardship as a result of divorce, but most men experience financial improvement. This is not surprising, given the number of women who stay in the home to care for children, especially when the children are young. Upon divorcing, many women face financial hardship because they have been out of the workforce for a period of time and because a majority of children of divorced parents live primarily with their mothers. It is estimated that one-fourth of those mothers receive only partial child support payments from their ex-husbands while another one-fourth receive nothing at all.

Alimony

Alimony, also called spousal support or maintenance, is money paid to help support an ex-wife or ex-husband after a divorce. It covers household and personal expenses, work-related costs, educational expenses, and recreation. Alimony has traditionally been paid by men to support their ex-wives. However, in 1980, the U.S. Supreme Court ruled that state laws restricting alimony to women were unconstitutional.

Alimony is based primarily on need, although the duration of the marriage is often a factor. As a result, alimony awards vary from case to case. When awarding alimony, courts consider the couple's standard of living, the financial status of both husband and wife, and the wage-earning capacity of each spouse. Sometimes *rehabilitative alimony* is awarded temporarily to help one spouse regain or develop job skills needed for future employment. Alimony is not awarded in all cases. The decision whether or not to award alimony is left to the discretion of the court, based on the circumstances of the case.

An important consideration in awarding alimony is how long the payments should continue. Many advocate that alimony should continue until the spouse no longer has the need for it, which may mean that payments could continue indefinitely. Others, however, feel that such an arrangement undermines the goal of ending the relationship for good. They say that the purpose of alimony is not to equalize incomes forever, but rather to give the disadvantaged spouse an opportunity to reestablish his or her life as an independent person. Under this theory, support payments should be made for a fixed period of time, thereby encouraging both parties to move on with their lives.

Dividing property owned by the couple is another important issue. It involves deciding who gets the house, the car, the furniture, the bank account, the life insurance, and so on. As you learned in Chapter 31, there are different categories of property, and state laws dictate how marital property (property acquired during marriage) will be treated upon divorce. In all states, property owned by one spouse prior to the marriage belongs to that person after divorce. In community property states, all the property acquired during the marriage is divided equally. In other states, marital property is divided based on what the court considers equitable, or fair.

Note that alimony and property division are separate concepts. Property includes all physical possessions and income that have been acquired by the family during the marriage. Alimony consists of future payments of support money after the end of the marriage.

Property division is an important issue for couples getting divorced. *How are property division and alimony different?*

The Medical School Degree

Roberto and Marta Flores sought a divorce to end their 11-year marriage. At first, the case seemed simple. The couple had no children, little property to divide, and, with California's no-fault divorce law, seemingly little to argue about. However, at the time of the divorce, Roberto argued that he deserved part of his ex-wife's income as a physician because he had worked to support the family (and pay some of her tuition) while she went to school to earn her medical degree.

Roberto claimed that he was entitled to a share of Marta's total projected lifetime income as a doctor. He estimated that Marta was likely to earn over $2 million in twenty

years of medical practice. She countered that while he might be entitled to reimbursement for part of the *cost* of her education, he is not entitled to share in the *potential future value* of her degree. She argues that there is no way to reasonably predict what she will earn in her career: she may decide to go abroad and donate her medical services, or HMOs may reduce her income considerably. In either case, her income could be far less than what Roberto predicts.

Problem 34.5

a. What happened in this case? What is Roberto asking for?

b. What is fair reimbursement: the cost of Marta's education or the value in terms of her potential increased earnings? Explain your answer.

Child Support

Both parents still have a legal duty to support their children after divorce. Therefore, divorcing couples with children need an agreement and court order regarding child support. Usually, only one parent actually makes child support payments. The other parent—the parent with physical custody—supports the child by taking care of daily needs such as food, clothing, and shelter. The level of support is based on the parent's ability to pay and the amount necessary to cover the child's needs. Child support is usually paid until the child becomes an adult or is emancipated, unless the parties agree to a longer period of support, such as through college.

When one spouse fails to provide the agreed-upon financial support, the other may seek a court order requiring payment. The *Family Support Act of 1988 (FSA)* was passed by Congress to help in enforcing support orders. This law requires states to have clear formulas for calculating child support and to expand their child support enforcement procedures and parent-locating services. The guidelines consider many factors, including both spouses' incomes and the number and ages of their children. Some deviation from these guidelines is allowed, but a court must provide clear reasons for such a variation. The *FSA* allows child support payments to be deducted from a parent's salary and permits states to track parents by means of their Social Security numbers.

Problem 34.6

Each of the following situations involves a divorce. Should either spouse pay alimony, child support, or both? If so, which spouse should pay what? How much should be paid, and for how long?

a. Miguel, a successful plumbing contractor, earns $75,000 per year. His wife, Carmen, stays at home and takes care of their four children. When Miguel and Carmen divorce, the two older children—a junior in high school and a freshman in college—wish to stay with Miguel. The two younger children prefer to stay with Carmen.

b. Angela, a government social worker, divorces her husband, Leroy, an occasionally employed freelance writer. He has been staying home, taking care of their two-year-old son. Angela's yearly salary is $33,000; Leroy has earned $6,000 in the past 12 months. The child will live with his mother.

Stepparents

After divorce, many people remarry and create new blended families. More and more families in the United States include stepparents who, especially when married to custodial parents, play important parts in the lives of children. The relationship that develops is different in every family. In many cases, a stepparent takes on a role that is different from a birth parent but that may be like an additional parent.

States have different laws about the rights and responsibilities of stepparents. In many places, stepparents are required to support their stepchildren as long as they are living with them. In some places, this responsibility may continue after the stepchild moves out if the stepparent has acted **in loco parentis,** or in place of the parent. If the marriage ends in divorce, stepparents usually cannot claim custody of the stepchild, though they may be able to seek visitation rights.

Stepparents are not considered full parents, however, unless they **adopt** their stepchildren. This is usually only possible if the child's noncustodial biological parent consents to the adoption. For example, assume that Jay and Marla marry and have a son, Brian. Then Jay and Marla divorce, Brian lives primarily with Marla, and she marries Larry. Larry, Brian's stepfather, will only be able to adopt Brian if Jay consents to the adoption because the adoption would end Jay's legal rights as Brian's parent.

Many stepparents play an important role in the lives of their spouse's children. *What can stepparents do to become full parents?*

Government Support for Families and Individuals

"We are trying to construct a more inclusive society. . . . We are going to make a country in which no one is left out."

— Franklin D. Roosevelt

Street Law
online

Visit the *Street Law* Web site at streetlaw.glencoe.com for chapter-based information and resources.

S ince the Great Depression of the 1930s, Congress has passed laws creating social programs that provide economic, educational, and health benefits to millions of Americans. Government social programs are a continuing source of controversy in the United States, a society that prizes individualism, self-reliance, and free enterprise. The New Deal programs that were created to relieve suffering brought on by the Depression were met with welcome arms by some and with outraged cries of "creeping Socialism" by others. Federal, state, and local governments today spend more than $300 billion a year on social services programs. This chapter discusses who benefits from these economic, education, and health programs, how much individuals receive, and how these programs operate.

There are many types of government support for families in need.

The U.S. government estimated that in 2001, there were nearly 33 million poor people living in the United States. Poor people are defined as those who live in households with less than a certain annual income. In 2001, that amount was $17,960 for a family of four. Many of these poor people are children. In 2001, more than 16 percent of American children were poor—the highest rate of any age group.

Most Americans correctly assume that government programs exist to help the poor. However, government programs offer benefits to families at all income levels. Programs that are directed toward poor Americans include Temporary Assistance to Needy Families (TANF), food stamps, Medicaid, and public housing. Programs that benefit Americans of all income levels include Social Security, Medicare, veterans' benefits, and unemployment compensation. In addition, millions of American families who are in the middle and upper class income levels receive mortgage interest deductions—tax breaks for owning a home.

Problem 35.1

a. List all of the causes of poverty in the United States that you can think of. Which of these problems can government programs help solve? How? Which of these problems can government not solve? Explain.

b. Should people receiving money under social programs receive the same amount no matter what state they live in? Why or why not?

Economic Benefits for Individuals and Families

People of all living situations and income levels need, and often rely on, economic benefits associated with government programs. For example, some people count on their Social Security benefits to help support them in their retirement. Others depend on the money and basic necessities supplied by welfare, food stamps, and Medicaid to provide for their children.

Social Security

When you apply for a job, the employer will ask for your Social Security number. This may seem unimportant now, but your Social Security number will be a valuable asset when you retire. Social Security works like an insurance policy. When you work, a percentage of your wages is deducted by your employer, who pays an equal amount to the federal government. Once you reach retirement age, you are entitled to benefits based on the amount paid into the Social Security fund. Because of the long-term investment nature of this retirement benefit, many legislators have argued for the privatization of Social Security. This continues to be a contested issue.

Almost all Americans—men, women, and children—have Social Security protection either as workers or as dependents of workers. The following list summarizes some of the major provisions of the Social Security law. For additional information, contact the nearest office of the U.S. Social Security Administration.

- **Retirement benefits.** Workers age 65 or older may retire and receive a monthly Social Security check. A worker's spouse and children may also be eligible. The amount a person receives is a percentage of earnings. In 2003, the maximum a retiring worker first claiming retirement benefits could receive was about $1,721 per month.

- **Disability benefits.** Workers who are blind, injured, or too ill to work can receive monthly checks if the disability is expected to last at least 12 months or to result in death. Spouses and children are also eligible.

- **Survivor's benefits.** When workers die, their families become eligible for payments. This is like a government life insurance policy.

Workers who are blind can receive Social Security benefits. *What other types of benefits are available through Social Security?*

To illustrate how Social Security works, consider the case of Melody Smith, age 28, a single parent with two children. She worked in a bakery for five years. Then she became seriously ill and had to stop working. After a required waiting period, Social Security will send Melody and her children a monthly check until Melody is able to return to work. If Melody dies, Social Security will continue to provide benefit checks to each of her children until they reach age 18, or until they reach age 22 if they are full-time students.

Supplemental Security Income

The federal Supplemental Security Income (SSI) program provides money for needy elderly, blind, and disabled people. This federal program provides monthly benefits at a standard rate all over the country. States may add their own benefits to those of the federal government. To receive SSI benefits, a person must be age 65 or older, be legally blind, or have a major disability that prevents employment for a year or more. Applications for SSI are handled by local Social Security offices.

The *Personal Responsibility and Work Opportunity Reconciliation Act of 1996* changed the definition of disability as it applies to children. Prior to the passage of this law, children were evaluated by a judge for their ability to function in a way similar to other children of the same age. After the law went into effect, the previous method for evaluation was discarded, and a child's impairment is now considered to be disabling only if it causes "marked and severe functional limitation." As a result of the change in the definition of disability, many children have become ineligible for monthly SSI benefits.

Welfare After Reform

Until 1996, Aid to Families with Dependent Children (AFDC)—often referred to as welfare—was the joint federal-state program that provided aid to needy families with dependent children. AFDC was controversial. Critics said that welfare discouraged people from working because welfare payments were reduced based on income received from employment. Others argued that it broke up the family, because many states would not pay AFDC benefits if the father lived in the home. Still others contended that the programs cost too much.

As a response to some of the controversy surrounding AFDC, Congress passed the *Personal Responsibility and Work Opportunity Reconciliation Act of 1996* as the primary federal welfare law. It replaced AFDC with Temporary Assistance to Needy Families (TANF). This law changed welfare dramatically.

TANF has a much stricter work requirement than AFDC had. After receiving aid for two years, most recipients must work or attend a vocational program for at least 20 hours a week or risk losing benefits (depending on the state's program). Although there is no additional funding for work programs, money is provided for child care under the law. Recipients also receive at least one year of health care benefits while they are making the transition from welfare to work.

There are restrictions on receiving TANF benefits. Families with an adult who has received federal assistance for a total of five years may not receive cash aid under TANF. Immigrants to the United States, regardless of whether they are here legally or illegally, are barred from receiving TANF benefits. Parents who are still minors are required to live in an adult-supervised home and to continue their education or receive vocational training in order to qualify for benefits.

Under the 1996 law, states were required to set up and maintain child-support payment enforcement programs. The law provides rules and procedures that make it easier to monitor and track parents who are delinquent on child-support payments. The law also makes it easier to establish paternity for child-support purposes.

Many welfare offices have been renamed "empowerment centers." *How does this change reflect changes in federal welfare law?*

Where You Live

What efforts have been made in your state to reform welfare programs? Are the reforms working?

Food Stamps

People with incomes below a certain level may be eligible for food stamps. Food stamps are coupons of various denominations that can be exchanged like money for food at authorized stores. Food stamps can be denied to immigrants who are in the country illegally and to people who refuse to seek employment. The program is funded chiefly by federal money through the U.S. Department of Agriculture. It is administered under uniform national standards, so eligibility requirements and the amount a household can receive are the same in all states. The *Personal Responsibility and Work Opportunity Reconciliation Act of 1996* reduced funding for the food stamp program.

The *Personal Responsibility and Work Opportunity Reconciliation Act of 1996* required all states to switch to an Electronic Benefit Transfer (EBT) system by the year 2002. This electronic system allows recipients to authorize automatic transfer of their benefits from their accounts to a retail store to pay for their purchases. There are many advantages to using an electronic system, including elimination of a bulky process for transmission and redemption of paper food stamps; cost-effectiveness; reduction of food stamp loss, theft, and fraud; and convenience.

Where You Live

What programs exist in your state to aid needy families? Are there any innovative programs in your state to deal with poverty?

Food stamps are just one of the economic benefits available to families in need. *What is the Electronic Benefit Transfer system? How does it work?*

Problem 35.2

Governments in Canada and many other developed nations in Europe provide their citizens with far more benefits than the U.S. government provides to its citizens. However, citizens in nations with more benefits pay higher taxes to finance these "safety net" programs that provide support for those in need. This difference reveals contrasting views about the role government should play in protecting citizens from hunger, homelessness, and illness.

a. What is your view of government safety net programs?

b. What costs would U.S. taxpayers face if the government were to expand our safety net programs?

c. What costs might we face if we decide not to provide safety net programs?

d. Do we, as a society, owe special protection to people who are to some degree helpless—for example, the elderly, children, or people with disabilities? Explain your answers.

e. Under the federal welfare reform laws, people do not have a "right" to government assistance. Should people be entitled to these benefits? Explain.

Earned Income Tax Credits

The federal government provides many tax advantages for families. One such benefit is the earned income tax credit. This credit is available to families with children whose income is below a certain level that is determined by the Internal Revenue Service (IRS) each year. The credit reduces the amount of tax that is owed to the federal government. It is intended to offset increases in living expenses and Social Security taxes, and to encourage people to work rather than receive welfare.

Tax Credits for Families with Children

Another tax credit that is available to families is the credit for child and dependent care expenses. This benefit is meant for families who must pay for child care in order for both parents to work. Anyone who cares for a dependent under age 13 or for any other dependent who is not able to care for himself or herself is eligible for a credit of up to 30 percent of the expenses for this care. Additionally, all adult taxpayers who have dependent children get a tax deduction for each child.

Housing Assistance and Mortgage Interest Deductions

Federal, state, and local governments offer programs designed to provide low-income people with housing assistance. These programs include government-operated housing projects, direct payments of portions of rent, and low-interest loans and insurance to help people buy homes.

The government also gives tax deductions for the amount of interest home owners pay on their home mortgages. This benefit was designed to encourage home ownership and make homes more affordable, so these deductions are enjoyed by those who are able to buy their own homes. Although there are a growing number of first-time home buyer programs to help lower-income families buy homes, the majority of households that benefit from this deduction are in middle and higher income brackets.

Home owners receive tax deductions on the interest paid as part of their mortgage loan. *Why was this benefit created? Does it help all home owners?*

Where You Live

What government job programs exist in your community? Are there any government-operated housing projects in your area?

Problem 35.3

- In 2000, the U.S. Department of Housing and Urban Development reported that housing assistance reached fewer than 30 percent of eligible low-income households, leaving 10 million households unassisted. And while 11.8 million households lived below the poverty level (about $17,400 for a family of four in 2000), only one in four received housing assistance.

- In 2000, advocacy organizations estimated that on any given night in February, nearly 700,000 Americans were homeless, and up to 3,500,000 might be homeless during the course of a year.

- The nation's stock of low-rent housing has decreased each decade since the 1970s.

  a. How are the three sets of statistics above related to each other?

  b. How might these data contradict the stereotype of poor Americans living on generous benefits from the government?

  c. Do you think that the government should act to increase affordable housing in the United States? Explain your answer.

  d. How might you expect government estimates of homelessness to differ from estimates by advocacy organizations? Why do you think it is so difficult to estimate the true size of the homeless population?

Health Benefits

Health care is a problem of great and growing importance in the United States. In 2000, more than 38 million Americans—many of them children—had no health insurance. Low-income and unemployed people are not the only people without health insurance. A significant portion of people without health insurance have jobs at higher salary levels, although jobs that do not include health insurance are more common among the working poor.

Medicare

Medicare is a federal health insurance program for people age 65 or older. It also aids people of any age with permanent kidney failure requiring dialysis or a transplant, as well as certain disabled people. Those receiving Medicare can usually obtain medical care through physicians of their own choosing. Medicare has two parts: hospital insurance and medical insurance. Hospital insurance helps pay for major hospital expenses and certain follow-up care, such as hospice care and some health care. Medical insurance helps pay for physician's office fees, physical and occupational therapists, and other medical expenses. An exception is most prescription medicine, which is not covered. Local Social Security Administration offices take applications for Medicare, assist people in filing claims, and provide information about the program.

Medicaid

Medicaid is a government program that provides private medical care to poor and disabled people. It covers most common medical services, including hospital and outpatient care, nursing-home services, hearing aids, eyeglasses, prescription drugs, dental care, physicians' office fees, medical supplies, and transportation to and from hospitals or doctors' offices.

Recipients of Temporary Assistance to Needy Families may also be eligible for Medicaid benefits, with a few exceptions. For example, a single adult who fails to meet the work requirement may not be eligible for Medicaid. Most Medicaid expenditures go to persons over age 65 or those who are blind or totally disabled. Elderly and disabled persons are eligible for Medicaid if they are U.S. citizens or legal immigrants, live in the state where they apply, and have an income below a set amount. Applications for Medicaid are processed through local social services offices.

In 1997, the federal government developed an essential new program for working families without health insurance. The State Children's Health Insurance Program (SCHIP) gives grants to states to provide health insurance coverage to uninsured children who live in families earning up to 200 percent of the federal poverty level. States may administer these grants through existing Medicaid programs or establish a special children's health insurance fund.

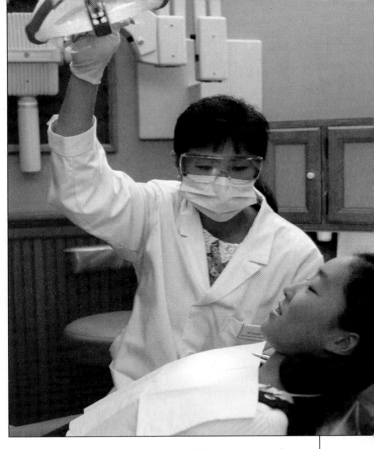

In addition to hospital care, Medicaid also provides dental care. *What other services are covered by Medicaid?*

Problem 35.4

Health care costs have risen dramatically during the past few decades. As a result, many Americans are going without necessary medical treatment. Medicare provides services to the elderly, and Medicaid provides services to the poor, but millions of others must go without any coverage.

a. Should government require that employers provide health care plans to all workers? How might such a requirement affect prices of goods and services? Explain.

b. Should government provide health care to Americans who do not qualify for Medicaid and cannot afford to buy health insurance? Explain.

c. Should government ensure that all children receive health care, regardless of family income? How would this affect taxpayers? What costs might we face if we do not ensure that children get adequate health care? Explain.

Where You Live

Where in your community does a person apply for Medicare benefits? For Social Security benefits? What is the procedure for applying?

Law in Action

Family and Medical Leave Act

In 1993, Congress passed the *Family and Medical Leave Act* to help parents who want to stay home with their babies, as well as workers who need time off to care for ailing relatives. The legislation guarantees working adults up to 12 weeks of unpaid leave during any 12-month period for any of the following reasons: (1) you give birth to a child and give care to the child, (2) you adopt a child or take a foster child into your home, (3) you must care for a spouse, child, or parent who is suffering from a "serious health condition," or (4) your own serious health condition makes you unable to perform your job.

The legislation does not apply to everyone. Only firms with 50 or more employees are covered, and there are "key exceptions" for "highly compensated" employees. This means if you are one of the most highly paid employees in your office or region, your employer may deny your request for leave.

Educational Benefits

Government support for educational benefits ranges from primary and secondary public education to child development programs. Some states also provide for higher education. In addition, grants and loans are available through the federal government.

Elementary and Secondary Public Schools

The government is involved in education at all levels. Both state and local governments are responsible for providing public elementary and secondary education for all students. Typically, less than ten percent of government support for elementary and secondary schools comes from the federal government. All 50 states provide for this right to a public education in their state constitutions. In fact, children between certain ages are required to attend school. In most states, students must attend school through age 16. Federal law requires schools to provide special educational services to students with disabilities.

Head Start and Early Head Start

Head Start and Early Head Start are comprehensive child development programs that serve children from birth to age 5, pregnant women, and their families. These programs are administered through a combined effort of local, state, and federal governments and aim to increase school readiness of young children in low-income families. Head Start and Early Head Start provide a range of services in the areas of education and early childhood development; medical, dental, and mental health; nutrition; and parental involvement. The programs are designed to respond to each child's and family's individual developmental, ethnic, cultural, and linguistic needs.

Colleges and Universities

States also provide funds for higher education. Many colleges and universities are run by the state. These institutions are generally less expensive than their private counterparts. Tuition is even cheaper for students who are residents of the state.

States generally provide some funding sources such as scholarships and grant and loan programs for college students to finance their college education. However, the vast majority of college students who seek financial aid to pay for college receive that aid through federal government loan and grant programs.

Grants Federal Pell Grants are available from the U.S. Department of Education to financially eligible students to obtain an undergraduate or professional degree. These grants do not have to be repaid. Federal Opportunity Grants are available to undergraduate students with exceptional financial need. A student who participates in this program may receive between $100 and $4,000 a year, depending upon a number of factors. The Federal Opportunity Grant program gives priority to students who also receive Pell Grants.

Many campus jobs are part of the Federal Work Study Program that helps college students earn money for school expenses. *What other options exist for college students in need of financial assistance?*

Law in Action

Economic Inequality and School Funding

The U.S. Constitution does not provide a legal right to education, and the responsibility for public education in this country has historically been left to the individual states. Although all state constitutions provide children in that state with the right to a public education, they do not necessarily provide children with any particular *quality* of education. Because public schools are funded largely from property tax revenue, wealthy communities are able to generate more revenue to spend on educating their children than are poorer communities. As a result, students in the wealthier districts are, on average, better prepared for college or for jobs. Some argue that this disparity violates the principle of "equal opportunity for all" and urge states to provide funds to equalize spending across the state regardless of local property tax revenues.

Problem 35.5

a. What are two arguments that would support such a policy?

b. What are two arguments that could be used to oppose such a policy?

c. What is your view? Explain.

d. Why do you think the writers of the U.S. Constitution felt that the "right" to an education should be left to the states to decide?

Schools in poor and wealthy communities

Federal Work Study   The Federal Work Study Program supplies colleges and universities with funds to provide jobs (usually on-campus) for financially needy undergraduate and graduate students. This program allows students to earn at least federal minimum wage to help them pay for their educational expenses while attending school. Students participating in this program are encouraged to do community service work. In addition, the Federal Work Study Program can help students get valuable work experience in their chosen course of study before they leave school.

Loans   Loan programs are also available from the U.S. Department of Education to help students finance their college degrees. (Visit the U.S. Department of Education online at **www.ed.gov/index.jsp** to learn about the loan programs available from the federal government.) Stafford Loans can be either subsidized and awarded on the basis of financial need, or unsubsidized and made available to anyone, regardless of financial need. The difference is that the subsidized loan does not accrue interest during the period the student is in school, whereas interest on the unsubsidized loan does accrue, even though the student is not required to make payments on the loan while in school. These loans must be used to pay for tuition, fees, room and board, and other school expenses. Other loan programs are available to parents to help their dependent children pay for school, to students who have been emancipated from their parents or guardians, and to students with exceptional financial need. All loans, regardless of the program or the source, must be repaid. Therefore, it is very important for students and their families to assess their true financial need, including other possible sources of income, such as college jobs, so that when the student graduates, he or she will not be overly burdened by student loan payments.

Problem 35.6

While all states provide a free elementary and secondary education for children, the government does not usually pay for students to attend college and pursue a higher education.

a. Should the state or federal government provide a free college education to all Americans?

b. Should students from poor families pay less tuition or get guaranteed loans at lower interest rates?

c. Should the state or federal government finance college for students who are willing to prepare for careers in which there is a shortage of qualified workers? If so, for how long should the graduate be required to work in that kind of job?

d. What is an appropriate penalty for a graduate who does not make the required payments on his or her guaranteed student loan? Explain your answer.

UNIT
6

Individual Rights and Liberties

Visit the *Street Law* Web site at streetlaw.glencoe.com for unit-based activities.

This final unit of *Street Law* provides information on individual rights and liberties. Unit 6 focuses primarily on constitutional law and federal civil rights laws passed by the U.S. Congress.

The topics in Unit 6 are controversial ones. Reasonable people often disagree about many of these issues and, over time, courts and legislatures change the laws in these areas. Abortion, sexual harassment, discrimination, the rights of gay and lesbian people, and conflicts over religious rights are among the most difficult public policy issues in the United States. These issues can be divisive, but at the same time, the Bill of Rights and our civil rights laws are the hallmarks of the extraordinary freedom Americans have in the area of political and social rights.

After Chapter 36 introduces the study of constitutional law, Chapter 37 focuses on freedom of expression. This freedom is critical to maintain a democracy: citizens must be free to communicate, particularly with their government. This chapter also deals with the scope and limits of the government's ability to regulate expression,

Dr. Martin Luther King, Jr. championed the cause of individual rights and liberties for everyone.

and in some instances, to prevent and punish it. Similar principles are discussed in Chapter 38, Freedom of the Press. Chapter 39 looks at speech and press issues in special settings.

Chapter 40 presents freedom of religion. This area of law is particularly challenging because the right of individuals to practice their religion sometimes clashes directly with the government's obligation not to establish—or unfairly favor—any specific religion.

Chapter 41 introduces the concept of due process, or legal fairness. Due process concerns both fair procedures and protection from government interference with certain rights. The most controversial of these, the right to privacy, is the subject of Chapter 42.

Chapter 43 looks at the ways in which the U.S. Constitution prevents the government, and civil rights laws prevent companies and individuals, from discriminating unlawfully.

The final chapter in this unit, Chapter 44, provides a link between school and the world of work with its focus on rights and responsibilities in the workplace.

439

Introduction to Constitutional Law

The U.S. Constitution is the framework of our government. It establishes the executive, legislative, and judicial branches. It is also the supreme law of the land, which all public officials are bound by oath to enforce. Moreover, the Constitution guarantees each American certain basic rights.

One remarkable feature of the U.S. Constitution is its endurance. It is the oldest written national constitution in the world that is still in use. Another remarkable feature of the Constitution is its ability to adapt itself to changing conditions.

"Injustice anywhere is a threat to justice everywhere."

— Dr. Martin Luther King, Jr.

Street Law online

Visit the *Street Law* Web site at streetlaw.glencoe.com for chapter-based information and resources.

The U.S. Constitution was signed in Independence Hall in Philadelphia, Pennsylvania.

Amendments to the Constitution

The Founders of the United States knew that the Constitution might have to be changed. Therefore, they provided two methods of proposing amendments, or additions, to the Constitution. The first method is by a two-thirds vote of both houses of Congress; the second is by a national convention called by Congress at the request of the legislatures in two-thirds of the states. Once proposed, an amendment does not take effect unless it is ratified either by the legislatures in three-fourths of the states or by special ratifying conventions in three-fourths of the states.

The original Constitution, adopted in 1787, contained only a few provisions guaranteeing individual rights. However, citizens pressured their leaders to add a Bill of Rights. In response, the first ten amendments were adopted by Congress in 1791 and quickly ratified by the states.

These first ten amendments contain most of our basic rights. The First Amendment protects the freedoms of religion, speech, press, assembly, and petition. The Second Amendment protects the right of the people to bear arms. The Third Amendment protects against the quartering of soldiers in private homes, and the Fourth Amendment protects against unreasonable searches and seizures.

The Fifth Amendment provides a right to due process of law—fair procedures that are required when government action affects your rights—and gives certain rights to accused people, including protection against self-incrimination. The Sixth Amendment provides the rights to a lawyer, an impartial jury, and a speedy trial in criminal cases.

The Seventh Amendment provides for jury trials in civil cases. The Eighth Amendment bars cruel and unusual punishment and excessive bail or fines. The Ninth Amendment declares that the rights spelled out in the Constitution are not the only rights that people have. Finally, the Tenth Amendment reserves to the states and the people any powers not belonging to the federal government. (The text of the entire Constitution can be found on pages 570–599.)

The Bill of Rights was designed to protect Americans against the overuse of power by the *federal* government. Nothing in the unamended Constitution specifically requires *state* governments to abide by the Bill of Rights. But in interpreting the Fourteenth Amendment, which was passed after the Civil War, the U.S. Supreme Court has applied most protections in the Bill of Rights to the state and local levels of government, including public schools.

Collection of Cheekwood Museum of Art, Nashville, Tennessee

As this painting *His First Vote* (1868) by Thomas Waterman Wood shows, African American men won the right to vote when the Fifteenth Amendment became law. *How did the Fourteenth and Fifteenth Amendments expand civil rights in the nation?*

In addition to the Bill of Rights, later amendments provide other important rights. The Thirteenth Amendment forbids slavery and outlaws involuntary servitude, except as a punishment for crime. The Fourteenth Amendment requires equal protection of the laws for all citizens. It also provides that no state can deprive any citizen of "life, liberty, or property without due process of law."

Several amendments protect and broaden the right to vote in federal and state elections. The Fifteenth Amendment forbids denying the right to vote based on race or color. The Nineteenth Amendment gives women the right to vote. The Twenty-third Amendment gives citizens of Washington, D.C., the right to vote in presidential elections. The Twenty-fourth Amendment prohibits poll taxes. The Twenty-sixth Amendment gives all people 18 years of age or older the right to vote.

Problem 36.1

a. Do we have any important rights not listed in the Bill of Rights? If so, what are they? Make a list.

b. Over the years, a number of new constitutional amendments have been suggested or proposed. Do you think we need any new amendments to the Constitution? If so, what amendments do you propose, and why?

c. The following are some of our most basic and important rights. Based on your opinion, rank these rights in order from the most important to the least important. Explain your rankings.

- Right to privacy
- Right to a jury trial
- Right to freedom of religion
- Right to travel freely
- Right to freedom of speech
- Right to be free from self-incrimination
- Right to bear arms
- Right to freedom of the press
- Right to be free from cruel and unusual punishment
- Right to legal counsel
- Right to assemble peacefully
- Right to vote

Basic Constitutional Law Principles

To understand constitutional law, there are three basic ideas to keep in mind. First, the rights guaranteed in the Constitution are not, and cannot be, absolute. The unrestricted exercise of certain rights would, in some instances, restrict the rights of others.

For example, freedom of speech does not mean that anyone can speak about any topic at any time and place. Freedom of the press does not allow a person to intentionally publish false or harmful information about another person. And, as you know, the right to vote does not extend to everyone, regardless of their age.

The courts have designed several "tests" to determine how cases should be decided. These tests are needed because the language of the Constitution is typically brief and often written in general terms. The words are not usually self-explanatory.

In this unit you will study many of the tests developed by the justices of the U.S. Supreme Court. These tests are not like those you have taken in school. Instead, they are rules that the Supreme Court requires courts to use in analyzing similar issues that arise in later cases.

For example, suppose someone, as a joke, yells "Fire!" in a crowded theater. The exact words protecting freedom of speech are: "Congress shall make no law . . . abridging the freedom of speech . . ." Do these words adequately explain whether the police can arrest the person for shouting "Fire!" falsely?

To analyze this particular case, the courts might use the **balancing test.** This means they would weigh the danger to the public of shouting "Fire!" falsely in a crowded theater (people might panic and be injured) against the benefit to an individual of being able to choose what to say and when and where to say it. In balancing one interest against the other, a court would probably decide that protecting the public is more important and would therefore restrict the speech of the person yelling "Fire!" We know this from analyzing the case using the balancing test, but we might not have been able to determine it simply from reading the language of the First Amendment.

The second idea basic to understanding constitutional law is that the Constitution protects citizens from certain actions by the *government.* Its protection usually does not extend to situations that are purely private in nature. This means that actions by private citizens, businesses, or organizations are generally not covered by the Constitution. For example, the Fourth Amendment protects against unreasonable searches and seizures by the government. It does not protect against searches and seizures by private individuals. Therefore, if a neighbor comes into your house and seizes your television, this act does *not* violate the Constitution. It may, however, constitute a tort, a crime, or both. As you will see later in this unit, many private actions, though not unconstitutional, have been made unlawful by congressional or state legislative action.

The rights guaranteed in the Constitution cannot be absolute. For example, the right to vote does not extend to everyone. *What other ideas basic to understanding constitutional law must you keep in mind?*

The third idea basic to understanding constitutional law is that enforcing one's rights can be time-consuming and expensive. Before trying to enforce a right, you should be aware of the time and money involved. You should then weigh these costs against the importance of protecting the right. However, remember that you can do many things to protect your rights. Therefore, if you are convinced that you are correct, do not give up.

Because of the importance of the U.S. Constitution, we sometimes assume that it contains all our rights. However, many basic rights are also protected by state constitutions, as well as by laws passed by the U.S. Congress and by state and local legislatures.

The U.S. Constitution does provide a so-called constitutional floor. This means that no government—federal, state, or local—can take away the basic rights protected by the federal Constitution. However, governments can grant citizens greater rights than those found in the U.S. Constitution. Federal courts, for example, have not interpreted the Constitution's equal protection clause to provide gay and lesbian people with the same degree of protection from government discrimination as is provided to African Americans. Some state and local governments, however, have laws and regulations forbidding discrimination based on sexual orientation. They are thus protecting more rights than those found in the U.S. Constitution.

The individual rights discussed in this chapter can also be called human rights. The world community has adopted a Universal Declaration of Human Rights, as well as a number of other international documents whereby participating countries promise to work to protect these human rights. Most of the human rights included in the U.S. Bill of Rights can be classified as political or civil rights. However, there are other rights, classified as social and economic rights, which are not included in the U.S. Constitution. These include the right to an adequate standard of living, housing, health care, and education.

Some people criticize the United States for acting as a leader in political and civil rights while ignoring the need for social and economic rights. Others say that such rights are not enforceable and that the government should consider them goals rather than enforceable rights.

> *"In respect of civil rights, all citizens are equal before the law. The humblest is the peer of the most powerful."*
>
> — John Marshall Harlan

Problem 36.2

a. What is meant by the statement, "Rights are not absolute"? Give an example of a right that is not absolute, and explain why this is so.

b. How does the U.S. Supreme Court use tests? What test does the Court use when determining whether the state can use a confession obtained by police from an accused person? (Hint: Look at Unit 2 and the material on criminal law.)

c. Give an example of an important economic right. Is it provided for in the Constitution? Should it be? Give your reasons.

Freedom of Speech

> *"Congress shall make no law . . . abridging the freedom of speech, or of the press; or the right of the people peaceably to assemble, and to petition the Government for a redress of grievances."*
>
> **— First Amendment to the U.S. Constitution**

The freedom of speech clause of the First Amendment guarantees the right to express information and ideas. It protects all forms of communication: speeches, books, art, newspapers, television, radio, and other media. The First Amendment exists to protect ideas that may be unpopular or different from those of the majority. The U.S. Constitution protects not only the person *making* the communication but also the person *receiving* it. Therefore, the First Amendment includes a right to hear, see, read, and in general be exposed to different points of view. While courts are very protective of this right, freedom of speech—like other constitutional rights—is not absolute.

Our democracy requires vigilant protection of freedom of speech.

Visit the *Street Law* Web site at streetlaw.glencoe.com for chapter-based information and resources.

The Importance of Freedom of Speech

The First Amendment's protection of speech and expression is central to U.S. democracy. The essential, core political purpose of the First Amendment is self-governance: enabling people to obtain information from a diversity of sources, make decisions, and communicate these decisions to the government. In this sense, the First Amendment is the heart of an open, democratic society.

Beyond the political purpose of free speech, the First Amendment provides us with a "marketplace of ideas." Rather than having the government establish the truth, freedom of speech enables the truth to emerge from diverse opinions. The people determine the truth by seeing which ideas have the power to be accepted in the marketplace of ideas. This underscores the United States's commitment to trusting the will of the people. The concept of a dynamic marketplace of ideas also encourages a variety of artistic and other creative expression that enriches our lives.

Related to self-government and the marketplace of ideas is the notion that a free, unfettered exchange of ideas and information gives society a safety valve that helps the people deal with change in a more orderly, stable way. Through discussion, society can adapt to changing circumstances without resorting to force. Those who disagree with a decision—and such disagreements are inevitable—may be more likely to go along with the majority if they have had a chance to express themselves. Sometimes, this self-expression is like letting off steam, hence the safety valve concept.

The language of the First Amendment seems absolute: "Congress shall make no law . . . abridging the freedom of speech." Yet as the example of shouting "Fire!" in a public place showed, freedom of speech

The need for peace and public order must be balanced against the right to express individual opinion. *Why are conflicts involving freedom of expression so difficult to resolve?*

is not absolute and was not intended to be. However, the expression of an opinion or point of view is usually protected under the First Amendment, even if most people disagree with the speaker's message. Remember that the First Amendment was designed to ensure a free marketplace of ideas—even unpopular ideas. Freedom of speech protects everyone, including people who criticize the government or express unconventional views. In some instances, the First Amendment provides people with a right *not* to speak and *not* to associate with others who propose a different message.

Problem 37.1

a. A Supreme Court justice once wrote that the most important value of free expression is "not free thought for those who agree with us, but freedom for the thought we hate." What did the justice mean by this? Do you agree or disagree?

b. Can you think of any public statements or expressions of public opinion that made you angry? How did you feel about protecting the speaker's right to freedom of expression? What is the value of hearing opinions you dislike? What is the danger of suppressing unpopular thought?

c. Assume that the United States is fighting a war and you disagree with the decision to be involved in this war. If you decide to join protests against the war, some people will call you unpatriotic. Is there some way that protest—even during a time of war—can be considered patriotic? Explain.

Conflicts involving freedom of expression are among the most difficult ones that courts are asked to resolve. Free speech cases frequently involve a clash of fundamental values. For example, how should the law respond to a speaker who makes an unpopular statement to which the listeners react violently? Should police arrest the speaker or try to control the crowd? Courts must balance the need for peace and public order against the fundamental right to express one's point of view.

As already noted, freedom of speech may at times be limited by government action. Sometimes government can limit or punish speech because the content of the speech is not fully protected. This idea will be explored in the sections that follow on obscenity, defamation, commercial speech, and fighting words and incitement. Government can also regulate speech even when the content is protected. The section on time, place, and manner restrictions deals with regulation of protected speech. Sometimes expressive conduct that communicates through actions rather than words is protected, and you will learn about this in the section on symbolic speech. Finally, you will study laws passed to restrict speech that are unenforceable either because they are unclear (vague) or because they are overinclusive—that is, they prohibit expression that should be protected.

The St. Patrick's Day Parade

Every year the City of Boston authorizes a group of Irish American war veterans to organize a St. Patrick's Day Parade. In 1993, this group refused to allow a gay, lesbian, and bisexual group of Irish Americans to march in the parade under its own banner. This group sued the veterans (the parade organizers) under a state law that prohibited discrimination based on sexual orientation in places of public accommodation. The Massachusetts courts said that the parade organizers had to allow the gay, lesbian, and bisexual group to participate.

The parade organizers appealed this decision to the U.S. Supreme Court. They argued that the state court order violated their First Amendment rights. The veterans contended that the parade was an example of protected, collective expression; that the gay, lesbian, and bisexual group had a message different from theirs; and that the government could not require them to endorse that message.

The U.S. Supreme Court reversed the decision of the Massachusetts courts, holding that a private speaker (the veterans group) has a right to express a point of view and that it is beyond the power of the government to control this point of view.

An Irish American war veteran

Problem 37.2

a. Do you agree or disagree with the decision of the Massachusetts courts? Give your reasons.

b. Why did the U.S. Supreme Court reverse the decision of the Massachusetts courts? Do you agree with this reversal? Explain.

c. Assume the parade was instead sponsored by a group of veterans and that another group of veterans who objected to U.S. foreign policy wanted to march and hold up banners expressing their critical views. Should the courts require that they be allowed to participate? Explain.

Obscenity

The portrayal of sex in art, literature, films, and on the Internet is a troublesome topic in American society. Although the First Amendment guarantees freedom of expression, the government has the power to prohibit the distribution of obscene materials. In general terms, obscenity is anything that treats sex or nudity in an offensive or lewd manner, exceeds recognized standards of decency, and lacks serious literary, artistic, political, or scientific value.

As you might expect, courts have had difficulty developing a precise legal definition of obscenity. For example, in speaking about pornography, Justice Potter Stewart once said that he could not define it, "but I know it when I see it." In 1957, the Supreme Court ruled that obscenity is not protected by the Constitution. Later, in the 1973 case of *Miller* v. *California,* the U.S. Supreme Court set out the following three-part test as a guideline for determining whether a work is obscene:

1. Would the average person applying contemporary community standards find that the material, taken as a whole, appeals to prurient interest (that is, an immoderate, unwholesome, or unusual interest in sex)?

2. Does the work depict or describe, in a patently offensive way, sexual conduct specifically outlawed by applicable state law?

3. Does the work, taken as a whole, lack serious literary, artistic, political, or scientific value?

Applying these standards, a medical textbook on anatomy with pictures of nudity is not obscene because it has scientific value. But a sex magazine filled only with nude photos of persons committing illegal acts may be obscene, depending on the standards of the local community.

Recently, state and local governments have developed new strategies for dealing with pornography. Some communities have tried to ban all pornographic works that degrade or depict sexual violence against women. Such works, they argue, are a form of sex discrimination that may lead to actual violence or abuse against women. Other communities regulate adult bookstores and movie theaters through their zoning laws. Such laws restrict these stores and theaters to special zones or ban them from certain neighborhoods. Finally, most communities have passed laws outlawing child pornography (depictions of children involved in sexual activity) and greatly restricting minors' access to sexually oriented material. The Supreme Court has held that laws against child pornography are constitutional, even when the laws ban material that is not technically obscene.

Lawmakers such as Senator Joe Lieberman from Connecticut testify before Congress in support of laws that protect children from adult content on the Internet. *Why has the Supreme Court found some efforts to do this unconstitutional?*

A more difficult problem arises in trying to protect children from pornography on Internet sites. The Supreme Court has found some of Congress's efforts to do this to be unconstitutional because those laws have not been sufficiently clear about exactly what expression is prohibited. Another problem with efforts to protect children from harmful material on the Internet is that such efforts may result in restricting adult access to material that is legal for adults to see.

Problem 37.3

a. Should the government be allowed to censor books, movies, the Internet, or magazines? If so, under what circumstances, and why?

b. Who should decide if a book or movie is obscene? What definition should be used?

c. Do you think books and movies that depict nude women and emphasize sex encourage violence against women? Should they be banned? Explain your answer.

d. Assume that filtering software is installed on the computers in your town's public school library. The software blocks pornographic sites, but some historical and religious sites are also blocked. Is the use of this software a violation of the First Amendment? Explain.

e. Is there a problem with indecent material on the Internet? If so, what should be done about it?

Defamation

The First Amendment does not protect defamatory expression. Defamation is a false expression about a person that damages that person's reputation. When defamation is spoken, it is called slander. Written defamation is called libel. For example, assume a patient said that her doctor was careless and had caused the death of patients. If others heard this remark, the doctor could sue the patient for slander if the statement had been false. If the patient had written the same thing in a letter, the suit would be for libel. However, if a statement—written or spoken, no matter how damaging or embarrassing—is proven to be true, the plaintiff cannot win a defamation suit in court. The U.S. Supreme Court has special rules that make it difficult for public officials or public figures to win defamation suits.

Commercial Speech

Another form of speech that is not fully protected by the Constitution is commercial speech. Most advertising is considered commercial speech, as distinguished from individual speech. At one time commercial speech received no protection by the courts. It was assumed that government could regulate commercial speech in much

The Public Official's Lawsuit for Libel

On March 29, 1960, the *New York Times* printed an advertisement placed by four African American clergymen. The ad was entitled "Heed Their Rising Voices." It called attention to the civil rights struggle in the South and appealed for funds for various causes, including a legal defense fund for Dr. Martin Luther King, Jr., who had been indicted for perjury in Montgomery, Alabama.

The ad focused on the violence with which the civil rights movement had been met in Montgomery. A portion of the advertisement contained factual errors. For example, the ad said that truckloads of armed police ringed the Alabama State College campus when, in fact, the police were deployed near the campus but did not surround it. The ad also said that Dr. King had been arrested seven times, but he had actually been arrested only four times.

L. B. Sullivan was an elected commissioner of the city of Montgomery, and he was responsible for the police department there. While the ad did not mention him by name, he contended that references to police included him. Sullivan sued the clergymen and the newspaper for libel in the Alabama courts and was awarded damages of $500,000.

On appeal, the U.S. Supreme Court reversed the decision. The Court did not analyze the ad as commercial speech, but instead viewed it as communicating information about a public issue of great concern. The Court said that debate on public issues must be "uninhibited, robust, and wide open" and that it may include "vehement, caustic, and sometimes unpleasantly sharp attacks on government and public officials." If critics had to guarantee the complete accuracy of every assertion, it would lead to self-censorship, not free debate.

In the case of *New York Times* v. *Sullivan,* the Court established a rule that a public official cannot recover damages for a defamatory

Dr. Martin Luther King, Jr. under arrest

falsehood relating to official conduct unless the official can prove the speaker either knew the statement was false or offered it recklessly. In this case, the Court said that the clergymen did not know the information in the ad was false and they did not offer it with reckless disregard for its truth. The newspaper had some information in its news files that could have resulted in catching some of the factual errors. However, the Court said that the newspaper did not act with malice.

In a later case, the Court extended this rule to cover lawsuits brought by all public figures—not just public officials.

Problem 37.4

a. Do you agree or disagree with the Supreme Court's decision in this case? Explain.

b. Does the rule about public officials and public figures reduce the privacy rights of these people? Explain.

c. What rights and interests were balanced by the Supreme Court in deciding this case?

the same way that it could regulate business itself. Today, commercial speech does not receive the same high level of protection accorded to political speech, but most commercial speech receives at least some First Amendment protection.

A case in point involves a state that passed a law making it unprofessional conduct for pharmacists to advertise prescription drug prices. The state's concern was that such advertising might lead to aggressive price competition and ultimately to unprofessional, shoddy services by pharmacists. While the information in these ads was purely commercial, the Supreme Court struck down the law based on the argument that society's interest in information about products was more important than the state's interest in regulating advertising of prescription drugs. In addition, when states tried to ban all advertising by lawyers as being inherently misleading, the Court said that such a concern could not support a total ban on advertising by lawyers.

In general, courts allow the government to ban commercial speech that is false or misleading or that provides information about illegal products. If information is not false or misleading and the product or service being advertised is legal, then the government is limited in the ways it can regulate commercial speech. The courts tend to look carefully at such government regulation to see if there is a good reason for it and if the regulation itself is consistent with that good reason.

In one case the government wanted to keep manufacturers of alcoholic beverages from competing with each other in "strength wars," so they banned statements about alcoholic content on beer cans. A beer company sued, arguing that this violated the company's freedom of speech. The Supreme Court agreed with the beer company. While the government had a good reason for its concern about "strength wars," it did not make sense to ban alcohol content from beer labels but not, for example, from wine labels.

Commercial speech includes advertising. *In what ways can states regulate commercial speech?*

The Case of . . .

The Offensive Speaker

In 1948, Father Terminiello arrived to make a speech at a Chicago auditorium. Outside the auditorium about 300 people were picketing his speech. Inside, Terminiello criticized Jews and African Americans, as well as the crowd outside. By the time his speech was finished, 1,500 people had gathered outside. A police line prevented the protesters from entering the building. However, the "howling mob" outside was throwing stones and bricks at the building, and the police were unable to maintain control. The crowd was also yelling at and harassing people who came to hear Terminiello speak.

Terminiello was arrested and charged under a statute that was interpreted to prohibit conduct "which stirs the public to anger, invites dispute, brings about a condition of unrest or creates a disturbance." The U.S. Supreme Court held that the statute was unconstitutional on grounds of vagueness and of being overly broad. Terminiello's conviction was reversed.

Problem 37.5

a. What happened in the Terminiello case? Why was Father Terminiello arrested?

b. Should the police have controlled the crowd instead of arresting Father Terminiello? Did the police violate his First Amendment rights? Why or why not?

c. What did the U.S. Supreme Court decide in this case? Why?

d. Under what circumstances, if any, should people be prohibited from voicing unpopular views? Explain your answer.

Fighting Words, Offensive Speakers, and Hostile Audiences

In addition to obscenity, defamation, and commercial speech, there are a few additional situations in which the U.S. Constitution does not protect the content of a person's speech. When a person speaks publicly, two elements are interacting: the speaker and the audience. Protection of a person's speech by the First Amendment depends on how these elements interact in different situations. There are times when certain words may be protected and other times when the same words may not be protected because the surrounding situation is different.

The First Amendment does not protect you if you use words that are so abusive or threatening that they amount to what the U.S. Supreme Court calls fighting words. These are words spoken face-to-face that are likely to cause an imminent breach of the peace between the speaker and the listener. Fighting words are like a verbal slap in the face. They do not convey ideas or contribute to the marketplace of ideas. Their value is outweighed by society's interest in maintaining order. Still, courts very rarely use the "fighting words" doctrine today. Even offensive, provocative speech that makes its listeners very angry is generally protected and not considered to be fighting words.

In the early 1950s, some people were accused of trying to organize the Communist Party in order to overthrow the U.S. government. *What test did the Supreme Court use to decide the* Dennis *case?*

In addition to analyzing face-to-face speech, the police must also decide how to handle the responses of a large audience to speech. Police action may depend on whether the audience is friendly or hostile toward the speaker and whether there is evidence that a serious danger exists if the speech continues.

In The Case of the Offensive Speaker on page 453, the police had to deal with an audience that disagreed with the speaker's message. The police must also deal with problems caused when the audience agrees with the message. For example, the government must decide how to deal with speakers who advocate illegal activities. Prior to the 1950s, the courts used the **clear and present danger** test. This test examined the circumstances under which a speech was made and determined whether a clear and present danger of unlawful action existed. The courts generally held that the unlawful action did not have to occur immediately after the speech (for example, when a speaker encourages the audience to overthrow the U.S. government). When there was a clear and present danger of unlawful activity, the government could punish the speaker.

In the early 1950s, the Supreme Court reflected the nation's concern with the Cold War and national security. In *Dennis* v. *United States* (1951), the defendants were convicted for attempting to organize the U.S. Communist Party, whose goal was to overthrow the government. In *Dennis,* the Court used a balancing test that downplayed the probability of the act. Instead, the Court balanced the right of the speaker against the harm the speaker proposed. When the speech advocated very dangerous acts, like overthrowing the government, the Court required less proof of clear and present danger.

In the late 1960s, however, the Supreme Court began using the **incitement test** for cases in which the speaker urged the audience to take unlawful action. This test allowed the government to punish advocacy only when it was directed toward inciting, or producing immediate lawless action from, the audience and when the advocacy was likely to produce such behavior. Unlike the clear and present danger test, the incitement test required that the unlawful action be likely to occur within a short period of time. Therefore, the incitement test gives speakers greater protection.

For example, if a speech causes members of an audience to talk to one another in disagreement, the speaker might not be arrested. However, if the speech urges the audience to throw objects at others and the audience begins to do this, the speaker could be arrested. In practice, the police can face a difficult dilemma in deciding whether to arrest an unpopular speaker or control a hostile audience.

Hate Speech

In recent years there has been an effort to punish those who express views—called **hate speech**—motivated by bigotry and racism. This effort has sometimes run afoul of the First Amendment.

Those who support punishment for hate speech argue that strong measures should be taken because of the emotional and psychological impact hate speech has on its victims and its victims' communities. Furthermore, supporters of punishment argue that hate speech amounts to fighting words, and thus does not qualify for First Amendment protection.

Others argue that so-called speech codes designed to promote tolerance for minorities, women, and gays, while well-intentioned, are vague and difficult to enforce fairly. They claim that such speech

White supremacists express views motivated by bigotry and racism. *What are the arguments in support of punishing hate speech? Against it?*

codes put the government into the censorship business—favoring certain content or viewpoints and disfavoring others—in violation of the First Amendment. Legal battles over speech codes, primarily on public college and university campuses, have usually resulted in courts striking them down as First Amendment violations. Supporters of the First Amendment argue that the preferred approach to hateful speech is more speech—speech that rebuts bigotry and racism.

The legal result has been different, however, for state laws that increase criminal punishments for bias-motivated violence and intimidation. In 1993 the U.S. Supreme Court unanimously upheld a Wisconsin law that provides enhanced sentencing when the defendant "intentionally selects the person against whom the crime (is committed) because of . . . race, religion, color, disability, sexual orientation, national origin or ancestry. . . ." Most states now have similar laws providing enhanced penalties for bias-motivated crimes.

Problem 37.6

A state university adopts the following policy: "A student or faculty member may be suspended or expelled for any behavior, verbal or physical, that stigmatizes an individual on the basis of race, ethnicity, religion, national origin, sex, sexual orientation, creed, ancestry, age, marital status, handicap, or veteran status."

a. Decide whether the following actions violate the above policy. If they do, should the student or faculty member be punished?

- After writing a limerick for an assignment, a student reads it aloud in an English class. It makes fun of the reported homosexual acts of a politician.
- A white student writes an article on race relations for the school newspaper. It states that African Americans are more likely than whites to become criminals in the United States, and says this is one reason why whites do not mix more with African Americans.
- The athletic director schedules the varsity club's awards dinner on a major Muslim holiday. Several Muslim athletes are unable to attend.
- An African American student hears that a group of Chinese students will not socialize with African Americans. She calls them "typical Chinese racists."
- Wearing white robes and hoods, a white supremacist student group stages a silent march on campus.

b. What are the arguments for and against the above policy? Do you support or oppose it? Can it be improved? If so, how? Are there ways for students to take a stand against hate speech even if there is no code? Explain.

c. Should television and radio stations be regulated by laws, or should they have their own rules similar to the above university policy? Should other private businesses have similar rules? Give your reasons.

d. Think about how racial and ethnic slurs compare with fighting words. In what ways are they the same? How do they differ?

Law in *Action*

International Forum on Hate Speech

Individuals from many different countries have gathered to discuss whether all countries should enact criminal laws against hate speech. The following speakers give their views.

A German: "Because of the experience of our country under Hitler, we are very worried about how speech can be used to condemn and abuse millions of people. If there had been laws forbidding anti-Semitic speech, could the Holocaust have been prevented? Today, we see strong antiforeigner feeling in our country. We are thankful that we have laws prohibiting 'incitement to hatred' laws and believe they are needed in all countries."

An American: "Our history includes a revolution that was at least partially a reaction to government censorship. We think it is dangerous to allow government to decide what speech will be allowed. It is true that racism is a serious problem in our country and that racist speech can have a very negative impact on the victims. However, it may be overly paternalistic for the government to try to protect people from such speech. Would it not be better to let the marketplace of ideas condemn the racists?"

An Israeli: "The continual conflict between Arabs and Jews in our region led the government to pass a criminal law governing incitement to racism. However, this law has done nothing but create the illusion of progress against racism. There have been few prosecutions, and the ones that have occurred have been against Arabs. Although the law has symbolic value, it may be better not to have prosecutions, because these just give racists on both sides a platform from which to speak."

A South African: "With its history of ethnic and racial division, my country seems a likely candidate

South Africa's Nelson Mandela

for a law against hate speech. In fact, for many years there has been such a law, which prohibited 'bringing any section of inhabitants of the country into ridicule or contempt.' This law was used principally by the white government to prosecute blacks. But many in my country think that the violence can only be stopped if people aren't allowed to promote racial hatred. My view is that while we work to undo racial injustice, it makes sense to ban racist speech."

Problem 37.7

a. Which of the speakers favor laws against hate speech? Why?

b. Which of the speakers oppose such laws? Why?

c. How do you think the history of each speaker's country affects the viewpoints expressed?

d. What are the pros and cons of encouraging countries to enact their own criminal laws against hate speech? What is your position? Give your reasons.

Time, Place, and Manner Restrictions

Laws may regulate expression in one of two ways. Some laws regulate expression based on its content. These laws prescribe *what* a speaker is allowed to say. Other laws regulate the time, place, and manner of expression. These laws prescribe *when, where,* and *how* speech is allowed.

As a general rule, government cannot regulate the content of expression—except in special situations, as noted in the preceding sections. However, government may make reasonable regulations governing the time, place, and manner of speech. For example, towns and cities may require citizens to obtain permits to hold a march, use sound trucks, or stage protests in parks, on streets, or on other public property. Towns and cities may also regulate the time during which loudspeakers may be used, the places where political posters may be displayed, and the manner in which demonstrations may be conducted. Such laws control when, where, and how expression is allowed.

The Case of . . .

The Nazis in Skokie

The American Nazi Party planned a demonstration in the town of Skokie, Illinois. A large number of Skokie's residents were Jewish, and many were survivors of Nazi concentration camps during World War II. Many others had lost relatives in the gas chambers. Because of this, many residents strongly opposed the Nazi demonstration in their town.

To prevent violence and property damage, the town passed a law that it hoped would keep the Nazis from demonstrating there. The law required anyone seeking a demonstration permit to obtain $300,000 in liability insurance. However, this requirement could be waived by the town. The law also banned distribution of material promoting racial or religious hatred and prohibited public demonstrations by people in military-style uniforms. The Nazis challenged the law as a violation of their First Amendment rights.

Problem 37.8

a. Why did Skokie's Jewish population feel so strongly about this demonstration?

b. Some people claimed that the purpose of the demonstration was to incite Skokie's Jews and to inflict emotional harm rather than to communicate ideas. Do you agree or disagree? Should the motive of the speaker influence whether a speech is protected by the Constitution?

c. Does the government have an obligation to protect the rights of Nazis and other unpopular groups, even if their philosophy would not permit free speech for others? Should Ku Klux Klan or Communist Party rallies have the same protection?

d. Was the law in this case neutral in its viewpoint? Explain.

e. How should this case be decided? In what ways, if any, should the town be able to regulate speech and assembly?

Courts analyze such regulations by first determining whether the site affected is a **public forum,** such as a street or park that is traditionally open to expression (or designated for this purpose), or whether the site is a non-public forum, such as a bus terminal or a school. If the site is a public forum, then the regulation will be overturned unless it serves an important government interest. For example, the government may prohibit loud-speakers from blaring in quiet hospital zones or keep marchers off busy main streets when commuters are driving to or from work. However, regulations for nonpublic forums are upheld if they are reasonable. For instance, a school district could choose to limit the use of school buildings (a nonpublic forum) to educational purposes.

Public forums, such as streets or parks, are places where First Amendment rights of expression are traditionally exercised. *How do the courts analyze time, place, and manner restrictions?*

Regulations for public and nonpublic forums must also be viewpoint-neutral—that is, they cannot promote or censor a particular point of view—and they must serve important government interests. The courts will also be more likely to uphold time, place, and manner restrictions if they leave open alternative ways for communicating the information in question.

Problem 37.9

Which of the following laws regulate the content of expression, and which regulate the time, place, and manner of expression? Which, if any, violate the First Amendment?

a. A city ordinance prohibits posting signs on public property such as utility poles, traffic signs, and streetlights.

b. A regulation prohibits people from sleeping in federal parks, even though the sleeping is part of a demonstration against homelessness.

c. A federal regulation prohibits public radio stations from airing editorials.

d. A town ordinance prohibits commercial billboards anywhere within the town limits.

e. A District of Columbia ordinance prohibits the display within 500 feet of a foreign embassy of any sign that tends to bring a foreign government into "public disrepute."

f. A town ordinance prohibits picketing outside abortion clinics.

g. A city ordinance prohibits political or religious organizations from passing out leaflets or asking for donations inside the airport terminal.

Where You Live

What are the rules in your town or city regarding permits for demonstrations, marches, or outdoor concerts? Have any groups been denied permits?

The Flag-Burning

While the Republican National Convention was taking place in Dallas in 1984, Gregory Lee Johnson participated in a political demonstration. Demonstrators marched through Dallas streets, stopping at several locations to stage "die-ins" intended to dramatize their opposition to nuclear weapons. One demonstrator took an American flag from a flagpole and gave it to Johnson.

The demonstration ended in front of the Dallas City Hall, where Johnson unfurled the American flag, doused it with kerosene, and set it on fire. While the flag burned, protesters chanted, "America, the red, white, and blue, we spit on you." There were no injuries or threats of injury during the demonstration.

Of the hundred or so demonstrators, only Johnson was arrested. He was charged under a Texas criminal statute that prohibited desecration of a venerated object (including monuments, places of worship or burial, or a state or national flag) "in a way that the actor knows will seriously offend one or more persons likely to observe or discover his action."

At Johnson's trial, several witnesses testified that they had been seriously offended by the flag-burning. He was convicted, sentenced to one year in jail, and fined $2,000. The case was appealed to the U.S. Supreme Court.

Problem 37.10

Assume that you are a justice on the U.S. Supreme Court. Study the two opinions that follow, decide which you would vote for, and in a letter to the editor of a national newspaper, give the reasons for your decision.

Opinion A

Johnson argues that his burning of the flag should be protected as symbolic speech under

The American flag

the First Amendment. The First Amendment literally protects speech itself. However, this Court has long recognized that First Amendment protection does not end with the spoken or written word. While we have rejected the idea that virtually all conduct can be labeled speech and so is protected by the First Amendment, we have recognized conduct as symbolic speech when the actor intended to convey a particular message and there was a great likelihood that those viewing the conduct would understand the message.

In this case, Johnson's conduct is similar to conduct protected as symbolic speech in our earlier cases. However, the First Amendment does not provide an absolute protection for speech. This Court will analyze the Texas law, along with the facts of the case, to determine whether the state's interest is sufficient to justify punishing Johnson's action.

In earlier cases, we upheld the conviction of a protester who burned his draft card. We reached that decision because the government had an important interest in requiring that everyone age 18 and older carry a draft card. In that case we did not punish the protester's speech, but rather his illegal act (burning his draft card). However, we have held that freedom of speech was violated when individuals were arrested for displaying a flag decorated with a peace symbol constructed of masking tape and for wearing pants with a small flag sewn into the seat.

In the *Johnson* case, the state argues that it has two important interests: preventing a breach of the peace and preserving the flag as a symbol of nationhood and national unity. The first interest is not involved in this case because there was no breach of the peace or even a threat of such a breach.

The state's other argument—the preservation of the flag as a symbol of nationhood and national unity—misses the major point of this Court's earlier First Amendment decisions: the government may not prohibit expression simply because society finds the ideas presented to be offensive or disagreeable. Johnson was prosecuted for burning the flag to express an idea—his dissatisfaction with the country's policies. His conviction must be reversed because his act deserves First Amendment protection as symbolic speech. The government has not provided sufficient justification for punishing his speech.

Opinion B

For more than 200 years the American flag has occupied a unique position as the symbol of the nation. Regardless of their own political beliefs, millions of Americans have an almost mystical reverence for the flag. Both Congress and the states have enacted many laws prohibiting the misuse and mutilation of the American flag. With the exception of Alaska and Wyoming, all the states have specific laws prohibiting the burning of the flag. We do not believe that the federal law and the laws in 48 states that prohibit burning of the flag are in conflict with the First Amendment. Although earlier cases have protected speech and even some symbolic speech related to the flag, none of our decisions has ever protected flag-burning.

The First Amendment is designed to protect the expression of ideas. Indeed, Johnson could have denounced the flag in public or even burned it in private without violating the Texas law. In fact, other methods of protest were used and permitted at the demonstration. The Texas statute did not punish him for the ideas that he conveyed but rather for the conduct he used to convey his message. Requiring that Johnson use some method other than flag-burning to convey his message places a very small burden on free expression.

We have never held that speech rights are absolute. If Johnson had chosen to spray-paint graffiti on the Washington Monument, there is no question that the government would have the power to punish him for doing so. The flag symbolizes more than national unity. It symbolizes to war veterans, for example, what they fought for and what many died for. It also symbolizes our shared values such as freedom, equal opportunity, and religious tolerance. If the great ideas behind our country are worth fighting for—and history demonstrates that they are—then the flag that uniquely symbolizes the power of those ideas is worth protecting from burning. The conviction should be affirmed.

Landmark Supreme Court Cases

Visit the Landmark Supreme Court Cases Web site at landmarkcases.org for information and activities about *Texas v. Johnson*.

Symbolic Speech

Expression may be symbolic as well as verbal. **Symbolic speech** is conduct that expresses an idea. Although speech is commonly thought of as verbal expression, we are all aware of nonverbal communication. Sit-ins, flag waving, demonstrations, and wearing armbands or protest buttons are examples of symbolic speech. While most forms of conduct could be said to express ideas in some way, only some conduct is protected as symbolic speech. In analyzing such cases, the courts ask whether the speaker intended to convey a particular message and whether it is likely that the message was understood by those who viewed it.

To convince a court that symbolic conduct should be punished and not protected as speech, the government must show it has an important reason. However, the reason cannot be merely that the government disapproves of the message conveyed by the symbolic conduct.

Vagueness and Overinclusive Laws

Courts have ruled that laws governing free speech must be clear and specific. This is so that a reasonable person can understand what expression is prohibited. Laws also need to be clear so they can be enforced in a uniform and nondiscriminatory way. Laws governing free speech that are not clear and specific can be struck down by courts on grounds of **vagueness.**

In addition, laws that regulate free speech must be narrowly drafted to prohibit only as much as is necessary to achieve the government's goals. Laws that prohibit both protected and unprotected expression are termed *overinclusive*. In specific cases, courts may strike down statutes that are overly vague or overinclusive, even if the expression in question could have been prohibited or punished under a clearer, more narrowly drafted law.

People often use sit-ins, a form of symbolic speech, to protest. *How do the courts determine whether conduct is protected as symbolic speech?*

The Cross-Burning Law

In the late 1980s, many states and localities passed laws against hate crimes. These laws defined the types of acts that constituted hate crimes and provided criminal penalties for them. St. Paul, Minnesota, was one of many cities to pass such a law. This city's ordinance read as follows:

Whoever places on public or private property a symbol . . . or graffiti, including but not limited to a burning cross or Nazi swastika, which one knows or has reasonable grounds to know arouses anger, alarm, or resentment in others on the basis of race, color, creed, religion, or gender, commits disorderly conduct and shall be guilty of a misdemeanor.

Russell and Laura Jones and their five children were an African American family who had just moved into a mostly white St. Paul neighborhood. Late one night they were awakened by noise outside their bedroom window. When they parted the curtains, they saw a cross burning on their front lawn. St. Paul police arrested a white 18-year-old factory worker. He was prosecuted and convicted under the local ordinance described above.

Surveying the damage

Problem 37.11

a. What happened in this case? Why was the 18-year-old prosecuted?

b. Could the state have prosecuted the defendant using some other law or ordinance? If so, which ones? Why do you think it used the hate crimes ordinance?

c. Can you identify words or phrases in the ordinance that are not clear and specific? What are they? Exactly what expression is prohibited?

d. On appeal, what legal arguments can the defendant raise? What legal arguments can the state make?

e. When interviewed by a national newspaper, the lawyer for the defendant said, "Everybody's gotten real thin-skinned lately, and I'm defending the right to express yourself in that kind of climate. . . . With an ordinance like this, you open up a doctrine that swallows the First Amendment." What did the lawyer mean by these comments? Do you agree or disagree with them? Give your reasons.

f. How should this case be decided? Give your reasons.

g. Assume that the ordinance is upheld. Could a man in St. Paul be prosecuted for wearing a sexist T-shirt, based on the language of the ordinance? Could a Native American family in St. Paul have a visitor from Washington, D.C., arrested because the visitor's car had a Washington Redskins bumper sticker? What steps can the government take to prevent hateful speech?

Law in Action

Advising Your City Council

Citizens have come to their representative on the city council and asked for her help in solving the following problem. They are concerned about people on their downtown streets who are approaching local citizens and tourists and asking for money. These people hold out a cup and say, "Help the homeless," to passersby. Some people report that they have had their path blocked and have felt harassed.

The council member is sympathetic to the concerns voiced by her constituents, but she also realizes that this issue might involve the First Amendment and the right to freedom of speech.

Problem 37.12

Assume that you work for this council member. Draft a paper advising her about possible approaches the council might take. Consider these points:

a. Should a new criminal law be drafted to address this problem? Can an existing criminal law be used? Remember that a criminal law that violates the First Amendment would be unconstitutional.

b. Are the words "Help the homeless" protected speech under the First Amendment? If so, would they be considered political speech? Commercial speech? Some other type of speech? If these words would not be protected, why not?

c. Even if the words are protected, is there some way to regulate this activity according to time, place, and manner that will improve the situation?

d. Draft a proposed law to regulate asking for money on downtown streets. Analyze the law

A homeless man

to be sure that it is not vague or overinclusive and that it is not designed to prohibit one particular point of view.

e. Would citizens support passing such a law? Would police support enforcement? Might the law be challenged in court? Explain your answers.

Freedom of the Press

> "If it were left to me to decide whether we should have a government without a free press or a free press without a government, I would prefer the latter."
>
> — Thomas Jefferson

The First Amendment to the U.S. Constitution guarantees freedom of the press. It protects us from government **censorship** of newspapers, magazines, books, radio, television, and film. Censorship occurs when the government examines publications and productions and prohibits the use of material it finds offensive. Traditionally, courts have protected the press from government censorship. For example, in 1966 the U.S. Supreme Court said that "justice cannot survive behind walls of silence." It said this to emphasize our system's distrust of secret trials. In addition to providing information about news events, the press subjects all of our political and legal institutions to public scrutiny and criticism.

The Framers of the Constitution provided the press with broad freedom. This freedom was considered necessary to the establishment of a strong, independent press sometimes called "the fourth branch" of government. An independent press can provide citizens with a variety of information and opinions on matters of public importance.

The right of the press to gather and publish information may conflict with other important rights.

Political debates are often televised so voters can find out where the candidates stand on issues that affect their lives and the nation's well-being. *Should all candidates be included in televised debates?*

However, freedom of the press sometimes clashes with other rights, such as a defendant's right to a fair trial or a citizen's right to privacy. In recent years there has been increasing concern about extremely aggressive journalism, including stories about people's sex lives and photographs of people when they believed they were in a private setting.

Among the difficult questions that government and the press have confronted are these: When can the government prevent the press from publishing information? When can the government keep the press from obtaining information? When can the government force the press to disclose information? Is freedom of the press limited in

The Case of . . .

The Gag Order

Six people were brutally murdered in their home in a small Nebraska town. The murders and the later arrest of a suspect received widespread news coverage. At a pretrial hearing that was open to the public, the prosecutor introduced a confession and other evidence against the accused. Both the trial judge and the lawyers believed that publication of the information would make it impossible for the suspect to have a fair trial before an unbiased jury. As a result, the trial judge issued a gag order, which prohibited the news media from reporting the confession or any other evidence against the accused. Members of the news media sued to have the gag order declared unconstitutional and removed.

Problem 38.1

a. What happened in this case? Why did the judge issue a gag order?

b. Should judges be able to close criminal trials to the press? If so, when and why?

c. Which is more important: the right to a fair trial or the right to freedom of the press? Explain your answer.

d. As a practical matter, how could the court protect the rights of the accused in this case without infringing on the rights of the press?

The Candidates' Televised Debate

The Arkansas Educational Television Commission, a state-owned public broadcaster, sponsored debates between the major political party candidates for the 1992 congressional election in Arkansas's Third Congressional District. Ralph Forbes, a ballot-qualified independent, sought permission to participate in the debate. The television station's staff determined that Forbes had not generated enough enthusiasm for his campaign from voters and did not include him in the debate. Forbes sued, contending that his exclusion violated his First Amendment rights.

The television station argued that its decision was a viewpoint-neutral exercise of journalistic discretion. The station staff did not invite Forbes because he lacked serious voter support, not because of his views.

Forbes argued that since the station is owned by the state, the government would actually be deciding who is and who is not a viable candidate. This, Forbes contends, is a decision that must be left to the voters. In addition, in an earlier campaign in which he ran as a Republican Party candidate for lieutenant governor, Forbes won a majority of the counties in the Third Congressional District.

Problem 38.2

a. What arguments can the television station make for keeping Forbes out of the debate?

b. What arguments can Forbes make that would enable him to participate in the debate?

c. How should this case be decided?

d. How important are televised debates between candidates?

e. Could a third-party candidate with only a modest level of support make a difference in the outcome of an election? Explain.

f. Should our political system do more to encourage participation from candidates who are not members of one of the two major parties? Why or why not?

g. Should a government-owned television station provide an automatic right of access for debates to all candidates who qualify to appear on the ballot? Give your reasons.

. . . .

places such as schools or prisons? Are there special limits on the press during wartime? What happens when the government is also the press, as in the case of publicly owned radio and television stations?

Prohibiting Publication

In The Case of the Gag Order on page 466, the judge was concerned about the defendant's Sixth Amendment right to a fair trial. The reporters were concerned about their First Amendment right to freedom of the press. This case presented a conflict between two important constitutional rights: free press and fair trial.

In 1976, the U.S. Supreme Court decided that the gag order was unconstitutional in this case. The Court held that the trial judge should have taken less drastic steps to lessen the effects of the pretrial publicity. The Court suggested postponing the trial until a later date,

Landmark Supreme Court Cases

Visit the Landmark Supreme Court Cases Web site at landmarkcases.org for information and activities about *U.S. v. Nixon.*

moving the trial to another county, questioning potential jurors to screen out those with fixed opinions, and carefully instructing the jury to decide the case based only on the evidence introduced at the trial.

If the gag order had been upheld, it would have amounted to a **prior restraint**—prohibition against any publication—on the press. Attempts to censor publications before they go to press are presumed unconstitutional by the courts. Prior restraint is only allowed if (1) publication would cause a certain, serious, and irreparable harm; (2) no lesser means would prevent the harm; and (3) the prior restraint would be effective in avoiding the harm.

A few years after the gag order case, the U.S. Supreme Court ruled that the public and the press usually have a right to attend criminal (and probably civil) trials. Trials can only be closed if there are vital government interests at stake and no less-restrictive way to protect those interests.

Another example of a government attempt to impose censorship before publication took place in 1971, when a government employee gave top-secret documents about origins of the Vietnam War to several newspapers. The documents outlined the past conduct of the United States regarding the Vietnam conflict. The government sued to block publication of the so-called Pentagon Papers, but the Supreme Court refused to stop publication. It said that the documents, although perhaps embarrassing to the government, would not cause "direct, immediate, and irreparable harm." However, if the documents had, for example, contained a secret plan of attack during a time of war, the Court might have blocked publication.

> After completing an analysis of the Vietnam War, Defense Department official Daniel Ellsberg released portions of the study to the *New York Times*. The government tried to block its publication, claiming that national security would be threatened. *Give an example of a government document whose release should be stopped by the courts.*

Problem 38.3

A state law made it a crime to publish the name of any youth charged as a juvenile offender. A newspaper later published an article containing the name of a juvenile charged with the murder of another youth. The newspaper learned the name of the arrested youth by listening to the police radio and by talking to several witnesses to the crime.

a. What is the state's interest in having and enforcing this law?

b. What is the newspaper's interest in publishing the juvenile's name?

c. How should the conflict be resolved?

Denying the Press Access to Information

Another way in which the government sometimes tries to control the press is by denying the public access to certain information. Some people argue that denying access to information does not violate the rights of the press. Others contend that freedom of the press implies a right to obtain information.

To protect the public's access to government information, Congress passed the *Freedom of Information Act (FOIA)* in 1966. This law requires federal agencies to release information in their files to the public. The law allows citizens to obtain government information and records unless the material falls into the category of a special exception. Exceptions include information affecting national defense or foreign policy, personnel and medical files, trade secrets, investigatory records, and other confidential information. The *FOIA* applies only to federal agencies and does not create a right of access to records held by Congress, the courts, or by local or state government agencies.

The purpose of the *FOIA* is to allow citizens to learn about the business of government. Federal agencies must respond to requests for information within 20 days. Agencies that refuse to release unprivileged information can be sued in federal court. If you want to request information under the *Freedom of Information Act,* send a letter to the head of the agency or to the agency's *FOIA* officer. You can find the contact information you need online at www.usdoj.gov/foia or by calling 202-514-FOIA.

Problem 38.4

The Defense Department has a policy restricting access to a U.S. Air Force base that serves as the main military mortuary for soldiers killed abroad. A group of veterans and photographers argued that this policy restricted needed public access to information. The federal court, as well as the court of appeals, however, agreed with the military's argument that the privacy of grieving families was of greater importance and should be protected. The policy did not interfere with protected First Amendment rights of the public or the press.

a. Why do you think the veterans and photographers wanted public access to a military base serving as a mortuary?

b. Do you agree with the decision of the court of appeals in this case? Give your reasons.

When you write to request information, identify the records you want as accurately as possible. Although you are not required to specify a document by its official name, your request must reasonably describe the information sought. The more specific and limited the request, the greater the likelihood that it will be processed without delay. You are not required to demonstrate a need or even a reason for

An embedded reporter during the 2003 Iraq war uses a laptop computer to write a story. *What were the advantages of allowing reporters to travel with the military troops in Iraq?*

wanting to see the information. However, you are more likely to receive the documents if you explain why you want them. Some states have laws similar to the *FOIA*. These laws provide citizens with access to state agency files.

During times of war, there may be special issues related to press access to information. For example, the Pentagon allowed hundreds of embedded reporters to accompany troops during the Iraq war in 2003. This strategy provided the public with a great deal of information, virtually in real time, about the war and its aftermath. However, the courts have not been particularly protective of the rights of the press in terms of access to information. In a leading case, the Supreme Court said: "It is one thing to say that the government cannot restrain the publication of news emanating from certain sources. It is quite another to suggest that the Constitution imposes upon the government the affirmative duty to make available to journalists sources of information not available to members of the public generally."

Problem 38.5

Rumors about a federal prison had circulated for years. Former prisoners claimed that rape, suicide, murder, and mistreatment were all common occurrences. The warden denied the allegations but refused to provide any information about prison conditions.

A newspaper asked permission to inspect the prison and interview the prisoners, but the warden denied the request. The newspaper then asked the federal government for information about the prison. The newspaper asked for a list of inmates and for information about anyone who had died or been injured while in custody. The government refused to provide any information.

The newspaper then did two things. It filed a suit seeking admission to the prison, and it filed a *Freedom of Information Act* request for information about the prison.

a. How would you decide this lawsuit? Explain.

b. What are the newspaper's rights under the *Freedom of Information Act*? How would you decide its request for information?

c. What rights or interests does the prison administration have in this case?

d. Give two examples of information held by the federal government that you could access using the *Freedom of Information Act*.

Where You Live

Does your state have a version of the *Freedom of Information Act*? If not, should it? If so, what information is covered by the act? How can a citizen get information under the act?

Requiring the Press to Disclose Information

The government and the press also sometimes disagree over the extent to which the First Amendment protects a reporter's sources of information. These conflicts arise because people may give reporters confidential information that is important to a news story. If the people thought they would be identified, they might be less likely to give journalists this information. In one case, a reporter was summoned before a grand jury and asked questions about a crime. The journalist knew this information based on a confidential conversation. The journalist requested a qualified privilege that would have allowed him not to reveal the identity of the source of the confidential information. The U.S. Supreme Court refused to extend any special First Amendment right to the journalist in this situation. The Court did say that states could pass "shield" laws that would give journalists such a privilege. More than half the states have done this, but even the shield laws can come into direct conflict with other very important constitutional rights.

The Reporters' Committee for Freedom of the Press was created in 1970 at a time when the U.S. news media faced a wave of government subpoenas asking reporters to name confidential sources. This organization, with its steering committee comprised of many of the nation's leading journalists, continues to provide free legal services to more than 2,000 journalists each year. The Reporters' Committee for Freedom of the Press also provides access to an updated collection of news stories on freedom of the press issues online at www.rcfp.org. Student journalists work with an affiliated group, the Student Press Law Center. Information about their work is available online at www.splc.org.

The Case of . . .

The Shield Law

In 1976, the *New York Times* published a story suggesting that a doctor had murdered several patients. As a result, New Jersey authorities investigated the case and charged the doctor with murder.

Defense attorneys asked the *New York Times* to turn over the names of all persons who had been interviewed during the investigation, as well as any other information it had. The defense contended that it could not properly prepare its case without this information. The *New York Times* and the reporter who conducted the investigation refused to turn over any information. They argued that the First Amendment and a New Jersey law that protected a reporter's sources of information allowed them to withhold any unpublished material in their possession.

Problem 38.6

a. What rights are in conflict in this case?

b. Should the judge allow the reporter to withhold the information sought by the defense attorney? Why or why not?

Expression in Special Places

"It can hardly be argued that either students or teachers shed their constitutional rights to freedom of speech or expression at the schoolhouse gate. . . ."

— *Tinker v. Des Moines* (1969), majority opinion

Schools, military bases, and prisons present special First Amendment problems. The rights of students, military personnel, or inmates often conflict with the rights of others or interfere with the need to preserve order. When this conflict occurs, courts must balance the competing interests in each case.

As a general rule, courts allow greater freedom of speech and assembly in public parks and on street corners than in schools, military bases, and prisons. Courts sometimes speak of places such as public parks and street corners, where First Amendment rights are traditionally exercised, as **public forums.** For the most part, however, courts have found that schools, military bases, and prisons (and their publications) provide only a limited forum for the exercise of First Amendment freedoms. In these places, you can usually exercise your rights, but only as long as the expression does not interfere with the purpose of the facility.

Street Law *online*

Visit the *Street Law* Web site at streetlaw.glencoe.com for chapter-based information and resources.

Schools provide only a limited forum for the exercise of First Amendment rights.

The Student Armbands

Mary Beth Tinker and her brother John were opposed to the Vietnam War. They decided to wear black armbands to school as symbols of their objection. When school administrators learned of this, they adopted a policy of asking anyone wearing armbands to remove them. Students who refused would be suspended until they returned to school without the armbands.

The Tinkers and three other students wore black armbands to school. Although some students argued the Vietnam issue in the halls, no violence occurred. The five protesting students were suspended from school until they came back without their armbands.

Should wearing armbands be considered a form of free expression protected by the Constitution?

Mary Beth and John Tinker

Landmark Supreme Court Cases

Visit the Landmark Supreme Court Cases Web site at landmarkcases.org for information and activities about *Tinker* v. *Des Moines*.

The First Amendment in Public Schools

In *Tinker* v. *Des Moines School District* (1969), the U.S. Supreme Court decided that the right to freedom of expression "does not end at the schoolhouse gate." The Court held that wearing armbands was a form of "symbolic speech" protected by the First Amendment. However, the Court also held that the students' right to free speech could be restricted when the school could show that the students' conduct would "materially and substantially disrupt" the educational process. Such a disruption did not occur in reaction to the Tinkers' armbands, nor could it reasonably have been predicted, so their suspensions were declared unconstitutional.

The *Tinker* case provides a standard that the courts use to determine whether punishment of student speech by public school officials violates the First Amendment. Although the *Tinker* case clearly involved expression not endorsed or sponsored by the school, in other cases the courts have been asked to determine the extent to which student speech can be controlled as part of school-sponsored activities. In these cases the courts have balanced students' First Amendment rights against the schools' duty to determine the educational program.

In *Hazelwood* v. *Kuhlmeier* (1988)—the school newspaper censorship case—the U.S. Supreme Court ruled that school officials could have editorial control over a school-sponsored newspaper produced in a journalism class. The justices found that such a publication should not be treated as a public forum for young journalists or students in general. The reasons given for allowing this control were that (1) schools should not have to permit student speech that is inconsistent with their basic educational mission (for example, schools could refuse to sponsor student speeches advocating drug or alcohol use), and (2) schools should be allowed to control expression that students, parents, and others in the community might reasonably believe the school has endorsed (for example, students could be stopped from printing vulgar or lewd material in the school newspaper).

This decision gives educators editorial control over the style and substance of school-sponsored student speech if they can show their actions are reasonably related to legitimate educational concerns.

The Case of . . .

Censorship of the School Newspaper

A high school principal deleted two pages from the year's final issue of the school newspaper because these pages contained one story on student experiences with pregnancy and another about the impact of divorce on students. The principal believed that the stories had been written in such a way that the privacy rights of some students might be violated. He also believed the topics might offend or be inappropriate for some of the younger students at the school.

The newspaper was written as part of the school's advanced journalism class. Following the school's regular practice, the journalism teacher had submitted the page proofs to the principal just before publication. The principal deleted the two pages on which the articles in question appeared. Those pages also contained several stories he did not object to. His reason for deleting the pages was that the school year was almost over, and he did not believe there would be enough time to rewrite the offensive stories.

The existing school board policy said, "School-sponsored student publications will not restrict free expression or diverse viewpoints within the rules of responsible journalism."

The student editors of the paper sued the principal and the school district, arguing that their First Amendment rights had been violated.

Problem 39.1

a. What arguments can the students make?

b. What arguments can the principal make?

c. How is this case similar to *Tinker*? Different?

d. How should the court decide this case?

e. Did the principal violate the school's policy? Give your reasons.

f. Is a new policy needed for student publications at this school? If so, draft one.

Landmark Supreme Court Cases

Visit the Landmark Supreme Court Cases Web site at landmarkcases.org for information and activities about *Hazelwood* v. *Kuhlmeier*.

Student Expression and the First Amendment

Based on the Supreme Court decisions in *Tinker* and *Hazelwood,* analyze each of the following cases. Give arguments both for permitting the expression and for supporting the school's need to regulate the expression. How should each case be decided?

a. At an assembly before student council elections, a student makes a campaign speech for a friend. While not legally obscene, the speech has many sexual references and makes some students uncomfortable. Others applaud, jeer, and shout additional sexual references. The principal meets with the speaker after the assembly, and then suspends him for several days. The student sues the school for violating his right to free speech.

b. Students publish, with their own money and equipment, an "underground newspaper" off school premises that contains the results of best/worst teacher and best/worst class surveys. The principal does not allow distribution of the newspaper at school. The students sue the school for violating freedom of the press.

c. A major project of a high school drama class is the production of a spring musical. Tickets are sold at the school and at several locations in the community. The students and their drama teacher select the musical *Hair,* which has several scenes with partially clothed actors and actresses. The drama class begins rehearsals, prints tickets, and starts to publicize the performances. When the school board learns which musical has been selected, it cancels the production. The students sue, alleging violation of their freedom of expression.

d. A few parents complain to the high school librarian that several of the school's library books contain negative stereotypes about

A high school radio station

women and certain racial and ethnic groups. The parents ask that the books be removed from the library. The principal agrees and removes the books, even though they are available in the community library. Other students and their parents sue the school for violating the rights of students who want access to those books.

e. Lakeside High School students operate a radio station each morning before school begins, playing music, reporting sports scores, and making other announcements from the student lounge. The faculty member responsible for supervising the student lounge believes that the lyrics of a popular song frequently played on the station are sexually suggestive. He complains to the principal, who removes the CD from the radio station and tells the student disc jockeys that they must submit an upcoming music playlist monthly for her approval. The student disc jockeys sue, claiming a violation of their rights.

Where You Live

What are your school's policies on student speech and press rights? Are they consistent with the decisions in *Tinker* and *Hazelwood*?

Therefore, even with the greater editorial control allowed by the *Hazelwood* decision, a principal who personally opposes (or supports) gun control, for example, cannot censor a student publication that fairly presents all points of view on that subject.

In addition to cases dealing directly with student speech and press rights, courts have had to consider whether student appearance—dress and grooming—is protected expression. In recent years students have worn shirts with messages promoting violence, gang membership, drug use, drinking, and sexism. Alarmed educators argue that these clothes transmit a message inconsistent with school and community values and that these messages can lead to school disruption, including violence. Parents also worry that their children may become targets for violence when wearing such clothing. Some principals have refused to allow students inside their schools wearing such clothing. Some students argue that their choice of clothing and personal grooming is a form of expression that should be protected by the First Amendment.

The First Amendment in Prisons and the Military

Compared with prisons and the military, schools are relatively open institutions. Schools are supposed to prepare students for life in our constitutional democracy, with its emphasis on individual freedom. By contrast, both prisons and the military closely regulate almost all aspects of life. Prisons, in particular, physically separate their members from society. In a 2001 case, the U.S. Supreme Court affirmed its existing rule that a prison regulation that interferes with an inmate's constitutional rights will be upheld as long as it is reasonably related to legitimate **penological** (corrections) objectives. In that case an inmate claimed a First Amendment right to provide legal assistance to a fellow inmate who had been charged with assaulting a correctional officer. The inmate offering the assistance was punished for violating prison rules. The Court explained that this inmate did not have a right to provide legal assistance and again emphasized the need to defer to prison authorities in the administration of the correctional system.

In 1976 the Court upheld a regulation on a large military base that prohibited all political speeches and the distribution of campaign literature. These cases show that individual rights are often very limited when balanced against the special needs of the military and prisons for order and discipline.

Individual rights and freedom of expression are limited on military bases. *Why is this so?*

Freedom of Religion

The first 16 words of the First Amendment to the U.S. Constitution deal with freedom of religion. These words reflect the deep concern that the Founders of the United States had about the relationship between church and state, and about the right of individuals to practice their religion freely. In addition, Article VI of the Constitution prohibits the government from requiring any religious test for public office.

Religious freedom is protected by two clauses in the First Amendment: the establishment clause and the free exercise clause. The **establishment clause** forbids the government from setting up a state religion. It also prohibits the government from endorsing or supporting religion and from preferring one religion over another. The **free exercise clause** protects the right of individuals to worship or believe as they choose. Government cannot prohibit or unduly burden religious practice.

Street Law *online*

Visit the *Street Law* Web site at streetlaw.glencoe.com for chapter-based information and resources.

People practice their religion in many different ways.

Taken together, the establishment and free exercise clauses prohibit the government from either endorsing religion or punishing religious belief or practice. Some people believe that the two clauses require the government to be neutral toward religion. This means that the government should not favor one religion over another or favor religion over nonreligion in its actions or its laws. Others believe that the First Amendment requires the government to accommodate religious belief and practice, as long as it does not establish or promote a state or national religion.

Between 1791 and 1940, the U.S. Supreme Court heard only five cases dealing with church-state relations. Since then, the Court has heard more than a hundred such cases, half of them since 1980.

Based on data about church membership and attendance, the United States is a religious country, and many Americans are religious people. Many national traditions have religious overtones. For example, U.S. money includes the words "In God We Trust." The Pledge of Allegiance contains references to God. And many state legislatures, Congress, and the Supreme Court begin their sessions with a brief prayer. Although these traditions are criticized by some people as violating the First Amendment, they have so far been upheld by the courts.

A Christmas tree and a Hanukkah menorah are displayed on government property. *Do either or both of these displays violate the First Amendment?*

The Establishment Clause

The establishment clause in the First Amendment forbids state and federal governments from setting up churches, from passing laws aiding one or all religions, or from favoring one religion over another. In addition, the establishment clause forbids the government from passing laws barring or requiring citizen attendance at any church or belief in any religious idea.

Thomas Jefferson once referred to the establishment clause as a "wall of separation between church and state." In the United States, there is a wall of separation, but it is not complete. Churches are indirectly aided by government in many ways. For example, churches do not have to pay real estate taxes, even though they receive government services such as police and fire protection.

The Rabbi's Invocation

For many years the Providence, Rhode Island school committee and superintendent have permitted, but not directed, school principals to include invocations and benedictions in the graduation ceremonies of the city's public middle schools. As a result, some public middle schools in Providence have included invocations and benedictions in their graduation ceremonies.

The invocations and benedictions are not written or delivered by public school employees, but by members of the clergy invited to participate in these ceremonies for that purpose. The schools provide the clergy with guidelines prepared by the National Conference of Christians and Jews. These guidelines stress inclusiveness and sensitivity in preparing nonreligious prayer for public, civic ceremonies. The clergy who have delivered these prayers in recent years at the graduations have included ministers of various Christian denominations, as well as rabbis.

Attendance at graduation ceremonies is voluntary, and parents and friends of the students are invited to attend. Middle school ceremonies are held at the schools.

A graduation ceremony

Daniel Weisman's daughter, Deborah, graduated from Nathan Bishop Middle School, a public school in Providence. Rabbi Leslie Gutterman, from a local synagogue in Providence, delivered the invocation and benediction at the ceremony. Both prayers were consistent with the guidelines that had been sent to him by the school principal.

The Weismans filed a case in federal court contending that inviting religious leaders to provide the invocation and benediction at public school graduations violated the separation of church and state required by the First Amendment.

Problem 40.1

a. What happened in this case? Why did the Weismans object to the rabbi's invocation and benediction?

b. What arguments can the Weismans make?

c. What arguments can the school make?

d. Compare this case to the decisions of the U.S. Supreme Court that have found public school-sponsored prayer to be unconstitutional. How is this case like the school prayer cases? How is it different?

e. How should this case be decided?

f. Assume that after the Weismans' complaint the school abandoned its policy of selecting different religious leaders each year and instead sponsored an election to select a student to deliver the prayers at graduation exercises. Would such a policy violate the First Amendment? Explain.

g. Could the school post information on its bulletin board about a community-based baccalaureate service sponsored by local churches for graduating seniors? Would it make a difference if the sign said "This is not a school sponsored or endorsed activity"?

Where You Live

How is the issue of religious holiday displays handled in your community? At your school?

Cases involving the establishment clause have been among the most controversial to reach the U.S. Supreme Court. In these cases, the justices tend to look closely at a very wide range of facts before rendering their decision, rather than being driven by one or two facts or rigid standards. In recent years they have relied on several tests. One of these, the *endorsement test,* asks whether the challenged law or government action has either the purpose or the effect of endorsing religion in the eyes of members of the community. When using this test, the Court analyzes whether the government has sent a message to nonbelievers that they are outsiders and not full members of the political community. As The Case of the Rabbi's Invocation illustrates, the test is not always easy to apply.

In addition to the endorsement test, the Supreme Court also uses the following three-part test from a case decided in 1971 to determine whether a government law or action meets the requirements of the establishment clause:

- The challenged law or government action must have a secular, or nonreligious, purpose.
- The primary effect of the law or action must be to neither advance nor inhibit (hold back) religion.
- The operation of the law or action must not foster excessive entanglement of government with religion.

Establishment clause cases are particularly controversial when they involve aid to parochial schools or prayer in public schools. Over the years, the Court has approved some forms of aid to parochial school students and their parents. For example, it has allowed states to provide bus transportation, computers, and loans of certain textbooks to parochial school students. In 2002 the Court approved a program from Ohio that provided vouchers to low-income parents to help pay tuition at a variety of nonpublic schools, including religiously affiliated schools. However, state or federal laws that provide financial aid directly to a religious institution or its instructors are less likely to be approved.

Although the topic continues to be very controversial, the Court has held that public school-sponsored prayer violates the establishment clause. Even *voluntary* school-sponsored prayer (or school-sponsored daily Bible readings or recitation of the Lord's Prayer) has been found to be unconstitutional.

The Free Exercise Clause

The free exercise clause in the First Amendment protects the right of individuals to worship as they choose. However, when an individual's right to free exercise of religion conflicts with other important interests, the First Amendment claim does not always win. As a rule, religious *belief* is protected. However, *actions* based on those beliefs may be restricted if they violate an important secular government interest. As long ago as 1878, the U.S. Supreme Court upheld the conviction of a Mormon man who had violated the criminal law against polygamy (having multiple spouses), even though his religion at that time encouraged this practice.

If the government intentionally acts to interfere with religious practice, the courts will almost always protect the religious practice. For example, a city in Florida passed an ordinance that banned religious animal sacrifice, a practice of followers of the Santeria religion. An analysis of the public debate behind this law showed that most local citizens disliked this religious practice. The Supreme Court unanimously agreed that the ordinance was passed in order to interfere with religious practice and therefore violated the free exercise clause of the First Amendment.

The Case of . . .

The Amish Children

Wisconsin had a law requiring all children to attend school until age 16. However, the Amish believe that children between the ages of 14 and 16 should devote that time to Bible study and to training at home in farmwork. The Amish believe that high school is "too worldly for their children." State officials prosecuted several Amish parents for not sending their children to school. The parents defended their actions as an exercise of their religion.

Wisconsin v. *Yoder* reached the U.S. Supreme Court in 1972. The Court weighed the rights of the Amish to practice their religion against the state's interest in requiring school attendance. The Court held that the Amish people's right to free exercise of religion was more important than the two additional years of required schooling. Among the factors the Court considered was the tendency for Amish children to become employed, law-abiding citizens after completing their religious education.

An Amish student

Problem 40.2

a. Do you agree with this decision? Give your reasons.

b. What arguments might the dissenters have put forward in their opinion?

c. This case began in Wisconsin as a prosecution of the parents for not sending their children to school. Their defense at trial, and their arguments in the appeals courts, focused primarily on the rights of the parents. Did the students have rights that might have been considered? What rights and interests might have been asserted on behalf of the students?

The more difficult problem arises when the government is not trying to harm religion, yet passes a law that happens to punish religious practice or forces someone to act in a way that violates his or her religious beliefs. In 1990, for example, the Court upheld the drug conviction of a Native American man even though his religion specifically required the sacramental use of peyote, an illegal drug. The Supreme Court's rule is that a valid, neutral law (that is, a law that does not specifically target a religious belief or practice)—in this case, the state's drug laws—will be upheld even if it interferes with religious practice.

The establishment and free exercise clauses are closely related. However, they often come into conflict with each other. Ensuring that a law does not establish a religion can interfere with free exercise of religion and sometimes with freedom of speech.

Consider the case of an evangelical Christian student group at a state university which applied for funding for its student publication. The university granted money to other student groups through this funding process. In order to avoid what it feared would be an establishment of religion (by funding the religious publication), the university refused the funding request. In 1995, the U.S. Supreme Court said that the university had to treat religious and nonreligious activities equally for funding purposes. The Court held that failure to treat the religious publication equally was a violation of freedom of speech (i.e., content-based discrimination).

That same year, the Court also allowed the Ku Klux Klan to display a cross on the lawn of a state-owned park across from the Ohio Statehouse. The state had treated the cross as a religious symbol rather than a political symbol and had denied the Klan permission to display it, even though the park had been made available to a wide range of expressive conduct in the past. In its decision, the Court reasoned that the expression should be viewed as private expression (the Klan's) in a public place and that a reasonable observer would not see the state as endorsing religion.

Although the free exercise clause protects people's right to worship as they choose, the government may pass laws that happen to punish certain religious practices. *How has the Supreme Court handled such cases?*

YOU BE THE JUDGE

Religion and Public Education

The following situations involve religion and public education. For each, determine whether the establishment clause, the free exercise clause, or both are involved. Then decide whether the government's action violates the First Amendment.

a. A high school student who has been deaf since birth asks his school district to pay for a sign language interpreter to accompany him to classes at a local religious school. A federal law requires school districts to provide for the education of all children with disabilities. The school district (which had provided the student with an interpreter while he attended the public school) refuses to pay.

b. A state law authorizes a one-minute period of silence in all public schools "for meditation or voluntary prayer."

c. A state law requires that the Ten Commandments be posted in each public school classroom.

d. A group of high school students requests permission from the school principal to form a prayer club. The group agrees to follow the rules required of all student clubs, which meet twice a week at the beginning of the school day during an activity period. A faculty member volunteers to supervise the group. The principal refuses the group's request.

e. A public high school coach gathers his players together before a game and leads them in a brief prayer. One of the players tells the coach he is uncomfortable with the prayer. The coach tells him that it is fine for him to either say nothing or leave the room while the prayer is being said.

f. Eid al-Fitr is an important religious holiday that Muslims celebrate in the days following

A Muslim holiday celebration

Ramadan. Muslim students stay home from school during the holiday. Unaware of the holiday, a public school system schedules standardized testing during that time.

g. In a science class, the instructor teaches about the theory of evolution. A student is concerned that evolution is different than the Biblical story she has learned in church and from her family. Her mother asks that the science teacher also provide a lesson on creationism in order to provide balance.

h. In December a school sets up a Christmas tree in the hallway outside the main office. The tree and ornaments are purchased using donations from students and their families, as opposed to the school's budget. Most students in the school celebrate Christmas.

i. A school district has a "no hats in school" rule to help keep outsiders out of the schools. A Jewish student wants to wear a yarmulke and a Muslim student wants to wear a headscarf as part of their religious practices.

Due Process

Street Law online

Visit the *Street Law* Web site at streetlaw.glencoe.com for chapter-based information and resources.

The phrase **due process** embodies society's basic notions of legal fairness. A first reading of the due process clauses in the Fifth and Fourteenth Amendments to the U.S. Constitution suggests a limitation that only relates to procedures. In fact, many due process cases do involve the question of fair procedures, or **procedural due process**. However, courts have also interpreted the language of these amendments as a limitation on the substantive powers of legislatures to pass laws affecting various aspects of life. When applying what is called **substantive due process**, courts look at whether a law or government action unreasonably infringes on a fundamental liberty.

In a case from 1833, the U.S. Supreme Court decided that the Fifth Amendment restricted only federal government actions and was not directly binding on state governments. As a result of that case, neither the Supreme Court nor the federal courts in general exercised much control over the substance of state laws or over the processes by which states administered their laws during the country's early years. This situation changed dramatically with the passage of the Civil War amendments (Thirteenth, Fourteenth, and Fifteenth Amendments), which were designed to prevent discrimination by states against blacks freed from slavery as a result of that war.

The Fifth and Fourteenth Amendments guarantee due process of law.

The Fourteenth Amendment's due process clause is almost identical to the Fifth Amendment's clause. However, the Fourteenth Amendment specifically limits the actions of the state governments. Courts have interpreted these two clauses identically: the Fifth Amendment now limits the power of the federal government and the Fourteenth Amendment limits the power of state and local governments.

Substantive Due Process

During the first third of the twentieth century, the U.S. Supreme Court used the due process clause to strike down certain social and economic legislation, such as child labor and minimum wage laws. In those cases, the Court believed that legislators were treating the property rights of businesses unfairly. Since the late 1930s, however, the courts have deferred much more to the legislative judgments of elected officials. It is common in current court opinions upholding economic regulations for judges to write that "we will not substitute our wisdom for that of the legislators." In reviewing social and economic welfare laws, the Court now simply requires that the law be rational in order to be constitutional. Only a law with no rational relationship to a legitimate legislative purpose will be declared unconstitutional. This is a fairly easy test to meet, hence the notion of deferring to the wisdom of state and federal lawmakers.

During the 1960s, the Court began to use a stricter test when social and economic welfare laws had an impact on fundamental rights. These fundamental rights, while not spelled out in the Constitution, include the right to marry, to bear and rear children, and to travel. Fundamental rights also include the controversial right to privacy—including a wide range of rights related to reproduction—which is the topic of the next chapter.

A law will not necessarily be struck down as unconstitutional because it affects a fundamental right. In some circumstances, the government may be able to show that it has a very strong, or compelling, interest when taking action that affects a fundamental right. For example, as noted above, parents have a fundamental right to bear and rear their children. However, the government has a compelling interest in protecting children and therefore may be able to remove children from abusive parents and place them in foster care.

Parents and children are guaranteed a choice between public and private schools because of substantive due process. *How is substantive due process different from procedural due process?*

The Right to Die

In 1983, Nancy Cruzan was severely injured in an automobile accident. As a result of the accident, she suffered permanent brain damage. She remained unconscious in a state hospital and almost totally unresponsive to the world around her for seven years. She was kept alive by a feeding tube that provided water and nutrition. Her parents asked the hospital to remove the tube, but the hospital refused to do so without a court order. All parties agreed that Nancy would soon die without the feeding tube.

State law required "clear and convincing" proof that Nancy would not want to continue her life in this persistent vegetative state. Both the trial court and the state supreme court found her parents unable to produce this evidence based on some conversations Nancy had had with friends before her accident. In a 5-to-4 decision in 1990, the U.S. Supreme Court affirmed the decision of the state supreme court. However, in holding that a state has a strong interest in preserving life, the Court also said that a competent adult has a liberty interest in not being forced to undergo unwanted medical procedures, such as artificial life-sustaining measures. In this case, Nancy Cruzan was found not competent to make this decision. Comments she had made to others before her accident were not considered by any of the reviewing courts as meeting the state's clear and convincing standard of proof.

Seven years later, a related case came to the U.S. Supreme Court. The State of Washington had passed a law that made promoting a suicide attempt a felony. The law provided: "A person is guilty of the crime when he knowingly causes or aids another person to attempt suicide." This law could be applied to a doctor who assisted a patient with a suicide attempt.

In January 1994, several doctors practicing in Washington, along with three gravely ill

Supporters of the right to die

patients and a nonprofit organization called Compassion in Dying, filed suit in federal court asking that their state's assisted suicide law be declared unconstitutional. They argued that the ban on physician-assisted suicide violates a liberty interest protected by the Fourteenth Amendment's due process clause, "which extends to a personal choice by a mentally competent, terminally ill adult to commit physician-assisted suicide." The state argued that its interest in preserving life outweighs an individual's interest in physician-assisted suicide.

Problem 41.1

a. How are the *Cruzan* and assisted suicide cases similar? How are they different?

b. What other arguments can you make in favor of allowing physician-assisted suicide?

c. What other arguments can you make against it?

d. How should the Court decide the physician-assisted suicide case?

e. Do you believe there should be a right to physician-assisted suicide? Give your reasons.

Procedural Due Process

Many modern due process cases deal with what is called procedural due process (fair administration of the law). Due process procedures do not guarantee that the *result* of government action will always be to a citizen's liking. However, fair procedures do help prevent arbitrary, unreasonable decisions. Due process requirements vary depending on the situation. At a minimum, due process means that citizens who will be affected by a government decision must be given notice of what the government plans to do and have a *chance to comment* on the action before it occurs.

Government takes many actions that may deprive people of life, liberty, or property. In each case, some form of due process is required. For example, a state might fire someone from a government job, revoke a prisoner's parole, or cut off someone's Social Security payments. Due process does not prohibit these actions, but it does require that certain procedures be followed before any action is taken.

If a person has a right to due process, the next issue is this: What process is due? Due process is a flexible concept. The procedures required in specific situations depend on several factors: (1) the seriousness of the harm that might be done to the citizen; (2) the risk of making an error without the procedures; and (3) the cost to the government, in time and money, of carrying out the procedures.

According to past decisions of the U.S. Supreme Court, the primary reason for establishing procedural safeguards—when a life, liberty, or property interest is affected by government action—is to prevent inaccurate or unjustified decisions. In a case decided by the Supreme Court in 2003, a sex offender released from prison complained that personal information about him was made available through a state-sponsored Internet site. The site provided information to residents about convicted sex offenders as part of their state's Megan's Law—a law passed in every state and the District of Columbia in memory of a New Jersey girl raped and killed in 1994 by a neighbor who, unbeknownst to the girl's parents, was a convicted sex offender. The former inmate in the 2003 case contended that listing his name and personal information without a court hearing to determine whether or not he was *currently* dangerous harmed his reputation—his interest in liberty—and therefore violated his procedural due process rights. The Court found that the operation of Megan's Law was valid because it simply provided residents with truthful information about convicted sex offenders without maintaining that they were currently dangerous. There was no need for individual hearings because there was no substantial risk of error.

In addition to providing notice and a chance to be heard, due process must follow certain procedures. These may include a hearing before an impartial person, representation by an attorney, calling witnesses on one's behalf, cross-examination of witnesses, a written decision with reasons based on the evidence introduced, a transcript of the proceeding, and an opportunity to appeal the decision.

Where You Live

What due process procedures are followed by schools in your area before a student is suspended?

If you believe that the government has not followed fair procedures when taking some action that affected your life, liberty, or property interest, you may want to consult an attorney. With the attorney's advice and assistance, you can file a complaint directly with the government agency. You may also be able to go to court and seek an order that the government follow due process in dealing with you.

Remember that when the U.S. Supreme Court decides a constitutionality issue, it sets out the minimum protection required. No government can offer less. For example, a state could not decide to do away with the notice requirement in the *Goss* decision. However, government agencies can, and sometimes do, offer greater due process protection than the Supreme Court requires.

The Case of . . .

The Deportation of Permanent Residents

Hyung Joon Kim came to the United States with his parents in 1984 when he was six. Two years later he got a "green card," which identifies legal aliens as permanent residents. He was convicted of burglary in 1996 and of petty theft the next year. After serving two years he was paroled. But soon he was arrested by immigration authorities and jailed as the federal government began deportation proceedings against him. Under the 1996 *Immigration and Naturalization Act,* immigrants—including legal permanent residents—who have already been convicted of certain crimes can be detained without a hearing while the government decides whether to deport them.

From jail, Kim asked a federal judge to release him and to provide him with a due process hearing before further detaining him. Kim wanted the government to have to show that he was unlikely to show up for his deportation hearing. Both the trial judge and the federal court of appeals sided with Kim. The government appealed the decision to the U.S. Supreme Court, which found the federal law to be constitutional, and not a violation of Kim's right to due process. Writing for the majority in this 5-to-4 decision, Chief Justice Rehnquist said: "This Court has firmly and repeatedly endorsed the proposition that Congress may make rules as to aliens that would be unacceptable if applied to citizens." In dissent, Justice Souter wrote that the Court was forgetting more than one hundred years of case precedents that protected the basic liberty interests of permanent residents by locking Kim up for no reason.

Congress had passed the 1996 law out of a concern that many immigrants, once released from jail, would continue to commit crimes and would be hard for authorities to locate. This decision affirms the wide-ranging power the federal government has over immigrants.

Problem 41.2

a. Do you agree with the Court's decision? Explain.

b. Should lawful permanent residents (green-card holders) have the exact same rights as citizens? Should immigrants in the country illegally have fewer rights than lawful permanent residents?

Goss v. Lopez

Ohio law provides for a free education for all children between the ages of 6 and 21. In 1971, widespread student unrest took place in the public schools of Columbus, Ohio. Students who either participated in, or were present at, demonstrations held on school grounds were suspended. Many suspensions were for a period of ten days. Students were not given a hearing before suspension, although at a later date some students and their parents were given informal conferences with the school principal. A number of students, through their parents, sued the board of education, claiming that their right to due process had been violated when they were suspended without a hearing.

In *Goss v. Lopez,* the U.S. Supreme Court decided that students who are suspended for ten days or less are entitled to certain rights before their suspension. These rights include (1) oral or written notice of the charges, (2) an explanation (if students deny the charges) of the evidence against them, and (3) an opportunity for students to present their side of the story.

The Court stated that in an emergency, students could be sent home immediately and a hearing could be held at a later date. The Court did not give students a right to a lawyer, a right to call or cross-examine witnesses, or a right to a hearing before an impartial person.

In *Goss,* the Court considered the due process interests of harm, cost, and risk. The Court ruled that reputations were harmed and educational opportunities were lost during the suspension; that an informal hearing would not be overly costly for the schools; and that while most disciplinary decisions were probably correct, an informal hearing would help reduce the risk of error.

Problem 41.3

a. What happened in the *Goss* case? What rights did the Supreme Court say the students should be given prior to a brief suspension?

b. What rights might the students want that they did not receive in this case? What are the arguments for and against providing these additional rights?

c. Do you think this case was decided correctly? Give your reasons.

Meeting with the principal

The Right to Privacy

Today, Justice Louis D. Brandeis's words from the *Olmstead* case continue to have meaning in our daily lives. Although the words *right to privacy* or *right to be let alone* do not appear anywhere in the U.S. Constitution, many people agree that privacy is a basic right that should be protected.

Development of the Right to Privacy

Since the mid-1960s, the U.S. Supreme Court has recognized a constitutional right to privacy. This right is protected when people seek to be let alone, such as in search and seizure cases. It is also protected when people want to make certain kinds of important decisions, such as marriage and family planning, free of undue government interference.

> *"The makers of our Constitution . . . conferred, against the Government, the right to be let alone—the most comprehensive of rights and the right most valued by civilized men."*
>
> — *Olmstead* v. *United States* (1928), dissenting opinion

Street Law online

Visit the *Street Law* Web site at streetlaw.glencoe.com for chapter-based information and resources.

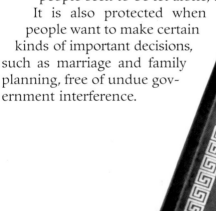

People expect privacy with their personal belongings.

The Supreme Court has said that the Constitution creates "zones of privacy." The zones are derived from the freedoms of speech and association (First Amendment), the freedom from unreasonable search and seizure (Fourth Amendment), the right to remain silent (Fifth Amendment), the right to have one's home free of soldiers during peacetime (Third Amendment), and the unspecified rights kept by the people (Ninth Amendment). In addition, because privacy has been found to be a fundamental right, the Court sometimes justifies privacy protection in terms of substantive due process. The right to privacy generally protects citizens from unreasonable interference by the government.

Courts have determined that protection of the public, as well as the public's right to know, often overrides a criminal's right to keep his or her criminal record private. *Do you agree with these court decisions?*

The right to privacy sometimes conflicts with important government interests. For example, the government may need information about individuals to solve a crime or to determine eligibility for government programs. In such cases, the government can regulate certain acts or activities, even though an individual's interest in privacy is affected. Deciding whether a constitutional right to privacy exists involves a careful weighing of competing private and government interests.

Several recent cases show how the courts weigh and balance these interests in privacy cases. In one case, the U.S. Supreme Court held in 1997 that a Georgia law requiring candidates for certain public offices to submit to drug tests before an election was unconstitutional. The Supreme Court balanced the individuals' privacy expectations against the state's interest in the drug testing program (i.e., ensuring that elected officials were not drug users). In that case the Court found that testing candidates in the absence of any suspicion that they were drug users could not be justified by the state's interest.

In another decision, the Supreme Court upheld a New Jersey law requiring that notice be given to local youth groups, day care centers, and neighbors that a convicted sex offender lived in the area. The Court determined that the public's right to know and to protect children overrode an offender's right to keep a criminal history private. Giving such notice did not violate the privacy rights of a sex offender.

Surveys regularly show popular support for protecting privacy, and some states have passed new privacy laws or added a right to privacy to their state constitutions. However, there has also been a movement to limit privacy protections that are based on the Constitution. Those who favor such limitations believe that the "zones of privacy" discussed above are the creation of some justices who have gone too far in reading privacy rights into the Constitution. Others point to popular

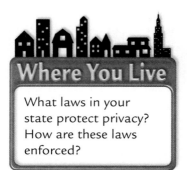

Where You Live

What laws in your state protect privacy? How are these laws enforced?

support for privacy, extensive state laws in this area, and the many U.S. Supreme Court decisions supporting privacy rights. They argue that privacy rights are settled law on which people have come to rely, and that these precedents should not be overruled.

In this chapter you will learn about privacy in a number of contexts: at home and at school, in gathering information, and in the areas of birth control and abortion. There is also information dealing with privacy on the job in Chapter 44.

Problem 42.1

For each of the following situations, decide what privacy rights or interests are in conflict and what arguments can be made for each side. Indicate whether you agree or disagree with the law or policy.

a. A public school requires students to obey a dress code and restricts the hair length of boys.

b. The government requires taxpayers to reveal the source of their income, even if it is from illegal activities.

c. A law forbids nude sunbathing anywhere at a community's beaches.

d. In a prison that has had several stabbings, inmates are strip-searched every day.

e. A state law requires motorcyclists to wear helmets.

f. The police place a small device in a phone that enables them to record all numbers dialed on that phone.

Privacy at home is protected by law. *What do police need in order to search a person's home?*

Privacy in the Home and at School

There is a saying that a person's home is his or her castle. Historically, the law has recognized that people may reasonably expect considerable privacy in their homes. For example, police usually need a valid search warrant in order to search a person's home.

In a 1986 case, the U.S. Supreme Court considered whether a state had the authority to prosecute consenting adult males for engaging in a sexual act in a bedroom of their own home. In a 5-to-4 decision, the Court held that there was no constitutionally protected right to engage in homosexual conduct—even in the privacy of one's home. The Court found that outlawing homosexual conduct was deeply rooted in the nation's history and traditions. The dissenters, basing their reasoning on the Georgia case that follows, believed that the sexual practices of consenting adults in their own bedrooms should be fully protected under previous

The Case of . . .

Possessing Obscene Materials at Home

Georgia had a law prohibiting the possession of obscene or pornographic films. A man was arrested in his own home for violating this law. He said—and the state prosecutor did not challenge him—that he had the films for his own use and did not offer them for sale.

In this case, the U.S. Supreme Court recognized the right to possess obscene materials in one's own home for private use. The Court indicated that individuals generally have the right to think, observe, and read whatever they please, especially in their own homes. However, the Court has held that states may prohibit the possession and viewing of child pornography, as long as the law is reasonably designed to protect the physical and psychological well-being of minors.

Problem 42.2

a. Do you agree or disagree with the Supreme Court's opinion? Give reasons for your answer.

b. Would you decide the case differently if the man had shown the obscene films to people outside his home?

c. Would your decision be different if people had to pay to see the films? Why?

d. Assume a person is arrested for possessing a small amount of marijuana in her home. Could she successfully argue, based on the Georgia case, that the law violates her right to privacy?

e. How is the case of possessing obscene materials similar to the case described in question **d.**? How are the two cases different? Be sure to provide supporting details to explain your answer.

. . . .

privacy decisions and the fundamental "right to be let alone" by the government. However, in 2003, the Court changed course, overruling the 1986 decision. For more information on this topic, see The Case of *Lawrence* v. *Texas* on page 528. This decision is an example of how the reasoning in the dissent in an earlier case (the 1986 case) can sometimes become the reasoning for the majority decision in a later case.

Government generally limits students' right to privacy in schools. For example, most courts have upheld searches of students' desks and lockers. The courts reason that lockers belong to the school and that students cannot reasonably expect privacy on school property. Likewise, the Supreme Court has upheld searches of students' belongings without a warrant and without probable cause, as long as school officials have some reasonable suspicion of wrongdoing. See the section on search and seizure in schools on pages 146 and 148.

There is, however, a federal law that protects students' right to some privacy. Known as the *Family Educational Rights and Privacy Act of 1974 (FERPA),* this law gives parents the right to inspect their children's school records. If parents find any inaccurate, misleading, or inappropriate information, they may insist on a written correction. The law also prohibits the release of school records to other parties without a parent's permission.

Where You Live

How do schools in your community notify people of their privacy rights? What written procedures have been developed to implement this law?

Students who reach age 18 or attend college have a right to see their own records. Requests to see school records must be honored within 45 days. Schools have a duty to inform parents and students of their rights under this law.

Information Gathering and Privacy

Computers have changed the way we live, work, and play. Computers allow businesses and organizations to collect, store, and examine detailed information about individuals. Some organizations sell the information collected to businesses or other organizations. Individuals are often unaware of this practice.

The Case of . . .

Peer Grading

The Owasso School District in Oklahoma does not have a formal policy telling teachers how student work is to be graded. Some teachers grade all assignments themselves, while others have students grade some of their own papers after the answers are provided. Still others use peer grading from time to time. This means that students exchange papers and grade each other's work from answers provided.

Mrs. Falvo has four children in the school system. She believes that peer grading humiliates her children and is a violation of their right to privacy under the federal *Family Educational Rights and Privacy Act of 1974 (FERPA)*. The school system believes that peer grading provides immediate feedback to students and avoids the problem of students cheating when they grade their own papers. The school system also contends that peer grading is done for the individual teacher and not for the school system, which does not maintain these educational records (i.e., grades for specific assignments during a semester). Mrs. Falvo wins her case in the lower courts, and the U.S. Supreme Court agrees to review the case in order to decide how *FERPA* applies to peer grading.

Grading a classmate's work

Problem 42.3

a. Must the Court decide that a grade on an assignment is part of a student's school record in order for the *Falvo* case to be upheld?

b. How should this case be decided? Explain.

The Candidate's Indiscretion

A married male state senator running for governor had a reputation for dating women in the state's capital city. The candidate's wife and two children lived in their hometown about 200 miles from the state capital. The members of the press who traveled with the senator on campaign trips noticed that his wife seldom came along and that he often dined late at night with one particular woman. The press decided to investigate further and discovered this woman leaving the candidate's hotel room one morning.

Problem 42.4

a. Is it reasonable for the candidate to expect the reporters not to disclose this personal information? Give arguments on both sides of this issue.

b. Suppose a reporter also had information that the candidate used cocaine at a social gathering. Would you analyze his privacy rights differently in this situation? Explain your reasons.

c. Some states have laws requiring that a political candidate reveal the source and amount of all campaign contributions. Do these laws violate the privacy rights of the contributors?

The federal government's computers contain enormous amounts of information. Today, there are more than 5,000 federal data banks. For example, the federal government requires financial institutions to microfilm large checks passing through customer accounts. In fact, most banks keep copies of all checks written or deposited by their customers. This information can be useful when authorities investigate white-collar crime, but it may be unfairly damaging if it falls into the hands of other investigators.

Courts have held that the right to privacy does not protect checks or deposit slips. However, limited protection is provided by a federal law that requires customers to receive notice whenever a federal agent seeks a copy of their financial records from a bank, savings and loan association, or credit card company. Individuals can then ask a federal court to decide whether the government's request should be honored. However, the law does not protect against requests from state and local governments, private investigators, or credit bureaus to see a person's financial records.

Although laws such as the *Freedom of Information Act* encourage the government to release information to the public, another law restricts access to federal records. The *Privacy Act of 1974* prevents the government from releasing most information about an individual without that person's written consent. It protects medical, financial, criminal, and employment records from unauthorized disclosure. The law also entitles individuals (with some exceptions) to see information about themselves and to correct any mistakes. If your rights are violated under this law, you may sue for damages in federal court.

After September 11, 2001, the federal government increased its methods of information gathering. Under the *USA Patriot Act,* if a federal law enforcement official alleges that requested records might be relevant to a terrorism investigation, the usual requirement of finding probable cause is waived (not needed). Under the act, warrants may be issued for library and bookstore records, as well as to search computer hard drives and discs. The *USA Patriot Act* is discussed in more detail in Chapter 17.

Reproductive Rights and Privacy

In 1965, the Supreme Court struck down a state law that prohibited the possession of contraceptives by married couples. In 1972, the Court declared that a law prohibiting the sale of birth control devices to unmarried people was also unconstitutional. In both cases, the Court found that these laws had interfered with the fundamental right to bear or not bear children and had violated the right to privacy.

Abortion laws have changed over time. In the early 1800s, abortion was legal in the United States prior to "quickening" (when the mother can first feel the fetus moving, usually about 16 weeks). However, by the late 1870s, attitudes changed, and almost every state had laws restricting abortions. As a result, abortion activity went underground. In the mid-1960s, some people became vocal about the need for legalized abortion. People proposed many arguments on both sides, giving medical, moral, religious, financial, political, and constitutional reasons.

Some people argue that abortion is wrong in all situations. These individuals believe that life begins at conception and must be protected from that moment on. This is often referred to as the "right to life," and supporters are said to be pro-life. Others argue that abortion is a constitutional right and a private matter to be decided by a

Women on both sides of the abortion issue show their support. *Why is abortion such a controversial issue?*

woman. These individuals believe that a woman must be allowed to control her own body and not have it regulated by laws that work against her personal choices. This is often referred to as the "right to choose," and supporters are said to be pro-choice.

The U.S. Supreme Court and many state courts have struggled with these issues. In 1973, a landmark Supreme Court decision in *Roe* v. *Wade* made abortion legal in certain circumstances. Based on a woman's constitutional right to privacy, *Roe* held that a woman had a fundamental, though not absolute, right to an abortion. This right was defined on a trimester basis. During the first trimester of pregnancy (the first three months), a woman could have an abortion on demand without interference from the state. During the second trimester of pregnancy (four through six months), the state could regulate abortions for safety but could not prohibit them entirely. During the third trimester of pregnancy (seven through nine months), the state could regulate or forbid all abortions except to save the life of the mother.

Problem 42.5

a. Why do you think abortion is so controversial?

b. Should abortion be allowed on demand? Totally banned? Regulated in some way? Would you allow late-term abortions under any circumstances? Explain.

c. What are the advantages and disadvantages of state laws that require minors to obtain consent from a parent before receiving an abortion?

d. Assume that a private organization wants to distribute condoms at a high school and that the school board passes a rule prohibiting condom distribution. Would such a rule violate the privacy rights of high school students? What are the arguments for and against such a rule?

The 1973 *Roe* decision did not end the debate over abortion. In some ways, the decision intensified the debate. Since 1973, the Supreme Court has held that states could not give a husband veto power over his wife's decision to have an abortion. Parents of minor-age, unwed girls also could not have absolute veto power over abortion decisions. However, the Supreme Court has said that states may require that pregnant unmarried minors obtain parental consent as long as the minor also has the option to avoid this by going before the court to obtain permission from a judge. While never actually overturning *Roe* v. *Wade,* the Supreme Court has allowed states additional authority to limit the right to an abortion. In 2000, however, the Supreme Court found a state law that criminalized the performance of partial-birth abortions (also called late-term abortions) to be unconstitutional because it did not contain an exception that would allow the procedure for the preservation of the health of the mother. This issue continues to be a very controversial topic.

The Case of . . .

Abortion Law Challenges

In 1992, the U.S. Supreme Court decided the case of *Planned Parenthood of Southeastern Pennsylvania* v. *Casey*. As a result of that case, a woman continues to have a right to an abortion before the fetus is viable (before the fetus could live independently outside the mother's womb). After fetal viability, however, states have increased power to restrict the availability of abortions. The state maintains the power to restrict some abortions because of its legitimate interests in protecting the health of the woman and the potential life of the fetus.

States can pass some laws that regulate abortion, but these laws cannot place a "substantial obstacle in the path of a woman seeking an abortion," the Court said in the *Casey* decision. However, the Court declined to define specifically what constitutes a substantial obstacle. This decision held that regulations were constitutional if they did not place an "undue burden" on obtaining an abortion. For example, the decision allowed a regulation that requires a woman to give "informed consent" at least 24 hours before the planned abortion takes place.

Problem 42.6

Which of the following laws, if any, would place an undue burden on the right to obtain an abortion? Give reasons for each answer.

a. A state law requires that the father of the baby provide written consent before a woman is able to obtain an abortion.

b. A poor woman is unable to obtain an abortion because her state does not provide public funds to cover such a medical procedure.

c. A state law requires a 24-hour waiting period between the time of the woman's decision to have the abortion and the actual procedure.

d. A state law requires a pregnant minor (someone under the age of 18) to obtain written consent from both parents in order to obtain an abortion.

e. A state law requires a pregnant minor to obtain written consent from one parent or from a judge in order to obtain an abortion.

Abortion has also been an important issue in elections and in judicial nominations. Depending on who is president as well as which party controls Congress, abortion counseling at federally funded clinics has sometimes been permitted and sometimes prohibited. In congressional district and U.S. Senate elections where the public is closely divided on this issue, candidates are often reluctant to take a strong stand either for or against abortion rights for fear of alienating an important segment of voters. And as long as the public believes that the U.S. Supreme Court is closely divided over abortion issues, advocacy groups on both sides will closely monitor presidential nominations to the Supreme Court and even to lower federal courts.

Abortion policies vary around the world. Some countries, including Canada, allow abortions on demand (i.e., without restrictions). Others ban abortion completely. Still others allow abortions only to preserve the health of the mother and in cases of rape or incest.

Discrimination

The promise of equality set out in the Declaration of Independence is one of our country's most ambitious ideals. But what does equality mean? Does it mean that every American receives the same *treatment?* Does it mean that everyone has equal *opportunities?* Or does it mean something else? Has equality been achieved only when *results*—in educational, financial, and occupational achievement, for example—are comparable among all groups? To the extent that neither treatment nor opportunities are equal, society must decide how to respond to the challenge of continuing discrimination in a way that is effective and fair to all.

Laws, regulations, amendments to the U.S. Constitution, and court decisions are among the ways in which government may respond to discrimination. The Thirteenth, Fourteenth, Fifteenth, Nineteenth, and Twenty-fourth Amendments were ratified in attempts to make equality a reality. Numerous decisions of the U.S. Supreme Court are regarded as landmarks because of the dramatic changes they called

Visit the *Street Law* Web site at streetlaw.glencoe.com for chapter-based information and resources.

Thurgood Marshall talks with students who integrated Central High School.

Changes in societal values forced the Supreme Court to declare that separate educational facilities were unequal and that schools should be integrated "with all deliberate speed." *What were Thurgood Marshall's arguments in the* Brown *case?*

Landmark Supreme Court Cases

Visit the Landmark Supreme Court Cases Web site at landmarkcases.org for information and activities about *Plessy* v. *Ferguson* and *Brown* v. *Board of Education.*

for in the struggle to halt discrimination. In addition, legislatures at local, state, and national levels have passed numerous laws prohibiting discrimination. However, U.S. history is also marked by long periods in which laws were not enforced, unconstitutional practices were permitted to go on, and court rulings had the effect of spreading rather than ending discrimination. Today the country still faces consequences of some of these unfortunate chapters in its history.

In 1896, for example, the Supreme Court ruled in *Plessy* v. *Ferguson* that segregation was permissible in facilities such as schools, restaurants, railroad cars, and restrooms, so long as those facilities were equal. This doctrine, known as "separate but equal," was in place for nearly 60 years. Because the idea of "separate but equal" lasted so long, many Americans came to think of segregation as appropriate or even desirable. The *Plessy* case is one example of the Supreme Court's power to interpret the Constitution in a manner that resulted in less equal opportunity, at least as this term is understood today.

The power of the Supreme Court to promote equal opportunity is illustrated by its 1954 reversal of the *Plessy* case in its *Brown* v. *Board of Education* decision. Thurgood Marshall, who later became the first African American Supreme Court justice, presented compelling arguments against separating schoolchildren by race, asserting that segregation is inherently unequal. He stated that equal facilities did not characterize the practice of Jim Crow laws (those that had enforced segregation) anywhere in the United States. In the *Brown* case, the Court ordered that schools be integrated "with all deliberate speed."

The *Brown* decision was followed by the civil rights movement, which resulted in significant legislation. The *Civil Rights Act of 1964* and the *Civil Rights Act of 1968* prohibited discrimination based on race, religion, sex, and national origin in employment and housing. Over the past 40 years Americans have also confronted issues of discrimination based on gender, age, disability, national origin (the status of being born in another country), citizenship status, and sexual orientation.

In studying discrimination, you will encounter some specific instances in which various civil rights laws collide with one another. For example, do some affirmative action laws protecting minorities actually discriminate against whites? Can the state require a private club to accept members of other races or the opposite sex without interfering with the existing members' freedom of association or their privacy? In recent years certain civil rights laws have come into conflict with the Supreme Court's initiative to return power to the states—sometimes called the Rehnquist Court's federalism revolution.

As a result, a series of controversial Court decisions have prohibited state government employees from being able to sue their employers for violating either the *Age Discrimination in Employment Act* (see page 530) or the *Americans with Disabilities Act* (see pages 532–535).

All of society suffers when discrimination takes place. If some citizens are prevented from developing their talents, they cannot apply their skills to solving the country's many complex problems. This wasted talent ultimately harms everyone. Hence, all Americans have an interest in halting discrimination—not just those who are its targets.

What Is Discrimination?

Discrimination occurs when some people are treated differently than others because of their membership in a group; for example, because of race, age, gender, or religion. However, not all types of discrimination are unfair or illegal. Many laws discriminate. In fact, discrimination is an unavoidable result of lawmaking. However, as long as the classifications are reasonable, they usually do not violate the Fourteenth Amendment's equal protection clause.

Everyone is familiar with laws that require a person to be a certain age to obtain a driver's license. These laws discriminate but are neither unreasonable nor unconstitutional. For example, in some states, people 16 or older qualify for a license; those under 16 do not. This classification is considered reasonable. However, what if the law required a person to be left-handed to get a license? Or what if whites but not African Americans, or Polish Americans but not Mexican Americans, could get a license? Would these laws be constitutional? Why are they unreasonable when an age requirement is not?

The Fourteenth Amendment provides that no state shall deny to any person the equal protection of the law. To determine whether a law or government practice meets the equal protection standard, courts use one of three different tests, depending upon the type of discrimination involved.

The Rational Basis Test

In most discrimination cases that go to court, judges use the rational basis test. Using this test, judges will uphold a law or practice that treats some people differently than others if there is a rational basis for the differential treatment or classification. A rational basis exists when there is a logical relationship between the treatment or classification and the purpose of the law.

For example, states require their citizens to be a certain age before they can marry. These laws discriminate against people below a certain age. However, is the discrimination unconstitutional? The reason for such a law is to ensure that those who marry are capable of accepting the responsibilities of marriage. In general, people become more responsible as they get older, so there is a rational relationship between

Where You Live

Does your state or local government have any laws against discrimination? What groups are protected by these laws? What state and local agencies are responsible for their enforcement?

Age requirements for marriage are laws that are upheld according to the rational basis test. *How do the courts apply the rational basis test?*

the classification and the purpose of the law. For the most part, courts uphold government laws and practices that are judged according to the rational basis test.

The Strict Scrutiny Test

Certain laws and practices discriminate based on race, national origin, citizenship status, or some fundamental right set out in the Constitution, such as freedom of religion. In these cases, the courts use a test called strict scrutiny. Judges applying strict scrutiny will find the law or practice unconstitutional *unless* the state can show that the discriminating classification serves a compelling (very important) interest and that there is no less discriminating way to satisfy that interest.

For example, a Florida town passed a law against ritual animal sacrifices by the members of a particular religion (see page 481). The law was challenged, and the Supreme Court used the strict scrutiny test. Although the government had a compelling interest in sanitation and in avoiding cruelty to animals, those interests had to be dealt with through laws applied fairly to everyone in the community, not simply by targeting the religious practices of one group. There was a nondiscriminating way—by not making one's religion determine whether or not the law applied—to satisfy that interest, so the Court determined that the ordinance was unconstitutional.

The Substantial Relationship Test

In gender discrimination cases, the Supreme Court uses the substantial relationship test. By this standard, there must be a close connection—not just a rational relationship—between the law or practice and its purpose. In addition, laws that classify based on gender must serve an important governmental purpose.

For example, a state law prohibited beer sales to males ages 18 to 20 but not to females, because more males had been arrested for drunk driving. Although this law served an important government purpose (reducing drunk driving), it was ruled unconstitutional. The Court held that there was not a close connection between the classification and the purpose, because females were legally free to buy beer and give it to males ages 18 to 20.

Potential Limits of Equal Protection

Equal protection cases are complicated and controversial. Some people have argued, for example, that when the Fourteenth Amendment was ratified in 1868, Congress intended it to protect only against racial discrimination. Others argue that it was intended to protect only African Americans—not women, other racial minorities, or whites—against racial discrimination. Still others contend that the amendment embodies the national commitment to the fundamental value of equality, and that all unfair forms of government discrimination should be prohibited by the equal protection clause.

Problem 43.1

The following situations involve some form of discrimination. For each, decide whether the discrimination is reasonable and should be permitted, or is unreasonable and should be prohibited. Explain your reasons.

a. An airline requires its pilots to retire at age 60.

b. A business refuses to hire a man with good typing skills for a secretarial position.

c. People who have AIDS cannot be hired as phone operators.

d. People under age 18 are not allowed into theaters showing X-rated movies.

e. A child with a disability is not permitted to play at a public playground.

f. In selecting applicants for government jobs, preference is given to veterans.

g. Girls are not allowed to try out for positions on an all-boy baseball team at a public high school.

h. Auto insurance rates are higher for young, unmarried drivers.

i. In order to project a classy image, an expensive seafood restaurant requires that its servers wear tuxedos. The restaurant hires only male wait staff.

Equal protection generally means that governments cannot draw unreasonable distinctions among different groups of people. *Why are equal protection cases controversial?*

Discrimination Based on Race

Most Americans believe that racial discrimination is both morally and legally wrong. Today, almost no one defends segregated public facilities or the operation of separate public school systems for children of different races or ethnic groups. Nevertheless, segregated schools and discrimination are still problems.

Americans are still coming to grips with their history of racial discrimination in light of the Constitution's guarantee of equal protection. In addition to enforcement of antidiscrimination laws, government faces the perplexing dilemma of helping those exposed to racial injustice while avoiding discrimination against others. The troubling issue of how to use just means to rid society of injustice raises complex questions. Does providing greater opportunities for some who have historically been denied equal protection result in fewer opportunities for others? Do antidiscrimination laws that were originally passed to protect minorities protect the majority as well? Must the disadvantaged be treated differently in order to be treated equally? Should there be reparation to make up for past injuries? Should minority groups be provided group rights, also known as collective rights?

Today, discrimination is usually more subtle than in the past. Moreover, reasonable people sometimes disagree as to what constitutes discrimination. For example, a town denied a request to rezone land to build townhouses for low- and moderate-income tenants. The town had mostly detached single-family houses, and almost all the town's residents were white. Critics of rezoning may have objected because the townhouses would have attracted a more diverse population. The Supreme Court upheld the zoning law because the Court found no *intent* to discriminate. However, when a school system redrew school attendance lines to keep African American and white children from attending the same schools, the Court found that this action violated the Fourteenth Amendment.

Reasonable people also sometimes disagree as to what constitutes a fair and effective remedy for discrimination. Controversy has often surrounded efforts to desegregate public schools, to eliminate unlawful discrimination in the workplace, and to ensure fair representation with respect to voting rights.

Discrimination in Education

Public school segregation was declared unconstitutional in the *Brown* case. In theory, the schools were then opened to students of all races. In many instances, however, segregation continued. Many methods were used to desegregate the schools, including allowing students to attend any school they desired, redrawing neighborhood school boundary lines, transferring teachers, and developing magnet schools and charter schools with special programs to attract a racially mixed student population.

Where You Live

What is the racial makeup of schools in your area? How has this changed over the past few years? Have there been court decisions where you live regarding school desegregation? Has busing been ordered? If so, has it worked?

Perhaps the most controversial method of school desegregation was busing. Busing as a means of transporting children to school has a long history. For many years busing was used to segregate schools. However, controversy arose in 1971 when the Supreme Court first allowed busing as a means of achieving school integration.

Supporters of busing claimed that requiring racially balanced schools would help provide equal educational opportunities and quality education for both African American and white children. Supporters believed that racially balanced schools weaken prejudices that are reinforced when children are separated. They also argued that busing, which was once used to support segregation by transporting students to separate African American and white schools, was an appropriate remedy.

Following the *Brown* case, schools used busing as a way to integrate schools. *What were the arguments of those people who supported busing? Of those people who opposed it?*

Opponents of busing contended that neighborhood schools are better because children are in school with their friends and are closer to home in case of an emergency. Critics also maintained that court-ordered busing has caused whites to flee city schools, resulting in even more segregation. Other critics said that it is patronizing to think that a minority student must sit next to a white student to learn.

By the late 1990s—after nearly 30 years of what some called a "noble but failed social experiment with busing"—school systems, parents, and courts began to reach a consensus that race should not be used as a factor to determine where students attend school. One reason for the move away from busing was a series of studies showing that African American students did not necessarily do better academically following a shift to integrated schools. Another reason to support neighborhood schools was that funds used to transport students away from local schools could be used to improve those schools. Part of the discussion also turned to giving parents, rather than politicians or courts, the power to determine where their children attended school. Although the pendulum has swung away from busing for integration and toward support for neighborhood schools in recent years, some contend that the educational value of a diverse student body is so great that race-based policies should be allowed to ensure this worthwhile outcome.

Problem 43.2

a. Should the government take steps to bring about greater integration of public schools? If so, what should the government do? If not, why not?

b. Some argue that the emphasis should not be on court-ordered integration, but instead on improving schools, regardless of their racial composition. Some also argue that young African American students might be better off being educated separately from white students. Do you agree with these statements? Give your reasons.

Affirmative action is another remedy for dealing with the effects of discrimination. Affirmative action means taking steps to remedy past and current discrimination in employment and education. It goes beyond merely stopping or avoiding discrimination. For example, a university might take affirmative action by starting a program to attract more applications from students who are members of minority groups.

Affirmative action plans can be either voluntary or mandatory. Voluntary plans are freely adopted. Mandatory plans are imposed by the government as a condition of government funding or as a court-imposed remedy in discrimination cases.

Affirmative action is controversial, and people in several states have voted to ban or limit these programs. Supporters of affirmative action say that preferential admissions to educational programs are needed to overcome the effects of past discrimination. Opponents of affirmative action say that it is a form of reverse discrimination. They argue that race should not be used as a basis for classification, because special treatment for some means discrimination against others.

Several methods are used to increase the number of minorities admitted to educational programs. These methods include **quotas** (which require a specific number of minorities to be admitted), **goals,** and **preferences** (which are given to minority applicants). These methods have been the source of considerable controversy. Each side in this debate claims that its position is fair.

The affirmative action issue was presented to the U.S. Supreme Court in the case of *Regents of the University of California* v. *Bakke* (1978). In this case, the medical school of the University of California at Davis had decided that the best way to increase minority enrollment was to give certain advantages to minority applicants. For each entering class, 16 of 100 places were reserved for minority applicants. Allan Bakke, a 33-year-old white engineer, was twice denied admission to the medical school. He claimed that without the special admissions program, he would have been admitted because his grades and test scores were higher than those of the minority students. Bakke sued the university, saying that its affirmative action program denied him equal protection of the laws.

After suing the University of California at Davis and its affirmative action program, Allan Bakke was admitted to the university's medical school. *What methods are used to increase the number of minorities admitted to educational programs?*

The Supreme Court held the medical school's special admissions program unconstitutional and ordered Bakke admitted to the university. However, the decision left many questions unanswered. The Court seemed to say that racial quotas were illegal but that race could be considered as one of the factors in the admissions decision as long as schools sought to obtain a diverse student body.

In the years following *Bakke,* it has been difficult to find an acceptable balance between ensuring diversity by using race as a factor in admissions policies and avoiding the use of racial quotas. As some courts struck down the way state universities used race to ensure diversity, new strategies have been developed to attract a diverse student body. One such approach required state universities to admit any student graduating in the top 10 percent of his or her high school class.

Landmark Supreme Court Cases

Visit the Landmark Supreme Court Cases Web site at landmarkcases.org for information and activities about *Regents of the University of California* v. *Bakke.*

Discrimination in Employment

In 1964, Congress passed a very significant law, the *Civil Rights Act of 1964. Title VII* of this act prohibits discrimination in employment based on race, color, sex, religion, or national origin by businesses with more than 15 employees or by labor unions. While the Fourteenth Amendment prohibited discrimination by government, *Title VII* extended protection to include discrimination by private employers. This law, enforced by the U.S. Equal Employment Opportunity Commission, does permit employment discrimination based on religion, sex, or national origin if it is a necessary qualification for the job. For example, a theatrical company may require that only women apply for female parts in a play.

Affirmative action has been just as controversial in employment as it has been in education. In 1979, the U.S. Supreme Court was called on to interpret the *Civil Rights Act of 1964* in a case involving a white employee at an aluminum plant in Louisiana. In that case, the employee's union and the plant voluntarily agreed to an affirmative action plan that reserved for African Americans 50 percent of the training slots for higher-paying, more skilled positions. The plan would operate until the level of African Americans in these higher-paying jobs reached the approximate level of African Americans in the local workforce. Before this agreement, African Americans had been dramatically underrepresented in the higher-paying jobs at the plant, compared to their percentage in the local workforce. Brian Weber, a white employee who was not admitted into the training program, brought a lawsuit against the plant because African American employees with less seniority had been admitted to the program.

Brian Weber lost his case against the plant. The Supreme Court found that *Title VII* had been passed to improve employment opportunities for minorities and that it did not prohibit employers in the private sector from establishing a *voluntary temporary* affirmative action plan designed to end racial imbalance.

The Case of . . .

Affirmative Action in Higher Education

The Law School Admissions Case

Barbara Grutter was a 49-year-old white mother of two and resident of Michigan who ran her own consulting firm when she applied to the University of Michigan Law School in 1996. She had a 3.8 grade point average and a 161 LSAT score (the 85th percentile) but was not accepted. She sued the law school in federal court, arguing that the law school had discriminated against her because of her race and had denied her equal protection of the law. Grutter objected to the admissions policy, which gave applicants belonging to certain racial minority groups a better chance of getting in than white students with the same credentials.

The University of Michigan Law School is highly competitive, admitting only 10 percent of applicants. Its admissions policy focuses on academic ability and a flexible assessment of the applicant's individual talents, experiences, and potential to contribute to law school life and diversity. Diversity is not defined solely in terms of race, but the policy does reaffirm the law school's commitment to achieving a critical mass of African American, Hispanic, and Native American students.

Barbara Grutter won her case before the federal court of appeals and the university appealed to the U.S. Supreme Court.

The Undergraduate Admissions Case

Jennifer Gratz, a white suburban resident of Michigan, applied for undergraduate admission to the University of Michigan in 1995. Although she met the entrance standards of the university, she was denied admission. The admissions process used a scoring system due to the large number of applications, assigning points to applicants based on high school courses and grades, standardized test scores, a personal essay, geographic diversity, special talents (athletic, musical, etc.), whether the applicant was the child of an alumnus, leadership, and race. This system automatically awarded 20 points toward the total of 150 (a score of 100 was generally required for admission) to students from underrepresented minority groups such as African Americans, Hispanics, and Native Americans. Virtually every qualified applicant from these groups has been admitted under this scoring system.

Gratz also sued the university in federal court, but lost. She appealed to the U.S. Supreme Court.

The Supreme Court Decides the Two Cases

Because the issues of diversity and affirmative action in higher education are so important and because federal courts of appeal had issued conflicting decisions, the Supreme Court granted **certiorari** and agreed to hear both Michigan cases in 2003. In analyzing both cases the justices agreed that racial discrimination was involved and that the Court had to apply strict judicial scrutiny. This meant that the state had to show a compelling governmental interest in support of the use of race and that race could only be used to further that interest if it did not unduly burden the disfavored groups. For example, a race-conscious admissions program cannot use a quota system which sets aside a certain number of places in the entering class for members of selected minority groups, although race or ethnicity could be considered a "plus" in a particular applicant's file.

A majority of the justices agreed that student body diversity is a compelling state interest that can justify using race in university admissions. In a 5-to-4 opinion, the Court found that

Michigan's law school admissions policy did not violate Barbara Grutter's rights. Having a critical mass (essential number) of students from underrepresented groups can enrich classroom discussion, produce cross-racial understanding, and break down racial stereotypes.

Rather than emphasizing diversity as justified by past or present discrimination, the Court's opinion in the law school case looked to the future and related diversity to the challenges the nation faces: "...because universities, and in particular, law schools, represent the training ground for a large number of the Nation's leaders, the path to leadership must be visibly open to talented and qualified individuals of every race and ethnicity." The Court also noted that "the Law School engaged in a highly individualized, holistic view of each applicant's file, giving serious consideration to all the ways an applicant might contribute to a diverse educational environment."

Four justices dissented in the law school case, believing that the "critical mass" notion was simply a disguise for an illegal quota. To the dissenters, the Constitution's prohibition against racial discrimination protects whites as well as minorities. They also believed there were nondiscriminatory ways to achieve diversity.

In contrast, Michigan's undergraduate admissions policy was found unconstitutional by a vote of 6 to 3. The majority objected to the program's failure to consider applicants on an individual basis as required by the Court's 1978 decision in the *Bakke* case. While the undergraduate admissions program could use race-conscious affirmative action, it had to be in a form that was individualized and not mechanical.

The dissenters would have allowed the use of automatic points to achieve diversity because it was an honest, open approach to the role race plays in the admissions process.

Barbara Grutter (left) and Jennifer Gratz

Problem 43.3

a. What are the key facts in each of the cases? How are the cases similar? Different?

b. What are the strongest arguments in favor of affirmative action based on race in higher education? Against it?

c. How were the cases decided? Do you agree with the two decisions? Give your reasons.

d. The majority opinion in the law school case includes the following sentence: "We expect that 25 years from now, the use of racial preferences will no longer be necessary to further the interest approved today." Why might this time frame be significant? Will affirmative action be needed in 2028? Explain.

e. Assume that African Americans, Hispanics, and Native Americans make up 30 percent of the high school students in your state but 12 percent of the undergraduates enrolled at your state's top public university. How would you advise the university's president to address this situation? Explain.

Courts have become skeptical of race-based programs in employment, such as those intended to increase the number of minorities in construction projects. *How do courts handle challenges to race-based programs?*

The Court reasoned that the purpose of *Title VII* was to end discrimination and to remedy the segregation and underrepresentation of minorities that discrimination had caused in the nation's workforce. Because the voluntary affirmative action plan examined in this case mirrored the purposes of *Title VII,* the Court allowed it to stand. The Court felt it was also important that no one lost a job as a result of the plan, and that the plan was designed to operate only temporarily—until underrepresentation was ended.

In recent years, courts have grown increasingly skeptical of race-based programs in employment (just as they have in the area of education). Typical of the kind of program that has come under attack is a requirement that a fixed percentage of a publicly funded project (for example, the building of a road or a school) be set aside for minority-owned firms. The purpose of these set-asides has generally been to increase the presence of minority contractors in the construction business. When this type of program is challenged as an illegal type of affirmative action, courts require proof that the program is necessary to achieve a compelling governmental interest. Most often, this has resulted in the program being struck down by the court. In other words, the same strict judicial scrutiny that was used to analyze actions that harmed minorities is now also used to analyze race-based federal, state, and local government programs designed to assist minorities. However, some race-conscious programs can still exist if, for example, they were designed to eradicate the results of past discrimination that a unit of government or a private party had engaged in.

Some people welcome what they consider to be this new era of race-neutral programs. They argue that we can never become a race-neutral society if we continue to rely on race-conscious programs. Others believe that there is no meaningful way to make up for past discrimination without effective affirmative action programs and that justice requires remedies for past injustice.

Problem 43.4

In a U.S. Supreme Court opinion, a justice once wrote that classifications based on race carry a danger of "stigmatic harm," meaning that the group benefited by the affirmative action program might be harmed in the long run because society might believe that this group cannot succeed without special protection. Do you agree or disagree with this notion? Give your reasons.

Discrimination in Voting Rights

The states have the power to control their elections, and in doing so, certain forms of discrimination are permitted. For example, states can set a minimum voting age and can also require citizenship and at least a minimal period of residency. They can discriminate against those who are too young, noncitizens (those who have lived in the United States for less than five years), and nonresidents. However, voting has been found by the Supreme Court to be a fundamental right—in fact, it is the right that helps protect all other rights in a democracy. For this reason, the Court closely scrutinizes any election rule that limits voting. In 1966, the Court found a state poll tax of $1.50 to be an unconstitutional infringement on the right to vote. The most important legal protections to the right to vote for persons of color are found in the Fifteenth Amendment and in the *Voting Rights Act of 1965* and its amendments.

Ratified in 1870, the Fifteenth Amendment to the U.S. Constitution provided the right to vote to nonwhite, male citizens. It states that, "the right of citizens of the United States to vote [shall not be] denied or abridged . . . by any State on account of race, color, or previous condition of servitude." However, obstacles to full voting rights continued well into the twentieth century through poll taxes, literacy tests, and intimidation of African Americans who wanted to exercise their voting rights. In addition, women did not win full voting rights until the ratification of the Nineteenth Amendment in 1920.

Congress passed the *Voting Rights Act of 1965* at the peak of the civil rights movement. The *Voting Rights Act,* promising equality in the area of political rights, was designed to help make good the unfulfilled promise of the Civil War amendments. Congress amended the *Voting Rights Act* several times during the 1970s and 1980s to address persistent obstacles to equal opportunity in voting.

One traditional way to strengthen voting power is to redraw voting district lines to ensure that a particular group of people is included in the same district. This is called gerrymandering. Often these gerrymandered districts are awkward in shape. In recent years, some states have redrawn voting districts to create districts in which underrepresented minority groups constitute the majority of voters. These are sometimes called majority-minority districts. Part of the rationale for the majority-minority districts is the fact that gerrymandering had once been widely used to divide minority communities and dilute their ability to elect representatives who would work for their interests.

The Oddly Shaped Voting District

In 1990, new data from the U.S. Census Bureau revealed that the state of North Carolina was entitled to one additional seat in the U.S. House of Representatives. The original districting plan drawn by the state was rejected by the U.S. attorney general, in favor of creating a plan that would better address the size of the African American population of North Carolina. Given a second chance, the state created a plan that included two districts in which African Americans were in the majority. One of the districts (the 12th District) snaked 160 miles across the state, along the Interstate 85 corridor. Both districts elected African American representatives to Congress.

Five white plaintiffs filed suit, claiming that the shape of the 12th District constituted an unconstitutional racial gerrymander in violation of the Fourteenth Amendment. They also claimed that their votes had been diluted as a result of the new redistricting plan.

Problem 43.5

Read the two opinions below. Then answer the questions that follow.

Opinion A

The purpose of the redistricting was "to create congressional districts along racial lines" and to ensure the election of two black representatives to Congress. These awkwardly shaped districts were not drawn to be compact or to respect traditional political borders, such as county or township lines.

In cases involving race, we automatically construe any such classification to be highly suspect. This district is so irregular on its face that it can be understood as nothing more than an effort to impermissibly segregate black and white voters. This type of race-based decision making violates the equal protection clause. It seeks to stigmatize individuals on account of their race, and brings about results such as racial bloc voting and social hostility and separatism.

Moreover, North Carolina's redistricting plan violates the equal protection clause because it has the effect of diluting the voting power of the five white plaintiffs. In this way, it significantly impacts their right to influence the political process.

Opinion B

Plaintiffs contend that North Carolina's redistricting plan unconstitutionally dilutes their votes as white individuals in a majority-black district. North Carolina's plan still has a disproportionate number of majority-white districts. In addition, prior to the passage of this plan, North Carolina had not sent an African American to Congress since Reconstruction. The mere notion that plaintiffs' votes were diluted as white voters in black districts is "both a fiction and a departure from settled equal protection principles."

In accordance with our precedents, plaintiffs did not prove a Fourteenth Amendment violation. Plaintiffs were neither denied the right to vote in any way, nor was their political strength as a group affected. Furthermore, race and ethnicity are a fact of the political process in the same way that religion, gender, or partisanship might be. For this reason, there is nothing wrong with drawing a district when the purpose is to provide a particular, previously disenfranchised interest group with the equal opportunity to influence the political process.

a. Summarize the reasoning of each decision.

b. With which decision do you agree? Explain your reasons.

c. Do you think allowing government to use race as a factor in drawing voting districts should be permitted or not? Explain.

Should Collective Rights Be Recognized?

Some believe that one remedy for discrimination is the recognition of collective rights. This occurs when a society recognizes that groups having a common culture, racial or ethnic heritage, religion, or language possess rights as a group. An example might be the French-speaking people of Canada who, under the Canadian constitution and laws, have been recognized as a group. They have been given certain rights, including the right, if they wish, to have their children educated in the French language. The U.S. Constitution and Bill of Rights do not specifically recognize collective rights. Instead, these documents are based principally on the concept of individual rights.

Those in favor of collective rights say that the U.S. system of protecting individual rights has failed to provide true equal rights for minorities, especially African Americans, Native Americans, and Hispanics. They also believe that American culture is too oriented toward the individual and that recognizing collective rights would move the country in a more community-oriented direction. This might result in people taking more responsibility for working together to solve society's problems.

Those opposed to recognizing collective rights see such rights as a threat to American culture and society. They say this would divide people into competing subgroups, do away with the common English language, and allow dangerous and sometimes illegal religious practices. Those opposed to collective rights feel it would also result in people voting for candidates based more on groups they belong to or support than on each candidate's position on the issues. In addition, they believe that every country needs a common culture, language, and laws that protect everyone, and that having laws giving special benefits to certain groups would undermine the accepted American principle of equal protection under the law.

The *Voting Rights Act of 1965* resulted in a dramatic increase in African American voter registration. *What obstacles to full voting rights existed before the passage of the* Voting Rights Act?

Human Rights USA

Would collective rights help end discrimination in the United States?

Problem 43.6

Examine each of the following situations. If the law were to recognize collective rights, how do you think each situation might be resolved? Would U.S. society as a whole be better off if collective rights were allowed in each circumstance?

a. Ninety percent of the students in a primary school in a small border town have parents who are immigrant farmworkers who speak Spanish, but little English. The parents want the school board to pass a regulation that all new teachers hired will be Spanish-speaking or be required to enroll in special courses to learn Spanish.

b. A Native American group has a strong cultural practice that a child is never removed from the "family." The family includes close and distant relatives. There are problems of child neglect and abuse in a number of families from this group, and the state government wants to place the children in foster care with families who are not Native American. The government agency says that these are the best families they can presently find. The law in the state requires that a neglected or abused child be removed from the family and placed in the best available foster care family.

c. Assume there is a law stating that a Native American group may live on land reserved for them, but a member of the group who marries a non-Native American loses the right to live on the reserved land.

A Native American family

d. Members of an ethnic group that has recently come to the United States from Southeast Asia wish to live near each other, because they speak the same language, practice the same religion, and have similar cultural practices. They get together and buy an apartment building and rent apartments in the building only to members of their ethnic group.

e. A group of African Americans in a large city apply to open a charter school with government money. They want the school to have an "Afrocentric" curriculum, which will be designed specifically to meet the needs of young, urban African American children.

Reparations

In cases involving property stolen from an individual, courts sometimes order offenders to make *restitution* to the rightful owner. When wrongs are committed on a large scale against a whole group, the wronged group often demands *reparations* from whoever committed the wrong. In addition, reparations can include a public acknowledgment of past wrongs.

In 1988, Congress made reparations to Japanese American citizens who had been interned in camps during World War II, authorizing a payment of $20,000 to each individual. Some governments in Europe also have paid some reparations to victims of the Holocaust.

One controversy regarding reparations today is whether the U.S. government, or companies who benefited from the forced labor of slaves, should make reparations to the slaves' descendants.

Problem 43.7

Congresswoman A has introduced a bill that would authorize payments to descendants of slaves who currently live in the United States. Read the comments from each member of Congress, and then answer the questions that follow.

Congresswoman A: "The time has come to pay the debt owed to African Americans for being kidnapped in Africa and forced to come to America to live as slaves. At the end of the Civil War, the government promised freed slaves 'forty acres and a mule,' but this promise was never fulfilled."

Congressman B: "This fund is not a workable idea. We do not have adequate records to prove who the descendants of slaves are. Even if we

assume all African Americans are descendants, you will find that some now have good opportunities and have acquired a piece of the American dream."

Congresswoman C: "African Americans deserve reparations, but so do other groups such as Latinos and women who have suffered discrimination. The best way to make reparations would be to establish an education fund for the poorest children of all races and other groups."

Congressman D: "Slavery was a crime against humanity. And even after slavery ended, its legacy carried on through discrimination in jobs and in many other aspects of life. We must at least set up a fund for better education for descendants of slaves."

Congressman E: "I don't see why my constituents, who have never owned slaves, should have to pay their tax dollars for things they didn't do. The United States may be wealthy, but we still don't have the money to pay every single slave descendant."

Congressman F: "Reparations will just reopen old wounds in this country. Different groups will all want reparations, and this will just cause more discontent."

a. Which Congressperson makes the strongest arguments in favor of reparations? Which Congressperson makes the strongest arguments against reparations? Explain.

b. Are there other arguments that should have been made but were not?

c. What is your position on the issue of reparations? Should Congress take any action? If yes, what should it be? If no, why not?

Discrimination Based on National Origin and Citizenship Status

Many remember the civil rights struggle in terms of cases in which African Americans brought lawsuits to end discriminatory practices. During the middle of the twentieth century, the National Association for the Advancement of Colored People (NAACP) and other organizations developed careful strategies for bringing important cases before the U.S. Supreme Court. At the same time, groups representing Hispanic and Asian plaintiffs brought significant cases in federal courts. While some of these cases dealt with racial discrimination, others analyzed discrimination based on national origin or citizenship status.

For the most part, the courts have not favored government laws and policies that discriminate based on national origin and citizenship status. The basic problem with these laws and policies is that they treat people as members of a group rather than considering their individual abilities and needs. For example, courts have struck down laws prohibiting noncitizens from becoming lawyers or engineers. State laws excluding noncitizens from all government jobs have also been held unconstitutional, although citizenship may be required for some jobs. Congress's power to exclude some noncitizens from receiving Medicare benefits has been upheld.

Public policy regarding persons from other countries who are in the United States illegally is controversial. Some current citizens want to discourage immigration of new workers who could compete for their jobs. They have at times expressed their negative sentiments toward immigrants by passing laws and referenda that severely limit benefits for which immigrants qualify. Others welcome persons from other countries who want to better their lives in the United States, so long as they are willing to work hard and play by the rules. Those who favor the rights of immigrants often make the case that the families of most Americans originally came here from other countries.

Racial oppression triggered the founding of the National Association for the Advancement of Colored People (NAACP). Today, the NAACP works for such causes as fair housing and employment, voter registration, and equal health care. *How do organizations like the NAACP work to make change possible?*

Educating the Children of Undocumented People

According to state law, local school districts receive no money for educating undocumented children not legally admitted into the United States. The same law also authorizes local school districts to deny enrollment to such children. A child of parents not legally admitted into the United States is excluded from his local school. That child's parents bring suit against the state, claiming that the law has denied their child equal protection.

Problem 43.8

Read the two opinions below, and decide which one should be the decision of the U.S. Supreme Court. Give your reasons.

Opinion A

The Fourteenth Amendment says that "No state shall . . . deny to any person within its jurisdiction the equal protection of the laws." This should be applied literally to all persons, even the children of undocumented people. While our past decisions have allowed states to treat undocumented people differently from those legally admitted, the idea of punishing innocent children for the misconduct of their parents does not fit with our basic idea of fairness. Although there is no federal constitutional right to an education, we recognize that economic opportunity is severely limited for those who are unable to obtain one. This law unconstitutionally places a lifetime hardship on the children of undocumented parents. It can place social and economic costs on other citizens if these children grow up to be unproductive members of society.

Opinion B

Undocumented people, as opposed to legal residents, are not a group receiving special judi-

Learning fractions

cial protection according to our past decisions, and this Court has never held that education is a fundamental right. Therefore, when we look at this new law, we should not be tempted to substitute our wisdom for that of the representatives elected by the state's citizens. Our precedents require only that state laws not violate the Constitution. In this case, the law must have a rational basis. It is certainly not irrational for the state to conclude, as it apparently has, that it does not have the responsibility to provide benefits for persons whose presence in this country is illegal. The state law in question is constitutional. The children of undocumented people need to address their problem to their state legislature.

As part of the war on terrorism that followed the September 11, 2001 tragedy in the United States, the federal government took numerous actions that have targeted noncitizens and even citizens who are from, or appear to be from, certain countries in the Middle East. The federal government used immigration law violations, rather than the traditional criminal justice process, to arrest thousands of Muslims, very few of whom were ever charged in connection with terrorist actions. These and other related issues are detailed in Chapter 17, which covers law and terrorism. In 2003, the U.S. Supreme Court upheld a federal law that required detention of noncitizens without bail or a hearing after their release from prison for commission of certain crimes while they were being processed for deportation.

Congress approved the Equal Rights Amendment (ERA) in 1972, but it ran into opposition when it was sent to the states for ratification. *What did the ERA propose?*

Discrimination Based on Gender

The movement to secure equal rights for women has a long history. From the nation's earliest days, women protested against unequal treatment. The first women's rights convention was held in 1848 in Seneca Falls, New York. It set out a list of demands for political, social, and economic equality. The most controversial issue to come out of the Seneca Falls Convention was women's demand for the right to vote. Over 70 years later, women finally won full voting rights in 1920 with the ratification of the Nineteenth Amendment.

Although women have made many gains, the U.S. Supreme Court was slow to recognize gender discrimination as a problem. Even after passage of the Nineteenth Amendment, it took another 50 years for the Court to find a government policy based on gender to be unconstitutional.

For many years, women fought to get the Equal Rights Amendment (ERA) passed. The ERA would have prohibited federal, state, and local governments from passing discriminatory laws or enforcing laws unequally based on gender. In 1982, the ERA failed to become part of the Constitution when the ratification deadline passed with the vote still 3 states short of the 38 total needed. While there is no federal ERA, at least 16 states have equal rights provisions for women in their state constitutions.

For Your Information . . .

Trends in the Status of Women

According to studies conducted by the Institute for Women's Policy Research— www.iwpr.org—there are some promising trends in terms of the status of women. Between 1996 and 2002, for example, the number of women governors jumped from 1 to 5, the number of women in the U.S. Senate increased from 9 to 13, and the number of women in the House of Representatives rose from 49 to 60. Also, in all but four states, the wage ratio between women's and men's earnings rose between 1989 and 1999. Studies also show significant differences for women among the states in areas such as employment, earnings, health, and political participation. In addition, many surveys continue to show that a majority of women—and many men—believe that discrimination in pay based on gender is a serious problem in the workplace.

The U.S. Supreme Court in recent years has not generally been sympathetic to claims of discrimination from people of color, from ethnic minorities, and from those who are not citizens. However, the story is somewhat different in the area of gender discrimination where those claiming discrimination have fared better. Some believe this is because there are now two women on the Court; others believe that the daughters of some of the male justices are also important influences. Still others claim that society is becoming more supportive of equal rights for women, despite the failure of the Equal Rights Amendment to be ratified on a national level.

The U.S. Supreme Court and Congress continue to handle gender discrimination issues. For example, in 1963 Congress passed the *Equal Pay Act,* which made it illegal to pay women less money than men for doing the same job. Under the *Equal Pay Act,* men and women must be given equal pay for equal work performed in the same establishment. If the job requires substantially equal skill, effort, and responsibility under the same working conditions, then equal pay is required, even if job titles are different. Nevertheless, today women as a whole still earn less than men.

One year after the *Equal Pay Act,* Congress passed the *Civil Rights Act of 1964. Title VII* of this act prohibits discrimination by private companies with more than 15 employees against women and minorities in all forms of employment: hiring, firing, working conditions, and promotion. In addition, employees who face discrimination by government because of their gender may sue under the Fourteenth Amendment to the U.S. Constitution, which guarantees "equal protection under the law." Women or men who think they have been discriminated against because of their gender can contact the U.S. Equal Employment Opportunity Commission (EEOC) or state or local antidiscrimination agencies. The EEOC is responsible for investigating charges of discrimination alleging a violation of *Title VII.*

The Single-Sex School

Virginia Military Institute (VMI) is a taxpayer-supported state military college in Lexington, Virginia. VMI's distinctive mission is to produce citizen-soldiers, men prepared for leadership in civilian life and in military service. In recent years, the military role of VMI has diminished somewhat, with only about 15 percent of VMI's graduates pursuing military careers.

Since its establishment in 1839, VMI has consistently produced an impressive corps of graduates who constitute a loyal, powerful alumni group, many of whom have become leaders in politics, business, and the military. VMI has the largest per-student endowment of any undergraduate college in the United States.

VMI uses a unique approach to instill physical and mental discipline in its cadets while imparting a strong moral code. Similar to a Marine boot camp, this "adversative method" breaks down the individual and then slowly builds him back up again by making him proud of himself and his capacity to survive. This approach includes physical rigor, mental stress, an absence of privacy, extreme regulation of behavior, and indoctrination in desirable values. One aspect of this method is the "rat line," where new cadets must run quickly through a line of more senior cadets while they receive physical punishment.

Between 1988 and 1990, 347 women wrote to VMI for admissions information. They received no response. In 1990, the U.S. Department of Justice brought suit to force VMI to admit women. The Justice Department argued that VMI was denying women the equal protection of the law. VMI argued that women would fundamentally change the character of their school.

Through a series of court decisions and negotiations, VMI agreed to establish a separate school, the Virginia Women's Institute for

A female cadet

Leadership (VWIL), rather than admit women to VMI. VWIL did not use the adversative method, but instead used cooperative methodology based on educational theories that this would be more appropriate for women. The Justice Department did not believe that this constituted equal protection of the law and sued a second time.

Problem 43.9

a. Why would Virginia want to keep VMI all male? What arguments can Virginia make that it is not denying women the equal protection of the law?

b. What arguments can the Justice Department make that Virginia's operation of VMI violates the Fourteenth Amendment?

c. How should this case be decided? Explain.

d. Assume VMI must be opened to members of both sexes. Does this mean that the exact same program should be offered to men and women? For example, should women have to run through the rat line and shave their heads the way men do? Explain.

e. Do you think that all single-sex schools operated by the government violate the U.S. Constitution? Give your reasons.

Problem 43.10

Based on your knowledge of gender discrimination law, analyze each of the following situations and decide whether illegal gender discrimination is occurring. Give reasons for your decisions.

a. A state-supported nursing school does not accept applications from men.

b. A man applies for a job as a used-car salesperson, but the woman who owns the business does not hire him. The reason she gives is that "he is not good-looking enough to entice the young women who come here looking for a car to buy one."

c. A state government provides three months of paid leave to women who become mothers. Paid disability leave for state-employed men who become fathers is limited to four weeks.

d. Women in the military are not allowed to fight in the infantry alongside men in the front line of battle.

Sexual Harassment

One type of gender discrimination that has been the subject of increased attention in recent years is **sexual harassment.** The federal Equal Employment Opportunity Commission (EEOC) has defined this as "unwelcome sexual advances, requests for favors, and other verbal or physical conduct of a sexual nature which takes place in the workplace." In one type of sexual harassment, a supervisor leads an employee to believe he or she will lose the job if he or she does not submit to the supervisor's sexual advances. Or a promotion is offered in exchange for sexual favors. This is called **quid pro quo** (literally, "this for that") sexual harassment. Employees of either sex are protected from harassment by supervisors of the opposite sex or of the same sex.

Increased attention has been given to the issue of sexual harassment in recent years. *Should the law protect women working in traditionally male job settings from sexual harassment?*

The Obnoxious Remarks

Theresa Harris worked as a manager at Forklift Systems. The president of the company, Charles Hardy, made comments to Harris on the job like, "You're a stupid woman," and "Let's go to the Highway Hotel to negotiate your raise." He made these comments to Harris in the presence of other employees. In addition, Hardy made sexual comments about Harris's clothes.

In a private meeting, Harris complained to Hardy about his behavior. He apologized, said he had only been joking, and promised to stop the behavior. But when the obnoxious comments continued, Harris quit her job. She filed a lawsuit under *Title VII* of the *Civil Rights Act of 1964*, claiming sexual harassment. At the trial, other female employees testified that they were not offended by Hardy's comments and considered them to be jokes. Harris testified that the comments upset her so much that she began drinking and had to quit her job.

The trial judge concluded that, while Hardy's behavior was annoying and insensitive, it did not create a hostile, abusive environment nor did it interfere with Harris's work performance. The court believed that the conduct did offend Harris and that it would offend a reasonable woman in the same position as Harris. The court found, however, that the conduct was not so severe as to seriously affect her psychological well-being. Therefore, the court decided that Harris could not win her lawsuit. The court of appeals upheld the trial court's decision, and Harris appealed to the U.S. Supreme Court.

In a unanimous decision, the Court established a new standard for deciding sexual harassment cases. It stated that *Title VII* is violated when a hostile or abusive work environment has been created. The victim must show only that he or she was offended by the conduct in question and that a reasonable person would find the conduct abusive as well.

Thus, Harris did not have to show psychological harm in order to win her sexual harassment suit.

The Court found it difficult to say exactly what conduct would be considered abusive or hostile. Instead, courts must look at all the circumstances surrounding the offensive conduct: How often did it occur? How severe was it? Did it unreasonably interfere with the victim's work performance? Was the victim physically threatened or humiliated? No single factor is required to make a case for a hostile or abusive environment. While the mere utterance of an offensive remark certainly does not violate the law, according to Justice Sandra Day O'Connor's opinion, "*Title VII* comes into play before the harassing conduct leads to a nervous breakdown."

Problem 43.11

a. Why is sexual harassment considered a form of gender discrimination? How is it related to *Title VII*'s goal of equal opportunity?

b. What was the standard decided by the U.S. Supreme Court in the *Harris* case? How does this differ from the standard used by the trial court when it first heard the case?

c. Assume the *Harris* case is tried again, this time using the standard announced by the U.S. Supreme Court. As Harris's attorney, what arguments would you make on her behalf? As Hardy's attorney, what arguments would you make on his behalf? If you were the trial judge, would you find sexual harassment in this case? Explain your reasons.

d. What steps should companies take to deal with the issue of sexual harassment in the workplace? What steps do you think an employee should take if he or she has been a victim of sexual harassment? Could mediation help?

The courts have also held that constant vulgar comments, unwelcome physical touching, or other sexual conduct affecting an employee's working conditions constitute sexual harassment. This is called hostile environment sexual harassment. The U.S. Supreme Court has defined a hostile work environment as unwelcome conduct of a sexual nature that is so severe or pervasive as to change the conditions of employment. When a hostile or offensive work environment exists, there is no need to show that the employee was in danger of losing his or her job or of being denied a promotion.

Surveys show a high incidence of sexual harassment in the workplace. A majority of women surveyed indicated that they had been the victims of sexual harassment. Men are victims less frequently. However, in 1998 the Supreme Court ruled that a male sexually harassed by other males while on the job can make a claim of sexual harassment. The Court said that just because the plaintiff and defendant are of the same sex does not mean there cannot be a claim.

Sexual harassment does not occur only in the workplace. Many types of sexual harassment occur in schools as well. There may be harassment from a teacher against a student, a student against a teacher, or harassment from one student against another. Studies indicate that a high percentage of both girls and boys are subject to sexual harassment in the school setting. The U.S. Supreme Court has ruled that a public school system can be sued for money damages for failing to respond to known acts of student-to-student harassment that were severe and pervasive.

Many instances of sexual harassment go unreported because of embarrassment or fear of retaliation. However, it is illegal for a supervisor to take punitive action against an employee because the worker complains of sexual harassment. An employee can file a complaint with the EEOC or a similar state agency or file a gender discrimination case in state or federal court.

In two important 1998 decisions, the U.S. Supreme Court ruled that an employer will be held liable for its employees' sexual harassment unless it can prove that it took reasonable steps to prevent harassment and that the alleged victim failed to take advantage of the available preventive measures. These decisions encourage employers to establish policies making it clear that harassment will not be tolerated in the workplace, communicate these policies to all employees, and provide a meaningful process for handling complaints. Although the courts have been protective of the rights of victims of harassment, some criticize the development of this area of the law as an attempt to excessively control the workplace and to try to regulate all aspects of male-female relationships.

There may be more than one way to handle a sexual harassment situation. It may be possible, for example, to use mediation to manage the conflict. In mediation, an impartial third party assists individuals in discussing and resolving their differences. (See the section on mediation in Chapter 4.)

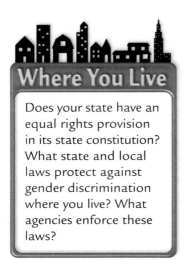

Where You Live

Does your state have an equal rights provision in its state constitution? What state and local laws protect against gender discrimination where you live? What agencies enforce these laws?

Problem 43.12

Which of the following situations, taken alone, constitutes sexual harassment? Why or why not? How should each situation be handled?

a. Fernando and Sylvia are police officers who share the same patrol car. Fernando is the senior officer in charge of the patrol. One night he tells Sylvia he is attracted to her and would like to start dating her.

b. Lois is one of a few female welders. Her male coworkers repeatedly display graphic photographs and drawings of nude women and also make derogatory sexual comments to her.

c. Bart likes to make sexual comments to Ella, who works with him on a construction crew. Ella says she hates his remarks and responds with similar comments only to get back at him for embarrassing her.

d. Stephanie supervises five computer programmers—Victor and four women. She often puts her arm on his shoulder when she is supervising him and calls him "honey." She often invites Victor, but never the other women, to lunch.

e. A gay male supervisor tells a new male employee, "We only hired you because you are nice to look at."

f. A male high-school teacher hugs a female student after she receives high college entrance exam scores. He tells her she has everything going for her, "including smarts and an attractive physique."

g. A female professor testifies before a government committee that her former male boss frequently made sexual remarks to her and asked her out on dates.

Title IX

In 1972, Congress acted to end gender discrimination in education. *Title IX* of the *Education Act of 1972* prohibits gender discrimination in most school activities, including curriculum, faculty hiring, and student athletic programs. Before the enactment of the law, fewer than 30,000 women participated in NCAA intercollegiate sports, and there were fewer than 300,000 female high school athletes. By 2000, nearly 151,000 women were NCAA athletes, and nearly 2.8 million females participated in high school athletics.

Title IX's impact on student athletes has been particularly controversial. The law requires equal opportunity in athletic programs. This means that sports programs must effectively accommodate the interests and abilities of both sexes. For example, assume a school has a men's basketball team and that it also has a number of women interested in playing basketball. The law requires the school either to establish a women's basketball team or to allow women to try out for the men's team. Moreover, if a separate women's team is established, the school cannot discriminate against the women by providing inferior facilities or equipment.

If only one woman is interested in baseball—or any other *noncontact* sport for which a men's team exists—the school must allow her to try out for the men's team. In *contact* sports, however, such as football or wrestling, schools can limit teams to members of one sex. Although athletic opportunities must be equal, the law does not require that total expenditures for men's and women's sports be equal.

Schools show their compliance with the law by ensuring that the percentage of male to female athletes is about equivalent to the percentage of males to females enrolled at the school. Schools can also comply by demonstrating that they are expanding sports opportunities for women.

As opportunities in sports for females have expanded, some lower-profile men's sports programs have been dropped. In 2002, college wrestling coaches brought a suit in federal court asking that *Title IX* be declared an illegal quota program. The coaches contended that 355 men's college athletic teams and 22,000 spots on these teams had been eliminated over the past decade. A federal court judge dismissed the case in 2003. Others argue that some of these sports were victims of lagging interest and overspending by athletic departments on men's football and basketball programs. In 2003, a commission was established to recommend changes in *Title IX* to the U.S. secretary of education.

If a school violates *Title IX*, the government or the person discriminated against can go to court. *Title IX* also allows the federal government to cut off financial aid to schools that discriminate on the basis of gender.

Title IX has increased the participation of females in high school and collegiate sports. *Why has* Title IX's *impact on student athletes been controversial?*

Problem 43.13

Title IX states: "No person in the United States shall, on the basis of sex, be excluded from participation in, be denied the benefits of, or be subjected to discrimination under any education program or activity receiving federal financial assistance."

Which, if any, of the following situations do you believe are in violation of *Title IX*? Assume each school receives federal funds.

a. The music department at the state college has two glee clubs, one for men and the other for women.

b. A school establishes a women's baseball team, which receives used equipment from the men's team.

c. A high-school grooming code requires that men's hair not reach the shirt collar, but women's hair length is not regulated.

d. A U.S. history textbook does not include important contributions made by American women.

e. A small public high school competes in volleyball and has a team of only female students. A male student wants to play interscholastic volleyball.

f. An eighth-grade curriculum offers shop class for boys and home economics for girls.

g. A large state university has established separate teams for women in all noncontact sports and has provided them with equivalent equipment. Twice as many males as females participate in the school's interscholastic programs, and 85 percent of the school's athletic scholarship funds go to males.

Where You Live

What effect, if any, has *Title IX* had on sports programs at high schools and colleges where you live?

Discrimination Based on Sexual Orientation

Throughout much of U.S. history, homosexuality has been a taboo subject. Often it has been a crime. Today, millions of gay, lesbian, and bisexual people are open about their sexuality and are campaigning for laws that would give them equal rights. These rights include the right to marry (or to have domestic-partner benefits like those granted to married couples), to be free from discrimination in employment and housing, and to be able to serve in the military without hiding their sexuality.

In the past two decades, American attitudes toward gays and lesbians have become more tolerant. However, gay rights remains a controversial issue because many people oppose the passing of specific laws that protect gays and lesbians. These people believe that rather than providing equal rights, such laws would give gays and lesbians special rights.

As of 2003, 23 states and more than 240 cities or towns had passed laws which in some way protected people from discrimination who are gay, lesbian, bisexual, uncertain about their sexual orientation,

and/or perceived to be any of the above. These laws vary from place to place and may protect individuals in the areas of employment, housing, education, family matters, and public accommodation. Laws in New York City, for example, allow individuals to inherit the rent-controlled status of apartments from their same-sex partner, prohibit discrimination in the workplace, and protect students from harassment and discrimination based on sexual orientation, real or perceived.

The Netherlands, Germany, and the Scandinavian countries have national domestic-partner laws that provide same-sex couples with many of the legal rights enjoyed by married couples. These rights include the right to medical decisions for an incapacitated partner, the right to share health insurance benefits, and the right to inherit under a will. However, many Americans, including prominent political and religious leaders, oppose legal recognition of same-sex couples, arguing that it is inconsistent with the country's religious teachings, traditions, and the morality of most people.

At the federal level, Congress has not passed laws to protect people based on their sexual orientation. Bills such as the Employment Non-Discrimination Act (ENDA) have been proposed to prohibit discrimination against gay, lesbian, and bisexual individuals, but have not passed. An executive order signed in 1998 prohibits discrimination in hiring and firing executive branch employees based on sexual orientation. Discrimination in the military has been particularly controversial. In 1993, President Bill Clinton created a compromise order known as "don't ask, don't tell." This policy declared that members of the armed services could not be forced to reveal their sexual orientation. However, a service member who reveals that he or she is gay, lesbian, or bisexual—or if it is discovered—can be discharged from service.

Cases dealing with discrimination based on sexual orientation have come before the U.S. Supreme Court with increasing frequency in recent years. In 1996, the Court heard a case from Colorado that dealt with a state constitutional amendment, adopted through a statewide

Many same-sex couples are fighting for laws that would give them equal rights, including the right to marry. *How do state and local laws reflect the changing attitudes toward gay and lesbian people in the United States?*

Lawrence v. Texas

On September 17, 1998, Houston police were called to the apartment of John Lawrence based on a report from a neighbor that an armed intruder was "going crazy" in Lawrence's apartment. When police arrived, they found Lawrence and Tyrone Garner engaged in a private consensual sex act. The neighbor later admitted that his allegations were false and was convicted of filing a false report.

Lawrence and Garner were arrested for violating a Texas law prohibiting two persons of the same sex from engaging in certain intimate sexual contact. They were convicted of this misdemeanor and fined $200 each. They appealed their convictions through the state court system, arguing that the Texas law violated their Fourteenth Amendment rights. Specifically, they believed the law denied them equal protection of the law because it prohibited sexual acts among gay and lesbian people that were permitted among heterosexual couples. They also believed that the due process clause of the Fourteenth Amendment protected the liberty and privacy interests of same-sex and opposite-sex couples and prohibited a state from criminalizing private, consensual sex acts among adults. Relying on the U.S. Supreme Court precedent in *Bowers* v. *Hardwick* (1986), which upheld the constitutionality of a similar law in Georgia, the Texas Court of Criminal Appeals—the highest state court for criminal cases—affirmed the convictions.

The U.S. Supreme Court agreed to hear the case and in June 2003 issued a 6-to-3 decision overturning the Texas law as well as its earlier precedent of *Bowers* v. *Hardwick*. The Court found support for Lawrence's due process argument in earlier privacy rights cases dealing with contraception and abortion.

Writing for the majority, Justice Anthony Kennedy said, "It is a promise of the Constitution that there is a realm of personal liberty which the government may not enter. … [This case does not involve minors or people paying for sex but rather] two adults who with full and mutual consent … engaged in sexual practices common to a homosexual lifestyle. [They] are entitled to respect for their private lives. The state cannot demean their existence … by making their private sexual conduct a crime." Four other justices signed Justice Kennedy's opinion. Justice O'Connor also agreed with the outcome but wrote in her own concurrence that it was their equal protection rather than due process rights that had been violated.

The dissenting justices and other critics of the decision argued that this decision takes away a state's traditional authority to pass laws that set moral standards and reflect the values and views of its citizens. This perspective sees outlawing such behavior as a logical outcome of democracy, not as discrimination. Critics also argued that the decision undermines family values and makes the military's ban on openly homosexual behavior harder to defend.

Problem 43.14

a. What arguments could Lawrence and Garner make for finding the Texas law unconstitutional? What arguments could Texas make for upholding its law?

b. Do you agree with the Supreme Court's decision in this case? Give your reasons.

c. One thing that supporters and critics of the decision agreed about was its importance. Why was the decision considered to be so important?

d. Explain the reason for Justice O'Connor's position.

e. Should states have authority over moral issues? Give reasons to support your answer.

referendum, which prohibited any level of government in the state from passing laws to protect people against discrimination based on sexual orientation. The Supreme Court said that disqualifying a class of persons from the right to obtain specific protection from the law is a denial of equal protection in its most basic sense. The Court also found that the amendment was "born of animosity toward the class that it affects." The Court did not say that the U.S. Constitution required strict judicial scrutiny in cases involving discrimination based on sexual orientation. Instead the Court used the rational basis test to strike down the law as having no legitimate legislative purpose.

Four years later, the Court heard a case from New Jersey in which a local Boy Scout troop dismissed an assistant scoutmaster who was gay, despite a state law that prohibited discrimination based on sexual orientation in places of public accommodation. The Court analyzed this case in terms of its First Amendment precedents in the area of "expressive association," ruling that the Boy Scouts did not have to keep as a member a person whose public views (favoring gay rights) were contrary to the organization's views (the values in the Scout Oath to be morally straight).

Where You Live

Are there laws that protect people based on sexual orientation in your town or state? If so, do you think these laws are necessary? If not, should there be such laws?

Problem 43.15

The organization Public Agenda—www.publicagenda.org—helps stimulate discussion about controversial public issues. Reasonable people have differing views about providing legal protections to gay and lesbian people. The following are adaptations of the three perspectives for framing the debate, developed by Public Agenda.

Perspective 1: *Protect and extend equal rights of all citizens.* The federal government has struggled to provide equal rights to citizens regardless of race, sex, or disability. As part of our overall effort to ensure that all citizens enjoy human rights, there is no legitimate reason to exclude gay and lesbian people who are victims of discrimination in housing, employment, and family matters.

Perspective 2: *Let states and communities choose solutions that work for them.* In a country as large and diverse as ours—and where diversity is part of our strength—it is best to let communities make their own decisions and fashion workable solutions at the grassroots level on issues as controversial as gay rights. In this area, the federal government should follow, not lead.

Perspective 3: *Support and protect traditional institutions and values.* Tolerating private behavior between consenting adults and granting legal protection for gay and lesbian people are very different. Many people are offended by the notion of same-sex relationships and believe that traditional marriage is a pillar of our civil society.

a. With which perspective do you most agree? Give your reasons.

b. What additional information would be helpful to you in determining your perspective? Where could you find this information?

c. Based on the perspective you have selected, what steps, if any, should be taken to prevent discrimination based on sexual orientation?

Discrimination Based on Age

Mario Campisi, age 55, worked for the same company for 20 years. His boss said that Mario was an excellent worker, but he wanted to bring in someone younger. Mario was given two choices: take a new, lower-paying job or quit. Mario might not have known it, but he had the law on his side.

The *Age Discrimination in Employment Act* protects workers age 40 or older. It forbids discrimination in hiring, firing, paying, promoting, and other aspects of employment. The law applies to private employers of 20 or more people, labor unions, government agencies, and employment agencies.

The law has several important exceptions. It does not apply if age is a bona fide job qualification. This means there must be a real and valid reason to consider age. For example, an older person could be refused a youthful role in a movie. The law also does not apply if an employment decision is made for a good reason other than age. For example, an older employee could be fired for misconduct. Any person who feels he or she has been discriminated against because of age can file a complaint with the Equal Employment Opportunity Commission.

Workers age 40 or older are protected by the *Age Discrimination in Employment Act*. Can you identify jobs in which an employer might be justified in refusing to hire an applicant over 40 years of age?

The Case of . . .

The Forced Retirement

Massachusetts required state police officers to retire at age 50. The law was designed to ensure that police officers were physically fit. The state police department required complete physical examinations every two years until an officer reached age 40. Then it required exams every year until the officer reached age 50, the mandatory retirement age. Officer Murgia passed all examinations and was in excellent health when the state police retired him on his 50th birthday. Murgia sued the state police, arguing that the mandatory retirement age denied him equal protection. Should the Fourteenth Amendment protect Officer Murgia in this case?

In deciding Officer Murgia's case, the U.S. Supreme Court said, "Drawing lines that create distinctions is . . . a legislative task and an unavoidable one. Perfection in making the classification is neither possible or necessary. Such action by a legislature is presumed to be valid." Although Officer Murgia was in good health, the Court accepted the fact that physical fitness generally declines with age. Therefore, it was rational for the state to draw a line at some age, and the Court upheld this law.

Age discrimination is not limited to older people. Many laws and practices discriminate against youths. However, restrictions on voting, running for public office, making a will, driving, and drinking are generally upheld by the courts as being reasonable.

Although the courts have not used the equal protection clause to protect the rights of youths, some state and local legislatures have passed laws or regulations forbidding age discrimination. In addition, the Twenty-sixth Amendment gives 18-year-olds the right to vote in federal and state elections.

Discrimination Based on Disability

According to the U.S. Census Bureau, about one in five Americans has some kind of disability. One in ten has a severe disability. A person is considered to have a disability if he or she has difficulty performing certain basic functions (seeing, hearing, talking, walking, etc.) or has regular difficulty performing basic activities of daily living. A person who is unable to perform one or more daily activities or who needs assistance from another person to perform basic activities is considered to have a severe disability.

Many people with disabilities regularly suffer discrimination in different areas of daily life. Discrimination often occurs because of prejudice, ignorance, or fear. For example, society may ignore or separate people who are different, believing it may not be appropriate or possible for people with disabilities to participate in certain activities. In addition, other people may not be comfortable seeing people with disabilities participating in society.

Since the 1970s, a number of laws have been passed to prohibit discrimination against people with disabilities. These laws requiring consideration of a person's special needs involve such issues as education, employment, building design, and transportation.

Early Legislation

The *Rehabilitation Act of 1973* prohibits discrimination by the federal government, federal contractors, and recipients of federal financial assistance. This act bans discrimination in employment and requires employers who receive federal benefits to set up programs to assist people with disabilities. Discrimination against people with disabilities is also prohibited in services, programs, or activities provided by all state and local governments.

The *Americans with Disabilities Act (ADA)* requires accommodations such as reserved parking for people with disabilities. *What is the primary purpose of the* ADA?

The Student with a Disability

Amy Rowley, who is deaf, was placed in kindergarten and first-grade classes with children who hear without assistance. She attended speech therapy and tutoring sessions in addition to her regular classes and also wore a special hearing aid provided by the school. Amy received passing grades in all her classes. Her parents believed that she would gain much more from her education if she had an interpreter, so they asked the school district to provide one. The school district denied the Rowleys' request, calling it unnecessary and an undue financial burden.

The Rowleys sued the school district under the federal *Education for All Handicapped Children Act.* This law entitles children with disabilities to "a free and appropriate education." The trial judge found that Amy understood only about 60 percent of what was said in class. The case was eventually appealed to the U.S. Supreme Court.

A hearing-impaired student

The Court held that under this law, schools were required to provide "specialized instruction and related services which are individually designed to provide an educational benefit to the handicapped child." A school is not required, however, to provide a program that will maximize the child's potential. With this language, the Court approved the program the school district was already providing to Amy. Do you agree with this decision? Explain.

Education is another area in which the law provides protection to people with disabilities. Historically, many children were excluded from attending public schools because of mental or physical disabilities. However, in 1975, Congress passed the *Education for All Handicapped Children Act.* This law, now known as the *Individuals with Disabilities Education Act (IDEA),* requires states to provide a free and appropriate education to children with special needs in the least restrictive setting possible.

The Americans with Disabilities Act

In 1990, the *Americans with Disabilities Act (ADA)* was passed to provide much broader protection against discrimination. Many people consider this the most important federal civil rights legislation since the *Civil Rights Act of 1964.* Now many more entities and businesses are prohibited from discriminating against people with disabilities. They include businesses in the private sector, public accommodations, services provided by state and local governments, transportation, and telecommunications.

The *ADA* defines a person with a disability as someone with "a mental or physical impairment that substantially limits one or more of the major life activities of a person; a record of such an impairment; or being regarded as having such an impairment." It is important to note that, with certain exceptions, the *ADA* does not list specific diseases and impairments that come under the definition of disability. This was done because a specific disease (such as diabetes) or a specific impairment (such as a hearing loss) may not be disabling for one person but may be severely disabling for another person.

People with HIV (the virus that causes AIDS) and AIDS, however, are protected under the *ADA*. Alcoholics who are in treatment or rehabilitated are also protected under the *ADA*, as are rehabilitated drug users and those in treatment for drug use.

The primary purpose of the *ADA* is to assist in bringing people with disabilities into the economic and social mainstream of society. For most Americans, a fundamental aspect of life is employment. However, many people with disabilities have been denied the opportunity to

The Case of . . .

The Dentist and His HIV-Infected Patient

Sidney Abbott became infected with HIV in 1986. On September 16, 1994, Ms. Abbott scheduled a dental appointment with Dr. Randon Bragdon of Bangor, Maine. She disclosed to him her HIV-positive status on a patient registration form. At the time of her visit, she had none of the virus's most serious symptoms. Dr. Bragdon informed Ms. Abbott that she had a cavity that needed a filling, but that he maintained a policy against filling cavities of HIV-infected patients in his office. As an alternative Dr. Bragdon offered to perform the procedure in a hospital at no extra charge. Ms. Abbott would, however, have to pay for the cost of using the hospital facilities.

Ms. Abbott filed suit under the *Americans with Disabilities Act*, alleging that she was discriminated against on the basis of her disability as an individual living with HIV. She contended that the major life activity limited by

her HIV-positive status was her ability to reproduce and bear children. She argued that the following section of the *ADA* protects her:

"No individual shall be discriminated against on the basis of disability in the full and equal enjoyment of the goods, services, facilities, privileges, advantages or accommodations of any place of public accommodation by any person who . . . operates a place of public accommodation."

Problem 43.16

a. Should a person who has HIV but who has not yet developed AIDS be considered a person with a disability under the *ADA*? Give your reasons.

b. Could the dentist successfully argue that treatment in his office of a person covered by the *ADA* is not required in this instance, because Ms. Abbott presents a "direct threat to the health and safety of others"?

c. How should this case be decided? Give your reasons.

The Golfer and His Golf Cart

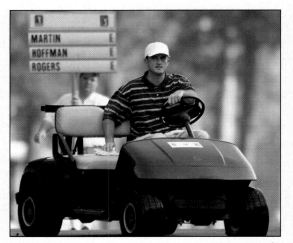

Casey Martin

Casey Martin is a professional golfer who suffers from a physical condition that makes it impossible for him to walk long distances. Due to the nature of his profession, Martin compensates for this inability by using a golf cart to maneuver around the course. Martin plays well enough to participate in the Professional Golfers' Association (PGA) Tour. However, PGA rules prohibit the use of a golf cart on the tour. The PGA's position is that walking is a basic part of the game of golf and that if Martin cannot walk the golf course, he must be excluded from the PGA Tour.

Martin, who could not play golf professionally without the use of a golf cart, brought a lawsuit against the PGA, claiming that the rule against carts violated his rights under the *Americans with Disabilities Act (ADA)*. The PGA argued that it was a private club, and could therefore make its own rules. In addition, famous golfers testified that walking was a critical part of the game of golf.

Problem 43.17

a. What arguments can Martin make that the PGA is violating his rights under the *ADA*?

b. What arguments can the PGA make supporting its decision that Martin not be allowed on the tour if he must use a cart to play golf?

c. How should this case be decided? Give your reasons.

participate fully in an employment situation, thus denying them full access to economic involvement in society. For this reason, a major portion of the *ADA* deals with employment.

A "qualified individual with a disability" is entitled to "reasonable accommodations" in order to overcome existing barriers. Some examples of reasonable accommodations include making facilities accessible for workers with mobility difficulties; modifying examinations and training materials, such as providing these items in large print; providing qualified readers or interpreters; and providing reserved parking. What constitutes a reasonable accommodation will be different for each person.

An employer is not required to make an accommodation if doing so would cause the employer significant difficulty or expense. Such a hardship must be "unduly costly"—not just inconvenient—and one that would "fundamentally alter" the business. An employer is not required to make changes ahead of time for any or all possible disabilities. A person with a disability must request an accommodation. In addition, an employer may not ask questions about a particular disability until after a job offer has been made. An employer, however, may ask if the person will be able to handle tasks that are essential to the job.

As noted previously, discrimination based on disability is prohibited in public accommodations. However, the *ADA* does provide a legal defense if the person claiming the protection of the law would "pose a direct threat to the health or safety of others."

Other federal, state, and local laws also assist people with disabilities. The *Architectural Barriers Act of 1968* requires that all public buildings be made accessible. Restrooms, elevators, drinking fountains, meeting rooms, and public telephones must be designed to accommodate people with disabilities. Similarly, many local laws require wheelchair ramps, Braille signs for the blind, designated parking spaces, and other accommodations for people with disabilities.

People with physical and mental disabilities now have more rights. However, some problems and conflicts still remain. For example, people who use wheelchairs need curb ramps, but people who are blind and use canes need curb markers to warn them where sidewalks end.

> *"It is the purpose of the* **Americans with Disabilities Act** *to provide a clear and comprehensive national mandate for the elimination of discrimination against individuals with disabilities."*
>
> — *Americans with Disabilities Act (1990)*

YOU BE THE JUDGE

Discrimination and Disabilities

Evaluate each of the following examples, and then answer these questions: Does the person have a disability? If so, describe the disability. Is there discrimination based on disability? Should an accommodation be provided? Explain.

a. A high-school student who uses a wheelchair needs a ramp installed to reach the stage during graduation. The principal says the diploma can be awarded down in front of the stage.

b. Doug applied for a position as a firefighter. He passed all the written and physical tests, and the city sent him a letter of appointment. Before he began work, the city learned that he was HIV positive and told him not to report for work.

c. A Little League baseball coach who uses a wheelchair is told that for safety reasons he can no longer coach his team from the playing field. He may now coach only from the dugout.

d. A 59-year-old executive director is fired from her job after her superiors learn that she has brain cancer.

e. A woman who is qualified to be a school lunchroom aide is overweight. When a position becomes available, she applies for it. She is denied the position because of her weight.

f. A man with only one hand is a major league baseball pitcher.

Housing Discrimination

Choice of housing is sometimes unfairly limited by unlawful discrimination. For various reasons, some property owners, real estate agents, and mortgage lenders prefer to sell or rent to certain types of people rather than to others.

The federal *Fair Housing Act of 1968* forbids discrimination in the selling, leasing, or financing of housing based on the race, color, religion, gender, or national origin of the applicant. The act was amended in 1988 to include persons with disabilities and families with children among the categories of people protected. The statute applies to the rental, sale, or financing of a privately owned house or a multifamily dwelling with four or more units. A presidential order prohibits similar forms of discrimination in federally owned, operated, or assisted housing, including public housing. Many states and cities also have antidiscrimination laws that may protect groups of people not mentioned in the federal act.

Accordingly, a landlord cannot discriminate against potential tenants because of a disability. A landlord must permit tenants with disabilities to reasonably modify a dwelling to accommodate their needs, at the tenants' expense. All new multifamily dwellings must be accessible to persons with disabilities.

The Case of . . .

The Unwanted Tenant

Since the death of her husband, Amy Weaver has operated a small, five-unit apartment house. She lives in one unit and makes a meager income by renting out the other four. She does not really dislike members of minority groups but knows that several of her regular tenants have threatened to move out if she rents to people in these groups. She feels she has the right to do whatever she wants in her own building.

Van Tran, an Asian immigrant, is looking for an apartment to rent. When a friend at work tells him about a vacancy at Mrs. Weaver's building, he calls and makes an appointment to see the apartment. When he arrives for the appointment, Mrs. Weaver takes one look at him and tells him the apartment has been rented. "After all," she thinks, "it's my property, and no one has the right to tell me whom I must allow to live here."

Problem 43.18

a. What happened in this case? Why did Mrs. Weaver refuse to rent the apartment to Van Tran?

b. Do you think what Mrs. Weaver did was legal or illegal? Why?

c. Should the law allow landlords to rent to whomever they want?

d. Which do you think is more important: the right to control one's own property or the right to live where one chooses?

e. Is there anything Van Tran can do? Explain.

A landlord also may not refuse to rent to a family because it has children under age 18. This is meant to end discrimination against families with children. In certain instances, landlords may still be able to exclude large families from homes that are clearly not large enough to provide them with adequate living space.

The 1988 amendments to the *Fair Housing Act* allow restriction of retirement housing to the elderly if certain criteria are met. Examples of such criteria include the existence of buildings in which all residents are over 62 years of age, or new housing in which over 80 percent of the units will be occupied by someone age 55 or older and in which specific facilities and services for the elderly will be provided. The act prohibits "adults only" housing except for the elderly.

Discrimination in housing can take many forms. For instance, a real estate agent can be guilty of **steering.** This means directing prospective buyers or renters to particular areas because of their race or some other factor. Some community groups and local governments employ "testers" to uncover steering practices. For example, prospective renters or buyers of different races but similar qualifications may approach an agent. Those agents who show housing to one person, but tell the other that the same housing is unavailable, are guilty of steering. Recent testing reveals that housing discrimination is still common in the United States.

Another type of housing discrimination is called redlining. This is the refusal by a bank or other mortgage lender to make loans for the purchase of homes in certain neighborhoods. Congress passed the *Community Reinvestment Act of 1977* to stop lenders from routinely

The *Fair Housing Act* does not allow "adults only" housing except for the elderly. *Why do some older people choose to live in retirement residences?*

Where You Live

What laws prohibit housing discrimination in your state or community? What state or local agencies enforce these laws and investigate complaints?

The Federal *Fair Housing Act*

Consider each of the following situations, and decide whether you think the action of the landlord, home owner, lender, or sales agent is legal or illegal under the federal *Fair Housing Act.* If the action is legal, do you think the law should be changed to prohibit the action?

a. A real estate company runs a series of advertisements in a major newspaper featuring photographs that portray all potential tenants as whites. The few nonwhites who appear are portrayed as janitors or door attendants.

b. A woman seeking a two-bedroom apartment is turned down by the landlord, who thinks the apartment is too small for her and her three children.

c. A landlord refuses to rent an apartment to two men who disclose they are gay and want to share a one-bedroom unit.

d. A home owner refuses to sell to a Hispanic couple because he thinks the neighbors will not approve.

e. A woman is rejected for a mortgage by a bank officer who believes her divorce makes her a financial risk.

f. A zoning change to allow a group home for persons with disabilities is blocked by a neighborhood association of home owners.

g. A landlord turns down a rental application from a man who is participating in a drug rehabilitation program, although the man says he no longer uses drugs.

h. A young musician is rejected as a tenant by a landlord who thinks the musician looks like a drug user and might make too much noise.

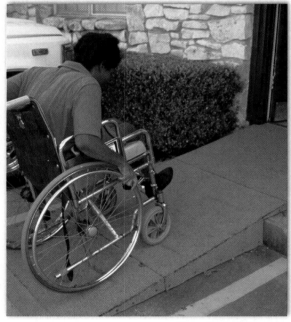

The wheelchair ramp

i. A credit union official discourages an elderly man from buying a house because the official thinks the man will not live long enough to pay off the mortgage.

j. After receiving permission from the landlord, a tenant who uses a wheelchair has a ramp built near the front door at her expense. She does this so that she can get to her car without assistance. Other tenants complain to the landlord that the ramp is an eyesore and a nuisance. Tired of the complaints, the owner removes the ramp and suggests that the disabled tenant might be happier living elsewhere.

rejecting loan applications from people attempting to buy homes in poor and minority neighborhoods. Under this act, a bank cannot purchase another bank or otherwise expand its business unless it can prove that it makes a sufficient number of loans to fund low-income housing. As a result, banks now invest over $1 billion a year to finance such housing.

Not all housing discrimination is illegal. For example, landlords and sellers can refuse to rent or sell to people who have poor credit ratings or whose income is not sufficient to meet the rent or mortgage payments. Other legitimate reasons for discriminating include poor rental references and unwillingness to follow reasonable rules (such as no pets).

FIGURE 43.1   Equal Housing Opportunity

EQUAL HOUSING
OPPORTUNITY

We Do Business in Accordance With the
Federal Fair Housing Law

(Title VIII of the Civil Rights Act of 1968, as Amended by the Fair Housing Act of 1988)

IT IS ILLEGAL TO DISCRIMINATE AGAINST
ANY PERSON BECAUSE OF RACE, COLOR,
RELIGION, SEX, OR NATIONAL ORIGIN

- In the sale or rental of housing or residential lots
- In advertising the sale or rental of housing
- In the financing of housing
- In the provision of real estate brokerage services

Blockbusting is also illegal

An aggrieved person may file a complaint of a housing discrimination act with the:
U.S. DEPARTMENT OF HOUSING AND URBAN DEVELOPMENT
Assistant Secretary for Fair Housing and Equal Opportunity
Washington, D.C. 20410

The *Fair Housing Act* declares a national policy of fair housing in which any discrimination in the sale or lease of housing is illegal. **ANALYZE THE DATA** *What is the purpose of this sign?*

Actions to Take If Your Rights Are Violated

No single procedure can be followed for all situations in which your rights have been violated. You should know that civil rights are protected by laws at both the state and federal levels. Federal law sometimes requires that you first try to solve your problem on a state or local level. Also, some civil rights laws have specific time limits for filing a case. Do not delay if you believe that some action should be taken. If you decide to act, you may wish to consider the following options:

- **Protest in some way.** You can protest verbally, by writing letters, or by demonstrating.

- **Contact an attorney.** Find an attorney who may be able to negotiate a settlement or file a case for you.

- **Contact a private organization with an interest in your type of problem.** For example, you may contact the ACLU for First Amendment problems or the NAACP for race discrimination.

- **Contact a state or local agency with the legal authority to help.** For example, a state fair-employment commission or a local human rights agency may be able to help you.

- **Contact a federal agency with the legal authority to help.** Although many federal agencies are based in Washington, D.C., most have regional offices and field offices in larger cities throughout the country. Look in the telephone directory under "U.S. Government" to find offices in your area.

- **Contact the U.S. Commission on Civil Rights.** The commission can provide general information on where to look for help, or suggest how to proceed if your complaint goes unanswered.

Usually, a major consideration of those who sell or rent is whether the money owed them will be paid in full and on time. To help ensure that this will occur, they usually want to know the following information about a potential tenant or buyer:

- Does the person have a steady income that is likely to continue into the future?

- Is the income high enough to enable the person to pay for the housing and meet other fixed expenses?

- Does the person have a record of paying bills on time and paying off previous bills or loans?

- Will the person take good care of the property?

If you think you have been illegally discriminated against, you may file a complaint with a state or local agency that deals with housing discrimination or with the U.S. Department of Housing and Urban Development's (HUD's) Fair Housing Office. The state or local agency or HUD has the authority to investigate your complaint and either resolve the problem or bring a lawsuit on your behalf. You also may be able to file a lawsuit in court.

State and Local Laws Against Discrimination

When the U.S. Supreme Court makes a decision regarding the Constitution, it determines the *minimum* protection that governments must extend to their citizens. However, governments may offer greater protection than what the Court says the Constitution requires.

For example, the various federal civil rights acts you have studied in this chapter prohibit discrimination based on race, national origin, citizenship, gender, sexual orientation, age, and disability. Housing discrimination is also prohibited by federal law. Some state and local governments have passed their own discrimination laws. These laws, which extend the protections offered by federal law, may cover discrimination based on one or more of the following characteristics:

- Age (young or old)
- Marital status
- Personal appearance
- Source of income
- Sexual orientation
- Family responsibility (having children)
- Physical handicap
- Matriculation (status of being a student)
- Political affiliation

Some states and municipalities have commissions that receive, investigate, and resolve complaints based on violations of these laws. In recent years there has been an increase in civil rights activity in state courts. This activity has made state and local laws and state supreme court decisions particularly important for those who claim to have been victims of unlawful discrimination.

Other controversial questions that often arise under state and local laws against discrimination involve private clubs that limit their membership based on race, gender, religion, or ethnic background. Small, selective, distinctly private clubs have generally been able to decide who their members will be without violating antidiscrimination laws. For example, prohibiting a church's youth group from requiring that its members be of the same religion might interfere with the basic purpose of the club. However, larger private clubs that regularly serve meals and rent out their facilities to nonmembers for business purposes have usually been deemed by the courts to have lost their "distinctly private" nature.

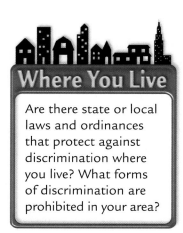

Where You Live

Are there state or local laws and ordinances that protect against discrimination where you live? What forms of discrimination are prohibited in your area?

Rights and Responsibilities in the Workplace

In previous chapters you have studied how the Bill of Rights and other important civil rights laws apply to individuals at home, at school, and on the street. Another important set of federal and state laws governs the workplace. In this chapter you will learn the rights and responsibilities of job applicants, employers, and employees during a job search, on the job, and in the event of job loss.

Looking for a Job

When looking for a job, you should keep a number of legal and practical considerations in mind. Important issues may arise during job interviews or when job applicants are tested. For example, employers

Visit the *Street Law* Web site at streetlaw.glencoe.com for chapter-based information and resources.

Everyone has certain rights and responsibilities in the workplace.

may ask questions about your race, gender, or age. In some instances, such questions are legitimate and necessary. In other instances, questions about a job applicant's race, gender, or age are illegal and constitute discrimination.

The Job Interview

Once you have obtained an appointment for an interview, it is important to be prepared for it. How you dress, act, and otherwise present yourself at an interview may determine whether you get the job. The interview is also a chance for you to learn as much as you can about the position and the organization so you can decide whether you really want to work there.

Employers ask many questions during job interviews to help them decide whether to hire applicants. Based on employment discrimination laws discussed earlier in this unit, as well as generally accepted employment practices, employers should not raise issues in job interviews that may infringe on an applicant's privacy or that could be viewed as evidence of illegal discrimination. Examples include inappropriate references to a person's gender, race, national origin, religion, disability, marital status, or personal practices outside the workplace. It *is* appropriate, however, for employers to ask applicants to identify their race, gender, or national origin for statistical purposes.

The *Americans with Disabilities Act* protects individuals with disabilities from discrimination in the workplace. *What does the act require of employers?*

In preemployment discussions, an employer cannot ask about a person's disability. An employer is allowed, however, to ask questions related to a person's ability to perform a particular task or assignment. The *Americans with Disabilities Act (ADA)* does not require employers to hire a person with a disability who is not qualified for the position. The *ADA,* however, does state that it is illegal to discriminate against a "qualified individual with a disability."

An inappropriate question does not necessarily constitute discrimination. To charge an employer with discrimination, a person must prove that he or she was actually denied the job for unlawful reasons. For example, it may be inappropriate to ask whether an applicant for a secretarial position is married, as such a question may be evidence of discrimination. However, the question would not constitute discrimination if the applicant was denied the job because he or she lacked the skills needed for the position.

Employers may legally raise issues such as religion, gender, and national origin in a work-related context. For example, a church could require that a minister it hires to lead the congregation be of a certain religion. In instances where religion, gender, and national origin are job requirements reasonably necessary to the normal operation of the business or enterprise, then the law recognizes what is called a **bona fide occupational qualification (BFOQ)** and allows the discrimination as reasonable. Turning down a male actor for a female role in a play would be another example of a reasonably necessary discrimination based on a BFOQ.

All employers must verify whether job applicants are U.S. citizens or have employment authorization. The *Immigration Reform and Control Act of 1986* made it unlawful for employers to knowingly hire or continue to employ persons without work authorization. Such employers are subject to fines under this law.

Whether employers have the right to ask questions about prior arrests and convictions is not as clear. Federal regulations provide, and some federal courts have found, that without proof of business necessity, an employer's use of arrest records to disqualify job applicants is unlawful discrimination. Making personnel decisions on the basis of records of arrests that did not result in criminal convictions has been found to have a disproportionate effect on employment opportunities for members of some minority groups. Some states have laws barring employers from turning down applicants because of prior arrests or convictions, while others allow this practice. In a number of states, ex-felons are barred from being hired as police or corrections officers or are denied the right to apply for barber or taxi driver licenses. Some federal courts have declared it illegal to have a blanket rule prohibiting employment of ex-felons without regard to the job or the nature of the offense.

Employers can inquire about the age of young applicants to determine whether they are old enough to work, to find out how long they have been working, or to help estimate their probable level of maturity. Some states require permits, or "working papers," before young people can be hired. Those between the ages of 12 and 14 may obtain permits in certain states to work during holidays and vacations. Older people are protected against discrimination based on age by the *Age Discrimination in Employment Act* (see page 530). Asking older people for their age may be evidence of unlawful discrimination unless there is another valid reason for not hiring them.

Employers are responsible for verifying that job applicants are U.S. citizens or have authorization to work. *What other information may an employer ask for from a job applicant?*

Problem 44.1

Jill Johnson, age 21, is applying for a job as an assistant hotel manager for a company that operates a chain of hotels throughout the country. She has scheduled a job interview with William Marconi, the regional manager of the company.

a. During the interview, Mr. Marconi asks Ms. Johnson the following questions. Which questions may be illegal? Legal but inappropriate? Legal and appropriate? Give reasons for each answer.

- How old are you?
- Why do you want this job?
- Are you a U.S. citizen?
- Do you plan to get married and have children in the near future?
- Are you willing to move to another area of the country?
- Have you ever been arrested?
- How tall are you? How much do you weigh?
- Have you ever worked with Hispanic Americans? Do you speak Spanish?
- Do you have a good credit rating?
- Will you have dinner with me tonight?
- Have you ever been treated for any mental problems?
- Have you ever had, or been treated for, any of the following conditions? (Ms. Johnson is given a checklist of diseases and conditions.)

b. Role-play the interview and have Ms. Johnson decide whether and how to answer each question. How did she answer or respond to any improper or illegal questions? How should she have answered each question? Should any of her answers be different for a better chance at getting the job? If so, which answers? How should she have answered differently? Which answers were particularly good and why?

c. Evaluate how well Ms. Johnson did in the interview.

d. If someone is asked an improper or illegal question in an interview and later is denied the job, can he or she file a lawsuit claiming discrimination? Where can this person go for assistance?

Testing Job Applicants

A controversial legal issue often arising in the job application process is whether applicants can be required to take psychological, lie detector, or drug tests. Some claim that such tests are an invasion of privacy and question the tests' accuracy. Others argue that employers should have a right to find out everything they can before hiring employees who might steal or otherwise harm their businesses.

The law allows aptitude, personality, or psychological tests that can be shown to relate to an applicant's ability to do the job. However, such tests have been successfully challenged when they have been

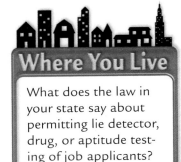

Where You Live

What does the law in your state say about permitting lie detector, drug, or aptitude testing of job applicants?

shown to be inaccurate or unnecessary for measuring a person's ability to succeed in the job. These tests have also been successfully challenged when they were actually used to discriminate based on such factors as race, gender, age, or national origin.

In addition, a test cannot be used if it screens out people with disabilities unless the tested activity is specifically job-related. Tests must also be given in a manner that does not require use of the impaired skill of a disabled person, unless that is the skill that the test was specifically designed to measure. For example, in a job that requires fast typing skills, an employer is not required to provide alternate testing for a person with cerebral palsy whose manual motor skills may be limited. In addition, some states have laws prohibiting the use of AIDS testing for hiring purposes. People with HIV and AIDS are protected under the *ADA* as individuals with disabilities.

Problem 44.2

a. Manuel has decided to apply for the following jobs. If you were the employer for each job, would you ask Manuel to take a lie detector, drug, or aptitude test? If you were Manuel, would you object to taking any of these tests? Why? Should the law allow these tests for these particular jobs?

- Cashier in a grocery store
- FBI agent
- Construction worker
- Secretary for the county government
- School bus driver

b. What are the arguments for and against allowing private employers to require lie detector testing of job applicants? Which position do you agree with, and why? Should the law allow such testing? Explain your position.

c. The mayor of your town proposes a new ordinance that would require all applicants for town jobs to submit to drug testing. As a member of the city council, will you support this legislation? Give reasons for your position. Will you support the proposal if it only covers police officers, firefighters, and ambulance drivers? Why or why not? Should the test also cover the use of alcohol and tobacco? If so, why?

Many employers argue that lie detector tests, called polygraph tests, are necessary to verify information on job applications and résumés, as well as to prevent the hiring of dishonest employees. However, many question the validity, or accuracy, of these tests and a number of states have passed laws restricting the use of lie detectors. In 1988, Congress passed the *Employee Polygraph Protection Act,* which makes it illegal for nearly all employers to use such tests to select job applicants. This law does not cover security guards and federal, state, and local government employees, who still may have to take these tests.

To reduce the hiring of workers who use drugs and alcohol, many people advocate drug testing of some or all job applicants. Generally, private corporations have been allowed to require drug testing. However, some states have passed laws prohibiting such testing or requiring that employers have reasonable grounds for suspicion before testing takes place. For many years the federal government has required drug testing for applicants for military, law enforcement, and certain other positions.

Conditions on the Job

Once on the job, you will find that various local, state, and federal laws apply in the workplace. These laws deal with wages and hours, taxes and benefits, Social Security, unions, health and safety, and privacy issues. Many of these laws exist to regulate the workplace and protect employees and employers.

Requiring job applicants to take aptitude, psychological, or lie detector tests is a controversial legal issue. *Should employers use these tests to screen potential employees?*

Wages and Hours

The vast majority of workers in the United States are covered by the *Fair Labor Standards Act,* which requires that a minimum hourly wage be paid to all employees. The federal minimum wage was $5.15 an hour in 2003. In addition, this law allows employers to pay a lower "training wage"—$4.25 an hour—for up to 90 days to certain workers under age 20. Some states have their own laws that set a minimum wage based on the type of job. When an employee is subject to both state and federal minimum-wage laws, the employee is entitled to the higher of the two minimum wages.

Certain jobs are not covered by the *Fair Labor Standards Act,* and some jobs are designated under federal or state law as having lower minimum wages. These include newspaper delivery and part-time retail, service, or agricultural jobs held by full-time students. Some jobs can pay less than the minimum wage if employees regularly receive tips to make up the difference.

Federal law also requires employers to pay overtime wages at a rate of one and one-half times the regular hourly pay when employees work more than 40 hours per week. For example, an employee who receives $6.00 per hour but works 50 hours in a week must receive $9.00 per hour for the 10 extra hours of work. Overtime pay rules do not apply to certain types of employees, including administrative and executive employees, professionals who receive fixed salaries and exercise discretion and control in their work, and those who work for commissions (for example, some salespeople).

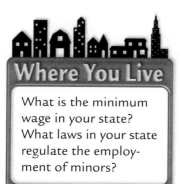

Where You Live

What is the minimum wage in your state? What laws in your state regulate the employment of minors?

Steps to Take

How to Complain About Wage and Hour Problems

- **Contact a government agency.** Employees who think their employer may not be paying them a fair wage should contact the Wage and Hour Division of the U.S. Department of Labor or their state or local government employment agency.

- **Contact the union.** If there is a union, it will have an established grievance procedure for members to follow.

- **File a complaint.** A complaint can be made to the union or to the appropriate government agency if an employer lays off or fires an employee who has complained about a wage and hour problem.

- **Take your case to court.** Employees can also file a case directly in court to enforce wage and hour laws or formal agreements with their employers.

Each state has its own laws concerning the employment of minors. These laws regulate how many hours a youth may work per day and per week, the minimum age (usually 15 or 16), which hours of the day they cannot work (for example, school hours), whether work permits are required, and what types of jobs minors are prohibited from holding (for example, dangerous activities or selling alcohol).

Employees sometimes have their wages reduced for reasons such as showing up late, leaving early, or not being productive while on the job. If workers believe they have been treated unfairly in such cases, they may be able to file a complaint or even sue their employer. Such a problem may occur, for example, when an employee who operates a cash register has less money in the register at the end of the shift than receipts indicate should be there. Whether the employer can reduce the employee's wages may depend on the employment contract, as well as federal and state laws concerning payment of wages.

Problem 44.3

a. Should all workers be covered by a minimum wage? Why? Some people favor a lower minimum wage for youths than for adults. What are the advantages and disadvantages of this idea? Do you support it? Explain.

b. As a fast-food cook who is paid $5.50 an hour, you hear that another cook at your restaurant, who is a good friend of the manager, is making $6.50 an hour. Also, last week you worked 42 hours and were paid your regular hourly wage ($5.50 × 42 = $231). What actions, if any, can you take to handle these problems?

c. Vana works as a waitress in a restaurant and is given her own cash bank from which to make change for her customers. At the end of her shift, she is $10 short based on her receipts. Should she have to pay this money to the restaurant owner?

Where You Live

Contact your state or local government employment agency to learn about the laws in your area governing young people in the workplace. What kinds of jobs may they hold at different ages, and what minimum wages apply to them? Where can you complain if you believe your employer is not following the wage and hour laws?

Taxes and Benefits

Employers must withhold federal and state taxes from the pay-checks of most employees. These taxes are used to provide government services, such as education, law enforcement, national defense, trash collection, and road building and maintenance. The law requires employers to provide workers with a W-2 form showing their earnings and the amounts withheld each year by January 31 of the following year. By April 15 of each year, most workers must file state, federal, and sometimes local tax returns based on the information reported on the W-2 form. Depending on the total income for the year, amounts withheld by the employer, and other factors, a worker may either receive a refund from the government or have to pay an additional amount.

Other items that employers may decide to provide to employees free of charge or at reduced cost are called **fringe benefits.** These benefits may include life, health, and disability insurance; pension plans; education and training; sick leave, vacations, holidays, and breaks; parking; meals; and severance pay in case of job loss. In 2003, it was estimated that more than 41 million workers did not have health care coverage. This issue has been part of the focus of national health care reform.

In recent years, a growing number of employers have begun to offer maternity and paternity leave to parents following the birth of a child. In 1993, Congress passed the *Family and Medical Leave Act (FMLA).* This act requires employers with over 50 employees working within a 75-mile radius to grant up to 12 weeks leave—usually unpaid—within a 12-month period to people who want to care for newborn babies, newly adopted children, or ailing relatives. Individual state laws may provide additional benefits. Employees may also bargain individually or collectively to include these fringe benefits as part of an employment contract.

Social Security

Social Security is the federal program that pays retirement, disability, or death benefits to eligible workers, their families, or both. Payroll deductions help to fund this program. The amount deducted is a percentage of an employee's salary. Employers pay a Social Security tax of 6.2 percent of each employee's salary up to $87,000 each year. The employer also pays a Medicare tax of 1.45 percent of each employee's salary, regardless of the amount.

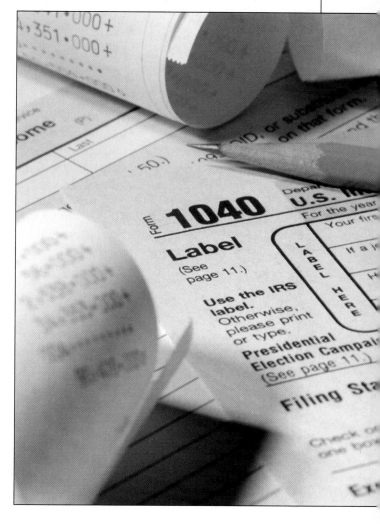

Workers must file tax returns based on the withholding information provided by their employers. *What are taxes withheld from workers used for?*

Problem 44.4

a. Bethany, age 22, has just graduated from college and is going to work for a computer company. Bethany is single and would like to return to school someday to acquire a master's degree in business. What company fringe benefits will interest Bethany most? Why?

b. The JKR Corporation has 40 employees—25 men and 15 women. The company gives women 10 days of paid maternity leave when they give birth but does not offer a similar benefit to men who become fathers. Chandler, whose wife just had a baby, asks Korey, the president of JKR, for paid paternity leave. Role-play this meeting. What reasons can Chandler present to support his request? What pros and cons might Korey consider in making his decision? If you were Korey, would you change JKR's policy? Explain why or why not.

c. Russell, age 18 and single, just graduated from high school and plans to work for several years to save money for college. He applies for a job delivering pizzas that requires him to wear a uniform. What fringe benefits might he want the company to provide? Why?

Unions

When a person begins a job, he or she should find out whether the company has a **union.** A union is an association of workers that seeks to secure favorable wages, improve working conditions and hours, and resolve grievances with employers. Although union membership has declined since 1983, it was estimated in 2002 that 16 million U.S. workers belonged to unions. This number had remained relatively constant from 1997 to 2002, with just over 13 percent of workers belonging to unions.

A union can be established only by an election in which more than 50 percent of the company's workers vote for it. Unions, which have been protected by federal law since 1935, are governed today principally by the federal *National Labor Relations Act.* This law is administered by the National Labor Relations Board, a federal agency.

The primary purpose of a union is to bargain as a group with an employer. Those who favor unions claim that unions accomplish much more for workers, through collective bargaining, than individual employees are likely to achieve separately. Collective bargaining is the process of settling labor disputes through negotiations between the employer and representatives of the employees. Union supporters cite higher wages, greater fringe benefits, and better working conditions as results of union activity. Those who criticize unions say they are costly, unnecessary, and disruptive. The critics believe that higher wages have resulted in higher prices and fewer jobs for workers. Some U.S. companies have begun to manufacture goods in other countries that have lower labor costs. In addition, foreign companies are sometimes able to produce items that can be sold at prices lower than those charged for similar items made in the United States.

A union contract is an employment contract negotiated between the owners of a company and the union representatives. The wages and benefits that union members receive are based on agreements written into the union contract. Although employees cannot be required to join a union, in a majority of the states a union contract can require everyone who works for a company to pay union dues and fees. This is based on the argument that the union is the sole bargaining agent for the workers, and all must pay equally for work done on their behalf. However, this is not the case in 22 **right-to-work states,** where it is illegal under state law to require workers to join unions or pay dues as a condition of employment. These states are Alabama, Arizona, Arkansas, Florida, Georgia, Iowa, Kansas, Louisiana, Mississippi, Nebraska, Nevada, North Carolina, North Dakota, Idaho, Oklahoma, South Carolina, South Dakota, Tennessee, Texas, Utah, Virginia, and Wyoming.

A branch of law known as labor relations determines how employees, unions, and employers may operate. Employees have the right to join and/or support a union, as well as the right not to engage in union activities. Unions have the right to take certain actions, such as organizing **strikes** (work stoppages) and **picketing** (public demonstrations) to publicize a dispute. They also can conduct group protests of hazardous and dangerous working conditions.

Neither employers nor unions are allowed to engage in acts that are classified as **unfair labor practices.** Examples of unfair practices by employers include firing a worker for trying to organize a union, questioning union members about their activities, and spying on union meetings. Refusing to bargain with a recognized union or to reinstate workers who take part in a legal strike are other examples of unfair labor practices.

Union members vote during a union meeting. *What are the arguments of those who support unions? Those who oppose unions?*

Unions commit unfair labor practices when they threaten workers to get them to join the union or to take part in a strike. A mass picketing action that makes it impossible for a nonstriking worker to enter the workplace is also an unfair practice. In addition, the use of violence during a strike is prohibited.

Problem 44.5

a. Why might some workers want to have a union in an auto manufacturing plant? Why might other workers in the plant prefer not to have a union? What information can you acquire to help you decide whether to support the formation of a union in an auto plant?

b. What is a right-to-work state? What are the arguments for and against a right-to-work law? Do you support or oppose such laws? Explain.

c. If city sanitation workers have had the same low salaries for five years and the city refuses to increase them, should the workers have the right to strike? Give reasons for your decision. If a public strike is illegal in their state, what else can the workers do to try to increase their wages?

d. Should any public employees be allowed to strike? Is your answer different depending on the jobs they do—for example, police officers, firefighters, schoolteachers, government clerks, or maintenance workers at city hall? Explain.

Union members may strike or picket in response to labor disputes. *Would you be willing to demonstrate for or against labor policies?*

The National Labor Relations Board (NLRB) considers charges of unfair labor practices filed by either unions or employers. After investigating a claim, the NLRB decides whether the case should be prosecuted or dismissed. A case that is prosecuted will receive a formal hearing before an administrative law judge.

Federal employees and some state and local government employees have the right to belong to unions, but they generally are not allowed to strike. The rights of federal employees are governed by the *Federal Labor Relations Act*. The rights of state and local public employees are established by state laws. State labor laws may also include special rules regarding the rights of private-sector employees, unions, strikes, and other labor issues.

Even if there is no union in the workplace, employees who engage in "protected concerted activity" are protected under the *National Labor Relations Act* and can file charges of unfair labor practices with the NLRB. Examples of protected behavior include circulating petitions for higher wages or better benefits, calling for improved safety at a company meeting, or joining with other employees to protest improper payments to managerial employees.

Problem 44.6

Taki works as a desk clerk at a local hotel. He is a member of a union that is about to go on strike. Examine the following actions or situations, and determine whether they are legal or illegal.

a. Before the strike begins, workers start to perform their job duties very slowly.

b. The union contract has a "no strike" clause.

c. When Taki comes to work one day, he finds that a strike has been called and a union picket line has been formed. Taki refuses to cross it.

d. The employer locks the door of the hotel during the strike, but the striking workers break it down.

e. Some employees tell Taki he may get hurt if he refuses to join the strike.

f. The strike demands are for better health insurance and more vacation days. Taki goes on strike and is not offered his job back after the strike.

Health and Safety in the Workplace

A government study estimated that there were more than 14,000 work-related deaths and 2.2 million injuries on the job in 1970. Many people became alarmed at the number of deaths and illnesses caused by the effects of lead and mercury poisoning, asbestos-containing materials, cotton dust, pesticides, new toxic substances, and new technologies. As a result, Congress passed the *Occupational Safety and Health Act*. This law requires that employers provide safe and healthy working conditions for all workers. Self-employed people and farm families are not covered. The law also does not cover state and local government employees, who usually receive protection under other laws. Many states have additional laws and standards to further protect the health and safety of workers.

The 1970 act established a federal agency, the Occupational Safety and Health Administration (OSHA), to issue safety regulations and standards that industries must follow. The act requires employers to keep records of all job-related illnesses and injuries among their workers. Workers may file complaints against their employers without making the workers' names known to employers. An employer who discovers the name of a complainant cannot take any disciplinary action against the employee. If agency inspections show that health or safety hazards exist, OSHA can issue citations requiring employers to take corrective action.

The Collapsed Building

A collapsed building

In 1986, a building under construction in Bridgeport, Connecticut, collapsed and killed 28 construction workers. A federal investigation showed that unsafe working conditions and practices caused the disaster. The construction site had been inspected once by OSHA six months before the accident because there had been a complaint. After the accident, OSHA issued fines totaling $5.1 million against three construction companies. What could be done to prevent this type of accident?

The Case of the Collapsed Building illustrates a number of problems with the government's attempts to reduce health and safety problems in the workplace. Some people say that OSHA does not administer the regulations properly. Others say that some people in business do not follow the standards. Many think that OSHA has too few inspectors and that it would take millions of additional dollars to do the job right.

To enforce the regulations, OSHA conducts on-site inspections, orders changes, and sometimes fines employers. For example, a large defense contractor was fined $1.5 million for willfully failing to record 251 employee illnesses and injuries and failing to tell workers in 88 instances that they were working with hazardous materials. OSHA also issues safety and health standards that industries must follow.

Standards have been issued for the use of such items as hand tools, power presses, electrical wiring, ladders, hazardous gases, and chemicals. OSHA does not assist workers in filing lawsuits and collecting money damages from employers. Generally, individuals can only receive compensation from their employers for injuries under the workers' compensation system. However, an injured worker may be able to sue a negligent coworker for tort damages. Also, workers are sometimes fired for making safety and health-related complaints to OSHA, to similar state or local agencies, or to their employer. Under the law, such employees are entitled to reinstatement (to get their job back) and to receive back pay with interest if they file a timely written complaint about the retaliation.

Some people criticize OSHA for overregulating businesses and industries and requiring companies to spend large sums of money to comply with unnecessary standards. OSHA has also been criticized for expending too much effort on concerns about accidents while neglecting the health issues that lead to many work-related illnesses and deaths. Examples of such illnesses include lung cancer resulting from asbestos exposure, black lung disease among coal miners, and brown lung disease in textile workers exposed to cotton dust.

In 2001, 5,900 workers suffered job-related deaths. The most common cause of death on the job was from vehicular accidents (i.e., in cars and trucks). The next most common causes were from falls, followed by homicides.

The U.S. Department of Labor reported that there were 5.2 million nonfatal workplace injuries and illnesses in private industry in 2001. Both injuries and illnesses are significantly higher in manufacturing than in service industries. Partly as a result of the *Occupational Safety and Health Act* and similar state laws, workplace injuries and illnesses have been declining in recent years, even as the population of workers has increased.

Problem 44.7

a. What is the purpose of OSHA, and how does it work? Some individuals say that people are safer in the workplace than in their cars. Do you think this is true? If so, is OSHA needed, or is it an example of overregulation by the government?

b. Jack works in a factory where there are strong fumes in the air. He and other workers cough a lot on the job. Jack complains to OSHA. He is laid off by the factory manager, who says the company has lost money due to the cost of controlling the fumes as ordered by OSHA. What actions can Jack take?

c. If workers have complained and reasonably believe that performing their duties exposes them to serious injury or possible death, can they refuse to work? What if their supervisor disagrees and orders them to work anyway? Should their supervisor be able to "dock" their paycheck or place an official reprimand in their personnel files? Does your answer change depending on whether the danger is long-term (such as the possibility of contracting lung disease from pollution) or short-term (such as the possibility of falling from an unsafe ladder)?

d. Should corporate executives who willfully or recklessly violate safety and health standards be prosecuted criminally for their actions? If convicted of a crime, should they be fined or sent to jail? If so, under what circumstances? What is the best way to motivate an employer to provide a safe workplace?

The *Occupational Safety and Health Act* requires that employers provide safe and healthy working conditions for workers. However, OSHA has been criticized for neglecting health issues, such as black lung disease, that lead to illnesses and death. *How does OSHA help to promote a safe and healthy working environment?*

Many workers have become concerned with the effects on their health of conditions in the workplace, such as noisy equipment and toxic substances. *How has the government responded to such concerns?*

In recent years, increasing numbers of workers have complained about health and safety conditions. These complaints include concerns about toxic substances within the workplace and about hearing damage caused by noisy equipment. The prolonged use of computer keyboards and monitors has also resulted in various health hazards, including eyestrain, neck and back pain, and wrist injuries.

In response to workers' concerns, the federal government and many state governments have enacted community "right-to-know" laws. These laws require employers using certain hazardous materials to inform their employees about the accident and health hazards of chemicals in the workplace. They must also train employees to properly handle such materials in order to minimize problems. Information about the materials and emergency response plans must be made available to employees and local officials. In addition, many employers offer training programs to inform employees of possible health hazards from assembly-line work or exposure to computer monitors.

A growing number of people also view cigarette smoke in the workplace as a serious health hazard. As a result, some states and cities have prohibited smoking inside office buildings. Others have restricted smoking to certain areas of the workplace.

Privacy at Work

The right to privacy is often referred to as "the right to be let alone." This means that individuals should be able to determine how much of their personal lives they wish to share with others. Some people say privacy is not possible at work, because an employer has an interest in monitoring, supervising, and evaluating employees' work to ensure that employees do their jobs properly. However, many employees believe that they do not give up all rights to privacy when they take a job.

The Smoking Insurance Agent

Arnold is an insurance agent who works in an office with glass partitions that do not reach all the way to the ceiling. There are 20 other agents on his floor with similar offices around his. Arnold says he must smoke because it is a habit he cannot break and it reduces the stress caused by his job. Sam, who occupies the office next to Arnold, claims that Arnold's smoking is unhealthy for him and everyone else in the office. He asks the office manager to issue a no-smoking rule for the entire office.

Problem 44.8

a. If you were the office manager, what would you do?

b. Would your answer change if Sam was allergic to cigarette smoke?

c. Role-play a mediation session (see Chapter 4, page 43) in which the office manager meets with Arnold and Sam and attempts to help them come to an agreement regarding Arnold's smoking.

d. Should there be a law prohibiting smoking in offices? If so, what should be included in the law?

Those who work for the federal and some state governments generally have greater privacy rights than those who work for private employers. For example, the federal *Privacy Act of 1974* gives federal government employees the right to be told what is in their personnel files, to correct an error in those files, and to limit others' access to the files. Some states provide similar protections for state government employees, but only a few states do so for private employees. However, union contracts often provide some privacy rights. In addition, some state and federal laws, such as the *Americans with Disabilities Act,* require employers to keep confidential sensitive personal information contained in employee personnel or health records. Most commonly, employers must protect the confidentiality of medical information about their employees.

In an attempt to cut down on theft, some employers use security guards and video monitoring to watch employees. *Should a person give up all privacy rights when he or she becomes an employee?*

557

Employee privacy rights have also become an issue in relation to certain actions that employers have taken to reduce workplace crime. In an effort to cut down on theft by employees, many employers hire private security guards to watch workers, and some use video monitoring as well. The courts have generally allowed employers to take such actions. They have also approved searches of employees' desks and of employees as they arrive at and depart from the workplace, based on the rationale that employers have the right to search their premises for business purposes. If an employer or security guard goes too far and detains employees against their will without good reason, the workers may have a tort claim for false imprisonment. Evidence of illegal activity found as a result of such searches can usually be used in court because the Fourth Amendment's exclusionary rule only prohibits the use in court of the fruits of unreasonable searches by the government.

Wiretapping without a warrant is usually prohibited by federal law, but the courts have allowed telephone monitoring of employees by employers on extension phones. Employers also have other methods of monitoring how much work an employee performs. For example, some firms use computers to determine how much word processing or e-mail an employee does per day. Employers are also allowed to read e-mail sent between company employees and to monitor employee use of the Internet. Employers argue that such monitoring is necessary to make sure employees are doing their jobs properly. Others claim that monitoring should be illegal and that it creates a negative work atmosphere.

Employers can also generally regulate how employees dress on the job unless such regulation is a cover-up for some form of illegal discrimination based on race, gender, national origin, or religion. Uniforms, if appropriate to the job, and a neat appearance can be required. This may even include rules regarding length of hair, wearing a beard or moustache, and modes of dress. In recent years, as styles have changed, many employers have relaxed such rules.

Drug testing is one of the most controversial issues involving privacy in the workplace, especially for those involved in providing services to the public. *Should a government or a private employer always have a reasonable suspicion of drug use before administering a drug test?*

Employee's Right to Privacy

Decide whether the law should protect the employee's right to privacy in each of the following situations. Explain your answers.

a. Judy, who works for a cement company, has applied for a new job with a construction firm. The manager of the construction firm calls the cement company's president, who reads the contents of Judy's personnel file over the phone, including many negative comments about her work and personality.

b. Lionel, an African American salesperson in a store frequented mostly by white people, begins to wear his hair in dreadlocks. His supervisor says Lionel will hurt business if he wears his hair that way and sends him home.

c. Jasper is missing some expensive jewelry from his store. He asks the police to come to the store and search the handbags of the three saleswomen who work for him.

d. Barnes, who owns a painting company, suspects Jenny, one of his painters, of not working very hard when he is not around. Without informing Jenny, he offers $20 to Sally, another of his painters, to spy on Jenny when he is not present and tell him how hard she works.

e. To reduce theft in his factory, Jay installs one-way mirrors that enable supervisors to watch employees.

f. Tami owns a business and begins monitoring the e-mail between her employees. She fires Hugo after discovering he has sent messages to other employees criticizing Tami and mentioning that he suspects her of stealing money.

A number of states have enacted laws that prohibit employers from interfering unreasonably with the privacy of their employees by penalizing them for engaging in lawful activities during nonbusiness hours. For example, under these laws someone who smokes cannot be discriminated against by an employer, unless that person works for an antismoking organization. In most states, employers can prohibit smoking on the job but must provide breaks to allow smoking off the premises or in a designated area.

One of the most controversial issues involving privacy in the workplace is that of testing employees for drug use. Recently, more private employers have begun to test their workers for drugs. These private testing programs are generally legal, unless they are conducted in a state with a strong privacy law or privacy protection in the state constitution. Some unions have been able to curtail drug testing through collective bargaining. Rulings under the *National Labor Relations Act* have held that companies must comply with union requests to negotiate about drug-testing policies.

In 1989, the U.S. Supreme Court addressed the drug-testing issue when it decided that blood and urine testing of railroad employees by

Testing Customs Agents for Drugs

U.S. customs agents work along the country's borders and at airports. One of their duties is to reduce the amount of drugs being smuggled into the United States. The customs commissioner establishes a drug-testing program for all employees who apply for promotion to "sensitive positions." In such positions, employees (1) stop shipments of drugs, (2) carry firearms, or (3) handle classified information. Employees who fail the required urinalysis test are fired, but the results are not turned over to law enforcement officials. Under this program, five customs employees out of 3,600 test positive for drugs. The customs agents' union files a lawsuit challenging the drug-testing program.

Problem 44.9

a. What are the arguments in favor of the drug-testing program?

b. What are the arguments against it?

c. If you were the judge in the case, how would you rule, and why?

the federal government after an accident was not a violation of the Fourth Amendment. This case made many references to public safety concerns regarding train accidents. Decisions in future cases will have to determine whether random drug testing of government employees will be allowed or whether some reasonable suspicion of the employees involved or some special public safety interest relating to the jobs involved will be required.

Losing a Job

Few things disturb people more than the thought of losing their jobs. Job loss can occur through firing for cause (for a specific reason) or, in some cases, for no reason at all. Workers also lose their jobs through layoffs, which may be the result of economic problems beyond the employer's control.

The fear of unemployment and the resulting loss of income needed to support workers and their families is a serious matter. The law provides some protection from job loss. It also provides some assistance for workers who have lost their jobs.

Employment Contracts

Most jobs are based on oral or written contracts between employees who promise to perform certain duties and employers who promise to pay them and provide benefits for doing so. Most employment agreements with private employers are referred to as **employment-at-will contracts.** Under this doctrine, the employees can quit anytime they wish, and the employer can discharge them anytime it wishes for any reason or for no reason at all, as long as discharging them does not violate some other law, such as an antidiscrimination law. This is not true for most government jobs, which often must follow specific standards and procedures in order to discharge an employee. It is also not true for some private employers who have negotiated contracts with unions or with nonunion employees that provide certain rights before job termination (for example, 30-day notice of termination).

Some written employment contracts specify that the employee must give the employer notice before resigning. If the failure to do so causes the employer to lose money, the employee may be liable.

Opinions differ on whether it is better to have the at-will approach to employment, in which the employer has great freedom to discharge employees, or whether the law should provide greater protection for workers, as it does in a number of other countries. Those in favor of keeping the at-will system argue that it gives businesses the freedom they need to achieve economic success and that restricting them would be inefficient and less profitable. They insist that employers must be able to get rid of workers who do not show up, are constantly late, do not follow the rules, or just cannot perform their jobs. Supporters of the at-will system say the government is not as efficient as private business at least partly because of restrictions on discharging employees.

Others call at-will employment very unfair. They claim that workers are often discharged without a good business reason or as a cover-up for illegal discrimination. Opponents of at-will employment argue that workers should be discharged only for a good reason, such as inability to do the job.

In recent years, courts and state legislatures have begun to carve out exceptions to the at-will doctrine by placing more restrictions on the employer's ability to discharge employees. Referring to employee handbooks or other personnel policies where an employer represents, for example, that "employees may only be fired for just cause," certain courts have forced employers to reinstate persons fired for no apparent reason or to provide just cause before firing. Other courts have said that there is an implied duty to treat the other party to a contract fairly and in good faith. For example, one state court would not allow an employer to end the employment contract of a salesperson in order to avoid paying him commissions he had already earned. The court held that the employer was not treating the worker fairly under his employment contract.

Employees who work for privately owned businesses such as salons and restaurants usually have employment-at-will contracts. *Should employers be able to discharge at-will employees for any reason or no reason at all?*

When a Firing May Be Illegal

As noted earlier, federal law provides that employees may not be discharged from their jobs based on race, gender, color, national origin, religion, age (if 40 or older), or physical disability. Federal law also prohibits discharge because of membership in a union or union activity. Some state laws go further and prohibit discrimination because of marital status, AIDS, and sexual orientation.

Courts have also held that discharges were unlawful when they determined that the employer's action violated a public policy. In one example, an employee was threatened with losing his job when he refused to lie before a grand jury as ordered by his supervisor. In another case, a discharged employee had been called for jury duty and was told by his supervisor not to serve.

Problem 44.10

Assume that the following situations occur at companies with employee handbooks stating that "any employee may be fired at any time for just cause." The following events occur in a state that has recognized such handbooks as implied terms-of-employment contracts. If employees are fired for the following reasons, which firings should the court allow, and which do you think should be declared illegal?

a. Warren is more than 30 minutes late for work two or three times a week and has been warned three times about it.

b. Michael, the owner of the restaurant at which Leona works, has instructed her not to ring up every check on the cash register so he can avoid paying the full sales tax. Leona refuses to follow Michael's instructions.

c. Pierre has an alcohol problem that makes it difficult for him to work most days after lunch.

d. While working on a computer, Naomi accidentally destroys an important company file. She has been warned about the importance of this file and has destroyed files before.

e. Winston and John's inability to get along is harming company operations. After starting a fistfight with Winston, John is fired. Winston does not lose his job.

f. The ice cream company that Chloe works for produces one flavor that is a big seller. She gives the recipe to her friend, who works at another ice cream company.

g. D'Angelo, a government scientist, gives a newspaper reporter classified information showing that a recently issued report to Congress contains false statements.

h. Marnie has been on the job for three months. One morning her son has a bad asthma attack, and she has to take him to the hospital. Marnie calls the boss from the hospital but misses her shift. The boss immediately fires her.

Closely related to the public policy exception are laws that protect **whistle-blowing.** This occurs when an employee "blows the whistle" on, or reports, an employer to the authorities for illegal acts. Some federal laws specifically protect this type of conduct. These include the *Fair Labor Standards Act, Title VII* of the *Civil Rights Act of 1964,* and the *Occupational Safety and Health Act,* each of which protects employees from being fired for making complaints about unfair labor practices, gender discrimination, and unsafe or hazardous conditions. Some states also have laws that forbid the firing of whistle-blowers.

Whistle-blowing might also take the form of telling someone other than the government about a problem. For example, a court ordered the reinstatement of a bank employee who was fired for telling bank vice presidents that the institution was illegally overcharging customers. The employee had done nothing wrong by reporting illegal business practices.

Whistle-blowing raises the conflict between employees' duty of loyalty to their employer and their obligation to act ethically and legally. In situations not involving whistle-blowing, loyalty is expected of employees. They can be legally fired for disloyal actions such as selling a company's trade secrets to a competing firm.

Former Enron executive Sherron Watkins testifies as to her knowledge of the corporation's financial instability. *How does whistle-blowing create a conflict between an employee's loyalty to his or her employer and an obligation to act ethically and legally?*

The Shoe Store Firing

Mr. Brady works as a salesperson at a shoe store in a mall. He has no written employment contract or employee handbook, and there is no union for store employees. Recently, Mr. Brady was fired by the owner, Mrs. Hinoshita, without a stated reason. Mr. Brady and his coworkers believe that he was fired because he often argued with Mrs. Hinoshita over the way the shoes were arranged in the storeroom, which shifts he worked, breaks, and other issues. The other salespeople in the store believe that Mrs. Hinoshita is a difficult supervisor and that Mr. Brady was a little outspoken, but they do not think he should have been fired.

Mrs. Hinoshita thinks Mr. Brady was more trouble than he was worth and was not a very good salesperson. She also thinks that because it is her store, she should not have to give reasons for firing him.

Problem 44.11

a. Does Mr. Brady have an at-will employment contract? If so, how does this affect his being fired by Mrs. Hinoshita without a stated reason?

b. Should the law allow at-will employment contracts? What are the arguments for and against them?

c. Role-play a meeting between Mrs. Hinoshita and the other shoe salespeople who want Mr. Brady reinstated in his job. If you were Mrs. Hinoshita, what would you do when confronted by the complaining salespeople? Why? What was the outcome of the meeting?

d. Assume that Mrs. Hinoshita agrees to issue an employee handbook listing the reasons for which an employee can be fired. Draft such a list. Are they fair to both Mrs. Hinoshita and the employees? How would you modify them to make them fairer?

e. If the employees and Mrs. Hinoshita disagreed on the acceptable reasons for firing people, what other process might be used to come to an agreement both sides can live with? Should Mrs. Hinoshita care whether the other employees support her firing decisions or think her rules are unfair? Explain your reasons.

At work in a shoe store

Employees must be careful when they complain to someone on the outside. For example, employees who call a newspaper to complain that their employer is breaking the law can be fired if they are acting unreasonably—that is, if the report is based on hearsay and no effort has been made to confirm its accuracy. Workers who complain are required to act reasonably and in good faith. If they do not, the courts are likely to let the firing stand.

Procedures Before Job Loss

If a government employee is about to lose his or her job, the U.S. Constitution, the state constitution, or state law will usually require that the employer follow certain procedures. This is not usually required in private employment. In general, most employees do not have to receive notice, and most employers do not have to follow due process.

Sometimes employees are not fired but are laid off. This often occurs when a company is in trouble financially or experiences a temporary lag in business. After a period of time, the laid-off workers may get their jobs back. Depending on the company's policies or its employment contracts, the workers may have rights to continued health insurance or other benefits during the layoff.

In recent years, a number of large factory closings have put many employees out of work. To protect such workers, Congress passed a law requiring that factories with more than 100 employees warn their workers at least 60 days in advance of an impending plant closing or large-scale layoff. If employers fail to provide such warnings, they can be liable for fines, back pay, and benefits. Notice is not required under some emergency and other special circumstances.

Employees who have been fired or laid off may be eligible for **severance pay.** This is pay to compensate for the loss of their jobs and for time they are not going to work. The amount is determined by the employer, by an employment contract, or by provisions in an employee handbook. Although such employees may be eligible for unemployment compensation, it may not begin for a period of time and may not provide sufficient financial support while they look for other jobs.

Under the *Consolidated Omnibus Budget Reconciliation Act (COBRA)*, employers of 20 or more employees are required to let terminated, covered employees elect to continue their health insurance under the employer's group health plan. However, the former employees must pay the full cost for such coverage, including a reasonable administrative fee. Coverage is usually available for up to 18 months, unless the employee gets another job that provides for health coverage without restrictions for preexisting medical conditions. The ability to purchase health insurance coverage at the employer's group cost can be important for terminated employees, since employers often get a better price than individuals for good health insurance.

Problem 44.12

a. Assume that you work for a computer software company. One morning the boss says, "I am sorry, but we have information that you use drugs and even bought some at work one day. We are going to have to let you go. The company has a clearly stated rule against drugs in the workplace." What procedures would you insist on before you were fired? If the employer refused to provide these procedures, what would you do?

b. If your employer is in financial trouble and going out of business, what are the arguments for and against requiring the owner to give you notice and severance pay? Which point of view do you agree with, and why?

c. Can you think of any jobs in which the employee should be required to give the employer notice of intent to leave the job? If so, which ones, and why should such notice be required? Should there be a penalty if the worker fails to do this? If so, what should the penalty be?

If You Lose Your Job

All states have a system of unemployment compensation—also called unemployment insurance—that protects you if you lose your job through no fault of your own. This system allows you to collect payments from the government while you look for another job. The pay will not be as much as you were earning while you were working, and it is only temporary. However, the money may keep you from using up your savings or going into debt during the period of unemployment. Typically, payments are for up to 26 weeks, although they can continue for longer periods in some states. Congress also has the power to extend unemployment benefits for up to 20 additional weeks. The unemployment payments come from payroll taxes collected from employers by the federal and state governments.

Some people do not qualify for unemployment compensation. For example, someone who cannot work due to an on-the-job injury is eligible for workers' compensation but probably not for unemployment benefits. To qualify for unemployment benefits, you must have worked for 20 to 40 weeks during the 12 months prior to your unemployment and earned a certain amount of wages, depending on the state.

Someone who was fired for misconduct is not eligible for unemployment compensation. An intentional action against the employer's interest would be considered misconduct. For example, theft would clearly constitute misconduct, whereas an error in filling out a form would not. Generally, a single incident would probably not be considered misconduct, but repeated incidents after being warned might make an employee ineligible for unemployment compensation. An employee fired for poor performance, such as slow typing, may still be able to obtain unemployment compensation. However, a typist who keeps showing up late for work after being warned would probably be ruled ineligible because of misconduct.

People who quit voluntarily are usually not are eligible for unemployment benefits unless they can show that the situation at work was unbearable. For example, a person who opposed war as part of his religion and who quit after being transferred to a job producing tanks was allowed to collect unemployment compensation. Someone who becomes physically unable to do a job can also quit and retain eligibility for benefits.

To apply for unemployment compensation, a person must file an application with the state agency that handles these claims. It is important to do this immediately after being discharged or quitting, because it can take a while to process the application. Agency staff must investigate all applications, and hearings are sometimes held if employers protest the claims. Employers may protest the payment of unemployment benefits to a former employee because it can result in higher payroll taxes for the employer in the future.

Problem 44.13

Assume that the following employees lose their jobs for the stated reasons. Should they be eligible to receive unemployment compensation? Explain.

a. Eric is injured on the job and is unable to return to work.

b. Maggie dislikes her boss and says she will no longer do any work he assigns. She is fired.

c. A fellow employee offers Phillip some marijuana. He is caught smoking it in the men's room and is fired.

d. Sybil stays home from work several times to care for her sick children. Her boss fires her, saying he needs someone he can count on.

e. When business declines, a company closes the plant where Alonzo works. The company offers him a job at its other plant, which is one and a half hours away by car. Alonzo turns down the new job because he does not want to drive that far.

Where You Live

Where is the office at which people can apply for unemployment compensation in your area? What are the rules that determine whether people are eligible? How much can they receive each week? For how many weeks can unemployment benefits be paid?

Unemployment compensation is handled by state agencies. *What steps should be taken to help reduce unemployment?*

APPENDIX

Contents

The Constitution of the United States

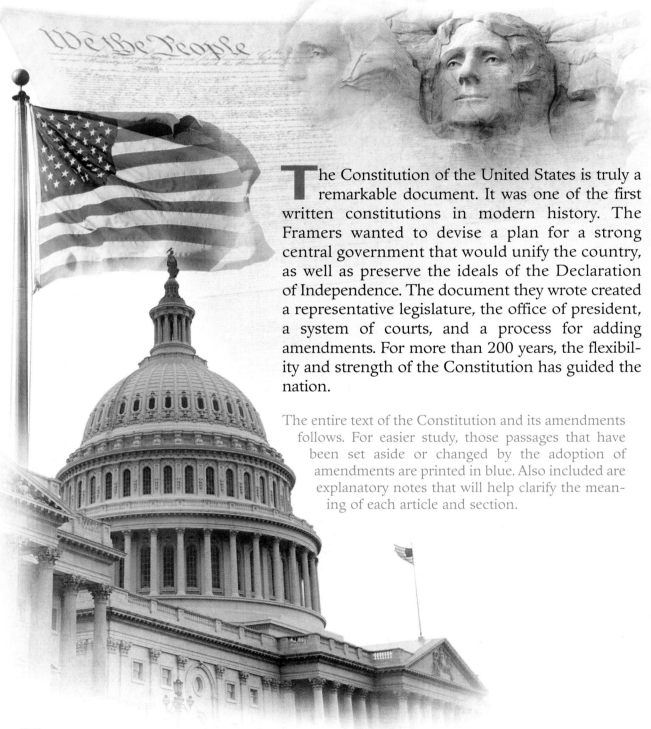

The Constitution of the United States is truly a remarkable document. It was one of the first written constitutions in modern history. The Framers wanted to devise a plan for a strong central government that would unify the country, as well as preserve the ideals of the Declaration of Independence. The document they wrote created a representative legislature, the office of president, a system of courts, and a process for adding amendments. For more than 200 years, the flexibility and strength of the Constitution has guided the nation.

The entire text of the Constitution and its amendments follows. For easier study, those passages that have been set aside or changed by the adoption of amendments are printed in blue. Also included are explanatory notes that will help clarify the meaning of each article and section.

Preamble

We, the people of the United States, in Order to form a more perfect Union, establish Justice, insure domestic Tranquility, provide for the common defence, promote the general Welfare, and secure the Blessings of Liberty to ourselves and our Posterity, do ordain and establish this Constitution for the United States of America.

Article I

Section 1

All legislative Powers herein granted shall be vested in a Congress of the United States, which shall consist of a Senate and House of Representatives.

Section 2

1. The House of Representatives shall be composed of Members chosen every second Year by the People of the several States, and the Electors in each State shall have the Qualifications requisite for Electors of the most numerous Branch of the State Legislature.

2. No Person shall be a Representative who shall not have attained to the Age of twenty-five Years, and been seven Years a Citizen of the United States, and who shall not, when elected, be an Inhabitant of that State in which he shall be chosen.

3. Representatives and direct Taxes shall be apportioned among the several states which may be included within this Union, according to the respective Numbers, which shall be determined by adding to the whole Number of free Persons, including those bound to Service for a Term of Years, and excluding Indians not taxed, three-fifths of all other Persons. The actual Enumeration shall be made within three Years after the first Meeting of the Congress of the United States, and within every subsequent Term of ten Years, in such Manner as they shall by Law direct. The Number of Representatives shall not exceed

The Preamble introduces the Constitution and sets forth the general purposes for which the government was established. The Preamble also declares that the power of the government comes from the people.

The printed text of the document shows the spelling and punctuation of the parchment original.

Article I THE LEGISLATIVE BRANCH

Section 1. Congress

The power to make laws is given to a Congress made up of two chambers to represent different interests: the Senate to represent the states; the House to be more responsive to the people's will.

Section 2. House of Representatives

1. **Election and Term of Office** "Electors" means voters. Every two years the voters choose new Congress members to serve in the House of Representatives. The Constitution states that each state may specify who can vote. But the 15th, 19th, 24th, and 26th Amendments have established guidelines that all states must follow regarding the right to vote.

2. **Qualifications** Representatives must be 25 years old, citizens of the United States for 7 years, and residents of the state they represent.

3. **Division of Representatives Among the States** The number of representatives from each state is based on the size of the state's population. Each state is divided into congressional districts, with each district required to be equal in population. Each state is entitled to at least one representative. The number of representatives in the House was set at 435 in 1929. Since then, there has been a reapportionment of seats based on population shifts rather than on addition of seats.

Only three-fifths of a state's slave population was to be counted in determining the number of representatives elected by the state. Native Americans were not counted at all.

The "enumeration" referred to is the census, the population count taken every 10 years since 1790.

4. **Vacancies** Vacancies in the House are filled through special elections called by the state's governor.

5. **Officers** The Speaker is the leader of the majority party in the House and is responsible for choosing the heads of various House committees. "Impeachment" means indictment, or bringing charges against an official.

Section 3. The Senate

1. **Number of Members, Terms of Office, and Voting Procedure** Originally, senators were chosen by the state legislators of their own states. The 17th Amendment changed this, so that senators are now elected directly by the people. There are 100 senators, 2 from each state.

2. **Staggered Elections; Vacancies** One-third of the Senate is elected every two years. The terms of the first Senate's membership was staggered: one group served two years, one four, and one six. All senators now serve a six-year term.

The 17th Amendment changed the method of filling vacancies in the Senate.

3. **Qualifications** Qualifications for the Senate are more restrictive than those for the House. Senators must be at least 30 years old, residents of the states they represent, and citizens of the United States for at least 9 years. The Framers of the Constitution made the Senate a more elite body to further check the powers of the House of Representatives.

one for every thirty Thousand, but each state shall have at Least one Representative; and until such enumeration shall be made, the State of New Hampshire shall be entitled to chuse three; Massachusetts eight, Rhode Island and Providence Plantations one, Connecticut five, New York six, New Jersey four, Pennsylvania eight, Delaware one, Maryland six, Virginia ten; North Carolina five, South Carolina five, and Georgia three.

4. When vacancies happen in the Representation from any State, the Executive Authority thereof shall issue Writs of Election to fill such Vacancies.

5. The House of Representatives shall chuse their Speaker and other Officers; and shall have the sole Power of Impeachment.

Section 3

1. The Senate of the United States shall be composed of two Senators from each State, chosen by the Legislature thereof; for six Years; and each Senator shall have one Vote.

2. Immediately after they shall be assembled in Consequence of the first Election, they shall be divided as equally as may be into three Classes. The Seats of the Senators of the first Class shall be vacated at the Expiration of the second Year, of the second Class at the Expiration of the fourth Year, and of the third Class at the Expiration of the sixth Year, so that one-third may be chosen every second Year; and if Vacancies happen by Resignations, or otherwise, during the Recess of the Legislature of any State, the Executive thereof may make temporary Appointments until the next Meeting of the Legislature, which shall then fill such Vacancies.

3. No person shall be a Senator who shall not have attained the Age of thirty Years, and been nine Years a Citizen of the United States, and who shall not, when elected, be an Inhabitant of that State in which he shall be chosen.

4. The Vice President of the United States shall be President of the Senate, but shall have no vote, unless they be equally divided.

5. The Senate shall chuse their Officers, and also a President pro tempore, in the absence of the Vice-President or when he shall exercise the Office of the President of the United States.

6. The Senate shall have the sole Power to try all impeachments. When sitting for that purpose they shall be on Oath or Affirmation. When the President of the United States is tried, the Chief Justice shall preside: And no person shall be convicted without the Concurrence of two-thirds of the Members present.

7. Judgment in Cases of Impeachment shall not extend further than to removal from Office, and disqualification to hold and enjoy any Office of Honor, Trust or Profit under the United States: but the Party convicted shall nevertheless be liable and subject to Indictment, Trial, Judgment and Punishment, according to Law.

Section 4

1. The Times, Places, and Manner of holding Elections for Senators and Representatives, shall be prescribed in each state by the Legislature thereof; but the Congress may at any time by Law make or alter such Regulations, except as to the Places of Chusing Senators.

2. The Congress shall assemble at least once in every Year, and such Meeting shall be on the first Monday in December, unless they shall by Law appoint a different Day.

Section 5

1. Each House shall be the Judge of the Elections, Returns and Qualifications of its own Members, and a Majority of each shall constitute a Quorum to do Business; but a smaller Number may adjourn from

4. President of the Senate The vice president's only duty listed in the Constitution is to preside over the Senate. The only real power the vice president has is to cast the deciding vote when there is a tie. However, modern presidents have given their vice presidents new responsibilities.

5. Other Officers The Senate selects its other officers, including a presiding officer (president pro tempore) who serves when the vice president is absent or has become president of the United States.

6. Trial of Impeachments When trying a case of impeachment brought by the House, the Senate convenes as a court. The chief justice of the United States acts as the presiding judge, and the Senate acts as the jury. A two-thirds vote of the members present is necessary to convict officials under impeachment charges.

7. Penalty for Conviction If the Senate convicts an official, it may only remove the official from office and prevent that person from holding another federal position. However, the convicted official may still be tried for the same offense in a regular court of law.

Section 4. Elections and Meetings

1. Holding Elections In 1842 Congress required members of the House to be elected from districts in states having more than one representative rather than at large. In 1845 it set the first Tuesday after the first Monday in November as the day for selecting presidential electors.

2. Meetings The 20th Amendment, ratified in 1933, has changed the date of the opening of the regular session of Congress to January 3.

Section 5. Organization and Rules of Procedure

1. Organization Until 1969 Congress acted as the sole judge of qualifications of its own members. In that year, the Supreme Court ruled that Congress could not legally exclude victorious candidates who met all the requirements listed in Article I, Section 2.

A "quorum" is the minimum number of members that must be present for the House or Senate to conduct sessions. For a regular House session, a quorum consists of the majority of the House, or 218 of the 435 members.

2. **Rules** Each house sets its own rules, can punish its members for disorderly behavior, and can expel a member by a two-thirds vote.

3. **Journals** In addition to the journals, a complete official record of everything said on the floor, as well as the roll call votes on all bills or issues, is available in the *Congressional Record,* published daily by the Government Printing Office.

4. **Adjournment** Neither house may adjourn for more than three days or move to another location without the approval of the other house.

Section 6. Privileges and Restrictions

1. **Pay and Privileges** To strengthen the federal government, the Founders set congressional salaries to be paid by the United States Treasury rather than by members' respective states. Originally, members were paid $6 per day. Salaries for senators and representatives were $154,700 beginning in 2003.

The "immunity" privilege means members cannot be sued or be prosecuted for anything they say in Congress. They cannot be arrested while Congress is in session, except for treason, major crimes, or breaking the peace.

2. **Restrictions** "Emoluments" means salaries. The purpose of this clause is to prevent members of Congress from passing laws that would benefit them personally. It also prevents the president from promising them jobs in other branches of the federal government.

day to day, and may be authorized to compel the Attendance of absent Members, in such Manner, and under such Penalties as each House may provide.

2. Each House may determine the Rules of its Proceedings, punish its Members for disorderly Behaviour, and, with the Concurrence of two-thirds, expel a Member.

3. Each House shall keep a Journal of its Proceedings, and from time to time publish the same, excepting such Parts as may in their Judgment require Secrecy; and the Yeas and Nays of the Members of either House on any question shall, at the desire of one-fifth of those Present, be entered on the Journal.

4. Neither House during the Session of Congress, shall, without the Consent of the other, adjourn for more than three days, nor to any other Place than that in which the two Houses shall be sitting.

Section 6

1. The Senators and Representatives shall receive a Compensation for their Services, to be ascertained by Law, and paid out of the Treasury of the United States. They shall in all Cases, except Treason, Felony and Breach of the Peace be privileged from Arrest during their attendance at the Session of their respective Houses, and in going to and returning from the same; and for any Speech or Debate in either House, they shall not be questioned in any other place.

2. No Senator or Representative shall, during the Time for which he was elected, be appointed to any civil Office under the Authority of the United States, which shall have been created, or the Emoluments whereof shall have been encreased, during such time; and no Person holding any Office under the United States, shall be a Member of either House during his continuance in Office.

Section 7

1. All Bills for raising Revenue shall originate in the House of Representatives; but the Senate may propose or concur with Amendments as on other bills.

2. Every Bill which shall have passed the House of Representatives and the Senate, shall, before it become a Law, be presented to the President of the United States; If he approve he shall sign it, but if not he shall return it, with his Objections, to that House in which it shall have originated, who shall enter the Objections at large on their Journal, and proceed to reconsider it. If after such Reconsideration two-thirds of that House shall agree to pass the bill, it shall be sent, together with the objections, to the other House, by which it shall likewise be reconsidered, and if approved by two-thirds of that House, it shall become a Law. But in all such Cases the Votes of both Houses shall be determined by Yeas and Nays, and the Names of the Persons voting for and against the Bill shall be entered on the Journal of each House respectively. If any Bill shall not be returned by the President within ten Days (Sundays excepted) after it shall have been presented to him, the Same shall be a Law, in like Manner as if he had signed it, unless the Congress by their Adjournment prevent its Return, in which Case it shall not be a Law.

3. Every Order, Resolution, or Vote to which the Concurrence of the Senate and House of Representatives may be necessary (except on a question of Adjournment) shall be presented to the President of the United States; and before the Same shall take Effect, shall be approved by him, or, being disapproved by him, shall be repassed by two-thirds of the Senate and House of Representatives, according to the Rules and Limitations prescribed in the case of a Bill.

Section 7. Passing Laws

1. **Revenue Bills** "Revenue" is income raised by the government. The chief source of government revenue is taxes. All tax laws must originate in the House of Representatives. This ensures that the branch of Congress which is elected by the people every two years has the major role in determining taxes. This clause does not prevent the Senate from amending tax bills.

2. **How Bills Become Laws** A bill may become a law only by passing both houses of Congress and by being signed by the president. If the president disapproves, or vetoes, the bill, it is returned to the house where it originated, along with a written statement of the president's objections. If two-thirds of each house approves the bill after the president has vetoed it, it becomes law. In voting to override a president's veto, the votes of all members of Congress must be recorded in the journals or official records. If the president does not sign or veto a bill within 10 days (excluding Sundays), it becomes law. However, if Congress has adjourned during this 10-day period, the bill does not become law. This is known as a "pocket veto."

3. **Presidential Approval or Veto** The Framers included this paragraph to prevent Congress from passing joint resolutions instead of bills to avoid the possibility of a presidential veto. A bill is a draft of a proposed law, whereas a resolution is the legislature's formal expression of opinion or intent on a matter.

Section 8. Powers Granted to Congress

1. **Revenue** This clause gives Congress the power to raise and spend revenue. Taxes must be levied at the same rate throughout the nation.

2. **Borrowing** The federal government borrows money by issuing bonds.

3. **Commerce** The exact meaning of "commerce" has caused controversy. The trend has been to expand its meaning and, consequently, the extent of Congress's powers.

4. **Naturalization and Bankruptcy** "Naturalization" refers to the procedure by which a citizen of a foreign nation becomes a citizen of the United States.

5. **Currency** Control over money is an exclusive federal power; the states are forbidden to issue currency.

6. **Counterfeiting** "Counterfeiting" means illegally imitating or forging.

7. **Post Office** In 1970 the United States Postal Service replaced the Post Office Department.

8. **Copyrights and Patents** Under this provision, Congress has passed copyright and patent laws.

9. **Courts** This provision allows Congress to establish a federal court system.

10. **Piracy** Congress has the power to protect American ships on the high seas.

11. **Declare War** While the Constitution gives Congress the right to declare war, the United States has sent troops into combat without a congressional declaration.

12. **Army** This provision reveals the Framers' fears of a standing army.

13. **Navy** This clause allows Congress to establish a navy.

Section 8
The Congress shall have the Power

1. To lay and collect Taxes, Duties, Imposts and Excises, to pay the Debts and provide for the common Defence and general Welfare of the United States; but all Duties, Imposts and Excises shall be uniform throughout the United States;

2. To borrow money on the credit of the United States;

3. To regulate Commerce with foreign Nations, and among the several States, and with the Indian Tribes;

4. To establish an uniform Rule of Naturalization, and uniform Laws on the subject of Bankruptcies throughout the United States.

5. To coin Money, regulate the Value thereof, and of foreign Coin, and fix the Standard of Weights and Measures;

6. To provide for the Punishment of counterfeiting the Securities and current Coin of the United States;

7. To establish Post Offices and post Roads;

8. To promote the Progress of Science and useful Arts, by securing for limited Times to Authors and Inventors the exclusive Right to their respective Writings and Discoveries;

9. To constitute Tribunals inferior to the Supreme Court;

10. To define and punish Piracies and Felonies committed on the high Seas, and Offenses against the Law of Nations.

11. To declare War, grant Letters of Marque and Reprisal, and make Rules concerning Captures on Land and Water;

12. To raise and support Armies, but no Appropriation of Money to that Use shall be for a longer Term than two Years;

13. To provide and maintain a Navy;

14. To make Rules for the Government and Regulation of the land and naval forces;

15. To provide for calling forth the Militia to execute the Laws of the Union, suppress Insurrections, and repel Invasions;

16. To provide for organizing, arming, and disciplining, the Militia, and for governing such Part of them as may be employed in the Service of the United States, reserving to the States respectively, the Appointment of the Officers, and the Authority of training the Militia according to the discipline prescribed by Congress;

17. To exercise exclusive Legislation in all Cases whatsoever, over such District (not exceeding ten Miles square) as may, by Cession of particular States, and the acceptance of Congress, become the Seat of Government of the United States, and to exercise like Authority over all Places purchased by the Consent of the Legislature of the State in which the Same shall be, for the Erection of Forts, Magazines, Arsenals, dock-Yards, and other needful Buildings;—And

18. To make all Laws which shall be necessary and proper for carrying into Execution the foregoing Powers, and all other Powers vested by this Constitution in the Government of the United States, or in any Department or Officer thereof.

Section 9

1. The Migration or Importation of such Persons as any of the States now existing shall think proper to admit, shall not be prohibited by the Congress prior to the Year one thousand eight hundred and eight, but a tax or duty may be imposed on such importation, not exceeding ten dollars for each Person.

2. The privilege of the Writ of Habeas Corpus shall not be suspended, unless when in Cases of Rebellion or Invasion the public Safety may require it.

14. Rules for Armed Forces Congress may pass regulations that deal with military discipline.

15. Militia The "militia" is now called the National Guard. It is organized by the states.

16. National Guard Even though the National Guard is organized by the states, Congress has the authority to pass rules for governing its behavior.

17. Nation's Capital This clause grants Congress the right to make laws for Washington, D.C.

18. Elastic Clause This is the so-called "elastic clause" of the Constitution and one of its most important provisions. The "necessary and proper" laws must be related to one of the 17 enumerated powers.

Section 9. Powers Denied to the Federal Government

1. Slave Trade This paragraph contains the compromise the Framers reached regarding regulation of the slave trade in exchange for Congress's exclusive control over interstate commerce.

2. Habeas Corpus "Habeas corpus" is a Latin term meaning "you may have the body." A writ of habeas corpus issued by a judge requires a law official to bring a prisoner to court and show cause for holding the prisoner. The writ may be suspended only during wartime.

3. **Bills of Attainder** A "bill of attainder" is a bill that punishes a person without a jury trial. An "ex post facto" law is one that makes an act a crime after the act has been committed.

4. **Direct Taxes** The 16th Amendment allowed Congress to pass an income tax.

5. **Tax on Exports** Congress may not tax goods that move from one state to another.

6. **Uniformity of Treatment** This prohibition prevents Congress from favoring one state or region over another in the regulation of trade.

7. **Appropriation Law** This clause protects against the misuse of funds. All of the president's expenditures must be made with the permission of Congress.

8. **Titles of Nobility** This clause prevents the development of a nobility in the United States.

Section 10. Powers Denied to the States

1. **Limitations on Power** The states are prohibited from conducting foreign affairs, carrying on a war, or controlling interstate and foreign commerce. States are also not allowed to pass laws that the federal government is prohibited from passing, such as enacting ex post facto laws or bills of attainder. These restrictions on the states were designed, in part, to prevent an overlapping in functions and authority with the federal government that could create conflict and chaos.

2. **Export and Import Taxes** This clause prevents states from levying duties on exports and imports. If states were permitted to tax imports and exports, they could use

3. No Bill of Attainder or ex post facto Law shall be passed.

4. No capitation, or other direct, Tax shall be laid unless in Proportion to the Census or Enumeration herein before directed to be taken.

5. No Tax or Duty shall be laid on Articles exported from any State.

6. No Preference shall be given by any Regulation of Commerce or Revenue to the Ports of one State over those of another: nor shall Vessels bound to, or from, one State, be obliged to enter, clear, or pay Duties in another.

7. No Money shall be drawn from the Treasury, but in Consequence of Appropriations made by Law; and a regular Statement and Account of the Receipts and Expenditures of all public Money shall be published from time to time.

8. No Title of Nobility shall be granted by the United States:—And no Person holding any Office of Profit or Trust under them, shall, without the Consent of the Congress, accept of any present, Emolument, Office, or Title, of any kind whatever, from any King, Prince, or foreign State.

Section 10

1. No State shall enter into any Treaty, Alliance, or Confederation; grant Letters of Marque and Reprisal; coin Money; emit Bills of Credit; make any Thing but gold and silver Coin a Tender in Payment of Debts; pass any Bill of Attainder; ex post facto Law, or Law impairing the Obligation of Contracts, or grant any Title of Nobility.

2. No State shall, without the Consent of the Congress, lay any Imposts or Duties on Imports or Exports, except what may be absolutely necessary for executing its inspection Laws: and the net Produce of all Duties and Imposts, laid by any State on Imports and Exports, shall be for the Use of the Treasury of the United States; and

all such Laws shall be subject to the Revision and Control of the Congress.

3. No State shall, without the Consent of Congress, lay any duty on Tonnage, keep Troops, or Ships of War in time of Peace, enter into any Agreement or Compact with another State, or with a foreign Power, or engage in War, unless actually invaded, or in such imminent Danger as will not admit of delay.

Article II

Section 1

1. The executive Power shall be vested in a President of the United States of America. He shall hold his Office during the Term of four years, and together with the Vice-President chosen for the same Term, be elected, as follows:

2. Each State shall appoint, in such Manner as the Legislature thereof may direct, a Number of Electors, equal to the whole Number of Senators and Representatives to which the State may be entitled in the Congress: but no Senator or Representative, or Person holding an Office of Trust or Profit under the United States, shall be appointed an Elector.

3. The Electors shall meet in their respective States, and vote by Ballot for two Persons, of whom one at least shall not be an Inhabitant of the same State with themselves. And they shall make a List of all the Persons voted for and of the Number of Votes for each; which List they shall sign and certify, and transmit sealed to the Seat of the Government of the United States, directed to the President of the Senate. The President of the Senate shall, in the Presence of the Senate and House of Representatives, open all the Certificates, and the Votes shall then be counted. The Person having the greatest Number of Votes shall be the President, if such Number be a Majority of the whole Number of Electors appointed; and if there be more

their taxing power in a way that weakens or destroys Congress's power to control interstate and foreign commerce.

3. **Duties, Armed Forces, War** This clause prohibits states from maintaining an army or navy and from going to war, except in cases where a state is directly attacked. It also forbids states from collecting fees from foreign vessels or from making treaties with other nations. All of these powers are reserved for the federal government.

Article II THE EXECUTIVE BRANCH

Section 1. President and Vice President

1. **Term of Office** The president is given power to enforce the laws passed by Congress. Both the president and the vice president serve four-year terms. The 22nd Amendment limits the number of terms the president may serve to two.

2. **Election** The Philadelphia Convention had trouble deciding how the president was to be chosen. The system finally agreed upon was indirect election by "electors" chosen for that purpose. The president and vice president are not directly elected. Instead, the president and vice president are elected by presidential electors from each state who form the electoral college. Each state has the number of presidential electors equal to the total number of its senators and representatives. State legislatures determine how the electors are chosen. Originally, the state legislatures chose the electors, but today they are nominated by political parties and elected by the voters. No senator, representative, or any other federal officeholder can serve as an elector.

3. **Former Method of Election** This clause describes the original method of electing the president and vice president. Accord-

ing to this method, each elector voted for two candidates. The candidate with the most votes (as long as it was a majority) became president. The candidate with the second highest number of votes became vice president. In the election of 1800, the two top candidates received the same number of votes, making it necessary for the House of Representatives to decide the election. To prevent such a situation from recurring, the 12th Amendment was added in 1804.

4. **Date of Elections** Congress selects the date when the presidential electors are chosen and when they vote for president and vice president. All electors must vote on the same day. The first Tuesday after the first Monday in November has been set as the date for presidential elections. Electors cast their votes on the Monday after the second Wednesday in December.

5. **Qualifications** The president must be a citizen of the United States by birth, at least 35 years old, and a resident of the United States for 14 years. See Amendment 22.

6. **Vacancies** If the president dies, resigns, is removed from office by impeachment, or is unable to carry out the duties of the office, the vice president becomes president. (Amendment 25 deals with presidential disability.) If both the president and vice president are unable to serve, Congress has the power to declare by law who acts as president. Congress set the line of succession in the Presidential Succession Act of 1947.

than one who have such Majority, and have an equal Number of Votes, then the House of Representatives shall immediately chuse by Ballot one of them for President; and if no Person have a Majority, then from the five highest on the List the said House shall in like Manner chuse the President. But in chusing the President, the Votes shall be taken by States, the Representation from each State having one Vote; a quorum for this Purpose shall consist of a Member or Members from two-thirds of the States, and a Majority of all the States shall be necessary to a Choice. In every Case, after the Choice of the President, the Person having the greatest Number of Votes of the Electors shall be the Vice-President. But if there should remain two or more who have equal votes, the Senate shall chuse from them by Ballot the Vice President.

4. The Congress may determine the Time of chusing the Electors, and the Day on which they shall give their Votes; which Day shall be the same throughout the United States.

5. No person except a natural born Citizen, or a Citizen of the United States, at the time of the Adoption of this Constitution, shall be eligible to the Office of President; neither shall any Person be eligible to that Office who shall not have attained to the Age of thirty-five years, and been fourteen Years a Resident within the United States.

6. In Case of the Removal of the President from Office, or of his Death, Resignation, or Inability to discharge the Powers and Duties of the said Office, the same shall devolve on the Vice-President, and the Congress may by Law provide for the Case of Removal, Death, Resignation or Inability, both of the President and Vice-President, declaring what Officer shall then act as President, and such Officer shall act accordingly, until the disability be removed, or a President shall be elected.

7. The President shall, at stated Times, receive for his Services a Compensation, which shall neither be encreased nor diminished during the Period for which he shall have been elected, and he shall not receive within that Period any other Emolument from the United States, or any of them.

8. Before he enter on the execution of his office, he shall take the following Oath or Affirmation "I do solemnly swear (or affirm) that I will faithfully execute the Office of President of the United States, and will to the best of my Ability, preserve, protect and defend the Constitution of the United States.

Section 2

1. The President shall be Commander in Chief of the Army and Navy of the United States, and of the Militia of the several States, when called into the actual Service of the United States; he may require the Opinion, in writing, of the principal Officer in each of the executive Departments, upon any subject relating to the Duties of their respective Offices, and he shall have Power to Grant Reprieves and Pardons for Offences against the United States, except in Cases of Impeachment.

2. He shall have Power, by and with the Advice and Consent of the Senate, to make Treaties, provided two-thirds of the Senators present concur; and he shall nominate, and by and with the Advice and Consent of the Senate, shall appoint Ambassadors, other public Ministers and Consuls, Judges of the supreme Court, and all other Officers of the United States, whose Appointments are not herein otherwise provided for, and which shall be established by Law. But the Congress may by Law vest the Appointment of such inferior Officers, as they think proper, in the President alone, in the Courts of Law, or in the Heads of Departments.

7. **Salary** Originally, the president's salary was $25,000 per year. The president's current salary of $400,000 plus a $50,000 taxable expense account per year was enacted in 1999. The president also receives numerous fringe benefits including a $100,000 non-taxable allowance for travel and entertainment, and living accommodations in two residences—the White House and Camp David. However, the president cannot receive any other income from the United States government or state governments while in office.

8. **Oath of Office** The oath of office is generally administered by the chief justice, but can be administered by any official authorized to administer oaths. All presidents-elect except Washington have been sworn into office by the chief justice. Only Vice Presidents John Tyler, Calvin Coolidge, and Lyndon Johnson in succeeding to the office have been sworn in by someone else.

Section 2. Powers of the President

1. **Military, Cabinet, Pardons** Mention of "the principal officer in each of the executive departments" is the only suggestion of the president's cabinet to be found in the Constitution. The cabinet is a purely advisory body, and its power depends on the president. Each cabinet member is appointed by the president and must be confirmed by the Senate. This clause also makes the president, a civilian, the head of the armed services. This established the principle of civilian control of the military.

2. **Treaties and Appointments** The president is the chief architect of American foreign policy. He or she is responsible for the conduct of foreign relations, or dealings with other countries. All treaties, however, require approval of two-thirds of the senators present. Most federal positions today are filled under the rules and regulations of the civil service system. Most presidential

appointees serve at the pleasure of the president. Removal of an official by the president is not subject to congressional approval. But the power can be restricted by conditions set in creating the office.

3. **Vacancies in Offices** The president can temporarily appoint officials to fill vacancies when the Senate is not in session.

Section 3. Duties of the President

Under this provision the president delivers annual State of the Union messages. On occasion, presidents have called Congress into special session to consider particular problems.

The president's duty to receive foreign diplomats also includes the power to ask a foreign country to withdraw its diplomatic officials from this country. This is called "breaking diplomatic relations" and often carries with it the implied threat of more drastic action, even war. The president likewise has the power of deciding whether or not to recognize foreign governments.

Section 4. Impeachment

This section states the reasons for which the president and vice president may be impeached and removed from office. (See annotations of Article I, Section 3, Clauses 6 and 7.)

Article III THE JUDICIAL BRANCH

Section 1. Federal Courts

The term *judicial* refers to courts. The Constitution set up only the Supreme Court but provided for the establishment of other federal courts. There are presently nine justices on the Supreme Court. Congress has created a system of federal district courts and courts of appeals, which review certain district court cases. Judges of these courts serve during "good behavior," which means that they usually serve for life or until they choose to retire.

Section 2. Jurisdiction

1. **General Jurisdiction** Use of the words *in law and equity* reflects the fact that American

3. The President shall have Power to fill up all Vacancies that may happen during the Recess of the Senate, by granting Commissions which shall expire at the End of their next Session.

Section 3
He shall from time to time give to Congress Information of the State of the Union, and recommend to their Consideration such Measures as he shall judge necessary and expedient; he may, on extraordinary occasions, convene both Houses, or either of them, and in Case of Disagreement between them, with respect to the Time of Adjournment, he may adjourn them to such Time as he shall think proper; he shall receive Ambassadors and other public Ministers; he shall take Care that the Laws be faithfully executed, and shall Commission all the Officers of the United States.

Section 4
The President, Vice-President and all civil Officers of the United States, shall be removed from Office on Impeachment for, and Conviction of, Treason, Bribery, or other high Crimes and Misdemeanors.

Article III

Section 1
The Judicial Power of the United States, shall be vested in one supreme Court, and in such inferior Courts as the Congress may from time to time ordain and establish. The judges, both of the supreme and inferior Courts, shall hold their Offices during good Behaviour, and shall, at stated Times, receive for their Services, a Compensation, which shall not be diminished during their Continuance in Office.

Section 2

1. The judicial Power shall extend to all Cases, in Law and Equity, arising under this Constitution, the Laws of the United

States, and treaties made, or which shall be made, under their Authority; to all Cases affecting ambassadors, other public ministers and consuls; to all cases of admiralty and maritime Jurisdiction; to Controversies to which the United States shall be a party; to Controversies between two or more states; between a State and Citizens of another State; between Citizens of different States; between Citizens of the same State claiming Lands under Grants of different States, and between a State, or the Citizens thereof, and foreign States, Citizens or Subjects.

2. In all Cases affecting Ambassadors, other public Ministers and Consuls, and those in which a State shall be Party, the supreme Court shall have original Jurisdiction. In all the other Cases before mentioned, the supreme Court shall have appellate Jurisdiction, both as to Law and Fact, with such Exceptions, and under such Regulations as the Congress shall make.

3. The trial of all Crimes, except in Cases of Impeachment, shall be by Jury; and such Trial shall be held in the State where the said Crimes shall have been committed; but when not committed within any State, the Trial shall be at such Place or Places as the Congress may by Law have directed.

Section 3

1. Treason against the United States, shall consist only in levying War against them, or in adhering to their Enemies, giving them Aid and Comfort. No Person shall be convicted of Treason unless on the Testimony of two Witnesses to the same overt Act, or on Confession in open Court.

2. The Congress shall have power to declare the Punishment of Treason, but no Attainder of Treason shall work Corruption of Blood, or Forfeiture except during the Life of the Person attainted.

courts took over two kinds of traditional law from Great Britain. The basic law was the "common law," which was based on over five centuries of judicial decisions. "Equity" was a special branch of British law developed to handle cases where common law did not apply.

Federal courts deal mostly with "statute law," or laws passed by Congress, treaties, and cases involving the Constitution itself. "Admiralty and maritime jurisdiction" covers all sorts of cases involving ships and shipping on the high seas and on rivers, canals, and lakes.

2. **The Supreme Court** When a court has "original jurisdiction" over certain kinds of cases, it means that the court has the authority to be the first court to hear a case. A court with "appellate jurisdiction" hears cases that have been appealed from lower courts. Virtually all Supreme Court cases are heard on appeal from lower courts.

3. **Jury Trials** Except in cases of impeachment, anyone accused of a crime has the right to a trial by jury. The trial must be held in the state where the crime was committed. Jury trial guarantees were strengthened in the 6th, 7th, 8th, and 9th Amendments.

Section 3. Treason

1. **Definition** Knowing that the charge of treason often had been used by monarchs to get rid of people who opposed them, the Framers of the Constitution defined treason carefully, requiring that at least two witnesses to the same treasonable act testify in court.

2. **Punishment** Congress is given the power to determine the punishment for treason. The children of a person convicted of treason may not be punished nor may the convicted person's property be taken away from the children. Convictions for treason have been relatively rare in the nation's history.

THE CONSTITUTION OF THE UNITED STATES   **583**

Article IV RELATIONS AMONG THE STATES

Section 1. Official Acts

This provision ensures that each state recognizes the laws, court decisions, and records of all other states. For example, a marriage license or corporation charter issued by one state must be accepted in other states.

Section 2. Mutual Duties of States

1. **Privileges** The "privileges and immunities," or rights of citizens, guarantee each state's citizens equal treatment in all states.

2. **Extradition** Described here, *extradition* means that a person convicted of a crime or a person accused of a crime must be returned to the state where the crime was committed. Thus, a person cannot flee to another state hoping to escape the law.

3. **Fugitive-Slave Clause** Formerly this clause meant that slaves could not become free persons by escaping to free states.

Section 3. New States and Territories

1. **New States** Congress has the power to admit new states. It also determines the basic guidelines for applying for statehood. One state, Maine, was created within the original boundaries of another state (Massachusetts) with the consent of Congress and the state.

2. **Territories** Congress has power over federal land. But neither in this clause nor anywhere else in the Constitution is the federal government explicitly empowered to acquire new territory.

Article IV

Section 1

Full Faith and Credit shall be given in each State to the public Acts, Records, and judicial Proceedings of every other State. And the Congress may by general Laws prescribe the Manner in which such Acts, Records, and Proceedings shall be proved, and the Effect thereof.

Section 2

1. The Citizens of each State shall be entitled to all Privileges and Immunities of Citizens in the several States.

2. A Person charged in any State with Treason, Felony, or other Crime, who shall flee from Justice, and be found in another State, shall on demand of the executive Authority of the State from which he fled, be delivered up, to be removed to the State having Jurisdiction of the crime.

3. No Person held to Service of Labour in one State, under the Laws thereof, escaping into another, shall, in Consequence of any Law or Regulation therein, be discharged from such Service or Labour, but shall be delivered up on Claim of the Party to whom such Service or Labour may be due.

Section 3

1. New States may be admitted by the Congress into this Union; but no new State shall be formed or erected within the Jurisdiction of any other State; nor any State be formed by the Junction of two or more States, or parts of States, without the Consent of the Legislatures of the States concerned as well as of the Congress.

2. The Congress shall have Power to dispose of and make all needful Rules and Regulations respecting the Territory or other Property belonging to the United States; and nothing in this Constitution shall be so construed as to Prejudice any Claims of the United States, or of any particular State.

Section 4

The United States shall guarantee to every State in this Union a Republican Form of Government, and shall protect each of them against Invasion; and on Application of the Legislature, or of the Executive (when the Legislature cannot be convened) against domestic Violence.

Article V

The Congress, whenever two-thirds of both Houses shall deem it necessary, shall propose Amendments to this Constitution, or, on the Application of the Legislatures of two-thirds of the several States, shall call a Convention for proposing Amendments, which, in either Case, shall be valid to all Intents and Purposes, as part of this Constitution, when ratified by the Legislatures of three-fourths of the several States, or by Conventions in three-fourths thereof, as the one or the other Mode of Ratification may be proposed by the Congress; Provided that no Amendment which may be made prior to the Year One thousand eight hundred and eight shall in any Manner affect the first and fourth clauses in the Ninth Section of the first Article; and that no State, without its Consent, shall be deprived of its equal Suffrage in the Senate.

Article VI

1. All Debts contracted and Engagements entered into, before the Adoption of this Constitution, shall be as valid against the United States under this Constitution as under the Confederation.

2. This Constitution, and the Laws of the United States which shall be made in Pursuance thereof; and all Treaties made, or which shall be made, under the Authority of the United States, shall be the supreme Law of the Land; and the Judges in every State shall be bound thereby, any Thing in the Constitution or Laws of any State to the Contrary notwithstanding.

Section 4. Federal Protection for States

This section allows the federal government to send troops into a state to guarantee law and order. The president may send in troops even without the consent of the state government involved.

Article V The Amending Process

There are now 27 amendments to the Constitution. The Framers of the Constitution deliberately made it difficult to amend the Constitution. Two methods of proposing and ratifying amendments are provided for. A two-thirds majority is needed in Congress to propose an amendment, and at least three-fourths of the states (38 states) must accept the amendment before it can become law. No amendment has yet been proposed by a national convention called by the states, though in the 1980s a convention to propose an amendment requiring a balanced budget had been approved by 32 states.

Article VI National Supremacy

1. **Public Debts and Treaties** This section promised that all debts the colonies had incurred during the Revolution and under the Articles of Confederation would be honored by the new United States government.

2. **The Supreme Law** The "supremacy clause" recognized the Constitution and federal laws as supreme when in conflict with those of the states. It was largely based on this clause that Chief Justice John Marshall wrote his historic decision in *McCulloch* v. *Maryland.* The 14th Amendment reinforced the supremacy of federal law over state laws.

3. Oaths of Office This clause also declares that no religious test shall be required as a qualification for holding public office.

Article VII RATIFICATION OF THE CONSTITUTION

Unlike the Articles of Confederation, which required approval of all thirteen states for adoption, the Constitution required approval of only nine of thirteen states. Thirty-nine of the 55 delegates at the Constitutional Convention signed the Constitution. The Constitution went into effect in June 1788.

3. The Senators and Representatives before mentioned, and the Members of the several State Legislatures, and all executive and judicial Officers, both of the United States and of the several States, shall be bound by Oath or Affirmation, to support this Constitution; but no religious Test shall ever be required as a Qualification to any Office or public Trust under the United States.

Article VII

The Ratification of the Conventions of nine States shall be sufficient for the Establishment of this Constitution between the States so ratifying the same.

Done in Convention, by the Unanimous Consent of the States present, the Seventeenth Day of September, in the Year of our Lord one thousand seven hundred and Eighty-seven, and of the Independence of the United States of America the Twelfth. In Witness whereof We have hereunto subscribed our Names.

Signers

George Washington, **President and Deputy from Virginia**

New Hampshire
John Langdon
Nicholas Gilman

Massachusetts
Nathaniel Gorham
Rufus King

Connecticut
William Samuel Johnson
Roger Sherman

New York
Alexander Hamilton

New Jersey
William Livingston
David Brearley
William Paterson
Jonathan Dayton

Pennsylvania
Benjamin Franklin
Thomas Mifflin
Robert Morris
George Clymer
Thomas FitzSimons
Jared Ingersoll
James Wilson
Gouverneur Morris

Delaware
George Read
Gunning Bedford, Jr.
John Dickinson
Richard Bassett
Jacob Broom

Maryland
James McHenry
Daniel of St. Thomas Jenifer
Daniel Carroll

Virginia
John Blair
James Madison, Jr.

North Carolina
William Blount
Richard Dobbs Spaight
Hugh Williamson

South Carolina
John Rutledge
Charles Cotesworth Pinckney
Charles Pinckney
Pierce Butler

Georgia
William Few
Abraham Baldwin

Attest:
William Jackson,
Secretary

Amendment I

Congress shall make no law respecting an establishment of religion, or prohibiting the free exercise thereof; or abridging the freedom of speech, or of the press; or the right of the people peaceably to assemble, and to petition the Government for a redress of grievances.

Amendment II

A well-regulated Militia, being necessary to the security of a free State, the right of the people to keep and bear Arms, shall not be infringed.

Amendment III

No soldier shall, in time of peace be quartered in any house, without the consent of the Owner, nor in time of war, but in a manner to be prescribed by law.

Amendment IV

The right of the people to be secure in their persons, houses, papers, and effects, against unreasonable searches and seizures, shall not be violated, and no Warrants shall issue, but upon probable cause, supported by Oath or affirmation, and particularly describing the place to be searched, and the persons or things to be seized.

Amendment V

No person shall be held to answer for a capital, or otherwise infamous crime, unless on a presentment or indictment of a Grand Jury, except in cases arising in the land or

Amendment 1.
Freedom of Religion, Speech, Press, and Assembly (1791)

The 1st Amendment protects the civil liberties of individuals in the United States. The 1st Amendment freedoms are not absolute, however. They are limited by the rights of other individuals.

Amendment 2.
Bearing Arms (1791)

This amendment is often debated. Some people argue that it protects the rights of states to have militias. Others argue that the Founders' original intent was to protect the right of individuals to have weapons.

Amendment 3.
Quartering Troops (1791)

This amendment is based on the principle that people have a right to privacy in their own homes. It also reflects the colonists' grievances against the British for quartering (housing) troops in private homes.

Amendment 4.
Searches and Seizures (1791)

Like the 3rd Amendment, the 4th Amendment reflects the colonists' desire to protect their privacy. Britain had used writs of assistance (general search warrants) to seek out smuggled goods. Americans wanted to make sure that such searches and seizures would be conducted only when a judge felt that there was "reasonable cause" to conduct them. The Supreme Court has ruled that evidence seized illegally without a search warrant may not be used in court.

Amendment 5.
Rights of Accused Persons (1791)

It is the function of a grand jury to bring a "presentment" or "indictment," which means to formally charge a person with committing a crime, if there is enough evidence to bring the accused person to trial. A person may not be tried more than once for the same crime (double jeopardy). Members of the armed services are subject to military law. They may be tried in a court martial. In times of war or a natural disaster, civilians may also be put under martial law. The 5th Amendment also guarantees that accused persons may refuse to answer questions on the grounds that the answers might tend to incriminate them.

Amendment 6.
Right to Speedy, Fair Trial (1791)

The requirement of a "speedy" trial ensures that an accused person will not be held in jail for a lengthy period as a means of punishing the accused without a trial. A "fair" trial means that the trial must be open to the public and that a jury must hear witnesses and evidence on both sides before deciding the guilt or innocence of a person charged with a crime. This amendment also provides that legal counsel must be provided to a defendant. In 1963, the Supreme Court ruled, in *Gideon* v. *Wainwright,* that if a defendant cannot afford a lawyer, the government must provide one to defend him or her.

Amendment 7.
Civil Suits (1791)

"Common law" means the law established by previous court decisions. In civil cases where one person sues another for more than $20, a jury trial is provided for. But customarily, federal courts do not hear civil cases unless they involve a good deal more money.

Amendment 8.
Bail and Punishment (1791)

"Bail" is money that an accused person provides to the court as a guarantee that he or she will be present for a trial. This amendment ensures that neither bail nor punishment for a crime shall be unreasonably severe.

naval forces, or in the Militia, when in actual service in time of War or public danger; nor shall any person be subject for the same offence to be twice put in jeopardy of life or limb; nor shall be compelled in any criminal case to be a witness against himself, nor be deprived of life, liberty, or property, without due process of law; nor shall private property be taken for public use, without just compensation.

Amendment VI

In all criminal prosecutions, the accused shall enjoy the right to a speedy and public trial, by an impartial jury of the State and district wherein the crime shall have been committed, which district shall have been previously ascertained by law, and to be informed of the nature and cause of the accusation; to be confronted with the witnesses against him; to have compulsory process for obtaining witnesses in his favor, and to have the Assistance of Counsel for his defence.

Amendment VII

In suits at common law, where the value in controversy shall exceed twenty dollars, the right of trial by jury shall be preserved, and no fact tried by a jury, shall be otherwise reexamined in any Courts of the United States, than according to the rules of common law.

Amendment VIII

Excessive bail shall not be required, nor excessive fines imposed, nor cruel and unusual punishments inflicted.

Amendment IX

The enumeration in the Constitution, of certain rights, shall not be construed to deny or disparage others retained by the people.

Amendment X

The powers not delegated to the United States by the Constitution, nor prohibited by it to the States, are reserved to the States respectively, or to the people.

Amendment XI

The Judicial power of the United States shall not be construed to extend to any suit in law or equity, commenced or prosecuted against one of the United States by Citizens of another State, or by Citizens or Subjects of any Foreign State.

Amendment 9.
Powers Reserved to the People (1791)

This amendment provides that the people's rights are not limited to those mentioned in the Constitution.

Amendment 10.
Powers Reserved to the States (1791)

This amendment protects the states and the people from an all-powerful federal government. It provides that the states or the people retain all powers except those denied them or those specifically granted to the federal government. This "reserved powers" provision is a check on the "necessary and proper" power of the federal government provided in the "elastic clause" in Article I, Section 8, Clause 18.

Amendment 11.
Suits Against States (1795)

This amendment provides that a lawsuit brought by a citizen of the United States or a foreign nation against a state must be tried in a state court, not in a federal court. This amendment was passed after the Supreme Court ruled that a federal court could try a lawsuit brought by citizens of South Carolina against a citizen of Georgia. This case, *Chisholm* v. *Georgia*, decided in 1793, was protested by many Americans, who insisted states would lose authority if they could be sued in federal courts.

Amendment 12.
Election of President and Vice President (1804)

This amendment changes the procedure for electing the president and vice president as outlined in Article II, Section 1, Clause 3.

To prevent the recurrence of the election of 1800 whereby a candidate running for vice president (Aaron Burr) could tie a candidate running for president (Thomas Jefferson) and thus force the election into the House of Representatives, the 12th Amendment specifies that the electors are to cast separate ballots for each office. The votes for each office are counted and listed separately. The results are signed, sealed, and sent to the president of the Senate. At a joint session of Congress, the votes are counted. The candidate who receives the most votes, providing it is a majority, is elected president. Other changes include: (1) a reduction from the five to three candidates receiving the most votes among whom the House is to choose if no candidate receives a majority of the electoral votes, and (2) provision for the Senate to choose the vice president from the two highest candidates if neither has received a majority of the electoral votes.

The 12th Amendment does place one restriction on electors. It prohibits electors from voting for two candidates (president and vice president) from their home state.

Amendment XII

The Electors shall meet in their respective States and vote by ballot for President and Vice-President, one of whom, at least, shall not be an inhabitant of the same State with themselves; they shall name in their ballots the person voted for as President, and in distinct ballots the person voted for as Vice-President, and they shall make distinct lists of all persons voted for as President, and of all persons voted for as Vice-President, and of the number of votes for each, which lists they shall sign and certify, and transmit sealed to the seat of the government of the United States, directed to the President of the Senate;—The President of the Senate shall, in the presence of the Senate and House of Representatives, open all the certificates and the votes shall then be counted;—The person having the greatest number of votes for President, shall be the President, if such number be a majority of the whole number of Electors appointed; and if no person have such majority, then from the persons having the highest numbers not exceeding three on the list of those voted for as President, the House of Representatives shall choose immediately, by ballot, the President. But in choosing the President, the votes shall be taken by states, the representation from each state having one vote; a quorum for this purpose shall consist of a member or members from two-thirds of the states, and a majority of all the states shall be necessary to a choice. And if the House of Representatives shall not choose a President whenever the right of choice shall devolve upon them, before the fourth day of March next following, then the Vice-President shall act as President, as in the case of the death or other constitutional disability of the President.—The person having the greatest number of votes as Vice-President, shall be the Vice-President, if such number be a majority of the whole number of Electors appointed, and if no person have a majority, then from the two highest numbers on the list, the Senate shall choose the Vice-President; a quorum for the purpose shall consist of two-thirds of the whole number of Senators, and a majority of the whole number shall be necessary to a choice. But no person constitutionally ineligible to the office of President shall be eligible to that of Vice-President of the United States.

Amendment XIII

Section 1

Neither slavery nor involuntary servitude, except as a punishment for crime whereof the party shall have been duly convicted, shall exist within the United States, or any place subject to their jurisdiction.

Section 2

Congress shall have power to enforce this article by appropriate legislation.

Amendment XIV

Section 1

All persons born or naturalized in the United States, and subject to the jurisdiction thereof, are citizens of the United States and of the State wherein they reside. No State shall make or enforce any law which shall abridge the privileges or immunities of citizens of the United States; nor shall any State deprive any person of life, liberty, or property, without due process of law, nor deny to any person within its jurisdiction the equal protection of the laws.

Amendment 13.
Abolition of Slavery (1865)

This amendment was the final act in ending slavery in the United States. It also prohibits the binding of a person to perform a personal service due to debt. In addition to imprisonment for crime, the Supreme Court has held that the draft is not a violation of the amendment.

This amendment is the first adopted to be divided into sections. It is also the first to contain specifically a provision granting Congress power to enforce it by appropriate legislation.

Amendment 14.
Rights of Citizens (1868)

The clauses of this amendment were intended (1) to penalize Southern states that refused to grant African Americans the vote, (2) to keep former Confederate leaders from serving in government, (3) to forbid payment of the Confederacy's debt by the federal government, and (4) to ensure payment of the war debts owed the federal government.

Section 1. Citizenship Defined By granting citizenship to all persons born in the United States, this amendment granted citizenship to former slaves. The amendment also guaranteed "due process of law." By the 1950s, Supreme Court rulings used the due process clause to protect civil liberties. The last part of Section 1 establishes the doctrine that all citizens are entitled to equal protection of the laws. In 1954 the Supreme Court ruled, in *Brown v. Board of Education of Topeka,* that segregation in public schools was unconstitutional because it denied equal protection.

Section 2. Representation in Congress
This section reduced the number of members a state had in the House of Representatives if it denied its citizens the right to vote. This section was not implemented, however. Later civil rights laws and the 24th Amendment guaranteed the vote to African Americans.

Section 3. Penalty for Engaging in Insurrection
The leaders of the Confederacy were barred from state or federal offices unless Congress agreed to revoke this ban. By the end of Reconstruction, all but a few Confederate leaders were allowed to return to public life.

Section 4. Public Debt
The public debt incurred by the federal government during the Civil War was valid and could not be questioned by the South. However, the debts of the Confederacy were declared to be illegal. And former slaveholders could not collect compensation for the loss of their slaves.

Section 2
Representatives shall be apportioned among the several States according to their respective numbers, counting the whole number of persons in each State, excluding Indians not taxed. But when the right to vote at any election for the choice of electors for President and Vice-President of the United States, Representatives in Congress, the Executive and Judicial officers of a State, or the members of the Legislature thereof, is denied to any of the male inhabitants of such State, being twenty-one years of age, and citizens of the United States, or in any way abridged, except for participation in rebellion, or other crime, the basis of representation therein shall be reduced in the proportion which the number of such male citizens shall bear to the whole number of male citizens twenty-one years of age in such State.

Section 3
No person shall be a Senator or Representative in Congress, or elector of President and Vice-President, or hold any office, civil or military, under the United States, or under any State, who, having previously taken an oath, as a member of Congress, or as an officer of the United States, or as a member of any State legislature, or as an executive or judicial officer of any State, to support the Constitution of the United States, shall have engaged in insurrection or rebellion against the same, or given aid or comfort to the enemies thereof. But Congress may by a vote of two-thirds of each House, remove such disability.

Section 4
The validity of the public debt of the United States incurred for payment of pensions and bounties for service, authorized by law, including debts in suppressing insurrections or rebellion, shall not be questioned. But neither the United States nor any State shall assume or pay any debt or obligation incurred in aid of insurrection or rebellion against the United

States, or any claim for the loss or emancipation of any slave; but all such debts, obligations and claims shall be held illegal and void.

Section 5

The Congress shall have power to enforce, by appropriate legislation, the provisions of this article.

Amendment XV

Section 1

The right of citizens of the United States to vote shall not be denied or abridged by the United States or by any State on account of race, color, or previous condition of servitude.

Section 2

The Congress shall have power to enforce this article by appropriate legislation.

Amendment XVI

The Congress shall have power to lay and collect taxes on incomes, from whatever source derived, without apportionment among several States, and without regard to any census or enumeration.

Amendment XVII

Section 1

The Senate of the United States shall be composed of two Senators from each State, elected by the people thereof, for six years; and each Senator shall have one vote. The electors in each state shall have the qualifications requisite for electors of the most numerous branch of the state legislatures.

Section 2

When vacancies happen in the representation of any State in the Senate, the executive authority of such State shall issue writs of election to fill such vacancies: Provided, that the legislature of any State may empower the executive thereof to make temporary appointments until the people fill the vacancies by election as the legislature may direct.

Section 5. Enforcement Congress was empowered to pass civil rights bills to guarantee the provisions of the amendment.

Amendment 15.
The Right to Vote (1870)

Section 1. Suffrage for All Citizens The 15th Amendment replaced Section 2 of the 14th Amendment in guaranteeing all citizens the right to vote; that is, the right to vote was not to be left to the states. During this prohibition, African Americans as well as other groups, including Hispanics and Asians, were often denied the right to vote by such means as poll taxes, literacy tests, and white primaries.

Section 2. Enforcement Congress was given power to enforce this amendment. During the 1950s and 1960s, it passed successively stronger laws to end racial discrimination in voting rights.

Amendment 16.
Income Tax (1913)

The origins of this amendment went back to 1895, when the Supreme Court declared a federal income tax unconstitutional. To overcome this Supreme Court decision, this amendment authorized an income tax that was levied on a direct basis.

Amendment 17.
Direct Election of Senators (1913)

Section 1. Method of Election The right to elect senators was given directly to the people of each state. It replaced Article I, Section 3, Clause 1, which empowered state legislatures to elect senators. This amendment was designed not only to make the choice of senators more democratic but also to cut down on corruption and to improve state government.

Section 2. Vacancies A state must order an election to fill a Senate vacancy. A state may empower its governor to appoint a person to fill a Senate seat if a vacancy occurs until an election can be held.

Section 3. Time in Effect This amendment was not to affect any Senate election or temporary appointment until it was in effect.

Amendment 18.
Prohibition of Alcoholic Beverages (1919)

This amendment prohibited the production, sale, or transportation of alcoholic beverages in the United States. This amendment was later repealed by the 21st Amendment.

Amendment 19.
Woman Suffrage (1920)

This amendment, extending the vote to all qualified women in federal and state elections, was a landmark victory for the woman suffrage movement, which had worked to achieve this goal for many years. The women's movement had earlier gained full voting rights for women in four Western states in the late nineteenth century.

Section 3
This amendment shall not be so construed as to affect the election or term of any Senator chosen before it becomes valid as part of the Constitution.

Amendment XVIII

Section 1
After one year from ratification of this article the manufacture, sale, or transportation of intoxicating liquors within, the importation thereof into, or the exportation thereof from the United States and all territory subject to the jurisdiction thereof for beverage purposes is hereby prohibited.

Section 2
The Congress and the several states shall have concurrent power to enforce this article by appropriate legislation.

Section 3
This article shall be inoperative unless it shall have been ratified as an amendment to the Constitution by the legislatures of the several States, as provided in the Constitution, within seven years from the date of the submission hereof to the states of the Congress.

Amendment XIX

Section 1
The right of citizens of the United States to vote shall not be denied or abridged by the United States or by any state on account of sex.

Section 2
Congress shall have power to enforce this article by appropriate legislation.

Amendment XX

Section 1

The terms of the President and Vice President shall end at noon on the 20th day of January, and the terms of the Senators and Representatives at noon on the 3rd day of January, of the years in which such terms would have ended if this article had not been ratified; and the terms of their successors shall then begin.

Section 2

The Congress shall assemble at least once in every year, and such meeting shall begin at noon on the 3rd day of January, unless they shall by law appoint a different day.

Section 3

If, at the time fixed for the beginning of the term of the President, the President elect shall have died, the Vice President elect shall become President. If a President shall not have been chosen before the time fixed for the beginning of his term, or if the President elect shall have failed to qualify, then the Vice President elect shall act as President until a President shall have qualified; and the Congress may by law provide for the case wherein neither a President elect nor a Vice President elect shall have qualified, declaring who shall then act as President, or the manner in which one who is to act shall be selected, and such person shall act accordingly until a President or Vice President shall have qualified.

Section 4

The Congress may by law provide for the case of the death of any of the persons from whom the House of Representatives may choose a President whenever the right of choice shall have devolved upon them, and for the case of the death of any of the persons from whom the Senate may choose a Vice President whenever the right of choice shall have devolved upon them.

Amendment 20.
"Lame-Duck" Amendment (1933)

Section 1. New Dates of Terms This amendment had two major purposes: (1) to shorten the time between the president's and vice president's election and inauguration, and (2) to end "lame-duck" sessions of Congress.

When the Constitution first went into effect, transportation and communication were slow and uncertain. It often took many months after the election in November for the president and vice president to travel to Washington, D.C., and prepare for their inauguration on March 4. This amendment ended this long wait for a new administration by fixing January 20 as Inauguration Day.

Section 2. Meeting Time of Congress "Lame-duck" sessions occurred every two years, after the November congressional election. That is, the Congress that held its session in December of an election year was not the newly elected Congress but the old Congress that had been elected two years earlier. This Congress continued to serve for several more months, usually until March of the next year. Often many of its members had failed to be reelected and were called "lame-ducks." The 20th Amendment abolished this lame-duck session, and provided that the new Congress hold its first session soon after the November election, on January 3.

Section 3. Succession of President and Vice President This amendment provides that if the president-elect dies before taking office, the vice president-elect becomes president. In the cases described, Congress will decide on a temporary president.

Section 4. Filling Presidential Vacancy If a presidential candidate dies while an election is being decided in the House, Congress may pass legislation to deal with the situation. Congress has similar power if this occurs when the Senate is deciding a vice-presidential election.

Section 5. Beginning the New Dates

Sections 1 and 2 affected the Congress elected in 1934 and President Roosevelt, elected in 1936.

Section 6. Time Limit on Ratification

The period for ratification by the states was limited to seven years.

Amendment 21.

Repeal of Prohibition Amendment (1933)

This amendment nullified the 18th Amendment. It is the only amendment ever passed to overturn an earlier amendment. It remained unlawful to transport alcoholic beverages into states that forbade their use. It is the only amendment ratified by special state conventions instead of state legislatures.

Amendment 22.

Limit on Presidential Terms (1951)

This amendment wrote into the Constitution a custom started by Washington, Jefferson, and Madison, whereby presidents limited themselves to two terms in office. Although both Ulysses S. Grant and Theodore Roosevelt sought third terms, the two-term precedent was not broken until Franklin D. Roosevelt was elected to a third term in 1940 and then a fourth term in 1944. The passage of the 22nd Amendment ensures that no president is to be considered indispensable. It

Section 5

Sections 1 and 2 shall take effect on the 15th day of October following the ratification of this article.

Section 6

This article shall be inoperative unless it shall have been ratified as an amendment to the Constitution by the legislatures of three-fourths of the several States within seven years from the date of its submission.

Amendment XXI

Section 1

The eighteenth article of amendment to the Constitution of the United States is hereby repealed.

Section 2

The transportation or importation into any State, Territory, or possession of the United States for delivery or use therein of intoxicating liquors, in violation of the laws thereof, is hereby prohibited.

Section 3

This article shall be inoperative unless it shall have been ratified as an amendment to the Constitution by conventions in the several States, as provided in the Constitution, within seven years from the date of the submission hereof to the States by the Congress.

Amendment XXII

Section 1

No person shall be elected to the office of the President more than twice, and no person who had held the office of President, or acted as President, for more than two years of a term to which some other person was elected President shall be elected to the office of the President more than once.

But this Article shall not apply to any person holding the office of President when this Article was proposed by the Congress, and shall not prevent any person who may be holding the office of President, or acting as President, during the term within which this Article becomes operative from holding the office of President or acting as President during the remainder of such term.

Section 2

This article shall be inoperative unless it shall have been ratified as an amendment to the Constitution by the legislatures of three-fourths of the several States within seven years from the date of its submission to the States by the Congress.

Amendment XXIII

Section 1

The District constituting the seat of Government of the United States shall appoint in such manner as the Congress may direct:

A number of electors of President and Vice President equal to the whole number of Senators and Representatives in Congress to which the District would be entitled if it were a State, but in no event more than the least populous State; they shall be in addition to those appointed by the States, but they shall be considered, for the purposes of the election of President and Vice President, to be electors appointed by a State; and they shall meet in the District and perform such duties as provided by the twelfth article of amendment.

Section 2

The Congress shall have power to enforce this article by appropriate legislation.

Amendment XXIV

Section 1

The right of citizens of the United States to vote in any primary or other election for President or Vice President, for electors for President or Vice President, or for Senator or Representative in Congress, shall not be denied or abridged by the United States or any State by reason of failure to pay any poll tax or other tax.

also provides that anyone who succeeds to the presidency and serves for more than two years of the term may not be elected more than one more time.

Amendment 23.
Presidential Electors for the District of Columbia (1961)

This amendment granted people living in the District of Columbia the right to vote in presidential elections. The District casts three electoral votes. The people of Washington, D.C., still are without representation in Congress.

Amendment 24.
Abolition of the Poll Tax (1964)

A "poll tax" was a fee that persons were required to pay in order to vote in a number of Southern states. This amendment ended poll taxes as a requirement to vote in any presidential or congressional election. In 1966 the Supreme Court voided poll taxes in state elections as well.

Amendment 25.
Presidential Disability and Succession (1967)

Section 1. Replacing the President The vice president becomes president if the president dies, resigns, or is removed from office.

Section 2. Replacing the Vice President The president is to appoint a new vice president in case of a vacancy in that office, with the approval of the Congress.

The 25th Amendment is unusually precise and explicit because it was intended to solve a serious constitutional problem. Sixteen times in American history, before passage of this amendment, the office of vice president was vacant, but fortunately in none of these cases did the president die or resign.

This amendment was used in 1973, when Vice President Spiro Agnew resigned from office after being charged with accepting bribes. President Richard Nixon then appointed Gerald R. Ford as vice president in accordance with the provisions of the 25th Amendment. A year later, President Nixon resigned during the Watergate scandal, and Ford became president. President Ford then had to fill the vice presidency, which he had left vacant upon assuming the presidency. He named Nelson A. Rockefeller as vice president. Thus both the presidency and vice presidency were held by men who had not been elected to their offices.

Section 3. Replacing the President With Consent If the president informs Congress, in writing, that he or she cannot carry out the duties of the office of president, the vice president becomes acting president.

Section 2
The Congress shall have power to enforce this article by appropriate legislation.

Amendment XXV

Section 1
In case of the removal of the President from office or his death or resignation, the Vice President shall become President.

Section 2
Whenever there is a vacancy in the office of the Vice President, the President shall nominate a Vice President who shall take the office upon confirmation by a majority vote of both houses of Congress.

Section 3
Whenever the President transmits to the President pro tempore of the Senate and the Speaker of the House of Representatives his written declaration that he is unable to discharge the powers and duties of his office, and until he transmits to them a written declaration to the contrary, such powers and duties shall be discharged by the Vice President as Acting President.

Section 4
Whenever the Vice President and a majority of either the principal officers of the executive departments or of such other body as Congress may by law provide, transmit to the President pro tempore of the Senate and the Speaker of the House of Representatives their written declaration that the President is unable to discharge the powers and duties of his office, the Vice President shall immediately assume the power and duties of the office of Acting President.

Thereafter, when the President transmits to the President pro tempore of the Senate and the Speaker of the House of Representatives his written declaration that no inability exists, he shall resume the powers and duties of his office unless the Vice President and a majority of either the principal officers of the executive departments or of such other body as Congress may by law provide, transmit within four days to the President pro tempore of the Senate and the Speaker of the House of Representatives their written declaration that the President is unable to discharge the powers and duties of his office. Thereupon Congress shall decide the issue, assembling within forty-eight hours for that purpose if not in session. If the Congress within twenty-one days after receipt of the latter written declaration, or, if Congress is not in session, within twenty-one days after Congress is required to assemble, determines by two-thirds vote of both houses that the President is unable to discharge the powers and duties of his office, the Vice President shall continue to discharge the same as Acting President; otherwise, the President shall resume the power and duties of his office.

Amendment XXVI

Section 1

The right of citizens of the United States, who are eighteen years of age or older, to vote shall not be denied or abridged by the United States or by any State on account of age.

Section 2

The Congress shall have power to enforce this article by appropriate legislation.

Amendment XXVII

No law, varying the compensation for the services of Senators and Representatives, shall take effect, until an election of Representatives shall have intervened.

Section 4. Replacing the President Without Consent If the president is unable to carry out the duties of the office but is unable or unwilling to so notify Congress, the cabinet and the vice president are to inform Congress of this fact. The vice president then becomes acting president. The procedure by which the president may regain the office if he or she recovers is also spelled out in this amendment.

Amendment 26.
Eighteen-Year-Old Vote (1971)

This amendment made 18-year-olds eligible to vote in all federal, state, and local elections. Until then, the minimum age had been 21 in most states.

Amendment 27.
Restraint on Congressional Salaries (1992)

Any increase in the salaries of members of Congress will take effect in the subsequent session of Congress.

The Universal Declaration of Human Rights

The Universal Declaration of Human Rights was written and adopted by the United Nations in 1948. It is a statement of basic human rights and standards for government that has been agreed upon by the international community. The declaration proclaims that all people have the right to liberty, education, political and religious freedom, and economic well-being. It also bans torture and says that all people have the right to participate in their country's governmental process.

Original Text

ARTICLE 1

All human beings are born free and equal in dignity and rights. They are endowed with reason and conscience and should act towards one another in a spirit of brotherhood.

ARTICLE 2

Everyone is entitled to all the rights and freedoms set forth in this Declaration, without distinction of any kind, such as race, colour, sex, language, religion, political or other opinion, national or social origin, property, birth or other status.

Furthermore, no distinction shall be made on the basis of the political, jurisdictional or international status of the country or territory to which a person belongs, whether it be independent, trust, non-self-governing or under any other limitation of sovereignty.

ARTICLE 3

Everyone has the right to life, liberty and security of person.

ARTICLE 4

No one shall be held in slavery or servitude; slavery and the slave trade shall be prohibited in all their forms.

Plain Language Version*

ARTICLE 1

When children are born, they are free and each should be treated in the same way. They have reason and conscience and should act towards one another in a friendly manner.

ARTICLE 2

Everyone can claim the following rights, despite

- a different sex
- a different skin colour
- speaking a different language
- thinking different things
- believing in another religion
- owning more or less
- being born in another social group
- coming from another country.

It also makes no difference whether the country you live in is independent or not.

ARTICLE 3

You have the right to live, and to live in freedom and safety.

ARTICLE 4

Nobody has the right to treat you as his or her slave and you should not make anyone your slave.

---

*   The plain language version is only given as a guide. This version is based in part on the translation of a text, prepared in 1978 for the World Association for the School as an Instrument of Peace, by a Research Group of the University of Geneva, under the responsibility of Prof. I Massarenu. In preparing the translation, the Group used a basic vocabulary of 2,500 words in use in the French-speaking part of Switzerland.

Original Text	Plain Language Version
## ARTICLE 5	## ARTICLE 5
No one shall be subjected to torture or to cruel, inhuman or degrading treatment or punishment.	Nobody has the right to torture you.
## ARTICLE 6	## ARTICLE 6
Everyone has the right to recognition everywhere as a person before the law.	You should be legally protected in the same way everywhere, and like everyone else.
## ARTICLE 7	## ARTICLE 7
All are equal before the law and are entitled without any discrimination to equal protection of the law. All are entitled to equal protection against any discrimination in violation of this Declaration and against any incitement to such discrimination.	The law is the same for everyone; it should be applied in the same way to all.
## ARTICLE 8	## ARTICLE 8
Everyone has the right to an effective remedy by the competent national tribunals for acts violating the fundamental rights granted him by the constitution or by law.	You should be able to ask for legal help when the rights your country grants you are not respected.
## ARTICLE 9	## ARTICLE 9
No one shall be subjected to arbitrary arrest, detention or exile.	Nobody has the right to put you in prison, to keep you there, or to send you away from your country unjustly, or without a good cause.
## ARTICLE 10	## ARTICLE 10
Everyone is entitled in full equality to a fair and public hearing by an independent and impartial tribunal, in the determination of his rights and obligations and of any criminal charge against him.	If you must go on trial this should be done in public. The people who try you should not let themselves be influenced by others.
## ARTICLE 11	## ARTICLE 11
1. Everyone charged with a penal offence has the right to be presumed innocent until proved guilty according to law in a public trial at which he has had all the guarantees necessary for his defence. 2. No one shall be held guilty of any penal offence on account of any act or omission which did not constitute a penal offence, under national or international law, at the time when it was committed. Nor shall a heavier penalty be imposed than the one that was applicable at the time the penal offence was committed.	You should be considered innocent until it can be proved that you are guilty. If you are accused of a crime, you should always have the right to defend yourself. Nobody has the right to condemn you and punish you for something you have not done.

Original Text	Plain Language Version

ARTICLE 12

No one shall be subjected to arbitrary interference with his privacy, family, home or correspondence, nor to attacks upon his honour and reputation. Everyone has the right to the protection of the law against such interference or attacks.

ARTICLE 13

1. Everyone has the right to freedom of movement and residence within the borders of each State.
2. Everyone has the right to leave any country including his own, and to return to his country.

ARTICLE 14

1. Everyone has the right to seek and enjoy in other countries asylum from persecution.
2. This right may not be invoked in the case of prosecutions genuinely arising from non-political crimes or from acts contrary to the purposes and principles of the United Nations.

ARTICLE 15

1. Everyone has the right to a nationality.
2. No one shall be arbitrarily deprived of his nationality nor denied the right to change his nationality.

ARTICLE 16

1. Men and women of full age, without any limitation due to race, nationality or religion, have the right to marry and to found a family. They are entitled to equal rights as to marriage, during marriage and at its dissolution.
2. Marriage shall be entered into only with the free and full consent of the intending spouses.
3. The family is the natural and fundamental group unit of society and is entitled to protection by society and the State.

ARTICLE 17

1. Everyone has the right to own property alone as well as in association with others.
2. No one shall be arbitrarily deprived of his property.

ARTICLE 12

You have the right to ask to be protected if someone tries to harm your good name, enter your house, open your letters, or bother you or your family without a good reason.

ARTICLE 13

You have the right to come and go as you wish within your country. You have the right to leave your country to go to another one; and you should be able to return to your country if you want.

ARTICLE 14

If someone hurts you, you have the right to go to another country and ask it to protect you.

You lose this right if you have killed someone and if you, yourself, do not respect what is written here.

ARTICLE 15

You have the right to belong to a country and nobody can prevent you, without a good reason, from belonging to another country if you wish.

ARTICLE 16

As soon as a person is legally entitled, he or she has the right to marry and have a family. In doing this, neither the colour of your skin, the country you come from nor your religion should be impediments. Men and women have the same rights when they are married and also when they are separated.

Nobody should force a person to marry.

The government of your country should protect your family and its members.

ARTICLE 17

You have the right to own things and nobody has the right to take these from you without a good reason.

Original Text

ARTICLE 18

Everyone has the right to freedom of thought, conscience and religion; this right includes freedom to change his religion or belief, and freedom, either alone or in community with others and in public or private, to manifest his religion or belief in teaching, practice, worship and observance.

ARTICLE 19

Everyone has the right to freedom of opinion and expression; this right includes freedom to hold opinions without interference and to seek, receive and impart information and ideas through any media and regardless of frontiers.

ARTICLE 20

1. Everyone has the right to freedom of peaceful assembly and association.
2. No one may be compelled to belong to an association.

ARTICLE 21

1. Everyone has the right to take part in the government of his country, directly or through freely chosen representatives.
2. Everyone has the right of equal access to public service in his country.
3. The will of the people shall be the basis of the authority of government; this will shall be expressed in periodic and genuine elections which shall be by universal and equal suffrage and shall be held by secret vote or by equivalent free voting procedures.

ARTICLE 22

Everyone, as a member of society, has the right to social security and is entitled to realization, through national effort and international co-operation and in accordance with the organization and resources of each State, of the economic, social and cultural rights indispensable for his dignity and the free development of his personality.

Plain Language Version

ARTICLE 18

You have the right to profess your religion freely, to change it, and to practice it either on your own or with other people.

ARTICLE 19

You have the right to think what you want, to say what you like, and nobody should forbid you from doing so.
You should be able to share your ideas also–with people from any other country.

ARTICLE 20

You have the right to organize peaceful meetings or to take part in meetings in a peaceful way. It is wrong to force someone to belong to a group.

ARTICLE 21

You have the right to take part in your country's political affairs either by belonging to the government yourself or by choosing politicians who have the same ideas as you.
Governments should be voted for regularly and voting should be secret. You should get a vote and all votes should be equal. You also have the same right to join the public service as anyone else.

ARTICLE 22

The society in which you live should help you to develop and to make the most of all the advantages (culture, work, social and welfare) which are offered to you and to all the men and women in your country.

Original Text

ARTICLE 23

1. Everyone has the right to work, to free choice of employment, to just and favourable conditions of work and to protection against unemployment.
2. Everyone, without any discrimination, has the right to equal pay for equal work.
3. Everyone who works has the right to just and favourable remuneration ensuring for himself and his family an existence worthy of human dignity, and supplemented, if necessary, by other means of social protection.
4. Everyone has the right to form and to join trade unions for the protection of his interests.

ARTICLE 24

Everyone has the right to rest and leisure, including reasonable limitation of working hours and periodic holidays with pay.

ARTICLE 25

1. Everyone has the right to a standard of living adequate for the health and well-being of himself and of his family, including food, clothing, housing and medical care and necessary social services, and the right to security in the event of unemployment, sickness, disability, widowhood, old age or other lack of livelihood in circumstances beyond his control.
2. Motherhood and childhood are entitled to special care and assistance. All children, whether born in or out of wedlock, shall enjoy the same social protection.

ARTICLE 26

1. Everyone has the right to education. Education shall be free, at least in the elementary and fundamental stages. Elementary education shall be compulsory. Technical and professional education shall be made generally available and higher education shall be equally accessible to all on the basis of merit.
2. Education shall be directed to the full development of the human personality and to the strengthening of respect for human rights

Plain Language Version

ARTICLE 23

You have the right to work, to be free to choose your work, to get a salary which allows you to live and support your family. If a man and a woman do the same work, they should get the same pay. All people who work have the right to join together to defend their interests.

ARTICLE 24

Each work day should not be too long, since everyone has the right to rest and should be able to take regular paid holidays.

ARTICLE 25

You have the right to have whatever you need so that you and your family do not fall ill; go hungry; have clothes and a house; and are helped if you are out of work, if you are ill, if you are old, if your wife or husband is dead, or if you do not earn a living for any other reason you cannot help. The mother who is going to have a baby, and her baby should get special help. All children have the same rights, whether or not the mother is married.

ARTICLE 26

You have the right to go to school and everyone should go to school. Primary schooling should be free. You should be able to learn a profession or continue your studies as far as you wish. At school, you should be able to develop all your talents and you should be taught to get on with others, whatever their race, religion or the country they

Original Text

and fundamental freedoms. It shall promote understanding, tolerance and friendship among all nations, racial or religious groups, and shall further the activities of the United Nations for the maintenance of peace.

3. Parents have a prior right to choose the kind of education that shall be given to their children.

ARTICLE 27

1. Everyone has the right freely to participate in the cultural life of the community, to enjoy the arts and to share in scientific advancement and its benefits.
2. Everyone has the right to the protection of the moral and material interests resulting from any scientific, literary or artistic production of which he is the author.

ARTICLE 28

Everyone is entitled to a social and international order in which the rights and freedoms set forth in this Declaration can be fully realized.

Plain Language Version

come from. Your parents have the right to choose how and what you will be taught at school.

ARTICLE 27

You have the right to share in your community's arts and sciences, and any good they do. Your works as an artist, a writer, or a scientist should be protected, and you should be able to benefit from them.

ARTICLE 28

So that your rights will be respected, there must be an "order" which can protect them. This "order" should be local and worldwide.

Original Text

ARTICLE 29

1. Everyone has duties to the community in which alone the free and full development of his personality is possible.
2. In the exercise of his rights and freedoms, everyone shall be subject only to such limitation as are determined by law solely for the purpose of securing due recognition and respect for the rights and freedoms of others and of meeting the just requirements of morality, public order and the general welfare in a democratic society.
3. These rights and freedoms may in no case be exercised contrary to the purposes and principles of the United Nations.

ARTICLE 30

Nothing in this Declaration may be interpreted as implying for any State, group or person any right to engage in any activity or to perform any act aimed at the destruction of any of the rights and freedoms set forth herein.

Plain Language Version

ARTICLE 29

You have duties towards the community within which your personality can only fully develop. The law should guarantee human rights. It should allow everyone to respect others and to be respected.

ARTICLE 30

In all parts of the world, no society, no human being, should take it upon her or himself to act in such a way as to destroy the rights which you have just been reading about.

Major Federal Civil Rights Laws

In the 1950s, a tide of protest began to rise in the United States against deeply rooted attitudes of racism and discrimination. The campaign for equality grew and gained momentum in the 1960s. For example, women and minority groups began to challenge predominant ethnic, racial, and gender stereotypes and worked to overturn laws that restricted their rights and freedoms. At the end of the twentieth century, an important civil rights law—the *Americans with Disabilities Act (ADA)*—was passed to protect persons with disabilities. The civil rights movement continues into the twenty-first century meeting both old and new challenges.

EQUAL PAY ACT OF 1963
(Amended in 1972)

- Requires equal pay for equal work, regardless of sex.
- Requires that equal work be determined by equal skill, effort, and responsibility under similar working conditions at the same place of employment.
- Requires equal pay when equal work is involved even if different job titles are assigned.

(Enforced by the Equal Employment Opportunity Commission and private lawsuit.)

CIVIL RIGHTS ACT OF 1964
(Amended in 1972, 1978, and 1991)

- Prohibits discrimination based on race, color, religion, or national origin in public accommodations (for example, hotels, restaurants, movie theaters, sports arenas). It does not apply to private clubs closed to the public.
- Prohibits discrimination in employment based on race, color, sex, religion, or national origin by businesses with more than 15 employees or by labor unions. (This section is commonly referred to as *Title VII.*)
- Prohibits discrimination based on race, color, religion, sex, or national origin by state and local governments and public educational institutions.
- Prohibits discrimination based on race, color, national origin, or sex in any program or activity receiving federal financial assistance. It authorizes ending federal funding when this ban is violated.
- Permits employment discrimination based on religion, sex, or national origin if it is a necessary qualification for the job.

(Enforced by the U.S. Equal Employment Opportunity Commission and private lawsuit.)

VOTING RIGHTS ACT OF 1965
(Amended in 1970, 1975, and 1982)

- Bans literacy and "good character" tests as requirements for voting.
- Requires bilingual election materials for most voters who don't speak English.
- Reduces residency requirements for voting in federal elections.
- Establishes criminal penalties for harassing voters or interfering with voting rights.

(Enforced by the U.S. Department of Justice and private lawsuit.)

AGE DISCRIMINATION IN EMPLOYMENT ACT OF 1967
(Amended in 1974, 1978, 1986, and 1990)

- Prohibits arbitrary age discrimination in employment by employers of 20 or more persons, employment agencies, labor organizations with 25 or more members, and federal, state, and local governments.
- Protects people aged 40 and older.
- Permits discrimination where age is a necessary qualification for the job.

(Enforced by the U.S. Equal Employment Opportunity Commission, a similar state agency, and private lawsuit.)

CIVIL RIGHTS ACT OF 1968
(Amended in 1988 and 1992)

- Prohibits discrimination based on race, color, religion or national origin in the sale, rental, or financing of most housing.

(Enforced by the U.S. Department of Justice, the U.S. Department of Housing and Urban Development, and private lawsuit.)

TITLE IX OF THE EDUCATION ACT AMENDMENTS OF 1972

- Prohibits discrimination against students and others on the basis of sex by educational institutions receiving federal funding.

- Prohibits sex discrimination in a number of areas, including student and faculty recruitment, admissions, financial aid, facilities, and employment.

- Requires that school athletic programs effectively accommodate the interest and abilities of members of both sexes; equal total expenditure on men's and women's sports is not required.

- Does not cover sex stereotyping in textbooks and other curricular materials.

(Enforced by the U.S. Department of Education's Office of Civil Rights.)

REHABILITATION ACT OF 1973
(Amended in 1998)

- Prohibits government employers and private employers receiving government assistance from discriminating on the basis of physical handicap.

- Requires companies that do business with the government to undertake affirmative action to provide jobs for the handicapped.

- Prohibits activities and programs receiving federal funds from excluding otherwise qualified handicapped people from participation or benefits.

(Enforced by lawsuit in federal court and, in some cases, state or local human rights or fair employment practices commissions.)

AMERICANS WITH DISABILITIES ACT OF 1990 (ADA)

- Prohibits discrimination against individuals with disabilities.

- Prohibits discrimination in employment. This covers such things as the application process, testing, hiring, evaluation, assignments, training, promotion, termination, compensation, leave, and benefits. (*Title I*)

- Prohibits discrimination in public services. This title covers state and local government

services and all services, programs, and activities provided or made available by these governments. This includes entities such as state metro rail systems and AMTRAK. (*Title II*)

- Prohibits discrimination in public accommodations and services operated by private entities. This includes entities such as private taxi companies, schools, restaurants, hotels, and grocery stores. (*Title III*)

- Prohibits discrimination in telecommunications. This covers relay services for hearing-impaired and speech-impaired individuals, and closed-captioning of public service announcements. (*Title IV*)

- Prohibits discrimination in such activities as construction, prohibits retaliation and coercion, and regulates the Architectural and Transportation Barriers Compliance Board. (*Title V*)

(Enforced by various methods including administrative complaint to a specific federal agency or private lawsuit.)

CIVIL RIGHTS ACT OF 1991

- Addresses discrimination in the workplace.

- Addresses discrimination at any point in the employment relationship, including private and governmental discrimination.

- Allows individuals who prove intentional employment discrimination on the basis of sex, disability, or religion to collect compensatory and punitive damages.

- Creates a limit on damages.

(Enforced by private lawsuit.)

INDIVIDUALS WITH DISABILITIES EDUCATION ACT OF 1991 (IDEA)
(Amended in 1997)

- Guarantees a "free appropriate public education" for all children with disabilities.

- Entitles each child with a disability to free special services, including medical services necessary to secure an appropriate education.

- Requires schools to develop an "individualized education program" (IEP) for each child with a disability.

- Requires parental approval of "individualized education programs" (IEP) and all changes in plan or placement.

- Includes learning disabilities, behavioral disorders, and mental and physical impairments within the definition of "disability."

(Enforced by private lawsuit and state and federal departments of education.)

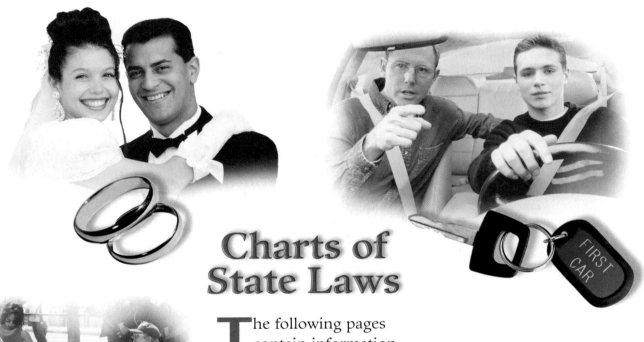

Charts of State Laws

The following pages contain information on state laws. The data is organized in tables according to topic, with each table consisting of the law as it applies in each of the 50 states. Online updates of this material can be found at streetlaw.glencoe.com.

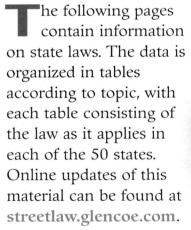

VOTER REGISTRATION INFORMATION

State or other jurisdiction	Closing date for registration before general election	Persons eligible for absentee registration	Cut-off for receiving absentee ballots	Residency requirements
Alabama	10	M/O	Close of polls	S, C (m)
Alaska	30	A	10 days after election	…
Arizona	29	A	7 p.m. Election day	S, C 29
Arkansas	30	A	7:30 p.m. Election day	(n)
California	15	A	8 p.m. Election day	S
Colorado	29	A	7 p.m. Election day	S, 30
Connecticut	14	A	8 p.m. Election day	S, T
Delaware	20	A	12 p.m. day before election	S (o)
Florida	29	A	7 p.m. Election day	S, C
Georgia	(b)	A	Close of polls	S, C
Hawaii	30	A	Close of polls	S
Idaho	25	A	8 p.m. Election day	S, C, 30
Illinois	28	M/O	Close of polls	S, P, 30
Indiana	29	C, D, E, M/O, O, P, T	Close of polls	S, P, 30
Iowa	10 (c)	A	Close of polls	S
Kansas	15	A	Close of polls	S
Kentucky	29	A	Close of polls	S, C, 28
Louisiana	30	A	12 a.m. day before election	S
Maine	Election day	A	10 days after election	S, M
Maryland	21	A	Friday after election	S, C
Massachusetts	20	A	10 days after election	S
Michigan	30	A	8 p.m. Election day	S, T, 30 (p)
Minnesota	Election day (d)	A	Election day	S, 20
Mississippi	30	A	5 p.m. day before election	S, C, 30
Missouri	28	A	Close of polls	S
Montana	30	A	Close of polls	S, C, 30
Nebraska	(f)	A	10 a.m. 2 days after election	S
Nevada	(k)	M/O	Close of polls	S, C, 30; P, 10 (t)
New Hampshire	Election day (d)	B, D, E, R, S, T	5 p.m. day before election	S (w)
New Jersey	29	A	8 p.m. Election day	S, C, 30 (q)
New Mexico	28	T	7 p.m. Election day	S
New York	25	A	Postmarked before election	S, C, 30 (r)
North Carolina	25	A	5 p.m. day before election	S, C, 30
North Dakota	(e)	(e)	2 days before election	(e)
Ohio	30	A	Close of polls	S, 30
Oklahoma	25	A	7 p.m. Election day	S
Oregon	21	A	8 p.m. Election day	S
Pennsylvania	30	B, D, M/O, O, P, R, S, T	5 p.m. Friday before election	S, P, 30
Rhode Island	30	D	9 p.m. Election day	S, 30
South Carolina	30	B, C, D, S (i)	Close of polls	S (v)
South Dakota	15	A	Close of polls	S
Tennessee	30	A	Close of polls	S
Texas	30	A	Close of polls	S, C
Utah	20	(g)	12 p.m. 1 day after election	S, 30
Vermont	(l)	(h)	Close of polls	S
Virginia	29	(j)	Close of polls	S, P
Washington	15 (c)	M/O	10 days after election	S, C, P, 30
West Virginia	20	A	Close of polls	S
Wisconsin	Election day (c) (u)	A	Close of polls	S, 10
Wyoming	Election day (d)	A	7 p.m. Election day	S (s)
District of Columbia	30	A	10 days after election	D, 30
American Samoa	30	A	N.A.	N.A.
Guam	10	A	N.A.	N.A.
Puerto Rico	50	A	N.A.	N.A.
U.S. Virgin Islands	30	M/O	N.A.	N.A.

Source: Federal Election Commission, http://www.fec.gov/ December 2002.

Key:
N.A. – Information not available.
Column 4: S–State, C–County, D–District, M–Municipality, P–Precinct, T–Town. Numbers represent the number of days before an election for which one must be a resident.

Note: Previous editions of this chart contained a column for "Automatic cancellation of registration for failure to vote for ____ years". However, the National Voter Registration Act requires a confirmation notice prior to any cancellation and thus effectively bans any automatic cancellation of voter registration.

(a) In this column: A–All of these; B–Absent on business; C–Senior citizen; D–Disabled persons; E–Not absent, but prevented by employment from registering; M/O–No absentee registration except military and overseas citizens as required by federal law; O–Out of state; P–Out of precinct (or municipality in PA); R–Absent for religious reasons; S–Students; T–Temporarily out of jurisdiction.

Source: The Book of the States, 2003.

(b) The 5th Monday before a general primary, general election, or presidential preference primary; the 5th day after the date of the call for all other special primaries and special elections.
(c) By mail: Iowa 15 days; Washington 30 days; Wisconsin 2nd Wednesday preceding election.
(d) Minnesota–delivered 21 days before an election or election-day registration at polling precincts; Wyoming–delivered 30 days before or election-day registration at polling precincts; New Hampshire–received by city or town clerk 10 days before election or election-day registration at precincts.
(e) No voter registration.
(f) Received by the 2nd Friday before election or postmarked by the 3rd Friday before the election.
(g) There are several criteria including religious reasons, disabled, etc., or if the voter otherwise expects to be absent from the precinct on Election day.
(h) Anyone unable to register in person.
(i) In South Carolina, all the following are eligible for absentee registration in addition to those categories already listed: electors with a death in the family within 3 days prior to the election; overseas military, Red

Cross, U.S.O. government employees, and their dependents and spouses residing with them; persons on vacation; persons admitted to the hospital as emergency patients 4 days prior to the election; persons confined to jail or pre-trial facility pending disposition or arrest/trial; and persons attending sick/disabled persons.
(j) In Virginia, the following temporarily out of jurisdiction persons are eligible for absentee registration: (1) uniformed services voters on active duty, merchant marine, and persons temporarily residing overseas by virtue of employment (and spouse/dependents of these persons residing with them), who are not normally absent from their locality, or have been absent and returned to reside within 28 days prior to an election, may register in person up to and including the day of the election; (2) members of uniformed services discharged from active duty during 60 days preceding election (and spouse/dependents) may register, if otherwise qualified, in person up to and including the day before the election.
(k) By 9 p.m. on the 5th Saturday preceding any primary or general election.
(l) Postmarked, submitted, or accepted by noon on the 2nd

Saturday before an election.
(m) At the time of registration.
(n) Must live in Arkansas at the address in Box 2 of your voter application.
(o) Must be a permanent state resident.
(p) Must be resident of the town or city at least 30 days before election day.
(q) Must be a resident of the state or county at your address for 30 days before election.
(r) Must be a resident of the county or the City of New York at least 30 days before election.
(s) Must be "an actual and physically bona fide resident."
(t) Must have continuously resided in the state and county at least 30 days and in precinct at least 10 days before election. Must claim no other place as legal residence.
(u) Registration may be completed in the local voter registration office 1 day before the election.
(v) Must claim the address on the application as your only legal place of residence.
(w) Must have a permanent established domicile in the state.
(x) Only if assisted by another party.
(y) If unable to sign.

CHARTS OF STATE LAWS 613

MOTOR VEHICLE LAWS

State or other jurisdiction	Plates transfer to new owner	Minimum age for driver's license (a) (b)			Must be child restraint if under ____ yrs./lbs. (c)	Seat belt law violations
		Unrestricted	Intermediate	Learner's		
Alabama	★(d)	16	...	15	4 yrs.	P
Alaska	★(e)	16	...	14	4 yrs.	S
Arizona	★	16	...	15 + 7 mo.	5 yrs.	S
Arkansas	...	18	16	14	6 yrs. & 60 lbs.	S
California	★(e)	17	16	15	6 yrs. or 60 lbs.	P
Colorado........................	...	17	16	15	(f)	S
Connecticut	...	16 + 6 mo.	...	16	4 yrs. & 40 lbs.	P
Delaware	★	16 + 10 mo.	16 + 4 mo.	15 + 10 mo.	7 yrs. & 60 lbs. (g)	S
Florida	...	18	16	15	3 yrs.	S
Georgia	...	18	16	15	4 yrs.	P
Hawaii	★	16	...	15	4 yrs.	P
Idaho	...	16	15	14 + 6 mo.	4 yrs. & 40 lbs.	S
Illinois	...	18	16	15	4 yrs.	S
Indiana..........................	...	18	15 + 2 mo.	15	4 yrs.	P
Iowa	...	17	16	14	3 yrs.	P
Kansas	...	16	15	14	4 yrs.	S
Kentucky	★	16 + 6 mo.	...	16	40 in.	S
Louisiana	...	17	16	15	3 yrs.	P
Maine	...	16 + 3 mo.	15 + 3 mo.	15	40 lbs. (h)	S
Maryland	...	17 + 7 mo.	16 + 1 mo.	15 + 9 mo.	6 yrs. or 40 lbs.	P
Massachusetts	...	18	16 + 6 mo.	16	5 yrs. & 40 lbs.	S
Michigan	...	17	16	14 + 9 mo.	4 yrs.	P
Minnesota	★(e)	18 (j)	16	15	4 yrs.	S
Mississippi	...	16	15 + 6 mo.	15	4 yrs.	S
Missouri	...	18	16	15	4 yrs.	S
Montana	...	15	...	15	2 yrs.	S
Nebraska	...	17	15 + 11 mo.	15	6 yrs.	S
Nevada	...	16	15 + 9 mo.	15 + 6 mo.	5 yrs. & 40 lbs.	S
New Hampshire	...	18	15 + 6 mo.	...	4 yrs.	(k)
New Jersey	...	18	16 + 6 mo.	16	(l)	P
New Mexico....................	...	16 + 6 mo.	15 + 6 mo.	15	(m)	P
New York.......................	...	18	16	16	4 yrs.	P
North Carolina	...	16 + 6 mo.	16	15	5 yrs. & 40 lbs. (n)	P
North Dakota	...	16	...	14	4 yrs.	S
Ohio	...	17	16	15 + 6 mo.	4 yrs. & 40 lbs.	S
Oklahoma......................	★	16	...	15 + 6 mo.	4 yrs. & 60 lbs.	P
Oregon	...	17	16	15	4 yrs. & 40 lbs. (o)	P
Pennsylvania	...	17	16 + 6 mo.	16	4 yrs.	S
Rhode Island	...	17 + 6 mo.	16 + 6 mo.	16	(p)	S
South Carolina	...	16 + 3 mo.	15 + 3 mo.	15	(q)	S
South Dakota	★(r)	16	14 + 6 mo.	14	5 yrs. & 40 lbs.	S
Tennessee......................	...	17	16	15	(s)	S
Texas	★	16 + 6 mo.	16	15	4 yrs. or 36 in.	P
Utah..............................	...	17	16	15 + 9 mo.	5 yrs.	S
Vermont	...	18	16	15	5 yrs.	S
Virginia	...	18	16 + 3 mo.	15 + 6 mo.	6 yrs.	S
Washington	★(d)	18	16	15 + 6 mo.	(t)	P
West Virginia	...	17	16	15	3 yrs.	S
Wisconsin	...	16 + 10 mo.	16	15 + 6 mo.	4 yrs.	S
Wyoming	...	16	...	15	5 yrs. & 40 lbs.	S
District of Columbia	...	21	16 + 6 mo.	16	8 yrs.	P
American Samoa.............	★	16	...	16	N.A.	P
Guam............................	...	16	...	15	2 yrs.	N.A.
Puerto Rico	★	18	...	16	4 yrs.	N.A.
U.S. Virgin Islands	★	18	...	16	5 yrs.	N.A.

See source, key, and footnotes on next page.

Source: American Automobile Association, *Digest of Motor Laws* (2003).

Key:

★—Provision.

…—No provision.

N.A.—Not Available.

P—Primary offense.

S—Secondary offense.

(a) Some states reduce the minimum age requirement if applicants meet certain criteria (e.g., they have completed a driver education course or financial hardship). Generally, this table lists the minimum age requirements without such exceptions.

(b) New drivers or permit holders are typically required to have a guardian or parental consent to get their license or permit. They must also be required to be enrolled in or have completed a driver education course. When they drive, they may be required to be accompanied by a licensed operator or adult over 21. Every state except for Alabama, Hawaii, Montana and Wyoming has a graduated driver's license system. A graduated system generally allows drivers to receive an intermediate license before receiving an unrestricted license. Intermediate licenses usually restrict driving between certain hours (e.g. 11 p.m.–6 a.m.) and carrying a certain number of passengers.

(c) All child restraint laws are primary enforcement. Every state except Connecticut, Kansas, Missouri, Nebraska, Oklahoma, Pennsylvania and Tennessee, indicates in their law that a child must be properly secured/restrained, which means that the seat must be used in accordance with manufacturer's instructions.

(d) Specialty plates apply.

(e) Specialty plates do not remain with the car upon transfer.

(f) Under one year and 20 pounds in rear-facing seat; one until four and 20–40 pounds in forward-facing seat; four through five years and less than 55 inches in a booster seat (The booster seat provision for four through five year olds in Colorado is secondary. The law is effective August 1, 2003.)

(g) No child who is 65 inches or less in height or is under 12 years of age shall occupy the front passenger seat of any vehicle equipped with a passenger-side airbag that has not been deliberately rendered inoperable.

(h) If 40–80 pounds and under eight, must be in a safety system that elevates the child so the seat belt fits properly. Children under 12 and 100 pounds must sit in rear seat if possible.

(i) In Maryland, vehicles registered out-of-state are required to restrain children under the age of four years or 40 pounds or less in a child restraint system. The law is effective October 1, 2003.

(j) Can be under 18 if driver has held an intermediate license for at least 12 consecutive months with no convictions for alcohol/controlled substance violations or crash-related moving violations, and with not more than one conviction for a moving violation that is not crash-related.

(k) Violation of the seat belt law is a secondary offense for passengers 12–18 and a primary offense for children under 12.

(l) Under eight years or under 80 pounds in a child seat or booster seat in rear seat of vehicle.

(m) If under one year, must be in rear-facing seat in rear seat if available; one to four years or less than 40 pounds.

(n) Must be restrained in a child safety seat in the rear seat if the vehicle has a passenger airbag, unless the child restraint system is designed for use with airbags.

(o) Four to six years or 40–60 pounds.

(p) Under seven years, under 54 inches, under 80 pounds must sit in rear seat.

(q) Under 20 pounds and one year in a rear-facing seat; one to five years and 20–40 pounds in a forward-facing seat; up to six and 40–60 pounds booster seat with lap/shoulder belt.

(r) In South Dakota, plates stay with vehicle unless organizational license plates obtained.

(s) Under four years; four to eight years and less than 40 pounds.

(t) Under 20 pounds or one year rear-facing safety seat; one to four years or 20–40 pounds in forward-facing child seat; four to five years or 40–60 pounds in booster seat.

MARRIAGE LAWS

| | Age with parental consent | | Age without consent | | Medical exam | | Marriage license | |
State	Male	Female	Male	Female	Maximum period between exam & license	Scope of exam	Waiting period before license	Duration of license validity (expiration)
Alabama*	14 a, b	14 a, b	18	18	---	---	---	30 days
Alaska	16 c	16 c	18	18	---	---	3 days, d	3 months
Arizona	16 c, z	16 c, z	18	18	---	---	---	1 year
Arkansas	17 c, e	16 c, e	18	18	---	---	f	---
California	b, g	b, g	18	18	30 days, d, h	---	---	90 days
Colorado*	16 c	16 c	18	18	---	---	---	30 days
Connecticut	16 c, z	16 c, z	18	18	---	i	4 days, d	65 days
Delaware	18 e	16 e	18	18	---	---	24 hours, j	30 days
Florida	16 a, e	16 a, e	18	18	---	---	---	60 days
Georgia^gg	16 e, k	16 e, k	18	18	---	i	3 days, l	30 days
Hawaii	15 k	15 k	18	18	---	---	---	30 days
Idaho^gg	16 c	16 c	18	18	---	m, n	---	---
Illinois	16 o	16 o	18	18	---	p	1 day	60 days
Indiana	17 e	17 e	18	18	---	q	---	60 days
Iowa*	16 k	16 k	18	18	---	---	3 days	20 days
Kansas*	14 k	12 k	18	18	---	---	3 days, d	6 months
Kentucky	18 k	18 k	18	18	---	---	---	30 days
Louisiana	18 c	18 c	18	18	10 days	---	---	---
Maine	16 c	16 c	18	18	---	---	3 days, d, f	90 days
Maryland	16 e, r	16 e, r	18	18	---	---	48 hours	6 months
Massachusetts	14 k	12 k	18	18	3–60 days	---	3 days, f	60 days
Michigan	16	16	18	18	---	---	3 days, d	33 days
Minnesota	16 k	16 k	18	18	---	---	5 days, d	6 months
Mississippi	g, k	g, k	17	15	30 days	t	3 days, d	---
Missouri	15 u	15 u	18	18	---	---	---	30 days
Montana*	16 k	16 k	18	18	---	t	---	180 days
Nebraska	17	17	19	19	---	i	---	1 year
Nevada	16	16	18	18	---	---	---	1 year
New Hampshire	14	13	18	18	---	b	3 days, d, f	90 days
New Jersey	16 c, e	16 c, e	18	18	---	---	72 hours, d	30 days
New Mexico	16 e, u	16 e, u	18	18	30 days	t	---	---
New York	16 v	16 v	18	18	---	w	24 hours	60 days
North Carolina	16 e	16 e	18	18	---	---	---	---
North Dakota	16	16	18	18	---	---	---	60 days
Ohio	18 k	16 c, e	18	18	---	---	5 days, d, x	60 days
Oklahoma*	16 c, e	16 c, e	18	18	30 days, d	t	y	30 days
Oregon	17 z	17 z	18	18	---	---	3 days, d	60 days
Pennsylvania*	16 u	16 u	18	18	30 days	t	3 days, d	60 days
Rhode Island*	18 u	16 u	18	18	---	aa	---	3 months
South Carolina*	16e	14 e	18	18	---	---	1 day	---
South Dakota	16 e	16 e	18	18	---	---	---	20 days
Tennessee	16 u	16 u	18	18	---	---	3 days, d, bb	30 days
Texas*	14 k, v	14 k, v	18	18	---	---	cc	30 days
Utah*	14 a	14 a	18 dd	18 dd	---	---	---	30 days
Vermont	16 k	16 k	18	18	30 days, d	t	1 day, d	---
Virginia	16 a, e	16 a, e	18	18	---	ee	---	60 days
Washington	17 u	17 u	18	18	---	ff	3 days	60 days
West Virginia	18 e	18 e	18	18	---	t	d	---
Wisconsin	16	16	18	18	---	n	5 days, d	30 days
Wyoming	16 u	16 u	18	18	---	i	---	---
Dist. of Columbia*	16 a	16 a	18	18	30 days	t	3 days, d	---
Puerto Rico	18 c, e, u	18 c, e, u	21	21 e	---	t	---	---

See source, key, and footnotes on next page.

MARRIAGE LAWS — Continued

Source: The Legal Information Institute Online at Cornell Law School, *http://www.law.cornell.edu/topics/Table_marriage.htm (retrieved December 31, 2002).*

* Indicates common-law marriage recognized.

---- Indicates that the authors of this table were unable to locate any information regarding the topic.

(a) Parental consent not required if minor was previously married.

(b) Other statutory requirements apply.

(c) Younger parties may marry with parental consent.

(c) (2) Younger parties may marry with parental and judicial consent.

(d) Waiting period may be avoided.

(e) Younger parties may obtain license in case of pregnancy or birth of child.

(f) Parties must file notice of intention to marry with local clerk.

(g) No age limits.

(h) When unmarried man and unmarried woman, not minors, have been living together as man and wife, they may, without health certificate, be married upon issuance of appropriate authorization.

(i) Venereal disease and rubella (for female).

(j) Residents, before expiration of 24 hour waiting period; non-residents, before expiration of 96 hour waiting period.

(k) Parental consent and/or permission of judge required.

(l) Unless parties are 18 years of age or more, or female is pregnant, or applicants are the parents of a living child born out of wedlock.

(m) Rubella for female; there are certain exceptions, and district judge may waive medical examination on proof that emergency exists.

(n) Applicants must receive information on AIDS and certify having read it.

(o) Judicial consent may be given when parents refuse to consent.

(p) Venereal diseases; test for sickle cell anemia given at request of examining physician.

(q) Any unsterilized female under 50 must submit with application for license a medical report stating whether she had immunological response to rubella, or a written record that the rubella vaccine was administered on or after her first birthday. Judge may by order dispense with these requirements.

(r) If parties are at least 16 years of age, proof of age and consent of parties in person are required. If a parent is ill, an affidavit by the incapacitated parent and a physician's affidavit required.

(s) Doctor's certificate must be filed 30 days prior to notice of intention.

(t) Venereal diseases. In WV and OK, Circuit court judge may waive requirement.

(u) Younger parties may obtain license in special circumstances.

(v) Below age of consent parties need parental consent and permission of judge, no younger than 14 for males and 13 for females.

(w) Tests for sickle cell may be required.

(x) Applicants under age 18 must state that they have had marriage counseling.

(y) If one or both parties are below the age for marriage without parental consent, three day waiting period.

(z) If a party has no parent residing within state, and one party has residence in state for six months, no permission required.

(aa) Physical examination and blood test required; offer of HIV counseling required.

(bb) Unless parties are over 18 years of age.

(cc) 72 hour waiting period following issuance of license.

(dd) Authorizes counties to provide for premarital counseling as a requisite to issuance of license to persons under 18 and persons previously divorced.

(ee) Required offer of HIV test, and/or must be provided with information on AIDS and tests available.

(ff) No exam required, but parties must file affidavit of non-affliction with contagious venereal disease.

(gg) No common-law marriage can be entered into, but these states recognize common-law marriages that were entered into before these dates: Georgia–entered into prior to January 1, 1997 are recognized, Idaho–entered into prior to January 1, 1997 are recognized, and Indiana–entered into prior to January 1, 1958 are recognized.

MINIMUM AGE FOR SPECIFIED ACTIVITIES

State or other jurisdiction	Age of majority (b)	Minimum age for marriage with consent (a) Male	Female	Minimum age for making a will	Minimum age for buying alcohol	Minimum age for serving on a jury	Minimum age for leaving school (c)
Alabama	19	14 (d, e)	14 (d, e)	19 (f)	21	19	16
Alaska	18	16 (g)	16 (g)	18 (h)	21	18	16
Arizona	18	16 (g)	16 (g)	18	21	18	16 (i)
Arkansas	18	17 (g, j)	16 (g, j)	18 (k)	21	18	17
California	18	(l)	(l)	18 (m)	21	18	18
Colorado	19	16 (g)	16 (g)	18	21	18	16
Connecticut	18	16 (g)	16 (g)	18 (f)	21	18	16
Delaware	18	18 (j)	16 (j)	18	21	18	16
Florida	18	16 (d, j)	16 (d, j)	18 (m)	21	18	16
Georgia	18	16 (j)	16 (j)	18 (h, m)	21	18	16
Hawaii	18	15 (g)	15 (g)	18 (m)	21	18	18 (n)
Idaho	18	16 (g)	16 (g)	18	21	18	16
Illinois	18	16 (o)	16 (o)	18 (k)	21	18	16
Indiana	18	17 (j)	17 (j)	18	21	18	18 (p)
Iowa	18	(l)	(l)	18 (m)	21	18	16
Kansas	18	(l)	(l)	18 (h, k)	21	18	16
Kentucky	18	(l)	(l)	18	21	18	16 (p)
Louisiana	18	18 (g)	18 (g)	18 (i, q)	21	18	17
Maine	18	16 (g)	16 (g)	18	21	18	17
Maryland	18	16 (j, r)	16 (j, r)	18	21	18	16
Massachusetts	18	14 (s)	14 (s)	18	21	18	16
Michigan	18	16	16	18 (k, l, t)	21	18	16
Minnesota	18	16 (g)	16 (g)	18	21	18	16 (u)
Mississippi	21	(l, s)	(l, s)	21 (f, k)	21	21	17
Missouri	18	16 (v)	16 (v)	18	21	21	16
Montana	18	16 (g)	16 (g)	18	21	18	16 (w)
Nebraska	19	17	17	19 (m)	21	19	16
Nevada	18	16 (g)	16 (g)	18	21	18	17
New Hampshire	18	14 (s)	14 (s)	18	21	18	16
New Jersey	18	16 (g, j)	16 (g, j)	18	21	18	16
New Mexico	18 (x)	16 (j, v)	16 (j, v)	18 (t, m)	21	18	18
New York	21	16 (s)	16 (s)	18 (m)	21	18	16 (y)
North Carolina	18	16 (j)	16 (j)	18 (m)	21	18	16
North Dakota	18	16	16	18 (t)	21	18	16
Ohio	18	18 (g, j)	18 (g, j)	18	21	18 (z)	18
Oklahoma	18	16 (g, j)	16 (g, j)	18 (k)	21	18	18
Oregon	18	17 (aa)	17 (aa)	18 (k)	21	18	18
Pennsylvania	18	16 (v)	16 (v)	18	21	18	17
Rhode Island	18	18 (v)	18 (v)	18	21	18	16
South Carolina	18	16 (j)	16 (j)	18	21	18	17
South Dakota	18	16 (j)	16 (j)	18	21	18	16 (w)
Tennessee	18	16 (v)	16 (v)	18 (k)	21	18	17
Texas	18	14 (s)	14 (s)	18 (k)	21	18	17
Utah	18	14 (d)	14 (d)	18 (m)	21	18	18
Vermont	18	14 (g)	14 (g)	18	21	18	16
Virginia	18	16 (d, j)	16 (d, j)	18	21	18	18
Washington	18	17 (v)	17 (v)	18	21	18	18 (bb)
West Virginia	18	18 (j)	18 (j)	21	21	18	16
Wisconsin	18	16 (e)	16 (e)	18	21	18	18
Wyoming	18	16 (v)	16 (v)	19	21	18	16
District of Columbia	21	16 (d)	16 (d)	18	21	18	18
Puerto Rico	21 (cc)	18 (g)	18 (g)	N.A.	N.A.	18	18

Sources: Distilled Spirits Council of the United States, Inc.; Education Commission of the States; National Center for State Courts; National Center for Youth Law; Gary Skoloff, Skoloff & Wolfe.

N.A.—Not Available.

(a) With parental consent. Minimum age for marrying without consent is 18 years in all states, except in Mississippi where the minimum age is 21.

(b) Generally, the age at which an individual has legal control over her own actions and business (e.g. ability to contract) except as otherwise provided by statute. In many states, age of majority is arrived at upon marriage if minimum legal marrying age is lower than prescribed age of majority.

(c) Without graduating.

(d) Parental consent not required if minor was previously married.

(e) Other statutory requirements apply.

(f) All married persons, widows and widowers over 18.

(g) Younger persons may marry with parental consent and/or permission of judge. In Connecticut and Puerto Rico, judicial approval.

(h) Married persons 16 and over.

(i) Or completed 10th grade.

(j) Younger person may obtain license in case of pregnancy or birth of child.

(k) Court may authorize minors to transact business.

(l) No age limits.

(m) By marriage.

(n) Students over the age of 16 can withdraw with the approval of both the principal and the student's guardian, and if an alternative education program exists.

(o) Judicial consent may be given when parents refuse to consent.

(p) In Indiana, students between 16 and 18 must submit to an exit interview and have written parental approval before leaving school. In Kentucky, must have parental signature for leaving school between 16 and 18.

(q) Parents may declare emancipation of minor at age 15.

(r) If under 16, proof of age and the consent of parents in person is required. If a parent is ill, an affidavit by the incapacitated parent and a physician's affidavit to the effect required.

(s) Parental consent and/or permission of judge required. In Texas, below age of consent, need parental consent and permission of judge.

(t) Age may be lower for a minor who is living apart from parents or legal guardians and managing own financial affairs, or who has contracted a lawful marriage, or on active duty in the military.

(u) Age 18, beginning in year 2000.

(v) Younger persons may obtain license in special circumstances.

(w) Or completion of eighth grade, whichever is earlier.

(x) Minors can be emancipated by valid marriage or by court issuance.

(y) Age 17 in New York City and Buffalo.

(z) Eligible to serve on a jury, if driver.

(aa) If a party has no parent residing within state, and one party has residence within state for six months, no permission required.

(bb) Can leave if age 15 and have completed grade eight, has a useful occupation, has met graduation requirements, or has certificate of education competency.

(cc) 21 or when minor is self-supporting through marriage.

Source: *The Book of the States*, 1998–1999.

STATE DEATH PENALTY (AS OF DECEMBER 2002)

State or other jurisdiction	Capital offenses	Minimum age	Prisoners under sentence of death	Method of execution
Alabama	Murder during kidnapping, robbery, rape, sodomy, burglary, sexual assault, or arson; murder of peace officer, correctional officer, or public official; murder while under a life sentence; murder for pecuniary gain or contract; aircraft piracy; murder by a defendant with a previous murder conviction; murder of a witness to a crime; murder when a victim is subpoenaed in a criminal proceeding, when the murder is related to the role of the victim as a witness; murder when a victim is less than 14 years old; murder in which a victim is killed while in a dwelling by a deadly weapon fired or otherwise used from outside the dwelling; murder in which a victim is killed while in a motor vehicle by a deadly weapon; murder in which a victim is killed by a deadly weapon fired or otherwise used in or from a motor vehicle.	16	186	Electrocution
Alaska	. . .			
Arizona	First-degree murder accompanied by at least one of 10 aggravating factors.	16	126	Lethal gas or lethal injection (a) (b)
Arkansas	Capital murder as defined by Arkansas statute. Felony murder; arson causing death; intentional murder of a law enforcement officer; teacher or school employee; murder of prison, jail, court or other correctional personnel, or military personnel acting in line of duty; multiple murders; intentional murder of public officeholder or candidate; intentional murder while under life sentence; contract murder.	16	40	Lethal injection or electrocution (a) (c)
California	Treason; homicide by a prisoner serving a life term; first-degree murder with special circumstances; train wrecking; perjury causing execution.	18	603	Lethal gas or lethal injection (a)
Colorado	First-degree murder; felony murder; intentionally killing a peace officer, firefighter, judge, referee, elected state, county or municipal official, federal law enforcement officer or agent; person kidnapped or being held hostage by the defendant or an associate of the defendant; being party to an agreement to kill another person; murder committed while lying in wait, from ambush, or by use of an explosive or incendiary device; murder for pecuniary gain; murder in an especially heinous, cruel, or depraved manner; murder for the purpose of avoiding or preventing a lawful arrest or prosecution or effecting an escape from custody, including the intentional killing of a witness to a criminal offense; killing two or more persons during the same incident and murder of a child less than 12 years old; treason. Capital sentencing excludes persons determined to be mentally retarded.	18	6	Lethal injection
Connecticut	Murder of a public safety or correctional officer; murder for pecuniary gain; murder in the course of a felony; murder by a defendant with a previous conviction for intentional murder; murder while under a life sentence; murder during a kidnapping; illegal sale of cocaine, methadone, or heroin to a person who dies from using these drugs; murder during first-degree sexual assault; multiple murders; the defendant committed the offense(s) with an assault weapon.	18	7	Lethal injection
Delaware	First-degree murder with aggravating circumstances, including murder of a child victim 14 years of age or younger by an individual who was at least 4 years older than the victim; killing of a nongovernmental informant who provides an investigative, law enforcement or police agency with information concerning criminal activity; and premeditated murder resulting from substantial planning.	16	14	Lethal injection or hanging (a) (d)
Florida	Felony murder, first-degree murder; sexual battery on a child under age 12; destructive devices (unlawful use resulting in death). Capital drug trafficking.	17	372	Lethal injection or electrocution (a)
Georgia	Murder; kidnapping with bodily injury when the victim dies; aircraft hijacking; treason; kidnapping for ransom when the victim dies.	17	116	Lethal injection
Hawaii	. . .			
Idaho	First-degree murder; aggravated kidnapping.	16	21	Lethal injection or firing squad (a)
Illinois	First-degree murder accompanied by at least one of 14 aggravating factors.	18	158	Lethal injection
Indiana	Murder with 14 aggravating circumstances.	18	36	Lethal injection

See source, key, and footnotes at end of table.

State or other jurisdiction	Capital offenses	Minimum age	Prisoners under sentence of death	Method of execution
Kansas	Capital murder, including intentional and premeditated killing of any person in the commission of kidnapping; contract murder; intentional and premeditated killing by a jail or prison inmate; intentional and premeditated killing in the commission of rape or sodomy; intentional and premeditated killing of a law enforcement officer; intentional and premeditated killing of a child under the age of 14 in the commission of kidnapping; killing two or more persons during the same incident.	18	4	Lethal injection
Kentucky	Murder with aggravating factor; kidnapping with aggravating factor.	16	36	Lethal injection or electrocution (a) (j)
Louisiana	First-degree murder; treason.	16	88	Lethal injection
Maine	. . .			
Maryland	First-degree murder, either premeditated or during the commission of a felony, provided that certain death eligibility requirements are satisfied.	18	16	Lethal injection
Massachusetts	. . .			
Michigan	. . .			
Minnesota	. . .			
Mississippi	Capital murder includes murder of a peace officer or correctional officer, murder while under a life sentence, murder by bomb or explosive, contract murder, murder committed during specific felonies (rape, burglary, kidnapping, arson, robbery, sexual battery, unnatural intercourse with a child, nonconsensual unnatural intercourse), and murder of an elected official. Capital rape is the forcible rape of a child under 14 years by a person 18 years or older. Aircraft piracy.	16	62	Lethal injection
Missouri..........................	First-degree murder.	16	73	Lethal injection or lethal gas (a)
Montana	Deliberate homicide; aggravated kidnapping when victim or rescuer dies; attempted deliberate kidnapping by a state prison inmate who has a prior conviction for deliberate homicide or who has been previously declared a persistent felony offender.	18	6	Lethal injection
Nebraska	First-degree murder.	18	7	Electrocution
Nevada	First-degree murder with nine aggravating circumstances.	16	86	Lethal injection
New Hampshire	Capital murder; including contract murder; murder of a law enforcement officer; murder of a kidnap victim; killing another after being sentenced to life imprisonment without parole.	17	0	Lethal injection or hanging (a) (g)
New Jersey	Purposeful or knowing murder; contract murder.	18	16	Lethal injection
New Mexico	First-degree murder; felony murder with aggravating circumstances.	18	3	Lethal injection
New York	First-degree murder with 1 of 12 aggravating factors. Capital sentencing excludes mentally retarded persons.	18	6	Lethal injection
North Carolina	First-degree murder.	17	216	Lethal injection
North Dakota	. . .			
Ohio	Aggravated murder, including assassination; contract murder; murder during escape; murder while in a correctional facility; murder after conviction for a prior purposeful killing or prior attempted murder; murder of a peace officer; murder arising from specified felonies (rape, kidnapping, arson, robbery, burglary); murder of a witness to prevent testimony in a criminal proceeding or in retaliation.	18	203	Lethal injection
Oklahoma	First-degree murder, including murder with malice aforethought; murder arising from specified felonies (forcible rape, robbery with a dangerous weapon, kidnapping, escape from lawful custody, first-degree burglary, arson); murder when the victim is a child who has been injured, tortured or maimed.	16	113	Lethal injection or electrocution or firing squad (a) (m)
Oregon	Aggravated murder.	18	26	Lethal injection
Pennsylvania	First-degree murder.	16	241	Lethal injection
Rhode Island	. . .			

See source, key, and footnotes at end of table.

State or other jurisdiction	Capital offenses	Minimum age	Prisoners under sentence of death	Method of execution
South Carolina	Murder with statutory aggravating circumstances.	16	73	Lethal injection or electrocution (a)
South Dakota	First-degree murder; kidnapping with gross permanent physical injury inflicted on the victim; felony murder.	16	5	Lethal injection
Tennessee	First-degree murder.	18	96	Lethal injection or electrocution (a) (l)
Texas	Murder of a public safety officer, fireman, or correctional employee; murder during the commission of specified felonies (kidnapping, burglary, robbery, aggravated rape, arson); murder for remuneration; multiple murders; murder during prison escape; murder of a correctional officer; murder by a state prison inmate who is serving a life sentence for any of five offenses; murder of an individual under 6 years of age.	17	453	Lethal injection
Utah..............................	Aggravated murder. Aggravated assault by a prisoner serving a life sentence, if serious bodily injury is intentionally caused.	16	11	Lethal injection or firing squad (a)
Vermont........................	. . .			
Virginia..........................	Murder during the commission or attempts to commit specified felonies (abduction, armed robbery, rape, forcible sodomy); contract murder; murder by a prisoner while in custody; murder of a law enforcement officer; multiple murders; murder of a child under 12 years during an abduction; murder arising from drug violations.	16	26	Lethal injection or electrocution (a)
Washington....................	Aggravated first-degree premeditated murder.	18	9	Lethal injection or hanging (a)
West Virginia.................	. . .			
Wisconsin......................	. . .			
Wyoming.......................	Premeditated murder; felony murder in the perpetration (or attempts) of sexual assault, arson, robbery, burglary escape, resisting arrest; kidnapping, or abuse of a child under 16 years of age.	16	2	Lethal injection or lethal gas (i)
Dist. of Columbia............	. . .			

Sources: U.S. Department of Justice, Bureau of Justice Statistics, *Capital Punishment, 2001.* December 2002; Death Penalty Information Center.

Key:

. . . — No capital punishment statute.

(a) Authorizes 2 methods of execution.

(b) State authorizes lethal injection for persons whose capital sentence was received after 11/15/92; for those sentenced before that date, the condemned may select lethal injection or lethal gas.

(c) State authorizes lethal injection for those whose capital offense occurred after 7/4/83; for those whose offense occurred before that date, the condemned prisoner may select lethal injection or electrocution.

(d) State authorizes lethal injection for those whose capital offense occurred after 6/13/86; for those whose offense occurred before that date, the condemned may select lethal injection or hanging.

(e) State authorizes lethal injection for those whose capital offense occurred after 3/25/94 and also for those whose offense occurred before that date, unless within 60 days from that date, the condemned selected lethal gas.

(f) State authorizes lethal injection for those convicted after 7/1/84 and lethal gas for those convicted prior to that date.

(g) State authorizes hanging only if lethal injection cannot be given.

(h) Juveniles may be transferred to adult court. Age may be a mitigating circumstance. No one under age 10 can commit a crime.

(i) State authorizes lethal gas if lethal injection is ever held to be unconstitutional.

(j) State authorizes lethal injection for persons whose capital sentence was received on or after 3/31/98; for those sentenced before that date, the condemned may select lethal injection or electrocution.

(k) State authorizes electrocution if lethal injection is ever held to be unconstitutional, and firing squad if both lethal injection and electrocution are held to be unconstitutional.

(l) State authorizes lethal injection for those whose capital offense occured after 12/31/98; those whose offense occurred before that date may select electrocution.

COUNTRIES WHOSE LAWS DO NOT
PROVIDE FOR THE DEATH PENALTY FOR ANY CRIME

Country	Date of abolition	Date of last execution
Andorra	1990	1943
Angola	1992	
Australia	1985	1967
Austria	1968	1950
Azerbaijan	1998	1993
Belgium	1996	1950
Bulgaria	1998	1989
Cambodia	1989	
Canada	1998	1962
Cape Verde	1981	1835
Colombia	1910	1909
Costa Rica	1877	
Cote D'Ivoire	2000	
Croatia	1990[1]	
Cyprus	2002	
Czech Republic	1990[2]	
Denmark	1978	1950
Djibouti	1995	Ind.[4]
Dominican Republic	1966	
East Timor	1999	
Ecuador	1906	
Estonia	1998	1991
Finland	1972	1944
France	1981	1977
Georgia	1997	1994[5]
Germany	1949/1987[3]	
Guinea-Bissau	1993	1986[5]
Haiti	1987	1972[5]
Honduras	1956	1940
Hungary	1990	1988
Iceland	1928	1830
Ireland	1990	1954
Italy	1994	1947
Kiribati	1979	Ind.[4]
Liechtenstein	1987	1785
Lithuania	1998	1995
Luxembourg	1979	1949
Macedonia	1991	
Malta	2000	
Marshall Islands	1986	Ind.[4]
Mauritius	1995	1987
Micronesia (Federated States)	1986	Ind.[4]
Moldova	1995	
Monaco	1962	1847
Mozambique	1990	1986
Namibia	1990	1988[5]
Nepal	1997	1979
Netherlands	1982	1952
New Zealand	1989	1957
Nicaragua	1979	1930
Norway	1979	1948
Palau		
Panama	1903	1930[5]
Paraguay	1992	1928
Poland	1997	1988
Portugal	1976	1849[5]
Romania	1989	1989
San Marino	1865	1468[5]
Sao Tome and Principe	1990	Ind.[4]
Seychelles	1993	Ind.[4]
Slovakia	1990[2]	
Slovenia	1989[1]	
Solomon Islands	1966	Ind.[4]
South Africa	1997	1991
Spain	1995	1975
Sweden	1972	1910
Switzerland	1992	1944
Turkmenistan	1999	
Tuvalu	1978	Ind.[4]
Ukraine	1999	
United Kingdom	1998	1964
Uruguay	1907	
Vanuatu	1980	Ind.[4]
Vatican City State	1969	
Venezuela	1863	
Yugoslavia	2002	

(1) Croatia and Slovenia abolished the death penalty while they were still republics of the Socialist Federal Republic of Yugoslavia. The two republics became independent in 1991.
(2) The death penalty was abolished in Czechoslovakia in 1990. On January 1, 1993 Czechoslovakia was divided into two states, the Czech Republic and Slovakia. The last execution in Czechoslovakia was in 1988.
(3) In 1990 the German Democratic Republic became unified with the Federal Republic of Germany, where the death penalty had been abolished in 1949. The date of the last execution in the Federal Republic of Germany was in 1949. The date of the last execution in the German Democratic Republic is not known.
(4) No executions since independence.
(5) Date of last known execution.

Sources: Amnesty International Online, *http://www.web.amnesty.org/ai.nsf/index/ACT500052000 (retrieved January 13, 2003);*
   Infoplease, *http://www.infoplease.com/ipa/A0777460.html (retrieved January 13, 2003).*

TRENDS IN STATE PRISON POPULATION (2000–2001)

State or other jurisdiction	Total population			Percent changes from		Incarceration rate June 2000 (a)
	June 2001	December 2000	June 2000	June 2000 to June 2001	December 2000 to June 2001	
United States	1,405,531	1,391,111	1,390,944	1.0%	1.0%	472
Federal	152,788	145,416	142,530	7.2	5.1	46
State	1,252,743	1,245,695	1,248,414	0.3	0.6	426
Eastern Region						
Connecticut (b)	18,875	18,355	18,616	1.4	2.8	384
Delaware (d)	7,122	6,921	7,043	1.1	2.9	505
Maine	1,693	1,679	1,715	-1.3	0.8	126
Massachusetts (c)	10,734	10,722	11,150	-3.7	0.1	247
New Hampshire	2,323	2,257	2,254	3.1	2.9	184
New Jersey (d)	28,108	29,784	31,081	-9.6	-5.6	331
New York	69,158	70,198	71,691	-3.5	-1.5	364
Pennsylvania	37,105	36,847	36,617	1.3	0.7	302
Rhode Island (b)	3,147	3,286	3,186	-1.2	-4.2	179
Vermont (b)	1,782	1,697	1,655	7.7	5.0	221
Regional total	180,047	181,746	185,008	-2.7	-0.9	2,843
Midwest Region						
Illinois (d)	45,269	45,281	44,819	1.4	1.3	370
Indiana	20,576	20,125	19,874	3.5	2.2	336
Iowa (c)	8,101	7,955	7,646	6.0	1.8	277
Kansas (d)	8,543	8,344	8,780	-2.7	2.4	317
Michigan	48,371	47,718	47,317	2.2	1.4	484
Minnesota	6,514	6,238	6,219	4.7	4.4	131
Nebraska	3,944	3,895	3,663	7.7	1.3	225
North Dakota	1,080	1,076	1,004	7.6	0.4	158
Ohio (d)	45,684	45,833	46,838	-2.5	-0.3	402
South Dakota	2,673	2,616	2,571	4.0	2.2	353
Wisconsin	29,931	20,612	20,781	0.7	1.5	373
Regional total	212,046	209,693	209,512	1.2	1.1	3,426
Southern Region						
Alabama	27,286	26,225	25,786	5.8	4.0	592
Arkansas	12,332	11,915	11,559	6.7	3.5	455
Florida (e)	72,007	71,319	71,233	1.1	1.0	439
Georgia (e)	45,363	44,232	43,626	4.0	2.6	540
Kentucky	15,400	14,919	15,444	-0.3	3.2	369
Louisiana	35,494	35,207	34,734	2.2	0.8	795
Maryland	23,970	25,538	23,704	1.1	1.8	432
Mississippi	20,672	20,241	19,264	7.3	2.1	689
Missouri	28,167	27,382	27,292	3.2	2.9	500
North Carolina	31,142	31,532	31,070	0.2	-1.2	329
Oklahoma (d)	23,139	23,181	23,009	0.6	-0.2	669
South Carolina	22,267	21,778	22,154	0.5	2.2	526
Tennessee	23,168	22,166	22,566	2.7	4.5	404
Texas	164,465	166,719	168,126	-2.2	-1.4	731
Virginia	30,473	30,168	29,890	2.0	1.0	415
West Virginia	4,130	3,856	3,800	8.7	7.1	225
Regional total	579,475	574,378	573,257	1.1	0.9	8,110
Western Region						
Alaska (b)	4,197	4,173	4,025	4.3	0.6	336
Arizona (e)	27,136	26,510	26,287	3.2	2.4	478
California	163,965	163,001	164,490	-0.3	0.6	468
Colorado (d)	17,122	16,833	16,319	4.9	1.7	338
Hawaii (b)	5,412	5,053	5,051	7.1	7.1	294
Idaho	5,688	5,535	5,465	4.1	2.8	431
Montana	3,250	3,105	3,039	6.9	4.7	359
Nevada	10,291	10,063	9,920	3.7	2.3	485
New Mexico	5,288	5,342	5,277	0.2	-1.0	281
Oregon	11,077	10,580	10,313	7.4	4.7	319
Utah	5,440	5,632	5,450	-0.2	-3.4	235
Washington	15,242	14,915	14,704	3.7	2.2	251
Wyoming	16,779	1,680	1,722	-2.5	-0.1	340
Regional total	275,787	272,422	272,062	1.4	1.2	4,615
Regional total without California	111,822	109,421	107,572	4.0	2.2	4,147
District of Columbia (b)	5,388	7,456	8,575	-37.2	-27.7	592

Source: U.S. Department of Justice, Bureau of Justice Statistics, *Bulletin, Prisoners and Jail Inmates at Midyear 2001* (June 2002).
Key:
(a) The number of prisoners with sentences of more than one year per 100,000 residents.
(b) Prisons and jails form one integrated system. Data include total jail and prison population.
(c) The incarceration rate includes an estimated 6,200 inmates sentenced to more than 1 year but held in local jails or houses of corrections.
(d) "Sentenced to more than 1 year" includes inmates "sentenced to 1 year or less."
(e) Population figures are based on custody counts.

Source: *The Book of the States, 2003.*

STATE PRISON CAPACITIES

State or other jurisdiction	Rated capacity	Operational capacity	Design capacity	Population as a percent of capacity: (a)	
				Highest capacity	Lowest capacity
Federal	100,199	...	...	131	131
Eastern Region					
Connecticut (b)	...	...	...	...	...
Delaware...	...	4,206	3,192	...	...
Maine	1,428	1,641	1,460	101	117
Massachusetts	...	...	8,926	114	114
New Hampshire	2,419	2,238	2,213	100	109
New Jersey	...	...	17,122	137	137
New York	61,844	64,492	54,527	105	124
Pennsylvania	33,757	33,757	26,186	110	142
Rhode Island	3,692	3,692	3,903	86	91
Vermont	1,311	1,361	1,220	103	115
Regional total	104,451	111,387	118,749	856	949
Midwest Region					
Illinois	34,575	34,575	27,791	128	149
Indiana	15,411	20,528	...	91	122
Iowa	6,772	6,772	6,772	118	118
Kansas	8,816	...	...	97	97
Michigan	...	49,324	...	98	98
Minnesota	6,582	6,582	6,582	97	97
Nebraska	...	3,923	3,331	100	118
North Dakota	1,005	952	1,005	103	109
Ohio	39,650	...	...	113	113
South Dakota	...	2,713	...	102	102
Wisconsin	...	13,772	...	126	126
Regional total	112,811	139,141	47,481	1,173	1,249
Southern Region					
Alabama	24,248	...	12,406	102	200
Arkansas (c)	12,046	11,382	10,647	95	108
Florida	...	76,518	56,607	89	121
Georgia	...	46,526	...	89	89
Kentucky	11,680	11,430	...	92	94
Louisiana	19,660	19,931	...	99	100
Maryland	...	23,874	...	99	99
Mississippi (c)	...	16,072	...	94	94
Missouri	...	29,162	...	98	98
North Carolina	29,254	...	29,254	110	110
Oklahoma (c)	...	23,304	...	93	93
South Carolina	...	23,325	21,861	93	99
Tennessee (c)	18,162	17,729	...	96	99
Texas (c) (d)	156,738	153,099	156,738	95	97
Virginia	32,117	...	...	93	93
West Virginia	...	3,593	3,189	96	107
Regional total	303,905	455,945	290,702	1,533	1,701
Western Region					
Alaska (e)	2,603	2,691	2,603	109	113
Arizona	...	27,948	...	99	99
California	...	150,536	79,957	101	191
Colorado	...	12,922	11,748	115	127
Hawaii	...	3,406	2,481	113	156
Idaho	3,981	3,781	3,194	99	123
Montana	...	1,370	896	125	191
Nevada (c)	10,548	...	8,312	93	118
New Mexico (c)	6,106	6,106	5,986	93	95
Oregon	...	11,298	11,008	97	99
Utah	...	4,286	4,509	92	96
Washington	9,898	12,793	12,793	119	154
Wyoming	1,114	1,052	1,141	89	97
Regional total	34,250	238,189	144,628	1,344	1,659
Regional total without California	34,250	87,653	64,671	1,243	1,468
District of Columbia	...	1,674	...	97	97

Source: U.S. Department of Justice, Bureau of Justice Statistics, *Prisoners in 2001* (August 2002).
Key:
... —Not available.
(a) Population counts are based on the number of inmates held in facilities operated by the jurisdiction. Excluded inmates held in local jails, in other states, or in private facilities.

(b) Connecticut no longer reports capacity due to a law passed in 1995.
(c) Includes capacity of private and contract facilities and inmates housed in them.
(d) Excludes capacity of county facilities and inmates housed in them.
(e) Capacity counts for 2000 were used as an estimate for capacity for 2001.

Source: *The Book of the States, 2003.*

ADULTS ON PROBATION (2001)

State or other jurisdiction	Probation population				Percent change during 2001	Number on probation on 12/31/01 per 100,000 adult residents
	1/1/01	2001 Entries	2001 Exits	12/31/01		
United States	3,826,209	2,110,550	1,999,164	3,932,751	2.8	1,849
Federal	31,669	13,828	13,893	31,561	-0.3	15
State	3,794,540	2,096,722	1,985,271	3,901,190	2.8	1,834
Eastern Region						
Connecticut	47,636	22,752	20,556	49,832	4.6	1,928
Delaware	20,052	11,792	11,849	19,995	-0.3	3,321
Maine	7,788	7,179	6,028	8,939	14.8	906
Massachusetts	45,233	39,871	40,985	44,119	-2.5	904
New Hampshire (a) (b)	3,629	2,798	2,762	3,665	1.0	385
New Jersey	130,610	55,010	52,774	132,846	1.7	2,075
New York	186,955	43,199	33,319	196,835	5.3	1,374
Pennsylvania (b)	121,176	48,245	43,493	125,928	3.9	1,344
Rhode Island (a)	20,922	8,482	4,645	24,759	...	3,049
Vermont	9,331	5,063	5,128	9,266	-0.7	1,988
Regional total	593,332	244,291	221,539	616,184	3.8	17,274
Midwest Region						
Illinois	139,029	62,911	60,432	141,508	1.8	1,532
Indiana	109,251	90,845	87,395	112,701	3.2	2,481
Iowa	21,147	18,870	19,220	20,797	-1.7	950
Kansas	15,992	21,338	22,080	15,250	-4.6	769
Michigan (b)	170,276	118,999	112,536	176,406	3.6	2,385
Minnesota	115,906	62,194	64,487	113,613	-2.0	3,081
Nebraska	21,483	14,570	15,206	20,847	-3.0	1,651
North Dakota	2,847	1,782	1,728	2,901	1.9	613
Ohio (b)	189,375	123,269	117,247	195,403	3.2	2,302
South Dakota	4,214	3,404	3,156	4,462	5.9	805
Wisconsin	53,242	25,817	24,108	54,951	3.2	1,362
Regional total	842,762	543,999	527,595	858,839	1.9	17,931
Southern Region						
Alabama	40,178	16,019	15,580	40,617	1.1	1,215
Arkansas	28,409	11,308	13,159	26,558	-6.5	1,319
Florida (b)	296,139	245,593	244,827	294,626	-0.5	2,304
Georgia (b) (d)	321,407	203,155	166,532	358,030	...	...
Kentucky	19,620	11,255	8,884	21,993	12.1	716
Louisiana	35,854	11,857	11,967	35,744	-0.3	1,101
Maryland	81,523	42,602	43,417	80,708	-1.0	2,006
Mississippi	15,118	8,074	7,757	15,435	2.1	741
Missouri	53,299	25,741	23,273	55,767	4.6	1,327
North Carolina	105,949	61,596	56,869	110,676	4.5	1,776
Oklahoma (a) (b)	30,969	15,086	15,786	30,269	-2.3	1,179
South Carolina	44,632	14,815	17,039	42,408	-5.0	1,388
Tennessee	40,682	24,374	23,070	41,089	1.0	946
Texas	441,848	202,476	200,640	443,684	0.4	2,873
Virginia	33,955	29,642	25,715	37,684	11.6	694
West Virginia (b)	6,216	3,102	3,142	6,176	-0.6	441
Regional total	1,595,798	926,695	877,657	1,641,662	2.8	20,026
Western Region						
Alaska	4,779	908	832	4,855	1.6	1,091
Arizona	59,810	39,464	36,192	63,082	5.5	1,598
California (a)	343,145	157,440	149,817	350,768	2.2	1,388
Colorado (b)	50,460	29,125	23,018	56,567	12.1	1,702
Hawaii	15,525	5,813	5,757	15,581	0.4	1,675
Idaho (c)	35,103	30,324	29,757	35,670	1.6	3,747
Montana	6,108	3,526	3,376	6,258	2.5	928
Nevada	12,189	5,528	7,263	10,454	-14.2	654
New Mexico	10,461	7,735	6,561	10,335	-1.2	782
Oregon (a)	46,023	17,419	16,902	46,540	1.1	1,770
Utah	9,800	5,036	4,505	10,331	5.4	667
Washington (b)	154,466	68,401	63,748	159,119	3.0	3,551
Wyoming	4,115	2,376	2,014	4,477	8.8	1,223
Regional total	751,984	373,095	349,742	774,037	2.9	20,772
Regional total without California	408,839	215,655	199,925	423,269	3.5	19,388
District of Columbia	10,664	8,542	8,738	10,468	-1.8	2,291

Source: U.S. Department of Justice, Bureau of Justice Statistics, *Probation and Parole in the United States, 2001,* (August 2002).
Note: Because of incomplete data, the population for some jurisdictions on December 31, 2001, does not equal the population on January 1, 2001, plus entries, minus exits.
Key:
...—Not calculated.

(a) All data were estimated.
(b) Data for entries and exits were estimated for nonreporting agencies.
(c) Counts include estimates for misdemeanors based on annual admissions.
(d) Counts include private agency cases and may overstate the number under supervision.

Source: *The Book of the States, 2003.*

MANDATORY WAITING PERIODS FOR ABORTION

State	Waiting period	Enforced	Enjoined/ Not enforced
Alabama	Min. 24 hours	X	
Arkansas	Min. 12 hours[1]	X	
Delaware	Min. 24 hours		X
Idaho	Min. 24 hours	X[2]	
Indiana	Min. 18 hours	X	
Kansas	Min. 24 hours	X	
Kentucky	Min. 24 hours	X	
Louisiana	Min. 24 hours	X	
Massachusetts	Min. 24 hours		X[3]
Michigan	Min. 24 hours	X	
Mississippi	Min. 24 hours	X	
Montana	Min. 24 hours		X[3]
Nebraska	Min. 24 hours	X	
North Dakota	Min. 24 hours	X	
Ohio	Min. 24 hours	X	
Pennsylvania	Min. 24 hours	X	
South Carolina	Min. 1 hour[4]	X	
South Dakota	Min. 24 hours	X	
Tennessee	Min. 48–72 hours[5]		X[3]
Utah	Min. 24 hours	X	
Virginia	Min. 24 hours	X	
Wisconsin	Min. 24 hours	X	
TOTAL ....22 states		18	4

Source: *Who Decides? A State-By-State Review of Abortion and Reproductive Rights 2003,* (The NARAL Foundation/NARAL), p. 211.
Mandatory waiting periods prohibit a woman from obtaining an abortion until a specified period of time after receiving a mandated lecture or materials.

1. This law provides that a woman may not obtain an abortion on the same day that she receives state-mandated information.
2. This law requires that a woman be provided with state-prepared materials at least 24 hours before an abortion, if reasonably possible.
3. A court has ruled that this waiting period provision is unconstitutional.
4. This law requires a one-hour waiting period if a woman chooses to review state-prepared materials.
5. This law provides that a woman may not obtain an abortion until the third day after her initial consultation.

RESTRICTIONS ON MINORS' ACCESS TO ABORTION

State	One Parent	Two Parent	Consent	Notice	Judicial Bypass	Enjoined/ Not Enforced	Enforced
Alabama	X		X		X	X[1]	X
Alaska	X		X		X	X[13]	
Arizona	X		X		X		
Arkansas		X		X	X		X
California	X		X		X	X[1]	
Colorado	X[11]			X		X[1]	
Connecticut							
Delaware	X[2]			X[3]	X		X
District of Columbia							
Florida	X			X	X	X[1]	
Georgia	X			X	X		X
Hawaii							
Idaho	X		X		X		X
Illinois	X[5]			X	X	X[1]	
Indiana	X		X		X		X
Iowa	X[2]			X	X		X
Kansas	X			X	X		X
Kentucky	X		X		X		X
Louisiana	X		X		X		X
Maine	X[6]		X[7]		X		X
Maryland	X			X[3]			X
Massachusetts	X[8]		X		X		X
Michigan	X		X		X		X
Minnesota		X		X	X		X
Mississippi		X	X		X		X
Missouri	X		X		X		X
Montana	X			X	X	X[1]	
Nebraska	X			X	X		X
Nevada	X			X	X	X[1]	
New Hampshire							
New Jersey	X			X	X	X[1]	
New Mexico	X		X			X[1]	
New York							
North Carolina	X[2]		X		X		X
North Dakota		X	X		X		X
Ohio	X[9]			X[12]	X		X
Oklahoma	X[12]			X[12]		X[1]	
Oregon							
Pennsylvania	X		X		X		X
Rhode Island	X		X		X		X
South Carolina	X[2]		X		X		X
South Dakota	X			X	X		X
Tennessee	X		X		X		X
Texas	X			X	X		X
Utah		X[4]		X			X
Vermont							
Virginia	X			X	X		X
Washington							
West Virginia	X			X[3]	X		X
Wisconsin	X[10]		X		X		X
Wyoming	X		X		X		X
TOTAL	38	5	22	21	38	11	32

Source: *Who Decides? A State-By-State Review of Abortion and Reproductive Rights 2003*, (The NARAL Foundation/NARAL), pp. 216–217.

1. This statute has been declared unenforceable by a court or attorney general.
2. This statute also allows consent of or notice to a grandparent under certain circumstances.
3. This requirement may be waived by a specified health professional under certain circumstances.
4. This statute requires notice to a minor's parents, if possible.
5. This statute also allows consent of or notice to a grandparent or step-parent.
6. This statute also allows consent of an adult family member.
7. This statute requires mandatory counseling and allows a minor to obtain an abortion without parental consent if the physician secures informed written consent of the minor and the minor is mentally and physically competent to give consent.
8. This statute requires two-parent consent, but a court has issued an order that the law be enforced as requiring the consent of one parent.
9. This statute also allows notice to a grandparent, step-parent, or adult sibling over the age of 21 under certain circumstances.
10. This statute allows consent of a grandparent or certain other adult family members over the age of 25.
11. This statute requires notice to both parents but states that if the parents reside together, delivery to one parent shall constitute delivery to both, and allows notice to one parent if the minor requests and if the parents do not reside together.
12. This statute provides that "(a)ny person who performs an abortion on a minor without parental consent or knowledge shall be liable for the cost of any subsequent medical treatment such minor might require because of the abortion." The law can be interpreted to require one- or two-parent involvement.
13. Although a court has ruled that this law is constitutional, the law is not in effect pending resolution of the case.

PUBLIC FUNDING FOR ABORTION

State*	Life endangerment only[1]	Life, rape, and incest only	Life, rape, incest, and some health circumstances	All or most circumstances
Alabama		X		
Alaska				X^3
Arizona				X^3
Arkansas		X^2		
California				X^3
Colorado		X^2		
Connecticut				X^3
Delaware		X		
District of Columbia		X		
Florida		X		
Georgia		X		
Hawaii				X
Idaho		X		
Illinois			$X^{2,4}$	
Indiana				X^3
Iowa			X^5	
Kansas		X		
Kentucky		X^2		
Louisiana		X^2		
Maine		X		
Maryland				X^5
Massachusetts				X^3
Michigan		X^2		
Minnesota				X^3
Mississippi			X^5	
Missouri		X^2		
Montana				X^3
Nebraska		X^2		
Nevada		X		
New Hampshire		X		
New Jersey				X^3
New Mexico				X^3
New York				X
North Carolina		X		
North Dakota		X^2		
Ohio		X		
Oklahoma		X^2		
Oregon				X^3
Pennsylvania		X		
Rhode Island		X		
South Carolina		X		
South Dakota	X			
Tennessee		X		
Texas		X^6		
Utah		X^2		
Vermont				X^3
Virginia			X^5	
Washington				X
West Virginia				$X^{3,5}$
Wisconsin			X^6	
Wyoming		X		
TOTAL	1	28	5	17

Source: Who Decides? A State-By-State Review of Abortion and Reproductive Rights 2003, (The NARAL Foundation/NARAL), pp. 218–219.

* This chart documents official state policies for public funding and may not necessarily reflect the actual implementation of these policies.

1. These states are not in compliance with federal law prohibiting participating states from excluding abortion from the Medicaid program in cases of life endangerment, rape and incest.
2. A court has ruled that this state must comply with federal law prohibiting the exclusion of abortion from the Medicaid program in cases of life endangerment, rape and incest.
3. A court has ruled that the state constitution prohibits the state from restricting funding for abortion while providing funds for costs associated with childbirth.
4. A court has ruled that the state constitution prohibits the enforcement of a state law restricting funding to the extent it bars funding for an abortion necessary to preserve the woman's health.
5. This statute includes funding for some cases of fetal anomaly.
6. A court has ruled that Texas must pay for all medically necessary abortions. However, this decision has been stayed pending appeal.

Glossary

A

abortion a premature end to a pregnancy. Abortion can result from a medical procedure performed in the early stages of pregnancy or as in a miscarriage, when the fetus leaves the womb before it can survive on its own. (pp. 496–498)

acceleration clause a provision in a contract that makes the entire debt due immediately if a payment is not made on time or if some other condition is not met (p. 301)

acceptance the act of agreeing to an offer and becoming bound to the terms of a contract (p. 276)

accessory a person who helps commit a crime but usually is not present. An accessory before the fact is one who encourages, orders, or helps plan a crime. An accessory after the fact is someone who, knowing a crime has been committed, helps conceal the crime or the criminal. (p. 103)

accomplice a person who voluntarily helps another person commit a crime; unlike an accessory, an accomplice is usually present or directly aids in the crime. (p. 102)

acquaintance rape sexual assault by someone known to the victim, such as a date or neighbor (also called date rape) (p. 114)

adjudicatory hearing the procedure used to determine the facts in a juvenile case; similar to an adult trial, but generally closed to the public (p. 199)

adoption the legal process of taking a child of other biological parents and accepting that child as your own, with all the legal rights and responsibilities there would be if the child were yours by birth (p. 408)

adultery voluntary sexual intercourse between a married person and someone other than his or her spouse (p. 418)

adversarial system the judicial system used in the United States. It allows opposing parties to present their legal conflicts before an impartial judge and jury. (p. 47)

advocacy active support or argument for a cause (p. 29)

advocate a person who speaks for the cause of another or on behalf of someone or something (p. 30)

affidavit a written statement of facts sworn to or made under oath before someone authorized to administer an oath (p. 141)

affirmative action steps taken to promote diversity in hiring, promotion, education, etc. by attempting to remedy past discrimination; for example, by actively recruiting minorities and women (p. 506)

aftercare the equivalent of parole in the juvenile justice system. A juvenile is supervised and assisted by a parole officer or social worker. (p. 202)

agency an administrative division of a government set up to make and carry out certain laws (p. 24)

age of majority the age (usually 18 or 21) at which a person becomes an adult, as specified by state law, and acquires both the rights and the responsibilities of adulthood (p. 190)

aggravating circumstances factors that tend to increase the seriousness of an offense. The presence of such circumstances must be considered by the judge and jury. (p. 180)

alibi a Latin word meaning "elsewhere;" an excuse or plea that a person was somewhere else at the time a crime was committed (p. 127)

alimony a court-ordered allowance a husband or wife (or an ex-husband/ex-wife) pays to his or her spouse after a legal separation, after a divorce, or while the case is being decided (p. 423)

Glossary

allegation a criminal accusation that has not been proven (p. 49)

amendment (1) one of the provisions of the U.S. Constitution enacted after the original Constitution became law; (2) an addition or change to an existing document or plan (pp. 17–18, 441)

annual percentage rate (APR) the interest rate paid per year on borrowed money (p. 293)

annulment a court or religious order that declares a marriage never legally existed (p. 379)

anti-miscegenation laws laws that prohibit marriage between people of different races (p. 374)

appeal to take a case to a higher court for a rehearing (pp. 51, 171–172)

appeals court a court in which appeals from trial-court decisions are heard (pp. 26, 51)

appellant one who signs or files an appeal of a trial decision (p. 172)

appellate court *see* appeals court

arbitration a way of settling a dispute without going to trial. The parties who disagree select one or more impartial persons to settle the argument. If the arbitration is binding, then all parties must accept the decision. (p. 43)

arraignment a court session at which a defendant is charged and enters a plea. For a misdemeanor this is also the defendant's initial appearance, at which the judge informs him or her of the charges and sets the bail. (p. 156)

arrest to take a person suspected of a crime into custody (p. 134)

arrest warrant a court-ordered document authorizing the police to arrest an individual on a specific charge (p. 134)

arson the deliberate and malicious burning of another person's property (p. 116)

assault an intentional threat, show of force, or movement that causes a reasonable fear of, or an actual physical contact with, another person. Can be a crime or a tort. (pp. 111, 233)

assumption of risk a legal defense to a negligence tort, whereby the plaintiff is considered to have voluntarily accepted a known risk of danger (p. 259)

attachment the act of taking a debtor's property or money to satisfy a debt, by court approval (p. 307)

attempt an effort to commit a crime that goes beyond mere preparation but does not result in the commission of the crime (p. 104)

attractive nuisance doctrine that says if a person keeps something on his or her premises that is likely to attract children, that person must take reasonable steps to protect children against dangers the condition might cause (p. 238)

B

bail money or property put up by the accused or his or her agent to allow release from jail before trial. The purpose of bail is to assure the court that the defendant will return for trial. If the defendant is present for trial, the money or property is returned. (p. 157)

bait and switch a deceptive sales technique in which customers are "baited" into a store by an ad promising an item at a low price and then "switched" to a more expensive item (p. 315)

balancing test used by judges to resolve legal issues by balancing the interests in conflict and deciding which is of higher importance (p. 443)

balloon payment a financing agreement in which the last payment of a loan is much higher than the regular monthly payments (p. 301)

bankruptcy the procedure under the *Federal Bankruptcy Act* by which a person is relieved of all debts once he or she has placed all property and money in a court's care (p. 305)

bar association an organization that licenses lawyers (p. 64)

battery any intentional, unlawful physical contact inflicted on one person by another without consent. In some states, this is combined with assault. *See also* assault. (pp. 111, 232)

bench trial trial that takes place before a judge without a jury (p. 61)

best interest of the child a doctrine used to determine custody by examining factors that will best benefit a child (p. 420)

beyond a reasonable doubt the level of proof required to convict a person of a crime. It does not mean "convinced 100 percent," but does mean there are no reasonable doubts as to guilt. (p. 14)

bigamy the crime of being married to more than one person at a time (p. 380)

bill (1) a draft of a proposed law being considered by a legislature (p. 21); (2) a written statement of money owed (pp. 293, 296)

bill consolidation a form of credit in which the lender combines all of a person's debts into a single monthly payment. In effect, this is a refinancing of a person's existing debts, often with an additional, higher interest charge (p. 301)

Bill of Rights the first ten amendments to the Constitution, which guarantee basic individual rights to all persons in the United States. (pp. 17, 570–599)

black-market adoption a form of adoption, illegal in many states, that bypasses licensed adoption agencies by using a go-between to negotiate between the expectant mother and the adopting parent(s) (p. 409)

bona fide a Latin term, meaning "in good faith"; (1) characterized by good faith and lack of fraud or deceit; (2) valid under or in compliance with the law (pp. 141, 283)

bona fide occupational qualification (BFOQ) an employment requirement that is considered reasonable because it is necessary to perform the job. For example, good vision is a BFOQ for a bus driver; the race or national origin of a bus driver is not a BFOQ. (p. 544)

bond a mandatory insurance agreement or obligation. A bail bond is the money a defendant pays to secure release from jail before the trial. (p. 157)

booking the formal process of making a police record of an arrest (p. 155)

breach the violation of a law, duty, or other form of obligation, including obligations formed through contracts or warranties, either by engaging in an action or failing to act (pp. 251, 281)

burden of proof the requirement that to win a point or have an issue decided in one party's favor, the party must show that a certain amount of the weight of the evidence is on his or her side. In a civil case, the burden of proof is on the plaintiff, who must usually prevail by a preponderance (majority) of the evidence. In a criminal case, the state must prove its case beyond a reasonable doubt. The weight of the evidence is more than the amount of evidence. It is also concerned with the believability of the evidence. (p. 152)

burglary breaking and entering a building with the intention of committing a crime (p. 119)

business necessity the legally acceptable reason for employee selection requirements. A business must show it can operate well only if these selection requirements are met by potential employees. (p. 544)

C

capital punishment the death penalty; putting a convicted person to death as punishment for a crime (p. 178)

Glossary

carjacking a crime in which the perpetrator uses force or intimidation to steal a car from a driver (p. 122)

causation the reason an event occurs; that which produces an effect. One of the four elements that must be proven in a negligence case, causation is subdivided into cause in fact and proximate cause. (p. 255)

cause in fact one of the elements a plaintiff must prove in order to establish causation in a negligence suit. It means that if the harm would not have occurred without the wrongful act, the act is the cause in fact. (p. 255)

caveat emptor Latin phrase meaning "let the buyer beware" (p. 274)

cease and desist order an order given by an administrative agency or a judge to stop some illegal or deceptive activity (p. 326)

censorship (1) the denial of freedom of speech or freedom of the press; (2) the process of examining publications or films for material that the government considers harmful or objectionable (p. 465)

certiorari *see* petition for certiorari

charge the formal accusation of a crime (p. 135)

checks and balances the power of each of the three branches of government (legislative, judicial, executive) to limit the other branches' power, so as to prevent an abuse (p. 16)

child abuse neglect or mistreatment of a child (p. 403)

child neglect the failure of a parent to properly feed, clothe, provide shelter for, educate, supervise, or provide for the medical needs of a child (p. 403)

child support a court-determined payment that the parent not living with the child must pay to help provide for the child's needs (pp. 422, 424)

civil action a noncriminal lawsuit, brought to enforce a right or redress a wrong (p. 13)

civil law all law that does not involve criminal matters, such as tort and contract law. Civil law usually deals with private rights of individuals, groups, or businesses. (pp. 13, 219)

class action a lawsuit brought by one or more persons on behalf of a larger group (pp. 222, 326)

clause a paragraph, sentence, or phrase in a legal document, such as a contract, lease, or will (p. 354)

clear and present danger test a test formerly used by courts to restrict speech when the government thought the speech would create an immediate danger of serious harm (p. 454)

closing statement at the end of a trial, the comments a lawyer makes to summarize the evidence presented (p. 49)

cohabitation agreement a written or oral contract outlining how unmarried couples want to deal with their money, property, or responsibilities during and after their relationship (p. 391)

collateral money or property given as security in case a person is unable to repay a debt (p. 292)

collective bargaining a required procedure in the *National Labor Relations Act* providing that under certain circumstances, employers must bargain with official union representatives regarding wages, hours, and other work conditions (p. 550)

collective rights rights that apply more to people acting together in a group than to individuals acting on their own; examples include the right to bear arms, freedom of assembly and of petition, and even freedom of the press (p. 513)

collision coverage insurance that pays for damage to the insured's own car caused by an automobile collision (p. 226)

commercial speech speech that is directed at buying or selling of goods and services. The law treats commercial speech differently from political speech and other forms of expression. (p. 450)

common law a system in which court decisions establish legal principles and rules of law (p. 216)

common-law marriage a marriage created without legal ceremony by a couple living together and publicly presenting themselves as husband and wife. Such a marriage can be formed only in certain states. (p. 380)

community policing a strategy whereby the community works actively with the local police to lower the crime rate in its area (p. 79)

community property property acquired during a marriage that is owned by both husband and wife, regardless of who earned it or paid for it (p. 383)

comparative negligence in a tort suit, a finding that the plaintiff was partly at fault and, therefore, does not deserve full compensation for his or her injuries. For example, if an accident was 40 percent the plaintiff's fault, the plaintiff's damages are reduced by 40 percent. (p. 259)

comparison shopping looking at several products and comparing quality and price before deciding which item best meets one's needs (p. 327)

compensatory damages in a civil case, money the court requires a defendant to pay a winning plaintiff to make up for harm caused. This harm can be financial (for example, lost wages, medical expenses, etc.), physical (for example, past, present, and future pain and suffering), and, in some jurisdictions, emotional (fright and shock, anxiety, etc.). (p. 231)

complaint (1) the first legal document filed in a civil lawsuit. It includes a statement of the wrong or harm done to the plaintiff by the defendant and a request for a specific remedy from the court. (p. 341); (2) A complaint in a criminal case is a sworn statement regarding the defendant's actions that constitute the crime charged. (p. 134)

comprehensive coverage the portion of an insurance policy that protects an individual against automobile damages or losses other than collisions. It includes damages and losses due to fire, vandalism, or theft. (p. 227)

computer crime the unauthorized access to, and tampering with, someone else's computer system (pp. 122–125)

concealment the crime of attempted shoplifting that is recognized by some states (p. 117)

concurring opinion an additional written court opinion in which a judge or judges agrees with the decision reached by the court, but for reasons different from those used to support the majority opinion (p. 51)

confession an accused person's voluntary admission of wrongdoing (p. 152)

consent written, spoken, or assumed agreement to something (p. 247)

consent decree a voluntary agreement to stop a practice that is claimed to be illegal (p. 326)

consideration something of value offered or received that must be present in every valid contract (p. 277)

conspiracy an agreement between two or more persons to commit a crime along with a substantial act toward committing the crime (p. 105)

consumer anyone who buys or uses a product or service (p. 274)

Glossary

consumer protection laws statutes that protect consumers by prohibiting unfair or misleading trade practices; setting standards for quality, safety, and reliability of many goods and services; and establishing agencies to enforce consumer laws and help consumers (pp. 324–326)

contempt of court any act to embarrass, hinder, or obstruct the court in the administration of justice (p. 169)

contingency fee the fee paid to an attorney based on a percentage of the sum the client is awarded or settles for in a lawsuit (pp. 68, 222)

continuance the postponement of the court proceedings in a case to a future time (p. 341)

contraband any items that are illegal to possess (p. 145)

contraceptive a precautionary item such as a condom or birth control pills designed to prevent or reduce the chance of pregnancy (p. 496)

contract a legally enforceable agreement between two or more people to exchange something of value (pp. 223, 276)

contributing to the delinquency of a minor the act, by an adult, of aiding or encouraging illegal or improper conduct by a minor (pp. 189, 402)

contributory negligence a legal defense in which it is determined that the plaintiff and defendant share the fault for a negligence tort. If proven, the plaintiff cannot recover damages. (p. 257)

conversion in tort law, the taking or controlling of another's property without consent. If the property is not returned to the rightful owner, the court can force the defendant to give the plaintiff the monetary value of the property. (p. 241)

conviction the finding that a person is guilty of a crime or wrongdoing (p. 126)

copyright the protection of a creative fixed expression giving the owner exclusive rights to the expression (For example, Matt Groening has exclusive rights to the *Simpsons* cartoon characters.) (p. 242)

corporal punishment physical punishment, such as spanking or paddling (p. 187)

corrective advertising a remedy imposed by the Federal Trade Commission requiring that any false claim in an advertisement be admitted and corrected in all future ads for a specified period of time (p. 313)

corroborate to confirm information (p. 136)

cosign to sign a legal document, guaranteeing to pay off the debt or contract if the original signer defaults (p. 278)

counterclaim a claim made by a defendant against the plaintiff in a civil lawsuit (p. 259)

covenant marriage a special type of marriage in which the couple surrenders, in advance, their right to a no-fault divorce (p. 418)

credit (1) a deduction from what is owed; (2) purchasing goods with delayed payment, as with a credit card; (3) money that is loaned (p. 287)

creditor a person who provides credit, loans money, or delivers goods or services before payment is made (p. 292)

credit property insurance insurance against theft or damage of items purchased with loans (p. 300)

credit life/disability insurance insurance that guarantees payment of owed balances should the buyer die or become disabled (p. 300)

crime an act or failure to act that violates a law and for which a government has set a penalty (usually a fine, jail, or probation) (p. 74)

crime of omission failing to perform an act required by criminal law (p. 103)

criminal fraud knowingly misstating or misrepresenting an important fact, with the intent to harm another person (p. 337)

criminal homicide the killing of another person intentionally and with malice (p. 107)

criminal justice process the system by which government enforces criminal law. It includes everything from the arrest of an individual to the individual's release from control by the state. (p. 133)

criminal law the branch of law dealing with crimes and their punishment (p. 13)

cross examination the questioning of the opposing side's witnesses during a hearing or trial (p. 49)

custodial interrogation questioning initiated by law enforcement officers after a person has been taken into custody or otherwise deprived of his or her freedom of action in any significant way (p. 154)

custody the care and keeping of something or someone, such as a child (p. 419)

D

damages (1) the injuries or losses suffered by one person due to the fault of another (p. 256); (2) money asked for or paid by court order to a plaintiff for injuries or losses suffered (p. 212)

date rape *see* acquaintance rape

death penalty a sentence to death for commission of a serious crime, such as murder; *see also* capital punishment (p. 178)

debit card also called a *check card;* a card used to make purchases in which the purchase price is deducted from your bank account (pp. 289–290)

debtor a person who owes money or buys on credit (p. 292)

decree an official decision of a court, setting out the facts found in a case and the legal results. It orders that the court's decision (for example, a divorce decree) be carried out. (p. 416)

deductible the amount an insured person agrees to pay toward repairs before the insurance company pays anything. (p. 226)

deep pockets a description of the person or organization, among many possible defendants, best able to pay damages and therefore most likely to be sued in a tort case (p. 220)

defamation written or spoken expression about a person that is false and damages that person's reputation (pp. 236, 450)

default failure to fulfill a legal obligation, such as making a loan payment or appearing in court on a specified date and time (p. 304)

default judgment a ruling against a party to a lawsuit who fails to take a required action (for example, failing to file a paper on time) (p. 306)

defendant the person against whom a claim is made. In a civil suit, the defendant is the person being sued; in a criminal case, the defendant is the person charged with committing a crime. (pp. 13, 46, 212)

defense a denial, answer, or plea by a defendant, disputing the correctness of charges against the defendant (p. 126)

defense of property the use of reasonable force, which would otherwise be illegal, to defend your home or other property (p. 248)

deinstitutionalization a policy of releasing a mentally ill patient from a mental hospital into the community (p. 195)

delegated powers the powers specifically granted to Congress by Article I, Section 8, of the Constitution; also called enumerated or expressed powers. They include the power to tax, regulate commerce, and declare war. (p. 56)

Glossary

deliberate intentional (p. 108)

delinquent offender a minor who has committed an act that, if committed by an adult, would be a crime under federal, state, or local law. Such offenders are usually processed through the juvenile justice system. (p. 188)

derivative work a work that is very similar to but slightly different from a copyrighted work (p. 245)

desegregate to end the policy of imposing legal and social separation of races, as in housing, schools, and jobs (p. 504)

desertion the act of abandoning one's spouse with no intention of returning or of reassuming the duties of marriage. Desertion is usually grounds for divorce. (p. 418)

deterrence measures taken to discourage criminal actions; usually some form of punishment. It is the belief that punishment will discourage the offender from committing future crimes and will serve as an example to keep others from committing crimes. (pp. 163, 177)

direct action an action that consumers take to make an impact on a business's or other organization's operations or profits (p. 337)

direct examination the questioning of a witness by the side calling the witness to the stand (p. 49)

disability a condition that makes performing certain basic functions or activities difficult (p. 531)

disbar to take away an attorney's license to practice law because of illegal or unethical conduct (p. 71)

disclaimer a clause or statement in a contract or agreement that limits responsibility for anything not expressly promised (p. 285)

discovery the pretrial process of exchanging information between the opposing sides (p. 161)

discrimination generally, choosing or selecting. In law, it may be the decision to treat or categorize persons based on race, color, creed, gender, or other characteristics rather than on individual merit. Also, the denial of equal protection of the law. (p. 501)

disposition the final sentence or result of a case (p. 200)

dispositional hearing the procedure in which a judge decides what type of punishment or sentence a juvenile offender should receive (p. 200)

dissenting opinion in a trial or appeal, the written opinion of the minority of judges who disagree with the decision of the majority (p. 51)

divorce the ending of a marriage by court order (pp. 379, 416)

DNA evidence biological evidence, derived from testing samples of human tissues and fluids, that genetically links an offender to a crime (p. 127)

domestic partnership laws laws that allow an employee's heterosexual or homosexual live-in partner to receive the same employment and health benefits a spouse would receive (p. 393)

down payment cash that must be paid up front when something is bought by paying in installments over time (p. 346)

drug courier profile using commonly held notions of what typical drug couriers look and act like in order to be able to question a person without establishing individualized suspicion (p. 134)

drunk driving the operation of a motor vehicle while intoxicated (overcome by alcohol to the point of losing control over one's conscious faculties). A drunk person's blood-alcohol concentration is above a predefined level, usually 0.10 percent. (p. 89)

due process the idea stated in the Fifth and Fourteenth Amendments that every person involved in a legal dispute is entitled to a fair hearing or trial. The requirements of due process vary with the situation, but they basically require notice and an opportunity to be heard. (pp. 441, 484)

duress unlawful pressure on a person to do something that he or she would not otherwise do. Duress may be a defense to a criminal charge. (p. 132)

duty a legal obligation (p. 251)

duty to mitigate (damages) the legal responsibility to make damages from a harm such as breaching a contract less severe if possible (p. 339)

E

elements the conditions that make an act unlawful (pp. 101, 251)

emancipated the condition of having reached legal adulthood; usually at age 16, 18, or 21 (p. 408)

emancipation the freeing of a child from the control of parents and allowing the child to live on his or her own or under the control of others. It usually applies to adolescents who leave the parents' household by agreement or demand. Emancipation may also end the responsibility of a divorced parent to pay child support. (p. 397)

embezzlement the taking of money or property by a person to whom it has been entrusted; for example, a bank teller or a company accountant (p. 119)

employment-at-will contract a work agreement in which the employee can quit at any time, and the employer can fire the employee for any reason or no reason at all (p. 560)

entrapment an act by law enforcement officials to persuade a person to commit a crime that the person would not otherwise have committed. If proven, entrapment is a valid defense to a criminal charge (p. 131)

equal protection a constitutional requirement of the Fourteenth Amendment that protects individuals against unlawful discrimination by government (pp. 442, 503)

Equal Rights Amendment a proposed amendment to the U.S. Constitution preventing gender discrimination. It was not ratified by enough states, so it was not added. (p. 518)

equitable distribution a system for dividing property at the end of a marriage in which each spouse is entitled to his or her separate property brought into or acquired during the marriage. Marital property is divided according to factors such as need and length of the marriage. (p. 384)

error of law a mistake made by a judge in legal procedures or rulings during a trial that may allow the case to be appealed (p. 51)

escrow money or property that a neutral party, such as a bank, holds for someone until that person fulfills some obligation or requirement (p. 319)

establishment clause part of the First Amendment to the U.S. Constitution that prohibits government from establishing a church or preferring one religion over another (p. 477)

estate an individual's personal property, including money, stocks, and all belongings (p. 317)

eviction the action by a landlord of removing a tenant from a rental unit (p. 358)

exclusionary rule a legal rule that generally prohibits the use of illegally obtained evidence against the defendant at trial; generally applies to violations of a defendant's Fourth, Fifth, or Sixth Amendment rights (p. 141)

Glossary

exclusive remedy the only solution, or compensation, available to a plaintiff in a particular legal situation (p. 229)

executive branch the administrative branch of a government; responsible for carrying out (enforcing) laws. This branch includes a chief executive (for example, the president), executive offices, and agencies. (p. 16)

expectation damages money the breaching party in a contract dispute must pay to make the other party as well off as if the contract had not been breached (p. 339)

express warranty a statement of fact or a demonstration concerning the quality or performance of goods offered for sale (p. 281)

extortion taking property illegally through threats of harm (often called blackmail) (p. 119)

F

fair use a clause of the copyright statute that allows limited reproduction of a copyrighted work for noncommercial purposes (p. 246)

false imprisonment the intentional or wrongful confinement of another person against his or her will (p. 235)

family car doctrine a legal rule stating that the owner of a car will be liable for damage done by any family member driving the car (p. 402)

family foster care a system of licensed families in each state who act as temporary parents for children who cannot live with their families (p. 407)

family mediator a professional who works directly with a divorcing couple, helping them preserve their relationship for the future. To save time and money, this person helps the couple reach some agreements out of court. (p. 417)

family responsibility laws laws that require adult children to care for their elderly parents (p. 397)

federalism the division of powers between the states and the federal government (p. 17)

felony a serious criminal offense punishable by a prison sentence of more than one year (pp. 13, 102)

felony murder the killing of someone during the commission of certain felonies, regardless of intent to kill (which is usually required for a murder charge) (p. 108)

fighting words a legal term applying to words spoken face-to-face that are so abusive that they are likely to cause an imminent fight between the speaker and the person spoken to. Such words are not usually entitled to First Amendment protection. (p. 453)

finance charge additional money owed to a creditor in exchange for the privilege of borrowing money (p. 292)

fine a monetary penalty imposed upon someone (p. 174)

first-degree murder *see* murder

first sale the first purchaser of a piece of copyrighted material may legally resell that particular copy of the protected work (p. 245)

fixture (1) anything attached to land or a building; (2) those things that, once attached, may not be removed by a tenant (p. 362)

food stamps coupons given to people with incomes below a certain level. The coupons can be exchanged like money for food at authorized stores. (p. 430)

foreseeable harm injury a person could reasonably predict. For instance, a person who leaves a banana peel on the floor could reasonably predict that someone might slip on the peel, fall, and break a bone. If this happens, the broken bone is a foreseeable harm. (p. 255)

forgery the act of making a fake document or altering a real one with the intent to commit fraud (p. 121)

foster parents a couple or family who take in and care for a child who is without parents or who has been removed from the custody of his or her parents (pp. 407–408)

fraud any deception, lie, or dishonest statement made to cheat someone or induce him or her to agree to a contract (pp. 280, 337)

free exercise clause part of the First Amendment to the U.S. Constitution that protects individuals' right to worship as they choose (p. 477)

fringe benefit an item provided by an employer to employees free of charge or at reduced cost (p. 549)

G

garnishment the legally authorized process of taking a person's money, generally by taking part of the person's wages in order to pay creditors (p. 307)

gerrymandering redrawing voting district lines to ensure that a particular group of people is included in the same districts (p. 511)

goals the number of minority applicants considered to be a fair proportion of the total employees selected for a business or of students accepted into an educational institution (p. 506)

grand jury a group of 16 to 23 people who hear preliminary evidence to decide if there is sufficient reason to formally charge a person with a crime (p. 160)

group home a residence in which several children in foster care live together under the supervision and care of licensed individuals (p. 408)

guilty but mentally ill a verdict that allows convicted criminal defendants to be sent to a hospital and later transferred to a prison after recovery from mental illness (p. 130)

H

habeas corpus Latin for "you have the body"; a writ (court order) which directs the law enforcement officials who have custody of a prisoner to appear in court with the prisoner to help the judge determine whether the prisoner is being held lawfully (p. 172)

hacker a person who illegally accesses government or corporate computer systems (p. 123)

hate speech bigoted speech attacking or disparaging a social or ethnic group or a member of such a group (p. 455)

hearing the process by which a judge or other court officer hears evidence to determine the factual or legal issues in a case (p. 156)

home confinement the type of sentence in which the defendant must serve the term at home and usually can leave only for essential purposes, such as work or school (p. 174)

homicide the killing of another person. Homicide can be criminal, noncriminal, or negligent. *See also* manslaughter *and* murder. (p. 107)

hostile environment an uncomfortable working environment in the context of sexual harassment (p. 522)

housing codes the municipal ordinances that regulate standards of safety and upkeep for buildings (p. 357)

human rights basic privileges a person has as a human being (p. 8)

hung jury the situation in which a jury cannot reach a unanimous decision (p. 49)

Glossary

immune—insanity defense

I

immune exempt from penalties, payments, or legal requirements; free from prosecution (p. 221)

immunity freedom from; protection from some action, such as being sued or prosecuted (p. 170)

implied consent an unwritten agreement to submit to forms of interrogation or searches in exchange for certain privileges, such as driving or flying (p. 90)

implied warranty the unwritten minimum standard of quality the law requires of products offered for sale (p. 283)

imprisonment confinement, usually in jail or prison. *See also* false imprisonment. (p. 174)

incapacitation a reason for criminal punishment that stresses keeping a convicted person confined to protect society (p. 177)

incarceration imprisonment by the state (p. 78)

incest sexual relations between people who are closely related to each other (p. 378)

incitement test a method used by courts to determine whether to restrict or punish expression based on its potential to cause immediate unlawful behavior (p. 454)

indictment a grand jury's formal charge or accusation of criminal action (p. 160)

infancy the legal defense of a person considered not yet legally responsible for his or her actions; the time before which a person becomes entitled to the legal rights and responsibilities normally held by citizens (p. 129)

infliction of emotional distress a tort in which a defendant purposely engages in an action that causes extreme emotional harm to the plaintiff (p. 233)

information a prosecuting attorney's formal accusation of the defendant, detailing the nature and circumstances of the charge (p. 158)

infringement the illegal use of someone's intellectual property, such as a copyright, patent, or trademark (p. 243)

inherent powers the powers that Congress is assumed to have because they result logically from the powers expressly listed in the U.S. Constitution. These powers are derived from the "necessary and proper clause" of the Constitution, which allows Congress to expand its power to carry out functions expressly delegated by the Constitution; also known as implied powers. *See also* delegated powers. (p. 56)

inheritance property received from a deceased person either by intestacy laws or from a will (pp. 386, 403)

initial hearing a preliminary examination of the validity of a youth's arrest, during which the state must prove that an offense was committed and that there is reasonable cause to believe the accused youth committed it. Decisions are made about further detention and legal representation, and a date is set for a hearing on the facts. (p. 199)

initiative a procedure by which voters can propose a law and submit it to the electorate or the legislature for approval (p. 34)

injunction a court order requiring a person to do, or refrain from doing, a particular act (p. 240)

in loco parentis Latin for "in place of a parent"; person or body (such as a school) that is entrusted with a minor's care and has intentionally assumed some or all of the rights of a parent over the minor (p. 425)

inquisitional system a European method for handling disputes in which the judge plays an active role in gathering and presenting evidence and questioning witnesses (p. 47)

insanity defense defense raised by a criminal defendant stating that because of mental disease or defect, the defendant should not be held responsible for the crime committed (p. 130)

insurance a contract in which one party pays money and the other party promises to reimburse the first party for specified types of losses if they occur (pp. 223–224)

intake the informal process in which court officials or social workers decide if a complaint against a juvenile should be referred to juvenile court (p. 196)

intellectual property a person's idea or invention that is given special ownership protections (pp. 238, 242)

intentionally with purpose (p. 230)

intentional tort an action taken deliberately to harm another person and/or his or her property; intentional wrong (p. 230)

intentional wrong *see* intentional tort (p. 217)

interest money paid for the use of someone's money; the cost of borrowing money. Money put in a savings account earns interest, while borrowing money costs interest. (p. 292)

interrogate to question a witness or suspected criminal (p. 152)

intoxication a state of drunkenness or similar condition created by the use of drugs or alcohol (p. 129)

involuntary manslaughter *see* manslaughter

irreconcilable differences disagreement between a couple that is grounds for a no-fault divorce (p. 418)

J

jail a place of short-term confinement for persons convicted of misdemeanors or awaiting trial (p. 182)

Jim Crow law a statute or law created to enforce segregation in such places as schools, buses, and hotels (p. 500)

joint custody a custody arrangement in which divorced or separated parents have equal rights in making important decisions concerning their children (p. 419)

judgment a court's decision in a civil case (p. 212)

judicial branch the branch of government that interprets laws and resolves legal questions (p. 16)

judicial integrity as used in discussing search and seizure, this is an argument for the use of the exclusionary rule, which emphasizes that courts should not permit lawbreaking by the police (p. 163)

judicial review the process by which courts decide whether the laws passed by Congress or state legislatures are constitutional (p. 16)

jurisprudence the study of law and legal philosophy (p. 4)

jury in a legal proceeding, a body of men and women selected to hear and examine certain facts and determine the truth (pp. 48–49, 166–168)

juvenile a person not yet considered an adult for the purposes of determining either criminal or civil liability; a minor (pp. 189–190)

K

kinship care placement of a vulnerable youth in the continuous care and supervision of relatives who are not his or her parents as directed by a social services or other child welfare agency. Such an arrangement also often occurs informally. (pp. 408, 421)

L

labor relations law the branch of law that determines how unions and employers may operate (p. 551)

landlord the property owner who leases or rents space (p. 349)

Glossary

larceny the unlawful taking of another's property with the intent to steal it. Grand larceny, a felony, is the theft of anything above a certain value (often $100 or more). Petty larceny, a misdemeanor, is the theft of any thing below a certain value (often $100). (p. 116)

lease a rental contract between a landlord and a tenant for the use of property for a specified length of time at a specified cost (p. 350)

lease application a form the landlord uses to determine whether someone qualifies for a rental property (p. 350)

legal authority (1) legal rights granted to officials, giving them certain powers; (2) the body of statutes, case law, and other sources that serve as legal guidance (pp. 247–248)

legal defense a legally recognized excuse for a defendant's actions, such as implied consent, privilege, and self defense, which may remove liability for certain offenses (p. 218)

legal malpractice the type of lawsuit brought against a lawyer for loss or injury to his or her client caused by the lawyer's error or failure to meet acceptable standards of practice for the legal profession (p. 71)

legal separation a situation in which the two spouses are separated but still maintain some marital obligations (p. 415)

legislative branch the branch of government that passes laws. The U.S. Senate and House of Representatives comprise the legislative branch of the federal government. (p. 16)

legislative intent what the lawmakers who passed a law wanted the law to mean. If the language of a statute is unclear, judges will often look at the legislative intent to help them interpret the law. (p. 21)

liability legal responsibility; the obligation to do or not do something. The defendant in a tort case incurs liability for failing to use reasonable care, resulting in harm to the plaintiff. (p. 214)

liability insurance the type of coverage or insurance that pays for injuries to other people or damage to property if the individual insured is responsible for an accident during the term of the contract (p. 223)

liable legally responsible (p. 213)

libel a written expression about a person that is false and damages that person's reputation (pp. 236, 450)

limited government a basic principle of our constitutional system. It limits government to powers provided to it by the people (p. 16)

litigator a trial attorney; a barrister (p. 63)

loan sharking lending money at high, often illegal, interest rates (p. 300)

lobbying influencing or persuading legislators to take action to introduce a bill or vote a certain way on a proposed law (p. 31)

loss leader something (as merchandise) sold at a loss (or for very little profit) in order to draw customers in to a store (p. 315)

M

malice ill will; deliberate intent to harm someone (p. 108)

malpractice failure to meet acceptable standards of practice in any professional or official position; often the basis for lawsuits by clients or patients against their attorney or physician (p. 223)

mandatory sentencing laws that require courts to sentence convicted criminals to prison terms of a certain specified length (p. 176)

manslaughter the killing of a person without malice or premeditation, but during the commission of an illegal act. Manslaughter can be either voluntary, when intentional but not premeditated, resulting from the heat of passion or the diminished mental capacity of the killer; or involuntary, when unintentional but done during an unlawful act of a lesser nature. *See also* homicide *and* murder (p. 108)

marital property property acquired during a marriage, including joint bank accounts, real estate, automobiles, etc. Such property is considered to be owned equally by both spouses. (p. 383)

marriage counselor a person who is trained to help couples settle their marital problems (p. 415)

mediation the act or process of resolving a dispute between two or more parties (p. 43)

Medicaid a government program that provides medical care to people with low incomes (p. 433)

medical coverage insurance which covers an individual's own medical expenses resulting from accidents (p. 226)

Medicare the federal health insurance program available to people who are eligible for Social Security or Social Security Disability Insurance (p. 432)

minor a child; a person under the legal age of adulthood, usually 18 or 21 (p. 220)

Miranda warnings rights that a person must be told of when arrested or taken into custody by police or other officials. These include the right to remain silent, to contact a lawyer, and to have a free lawyer provided if the person arrested cannot afford one. (pp. 152–153)

misdemeanor a criminal offense, less serious than a felony, punishable by a prison sentence of one year or less (pp. 13, 102)

misprision of felony federal crime, punishable by up to three years in prison, for not providing the government with information a person knows regarding the commission of another crime (p. 106)

mistrial the termination of a trial before its normal conclusion because of procedural error, statements by a witness, judge, or attorney which prejudice a jury, a deadlock by a jury without reaching a verdict after lengthy deliberation (a "hung jury"), or the failure to complete a trial within the time set by the court. A new trial must be ordered and the case starts over from the beginning. (p. 171)

mitigating circumstances factors that tend to lessen the seriousness of an offense. The presence of these factors must be considered by the judge or jury (p. 180)

monopoly exclusive ownership or possession (p. 244)

month-to-month lease a lease enabling the tenant to leave with 30 days' notice and the landlord to raise the rent or evict the tenant with 30 days' notice (p. 351)

mortgage a loan in which land or buildings are put up as security (p. 349)

motion a request made by one party to a lawsuit that a judge take specific action or make a decision (p. 161)

motion for change of venue a request to change the location of a trial to avoid community hostility, for the convenience of a witness, or for other reasons (p. 162)

motion for a continuance a request to postpone a lawsuit to gain more time to prepare the case (p. 162)

motion for discovery of evidence a request by the defendant to examine, before trial, certain evidence possessed by the prosecution (p. 161)

motion to suppress evidence a motion filed by a criminal defense attorney, asking the court to exclude any evidence that was illegally obtained from the attorney's client (p. 162)

motive the reason a person commits a crime (p. 100)

Glossary

murder the unlawful killing of a person with malice aforethought. Murder in the first degree is planned in advance and done with malice or during the commission of a dangerous felony. Murder in the second degree does not require malice or premeditation but is the result of a desire to inflict bodily harm. It is done without excuse, and is therefore more serious than manslaughter. *See also* manslaughter, homicide, *and* malice. (p. 108)

N

national origin country where one was born or from which one's ancestors came (p. 500)

necessities those things that parents have a legal obligation to provide to their children and that one spouse has the responsibility to provide to the other. These usually include food, clothing, housing, and medical care. (p. 394)

necessity a defense to a criminal charge that shows a just or lawful reason for the defendant's conduct (p. 132)

neglect the failure of a parent or guardian to properly feed, clothe, shelter, educate, or tend to the medical needs of a child (p. 188)

negligence the failure to exercise a reasonable amount of care in either doing or not doing something, resulting in harm or injury to another person (pp. 108, 218, 250)

negligent homicide causing death through criminally negligent behavior (p. 108)

negotiation the process of discussing an issue to reach a settlement or agreement (p. 41)

no-fault divorce a divorce in which neither party is charged with any wrongdoing. The marriage is ended on the grounds that there are irreconcilable differences (i.e., basic disagreements) that caused the marriage to break down. (p. 418)

no-fault insurance a form of automobile or accident insurance (available in only a few states) in which each person's insurance company pays up to a certain share of damages, regardless of fault (p. 227)

nolo contendere Latin phrase meaning "no contest"; a defendant's plea to criminal charges that does not admit guilt but also does not contest the charges. It is equivalent to a guilty plea, but cannot be used as evidence in a later civil trial for damages based on the same facts. (p. 161)

nominal damages a token amount of money awarded by a court to a plaintiff to show that the claim was justified, even if the plaintiff is unable to prove economic harm (p. 231)

nonbinding arbitration a method in which disputants agree to have a third party listen to arguments from both sides and make a decision that is not final (i.e., either party may still take other steps to settle the dispute) (p. 43)

notice a written statement intended to inform a person of some proceeding in which his or her interests are involved (p. 487)

novel truly new or unique (p. 243)

nuisance an unreasonable interference with the use and enjoyment of one's property, usually repeated or continued for prolonged periods of time (p. 240)

O

obscenity a general term applying to anything that is immoral, indecent, or lewd (p. 448)

offer a specific proposal by one person to another to make a deal or contract (p. 276)

ombudsperson a person who has the power to investigate reported complaints and help achieve fair settlements (p. 44)

opening statement at the start of a trial, one side's explanation of what it expects to prove and how it intends to prove it (p. 49)

ordinance a county or city law (p. 21)

overt open; clear (For example, an overt act in criminal law is more than mere preparation to do something; it is at least the first step of actually attempting the crime.) (p. 106)

P

palimony the support payment that one partner may make or be ordered by a court to make to the other when an unmarried couple, romantically involved and living together, breaks up and no longer cohabitates (p. 391)

parens patriae Latin for "parent of the country"; the doctrine that allows the government to take care of minors and others who cannot legally take care of themselves (p. 188)

parental responsibility laws statutes in which parents are held responsible and may be prosecuted for crimes committed by their children (p. 189)

parochial school a private school supported and controlled by a religious organization (p. 480)

parole release from prison before the full sentence has been served, granted at the discretion of a parole board (p. 177)

parties the people directly concerned with or taking part in any legal matter (p. 46)

patent federal protection for an invention or design, giving the inventor exclusive ownership rights for a period of time (p. 242)

paternity fatherhood (p. 395)

paternity leave a temporary absence from work for men to care for their infants (p. 434)

paternity suit a lawsuit brought by a woman against a man she claims is the father of her child. If paternity is proven, the man is legally responsible for contributing to the support of the child. (p. 395)

penological of or relating to the criminal corrections process (p. 476)

peremptory challenge part of the pretrial jury selection. Attorneys on opposing sides may dismiss a certain number of possible jurors without giving any reason. There is one exception: peremptory challenges cannot be used to discriminate based on race. (pp. 50, 167)

personal property property or belongings that can be moved, such as cars, clothing, furniture, and appliances (p. 238)

personal recognizance a release from legal custody based on a defendant's promise to show up for trial. An alternative to cash bail, this practice is used if the judge decides that the defendant is likely to return. (p. 157)

petition (1) to file charges in a juvenile court proceeding (p. 195); (2) a request to a court or public official (p. 34)

petitioner one who signs and/or files a petition. The party initiating or appealing a case to the Supreme Court is referred to as the petitioner. (p. 172)

petition for certiorari *Certiorari* is a Latin word meaning "to be informed of." It is a formal application by a party to have a lower-court decision reviewed by the U.S. Supreme Court, which has discretion to approve or deny any such application. (p. 57)

picketing a gathering of individuals in a public place to express their opposition to certain views or practices (p. 551)

plaintiff in a civil case, the injured party who brings legal action against the alleged wrongdoer (pp. 13, 46, 212)

plea bargaining in a criminal case, the negotiations between the prosecutor, defendant, and defendant's attorney. In exchange for the defendant agreeing to plead guilty, the prosecutor agrees to charge the defendant with a

Glossary

less serious crime, which usually results in a lesser punishment. (p. 164)

polygamy the practice of having more than one spouse at the same time. Polygamy is illegal in the United States. (p. 379)

polygraph test a lie-detector instrument (p. 546)

precedent court decision on a legal question that guides future cases with similar questions (pp. 26, 51)

preference a method used to increase the number of minorities admitted to educational programs and hired for jobs. It involves giving some advantage to minority applicants. (p. 506)

preliminary hearing pretrial proceeding at which the prosecutor must prove that a crime was committed and establish the probable guilt of the defendant. If the evidence presented does not show probable guilt, the judge may dismiss the case. (p. 160)

premiums payments made for insurance coverage (p. 223)

prenuptial agreement a contractual agreement between a couple prior to marriage. It often includes provisions for the disposal of property in the event of separation, divorce, or death. (p. 385)

preponderance of the evidence usually the standard of proof used in a civil suit; the burden of proof that a party must meet in order to win the lawsuit. To win, a party must provide evidence that is more convincing than the other side's evidence. (pp. 14, 219)

presentence report a probation officer's written report that gives the sentencing judge information about the defendant's background and prospects for rehabilitation (p. 176)

pretrial motion a document by which a party asks the judge to make a decision or take some action before the trial begins (p. 161)

preventive detention holding a person (such as a juvenile) against his or her will without bail until trial because of the likelihood that the individual will commit another crime (p. 199)

principal the person who commits a crime (p. 102)

prior restraint any effort to censor a publication before it goes to press (p. 468)

prison a place of confinement for criminals who are serving long-term sentences (p. 182)

privacy the state of being left alone (p. 490)

privilege (1) an advantage, right to preferential treatment, or excuse from a duty others must perform; (2) a right that cannot be taken away; (3) the right to speak or write personally damaging words because the law specially allows it (p. 247); (4) the right and the duty to withhold information from others because of some special status or relationship of confidentiality. These privileges include husband-wife, doctor-patient, and attorney-client. (p. 69)

privilege against self-incrimination the rule, derived from the Fifth Amendment, that says suspects have a right to remain silent and cannot be forced to testify against themselves. (p. 152)

probable cause a reasonable belief, known personally or through reliable sources, that a specific person has committed a crime (p. 134)

probate the process of proving to a court that a will is genuine; distributing property according to the terms of a will (p. 53)

probation a system of supervised freedom, usually by a probation officer, for persons convicted of a criminal offense. Typically, the probationee must agree to certain conditions such as getting a job, avoiding drugs, and not traveling outside a limited area. (pp. 174, 200)

procedural due process a citizen's right to fair access to the courts and to fair treatment in those courts. Generally, a right to fair treatment when government action affects a person's interests. (p. 484)

product liability the legal responsibility of manufacturers and sellers for injuries caused by defective products they produce or sell (p. 264)

pro se Latin term meaning "for oneself" or "on one's own behalf"; typically used to describe a person who represents himself or herself in court (p. 417)

prosecution the side bringing a criminal case against another party (pp. 46, 49)

prosecutor the state or federal government's attorney in a criminal case (pp. 14, 46)

protective order in family law, a court order directing one spouse not to abuse the other spouse or the children. The penalty for violating a protective order is jail. (p. 390)

proximate cause in negligence law, this concept limits damages the defendant must pay to only those harms that are reasonably predictable consequences of the defendant's wrongful acts. *See also* foreseeable harm. (p. 255)

public domain property that belongs to the public; the point at which an unprotected idea or invention reaches the public and no longer belongs to the creator (p. 245)

public forum any place, such as a park or street, where First Amendment expression rights are traditionally exercised (pp. 459, 472)

public hearings proceedings that are open to the public. During these proceedings, evidence is considered and then a decision is reached based on this evidence. (p. 25)

puffing an exaggerated statement or advertisement as to the desirability or reliability of a product or service (pp. 282, 314)

punitive damages awards in excess of the proven economic loss. In a tort action, they are awarded to the plaintiff to punish the defendant and to warn others not to engage in such conduct. (p. 232)

Q

quid pro quo Latin for "this for that"; an exchange of things or favors (p. 520)

quotas a system that requires a certain number of minority applicants be selected for educational programs or jobs; such a system is generally unconstitutional in government-funded programs (p. 506)

R

racial profiling the inappropriate use of race as a factor in identifying people who may break or who may have broken the law (p. 148)

rape unlawful sexual intercourse. It is committed when one party forces another party to have sexual intercourse. It implies lack of consent. (p. 112)

ratify to confirm a previous act of another even though it was not approved beforehand. For example, when the president negotiates a treaty, the Senate must ratify it for it to become law. (p. 278)

real property land and all items attached to it, such as houses, crops, and fences (p. 238)

reasonable-person standard the idealized standard of how a community expects its members to act. It is based on how much care a person of ordinary prudence would exercise in a particular situation. (p. 253)

reasonable suspicion evidence that justifies an officer in stopping and questioning an individual believed to be involved in criminal activity; based on less evidence than probable cause but more than a mere hunch (p. 136)

Glossary

rebuttal argument the presentation of facts to a court, demonstrating that the testimony of a witness or evidence presented by the opposing party is not true (p. 49)

recall the removal of an elected official from office by a vote of the people (p. 34)

receiving stolen property receiving or buying property that is known or reasonably believed to be stolen (p. 121)

recidivist a repeat criminal offender, convicted of a crime after having been previously convicted (p. 92)

redlining a discriminatory practice in which certain geographical areas in a community are designated by a bank or other lender as ineligible for mortgage loans (p. 537)

referendum a procedure in which issues are voted on directly by the citizens rather than by their representatives in government (p. 34)

referral sale a selling technique in which a seller offers customers incentives (usually in the form of a discount) for generating additional sales by referring other potential customers to the seller. The consumer generally will receive the incentives only in cases where a referral results in a sale. (p. 311)

regulation a rule made by a government agency (p. 21)

rehabilitation the process through which a convicted person is changed or reformed, in order to lead a productive life rather than commit another crime (p. 177)

rehabilitative alimony after a divorce, money awarded to a spouse for the purpose of regaining or developing job skills (p. 423)

release (1) the giving up of a claim or right by a person; (2) a landlord's act of excusing a tenant from all duties related to the apartment or house and the lease (p. 364)

remedy what is done to compensate for an injury or to enforce some right (pp. 213, 326)

removal for cause part of the jury selection process. After voir dire, opposing attorneys may request removal of any juror who does not appear capable of rendering a fair and impartial verdict. (p. 50)

rent control a law that limits how much existing rents can be raised. Large cities often have such laws. (p. 356)

repossess to take back a debtor's property because the debtor failed to repay a debt (p. 306)

rescission the act of canceling a contract and treating it as if it never existed (p. 339)

restitution the act of restoring something to its owner; the act of making good for loss or damage; repaying or refunding illegally obtained money or property (pp. 95, 326, 339)

restorative justice a concept in criminal justice that emphasizes reparation to the victim or the affected members of the community by the offender, as by cash payment or by community service (p. 198)

retainer a down payment by which a client hires an attorney to act in his or her behalf (p. 68)

retribution punishment given as a kind of revenge for wrongdoing (p. 176)

revoke to take back or cancel (p. 334)

right of entry or access the provision of a lease that allows a landlord and his or her agents to enter a tenant's premises to make repairs, collect rent, or enforce other provisions of the lease (p. 363)

right to die the right of terminally ill (or comatose) patients not to be kept alive by artificial or extraordinary means (p. 486)

right to quiet enjoyment a tenant's basic right to use and enjoy a rented or leased property without unnecessary disturbance by the landlord or other tenants (p. 365)

right-to-work state a state in which it is illegal to require workers to pay union dues as a condition of employment (p. 551)

robbery the unlawful taking of property from a person's immediate possession by force or intimidation (p. 119)

S

search warrant a court order issued by a judge or magistrate, giving police the power to search a person or to enter a building to search for and seize items related to a crime (p. 141)

second-degree murder *see* murder

secular not of a religious nature (p. 480)

secured credit credit for which the consumer must put up some kind of property as protection in the event a debt is not repaid (p. 292)

security deposit refundable money that a landlord requires a tenant to pay before moving in; used to cover any damages, cleaning costs, or unpaid rent, if such fees arise (pp. 360–361)

segregation the now unconstitutional practice of separating persons in housing, education, public facilities, and other ways based on their race, color, nationality, or other arbitrary categorization (p. 500)

self-defense the right to defend oneself with whatever force is reasonably necessary against an actual or reasonably perceived threat of personal harm (p. 248)

self-incrimination giving evidence and answering questions that would tend to subject one to criminal prosecution (p. 152)

separate-but-equal doctrine the rule, now unconstitutional, that allowed facilities to be racially segregated as long as they were basically equal (p. 500)

separate property a system under which property owned by either spouse before the marriage remains that person's property throughout the marriage, and any property acquired during the marriage belongs to the person who acquired it (p. 383)

separation agreement a written document that lists the continuing legal rights and duties of each spouse when a couple separates, including alimony, child custody, support, and division of property (p. 415)

separation of powers the division of power among the branches of government (executive, legislative, and judicial) (p. 16)

service charge a fee for service, such as using a bank's ATM (p. 300)

set-asides certain amounts of government money and work reserved for companies owned by members of minority groups (p. 510)

settlement a mutual agreement between two sides in a civil lawsuit, made either before the case goes to trial or before a final judgment is entered, that settles or ends the dispute (pp. 41, 215)

severance pay money paid to employees who have been dismissed (generally through no fault of their own) to compensate for the time they are not going to work because of the job loss (p. 565)

sexual assault unwelcome sexual contact against another individual committed through the use of force, threat, or intimidation, or enabled because the victim is incapacitated due to drugs, alcohol, or mental disability (p. 112)

sexual harassment unwelcome sexual advances, requests for sexual favors, and other verbal or physical conduct of a sexual nature that occurs in the workplace (p. 520)

Glossary

shoplifting a form of larceny in which a person takes items from a store without paying or intending to pay (p. 117)

slander spoken expression about a person that is false and damages that person's reputation (pp. 236, 450)

small claims court a court that handles civil claims for small amounts of money. People usually represent themselves in this type of court rather than hire an attorney. (pp. 53, 340–341)

solicitation the act of requesting or strongly urging someone to do something. If the request is to do something illegal, solicitation is considered a crime. (p. 104)

specific performance a remedy available in civil court in which the breaching party must do exactly what he or she promised under the contract (p. 339)

spouse abuse the physical, sexual, psychological, or emotional harm by one spouse against the other (pp. 386–389)

stalking the act of following or harassing another person, causing the fear of death or injury (p. 112)

standard of proof the level of certainty and the degree of evidence necessary to establish proof in a criminal or civil proceeding. The standard of proof in a criminal trial is generally beyond a reasonable doubt, whereas a civil case generally requires the lesser standard of preponderance of the evidence. *See* preponderance of the evidence. (p. 219)

state of mind what you are thinking; most crimes require that the actor have a guilty state of mind, meaning that he or she purposefully commits the prohibited act (p. 100)

status offender a minor who has committed an act that would not be a crime if committed by an adult, such as truancy from school, running away from home, or being habitually disobedient. They are considered beyond the control of their legal guardians. (p. 188)

status offense an illegal act that can only be committed by a juvenile (for example, truancy or running away from home) (pp. 191–192)

statutes written laws enacted by legislatures (pp. 16, 20, 216)

statutory rape the act of unlawful sexual intercourse by an adult with someone under the age of consent, even if the minor is a willing and voluntary participant in the sexual act (p. 112)

steering a discriminatory practice in which real estate agents direct buyers or renters to particular areas because of their race or for other unlawful reasons (p. 537)

stop and frisk to "pat down" or search the outer clothing of someone whom the police believe is acting suspiciously (p. 136)

stop payment a depositor's order to a bank to refuse to honor a specified check drawn by him or her (p. 290)

strict liability the legal responsibility for damage or injury even if you are not negligent (pp. 101, 218, 284)

strike the act in which employees stop, slow down, or disrupt work to win demands from an employer (p. 551)

sublease clause the provision of most standard leases that requires the tenant to obtain the landlord's permission before allowing someone else to live on the premises and pay all or part of the rent (p. 364)

subpoena a court order to appear in court or turn over documents on a specified date and time (p. 169)

substance a chemical, often mind-altering, that people abuse, such as alcohol, drugs, and tobacco (p. 88)

Glossary

substance abuse the harmful overuse of chemicals, such as drugs or alcohol (p. 88)

substantive due process used by courts to protect basic freedoms by making sure that government does not violate a fundamental right without good reason (p. 484)

suicide the deliberate taking of one's own life (p. 110)

supremacy clause the provision in Article VI of the Constitution stating that U.S. laws and treaties must be followed even if state and local laws disagree with the Constitution and these treaties (p. 21)

surrogate mother a woman, other than the wife, who agrees to be artificially inseminated with the sperm of the husband of a couple desiring a child, to carry the resulting child to term, and to release legal custody to the couple immediately following birth (p. 411)

suspended sentence a sentence issued by the court but not actually served. The individual is usually released by the court with no conditions attached. (p. 174)

symbolic speech conduct that expresses an idea (for example, wearing a black armband to protest a war) (p. 462)

T

temporary legal guardian the state's role in making most decisions for children whose parents are temporarily unable to care for them. The parents usually retain limited rights. (p. 407)

tenancy at will an arrangement in which a tenant remains on rented property beyond the end of the lease with the understanding that the tenant may leave, or be asked to leave, at any time. (p. 351)

tenancy for years any lease for a fixed period of time. This type of lease specifies that the tenant may live on the property for a single definite period of time, during which the landlord may not raise the rent or evict the tenant. (p. 352)

tenant a person who rents property (p. 349)

tender years doctrine the presumption (now rejected by most states) that a young child is always better off living with his or her mother (p. 420)

term (1) a word; (2) a condition of an agreement; (3) a length or duration of time (p. 349)

terminate parental rights a court decision ending the rights of an unfit parent, leaving the child available for adoption by the foster family, relatives, or others (p. 408)

testify to provide evidence under oath (pp. 169–170)

throwaways children, usually older teenagers, whose parents have refused to continue to care for them (p. 403)

tort a breach of some obligation, causing harm or injury to someone; a civil wrong, such as negligence or libel (p. 212)

tort action a civil lawsuit for damages (p. 212)

tort reform the movement that focuses on changing the process of settling tort claims. It emphasizes methods other than going to court or establishes limitations on how much money the winning party may receive. (p. 269)

toxic torts a lawsuit against a manufacturer of a toxic substance for harm caused by the manufacture or disposal of that substance (p. 262)

transfer hearing to move a juvenile felony case to adult criminal court. Also called waiver hearing. (p. 190)

Glossary

treaty a pact between nations; if entered into by the United States through its executive branch, the pact must be approved by "two-thirds of the senators present," under Article II, Section 2 of the Constitution, to become effective. (p. 26)

trespass the unauthorized intrusion on, or improper use of, property belonging to another person. This can be the basis of an intentional tort case or a criminal prosecution. (p. 238)

trial a court proceeding (p. 26)

trial courts courts that listen to testimony, consider evidence, and decide the facts in a disputed situation (p. 46)

truant a child who stays away from school without permission (p. 398)

U

unauthorized use of a vehicle unlawful taking of a car by someone who intends only to use it temporarily (p. 121)

unconscionable (1) unfair, harsh, oppressive; (2) a sales practice or term in a contract that is so unfair that a judge will not permit it (p. 279)

unconstitutional conflicting with some provision of the Constitution (p. 16)

unemployment compensation the government system that protects employees who lose their jobs through no fault of their own, by providing them with payments while they look for other jobs (p. 566)

unfair labor practices the failure on the part of an employer or a union to abide by the regulations of the *National Labor Relations Act* (p. 551)

uninsured motorist coverage insurance that protects drivers from those with no insurance or inadequate insurance. It compensates the insured for the personal injuries or damage the uninsured driver caused. (p. 227)

union an association of workers that seeks to secure favorable wages, improve working conditions and hours, and resolve grievances with employers (p. 550)

unsecured credit credit based only on a promise to repay in the future (p. 292)

U.S. Constitution the written document that contains the fundamental laws of the nation and the principles of a free, representative democracy (pp. 15, 570–599)

usury the unlawful act of charging interest for various types of credit at rates higher than the state's legal limit (p. 299)

uttering offering to someone as genuine a document known to be a fake (p. 121)

V

vagueness indefiniteness, uncertainty, imprecision; not clear or specific (p. 462)

vandalism the deliberate destruction or defacement of another person's property; also known as malicious mischief (p. 116)

variable interest rate interest charged for credit at a rate that changes slightly from time to time, going up or down within certain limits, depending on changes in the economy (p. 299)

verdict a jury's decision on a trial case (p. 49)

veto prohibit; in government, the veto is the power of a chief executive to prevent enactment of a bill (i.e., to prevent the bill from becoming a law) (p. 16)

visitation rights following a divorce or separation, the right of the parent without custody of the children to visit and spend time with those children (p. 419)

voir dire from the French phrase meaning "to speak the truth." It is the screening process in which opposing lawyers question prospective jurors to ensure as favorable or as fair a jury as possible (p. 50)

voluntary manslaughter *see* manslaughter

W

waive to give up some right, privilege, or benefit voluntarily (pp. 167, 221, 362)

waiver hearing *see* transfer hearing

waiver of tort liability a lease clause in which the tenant agrees to give up the usual right to hold the landlord responsible for personal injuries (p. 362)

warrant a paper signed by a judge authorizing some action, such as an arrest or search and seizure (pp. 134, 141, 143)

warranty a guarantee or promise made by a seller or manufacturer concerning the quality or performance of goods offered for sale (p. 281)

warranty of fitness for a particular purpose a seller's promise, implied by law, that the item sold will meet the buyer's stated purpose (p. 284)

warranty of habitability the implied, or unwritten, obligation of a landlord to provide a unit fit for human habitation (p. 357)

warranty of merchantability an implied promise that the item sold is of at least average quality for that type of item (p. 284)

warranty of title the seller's promise that he or she owns and may transmit title to the item being offered for sale (p. 284)

waste damages caused by a tenant's misuse or neglect of property. The landlord can force the tenant to make repairs or can sue for damages. (p. 360)

welfare financial or other aid provided, especially by the government, to people in need (p. 429)

whistle blowing when an employee tells authorities about his or her employer's illegal acts (p. 563)

will a legal document that states what a person wants done with his or her belongings after death (p. 371)

workers' compensation system a system of compensating employees who are injured on the job. These benefits are paid no matter who caused the accident, but limit a worker's ability to collect damages through the tort system. (pp. 228–229)

work release the type of sentence in which a defendant is allowed to work in the community but is required to return to prison at night or on weekends (p. 174)

writ a judge's order, or authorization, for something to be done (p. 172)

wrongful conduct unreasonable behavior that violates an individual's duty to others (p. 251)

Y

youth court a court proceeding for sentencing minors who have taken responsibility for their actions. The system aims to involve the community directly and to teach the young offenders the impact of their acts. *See also* restorative justice. (p. 198)

Index

Index

Index

Index

Index

Index

Index

Index

Index

Index

Index

Index

Index

Photo Credits

Cover (t)Getty Images, (b)Michael Dunning/Getty Images; **i** Michael Dunning/Getty Images; **iv** (t)Mark Burnett/Stock Boston, (b)Mike Powell/AllSport/Getty Images; **v** (t)SuperStock, (b)A. Ramey/PhotoEdit; **vi** (t)Kathy McLaughlin/The Image Works, (b)AP/Wide World Photos; **vii** (t)Thinkstock/Getty Images, (b)AP/Wide World Photos; **viii** Chabruken/Getty Images; **ix** (t)Digital Vision, (b)Frank Siteman/PhotoEdit; **x** (t)Spencer Grant/PhotoEdit, (b)Image Source/elektraVision/PictureQuest; **xi** (t)Image Source/elektraVision/PictureQuest, (b)Myrleen Ferguson Cate/PhotoEdit; **xii** (t)Jonathan Nourok/PhotoEdit, (b) John Neubauer/Rainbow; **xiii** (t)Robert W. Kelley/Time Life Pictures/Getty Images, (b)David J. & Janice L. Frent Collection/CORBIS; **2** Getty Images; **2-3** Elliott Teel/DCstockphoto.com; **4** Jon Feingersh/Stock Boston/PictureQuest; **5** Bob Rowan/Progressive Image/CORBIS; **7** Peter Turnley/CORBIS; **9** Courtesy of the Franklin D. Roosevelt Library; **11** AP/Wide World Photos; **12** Arthur Schatz/Time Life Pictures/Getty Images; **14** Time Inc./Time Life Pictures/Getty Images; **15** Bettmann/CORBIS; **17** Francis Miller/Time Life Pictures/Getty Images; **19** Mark Burnett/Stock Boston; **20** Bettmann/CORBIS; **22** Corey Lynn; **24** Digital Vision; **25** Mike Theiler/Getty Images; **27** Stuart Franklin/Magnum Photos; **28** Henryk Kaiser/eStock Photography, (inset) SuperStock; **29** Bob Daemmrich/Stock Boston/PictureQuest; **31** Bob Daemmrich/Stock Boston; **34** Bob Daemmrich/The Image Works; **35** Library of Congress; **38** AP/Wide World Photos; **40** Mike Powell/AllSport/Getty Images; **42** Michael Newman/PhotoEdit; **45** CORBIS; **46** John Neubauer/PhotoEdit; **47** (l)Manuel H. De Leon/AFP/Getty Images, (r)Jeff Cadge/Getty Images; **49** Brand X Pictures; **50** John Neubauer/PhotoEdit; **51** AP/Wide World Photos; **53** Kevin R. Morris/CORBIS; **56** AP/Wide World Photos; **59** The Supreme Court Historical Society; **61** Image Ideas/PictureQuest; **62** (t)AP/Wide World Photos, (b)Dave Bartruff/CORBIS; **63** Wolfgang Kaehler/CORBIS; **64** Davis Barber/PhotoEdit; **66** Bob Daemmrich/Stock Boston; **67** Jeff Greenberg/Rainbow; **69** Brand X Pictures; **72** Doug Martin; **72–73** A. Ramey/Stock Boston; **74** Seth Resnick/Stock Boston/PictureQuest; **77** David Simson/Stock Boston/PictureQuest; **79** AP/Wide World Photos; **80** Frank Siteman/PhotoEdit; **82** Mark Richards/PhotoEdit; **83** Michael Newman/PhotoEdit; **85 87** Reuters NewMedia Inc./CORBIS; **89** Richard Hutchings/CORBIS; **90** Catherine Karnow/CORBIS; **93** Charles Gupton/Stock Boston/PictureQuest; **95** Rubberball Productions/Getty Images; **97** AP/Wide World Photos; **98** Rhoda Sidney/PhotoEdit; **100** Tom Carter/PhotoEdit; **103** Klaus Lahnstein/Getty Images; **105** (l)Steve Spak/911 Pictures, (r)Reuters NewMedia Inc./CORBIS; **107** A. Ramey/PhotoEdit; **109** Michael Newman/PhotoEdit; **110** Mary Kate Denny/PhotoEdit; **112** Brand X Pictures; **113** Mark Burnett/Stock Boston/PictureQuest; **115** Kathy McLaughlin/The Image Works; **117** (l)Getty Images, (r)Tony Freeman/PhotoEdit; **119** Reuters NewMedia Inc./CORBIS; **120** Getty Images; **121** CORBIS; **122** Touhig Sion/CORBIS Sygma; **123** Getty Images; **124** David W. Hamilton/Getty Images; **126** David Young-Wolff/Getty Images; **127** SIU/Visuals Unlimited; **129** Yellow Dog Productions/Getty Images; **130** Bettmann/CORBIS; **131** Ed Gifford/Masterfile; **133 135** CORBIS; **136** Brand X Pictures; **138** John Griffin/The Image Works; **140** Mikael Karlsson/911 Pictures; **142** William McCoy/Rainbow/PictureQuest; **143** Mark Burnett/Stock Boston; **144** Mark Burnett; **146 147** AP/Wide World Photos; **150** Shepard Sherbell/CORBIS Saba; **152** Bonnie Kamin/PhotoEdit; **155** Thinkstock/Getty Images; **156** Spencer Grant/PhotoEdit; **157** AP/Wide World Photos; **158** Jon Feingersh/Stock Boston/PictureQuest; **161** Jeff Greenberg/PhotoEdit; **162** CORBIS; **164** Michael Newman/PhotoEdit; **166** CORBIS; **171** Bob Daemmrich/Stock Boston/PictureQuest; **172** Getty Images; **173** Fabian Falcon/Stock Boston/PictureQuest; **174** Polak Matthew/CORBIS Sygma; **177** A. Ramey/PhotoEdit; **179** Tim Boyle/Getty Images; **180** Reuters NewMedia Inc./CORBIS; **183** AP/Wide World Photos; **186** Bob Daemmrich/The Image Works; **187** Alon Reininger/Contact Press/PictureQuest; **188** James Shaffer/PhotoEdit; **191** CLEO Photography/PhotoEdit; **193** AP/Wide World Photos; **196** Mitch Wojnarowicz/The Image Works; **198** Bob Daemmrich/Stock Boston/PictureQuest; **200** David Young-Wolff/PhotoEdit; **202** AP/Wide World Photos; **203** (l)David Young-Wolff/PhotoEdit, (r)Robert Clare/Getty Images; **204** Reuters NewMedia Inc./CORBIS; **205** CORBIS; **206** Steve Starr/CORBIS; **208** AFP/CORBIS; **210** Getty Images; **210–211** Tony Freeman/PhotoEdit; **212** Michael Heller/911 Pictures; **213** Chabruken/Getty Images; **215** Ron Chapple/Getty Images; **216** (l)Laura Dwight/CORBIS, (r)Joseph Devenney/Getty Images; **219** Kathleen Kliskey-Geraghty/Index Stock; **221** Lester Sloan; **222** AFP/CORBIS; **224** Getty Images; **225** Digital Vision; **227** Getty Images; **228** (l)David Weintraub/Stock Boston/PictureQuest, (r)Robert Brenner/PhotoEdit; **230** Reuters NewMedia Inc./CORBIS; **232** Bill Aron/PhotoEdit; **236** AP/Wide World Photos; **238** Dewitt Jones/CORBIS; **239** Martin Jones/Ecoscene/CORBIS; **241** Bertram Henry/Getty Images; **243** (l)Getty Images, (r)AP/Wide World Photos; **245** Arthur Tilley/i2i Images/PictureQuest; **246** Tom Prettyman/PhotoEdit; **250** Getty Images; **252** David R. Frazier Photolibrary; **254** Courtesy of Chicago Historical Society, negative #ICHi-02811; **258** Viviane Moos/CORBIS; **259** Jeff Greenberg/PhotoEdit; **260** ATABOY/Getty Images; **261** Gary Knight/Picturesque/PictureQuest; **263** Lester Lefkowitz/Getty Images; **263** Aneal Vohra/Unicorn Stock Photos; **266** (t)David Woo/Stock Boston/PictureQuest, (b)David Butow/CORBIS Saba; **268** Najlah Feanny/CORBIS; **270** Don Johnston/Getty Images; **272** AP/Wide World Photos; **274** Courtesy the Federal Trade Commission; **274–275** Elliott Teel/DCstockphoto.com; **276** Susan Van Etten/PhotoEdit; **278** Frank Siteman/PhotoEdit; **279** SuperStock; **280** Steve Peters/Getty Images; **281** Aaron Haupt; **284** Shawn Calvert; **286** Darrell Gulin/Getty Images; **287** Ed Taylor/Getty Images; **288** Michael Newman/PhotoEdit; **289** Getty Images; **292** Dennis MacDonald/PhotoEdit; **294** Aaron Haupt; **295** Getty Images; **297** David Young-Wolff/PhotoEdit; **301** Michael Newman/PhotoEdit; **302** Digital Vision; **305** CORBIS; **306** Jeff Greenberg/PhotoEdit; **308** Spencer Grant/PhotoEdit; **311 314** Shawn Calvert; **316** (l)Getty Images, (r)Brand X Pictures; **318** Getty Images, (inset)Ed Bock/CORBIS; **320** Francisco Cruz/SuperStock; **321** Image Source/elektraVision/PictureQuest; **323** (l)George DeSota/Getty Images, (r)Shawn Calvert/General Motors Corp. Used with permission, GM Media Archives; **325** (l)David Young-Wolff/PhotoEdit, (r)Shawn Calvert; **326** Michael Newman/PhotoEdit; **328** James Leynse/CORBIS Saba; **330** Bob Daemmrich/Stock Boston/PictureQuest; **332** AP/Wide World Photos; **334** David Joel/Getty Images; **336** Lawrence Migdale/Getty Images; **337** AP/Wide World Photos; **339** Ed Bock/CORBIS; **341** Dennis MacDonald/Index Stock; **343** Rob Crandall; **344** Christopher Bissell/Getty Images; **348** Tony Freeman/PhotoEdit; **349** Jeff Greenberg/PhotoEdit; **352** Michael Newman/PhotoEdit; **356** Tom Carter/PhotoEdit; **359** Chronoscope/Getty Images; **361** Amy Etra/PhotoEdit; **362** Ariel Skelley/CORBIS; **364** Robert Melnychuk/firstlight/PictureQuest; **365** Ellen Senisi/The Image Works; **366** Michael J. Doolittle/The Image Works; **368** Image Source/elektraVision/PictureQuest; **368–369** Stewart Cohen/Getty Images; **370** Myrleen Ferguson Cate/PhotoEdit; **371** Sean Cayton/The Image Works; **373** (t)(cl)Getty Images, (cr)Digital Vision, (b)Dennie Cody/Getty Images; **375** Walter Hodges/Getty Images; **376** SuperStock; **377** A. Ramey/PhotoEdit; **379** (t)AP/Wide World Photos, (b)Spencer Grant/PhotoEdit; **381** Omni Photo Communications/Index Stock; **382** Gary Conner/PhotoEdit; **383** Pixtal/SuperStock; **384** Robin Sachs/PhotoEdit; **387 388** Michael Newman/PhotoEdit; **390** Dwayne Newton/PhotoEdit; **391** Bill Lai/The Image Works; **393** Dana White/PhotoEdit; **394** Andre Jenny/Focus Group/PictureQuest; **395** Geoff Tompkinson/SPL/Custom Medical Stock Photo; **396** Will Hart/PhotoEdit; **397** Jose Galvez/PhotoEdit; **398** Paul Conklin/PhotoEdit; **400 402** Getty Images; **406** Tony Freeman/PhotoEdit; **407** Ellen Senisi/The Image Works; **408** Myrleen Ferguson Cate/PhotoEdit; **411** CORBIS; **413** SW Production/Index Stock; **414** Larry Dale Gordon/Getty Images; **415** Getty Images; **416** Patrick Sheandell O'Carroll/PhotoAlto/PictureQuest; **417** Don Milici; **418** Dave L. Ryan/Index Stock; **420** Spencer Grant/PhotoEdit; **422** AP/Wide World Photos; **423** Getty Images; **425** Frank Siteman/Index Stock; **426** Tony Freeman/PhotoEdit; **428** Mark Richards/PhotoEdit; **429** Michael Newman/PhotoEdit; **430** Courtesy Louisiana Department of Social Services, (inset)Getty Images; **431** CORBIS; **433** Getty Images; **435** Dana White/PhotoEdit; **436** (l)Mary Kate Denny/PhotoEdit, (r)Life Images; **438** David J. & Janice L. Frent Collection/CORBIS; **438–439** Robert W. Kelley/Time Life Pictures/Getty Images; **440** Dennis Degnan/CORBIS; **441** Collection of Cheekwood Museum of Art, Nashville, TN; **443** Dennis MacDonald/PhotoEdit; **445** David Young-Wolff/PhotoEdit; **446** Lichtenstein Andrew/CORBIS Sygma; **448** Joseph Sohm; ChromoSohm/CORBIS; **449 451** AP/Wide World Photos; **452** Barbara Sitzer/PhotoEdit; **454** Bettmann/CORBIS; **455** J.B. Diederich/Contact Press Images/PictureQuest; **457** Brauchli David/CORBIS Sygma; **459** Sorbo Robert/CORBIS Sygma; **460** Getty Images; **462 463** AP/Wide World Photos; **464** Paul Colangelo/CORBIS; **465** J.P. Williams/Getty Images; **466** CORBIS Sygma; **468 470** AP/Wide World Photos; **472** David Kelly Crow/PhotoEdit; **473** Bettmann/CORBIS; **475** Mark Burnett/Stock Boston/PictureQuest; **476** Leif Skoogfors/CORBIS; **477** Bob Daemmrich/Stock Boston/PictureQuest; **478** (t)Richard T. Nowitz/National Geographic Society/Getty Images, (b)Mark Thiessen/CORBIS; **479** Jonathan Nourok/PhotoEdit; **481** John Neubauer/Rainbow; **482** Wolfgang Kaehler/CORBIS; **483** Jim West/The Image Works; **484** Chris Collins/CORBIS; **485** Ed Bock/CORBIS; **486** AP/Wide World Photos; **489** Michael Newman/PhotoEdit; **490** David Young-Wolff/PhotoEdit; **491** AP/Wide World Photos; **492** Getty Images; **494** Sean Justice/Getty Images; **496** AP/Wide World Photos; **499 500** Bettmann/CORBIS; **502** C/B Productions/CORBIS; **503** Jim West/The Image Works; **505** Bettmann/CORBIS; **506** Roger Ressmeyer/CORBIS; **509** AP/Wide World Photos; **510** Sergio Dorantes/CORBIS; **513** Bettmann/CORBIS; **514** Robert Huntzinger/CORBIS; **516** (l)CORBIS, (r)AP/Wide World Photos; **517** David Young-Wolff/Getty Images; **518** Bettmann/CORBIS; **520** Jim West/The Image Works; **521** Steve Dunwell Photography, Inc./Index Stock; **525** Monika Graff/The Image Works; **527** Patrizia Savarese/CORBIS; **530** Zefa Visual Media-Germany /Index Stock; **531** Joseph Sohm; ChromoSohm/CORBIS; **532** Mug Shots/CORBIS; **534** AFP/CORBIS; **537** Rob Crandall/The Image Works; **538** Bob Daemmrich/Stock Boston/PictureQuest; **542** Getty Images; **543** Billy Hustace/Getty Images; **544** Don Smetzer/Getty Images; **547** Bill Aron/PhotoEdit; **549** Elizabeth Simpson/Getty Images; **551** AP/Wide World Photos; **552** Bob Daemmrich/The Image Works; **554** AFP/CORBIS; **555** Vince Streano/CORBIS; **556** Andy Sacks/Getty Images; **557** Bill Varie/CORBIS; **558** Greg Kiger/Index Stock; **561** Cat Gwynn/CORBIS; **563** AFP/CORBIS; **564** Jose Galvez/PhotoEdit; **567** James Leynse/CORBIS Saba; **569** (t)Getty Images, (b)Michael Dunning/Getty Images; **570** (l)(r)(c)Getty Images, (b)CORBIS; **570–599** Getty Images; **600** (tl)CORBIS, (tr)Getty Images, (b)Index Stock; **606** Ewing Galloway/Index Stock; **607** Jan Halaska/Index Stock; **608** (t)file photo, (c)Bob Adelman/Magnum, (b)Library of Congress; **610** Allen Russell/Index Stock; **612** (cw from tr)Getty Images, Getty Images, CORBIS, Getty Images, Gary Hofheimer/Index Stock, Getty Images, Getty Images, Jonathan Nourok/Getty Images, Image Source/elektraVision/PictureQuest, Getty Images; **Design elements:** (gavel, Capitol Building, Constitution, U.S. Flag) Getty Images; (Supreme Court)CORBIS; **Silhouette people:** Michael Dunning/Getty Images.